ARCHER'S COMPOUND INTEREST AND ANNUITY TABLES

ARCHER, Joseph Alfred

ARCHER'S
COMPOUND INTEREST
AND
ANNUITY TABLES

VOLUME 2

EFFECTIVE RATES 3% to 6%

ORIGINALLY COMPILED BY

J. A. ARCHER

ELEVENTH EDITION

BY

A. C. JAMES

SHAW & SONS LTD.
SHAWAY HOUSE, LONDON, SE26 5AE, ENGLAND
1974

First published *1886*

Eleventh edition *1974*

ISBN 0 7219 0272 3

Printed in Great Britain by SHAW & SONS LTD., London.

PREFACE TO THE ELEVENTH EDITION

This edition shows considerable departures from all previous editions, both in the range of values of the variables and the manner of display.

The very comprehensive range of interest rates presented necessitates three volumes to cover all annual or "effective" rates from $\frac{1}{2}\%$ to $12\frac{1}{8}\%$ at intervals of one sixteenth per cent.

Since the number of new tables to be calculated was very large it was practical to use a computer and to reproduce the print out by photography; To achieve a uniform presentation all the tables, including those previously published, have been recalculated to extend the number of significant figures to include ten decimal places for all functions, conveniently displayed in sets of 3–3–4.

It was thought desirable to retain the traditional grouping by functions with which users are familiar, rather than present the six main functions side by side (i.e. grouped by rate of interest). Distinction between the functions has, however, been facilitated by the use of contrasting paper tints. It was not possible without unduly increasing the size of the whole work to display the period variable to the standard of 200 or 100 used in previous editions, and it is believed that the reduced standard of 180 at effective rates up to 6% and 60 at effective rates from 6% to $12\frac{1}{8}\%$ will cover the requirements of the great majority of users.

The function "Accumulation of a Sinking Fund" has been omitted because this can be directly and simply calculated from the values shown, as explained within, and all references to currency have been removed together with the examples formerly given at the foot of each table; it is hoped the extended explanation of the tables and the additional appendices will in conjunction with the new page headings, assist users in resolving their practical problems involving compound interest.

The editor wishes to express his indebtedness to the late J. A. Archer and to the editors who succeeded him, and to acknowledge the help and encouragement given in preparing the present edition by Gordon Morris of Shaw & Sons Ltd.

CONTENTS

SYNOPSIS OF TABLES

in order of display

REPAYMENT OF A LOAN BY WAY OF ANNUITY
SINKING FUND
AMOUNT OF 1
PRESENT VALUE OF 1
AMOUNT OF 1 PER PERIOD
PRESENT VALUE OF 1 PER PERIOD

	Interest Compounded	Nominal Annual Rate of Interest %	No. of Periods
Volume 1	Yearly (Effective Rates) Half yearly Quarterly Monthly	$\frac{1}{2}$ increasing by $\frac{1}{16}$ to 3 1 ,, $\frac{1}{8}$ to 6 2 ,, $\frac{1}{4}$ to 12 6 ,, $\frac{3}{4}$ to 36	1 to 180
Volume 2	Yearly (Effective Rates) Half yearly Quarterly	3 increasing by $\frac{1}{16}$ to 6 6 ,, $\frac{1}{8}$ to 12 12 ,, $\frac{1}{4}$ to 24	1 to 180
Volume 3	Yearly (Effective Rates) Half yearly Quarterly	6 increasing by $\frac{1}{16}$ to $12\frac{1}{8}$ 12 ,, $\frac{1}{8}$ to $24\frac{1}{4}$ 24 ,, $\frac{1}{4}$ to $48\frac{1}{2}$	1 to 60

Supplementary tables of value of the annuity for use with quarterly or monthly compounding			
	Nominal annual rate of interest %	No. of years	No. of periods
Interest Compounded Quarterly	$3\frac{1}{8}$% increasing by $\frac{1}{4}$ to $5\frac{7}{8}$%	5, 10, 15, 20, 25, 30	20, 40, 60, 80, 100, 120
Interest Compounded Monthly	3% increasing by $\frac{1}{8}$ to 6%	5, 10, 15, 20, 25, 30	60, 120, 180, 240, 300, 360

EXPLANATION OF THE TABLES

1.1 The information in the following paragraphs is given for the guidance of users of the tables, and especially those who have had no technical training in the theory of compound interest. Those who require to calculate any special value or table of values not given in this work are referred to Appendix 1 which gives Mr. Archer's description of the methods he adopted in the calculation of the values in the tables published in the early editions, and Appendix 2 which gives a simple explanation of the method of calculating values, the relationship between the functions, and a numerical approach to problems arising. In the examples given, the answers are expressed to two decimals of a currency unit, e.g. pounds/pence, dollars/cents.

Particulars of the functions tabulated

2.1 The functions tabulated are, with the approved actuarial symbol:

1.	Repayment of a loan by way of annuity	$\frac{1}{a_{\overline{n}\mid}}$
2.	Sinking fund	$\frac{1}{s_{\overline{n}\mid}}$
3.	Amount of 1	$s = (1 + i)^n$
4.	Present value of 1	v^n
5.	Amount of 1 per period	$s_{\overline{n}\mid}$
6.	Present value of 1 per period	$a_{\overline{n}\mid}$
7.	Nominal rates of interest equivalent to effective rates	$i^{(m)} = m\,[(1 + i)^{1/m} - 1]$
8.	Ratio of effective rates of interest to nominal rates	$\frac{i}{i^{(m)}} = \frac{i}{m\,[(1 + i)^{1/m} - 1]}$

2.2 It should be noted that, as explained in the Appendices the basic value from which all the other values are derived is the amount of 1, viz. $(1 + i)^n$ where

$1 =$ unity

$i =$ interest on 1 for one period

$n =$ the number of periods

The title page to each function gives algebraically the relationship between the amount of 1 and the tabulated function using the above symbols, and each page heading shows the effective annual interest rate, i.e. the " periodical " rate together with the corresponding " nominal " annual rate for periods of:

Half years : at twice the effective annual rate

Quarters : at four times the effective annual rate (Vol. 1 and 2)

Months : at twelve times the effective annual rate (Vol. 1 only)

It is important to note the substitution of the word " periods " for " years " shown in earlier editions, and to bear in mind the difference between an " effective " rate related to the period and a " nominal " **annual** rate.

Methods of repayment of a loan

3.1 Repayment of a loan may be effected by any of the following methods: (i) by equal yearly or other periodical payments including both principal and interest, known as the " annuity " method, (ii) by a " sinking fund ", and (iii) by equal yearly or other periodic payments of principal with interest on the reducing balance, referred to as the " instalment " method. These methods are explained in paras. 4, 5, 6 and 7.

Annuity Method

4.1 The annual, half yearly, etc. payments for repayment of a loan by the annuity method are given in the first set of tables. Each payment is of the same amount throughout the term, and consists partly of interest and partly of repayment of principal; in each successive payment the interest portion decreases and the principal repayment portion increases. A schedule of repayments showing the apportionment of each payment to interest and principal can be prepared by two methods, taking as an example a loan of 1000 repayable over 10 years by equal annual payments to include principal and interest at 6 per cent. The appropriate table (page 315) shows the periodical payment at 6% to repay 1 in 10 periods = ·1358679582 and the required annual payment is therefore

$$\cdot 1358679582 \times 1000 = 135{\cdot}8679582 \text{ say } 135{\cdot}87$$

It is customary to round up any fraction of the smallest unit of currency to ensure complete amortisation, any excess being appropriated to interest.

Method 1. Calculation of interest on reducing balance.

4.2 Using the example above, the interest due at the end of the first year is:

$1000 \times \frac{6}{100} = 60$ and the difference, viz. 75·87 between the interest and the annual payment represents the first repayment of principal which is thus reduced to 924·13. In the second and subsequent periods the interest is calculated upon the balance outstanding at the end of the preceding year, and deducting as before the interest from 135·87 the remainder is apportioned to principal.

The schedule will appear as follows:

Table for repayment of a loan of 1000 with interest at 6% by 10 equal annual payments of 135·87.

Instalment No.	Interest at 6%	Principal	Balance outstanding
1	60·00	75·87	924·13
2	55·45	80·42	843·71
3	50·62	85·25	758·46
4	45·51	90·36	668·10
5	40·09	95·78	572·32
6	34·34	101·53	470·79
7	28·25	107·62	363·17
8	21·79	114·08	249·09
9	14·95	120·92	128·17
10	7·70	128·17	—
	358·70	1000·00	

Because the periodical payment has been rounded up, and the calculation of interest is worked to two decimals it is probable that when the final payment is reached, the principal portion so computed will be more or less than the balance, and the discrepancy must be corrected by adjusting the final payment of interest. In this example the interest calculated on the balance of 128·17 is 7·69 and this has been adjusted to 7·70.

Method 2. Calculation of accretion to principal.

4.3 This method is much to be preferred, particularly when a calculating machine is available, and involves multiplying the sinking fund, i.e. the first payment of principal by (1 plus the interest on 1 for 1 period) and proceeding successively as in this example:

The annuity as para. 4.1 is ·1358679582 to repay 1.

Deduct interest at 6% ·06 on 1.

∴ Sinking fund which at 6% p.a. accumulates to 1 in 10 years = ·0758679582. See page 367.

and sinking fund which accumulates to 1000 = 75·8679582. First payment.

The maximum capacity of the machine should be used to ensure accuracy; most machines will retain 10 figures in the product, but only 4 decimals need be written, for rounding to 2.

(1)		(2)	Reduce to two decimals (3)
First payment of principal	=	75·8680	75·87
2nd—multiply by 1·06	=	80·4200	80·42
3rd ,,		85·2452	85·24
4th ,,		90·3600	90·36
5th ,,		95·7815	95·78
6th ,,		101·5284	101·53
7th ,,		107·6201	107·62
8th ,,		114·0774	114·08
9th ,,		120·9220	120·92
10th ,,		128·1773	128·18
10th + 1 ,, i.e. annuity	=	135·8679582	—
Total			1000·00

4.4 The advantage of this method of calculation is that it is continuous, i.e. without the interruption involved in the first method, whereby the balance outstanding must be obtained between each interest calculation. Furthermore by carrying the calculation to the term $n + 1$ (No. 11 in this case), the amount of the annuity appears, thus proving the correctness of the whole. The table can now be quickly prepared, with confidence, by a series of continuous calculations after rounding each amount to 2 decimals, noting that as with the example for method I a correction is required on adding column 3; this correction is made at payment No. 3. In a lengthy series a number of corrections will be required and these should properly be made to the amounts showing the least difference over (or under if the total is deficient) the critical digit of 5 in the third decimal.

The balance is inserted either by continuous subtraction, or by addition starting by inserting the final payment of principal against the penultimate instalment.

The interest is inserted by deducting each instalment of principal from the periodical payment, the total being proved by comparison with the product of the periodical payment times the number of payments, minus the principal.

4.5 If the schedule is lengthy it is desirable to check the values or prepare check values in advance at suitable intervals, e.g. at every tenth period, as a precaution against continuing an error in multiplication. This involves multiplying the first payment of principal, i.e. the sinking fund, by appropriate values of the amount of 1; for example the fifth payment of principal in the table at para. 4.3 is:

75·86796 × 1·26247696 (page 419—amount of 1 at 6% for 4 periods) = 95·78155.

The appropriate values of the amount of 1 are those given for a period of one less than the number of the instalment to be checked or calculated.

Sinking Fund Method

5.1 It is sometimes required to raise a loan repayable at maturity, i.e. where the principal is repaid at the end of an agreed term instead of by periodic payments. The borrower will pay throughout the whole of the term the interest on the full sum borrowed at agreed intervals and can secure the whole of the principal for repayment at the end of the term by means of a sinking fund. If the rate of interest at which the sinking fund can be accumulated is the same as that paid to the lender, then the cost to the borrower is the same as if the loan was repaid by annuity.

If, however, the borrower cannot accumulate the sinking fund at the same rate as that charged by the lender (and in many cases it will be a lower rate) the sinking fund calculation must be made at the " accumulation " rate regardless of the rate charged by the lender.

It is important to see that the sinking fund accumulations are maintained at the correct value from time to time and for this purpose the table of values of amount of 1 per period can be used. For example, a sinking fund is required to accumulate to 20,000 at the end of a term of 30 years at a rate of $7\frac{1}{2}\%$ per annum. The annual contribution is 20,000 $\times$ ·0096712358 (page 623) $=$ 193·424716.

At the end of a period of 10 years the fund will have accumulated to:

193·424716 $\times$ 14·1470874955 (Vol. 3—amount of 1 p.p. at $7\frac{1}{2}\%$ for 10 periods)$=$ 2736·3964; if at the end of this period the accumulation rate is reduced to 6% it will be required to ascertain the revised contribution.

The balance remaining to be accumulated is 20,000 — 2736·3964 $=$ 17263·6036 and the revised annual contribution is the sinking fund which will accumulate at 6% p.a. to that amount in 20 years, viz.:

17263·6036 $\times$ ·027184557 (page 367) $=$ 469·303416.

A similar procedure can be used to check the amount of the fund at the end of any period.

5.2 In the case of some internal transactions the rate of accumulation is fixed on the assumption that the fund can be invested internally, e.g. to finance expenditure without recourse to external borrowing. In such cases the interest is notional and it is unnecessary to construct a table of the periodical payments of sinking fund contributions and interest, neither is there any particular advantage in using tables showing the " accumulation of a sinking fund " to check the rate of accumulation; such tables are merely the appropriate sinking fund contribution to repay 1 multiplied successively by the amount of 1 per period. On the assumption that a contribution has to be made annually with interest it is only necessary to make the calculation from the table of the amount of 1 per period once yearly, irrespective of the frequency of compounding interest.

For example, a loan of 125,000 is to be repaid in 30 years by 60 half yearly contributions to a sinking fund to accumulate at a *nominal* rate of 12% p.a., i.e. an *effective* rate of 6% per half year. The amount which will accumulate to 125,000 in 60 periods at 6% is:

·0018757215 (page 367) × 125,000 = 234·46519, say 234·47.

The accumulation of the fund is calculated once yearly by multiplying this sum by values of the amount of 1 per period appropriate to the number of elapsed periods; half years in this example:

Year No.	Elapsed periods	Calculation Sinking fund	×	Amount of 1 p.p. Page 523	Amount of fund
1	2	234·47	×	2·06	483
2	4	,,	×	4·37	1025
3	6	,,	×	6·98	1637
4	8	,,	×	9·90	2321
5	10	,,	×	13·18	3090
.	.	.	.	.	.
10	20	234·47	×	36·79	8626
.	.	.	.	.	.
30	60	234·46519	×	533·12818	125000

The use of unnecessary decimals should be avoided; each calculation is independent and any error will be rectified in a following calculation. Working the final calculation with an appropriate number of decimals in the multiplier and multiplicand will produce the exact sum required. This procedure has particular advantages:

(i) When a number of loans can be merged at suitable time intervals to produce standard periods, and repaid by one accumulating sinking fund at a common rate.

(ii) On a change in the rate of accumulation. (See para. 5.1.)

(iii) When it is unnecessary to calculate the periodic contributions to a degree of accuracy greater than one whole unit of currency.

Quarterly, Monthly or Weekly Instalments

6.1 Repayment of loans is sometimes required to be made by payments of principal and interest at more frequent intervals than yearly or half yearly, e.g. quarterly, monthly or weekly, and such payments may be on account of the yearly or half yearly payments for which the tables are primarily intended, or independently calculated at an effective rate related to the period for compounding interest.

6.2 The construction of repayment tables where quarterly, monthly or weekly payments are on account of the yearly or half yearly annuity is straightforward, each instalment being the appropriate fraction of the periodic payment; the calculation is best done by division of the principal followed by insertion of the balance and interest as suggested in para. 4.3. Any remainder arising from the division of principal should be allocated to the later of the weekly, monthly or quarterly payments.

6.3 For quarterly or monthly payments independently calculated, nominal annual rates are shown in the Synopsis of tables, the interest intervals being $\frac{1}{2}\%$ for quarterly and $\frac{3}{4}\%$ for monthly compounding. Supplementary Tables of values of the annuity function for a range of commonly used periods are set out on pages 576A to E and these will in conjunction with the main set of tables provide a range of nominal annual interest rates for quarterly and monthly compounding from 3% to 6% at intervals of $\frac{1}{8}\%$. Nominal rates from 6% to $12\frac{1}{4}\%$ are shown in Volume 3.

6.4 In constructing repayment schedules when using quarterly or monthly compounding the factor to be used as the continuous multiplier (see para. 4.3) will be 1 plus the periodical *effective* rate as shown in the first column of the Supplementary Tables, or the yearly rate shown in the main tables applied to the compounding period. It is worth noting that whereas the work involved in constructing repayment tables increases in proportion to the frequency of compounding, the difference in the repayments becomes less significant with each successive proportional increase in frequency of compounding. For example consider the differences in annual cost of repaying a loan of 1000 at a nominal annual rate of $6\frac{1}{2}\%$ over a period of 5 years by:

Annual payments at $6\frac{1}{2}\%$			=	240·64
Half yearly payments at $3\frac{1}{4}\%$ effective	=	118·74 × 2	=	237·48
Quarterly payments at $1\frac{5}{8}\%$ effective	=	58·97 × 4	=	235·88
Monthly payments at $\frac{13}{24}\%$ effective	=	19·57 × 12	=	234·84
Weekly payments at $\frac{1}{8}\%$ effective	=	4·51 × 52	=	234·52
Daily payments at ·01781% effective	=	·64 × 365	=	233·60

(Each periodical payment has been rounded up as suggested in para. 4.1.)

Repayment by equal instalments of principal

7.1 Under this arrangement each periodical payment includes principal and interest as with annuity repayment, but the principal repaid is the same amount in each payment, being simply the amount of the loan divided by the number of payments, whilst the interest is calculated on the balance outstanding. Preparation of a repayment schedule is simple since the items of principal are of uniform amount and each successive item of interest decreases uniformly by the amount of the interest on each payment of principal. The total interest charge is less than that payable under annuity repayment, and can be found by multiplying the interest on the loan for 1 period by the number of periods plus 1 and dividing the product by 2.

Valuation of an annuity or other periodic payment

8.1 This is the reverse process of finding the annual payment to repay a loan either by way of annuity to include principal and interest or by way of a sinking fund. The periodic payment is given and it is required to find the present value of a series of future payments, or the amount of a series of past payments. The appropriate tables are Present value of 1 per period and Amount of 1 per period respectively.

8.2 For example the present value at 6 per cent. of an annual payment of 100 for 8 years is:

$$100 \times 6{\cdot}20979 \text{ (Page 575)} = 620{\cdot}98$$

And a half yearly payment of 20 for 30 years will accumulate at 12 per cent. nominal per annum, i.e. an effective rate of 6 per cent. per half year to

$$20 \times 533{\cdot}12818 \text{ (Page 523 60 periods)} = 10662{\cdot}56$$

8.3 Single payments or irregular series of payments are valued by using Present value of 1 or Amount of 1 as the case may be. For example an irregular series of payments of 100 at the end of 1 year, 200 at the end of 2 years and 300 at the end of 3 years will amount at 6 per cent. per annum to:

100 × 1·1236	(Amount of 1 in 2 periods at 6%)	=	112·36
200 × 1·060	(Amount of 1 in 1 period at 6%)	=	212·00
300 × 1	(Paid at end of period)	=	300·00
	Total		624·36

And the present value of this series of payments will, at 6 per cent. per annum, be:

100 × ·943396	(Present value of 1 due in 1 year)	=	94·34
200 × ·889996	(Present value of 1 due in 2 years)	=	178·00
300 × ·839619	(Present value of 1 due in 3 years)	=	251·89
	Total		524·23

Payments made at the beginning of each year or other period

9.1 Each of the tables concerned with periodic payments assumes the payments are to be made at the *end* of each period. If it is required to find values where the periodic payments are to be made at the *beginning* of each period (i.e. where the first payment is to be made immediately, as for example in the case of insurance premiums) the following adjustments should be made to the values given in the respective tables.

9.2 Repayment of a loan by way of annuity and Sinking Fund—divide by (1 plus the interest on 1 for 1 period).

Examples:

(i) The payment to be made at the beginning of each half year to include principal and interest at a nominal rate of 12% per annum to repay a loan of 1000 over 10 years will be:

$$1000 \times \frac{\cdot 087184557}{1\cdot 06} \text{ (p. 315)} = 82\cdot 249, \text{ say } 82\cdot 25.$$

(ii) The sinking fund payment to be made at the beginning of each year for 15 years to accumulate at 3% p.a. to 1000 will be:

$$1000 \times \frac{\cdot 0537665805}{1\cdot 03} \text{ (p. 319)} = 52\cdot 20056 \text{ say } 52\cdot 21$$

The payments accumulate to the *end* of the period of 15 years, i.e. to the end of the last period in which the payment is made.

9.3 Amount of 1 per period: either multiply by (1 plus the interest on 1 for 1 period) or take the value for one period greater than the number of periods and deduct 1 (unity) from that value.

Present value of 1 per period: either multiply by (1 plus the interest on 1 for 1 period) or take the value for one period less than the number of periods and add 1 (unity) to that value.

Examples:

(i) 10000 payable at the beginning of each year for 20 years at 6% per annum will amount to:

$$10000 \times 36\cdot 7855912035 \text{ (p. 523)} \times 1\cdot 06 = 389927\cdot 27.$$

$$\text{or } 10000 \times (39\cdot 9927266758 \text{ (p. 523)} - 1) = 389927\cdot 27.$$

(ii) The present value of 500 payable at the beginning of each half year for 15 years at 6% per annum (3% effective) is:

$$500 \times 19\cdot 6004413495 \text{ (p. 527)} \times 1\cdot 03 = 10094\cdot 23$$

$$\text{or } 500 \times (19\cdot 18845459 \text{ (p. 527)} + 1) = 10094\cdot 23.$$

Payments commencing after a fractional period

10.1 It sometimes happens that a loan is to be repaid by way of annuity and that the repayments are to commence on a date prior to the anniversary of the date of the advance. If interest is added to the loan for the fractional period from the date of the advance to the date of the first payment the position is then that the loan so increased by interest is to be repaid by periodic payments made at the beginning of each period. Following the method of para. 9.2 the rule to calculate the periodic payment is:

> Increase the loan by interest for the fractional period. Multiply by the tabulated value for repayment of 1. Divide the product by (1 plus interest on 1 for 1 period) (i.e. the first entry in the table of the annuity, relating to 1 period).

Example: A loan of 1000 is to be repaid by 60 equal half yearly payments to include principal and interest at 12% p.a. nominal. The loan is advanced on 1st January and it is desired that repayments shall be made on 31st March and 30th September in each year.

Interest for 89 days on 1000 at 12% $=$ 29·26

Loan plus interest $=$ 1029·26

$$\text{Half yearly payment} = \frac{1029{\cdot}26 \times {\cdot}0618757215 \text{ (p. 315)}}{1{\cdot}060} = 59{\cdot}111, \text{ say } 59{\cdot}12.$$

Payments made more frequently than once a year or other period at effective annual or periodical rates of interest

11.1 The values of the periodic payments in the tables and used in the examples in previous paragraphs are shown at annual rates of interest, i.e. the unit of time for calculation of interest is taken as a year; but the unit interval can be any period of time and the use of the tabulated values where the interval is less than a year is simply a matter of applying the tabulated rate to the selected period, when the nominal annual rate is the effective or tabulated annual rate times the number of time intervals in a year for compounding, e.g. the tabulated annual rate of 6% applied to half yearly compounding gives a nominal annual rate of 12%. But 6% per half year is not the same as 12% per annum as will be evident from the following example:

(a) The amount of 1 in 4 years at 12% p.a. (p. 683, Vol. 3) $=$ 1·573519.

(b) The amount of 1 in 8 half years at 6% per h.y. (p. 419) $=$ 1·593848.

The effective annual rate (a) is therefore slightly more than the nominal annual rate compounded half yearly (b) since a marginally higher rate than 12% would be required to produce the amount of 1·593848. Conversely, the nominal rate compounded half yearly is slightly less than the corresponding effective annual rate since a marginally lower rate than 6% per half year would be sufficient to produce 1·573519.

11.2 The tables on pages liii to lv give the nominal rates of interest, $i^{(m)}$ which, compounded m times a year, e.g. half yearly, quarterly, monthly or " momently ", correspond to the effective annual rates of interest used in the tables; the values are of course valid for any period and period fractions. The outstanding use of these tables is to calculate the amount or present value of an annuity payable more frequently than once per period at a specified effective periodical rate of interest: thus the amount of 1 payable by m equal payments per annum for n years is

$$\frac{\text{amount of 1 accumulated for } n \text{ years} - 1}{i^{(m)}}$$

and the present value of 1 payable by m equal payments per annum for n years is

$$\frac{1 - \text{present value of 1 due in } n \text{ years}}{i^{(m)}}$$

Example (i): The amount of 100 per annum payable quarterly for 15 years at an effective annual rate of 6 per cent.

$$= 100 \times \frac{2{\cdot}3965581931 \text{ (Amount of 1, p. 419)} - 1}{{\cdot}0586953847 \text{ (nominal rate where } m = 4)} = 2379{\cdot}332$$

Compare the amount of 25 per quarter payable for 60 quarters at an effective quarterly rate of $1\frac{1}{2}$ per cent.

= 25 × 96·2146517126 (Amount of 1 per period at $1\frac{1}{2}\%$ for 60 periods, see Volume I) = 2405·365

The effective annual rate in the latter case is thus slightly greater than 6 per cent.

Example (ii): The present value of 100 per annum payable half yearly for 30 years at an effective annual rate of 6 per cent.

$$= 100 \times \frac{1 - {\cdot}1741101309 \text{ (Present value of 1, p. 471)}}{{\cdot}0591260282 \text{ (nominal rate where } m = 2)} = 1396{\cdot}830$$

Compare the present value of 50 per half year for 60 half years at an effective half yearly rate of 3 per cent.

= 50 × 27·6755636661 (Present value of 1 per period at 3% for 60 periods, see page 527) = 1383·778

The effective annual rate in the latter case is slightly greater than 6 per cent. since the effect of discounting future payments at the higher rate is to reduce their present value.

11.3 The calculations illustrated in para. 11.2 can be done more easily by using the tables on pages lvi to lviii which give the values $\frac{i}{i^{(m)}}$ as factors to convert the amount or present value of a periodical payment made at the end of each period to the amount or present value of the same periodical payment made in m equal payments at the end of each one mth of a period; thus the amount of 1 payable by m equal payments per annum for n years is Amount of 1 per annum for n years $\times \frac{i}{i^{(m)}}$, and the present value of 1 payable by m equal payments per annum for n years is Present value of 1 per annum for n years $\times \frac{i}{i^{(m)}}$.

The examples in para. 11.2 then become:

Example (i): 100 × 23·275969885 (Amount of I p.p. for 15 periods at 6%) × 1·02222688 (factor where $m = 4$) = 2379·332 as before.

Example (ii): 100 × 13·7648311515 (Present value of I p.p. for 30 periods at 6%) × 1·014781507 (factor where $m = 2$) = 1396·830 as before.

11.4 The table of $i^{(m)}$ has other applications, e.g. it gives m times the interest on I for one mth of a period at an effective periodical rate of interest; hence, dividing by m and adding I we obtain the amount of I for one mth of a period at an effective periodical rate; viz. $(1 + i)^{1/m}$.

Example: The amount of I in one quarter at an effective annual rate of 6% =

$$\frac{\cdot 0586953847 \text{ (Nominal rate where } m = 4)}{4} + 1 = 1\cdot 0146738462.$$

From the value of $(1 + i)^{1/m}$ can be calculated the payment at the end of each one mth of a period which is equivalent to I at the end of each period, by deducting 1 and dividing by i; viz. $\frac{(1 + i)^{1/m} - 1}{i}$ thus: $\frac{1\cdot 0146738462 - 1}{\cdot 06} = \cdot 2445641033.$

This is in fact, the quarterly payment which will amount to I at the end of four quarters at a nominal annual rate of 5·86953847 per cent.

And the reciprocal of this value, viz. $\frac{i}{(1 + i)^{1/m} - 1}$ represents the payment at the end of each period which is equivalent to I at the end of each one mth of a period; thus where $m = 4$ and the effective annual rate = 6%

$$\frac{1}{\cdot 2445641033} = 4\cdot 0889075236$$

This value can be obtained more easily by multiplying the appropriate factor $\frac{i}{i^{(m)}}$ by m, e.g.

1·0222268809 (factor where $m = 4$) × 4 = 4·0889075236 = the amount to which a payment of I made at the end of each quarter will accumulate at the end of the fourth quarter at an effective annual rate of 6%, with interest compounded quarterly; compare the amount of I per quarter for 4 quarters at a nominal annual rate of 6%, i.e. an effective rate of $1\frac{1}{2}$% per quarter = 4·090903375.

11.5 As an annuity to repay a loan and a sinking fund are the reciprocals respectively of the present value of I per period and the amount of I per period the function $i^{(m)}$ can also be used to find the annuity or sinking fund payments to be made more frequently than once per period at an effective periodical rate of interest. The annuity payable by m equal payments per period required to repay a loan of 1 in n periods at an effective periodical rate is:

$$\frac{i^{(m)}}{1 - \text{present value of 1 due in } n \text{ periods}} \text{ per period}$$

and the sinking fund payable by m equal payments per period required to accumulate to 1 in n periods at an effective periodical rate is:

$$\frac{i^{(m)}}{\text{amount of 1 accumulated for } n \text{ periods} - 1} \text{ per period.}$$

Example (i). The annuity payable by quarterly payments to repay a loan of 1000 at the end of 15 years at an effective annual rate of 6 per cent.

$$= 1000 \times \frac{\cdot 0586953847, \textit{ viz. } i^{(m)} \text{ where } m = 4}{1 - \cdot 4172650607, \textit{ viz. } \text{p.v. of 1 for 15 periods}}$$

$= 100{\cdot}724$ per annum $= 25{\cdot}181$ per quarter.

Compare the quarterly payment at a nominal annual rate of 6%, i.e. a quarterly effective rate of $1\frac{1}{2}\%$:

$$\cdot 0253934274 \times 1000 = 25{\cdot}393 \text{ per quarter.}$$

Example (ii). The sinking fund payable by half yearly payments to accumulate to 5000 at the end of 12 years at an effective annual rate of 6 per cent.

$$= 5000 \times \frac{\cdot 0591260282, \textit{ viz. } i^{(m)} \text{ where } m = 2}{2{\cdot}0121964718, \text{ (Amount of 1 for 12 periods)} - 1}$$

$= 292{\cdot}068$ per annum $= 146{\cdot}034$ per half year.

Compare the half yearly sinking fund payment at a nominal annual rate of 6%, i.e. a half yearly effective rate of 3%:

$$\cdot 0290474159 \times 5000 = 145{\cdot}237 \text{ per half year.}$$

The advantage gained by using the factor $\frac{i}{i^{(m)}}$ as in the examples in para. 10.3, in having a straightforward multiplication to perform is lost in the present case, as the annuity to repay a loan and the sinking fund would have to be divided by this factor.

11.6 When m is infinitely great, i.e. when interest is compounded continuously, the time intervals for compounding interest are infinitesimal and (assuming the rate of interest per finite time interval is finite) then the amount of 1 after an infinite number of infinitesimal time intervals will be 2·7182818 . . . the irrational number e and the base of natural or Naperian logarithms. The function $i^{(m)}$ when $m = \infty$ is called "the nominal rate of interest compounded momently" and is represented in actuarial notation by the symbol δ. It is often used to value approximately payments made at very frequent intervals, or a group of annuities the payments of which are spread more or less uniformly over a number of years. The factor $\frac{i}{i^{(\infty)}}$ or $\frac{i}{\delta}$ is similarly used in the appropriate formulæ for the valuation of very frequent payments.

11.7 It should be noted that, as illustrated in para. 6.4, successive increases in the frequency of compounding produce progressively smaller proportional decreases in the nominal rate. The tables of values of $i^{(m)}$ and $\frac{i}{i^{(m)}}$ show the frequencies usually required, i.e. 2, 4 and 12, corresponding to half years, quarters and months when the effective rate is " per annum ". For frequencies greater than 12 a close approximation can usually be made by using the tabulated values where $m = \infty$. This is illustrated by the following table of nominal rates compounded at various time intervals using an effective annual rate of 6%.

Frequency of compounding in a period of a year	Nominal annual rate %
Once, i.e. effective rate	6·0000
Twice	5·9126
Four times	5·8695
Twelve times	5·8411
Fifty two times	5·8302
Three hundred and sixty five times	5·8274
Continuously	5·8269

Discounted Cash Flow

12.1 D.C.F. is a method used in investment appraisal or capital budgeting for evaluating the profitability of capital outlay, comparing the cost of renting or leasing assets with outright purchase, or comparing different methods of achieving an objective, e.g. capital outlay with a non-capital alternative.

Having estimated the periodical expected cash flow, the present value of the flows can be equated with outlay at a given rate per cent. (in which case the time in which the equation occurs is calculated), or the present value of the flows can be equated over a given period (in which case the rate per cent. is calculated). The equation is achieved when the net present value (N.P.V.) of outlays and cash flow is nil.

12.2 The use of the present value method is illustrated by the following examples:

Example 1.

Capital outlay		1000
Required rate of return		6% per annum
Cash flows:	year 1	100
	2	200
	3	220
	4	350
	5	400

It is required to find the time in which the present value of the cash flows discounted at 6% will equate with the outlay

Year	Cash flow	Present value of 1 @ 6%	Present value of cash flows −	+
0	− 1000	1·	1000	
1	+ 100	·94340		94·34
2	+ 200	·89000		178·00
3	+ 220	·83962		184·72
4	+ 350	·79209		277·23
5	+ 400	·74726		298·90
			1000	1033·19
		N.P.V.:		+ 33·19

Since the N.P.V. is positive, the required period is somewhat less than 5 years; a cash flow in year 5 of $400 - \frac{33 \cdot 19}{\cdot 74726} = 356$ would produce a nil N.P.V., leading to the conclusion that, providing the flow in year 5 is regular, the period could be interpolated as approximately 4·9 years.

Example 2.

Capital outlay		1000
Cash flows: year	1	100
	2	150
	3	200
	4	300
	5	400

It is required to find the rate at which the cash flow should be discounted to equate with the outlay over a period of 5 years. A trial rate of 5% shows:

Year	Cash flow	Present value of 1 @ 5%	Present value of cash flows −	+
0	− 1000	1·	1000	
1	+ 100	·95238		95·24
2	+ 150	·90703		136·05
3	+ 200	·86384		172·77
4	+ 300	·82270		246·81
5	+ 400	·78353		313·41
			1000	964·28
		N.P.V.:		− 35·72

A negative N.P.V. indicates that the rate is too high, and further trial will show the required rate to be $3\frac{15}{16}$%.

Example 3.

It is required to find the rate at which the payment of a capital sum of 5000 equates with 60 monthly payments of 100.

The cash flow of 100 per month being regular, the appropriate function is present value of 1 per period, and it is necessary to search the tables to find the present value of 1 per period for 60 periods which most closely approximates $\frac{5000}{100} = 50.$

At $\frac{9}{16}\%$ the value is	50·804074
At $\frac{5}{8}\%$ the value is	49·905308
Difference (a)	·898766

An approximate rate between $\frac{9}{16}\%$ and $\frac{5}{8}\%$ can be found by first difference interpolation:

The higher value is	50·804074
The value required is	50
Difference (b)	·804074

$$\frac{\cdot804074 \text{ (difference b)}}{\cdot898766 \text{ (difference a)}} = \cdot894642$$

Interest interval $\frac{1}{16}\%$ = ·0625%

$\cdot0625 \times \cdot894642 = \cdot0559\%$

The rate required is higher than $\frac{9}{16}\%$

$\frac{9}{16}\%$	=	·5625%
Add		·0559%
		·6184%

·6184% = approximate monthly effective rate, equivalent to 7·421% nominal annual. Since the annuity is the reciprocal of present value of 1 per period, a monthly payment of 100 would repay 5000 over 60 months at an effective monthly rate of ·6184%. If the alternative to monthly payments of 100 over 5 years was the repayment of 5000 by 10 half yearly payments, then the appropriate rate to equate would be found by searching the annuity tables for the value for 10 periods which is nearest to $\frac{100 \times 6}{5000} = \cdot12.$

At $3\frac{7}{16}\%$ the value is	·11986288
At $3\frac{1}{2}\%$ the value is	·12024137

The rate is therefore between $3\frac{7}{16}\%$ and $3\frac{1}{2}\%$ per half year, giving a nominal annual rate between $6\frac{7}{8}\%$ and 7%.

Example 4.

It is required to find the rate at which a monthly cash flow of 100 equates with a single payment made at the commencement of a year of 1200 less $2\frac{1}{2}\%$ discount.

$$1200 - 2\tfrac{1}{2}\% = 1170 = \text{present value of single payment.}$$

It is necessary to search the tables of present value of 1 per period to find the value for 12 periods which most closely approximates to $\frac{1170}{100} = 11{\cdot}7$.

At $\frac{3}{8}\%$ the value is 11·7125476

At $\frac{7}{16}\%$ the value is 11·6656045

The rate is therefore between $\frac{3}{8}\%$ and $\frac{7}{16}\%$ monthly, equivalent to a nominal annual rate between $4\frac{1}{2}\%$ and $5\frac{1}{4}\%$. Simple interpolation would refine this to:

11·7125476 − 11·6656045	=	·0469431
11·7125476 − 11·7	=	·0125476
Interval $\frac{1}{16}\%$	=	·0625

$$\frac{{\cdot}0125476}{{\cdot}0469431} \times {\cdot}0625 = {\cdot}0167$$

$\frac{3}{8}\%$ = ·375

Add ·0167

Required rate: ·3917% = approximate monthly effective rate, equivalent to a nominal annual rate of 4·7%.

Example 5.

It is required to find the rate of discount which can be allowed for prompt settlement of an account within one month, in lieu of settlement within three months, assuming a D.C.F. rate of $8\frac{1}{4}\%$ per annum nominal = $\frac{11}{16}\%$ monthly effective.

The distance between the two payment dates is two months, the present value of 1 in two periods at $\frac{11}{16}\%$ is ·9863905, and the required rate is:
$1 - {\cdot}9863905 \times 100 = 1{\cdot}36095$ say 1·36%.

12.3 The examples given above illustrate the use of the present value tables to evaluate and compare known cash flows. Problems arising when using D.C.F. techniques, e.g. the comparison of yield from capital investments having different lives, where depreciation or maintenance costs are involved or under conditions of uncertainty are not within the scope of this explanation, and the reader is referred to the numerous publications on the subject of capital budgeting, investment appraisal and economic analysis.

PRACTICAL EXAMPLES

With Calculations illustrating the use of the Tables

EXAMPLE 1. *A loan of* 3000 *is to be repaid in* 30 *years by equal annual payments to include principal and interest at* 3%. *What is the required annual payment ?*

The annual payment by annuity with interest at 3% to repay 1 in 30 periods = ·0510192593 (p. 267).

3000 × ·0510193 = 153·0579, say 153·06

EXAMPLE 2. *What is the total amount of principal repaid up to the* 23*rd annual payment in the case of the loan referred to at example* 1 *?*

The sinking fund contribution to provide a sum of 3000 by annual contributions at 3% over 30 years = ·0210192593 (p. 319) × 3000 = 63·0577779.

The amount of 1 per period accumulated for 23 periods at 3% = 32·4528837042 (p. 475).

63·0577779 × 32·4528837 = 2046·41

EXAMPLE 3. *What are the amounts of principal and interest included in the* 23*rd annual payment in the case of the loan referred to at example* 1 *?*

The amount of 1 accumulated for 23 — 1 = 22 periods at 3% = 1·9161034089 (p. 371).

63·0577779 × 1·9161034089 = 120·83

Interest = 153·06 — 120·83 = 32·23

Proof: $3000 - 2046{\cdot}41 + 120{\cdot}83 = 1074{\cdot}42 \times \frac{3}{100} = 32{\cdot}23$

EXAMPLE 4. *A loan of* 3000 *is to be repaid in* 30 *years by equal half yearly payments to include principal and interest at* 6% *p.a. nominal, i.e.* 3% *per half year. What is the required semi annual payment ?*

The periodical payment by annuity with interest at 3% effective to repay 1 in 60 periods = ·0361329587 (p. 267).

3000 × ·0361329587 = 108·3989, say 108·40

EXAMPLE 5. *A loan of 5000 is to be repaid by 20 equal annual payments to include principal and interest at 3%. The money is advanced on 20th July and the annual payments are to be made on 15th March in each year the first becoming due on 15th March next following the date of advance. What is the annual payment required ?*

The interest due 20th July to 15th March is for 238 days on 5000 at 3%:

$$\frac{238}{365} \times 5000 \times \cdot 03 = 97 \cdot 81.$$

$$\text{Annual payment} = \frac{5097 \cdot 81 \times \cdot 0672157076 \text{ (p. 267)}}{1 \cdot 03}$$

$$\text{or } \frac{5097 \cdot 81}{1 + 14 \cdot 3237991063 \text{ (p. 527)}} = 332 \cdot 672, \text{ say } \underline{332 \cdot 68}$$

EXAMPLE 6. *A loan of 8000 is to be repaid by 55 equal half yearly payments to include principal and interest at a nominal rate of 12% per annum, i.e. an effective rate of 6% per half year. The loan is to be advanced on 6th January and the half yearly payments are to be made on 20th March and 20th September, the first falling due on 20th March following the date of the advance. What is the half yearly payment required ?*

The interest due 6th January to 20th March is for 73 days on 8000 at 12%

$$= \frac{73}{365} \times 8000 \times \cdot 12 = 192.$$

$$\text{Half yearly payment} = \frac{8192 \times \cdot 0625369634 \text{ (p. 315)}}{1 \cdot 06}$$

$$\text{or } \frac{8192}{1 + 15 \cdot 9499755436 \text{ (p. 575)}} = 483 \cdot 304, \text{ say } \underline{483 \cdot 31}$$

EXAMPLE 7. *What annuity payable at the end of each year for 20 years will 500 purchase at an effective rate of 3% per annum ?*

The purchase of an annuity is the same transaction as the making of a loan to be repaid by equal payments of principal and interest. The annuity is:

$$\cdot 0672157076 \text{ (p. 267)} \times 500 = 33 \cdot 608 \text{ say } \underline{33 \cdot 60}$$

EXAMPLE 8. *What annuity payable at the beginning of each year for 21 years (first payment immediately) will 25000 purchase at an effective rate of 3% per annum ?*

The annuity required is

$$\frac{25000 \times \cdot 0648717765 \text{ (p. 267)}}{1 \cdot 03} = 1574 \cdot 557$$

Or: 25000 ÷ (1 + present value of 1 per period for 20 periods at 3%)

$$\text{viz. } \frac{25000}{1 + 14 \cdot 8774748605 \text{ (p. 527)}} = 1574 \cdot 557 \text{ say } \underline{1574 \cdot 55}$$

EXAMPLE 9. *What half yearly payment by way of annuity at a nominal annual rate of 6%, i.e. an effective rate of 3% per half year will 12000 purchase if the first payment is to be made immediately and further payments are to be made at the end of each succeeding half year for a term of 15 years (31 payments) ?*

This is the same as an annuity payable at the beginning of each half year for 31 half years.

The half yearly payment is

$$\frac{12000 \times \cdot 0499989288 \text{ (p. 267)}}{1 \cdot 03} = 582 \cdot 512$$

Or:

12000 ÷ (1 + present value of 1 per period for 30 periods at 3%)

$$\text{viz.} \frac{12000}{1 + 19 \cdot 6004413495 \text{ (p. 527)}} = 582 \cdot 512 \text{ say } \underline{582 \cdot 51}$$

EXAMPLE 10. *What is the present value at an effective annual rate of 3% of an annuity of 965·45 payable for 31 years ?*

The present value of 1 per period for 31 periods at 3% is 20·0004284946 (p. 527).

$$965 \cdot 45 \times 20 \cdot 0004284946 = \underline{19309 \cdot 414}$$

EXAMPLE 11. *A loan of 30000 was borrowed at 3% (interest payable yearly) and is repayable by means of a sinking fund at the end of 50 years. The unexpired term is 26 years and assuming the loan cannot be repaid before the expiration of the full term, what is the value of the interest payments and principal at an effective annual rate of $3\frac{1}{2}$% ?*

The present value of the interest payments of 30000 × ·03; viz. 900 for 26 years at $3\frac{1}{2}$% is:

$$16 \cdot 8903522631 \text{ (p. 535)} \times 900 = 15201 \cdot 317.$$

The present value of the principal sum of 30000 to be repaid at the end of 26 years is

$$\cdot 4088376708 \text{ (p. 431)} \times 30000 = 12265 \cdot 130$$

$$15201 \cdot 317 + 12265 \cdot 130 = \underline{27466 \cdot 447}$$

EXAMPLE 12. *A loan of 10000 is to be repaid in 30 years by annual payments into a sinking fund at an effective annual rate of 3%. What is the annual payment ?*

The sinking fund required to repay 1 by periodic contributions over 30 periods at 3% is (p. 319) ·0210192593; the annual payment is therefore 210·193, say 210·20.

EXAMPLE 13. *In the foregoing example what should be the aggregate amount of the fund with accumulations of interest at the end of the 15th year ?*

The accumulation of the annual payments is found by multiplying the periodic contribution by the amount of 1 per period for the number of elapsed periods.

$$210{\cdot}2 \times 18{\cdot}5989138867 \text{ (p. 475)} = 3909{\cdot}4917 \text{ say } \underline{3909{\cdot}50}$$

EXAMPLE 14. *An amount of 500, being the unexpended balance of a loan of 10000 borrowed for a period of 25 years is paid into the sinking fund provided for the repayment of the loan in the 3rd year of the loan period. The annual payment into the sinking fund at 6% is 182·27. What is the appropriate reduction in the annual payment in the 4th and succeeding years ?*

The annuity to repay 1 in 22 years at 6% is ·0830455685

$$500 \times {\cdot}0830456 = 41{\cdot}523, \text{ say } \underline{41{\cdot}52}$$

The annual payment is therefore reduced to 140·75.

Note: The fund will accumulate to 10000 as follows:

182·27 (Sinking fund payment) × 3·1836 (Amount of 1 per period at 6% for 3 periods)	=	580·2747
Add payment into Sinking fund:		500·
Amount in Sinking fund at end of 3rd year:		1080·2747
1080·2747 × 3·603537 (Amount of 1 at 6% in 22 periods)	=	3892·8098
140·75 × 43·39229 (Amount of 1 per period for 22 periods at 6%)	=	6107·4648
Amount in fund at end of 25 years:		10000·2746

The excess of 0·2746 is due to rounding up the sinking fund payments used in the calculation.

EXAMPLE 15. *In the foregoing example the annual payment is to be reduced at the end of the 3rd year as well as the succeeding payments. What is the appropriate reduction ?*

500 ÷ (1 plus present value of 1 per period for 22 periods at 6%)

$$\frac{500}{1 + 12{\cdot}0415817182 \text{ (p. 575)}} = 38{\cdot}3389 \text{ say } \underline{38{\cdot}34}$$

The annual payment is therefore reduced to 143·93.

EXAMPLE 16. *Owing to a fall in the value of investments a loss of 400 has occurred in the securities in which the sinking fund is invested, in the 28th year of the term of a loan of 10000 repayable at the end of 48 years. Annual payments of 95·78 are made into the fund at 3%. What is the appropriate increase in the annual payments in the 29th and succeeding years ?*

The annual payment to include principal and interest at 3% for a period of 20 years, i.e. the remaining period of the loan is ·0672157076 to repay 1 (p. 267).

$400 \times \cdot 067216 = 26 \cdot 886$, say $\underline{26 \cdot 89}$.

The annual payment is therefore increased to 122·67.

EXAMPLE 17. *In the foregoing example the annual payment at the end of the 28th year is to be increased as well as the succeeding payments. What is the increase in the annual payments ?*

400 ÷ (1 plus present value of 1 per period for 20 periods at 3%).

$$\frac{400}{1 + 14 \cdot 8774748605 \text{ (p. 527)}} = 25 \cdot 1929, \text{ say } \underline{25 \cdot 20}.$$

The annual payment is therefore increased from 95·78 to 120·98.

EXAMPLE 18. *A loan of 100000 is repayable by 60 annual payments into a sinking fund at 6%. At the end of the 15th year the interest rate which is the basis of accumulation is to be reduced to 3%. What is the annual payment for the 16th and succeeding years ?*

The sinking fund would amount at the end of the 15th year to:

100000 × ·0018757215 (Sinking fund to repay 1 at 6% per period for 60 periods)
× 23·275969885 (Amount of 1 per period at 6% for 15 periods)
= 187·57215 × 23·2759699 = 4365·9237.

This sum will continue to accumulate, but at 3% and will amount at the end of a further 45 years to:

4365·9237 × 3·7815958417 (Amount of 1 for 45 periods at 3%) = 16510·1587.

It is now required to find the sinking fund at 3% to amount to 100000 − 16510·1587 = 83489·8413 in 45 years:

$83489 \cdot 8413 \times \cdot 0107851757$ (p. 319) $= \underline{900 \cdot 453}$.

EXAMPLE 19. *What weekly payment will accumulate to 500 in 4 years at an effective annual rate of interest of 8% ?*

The equivalent nominal rate compounded weekly, i.e. where $m = 52$ is not given in the tables. An approximation can be made using the rate compounded momently, i.e. where $m = \infty$.

The annual sum is $\dfrac{500 \times \cdot 0769610411 \text{ (p. lv)}}{1 \cdot 36048896 - 1 \text{ (p. 661 Vol. 3)}}$

$= 106 \cdot 745$ and dividing by 52, the weekly payment is $2 \cdot 053$, say $2 \cdot 06$.

(The equivalent nominal rate compounded weekly is ·0770180216 which, substituted for the figure of ·0769610411 applicable to continuous compounding would give an annual sum of 106·824 which, divided by 52 = 2·054.)

EXAMPLE 20. *A loan is made at a nominal annual rate of 12%. If repayments are made monthly on account of the annual repayment what is the effective annual rate ?*

The equivalent effective monthly rate is 1% and the amount of 1 for 12 periods at 1% per period is 1·1268250301 (see Volume 1). The effective annual rate is therefore $(1 \cdot 1268 - 1) \times 100 = 12 \cdot 68\%$. (And see example 28.)

EXAMPLE 21. *A loan of 1000 is made at an effective annual rate of 10% for a period of 5 years, calling for annual repayments of:*

$$1000 \times \cdot 2637974808 \text{ (p. 600, Vol. 3)} = 263 \cdot 80.$$

If the borrower agrees to make repayments monthly, what is the appropriate monthly payment ?

See Explanation of Tables, para. 11.4.

The nominal rate compounded 12 times in a period where the effective rate is 10% is ·956896851 (p. lv). Dividing by 12 and adding 1 gives the amount of 1 for 1 month at an effective annual rate of 10%:

$$\frac{\cdot 956896851}{12} + 1 = 1 \cdot 0079741404.$$

Deducting 1 and dividing by ·1 (interest on 1) gives the monthly payment equivalent to an annual payment of 1:

$$\frac{\cdot 0079741404}{\cdot 10} = \cdot 079741404.$$

The monthly payment is therefore

$$263 \cdot 80 \times \cdot 079741404 = 21 \cdot 04.$$

EXAMPLE 22. *How long will it take for a deposit of money to double at 6% per period ?*

The table of the amount of 1 at 6% shows that 1 will accumulate to 1·898298 at the end of the 11th period and 2·012196 at the end of the 12th period; the answer is between 11 and 12 periods.

EXAMPLE 23. *A deposit of 1200 has accumulated over a period of 10 years to 2160; interest has been compounded half yearly and it is required to find the effective half yearly and the nominal annual rate of interest.*

It is necessary to search the tables of Amount of 1 to find the entry for 20 periods (i.e. 20 half years) which most closely approximates $\frac{2160}{1200} = 1{\cdot}8$.

At $2\frac{15}{16}$% per period the amount of 1 in 20 periods = 1·7843.

At 3% per period the amount of 1 in 20 periods = 1·8061.

The effective half yearly rate is therefore between $2\frac{15}{16}$% and 3% giving a nominal annual rate of between $5\frac{7}{8}$% and 6%. If a closer approximation is required, the method of first difference interpolation can be used:

The entry at 3% is	1·8061112347	**(a)**
The entry at $2\frac{15}{16}$% is	1·7843183026	**(b)**
The difference is	·0217929321	

The difference between the required amount and the entry at 3% is

1·8061112347
1·8
·0061112347

Dividing this by ·0217929321 = ·2804227844.

The interest interval between **(a)** and **(b)** is ·0625 so the proportional difference is:

·0625 × ·2804227844 = ·017526424.

Since 3% is higher than the required rate the rate required is 3 — ·017526424 = 2·98247% effective half yearly, or 5·96494% nominal annual.

EXAMPLE 24. *A deposit of 20 per month with interest compounded monthly has accumulated to 3600 over a period of 10 years. What is the average effective monthly interest rate?*

In this case the tables to search are the Amounts of 1 per period to find the entry for 120 periods which most closely approximates $\frac{3600}{20} = 180.$

At $\frac{11}{16}$% per period the amount of 1 per period in 120 periods	=	185·5197216015 **(a)**
At $\frac{5}{8}$% the amount	=	177·9303419404 **(b)**

The effective monthly rate is between $\frac{11}{16}$% and $\frac{5}{8}$%. First difference interpolation will give a closer approximation:

The difference between **(a)** and **(b)** is	7·5893796611
The amount at **(a)** is	185·5197216015
The required amount is	180·
Difference	5·5197216015

$$\frac{5\cdot5197216015}{7\cdot5893796611} = \cdot7272954903$$

The interest interval $\frac{1}{16}$% = ·0625.

·0625 × ·7272954903 = ·0454559681.

The higher amount **(a)** is produced by interest at $\frac{11}{16}$%	=	·6875
∴ Deduct		·04545
∴ Rate %	=	·64205 compounded monthly

EXAMPLE 25. *To what amount would the following sums paid at the beginning of each year, accumulate at the end of 15 years at 6% effective rate:*

10 for the first 5 years.

20 for the second 5 years.

30 for the third 5 years.

The sums are converted to

10 for 15 years.

10 for 10 years.

10 for 5 years.

Since the payments are made at the beginning of each year, values for one period more than the stated periods must be used, and 1 (unity) deducted from each.

The amount is therefore (page 523)

10 (24·6725280781 + 13·9716426389 + 5·9753185376) = 446·195.

EXAMPLE 26. *What is the value of the sums payable in the preceding example at the beginning of the period of 15 years ?*

Having obtained the previous result, the present value is

$$\cdot 4172650607 \text{ (p. 471)} \times 446\cdot 195 = \underline{186\cdot 182.}$$

To obtain the value independently we can value 30 for 15 years, less 10 for 10 years and less 10 for 5 years. As the payments are made at the beginning of each year, the values for one period less than the stated periods must be used and 1 (unity) added to each.

The present value is therefore (see page 575)

$$[30 \times (1 + 9\cdot 294983927)] - [10 \times (1 + 6\cdot 8016922745)] - [10 \times (1 + 3\cdot 4651056127)] = \underline{186\cdot 182.}$$

EXAMPLE 27. *What is the present value at 6% of payments of 100 per annum to commence in 5 years hence and to end with the final payment 12 years hence ?*

This is a deferred annuity. As the tables are designed to value payments made at the end of each year, this example can be regarded as an annuity payable at the end of each year for 8 years and deferred 4 years. Then, either the present value of 1 per period for 8 periods can be multiplied by the present value of 1 due in 4 periods, or the present value of 1 per period for 4 periods can be deducted from the present value of 1 per period for 12 periods;

$$100 \times 6\cdot 209793811 \text{ (p. 575)} \times \cdot 7920936632 \text{ (p. 471)} = \underline{491\cdot 874.}$$

$$100 \times (8\cdot 3838439404 - 3\cdot 4651056127) \text{ (p. 575)} = \underline{491\cdot 874.}$$

EXAMPLE 28. *A loan of 100 is made subject to monthly repayments to include a flat charge of 12% per annum. Assuming the term of the loan is 2 years what is the true compound interest rate per annum ?*

The total charge will be $12 \times 2 = 24$, and the monthly repayment will be $\frac{124}{24} = 5\cdot 1666$, say $5\cdot 17$. It is required to know at what monthly effective rate this amount would repay 100 in 24 periods. A search of the tables for repayment of a loan by annuity shows:

At $1\frac{3}{4}\%$ the annuity to repay 1 in 24 periods = ·0513856510

At $1\frac{13}{16}\%$,, ,, ,, ,, = ·0517547802

The effective monthly rate is therefore between $1\frac{3}{4}\%$ and $1\frac{13}{16}\%$.

These rates are converted to equivalent annual rates by extracting the amount of 1 for 12 periods at the effective rates:

At $1\frac{3}{4}$% the amount of 1 for 12 periods = 1·2314393149

At $1\frac{13}{16}$% ,, ,, ,, = 1·2405469915

Subtracting 1 and multiplying by 100 gives the annual rate as between 23·144% and 24·055%.

The rate will vary with the period of the loan, notwithstanding the flat annual charge being constant.

Alternatively, the following formula can be used to calculate the true annual rate %:

$$\frac{200\ mc}{p\ (n + 1) + \frac{c}{3}\ (n - 3\ m + 2)}$$

where m = number of payments in year

n = total number of payments

p = amount borrowed

c = total charge or interest

Applying this formula to the above example gives:

$$\frac{200 \times 12 \times 24}{(100 \times 25) + \frac{24}{3}\ (24 - 36 + 2)} = \frac{57600}{2500 + 8\ (-10)}$$

$$= \frac{57600}{2420} = 23{\cdot}8016\%$$

APPENDIX I

Methods used in constructing the original Archer's Tables

In giving the following brief description of the methods employed in the construction of the Tables, it is assumed that the reader possesses an acquaintance with the elements of actuarial science so far as it relates to compound interest and annuities.

Let i = the interest on 1 for one year,

and n = the period in years,

then $(1 + i)^n$ = the amount of 1 in n years,

and $\frac{1}{(1 + i)^n} = v^n$ = the present value of 1 due n years hence.

$$s_{\overline{n|}} = 1 + (1 + i) + (1 + i)^2 + \ldots \ldots + (1 + i)^{n-1} =$$

$\frac{(1 + i)^n - 1}{i}$ = the amount of an annuity of 1 in n years,

$a_{\overline{n|}} = v + v^2 + v^3 + \ldots \ldots + v^n = \frac{1 - v^n}{i}$ = the present value of an annuity of 1 for n years,

$\frac{1}{s_{\overline{n|}}}$ = the annuity which will amount to 1 in n years,

and $\frac{1}{a_{\overline{n|}}}$ = the annuity for n years which 1 will purchase or the annuity required to repay a loan of 1 with interest in n years.

Compound interest is assumed, and all payments are taken to be due at the end of the year.

It may be stated briefly that the values of $(1 + i)^n$ were first computed and $s_{\overline{n}|}$ obtained from these by summation. The values of v^n were next calculated, and $a_{\overline{n}|}$ formed by summation. The values of $\frac{1}{s_{\overline{n}|}}$ and $\frac{1}{a_{\overline{n}|}}$ were computed, with the aid of the arithmometer, from the corresponding values of $s_{\overline{n}|}$ and $a_{\overline{n}|}$ by simple division.

While there is little or nothing original in the methods indicated above, a description of the details of the work may prove interesting.

A preparatory table of the values of $(1 + i)^n$ and $s_{\overline{n}|}$ for intervals of ten years was first constructed, mainly by means of the arithmometer. The following are the actual figures obtained in computing these functions in the case where $i = \cdot 0425$ ($4\frac{1}{4}$ per cent.), which rate will be taken to illustrate the various processes throughout:—

n	$(1 + i)^n$	$s_{\overline{n}|}$
10	1·516214468055965	12·1462227777874
20	2·298906313142233	30·5625014856996
30	3·485635012691450	58·4855297103871
40	5·284970236605214	100·8228290965933
50	8·013148335985982	165·0152549643760

The initial value, $(1 + i)^{10}$, was obtained by commencing with $(1 + i)$ and multiplying successively by the same value $(1 + i)$ in the manner shown hereafter,* the figures, however, for this particular purpose being carried to sixteen places of decimals. The result was then checked by squaring the value of $(1 + i)^5$ on the arithmometer. The

---

**Vide* p. xliv

value of $(1 + i)^{10}$ was then reduced to fifteen places of decimals so as to retain sixteen figures in all. The arithmometer was then again utilized for computing the remaining values $(1 + i)^{20}$, $(1 + i)^{30}$ . . . $(1 + i)^{50}$. Although the fixed plate of the machine only carried ten figures, it could be used to multiply one set of sixteen figures by another set of equal dimensions by splitting each set into two sections of ten and six figures. Let the two sections of the multiplicand be represented by a and b respectively, and the two sections of the multiplier by c and d. Then remembering that $(a + b)(c + d) = ac + ad + bc + bd$, it is only necessary to perform the operations indicated by the first three terms of the product, the fourth term having no significant value, thus: place a upon the fixed plate and multiply in turn by c and d, taking down each result; then place b on the fixed plate and multiply by c, again taking down the product, and finally add together the three results, having taken care to assign each to its proper position. Similarly, if it were required to square a quantity containing sixteen figures, the first two terms of the latter part of the equation $(a + b)^2 = a^2 + 2\,ab + b^2$ would suggest the necessary operations. For the purposes of the above Table only sixteen figures were required to be retained (in fact, it was unnecessary to work to such a degree of accuracy, but this involved very little additional labour), and these were obtained with great facility in the following manner:—

Firstly, $(1 + i)^{20}$ was obtained by squaring $(1 + i)^{10}$.

	a	b	
$(1 + i)^{10} =$	1·516214468	055965	
	2·298906312	972523	$= a^2$
		84855	$= ab$
		84855	$= ab$
		0	$= b^2$
$(1 + i)^{20} =$	2·298906313	142233	$= (a + b)^2$.

The value of $(1+i)^{30}$ was then obtained by multiplying $(1+i)^{20}$ by $(1+i)^{10}$.

	a	b	
$(1+i)^{20} =$	2·298906313	142233	
	c	d	
$(1+i)^{10} =$	1·516214468	055965	
	3·485635012	347136	$= ac$
		128658	$= ad$
		215656	$= bc$
		0	$= bd$
$(1+i)^{30} =$	3·485635012	691450	$= (a+b)(c+d)$.

The values of $(1+i)^{40}$ and $(1+i)^{50}$ were calculated in a similar way by multiplying successively by $(1+i)^{10}$.

The values of $s_{\overline{n}|}$ were then easily obtainable from the corresponding values of $(1+i)^n$ by deducting unity from the latter and dividing the result by i.

Thus $s_{\overline{10}|} = \dfrac{(1+i)^{10}-1}{i} = \dfrac{\cdot 516214468055965}{\cdot 0425} =$

$\cdot 516214468055965 \times \dfrac{400}{17} = \dfrac{206\cdot 4857872223860}{17} = 12\cdot 1462227777874$

The following preparatory Table of the values of v^n and $a_{\overline{n}|}$ was next computed:—

n	v^n	$a_{\overline{n}\vert}$
50	·1247948943499689	20·59306130941250
40	·1892158243529384	19·07727472110733
30	·2868917704690615	16·77901716543385
20	·4349894531513820	13·29436580820278
10	·6595373023198778	8·01088700423817

The value of v^{50} was first obtained by dividing unity by $(1 + i)^{50}$. Since $\frac{1}{a+b} = \frac{1}{a} - \frac{b}{a^2} + \frac{b^2}{a^3} - \ldots$ it is evident that by dividing the value of $(1 + i)^{50}$ into two sections, a and b, of ten and six figures respectively, the operation can be readily performed on the arithmometer, the first two terms only of the latter part of the equation having a significant value,

$$\text{Thus } (1+i)^{50} = \overset{a}{8{\cdot}013148335}\quad \overset{b}{985982}$$

$$\frac{1}{a} = \frac{1}{8{\cdot}013148335} = {\cdot}1247948943653244$$

$$\frac{b}{a^2} = {\cdot}000000000985982 \times ({\cdot}12479489)^2 = 153555$$

$$\therefore \frac{1}{a} - \frac{b}{a^2} = \frac{1}{(1+i)^{50}} = v^{50} = {\cdot}1247948943499689$$

The result was checked by multiplying the quotient into the divisor to obtain unity. The values of v^{40}, v^{30}, ... v^0 were then in turn deduced by multiplying v^{50} and the resultant values successively by $(1 + i)^{10}$, and the final result v^0 proving $= 1$ was evidence of the accuracy of the whole of the work. The values of $a_{\overline{n}|}$ were next prepared from the corresponding values of v^n by deducting the latter from unity and dividing by i.

$$\text{Thus } a_{\overline{50}|} = \frac{1 - v^{50}}{i} = \frac{{\cdot}875205105650031\,1}{{\cdot}0425} =$$

$${\cdot}875205105650031\,1 \times \frac{400}{17} = \frac{350{\cdot}08204226001244}{17}$$

$$= 20{\cdot}59306130941250.$$

Having completed the preparatory Tables as above and so obtained the values of the functions $(1 + i)^n$, $s_{\overline{n}|}$, v^n, and $a_{\overline{n}|}$ for intervals of ten years, the calculation of the consecutive values of these functions from $n = 1$ to $n = 50$ was then entered upon with confidence, as these could be periodically checked and corrected (if necessary) so as to prevent a serious accumulation of errors. The ultimate values of $(1 + i)^n$ were required to be correct to ten places of decimals, and it was considered necessary therefore to work to two places beyond, viz., to twelve places. The following shows the *modus operandi*:—

n	$(1 + i)^n$
1	1·0425 41700 260625
2	1·08680625 434722500 2717015625
3	1·132995515625 45319820625 2832488789
4	1·181147825039 47245913001 2952869563
5	1·231346607603
*	*

n	$(1 + i)^n$	$s_{\overline{n}\rceil}$	$\frac{1}{s_{\overline{n}\rceil}}$
1	1·0425	1·	1·
2	1·08680625	2·0425	·48959608
3	1·1329955156	3·12930625	·31955965
4	1·1811478250	4·2623017656	·23461502
5	1·2313466076	5·4434495906	·18370704
*	*	*	*

The values of $(1 + i)^n$ were computed by the contracted method of multiplication as shown above and the results, after being reduced to ten places of decimals, were entered in the proper column of a Table of the above form so that the corresponding column of $s_{\overline{n}|}$ could be readily formed by summation according to the formula $s_{\overline{n}|} = 1 + (1 + i) + (1 + i)^2 + \ldots\ldots + (1 + i)^{n-1}$. The values of $\frac{1}{s_{\overline{n}|}}$ were subsequently calculated on the arithmometer by dividing unity by the successive values of $s_{\overline{n}|}$.

The following specimens of the actual work illustrate the methods of obtaining the values of v^n and $a_{\overline{n}|}$:—

n	v^n
50	·124794894350
	4991795774
	311987236
49	·130098677360
	5203947094
	325246693
48	·135627871147
	5425114846
	339069678
47	·141392055671
	5655682227
	353480139
46	·147401218037
*	*

n	v^n	$a_{\overline{n}|}$	$\frac{1}{a_{\overline{n}|}}$
1	·9592326139	·9592326139	1·0425
2	·9201272076	1·8793598215	·53209608
3	·8826160265	2·7619758480	·36205965
4	·8466340781	3·6086099261	·27711502
5	·8121190198	4·4207289459	·22620704
*	*	*	*

The values of v^n were calculated to twelve places of decimals by the contracted method of multiplication, and the results, after being cut down to ten places, were entered in the proper column of a Table as shown above, so that the corresponding values of $a_{\overline{n}|}$ could be obtained by summation according to the formula $a_{\overline{n}|} = v + v^2 + v^3 + \ldots\ldots + v^n$. The values of $\frac{1}{a_{\overline{n}|}}$ were obtained with the help of the arithmometer by simple division.

The functions of $(1 + i)^n$, $s_{\overline{n}|}$, v^n and $a_{\overline{n}|}$ having been computed by a continuous method, and the results having agreed at intervals with the values in the preparatory Tables, all the preceding values might be confidently assumed to be correct. The values of $\frac{1}{s_{\overline{n}|}}$ and $\frac{1}{a_{\overline{n}|}}$ were however, in each case calculated independently, but a final and valuable check on the values of these two functions, and at the same time upon the whole of the work, was applied by adding i to $\frac{1}{s_{\overline{n}|}}$ throughout to prove the correctness of $\frac{1}{a_{\overline{n}|}}$. The last operation thus formed a link which not only confirmed the values of $\frac{1}{s_{\overline{n}|}}$ and $\frac{1}{a_{\overline{n}|}}$, but gave additional security to the other values with which they were brought into relationship as illustrated by the following diagram:—

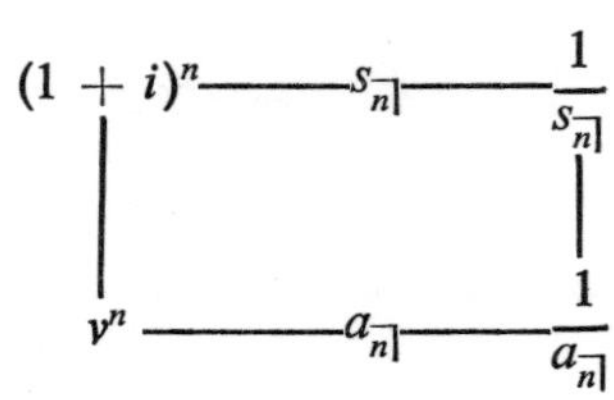

APPENDIX 2

Methods of calculating and extending the tables

1.1 The relationship of the values of the tabulated functions is shown on the title page for each function in terms of $(1 + i)^n$, i.e. the amount of 1, and can be illustrated by arranging the six functions diagrammatically, in the form of a six spoked wheel.

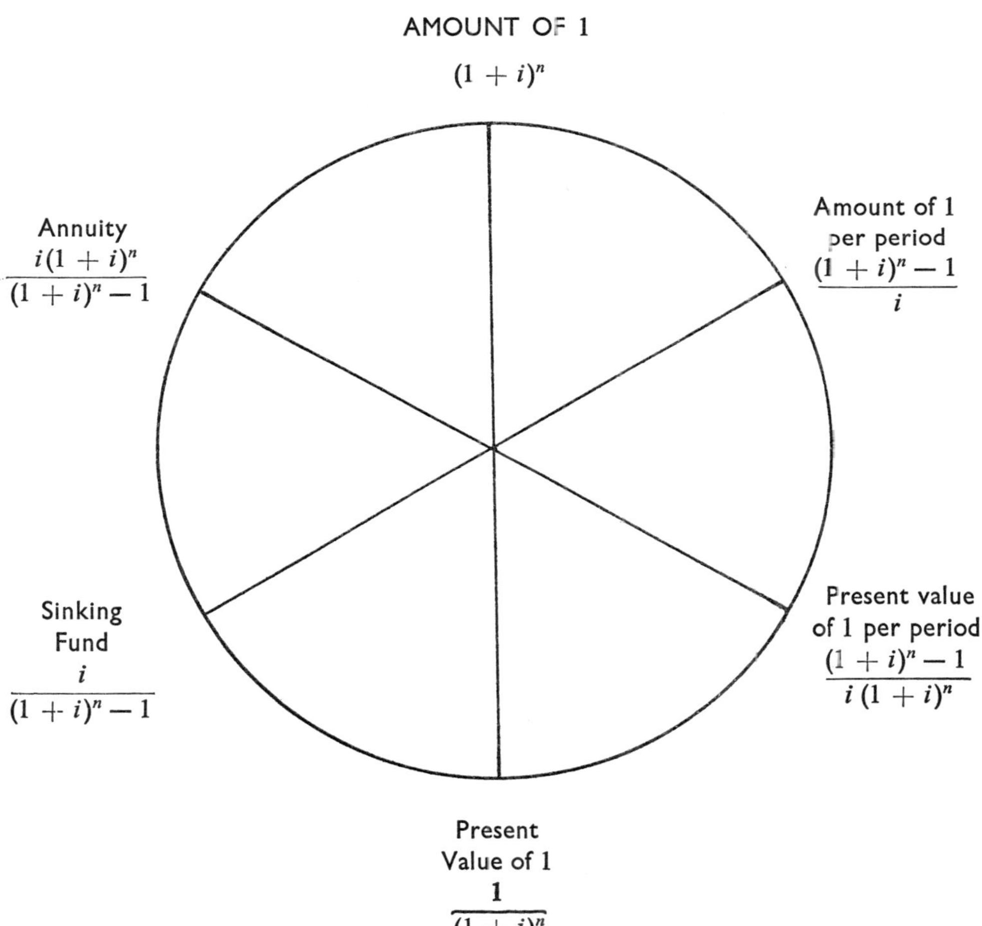

1.2 In this diagram each function is the product of the functions on either side, and each is the reciprocal of the function opposite.

2.1 If a value is required for a greater number of periods than the tabulated periods, this can be readily calculated preferably by doubling the term of an appropriate tabulated term (see para. 2.4). The functions to be used for this purpose are amount of 1, amount of 1 per period and present value of 1 per period; these three are chosen because they contain a greater number of significant figures than the other three, the values of which can be obtained by taking the appropriate reciprocal.

2.2 The extension of a term is accomplished in the following manner:

(a) *Amount of 1*

By direct multiplication of the values tabulated for the two terms which, when added give the required term. Example:

What is the amount of 1 for 240 periods at an effective rate of 3% per period ?

The tabulated value for 180 periods (page 371) is 204·5033595526 and for 60 periods 5·891603104

$$204{\cdot}5033595526 \times 5{\cdot}891603104 = \underline{\underline{1204{\cdot}8526279279}}$$

Alternatively, the value for 120 periods can be squared:

$$34{\cdot}7109871356^2 = \underline{\underline{1204{\cdot}8526279279}}$$

(b) *Amount of 1 per Period*

By separating the required term into two terms for which values are tabulated, extending the first term by multiplying this by the amount of 1 for the number of periods in the second term, and adding the result to the value for the second term. Example:

What is the amount of 1 per period for 185 periods at an effective rate of 3% per period ?

The tabulated value for 180 periods (page 475) is 6783·44531842.

The amount of 1 for 5 periods (page 371) is 1·1592740743.

6783·44531842 × 1·1592740743	=	7863·872292076
Amount of 1 per period for 5 periods	=	5·309135810
Amount of 1 per period for 185 periods :		7869·181427886

(c) *Present value of 1 per Period*

By separating the required term into two terms for which values are tabulated. The second term is extended by multiplying by the present value of 1 for the number of periods in the first term; adding the result to the value for the first term will give the required value. Example:

What is the present value of 1 per period for 195 periods at 3% per period ?

The tabulated values are (page 527)

for 180 periods	33·1703368261
for 15 periods	11·9379350868

and the present value of 1 for 180 periods (page 423) is ·0048898952

11·9379350868 × ·0048898952 =	·0583752517
Add present value of 1 per period for 180 periods	33·1703368261
Present value of 1 per period for 195 periods:	33·2287120778

2.3 The method of obtaining the values for extended periods of the present value of 1, sinking fund to provide 1 and annuity to repay 1 will be apparent by reference to the diagram in para. 1.1. For example if the annuity is required for 195 periods at 3% per period it will be necessary first to calculate the present value of 1 per period for 195 periods as in the example at para. 2.2 (c) and divide this into 1:

$$\frac{1}{33{\cdot}2287120778} = {\cdot}0300944556.$$

2.4 Para. 2.2 gives the rules to be followed when extending a term, whether or not the required term can be obtained by doubling a tabulated term. If a tabulated term can be doubled the required value can be obtained more directly by the following procedures:

(a) *Amount of 1*
By squaring the value of the term to be doubled.

(b) *Amount of 1 per period*
By multiplying the value of the term to be doubled by the [amount of 1 for the same term plus 1 (unity)].

(c) *Present value of 1 per period*
By multiplying the value of the term to be doubled by the [present value of 1 for the same term plus 1 (unity)].

(d) *Present value of 1*
By squaring the value of the term to be doubled.

(e) *Sinking Fund*
By dividing the value of the term to be doubled by the [amount of 1 for the same term plus 1 (unity)].

(f) *Annuity*
By dividing the value of the term to be doubled by the [present value of 1 for the same term plus 1 (unity)].
If necessary a doubled term can of course be re-doubled.

3.1 For the calculation of values at rates of interest which are not tabulated, Appendix 1 describes Archer's methods of constructing the original tables, firstly by computation of successive powers of $1 + i$, using values of $(1 + i)^n$ at intervals of $n = 10$ as a check. When calculating individual values for any of the functions a similar method must be

I

used, and the values of any of the other functions may be deduced directly from the value of $(1+i)^n$ thus:

Where $1 =$ Unity

$i =$ Interest on I for I period

$n =$ Number of periods

Annuity: $i \div \left[1 - \frac{1}{(1+i)^n}\right]$

Deduct from I the reciprocal of $(1+i)^n$ and divide the result into i.

OR $i + \left[\frac{i}{(1+i)^n - 1}\right]$

Deduct I from $(1+i)^n$, divide result into i (giving Sinking Fund) and add i.

Sinking Fund: $\frac{i}{(1+i)^n - 1}$

Deduct I from $(1+i)^n$ and divide result into i

Present Value of I: $\frac{1}{(1+i)^n}$

Reciprocal of $(1+i)^n$

Amount of I per Period: $\frac{(1+i)^n - 1}{i}$

Deduct I from $(1+i)^n$ and divide result by i

Present Value of I per Period: $\left[1 - \frac{1}{(1+i)^n}\right] \div i$

Deduct from I the reciprocal of $(1+i)^n$ and divide the result by i

3.2 The use of the formulæ and the method of computing values of $(1+i)^n$ are illustrated by the following example.

It is required to calculate the amount of the half yearly payment by annuity to repay a loan over 60 years at a nominal annual rate of $4\frac{3}{16}$%.

The effective rate is therefore $2\frac{3}{32}$% and the term is 120 periods of half years, therefore

$$i = \cdot 0209375$$

$$1 + i = 1 \cdot 0209375$$

$$n = 120$$

It is assumed that the result is required to be expressed correct to ten decimal places, and that the reader has access to a calculating machine capable of multiplying 10 × 10 digits and showing the product to at least 16 digits, this being required to ensure accuracy.

The first step is to calculate successive values of $(1+i)^n$ to the power of $n = 5$ by multiplying the successive values by the constant $1+i$. After calculating $(1+i)^2$ the product exceeds 10 digits and must be split into two sets each of which is multiplied by the constant and the results added; the first set should contain the maximum digits accepted by the machine, in this example 10. The calculation then proceeds as indicated.

n	First set	Second set	Operation
1	1·0209375		
2	1·042313378	906250	(1·0209375^2)
	1·064136814	351875	(1·042313378 × 1·0209375)
		925224	(906250 × 1·0209375)
	1	277099	Addition
3	1·064136815		
	1·086417179	564063	(1·064136815 × 1·0209375)
		282901	(277099 × 1·0209375)
	·	846964	Addition
4	1·086417179		
	1·109164038	685312	(1·086417179 × 1·0209375)
		864697	(846964 × 1·0209375)
	1	550009	Addition
5	1·109164039		

The shortest way to $n = 120$ is by squaring $(1 + i)^5$ to obtain $(1 + i)^{10}$, squaring again to obtain $(1 + i)^{20}$, multiplying $(1 + i)^{20}$ by $(1 + i)^{10}$ to obtain $(1 + i)^{30}$, thence by squaring to $(1 + i)^{60}$ and finally $(1 + i)^{120}$.

n	First set	Second set	Operation
	1·230244865	410794	(1·109164039^2)
		610050	(550009 × 1·109164039)
		610050	,, ,,
	1	630894	Addition
10	1·230244866		
	1·513502430	319358	(1·230244866^2)
		776154	(630894 × 1·230244866)
		776154	,, ,,
	1	871666	Addition
20	1·513502431		
	1·861978595	416269	(1·513502431 × 1·230244866)
	1	072363	(1·230244866 × 871666)
		954860	(1·513502431 × 630894)
	1	443492	Addition
30	1·861978597		
	3·466964295	686088	(1·861978597^2)
		825773	(443492 × 1·861978597)
		825773	,, ,,
	2	337634	Addition
60	3·466964297		
	12·019841436	672704	(3·466964297^2)
	1	170565	(337634 × 3·466964297)
	1	170565	,, ,,
	1	013834	Addition
120	12·019841439		

The amount of 1 at $2\frac{3}{32}\%$ for 120 periods, correct to 10 decimal places is 12·0198414390. The other functions are derived as follows:

Annuity:

(i) $\frac{1}{12 \cdot 019841439} = \cdot 083195773$

(ii) $1 - \cdot 083195773 = \cdot 916804227$

(iii) $\frac{\cdot 0209375}{\cdot 916804227} = \cdot 0228374820$

Sinking Fund:

(i) $12 \cdot 019841439 - 1 = 11 \cdot 019841439$

(ii) $\frac{\cdot 0209375}{11 \cdot 019841439} = \cdot 0018999820$

Present value of 1:

$\frac{1}{12 \cdot 019841439} = \cdot 0831957730$

Amount of 1 per period:

(i) $12 \cdot 019841439 - 1 = 11 \cdot 019841439$

(ii) $\frac{11 \cdot 019841439}{\cdot 0209375} = 526 \cdot 3207851463$

Present value of 1 per period:

(i) $\frac{1}{12 \cdot 019841439} = \cdot 083195773$

(ii) $1 - \cdot 083195773 = \cdot 916804227$

(iii) $\frac{\cdot 916804227}{\cdot 0209375} = 43 \cdot 7876645731$

All the values given relate to an effective rate of $2\frac{3}{32}\%$ for a term of 120 periods.

3.3 Although powerful desk computers are available which will compute any required value almost instantly, the example illustrates how the calculations can be done with relatively simple machines; an understanding of the method of calculating the values, and of the relationship between them will assist in the manipulation of values for the more complicated calculations involving compound interest.

NOMINAL RATES OF INTEREST convertible m times per period, $i^{(m)}$, equivalent to effective periodical rates of interest, i.

$$i^{(m)} = m\ [(1+i)^{1/m} - 1]$$

(*See:* Explanation of Tables para. 11.2.)

Effective annual (or other periodical) rates of interest per cent.	Equivalent nominal rates of interest convertible m times a year (or other period), $i^{(m)}$			
	$m = 2$	$m = 4$	$m = 12$	$m = \infty$
0·5000	·004 993 7656	·004 990 6523	·004 988 5781	·004 987 5415
0·5625	·005 617 1120	·005 613 1735	·005 610 5500	·005 609 2388
0·6250	·006 240 2648	·006 235 4047	·006 232 1675	·006 230 5498
0·6875	·006 863 2240	·006 857 3461	·006 853 4313	·006 851 4749
0·7500	·007 485 9900	·007 478 9981	·007 474 3416	·007 472 0148
0·8125	·008 108 5628	·008 100 3608	·008 094 8990	·008 092 1699
0·8750	·008 730 9427	·008 721 4347	·008 715 1038	·008 711 9406
0·9375	·009 353 1297	·009 342 2201	·009 334 9564	·009 331 3274
1·0000	·009 975 1242	·009 962 7173	·009 954 4574	·009 950 3309
1·0625	·010 596 9263	·010 582 9265	·010 573 6070	·010 568 9513
1·1250	·011 218 5361	·011 202 8481	·011 192 4057	·011 187 1894
1·1875	·011 839 9539	·011 822 4825	·011 810 8540	·011 805 0454
1·2500	·012 461 1797	·012 441 8299	·012 428 9522	·012 422 5200
1·3125	·013 082 2139	·013 060 8906	·013 046 7007	·013 039 6135
1·3750	·013 703 0566	·013 679 6649	·013 664 1000	·013 656 3264
1·4375	·014 323 7078	·014 298 1532	·014 281 1505	·014 272 6593
1·5000	·014 944 1680	·014 916 3558	·014 897 8526	·014 888 6125
1·5625	·015 564 4371	·015 534 2729	·015 514 2067	·015 504 1865
1·6250	·016 184 5154	·016 151 9049	·016 130 2132	·016 119 3819
1·6875	·016 804 4030	·016 769 2520	·016 745 8725	·016 734 1990
1·7500	·017 424 1002	·017 386 3147	·017 361 1850	·017 348 6383
1·8125	·018 043 6071	·018 003 0931	·017 976 1512	·017 962 7004
1·8750	·018 662 9238	·018 619 5377	·018 590 7714	·018 576 3856
1·9375	·019 282 0506	·019 235 7986	·019 205 0461	·019 189 6944
2·0000	·019 900 9877	·019 851 7263	·019 818 9756	·019 802 6273
2·0625	·020 519 7351	·020 467 3710	·020 432 5604	·020 415 1847
2·1250	·021 138 2931	·021 082 7329	·021 045 8009	·021 027 3672
2·1875	·021 756 6619	·021 697 8125	·021 658 6974	·021 639 1751
2·2500	·022 374 8416	·022 312 6100	·022 271 2504	·022 250 6089
2·3125	·022 992 8324	·022 927 1258	·022 883 4603	·022 861 6691
2·3750	·023 610 6345	·023 541 3600	·023 495 3275	·023 472 3562
2·4375	·024 228 2480	·024 155 3131	·024 106 8523	·024 082 6705
2·5000	·024 845 6731	·024 768 9853	·024 718 0352	·024 692 6126
2·5625	·025 462 9101	·025 382 3769	·025 328 8766	·025 302 1829
2·6250	·026 079 9589	·025 995 4883	·025 939 3769	·025 911 3818
2·6875	·026 696 8200	·026 608 3196	·026 549 5365	·026 520 2098
2·7500	·027 313 4933	·027 220 8713	·027 159 3557	·027 128 6674
2·8125	·027 929 9791	·027 833 1436	·027 768 8350	·027 736 7550
2·8750	·028 546 2775	·028 445 1368	·028 377 9748	·028 344 4730
2·9375	·029 162 3888	·029 056 8512	·028 986 7754	·028 951 8219
3·0000	·029 778 3130	·029 668 2871	·029 595 2373	·029 558 8022
3·0625	·030 394 0504	·030 279 4448	·030 203 3608	·030 165 4143
3·1250	·031 009 6012	·030 890 3246	·030 811 1464	·030 771 6587
3·1875	·031 624 9654	·031 500 9268	·031 418 5944	·031 377 5357
3·2500	·032 240 1433	·032 111 2517	·032 025 7052	·031 983 0459
3·3125	·032 855 1350	·032 721 2996	·032 632 4793	·032 588 1896
3·3750	·033 469 9408	·033 331 0707	·033 238 9169	·033 192 9674
3·4375	·034 084 5607	·033 940 5654	·033 845 0186	·033 797 3796
3·5000	·034 698 9949	·034 549 7840	·034 450 7846	·034 401 4267
3·5625	·035 313 2437	·035 158 7267	·035 056 2154	·035 005 1092
3·6250	·035 927 3071	·035 767 3938	·035 661 3114	·035 608 4275
3·6875	·036 541 1854	·036 375 7857	·036 266 0730	·036 211 3820
3·7500	·037 154 8787	·036 983 9026	·036 870 5004	·036 813 9731
3·8125	·037 768 3872	·037 591 7448	·037 474 5942	·037 416 2014
3·8750	·038 381 7111	·038 199 3126	·038 078 3547	·038 018 0672
3·9375	·038 994 8504	·038 806 6063	·038 681 7823	·038 619 5710

Effective annual (or other periodical) rates of interest per cent.	Equivalent nominal rates of interest convertible *m* times a year (or other period), $i^{(m)}$			
	$m = 2$	$m = 4$	$m = 12$	$m = \infty$
4·0000	·039 607 8054	·039 413 6262	·039 284 8774	·039 220 7132
4·0625	·040 220 5763	·040 020 3725	·039 887 6403	·039 821 4942
4·1250	·040 833 1632	·040 626 8456	·040 490 0715	·040 421 9145
4·1875	·041 445 5663	·041 233 0458	·041 092 1713	·041 021 9745
4·2500	·042 057 7857	·041 838 9732	·041 693 9400	·041 621 6747
4·3125	·042 669 8216	·042 444 6283	·042 295 3782	·042 221 0154
4·3750	·043 281 6742	·043 050 0112	·042 896 4861	·042 819 9972
4·4375	·043 893 3436	·043 655 1224	·043 497 2642	·043 418 6204
4·5000	·044 504 8300	·044 259 9620	·044 097 7128	·044 016 8854
4·5625	·045 116 1336	·044 864 5304	·044 697 8323	·044 614 7928
4·6250	·045 727 2545	·045 468 8278	·045 297 6231	·045 212 3428
4·6875	·046 338 1930	·046 072 8545	·045 897 0855	·045 809 5360
4·7500	·046 948 9490	·046 676 6108	·046 496 2199	·046 406 3728
4·8125	·047 559 5229	·047 280 0970	·047 095 0267	·047 002 8536
4·8750	·048 169 9148	·047 883 3134	·047 693 5064	·047 598 9788
4·9375	·048 780 1249	·048 486 2602	·048 291 6591	·048 194 7488
5·0000	·049 390 1532	·049 088 9377	·048 889 4854	·048 790 1642
5·0625	·050 000 0000	·049 691 3463	·049 486 9856	·049 385 2252
5·1250	·050 609 6654	·050 293 4861	·050 084 1600	·049 979 9323
5·1875	·051 219 1497	·050 895 3575	·050 681 0091	·050 574 2860
5·2500	·051 828 4529	·051 496 9607	·051 277 5332	·051 168 2866
5·3125	·052 437 5752	·052 098 2961	·051 873 7327	·051 761 9346
5·3750	·053 046 5168	·052 699 3639	·052 469 6079	·052 355 2303
5·4375	·053 655 2778	·053 300 1644	·053 065 1592	·052 948 1743
5·5000	·054 263 8584	·053 900 6978	·053 660 3870	·053 540 7669
5·5625	·054 872 2588	·054 500 9644	·054 255 2917	·054 133 0086
5·6250	·055 480 4791	·055 100 9646	·054 849 8735	·054 724 8997
5·6875	·056 088 5195	·055 700 6985	·055 444 1330	·055 316 4407
5·7500	·056 696 3801	·056 300 1665	·056 038 0704	·055 907 6319
5·8125	·057 304 0611	·056 899 3689	·056 631 6861	·056 498 4739
5·8750	·057 911 5627	·057 498 3058	·057 224 9805	·057 088 9670
5·9375	·058 518 8850	·058 096 9777	·057 817 9539	·057 679 1116
6·0000	·059 126 0282	·058 695 3847	·058 410 6068	·058 268 9081
6·0625	·059 732 9924	·059 293 5271	·059 002 9394	·058 858 3570
6·1250	·060 339 7778	·059 891 4053	·059 594 9521	·059 447 4586
6·1875	·060 946 3846	·060 489 0194	·060 186 6453	·060 036 2134
6·2500	·061 552 8128	·061 086 3697	·060 778 0194	·060 624 6218
6·3125	·062 159 0627	·061 683 4566	·061 369 0747	·061 212 6842
6·3750	·062 765 1345	·062 280 2803	·061 959 8115	·061 800 4009
6·4375	·063 371 0282	·062 876 8411	·062 550 2303	·062 387 7724
6·5000	·063 976 7441	·063 473 1391	·063 140 3313	·062 974 7992
6·5625	·064 582 2822	·064 069 1748	·063 730 1150	·063 561 4815
6·6250	·065 187 6428	·064 664 9484	·064 319 5817	·064 147 8198
6·6875	·065 792 8260	·065 260 4601	·064 908 7317	·064 733 8146
6·7500	·066 397 8320	·065 855 7102	·065 497 5655	·065 319 4661
6·8125	·067 002 6609	·066 450 6989	·066 086 0833	·065 904 7749
6·8750	·067 607 3128	·067 045 4267	·066 674 2855	·066 489 7413
6·9375	·068 211 7880	·067 639 8936	·067 262 1725	·067 074 3657
7·0000	·068 816 0866	·068 234 1000	·067 849 7446	·067 658 6485
7·0625	·069 420 2087	·068 828 0462	·068 437 0022	·068 242 5901
7·1250	·070 024 1544	·069 421 7323	·069 023 9457	·068 826 1909
7·1875	·070 627 9241	·070 015 1588	·069 610 5753	·069 409 4514
7·2500	·071 231 5177	·070 608 3258	·070 196 8914	·069 992 3718
7·3125	·071 834 9355	·071 201 2336	·070 782 8945	·070 574 9527
7·3750	·072 438 1776	·071 793 8824	·071 368 5847	·071 157 1943
7·4375	·073 041 2442	·072 386 2726	·071 953 9625	·071 739 0972
7·5000	·073 644 1353	·072 978 4044	·072 539 0283	·072 320 6616
7·5625	·074 246 8513	·073 570 2780	·073 123 7823	·072 901 8880
7·6250	·074 849 3921	·074 161 8938	·073 708 2250	·073 482 7768
7·6875	·075 451 7581	·074 753 2520	·074 292 3566	·074 063 3283
7·7500	·076 053 9492	·075 344 3528	·074 876 1775	·074 643 5430
7·8125	·076 655 9657	·075 935 1965	·075 459 6881	·075 223 4212
7·8750	·077 257 8078	·076 525 7833	·076 042 8887	·075 802 9634
7·9375	·077 859 4755	·077 116 1136	·076 625 7797	·076 382 1699

Effective annual (or other periodical) rates of interest per cent.	Equivalent nominal rates of interest convertible m times a year (or other period), $i^{(m)}$			
	$m = 2$	$m = 4$	$m = 12$	$m = \infty$
8·0000	·078 460 9691	·077 706 1876	·077 208 3613	·076 961 0411
8·0625	·079 062 2886	·078 296 0056	·077 790 6340	·077 539 5775
8·1250	·079 663 4343	·078 885 5677	·078 372 5980	·078 117 7793
8·1875	·080 264 4063	·079 474 8743	·078 954 2538	·078 695 6469
8·2500	·080 865 2047	·080 063 9256	·079 535 6017	·079 273 1809
8·3125	·081 465 8296	·080 652 7220	·080 116 6419	·079 850 3815
8·3750	·082 066 2814	·081 241 2635	·080 697 3749	·080 427 2491
8·4375	·082 666 5600	·081 829 5505	·081 277 8009	·081 003 7842
8·5000	·083 266 6656	·082 417 5833	·081 857 9204	·081 579 9870
8·5625	·083 866 5984	·083 005 3621	·082 437 7336	·082 155 8580
8·6250	·084 466 3586	·083 592 8872	·083 017 2410	·082 731 3976
8·6875	·085 065 9462	·084 180 1588	·083 596 4427	·083 306 6061
8·7500	·085 665 3615	·084 767 1772	·084 175 3392	·083 881 4840
8·8125	·086 264 6045	·085 353 9426	·084 753 9309	·084 456 0315
8·8750	·086 863 6755	·085 940 4552	·085 332 2180	·085 030 2492
8·9375	·087 462 5745	·086 526 7155	·085 910 2008	·085 604 1373
9·0000	·088 061 3018	·087 112 7235	·086 487 8798	·086 177 6962
9·0625	·088 659 8574	·087 698 4795	·087 065 2552	·086 750 9264
9·1250	·089 258 2416	·088 283 9839	·087 642 3274	·087 323 8282
9·1875	·089 856 4544	·088 869 2367	·088 219 0967	·087 896 4019
9·2500	·090 454 4960	·089 454 2384	·088 795 5634	·088 468 6480
9·3125	·091 052 3666	·090 038 9892	·089 371 7280	·089 040 5668
9·3750	·091 650 0663	·090 623 4892	·089 947 5906	·089 612 1587
9·4375	·092 247 5953	·091 207 7388	·090 523 1517	·090 183 4241
9·5000	·092 844 9536	·091 791 7382	·091 098 4115	·090 754 3633
9·5625	·093 442 1415	·092 375 4877	·091 673 3704	·091 324 9767
9·6250	·094 039 1591	·092 958 9875	·092 248 0288	·091 895 2647
9·6875	·094 636 0066	·093 542 2378	·092 822 3869	·092 465 2277
9·7500	·095 232 6840	·094 125 2389	·093 396 4451	·093 034 8660
9·8125	·095 829 1915	·094 707 9911	·093 970 2036	·093 604 1800
9·8750	·096 425 5293	·095 290 4945	·094 543 6630	·094 173 1700
9·9375	·097 021 6976	·095 872 7495	·095 116 8234	·094 741 8365
10·0000	·097 617 6963	·096 454 7563	·095 689 6851	·095 310 1798
10·0625	·098 213 5258	·097 036 5152	·096 262 2486	·095 878 2003
10·1250	·098 809 1862	·097 618 0263	·096 834 5142	·096 445 8983
10·1875	·099 404 6775	·098 199 2900	·097 406 4821	·097 013 2742
10·2500	·100 000 0000	·098 780 3064	·097 978 1526	·097 580 3283
10·3125	·100 595 1538	·099 361 0758	·098 549 5262	·098 147 0611
10·3750	·101 190 1389	·099 941 5986	·099 120 6031	·098 713 4729
10·4375	·101 784 9557	·100 521 8748	·099 691 3837	·099 279 5641
10·5000	·102 379 6042	·101 101 9048	·100 261 8682	·099 845 3350
10·5625	·102 974 0845	·101 681 6888	·100 832 0570	·100 410 7859
10·6250	·103 568 3968	·102 261 2270	·101 401 9505	·100 975 9173
10·6875	·104 162 5412	·102 840 5197	·101 971 5488	·101 540 7296
10·7500	·104 756 5180	·103 419 5671	·102 540 8525	·102 105 2229
10·8125	·105 350 3271	·103 998 3695	·103 109 8617	·102 669 3978
10·8750	·105 943 9689	·104 576 9272	·103 678 5768	·103 233 2546
10·9375	·106 537 4433	·105 155 2402	·104 246 9981	·103 796 7937
11·0000	·107 130 7506	·105 733 3090	·104 815 1259	·104 360 0153
11·0625	·107 723 8908	·106 311 1337	·105 382 9605	·104 922 9199
11·1250	·108 316 8642	·106 888 7146	·105 950 5024	·105 485 5078
11·1875	·108 909 6709	·107 466 0519	·106 517 7517	·106 047 7794
11·2500	·109 502 3110	·108 043 1458	·107 084 7087	·106 609 7351
11·3125	·110 094 7846	·108 619 9966	·107 651 3739	·107 171 3751
11·3750	·110 687 0919	·109 196 6046	·108 217 7475	·107 732 6998
11·4375	·111 279 2331	·109 772 9700	·108 783 8299	·108 293 7096
11·5000	·111 871 2082	·110 349 0929	·109 349 6212	·108 854 4049
11·5625	·112 463 0174	·110 924 9737	·109 915 1220	·109 414 7860
11·6250	·113 054 6609	·111 500 6126	·110 480 3324	·109 974 8532
11·6875	·113 646 1388	·112 076 0098	·111 045 2528	·110 534 6069
11·7500	·114 237 4512	·112 651 1655	·111 609 8834	·111 094 0475
11·8125	·114 828 5983	·113 226 0801	·112 174 2247	·111 653 1753
11·8750	·115 419 5801	·113 800 7537	·112 738 2769	·112 211 9906
11·9375	·116 010 3969	·114 375 1865	·113 302 0403	·112 770 4938
12·0000	·116 601 0489	·114 949 3789	·113 865 5152	·113 328 6853

FACTORS to convert the amount or present value of a periodical payment made at the end of each period to the amount or present value of the same periodical payment made in m equal payments at the end of each $1/m$ of a period at effective annual rates of interest, i.

$$\frac{i}{i^{(m)}} = \frac{i}{m\,[(1+i)^{1/m} - 1]}$$

(*See:* Explanation of Tables para. 11.3.)

Effective annual (or other periodical) rates of interest per cent.	FACTORS, $\frac{i}{i^{(m)}}$			
	$m = 2$	$m = 4$	$m = 12$	$m = \infty$
0·5000	1·001 248 4414	1·001 873 0517	1·002 289 6030	1·002 497 9219
0·5625	1·001 404 2780	1·002 106 9100	1·002 575 5139	1·002 809 8707
0·6250	1·001 560 0662	1·002 340 7077	1·002 861 3608	1·003 121 7549
0·6875	1·001 715 8060	1·002 574 4450	1·003 147 1436	1·003 433 5747
0·7500	1·001 871 4975	1·002 808 1219	1·003 432 8624	1·003 745 3300
0·8125	1·002 027 1407	1·003 041 7384	1·003 718 5173	1·004 057 0209
0·8750	1·002 182 7357	1·003 275 2946	1·004 004 1083	1·004 368 6475
0·9375	1·002 338 2824	1·003 508 7905	1·004 289 6355	1·004 680 2099
1·0000	1·002 493 7811	1·003 742 2263	1·004 575 0990	1·004 991 7081
1·0625	1·002 649 2316	1·003 975 6020	1·004 860 4987	1·005 303 1421
1·1250	1·002 804 6340	1·004 208 9175	1·005 145 8349	1·005 614 5120
1·1875	1·002 959 9885	1·004 442 1731	1·005 431 1074	1·005 925 8179
1·2500	1·003 115 2949	1·004 675 3687	1·005 716 3164	1·006 237 0599
1·3125	1·003 270 5535	1·004 908 5043	1·006 001 4620	1·006 548 2380
1·3750	1·003 425 7641	1·005 141 5802	1·006 286 5442	1·006 859 3522
1·4375	1·003 580 9270	1·005 374 5962	1·006 571 5630	1·007 170 4026
1·5000	1·003 736 0420	1·005 607 5525	1·006 856 5185	1·007 481 3893
1·5625	1·003 891 1093	1·005 840 4491	1·007 141 4109	1·007 792 3123
1·6250	1·004 046 1288	1·006 073 2860	1·007 426 2400	1·008 103 1718
1·6875	1·004 201 1007	1·006 306 0634	1·007 711 0061	1·008 413 9676
1·7500	1·004 356 0250	1·006 538 7813	1·007 995 7090	1·008 724 7000
1·8125	1·004 510 9018	1·006 771 4397	1·008 280 3491	1·009 035 3690
1·8750	1·004 665 7309	1·007 004 0387	1·008 564 9261	1·009 345 9746
1·9375	1·004 820 5127	1·007 236 5783	1·008 849 4403	1·009 656 5168
2·0000	1·004 975 2469	1·007 469 0586	1·009 133 8917	1·009 966 9958
2·0625	1·005 129 9338	1·007 701 4797	1·009 418 2803	1·010 277 4116
2·1250	1·005 284 5733	1·007 933 8416	1·009 702 6062	1·010 587 7643
2·1875	1·005 439 1655	1·008 166 1443	1·009 986 8695	1·010 898 0539
2·2500	1·005 593 7104	1·008 398 3879	1·010 271 0702	1·011 208 2804
2·3125	1·005 748 2081	1·008 630 5726	1·010 555 2083	1·011 518 4440
2·3750	1·005 902 6586	1·008 862 6982	1·010 839 2840	1·011 828 5447
2·4375	1·006 057 0620	1·009 094 7649	1·011 123 2973	1·012 138 5825
2·5000	1·006 211 4183	1·009 326 7727	1·011 407 2482	1·012 448 5576
2·5625	1·006 365 7275	1·009 558 7218	1·011 691 1368	1·012 758 4699
2·6250	1·006 519 9897	1·009 790 6120	1·011 974 9631	1·013 068 3195
2·6875	1·006 674 2050	1·010 022 4436	1·012 258 7273	1·013 378 1065
2·7500	1·006 828 3733	1·010 254 2165	1·012 542 4293	1·013 687 8309
2·8125	1·006 982 4948	1·010 485 9308	1·012 826 0693	1·013 997 4928
2·8750	1·007 136 5694	1·010 717 5866	1·013 109 6472	1·014 307 0923
2·9375	1·007 290 5972	1·010 949 1838	1·013 393 1632	1·014 616 6293
3·0000	1·007 444 5783	1·011 180 7226	1·013 676 6172	1·014 926 1041
3·0625	1·007 598 5126	1·011 412 2030	1·013 960 0095	1·015 235 5165
3·1250	1·007 752 4003	1·011 643 6251	1·014 243 3399	1·015 544 8667
3·1875	1·007 906 2413	1·011 874 9889	1·014 526 6086	1·015 854 1548
3·2500	1·008 060 0358	1·012 106 2945	1·014 809 8156	1·016 163 3807
3·3125	1·008 213 7837	1·012 337 5419	1·015 092 9610	1·016 472 5446
3·3750	1·008 367 4852	1·012 568 7312	1·015 376 0448	1·016 781 6465
3·4375	1·008 521 1402	1·012 799 8624	1·015 659 0671	1·017 090 6864
3·5000	1·008 674 7487	1·013 030 9356	1·015 942 0279	1·017 399 6645
3·5625	1·008 828 3109	1·013 261 9508	1·016 224 9274	1·017 708 5807
3·6250	1·008 981 8268	1·013 492 9081	1·016 507 7655	1·018 017 4351
3·6875	1·009 135 2963	1·013 723 8075	1·016 790 5423	1·018 326 2279
3·7500	1·009 288 7197	1·013 954 6491	1·017 073 2578	1·018 634 9589
3·8125	1·009 442 0968	1·014 185 4330	1·017 355 9122	1·018 943 6284
3·8750	1·009 595 4278	1·014 416 1592	1·017 638 5055	1·019 252 2363
3·9375	1·009 748 7126	1·014 646 8277	1·017 921 0377	1·019 560 7827

Effective annual (or other periodical) rates of interest per cent.	FACTORS, $\frac{i}{i^{(m)}}$ $m=2$	$m=4$	$m=12$	$m=\infty$
4·0000	1·009 901 9514	1·014 877 4386	1·018 203 5089	1·019 869 2676
4·0625	1·010 055 1441	1·015 107 9920	1·018 485 9191	1·020 177 6912
4·1250	1·010 208 2908	1·015 338 4878	1·018 768 2684	1·020 486 0534
4·1875	1·010 361 3916	1·015 568 9262	1·019 050 5568	1·020 794 3544
4·2500	1·010 514 4464	1·015 799 3073	1·019 332 7845	1·021 102 5942
4·3125	1·010 667 4554	1·016 029 6309	1·019 614 9514	1·021 410 7727
4·3750	1·010 820 4185	1·016 259 8973	1·019 897 0577	1·021 718 8902
4·4375	1·010 973 3359	1·016 490 1065	1·020 179 1033	1·022 026 9466
4·5000	1·011 126 2075	1·016 720 2584	1·020 461 0883	1·022 334 9420
4·5625	1·011 279 0334	1·016 950 3533	1·020 743 0128	1·022 642 8765
4·6250	1·011 431 8136	1·017 180 3910	1·021 024 8768	1·022 950 7500
4·6875	1·011 584 5482	1·017 410 3717	1·021 306 6804	1·023 258 5628
4·7500	1·011 737 2372	1·017 640 2954	1·021 588 4237	1·023 566 3147
4·8125	1·011 889 8807	1·017 870 1622	1·021 870 1066	1·023 874 0059
4·8750	1·012 042 4787	1·0 8 099 9721	1·022 151 7293	1·024 181 6364
4·9375	1·012 195 0312	1·018 329 7252	1·022 433 2918	1·024 489 2064
5·0000	1·012 347 5383	1·018 559 4214	1·022 714 7941	1·024 796 7157
5·0625	1·012 500 0000	1·018 789 0610	1·022 996 2364	1·025 104 1645
5·1250	1·012 652 4163	1·019 018 6439	1·023 277 6186	1·025 411 5529
5·1875	1·012 804 7874	1·019 248 1701	1·023 558 9408	1·025 718 8809
5·2500	1·012 957 1132	1·019 477 6398	1·023 840 2031	1·026 026 1485
5·3125	1·013 109 3938	1·019 707 0529	1·024 121 4055	1·026 333 3558
5·3750	1·013 261 6292	1·019 936 4096	1·024 402 5481	1·026 640 5029
5·4375	1·013 413 8194	1·020 165 7098	1·024 683 6309	1·026 947 5898
5·5000	1·013 565 9646	1·020 394 9537	1·024 964 6540	1·027 254 6165
5·5625	1·013 718 0647	1·020 624 1412	1·025 245 6174	1·027 561 5832
5·6250	1·013 870 1198	1·020 853 2725	1·025 526 5212	1·027 868 4898
5·6875	1·014 022 1299	1·021 082 3475	1·025 807 3655	1·028 175 3365
5·7500	1·014 174 0950	1·021 311 3663	1·026 088 1502	1·028 482 1232
5·8125	1·014 326 0153	1·021 540 3290	1·026 368 8755	1·028 788 8501
5·8750	1·014 477 8907	1·021 769 2357	1·026 649 5414	1·029 095 5171
5·9375	1·014 629 7212	1·021 998 0863	1·026 930 1479	1·029 402 1244
6·0000	1·014 781 5070	1·022 226 8809	1·027 210 6952	1·029 708 6719
6·0625	1·014 933 2481	1·022 455 6196	1·027 491 1832	1·030 015 1598
6·1250	1·015 084 9444	1·022 684 3024	1·027 771 6119	1·030 321 5881
6·1875	1·015 236 5961	1·022 912 9294	1·028 051 9816	1·030 627 9569
6·2500	1·015 388 2032	1·023 141 5006	1·028 332 2922	1·030 934 2661
6·3125	1·015 539 7657	1·023 370 0161	1·028 612 5437	1·031 240 5159
6·3750	1·015 691 2836	1·023 598 4758	1·028 892 7362	1·031 546 7063
6·4375	1·015 842 7570	1·023 826 8800	1·029 172 8698	1·031 852 8373
6·5000	1·015 994 1860	1·024 055 2286	1·029 452 9446	1·032 158 9090
6·5625	1·016 145 5705	1·024 283 5216	1·029 732 9605	1·032 464 9215
6·6250	1·016 296 9107	1·024 511 7591	1·030 012 9176	1·032 770 8749
6·6875	1·016 448 2065	1·024 739 9412	1·030 292 8160	1·033 076 7690
6·7500	1·016 599 4580	1·024 968 0679	1·030 572 6557	1·033 382 6041
6·8125	1·016 750 6652	1·025 196 1392	1·030 852 4368	1·033 688 3802
6·8750	1·016 901 8282	1·025 424 1553	1·031 132 1593	1·033 994 0972
6·9375	1·017 052 9470	1·025 652 1161	1·031 411 8233	1·034 299 7554
7·0000	1·017 204 0216	1·025 880 0218	1·031 691 4288	1·034 605 3547
7·0625	1·017 355 0522	1·026 07 8722	1·031 970 9759	1·034 910 8951
7·1250	1·017 506 0386	1·026 335 6676	1·032 250 4646	1·035 216 3767
7·1875	1·017 656 9810	1·026 563 4079	1·032 529 8950	1·035 521 7997
7·2500	1·017 807 8794	1·026 791 0932	1·032 809 2672	1·035 827 1639
7·3125	1·017 958 7339	1·027 018 7236	1·033 088 5811	1·036 132 4696
7·3750	1·018 109 5444	1·027 246 2990	1·033 367 8369	1·036 437 7166
7·4375	1·018 260 3110	1·027 473 8196	1·033 647 0346	1·036 742 9052
7·5000	1·018 411 0338	1·027 701 2854	1·033 926 1742	1·037 048 0353
7·5625	1·018 561 7128	1·027 928 6964	1·034 205 2558	1·037 353 1069
7·6250	1·018 712 3480	1·028 156 0526	1·034 484 2794	1·037 658 1202
7·6875	1·018 862 9395	1·028 383 3543	1·034 763 2451	1·037 963 0752
7·7500	1·019 013 4873	1·028 6 0 6012	1·035 042 1529	1·038 267 9719
7·8125	1·019 163 9914	1·028 837 7937	1·035 321 0030	1·038 572 8104
7·8750	1·019 314 4519	1·029 064 9316	1·035 599 7952	1·038 877 5907
7·9375	1·019 464 8689	1·029 292 0150	1·035 878 5298	1·039 182 3129

Effective annual (or other periodical) rates of interest per cent.	FACTORS, $\frac{i}{i^{(m)}}$			
	$m = 2$	$m = 4$	$m = 12$	$m = \infty$
8·0000	1·019 615 2423	1·029 519 0439	1·036 157 2067	1·039 486 9770
8·0625	1·019 765 5722	1·029 746 0185	1·036 435 8260	1·039 791 5832
8·1250	1·019 915 8586	1·029 972 9388	1·036 714 3877	1·040 096 1313
8·1875	1·020 066 1016	1·030 199 8047	1·036 992 8919	1·040 400 6216
8·2500	1·020 216 3012	1·030 426 6164	1·037 271 3387	1·040 705 0540
8·3125	1·020 366 4574	1·030 653 3739	1·037 549 7280	1·041 009 4285
8·3750	1·020 516 5703	1·030 880 0773	1·037 828 0600	1·041 313 7453
8·4375	1·020 666 6400	1·031 106 7265	1·038 106 3347	1·041 618 0044
8·5000	1·020 816 6664	1·031 333 3217	1·038 384 5521	1·041 922 2058
8·5625	1·020 966 6496	1·031 559 8629	1·038 662 7123	1·042 226 3496
8·6250	1·021 116 5896	1·031 786 3501	1·038 940 8153	1·042 530 4359
8·6875	1·021 266 4865	1·032 012 7834	1·039 218 8612	1·042 834 4646
8·7500	1·021 416 3404	1·032 239 1628	1·039 496 8500	1·043 138 4359
8·8125	1·021 566 1511	1·032 465 4884	1·039 774 7818	1·043 442 3497
8·8750	1·021 715 9189	1·032 691 7603	1·040 052 6567	1·043 746 2062
8·9375	1·021 865 6436	1·032 917 9783	1·040 330 4746	1·044 050 0054
9·0000	1·022 015 3254	1·033 144 1427	1·040 608 2357	1·044 353 7473
9·0625	1·022 164 9643	1·033 370 2535	1·040 885 9399	1·044 657 4319
9·1250	1·022 314 5604	1·033 596 3106	1·041 163 5874	1·044 961 0594
9·1875	1·022 464 1136	1·033 822 3143	1·041 441 1781	1·045 264 6298
9·2500	1·022 613 6240	1·034 048 2644	1·041 718 7122	1·045 568 1431
9·3125	1·022 763 0916	1·034 274 1610	1·041 996 1896	1·045 871 5994
9·3750	1·022 912 5166	1·034 500 0043	1·042 273 6105	1·046 174 9987
9·4375	1·023 061 8988	1·034 725 7941	1·042 550 9748	1·046 478 3411
9·5000	1·023 211 2384	1·034 951 5307	1·042 828 2826	1·046 781 6266
9·5625	1·023 360 5354	1·035 177 2140	1·043 105 5340	1·047 084 8552
9·6250	1·023 509 7898	1·035 402 8440	1·043 382 7290	1·047 388 0271
9·6875	1·023 659 0016	1·035 628 4209	1·043 659 8677	1·047 691 1423
9·7500	1·023 808 1710	1·035 853 9446	1·043 936 9501	1·047 994 2007
9·8125	1·023 957 2979	1·036 079 4152	1·044 213 9762	1·048 297 2026
9·8750	1·024 106 3823	1·036 304 8328	1·044 490 9462	1·048 600 1478
9·9375	1·024 255 4244	1·036 530 1974	1·044 767 8600	1·048 903 0365
10·0000	1·024 404 4241	1·036 755 5090	1·045 044 7177	1·049 205 8687
10·0625	1·024 553 3814	1·036 980 7677	1·045 321 5193	1·049 508 6445
10·1250	1·024 702 2965	1·037 205 9735	1·045 598 2650	1·049 811 3639
10·1875	1·024 851 1694	1·037 431 1265	1·045 874 9547	1·050 114 0269
10·2500	1·025 000 0000	1·037 656 2267	1·046 151 5885	1·050 416 6336
10·3125	1·025 148 7884	1·037 881 2742	1·046 428 1664	1·050 719 1841
10·3750	1·025 297 5347	1·038 106 2691	1·046 704 6885	1·051 021 6783
10·4375	1·025 446 2389	1·038 331 2112	1·046 981 1548	1·051 324 1164
10·5000	1·025 594 9010	1·038 556 1008	1·047 257 5654	1·051 626 4984
10·5625	1·025 743 5211	1·038 780 9378	1·047 533 9204	1·051 928 8244
10·6250	1·025 892 0992	1·039 005 7223	1·047 810 2197	1·052 231 0943
10·6875	1·026 040 6353	1·039 230 4543	1·048 086 4634	1·052 533 3082
10·7500	1·026 189 1295	1·039 455 1339	1·048 362 6516	1·052 835 4663
10·8125	1·026 337 5818	1·039 679 7612	1·048 638 7844	1·053 137 5684
10·8750	1·026 485 9922	1·039 904 3361	1·048 914 8616	1·053 439 6148
10·9375	1·026 634 3608	1·040 128 8587	1·049 190 8835	1·053 741 6053
11·0000	1·026 782 6876	1·040 353 3290	1·049 466 8501	1·054 043 5401
11·0625	1·026 930 9727	1·040 577 7472	1·049 742 7613	1·054 345 4193
11·1250	1·027 079 2160	1·040 802 1132	1·050 018 6173	1·054 647 2427
11·1875	1·027 227 4177	1·041 026 4271	1·050 294 4181	1·054 949 0106
11·2500	1·027 375 5777	1·041 250 6889	1·050 570 1637	1·055 250 7230
11·3125	1·027 523 6961	1·041 474 8987	1·050 845 8542	1·055 552 3799
11·3750	1·027 671 7730	1·041 699 0565	1·051 121 4897	1·055 853 9813
11·4375	1·027 819 8083	1·041 923 1624	1·051 397 0701	1·056 155 5273
11·5000	1·027 967 8020	1·042 147 2164	1·051 672 5956	1·056 457 0179
11·5625	1·028 115 7544	1·042 371 2185	1·051 948 0661	1·056 758 4532
11·6250	1·028 263 6652	1·042 595 1688	1·052 223 4818	1·057 059 8333
11·6875	1·028 411 5347	1·042 819 0673	1·052 498 8426	1·057 361 1581
11·7500	1·028 559 3628	1·043 042 9142	1·052 774 1486	1·057 662 4278
11·8125	1·028 707 1496	1·043 266 7093	1·053 049 3999	1·057 963 6423
11·8750	1·028 854 8950	1·043 490 4528	1·053 324 5964	1·058 264 8018
11·9375	1·029 002 5992	1·043 714 1448	1·053 599 7384	1·058 565 9062
12·0000	1·029 150 2622	1·043 937 7851	1·053 874 8257	1·058 866 9557

Repayment of a Loan by way of an Annuity

Periodical payment to include principal and interest

$$\frac{1}{a_{\overline{n}|}} = \frac{i}{1-v^n} = \frac{i\,(1+i)^n}{(1+i)^n-1}$$

Nominal rate of interest per annum	*Number of periods*
3% increasing by $\frac{1}{16}$% to 6%	180 years
6% increasing by $\frac{1}{8}$% to 12%	180 half years (90 years)
12% increasing by $\frac{1}{4}$% to 24%	180 quarters (45 years)

NOTE

This set of tables gives values for the repayment of loans by annual payments made at the end of each year at the effective rates of interest shown, for any number of years up to 180.

The tables also give the values for the repayment of loans by half yearly payments made at the end of each half year at effective interest rates compounded half yearly from 3% to 6% i.e. at nominal annual interest rates of twice the effective annual rates.

Similarly the tables may be used for ascertaining quarterly payments made at the end of each quarter at effective interest rates compounded quarterly from 3% to 6%, i.e. at nominal annual interest rates of four times the effective annual rates.

NOMINAL INTEREST RATE COMPOUNDED

YEARLY	HALF-YEARLY	QUARTERLY
@	@	@
3%	6%	12%
3.0000%	6.0000%	12.0000%
PER ANNUM	PER ANNUM	PER ANNUM

Periods	Loan of 1	Periods	Loan of 1	Periods	Loan of 1
1	1.030 000 0000	61	.035 919 0847	121	.030 863 2518
2	.522 610 8374	62	.035 713 8485	122	.030 837 4067
3	.353 530 3633	63	.035 516 8216	123	.030 812 3558
4	.269 027 0452	64	.035 327 6021	124	.030 788 0734
5	.218 354 5714	65	.035 145 8128	125	.030 764 5348
6	.184 597 5005	66	.034 971 0995	126	.030 741 7163
7	.160 506 3538	67	.034 803 1288	127	.030 719 5947
8	.142 456 3888	68	.034 641 5871	128	.030 698 1479
9	.128 433 8570	69	.034 486 1787	129	.030 677 3543
10	.117 230 5066	70	.034 336 6251	130	.030 657 1934
11	.108 077 4478	71	.034 192 6632	131	.030 637 6450
12	.100 462 0855	72	.034 054 0446	132	.030 618 6898
13	.094 029 5440	73	.033 920 5345	133	.030 600 3091
14	.088 526 3390	74	.033 791 9109	134	.030 582 4849
15	.083 766 5805	75	.033 667 9634	135	.030 565 1997
16	.079 610 8493	76	.033 548 4929	136	.030 548 4366
17	.075 952 5294	77	.033 433 3105	137	.030 532 1794
18	.072 708 6959	78	.033 322 2371	138	.030 516 4122
19	.069 813 8806	79	.033 215 1027	139	.030 501 1198
20	.067 215 7076	80	.033 111 7457	140	.030 486 2875
21	.064 871 7765	81	.033 012 0127	141	.030 471 9010
22	.062 747 3948	82	.032 915 7577	142	.030 457 9465
23	.060 813 9027	83	.032 822 8417	143	.030 444 4106
24	.059 047 4159	84	.032 733 1325	144	.030 431 2805
25	.057 427 8710	85	.032 646 5042	145	.030 418 5437
26	.055 938 2903	86	.032 562 8365	146	.030 406 1881
27	.054 564 2103	87	.032 482 0151	147	.030 394 2019
28	.053 293 2334	88	.032 403 9306	148	.030 382 5739
29	.052 114 6711	89	.032 328 4787	149	.030 371 2930
30	.051 019 2593	90	.032 255 5599	150	.030 360 3488
31	.049 998 9288	91	.032 185 0789	151	.030 349 7308
32	.049 046 6183	92	.032 116 9449	152	.030 339 4292
33	.048 156 1219	93	.032 051 0708	153	.030 329 4344
34	.047 321 9633	94	.031 987 3733	154	.030 319 7369
35	.046 539 2916	95	.031 925 7729	155	.030 310 3279
36	.045 803 7942	96	.031 866 1932	156	.030 301 1985
37	.045 111 6244	97	.031 808 5613	157	.030 292 3402
38	.044 459 3401	98	.031 752 8070	158	.030 283 7449
39	.043 843 8516	99	.031 698 8633	159	.030 275 4046
40	.043 262 3779	100	.031 646 6659	160	.030 267 3117
41	.042 712 4089	101	.031 596 1530	161	.030 259 4585
42	.042 191 6731	102	.031 547 2653	162	.030 251 8381
43	.041 698 1103	103	.031 499 9461	163	.030 244 4432
44	.041 229 8469	104	.031 454 1408	164	.030 237 2672
45	.040 785 1757	105	.031 409 7968	165	.030 230 3034
46	.040 362 5378	106	.031 366 8639	166	.030 223 5456
47	.039 960 5065	107	.031 325 2936	167	.030 216 9875
48	.039 577 7738	108	.031 285 0394	168	.030 210 6231
49	.039 213 1383	109	.031 246 0565	169	.030 204 4466
50	.038 865 4944	110	.031 208 3018	170	.030 198 4525
51	.038 533 8232	111	.031 171 7340	171	.030 192 6352
52	.038 217 1837	112	.031 136 3131	172	.030 186 9895
53	.037 914 7059	113	.031 102 0009	173	.030 181 5102
54	.037 625 5841	114	.031 068 7603	174	.030 176 1925
55	.037 349 0710	115	.031 036 5558	175	.030 171 0314
56	.037 084 4726	116	.031 005 3531	176	.030 166 0223
57	.036 831 1432	117	.030 975 1192	177	.030 161 1607
58	.036 588 4819	118	.030 945 8222	178	.030 156 4423
59	.036 355 9281	119	.030 917 4315	179	.030 151 8626
60	.036 132 9587	120	.030 889 9176	180	.030 147 4177

Repayment of a Loan by way of an Annuity

NOMINAL INTEREST RATE COMPOUNDED

	YEARLY	HALF-YEARLY	QUARTERLY
	@	@	@
	$3\frac{1}{16}\%$	$6\frac{1}{8}\%$	$12\frac{1}{4}\%$
	3.0625%	6.1250%	12.2500%
	PER ANNUM	PER ANNUM	PER ANNUM

Periods	Loan of 1	Periods	Loan of 1	Periods	Loan of 1
1	1.030 625 0000	61	.036 406 4580	121	.031 442 2061
2	.523 084 2182	62	.036 203 3693	122	.031 417 2946
3	.353 955 2613	63	.036 008 4696	123	.031 393 1610
4	.269 429 2430	64	.035 821 3568	124	.031 369 7800
5	.218 744 3807	65	.035 641 6534	125	.031 347 1271
6	.184 980 0753	66	.035 469 0051	126	.031 325 1785
7	.160 884 6377	67	.035 303 0783	127	.031 303 9115
8	.142 832 2198	68	.035 143 5592	128	.031 283 3040
9	.128 808 4585	69	.034 990 1523	129	.031 263 3347
10	.117 604 7331	70	.034 842 5785	130	.031 243 9833
11	.108 451 9191	71	.034 700 5750	131	.031 225 2297
12	.100 837 2643	72	.034 563 8931	132	.031 207 0549
13	.094 405 7845	73	.034 432 2981	133	.031 189 4404
14	.088 903 9175	74	.034 305 5677	134	.031 172 3683
15	.084 145 7162	75	.034 183 4916	135	.031 155 8213
16	.079 991 7183	76	.034 065 8706	136	.031 139 7828
17	.076 335 2749	77	.033 952 5159	137	.031 124 2367
18	.073 093 4352	78	.033 843 2483	138	.031 109 1674
19	.070 200 7106	79	.033 737 8977	139	.031 094 5598
20	.067 604 7088	80	.033 636 3027	140	.031 080 3993
21	.065 263 0158	81	.033 538 3097	141	.031 066 6720
22	.063 140 9282	82	.033 443 7729	142	.031 053 3641
23	.061 209 7770	83	.033 352 5532	143	.031 040 4626
24	.059 445 6702	84	.033 264 5185	144	.031 027 9547
25	.057 828 5377	85	.033 179 5429	145	.031 015 8281
26	.056 341 3961	86	.033 097 5062	146	.031 004 0709
27	.054 969 7774	87	.033 018 2942	147	.030 992 6716
28	.053 701 2794	88	.032 941 7975	148	.030 981 6190
29	.052 525 2101	89	.032 867 9119	149	.030 970 9024
30	.051 432 3022	90	.032 796 5380	150	.030 960 5113
31	.050 414 4835	91	.032 727 5806	151	.030 950 4357
32	.049 464 6903	92	.032 660 9489	152	.030 940 6657
33	.048 576 7143	93	.032 596 5561	153	.030 931 1919
34	.047 745 0772	94	.032 534 3188	154	.030 922 0052
35	.046 964 9261	95	.032 474 1578	155	.030 913 0966
36	.046 231 9470	96	.032 415 9966	156	.030 904 4577
37	.045 542 2916	97	.032 359 7626	157	.030 896 0802
38	.044 892 5162	98	.032 305 3857	158	.030 887 9558
39	.044 279 5300	99	.032 252 7990	159	.030 880 0770
40	.043 700 5508	100	.032 201 9384	160	.030 872 4362
41	.043 153 0673	101	.032 152 7421	161	.030 865 0260
42	.042 634 8073	102	.032 105 1512	162	.030 857 8394
43	.042 143 7093	103	.032 059 1089	163	.030 850 8696
44	.041 677 8992	104	.032 014 5608	164	.030 844 1098
45	.041 235 6688	105	.031 971 4547	165	.030 837 5538
46	.040 815 4584	106	.031 929 7402	166	.030 831 1952
47	.040 415 8408	107	.031 889 3692	167	.030 825 0281
48	.040 035 5072	108	.031 850 2953	168	.030 819 0466
49	.039 673 2557	109	.031 812 4739	169	.030 813 2451
50	.039 327 9801	110	.031 775 8622	170	.030 807 6181
51	.038 998 6610	111	.031 740 4188	171	.030 802 1602
52	.038 684 3568	112	.031 706 1041	172	.030 796 8663
53	.038 384 1973	113	.031 672 8799	173	.030 791 7315
54	.038 097 3761	114	.031 640 7094	174	.030 786 7509
55	.037 823 1457	115	.031 609 5574	175	.030 781 9199
56	.037 560 8115	116	.031 579 3895	176	.030 777 2338
57	.037 309 7277	117	.031 550 1731	177	.030 772 6884
58	.037 069 2929	118	.031 521 8765	178	.030 768 2793
59	.036 838 9463	119	.031 494 4692	179	.030 764 0024
60	.036 618 1644	120	.031 467 9218	180	.030 759 8538

Repayment of a Loan by way of an Annuity

NOMINAL INTEREST RATE COMPOUNDED

YEARLY @ $3\frac{1}{8}\%$ 3.1250% PER ANNUM	HALF-YEARLY @ $6\frac{1}{4}\%$ 6.2500% PER ANNUM	QUARTERLY @ $12\frac{1}{2}\%$ 12.5000% PER ANNUM

Periods	Loan of 1	Periods	Loan of 1	Periods	Loan of 1
1	1.031 250 0000	61	.036 896 5642	121	.032 023 4437
2	.523 557 6923	62	.036 695 6389	122	.031 999 4439
3	.354 380 3250	63	.036 502 8810	123	.031 976 2057
4	.269 831 6739	64	.036 317 8885	124	.031 953 7039
5	.219 134 4880	65	.036 140 2837	125	.031 931 9142
6	.185 363 0120	66	.035 969 7120	126	.031 910 8132
7	.161 263 3465	67	.035 805 8397	127	.031 890 3782
8	.143 208 5380	68	.035 648 3530	128	.031 870 5875
9	.129 183 6090	69	.035 496 9560	129	.031 851 4198
10	.117 979 5701	70	.035 351 3699	130	.031 832 8551
11	.108 827 0617	71	.035 211 3314	131	.031 814 8735
12	.101 213 1750	72	.035 076 5920	132	.031 797 4563
13	.094 782 8169	73	.034 946 9168	133	.031 780 5850
14	.089 282 3475	74	.034 822 0835	134	.031 764 2421
15	.084 525 7624	75	.034 701 8817	135	.031 748 4105
16	.080 373 5563	76	.034 586 1124	136	.031 733 0737
17	.076 719 0473	77	.034 474 5865	137	.031 718 2157
18	.073 479 2588	78	.034 367 1249	138	.031 703 8213
19	.070 588 6816	79	.034 263 5576	139	.031 689 8756
20	.067 994 9071	80	.034 163 7230	140	.031 676 3642
21	.065 655 5078	81	.034 067 4678	141	.031 663 2732
22	.063 535 7692	82	.033 974 6461	142	.031 650 5892
23	.061 607 0130	83	.033 885 1188	143	.031 638 2993
24	.059 845 3396	84	.033 798 7540	144	.031 626 3909
25	.058 230 6721	85	.033 715 4257	145	.031 614 8520
26	.056 746 0216	86	.033 635 0139	146	.031 603 6707
27	.055 376 9152	87	.033 557 4043	147	.031 592 8359
28	.054 110 9465	88	.033 482 4878	148	.031 582 3364
29	.052 937 4197	89	.033 410 1603	149	.031 572 1618
30	.051 847 0642	90	.033 340 3223	150	.031 562 3018
31	.050 831 8051	91	.033 272 8789	151	.031 552 7464
32	.049 884 5760	92	.033 207 7392	152	.031 543 4861
33	.048 999 1664	93	.033 144 8167	153	.031 534 5116
34	.048 170 0958	94	.033 084 0281	154	.031 525 8140
35	.047 392 5095	95	.033 025 2943	155	.031 517 3844
36	.046 662 0918	96	.032 968 5390	156	.031 509 2147
37	.045 974 9929	97	.032 913 6896	157	.031 501 2965
38	.045 327 7676	98	.032 860 6763	158	.031 493 6221
39	.044 717 3239	99	.032 809 4323	159	.031 486 1838
40	.044 140 8783	100	.032 759 8935	160	.031 478 9743
41	.043 595 9186	101	.032 711 9986	161	.031 471 9864
42	.043 080 1714	102	.032 665 6886	162	.031 465 2132
43	.042 591 5744	103	.032 620 9070	163	.031 458 6480
44	.042 128 2525	104	.032 577 5995	164	.031 452 2845
45	.041 688 4969	105	.032 535 7140	165	.031 446 1161
46	.041 270 7470	106	.032 495 2005	166	.031 440 1371
47	.040 873 5749	107	.032 456 0110	167	.031 434 3414
48	.040 495 6713	108	.032 418 0991	168	.031 428 7233
49	.040 135 8335	109	.032 381 4206	169	.031 423 2774
50	.039 792 9549	110	.032 345 9328	170	.031 417 9984
51	.039 466 0153	111	.032 311 5945	171	.031 412 8810
52	.039 154 0731	112	.032 278 3663	172	.031 407 9202
53	.038 856 2571	113	.032 246 2103	173	.031 403 1113
54	.038 571 7609	114	.032 215 0898	174	.031 398 4496
55	.038 299 8363	115	.032 184 9697	175	.031 393 9304
56	.038 039 7885	116	.032 155 8160	176	.031 389 5494
57	.037 790 9713	117	.032 127 5962	177	.031 385 3023
58	.037 552 7830	118	.032 100 2788	178	.031 381 1850
59	.037 324 6626	119	.032 073 8335	179	.031 377 1935
60	.037 106 0861	120	.032 048 2312	180	.031 373 3240

Repayment of a Loan by way of an Annuity

NOMINAL INTEREST RATE COMPOUNDED

YEARLY @ $3\frac{3}{16}\%$ 3.1875% PER ANNUM	HALF-YEARLY @ $6\frac{3}{8}\%$ 6.3750% PER ANNUM	QUARTERLY @ $12\frac{3}{4}\%$ 12.7500% PER ANNUM

Periods	Loan of 1	Periods	Loan of 1	Periods	Loan of 1
1	1.031 875 0000	61	.037 389 3658	121	.032 606 8652
2	.524 031 2596	62	.037 190 6182	122	.032 583 7549
3	.354 805 5544	63	.037 000 0157	123	.032 561 3897
4	.270 234 3375	64	.036 817 1559	124	.032 539 7447
5	.219 524 8930	65	.036 641 6610	125	.032 518 7958
6	.185 746 3101	66	.036 473 1761	126	.032 498 5197
7	.161 642 4796	67	.036 311 3677	127	.032 478 8940
8	.143 585 3428	68	.036 155 9216	128	.032 459 8972
9	.129 559 3080	69	.036 006 5419	129	.032 441 5084
10	.118 355 0168	70	.035 862 9496	130	.032 423 7075
11	.109 202 8749	71	.035 724 8815	131	.032 406 4751
12	.101 589 8165	72	.035 592 0890	132	.032 389 7925
13	.095 160 6400	73	.035 464 3370	133	.032 373 6416
14	.089 661 6275	74	.035 341 4033	134	.032 358 0050
15	.084 906 7174	75	.035 223 0775	135	.032 342 8658
16	.080 756 3615	76	.035 109 1604	136	.032 328 2077
17	.077 103 8445	77	.034 999 4631	137	.032 314 0152
18	.073 866 1643	78	.034 893 8065	138	.032 300 2729
19	.070 977 7911	79	.034 792 0206	139	.032 286 9663
20	.068 386 2997	80	.034 693 9438	140	.032 274 0811
21	.066 049 2493	81	.034 599 4229	141	.032 261 6039
22	.063 931 9142	82	.034 508 3118	142	.032 249 5212
23	.062 005 6068	83	.034 420 4719	143	.032 237 8204
24	.060 246 4197	84	.034 335 7710	144	.032 226 4892
25	.058 634 2695	85	.034 254 0833	145	.032 215 5155
26	.057 152 1616	86	.034 175 2890	146	.032 204 8880
27	.055 785 6181	87	.034 099 2738	147	.032 194 5955
28	.054 522 2285	88	.034 025 9287	148	.032 184 6272
29	.053 351 2931	89	.033 955 1497	149	.032 174 9727
30	.052 263 5382	90	.033 886 8374	150	.032 165 6219
31	.051 250 8859	91	.033 820 8971	151	.032 156 5652
32	.050 306 2671	92	.033 757 2382	152	.032 147 7931
33	.049 423 4691	93	.033 695 7739	153	.032 139 2966
34	.048 597 0094	94	.033 636 4214	154	.032 131 0668
35	.047 822 0314	95	.033 579 1015	155	.032 123 0952
36	.047 094 2175	96	.033 523 7384	156	.032 115 3736
37	.046 409 7164	97	.033 470 2593	157	.032 107 8942
38	.045 765 0816	98	.033 418 5948	158	.032 100 6490
39	.045 157 2198	99	.033 368 6782	159	.032 093 6309
40	.044 583 3462	100	.033 320 4456	160	.032 086 8324
41	.044 040 9475	101	.033 273 8357	161	.032 080 2467
42	.043 527 7494	102	.033 228 7899	162	.032 073 8670
43	.043 041 6886	103	.033 185 2519	163	.032 067 6868
44	.042 580 8890	104	.033 143 1674	164	.032 061 6997
45	.042 143 6412	105	.033 102 4847	165	.032 055 8998
46	.041 728 3837	106	.033 063 1538	166	.032 050 2810
47	.041 333 6879	107	.033 025 1270	167	.032 044 8376
48	.040 958 2440	108	.032 988 3582	168	.032 039 5642
49	.040 600 8485	109	.032 952 8033	169	.032 034 4553
50	.040 260 3944	110	.032 918 4196	170	.032 029 5058
51	.039 935 8610	111	.032 885 1666	171	.032 024 7107
52	.039 626 3059	112	.032 853 0047	172	.032 020 0650
53	.039 330 8578	113	.032 821 8963	173	.032 015 5641
54	.039 048 7096	114	.032 791 8050	174	.032 011 2035
55	.038 779 1129	115	.032 762 6959	175	.032 006 9787
56	.038 521 3725	116	.032 734 5352	176	.032 002 8855
57	.038 274 8418	117	.032 707 2906	177	.031 998 9197
58	.038 038 9188	118	.032 680 9307	178	.031 995 0773
59	.037 813 0421	119	.032 655 4257	179	.031 991 3546
60	.037 596 6877	120	.032 630 7465	180	.031 987 7476

Repayment of a Loan by way of an Annuity

	NOMINAL INTEREST RATE COMPOUNDED				
	YEARLY @ $3\frac{1}{4}\%$ 3.2500% PER ANNUM		HALF-YEARLY @ $6\frac{1}{2}\%$ 6.5000% PER ANNUM		QUARTERLY @ 13% 13 0000% PER ANNUM
Periods	Loan of 1	Periods	Loan of 1	Periods	Loan of 1
1	1,032 500 0000	61	,037 884 8252	121	,033 192 3744
2	,524 504 9200	62	,037 688 2685	122	,033 170 1312
3	,355 230 9493	63	,037 499 8335	123	,033 148 6165
4	,270 637 2337	64	,037 319 1174	124	,033 127 8056
5	,219 915 5954	65	,037 145 7424	125	,033 107 6747
6	,186 129 9692	66	,036 979 3534	126	,033 088 2007
7	,162 022 0366	67	,036 819 6168	127	,033 069 3616
8	,143 962 6337	68	,036 666 2182	128	,033 051 1359
9	,129 935 5546	69	,036 518 8618	129	,033 033 5030
10	,118 731 0724	70	,036 377 2684	130	,033 016 4431
11	,109 579 3576	71	,036 241 1746	131	,032 999 9369
12	,101 967 1878	72	,036 110 3320	132	,032 983 9661
13	,095 539 2525	73	,035 984 5053	133	,032 968 5127
14	,090 041 7561	74	,035 863 4724	134	,032 953 5595
15	,085 288 5797	75	,035 747 0229	135	,032 939 0899
16	,081 140 1319	76	,035 634 9575	136	,032 925 0879
17	,077 489 6646	77	,035 527 0874	137	,032 911 5380
18	,074 254 1496	78	,035 423 2334	138	,032 898 4252
19	,071 368 0366	79	,035 323 2256	139	,032 885 7351
20	,068 778 8839	80	,035 226 9026	140	,032 873 4538
21	,066 444 2371	81	,035 134 1111	141	,032 861 5678
22	,064 329 3596	82	,035 044 7051	142	,032 850 0642
23	,062 405 5544	83	,034 958 5461	143	,032 838 9303
24	,060 648 9063	84	,034 875 5020	144	,032 828 1541
25	,059 039 3253	85	,034 795 4471	145	,032 817 7238
26	,057 559 8109	86	,034 718 2617	146	,032 807 6281
27	,056 195 8805	87	,034 643 8316	147	,032 797 8562
28	,054 935 1193	88	,034 572 0479	148	,032 788 3973
29	,053 766 8238	89	,034 502 8068	149	,032 779 2415
30	,052 681 7169	90	,034 436 0091	150	,032 770 3787
31	,051 671 7179	91	,034 371 5600	151	,032 761 7994
32	,050 729 7552	92	,034 309 3692	152	,032 753 4945
33	,049 849 6135	93	,034 249 3501	153	,032 745 4550
34	,049 025 8084	94	,034 191 4200	154	,032 737 6723
35	,048 253 4812	95	,034 135 5000	155	,032 730 1381
36	,047 528 3128	96	,034 081 5142	156	,032 722 8444
37	,046 846 4502	97	,034 029 3902	157	,032 715 7833
38	,046 204 4456	98	,033 979 0588	158	,032 708 9474
39	,045 599 2041	99	,033 930 4533	159	,032 702 3294
40	,045 027 9400	100	,033 883 5102	160	,032 695 9223
41	,044 488 1388	101	,033 838 1683	161	,032 689 7193
42	,043 977 5251	102	,033 794 3693	162	,032 683 7137
43	,043 494 0347	103	,033 752 0568	163	,032 677 8993
44	,043 035 7906	104	,033 711 1771	164	,032 672 2699
45	,042 601 0826	105	,033 671 6784	165	,032 666 8195
46	,042 188 3484	106	,033 633 5112	166	,032 661 5425
47	,041 796 1588	107	,033 596 6278	167	,032 656 4331
48	,041 423 2032	108	,033 560 9823	168	,032 651 4861
49	,041 068 2777	109	,033 526 5309	169	,032 646 6963
50	,040 730 2745	110	,033 493 2313	170	,032 642 0585
51	,040 408 1725	111	,033 461 0429	171	,032 637 5680
52	,040 101 0288	112	,033 429 9266	172	,032 633 2200
53	,039 807 9716	113	,033 399 8448	173	,032 629 0100
54	,039 528 1935	114	,033 370 7615	174	,032 624 9336
55	,039 260 9455	115	,033 342 6419	175	,032 620 9864
56	,039 005 5322	116	,033 315 4526	176	,032 617 1644
57	,038 761 3066	117	,033 289 1613	177	,032 613 4635
58	,038 527 6664	118	,033 263 7372	178	,032 609 8800
59	,038 304 0499	119	,033 239 1503	179	,032 606 4099
60	,038 089 9328	120	,033 215 3719	180	,032 603 0499

Repayment of a Loan by way of an Annuity

NOMINAL INTEREST RATE COMPOUNDED

YEARLY	HALF-YEARLY	QUARTERLY
@	@	@
$3\frac{5}{16}\%$	$6\frac{5}{8}\%$	$13\frac{1}{4}\%$
3.3125%	6.6250%	12.2500%
PER ANNUM	PER ANNUM	PER ANNUM

Periods	Loan of 1	Periods	Loan of 1	Periods	Loan of 1
1	1.033 125 0000	61	.038 382 9047	121	.033 779 8785
2	.524 978 6735	62	.038 188 5509	122	.033 758 4796
3	.355 656 5095	63	.038 002 2941	123	.033 737 7926
4	.271 040 3622	64	.037 823 7316	124	.033 717 7931
5	.220 306 5949	65	.037 652 4852	125	.033 698 4574
6	.186 513 9891	66	.037 488 1999	126	.033 679 7627
7	.162 402 0169	67	.037 330 5417	127	.033 661 6872
8	.144 340 4100	68	.037 179 1963	128	.033 644 2098
9	.130 312 3483	69	.037 033 8678	129	.033 627 3099
10	.119 107 7361	70	.036 894 2769	130	.033 610 9681
11	.109 956 5090	71	.036 760 1603	131	.033 595 1654
12	.102 345 2878	72	.036 631 2692	132	.033 579 8835
13	.095 918 6533	73	.036 507 3688	133	.033 565 1049
14	.090 422 7320	74	.036 388 2366	134	.033 550 8124
15	.085 671 3477	75	.036 273 6623	135	.033 536 9898
16	.081 524 8659	76	.036 163 4467	136	.033 523 6213
17	.077 876 5054	77	.036 057 4010	137	.033 510 6915
18	.074 643 2122	78	.035 955 3461	138	.033 498 1858
19	.071 759 4153	79	.035 857 1120	139	.033 486 0899
20	.069 172 6566	80	.035 762 5376	140	.033 474 3902
21	.066 840 4681	81	.035 671 4694	141	.033 463 0734
22	.064 728 1019	82	.035 583 7617	142	.033 452 1268
23	.062 806 8520	83	.035 499 2760	143	.033 441 5379
24	.061 052 7951	84	.035 417 8804	144	.033 431 2949
25	.059 445 8346	85	.035 339 4493	145	.033 421 3863
26	.057 968 9644	86	.035 263 8631	146	.033 411 8010
27	.056 607 6968	87	.035 191 0077	147	.033 402 5283
28	.055 349 6126	88	.035 120 7744	148	.033 393 5578
29	.054 184 0049	89	.035 053 0594	149	.033 384 8795
30	.053 101 5931	90	.034 987 7639	150	.033 376 4838
31	.052 094 2934	91	.034 924 7931	151	.033 368 3612
32	.051 155 0316	92	.034 864 0569	152	.033 360 5029
33	.050 277 5903	93	.034 805 4690	153	.033 352 9000
34	.049 456 4827	94	.034 748 9467	154	.033 345 5442
35	.048 686 8484	95	.034 694 4113	155	.033 338 4274
36	.047 964 3664	96	.034 641 7873	156	.033 331 5416
37	.047 285 1823	97	.034 591 0024	157	.033 324 8793
38	.046 645 8466	98	.034 541 9873	158	.033 318 4332
39	.046 043 2632	99	.034 494 6760	159	.033 312 1961
40	.045 474 6453	100	.034 449 0049	160	.033 306 1612
41	.044 937 4771	101	.034 404 9132	161	.033 300 3219
42	.044 429 4822	102	.034 362 3425	162	.033 294 6718
43	.043 948 5954	103	.034 321 2370	163	.033 289 2047
44	.043 492 9391	104	.034 281 5430	164	.033 283 9145
45	.043 060 8018	105	.034 243 2091	165	.033 278 7956
46	.042 650 6210	106	.034 206 1858	166	.033 273 8423
47	.042 260 9663	107	.034 170 4258	167	.033 269 0492
48	.041 890 5267	108	.034 135 8835	168	.033 264 4112
49	.041 538 0976	109	.034 102 5151	169	.033 259 9230
50	.041 202 5707	110	.034 070 2787	170	.033 255 5799
51	.040 882 9243	111	.034 039 1339	171	.033 251 3772
52	.040 578 2150	112	.034 009 0419	172	.033 247 3102
53	.040 287 5707	113	.033 979 9654	173	.033 243 3746
54	.040 010 1834	114	.033 951 8684	174	.033 239 5660
55	.039 745 3038	115	.033 924 7165	175	.033 235 8804
56	.039 492 2361	116	.033 898 4766	176	.033 232 3137
57	.039 250 3330	117	.033 873 1165	177	.033 228 8622
58	.039 018 9919	118	.033 848 6058	178	.033 225 5219
59	.038 797 6507	119	.033 824 9146	179	.033 222 2894
60	.038 585 7851	120	.033 802 0147	180	.033 219 1612

Repayment of a Loan by way of an Annuity

NOMINAL INTEREST RATE COMPOUNDED

YEARLY	HALF-YEARLY	QUARTERLY
@	@	@
$3\frac{3}{8}\%$	$6\frac{3}{4}\%$	$13\frac{1}{2}\%$
3.3750%	6.7500%	13.5000%
PER ANNUM	PER ANNUM	PER ANNUM

Periods	Loan of 1	Periods	Loan of 1	Periods	Loan of 1
1	1.033 750 0000	61	.038 883 5668	121	.034 369 2875
2	.525 452 5200	62	.038 691 4265	122	.034 348 7102
3	.356 082 2349	63	.038 507 3576	123	.034 328 8282
4	.271 443 7228	64	.038 330 9570	124	.034 309 6172
5	.220 697 8913	65	.038 161 8467	125	.034 291 0539
6	.186 898 3691	66	.037 999 6714	126	.034 273 1157
7	.162 782 4202	67	.037 844 0971	127	.034 255 7810
8	.144 718 6713	68	.037 694 8093	128	.034 239 0289
9	.130 689 6884	69	.037 551 5121	129	.034 222 8394
10	.119 485 0071	70	.037 413 9261	130	.034 207 1929
11	.110 334 3281	71	.037 281 7880	131	.034 192 0709
12	.102 724 1154	72	.037 154 8492	132	.034 177 4553
13	.096 298 8410	73	.037 032 8745	133	.034 163 3288
14	.090 804 5536	74	.036 915 6417	134	.034 149 6746
15	.086 055 0197	75	.036 802 9404	135	.034 136 4765
16	.081 910 5616	76	.036 694 5715	136	.034 123 7191
17	.078 264 3650	77	.036 590 3462	137	.034 111 3872
18	.075 033 3498	78	.036 490 0855	138	.034 099 4664
19	.072 151 9248	79	.036 393 6196	139	.034 087 9428
20	.069 567 6149	80	.036 300 7873	140	.034 076 8027
21	.067 237 9389	81	.036 211 4352	141	.034 066 0333
22	.065 128 1376	82	.036 125 4179	142	.034 055 6220
23	.063 209 4955	83	.036 042 5969	143	.034 045 5566
24	.061 458 0816	84	.035 962 8404	144	.034 035 8255
25	.059 853 7926	85	.035 886 0229	145	.034 026 4174
26	.058 379 6167	86	.035 812 0251	146	.034 017 3215
27	.057 021 0610	87	.035 740 7329	147	.034 008 5271
28	.055 765 7023	88	.035 672 0378	148	.034 000 0241
29	.054 602 8296	89	.035 605 8364	149	.033 991 8028
30	.053 523 1592	90	.035 542 0297	150	.033 983 8537
31	.052 518 6042	91	.035 480 5234	151	.033 976 1676
32	.051 582 0878	92	.035 421 2273	152	.033 968 7358
33	.050 707 3902	93	.035 364 0555	153	.033 961 5498
34	.049 889 0225	94	.035 308 9256	154	.033 954 6012
35	.049 122 1224	95	.035 255 7588	155	.033 947 8822
36	.048 402 3670	96	.035 204 4800	156	.033 941 3851
37	.047 725 9003	97	.035 155 0172	157	.033 935 1024
38	.047 089 2716	98	.035 107 3012	158	.033 929 0271
39	.046 489 3833	99	.035 061 2662	159	.033 923 1522
40	.045 923 4473	100	.035 016 8489	160	.033 917 4711
41	.045 388 9467	101	.034 973 9886	161	.033 911 9772
42	.044 883 6041	102	.034 932 6274	162	.033 906 6644
43	.044 405 3535	103	.034 892 7096	163	.033 901 5267
44	.043 952 3160	104	.034 854 1817	164	.033 896 5581
45	.043 522 7797	105	.034 816 9925	165	.033 891 7532
46	.043 115 1810	106	.034 781 0930	166	.033 887 1064
47	.042 728 0891	107	.034 746 4359	167	.033 882 6125
48	.042 360 1920	108	.034 712 9759	168	.033 878 2665
49	.042 010 2848	109	.034 680 6696	169	.033 874 0635
50	.041 677 2584	110	.034 649 4752	170	.033 869 9986
51	.041 360 0907	111	.034 619 3526	171	.033 866 0674
52	.041 057 8378	112	.034 590 2632	172	.033 862 2655
53	.040 769 6271	113	.034 562 1700	173	.033 858 5884
54	.040 494 6503	114	.034 535 0374	174	.033 855 0322
55	.040 232 1576	115	.034 508 8312	175	.033 851 5927
56	.039 981 4528	116	.034 483 5183	176	.033 848 2663
57	.039 741 8884	117	.034 459 0672	177	.033 845 0490
58	.039 512 8614	118	.034 435 4473	178	.033 841 9374
59	.039 293 8096	119	.034 412 6294	179	.033 838 9279
60	.039 084 2082	120	.034 390 5851	180	.033 836 0172

Repayment of a Loan by way of an Annuity

NOMINAL INTEREST RATE COMPOUNDED

YEARLY	HALF-YEARLY	QUARTERLY
@	@	@
$3\frac{7}{16}\%$	$6\frac{7}{8}\%$	$13\frac{3}{4}\%$
3.4375%	6.8750%	13.7500%
PER ANNUM	PER ANNUM	PER ANNUM

Periods	Loan of 1	Periods	Loan of 1	Periods	Loan of 1
1	1.034 375 0000	61	.039 386 7739	121	.034 960 5149
2	.525 926 4593	62	.039 196 8565	122	.034 940 7365
3	.356 508 1253	63	.039 014 9837	123	.034 921 6366
4	.271 847 3153	64	.038 840 7525	124	.034 903 1913
5	.221 089 4841	65	.038 673 7844	125	.034 885 3775
6	.187 283 1091	66	.038 513 7243	126	.034 868 1729
7	.163 163 2460	67	.038 360 2379	127	.034 851 5563
8	.145 097 4170	68	.038 213 0109	128	.034 835 5069
9	.131 067 5743	69	.038 071 7471	129	.034 820 0049
10	.119 862 8846	70	.037 936 1672	130	.034 805 0313
11	.110 712 8140	71	.037 806 0079	131	.034 790 5674
12	.103 103 6696	72	.037 681 0205	132	.034 776 5957
13	.096 679 8146	73	.037 560 9699	133	.034 763 0989
14	.091 187 2197	74	.037 445 6339	134	.034 750 0606
15	.086 439 5941	75	.037 334 8023	135	.034 737 4650
16	.082 297 2171	76	.037 228 2758	136	.034 725 2966
17	.078 653 2411	77	.037 125 8658	137	.034 713 5406
18	.075 424 5602	78	.037 027 3934	138	.034 702 1829
19	.072 545 5623	79	.036 932 6888	139	.034 691 2098
20	.069 963 7560	80	.036 841 5910	140	.034 680 6079
21	.067 636 6463	81	.036 753 9468	141	.034 670 3645
22	.065 529 4629	82	.036 669 6108	142	.034 660 4672
23	.063 613 4809	83	.036 588 4446	143	.034 650 9042
24	.061 864 7615	84	.036 510 3167	144	.034 641 6641
25	.060 263 1945	85	.036 435 1018	145	.034 632 7357
26	.058 791 7624	86	.036 362 6804	146	.034 624 1084
27	.057 435 9675	87	.036 292 9390	147	.034 615 7719
28	.056 183 3820	88	.036 225 7692	148	.034 607 7162
29	.055 023 2912	89	.036 161 0675	149	.034 599 9318
30	.053 946 4079	90	.036 098 7354	150	.034 592 4095
31	.052 944 6424	91	.036 038 6787	151	.034 585 1402
32	.052 010 9152	92	.035 980 8075	152	.034 578 1155
33	.051 139 0040	93	.035 925 0360	153	.034 571 3268
34	.050 323 4178	94	.035 871 2820	154	.034 564 7664
35	.049 559 2923	95	.035 819 4671	155	.034 558 4263
36	.048 842 3030	96	.035 769 5163	156	.034 552 2991
37	.048 168 5922	97	.035 721 3577	157	.034 546 3776
38	.047 534 7076	98	.035 674 9227	158	.034 540 6548
39	.046 937 5504	99	.035 630 1455	159	.034 535 1240
40	.046 374 3312	100	.035 586 9631	160	.034 529 7787
41	.045 842 5321	101	.035 545 3151	161	.034 524 6127
42	.045 339 8745	102	.035 505 1438	162	.034 519 6197
43	.044 864 2913	103	.035 466 3937	163	.034 514 7941
44	.044 413 9031	104	.035 429 0117	164	.034 510 1301
45	.043 986 9968	105	.035 392 9468	165	.034 505 6223
46	.043 582 0081	106	.035 358 1503	166	.034 501 2654
47	.043 197 5056	107	.035 324 5750	167	.034 497 0544
48	.042 832 1767	108	.035 292 1762	168	.034 492 9843
49	.042 484 8156	109	.035 260 9105	169	.034 489 0504
50	.042 154 3129	110	.035 230 7364	170	.034 485 2480
51	.041 839 6459	111	.035 201 6142	171	.034 481 5728
52	.041 539 8703	112	.035 173 5055	172	.034 478 0205
53	.041 254 1128	113	.035 146 3736	173	.034 474 5869
54	.040 981 5649	114	.035 120 1831	174	.034 471 2681
55	.040 721 4763	115	.035 094 9001	175	.034 468 0602
56	.040 473 1506	116	.035 070 4919	176	.034 464 9595
57	.040 235 9399	117	.035 046 9271	177	.034 461 9624
58	.040 009 2409	118	.035 024 1755	178	.034 459 0653
59	.039 792 4912	119	.035 002 2080	179	.034 456 2650
60	.039 585 1658	120	.034 980 9968	180	.034 453 5582

NOMINAL INTEREST RATE COMPOUNDED

YEARLY	HALF-YEARLY	QUARTERLY
@	@	@
$3\frac{1}{2}\%$	7%	14%
3.5000%	7.0000%	14.0000%
PER ANNUM	PER ANNUM	PER ANNUM

Periods	Loan of 1	Periods	Loan of 1	Periods	Loan of 1
1	1.035 000 0000	61	.039 892 4882	121	.035 553 4772
2	.526 400 4914	62	.039 704 8020	122	.035 534 4748
3	.356 934 1806	63	.039 525 1325	123	.035 516 1342
4	.272 251 1395	64	.039 353 0765	124	.035 498 4319
5	.221 481 3732	65	.039 188 2558	125	.035 481 3449
6	.187 668 2087	66	.039 030 3148	126	.035 464 8513
7	.163 544 4938	67	.038 878 9193	127	.035 448 9301
8	.145 476 6465	68	.038 733 7550	128	.035 433 5608
9	.131 446 0051	69	.038 594 5255	129	.035 418 7239
10	.120 241 3679	70	.038 460 9517	130	.035 404 4006
11	.111 091 9658	71	.038 332 7702	131	.035 390 5726
12	.103 483 9493	72	.038 209 7323	132	.035 377 2225
13	.097 061 5726	73	.038 091 6030	133	.035 364 3334
14	.091 570 7287	74	.037 978 1601	134	.035 351 8891
15	.086 825 0694	75	.037 869 1934	135	.035 339 8739
16	.082 684 8306	76	.037 764 5038	136	.035 328 2727
17	.079 043 1317	77	.037 663 9029	137	.035 317 0712
18	.075 816 8408	78	.037 567 2117	138	.035 306 2551
19	.072 940 3252	79	.037 474 2606	139	.035 295 8112
20	.070 361 0768	80	.037 384 8887	140	.035 285 7262
21	.068 036 5870	81	.037 298 9429	141	.035 275 9878
22	.065 932 0742	82	.037 216 2781	142	.035 266 5838
23	.064 018 8042	83	.037 136 7560	143	.035 257 5025
24	.062 272 8303	84	.037 060 2452	144	.035 248 7328
25	.060 674 0354	85	.036 986 6205	145	.035 240 2638
26	.059 205 3963	86	.036 915 7629	146	.035 232 0851
27	.057 852 4103	87	.036 847 5589	147	.035 224 1865
28	.056 602 6452	88	.036 781 9002	148	.035 216 5585
29	.055 445 3825	89	.036 718 6838	149	.035 209 1915
30	.054 371 3316	90	.036 657 8111	150	.035 202 0765
31	.053 372 3998	91	.036 599 1884	151	.035 195 2049
32	.052 441 5048	92	.036 542 7259	152	.035 188 5682
33	.051 572 4221	93	.036 488 3379	153	.035 182 1583
34	.050 759 6583	94	.036 435 9428	154	.035 175 9674
35	.049 998 3473	95	.036 385 4621	155	.035 169 9879
36	.049 284 1628	96	.036 336 8213	156	.035 164 2125
37	.048 613 2454	97	.036 289 9487	157	.035 158 6343
38	.047 982 1414	98	.036 244 7758	158	.035 153 2464
39	.047 387 7506	99	.036 201 2372	159	.035 148 0422
40	.046 827 2823	100	.036 159 2702	160	.035 143 0155
41	.046 298 2174	101	.036 118 8147	161	.035 138 1601
42	.045 798 2765	102	.036 079 8131	162	.035 133 4702
43	.045 325 3914	103	.036 042 2104	163	.035 128 9401
44	.044 877 6816	104	.036 005 9536	164	.035 124 5643
45	.044 453 4334	105	.035 970 9921	165	.035 120 3375
46	.044 051 0817	106	.035 937 2773	166	.035 116 2546
47	.043 669 1944	107	.035 904 7626	167	.035 112 3107
48	.043 306 4580	108	.035 873 4032	168	.035 108 5009
49	.042 961 6665	109	.035 843 1564	169	.035 104 8208
50	.042 633 7096	110	.035 813 9807	170	.035 101 2659
51	.042 321 5641	111	.035 785 8368	171	.035 097 8319
52	.042 024 2854	112	.035 758 6865	172	.035 094 5146
53	.041 740 9997	113	.035 732 4935	173	.035 091 3102
54	.041 470 8979	114	.035 707 2227	174	.035 088 2146
55	.041 213 2297	115	.035 682 8404	175	.035 085 2242
56	.040 967 2981	116	.035 659 3142	176	.035 082 3355
57	.040 732 4549	117	.035 636 6130	177	.035 079 5448
58	.040 508 0966	118	.035 614 7069	178	.035 076 8490
59	.040 293 6605	119	.035 593 5672	179	.035 074 2447
60	.040 088 6213	120	.035 573 1662	180	.035 071 7289

Repayment of a Loan by way of an Annuity

NOMINAL INTEREST RATE COMPOUNDED

YEARLY @ $3\frac{9}{16}\%$ 3.5625% PER ANNUM		HALF-YEARLY @ $7\frac{1}{8}\%$ 7.1250% PER ANNUM		QUARTERLY @ $14\frac{1}{4}\%$ 14.2500% PER ANNUM	
Periods	Loan of 1	Periods	Loan of 1	Periods	Loan of 1
1	1.035 625 0000	61	.040 400 6723	121	.036 148 0941
2	.526 874 6162	62	.040 215 2242	122	.036 129 8449
3	.357 360 4005	63	.040 037 7639	123	.036 112 2409
4	.272 655 1951	64	.039 867 8881	124	.036 095 2588
5	.221 873 5581	65	.039 705 2184	125	.036 078 8761
6	.188 053 6673	66	.039 549 3993	126	.036 063 0710
7	.163 926 1631	67	.039 400 0965	127	.036 047 8227
8	.145 856 3593	68	.039 256 9955	128	.036 033 1112
9	.131 824 9804	69	.039 119 8002	129	.036 018 9171
10	.120 620 4561	70	.038 988 2313	130	.036 005 2219
11	.111 471 7826	71	.038 862 0254	131	.035 992 0077
12	.103 864 9533	72	.038 740 9339	132	.035 979 2573
13	.097 444 1139	73	.038 624 7218	133	.035 966 9540
14	.091 955 0793	74	.038 513 1672	134	.035 955 0820
15	.087 211 4438	75	.038 406 0598	135	.035 943 6258
16	.083 073 4003	76	.038 303 2006	136	.035 932 5706
17	.079 434 0348	77	.038 204 4013	137	.035 921 9021
18	.076 210 1894	78	.038 109 4831	138	.035 911 6067
19	.073 336 2109	79	.038 018 2766	139	.035 901 6710
20	.070 759 5744	80	.037 930 6208	140	.035 892 0823
21	.068 437 7576	81	.037 846 3632	141	.035 882 8283
22	.066 335 9678	82	.037 765 3584	142	.035 873 8971
23	.064 425 4613	83	.037 687 4685	143	.035 865 2774
24	.062 682 2834	84	.037 612 5623	144	.035 856 9582
25	.061 086 3103	85	.037 540 5149	145	.035 848 9288
26	.059 620 5130	86	.037 471 2073	146	.035 841 1790
27	.058 270 3836	87	.037 404 5263	147	.035 833 6990
28	.057 023 4856	88	.037 340 3640	148	.035 826 4792
29	.055 869 0967	89	.037 278 6173	149	.035 819 5106
30	.054 797 9228	90	.037 219 1882	150	.035 812 7843
31	.053 801 8682	91	.037 161 9829	151	.035 806 2917
32	.052 873 8479	92	.037 106 9121	152	.035 800 0247
33	.052 007 6350	93	.037 053 8904	153	.035 793 9754
34	.051 197 7339	94	.037 002 8362	154	.035 788 1361
35	.050 439 2765	95	.036 953 6716	155	.035 782 4995
36	.049 727 9347	96	.036 906 3220	156	.035 777 0585
37	.049 059 8475	97	.036 860 7163	157	.035 771 8062
38	.048 431 5596	98	.036 816 7862	158	.035 766 7360
39	.047 839 9696	99	.036 774 4665	159	.035 761 8416
40	.047 282 2854	100	.036 733 6949	160	.035 757 1169
41	.046 755 9869	101	.036 694 4114	161	.035 752 5559
42	.046 258 7934	102	.036 656 5590	162	.035 748 1528
43	.045 788 6359	103	.036 620 0827	163	.035 743 9023
44	.045 343 6329	104	.036 584 9300	164	.035 739 7989
45	.044 922 0700	105	.036 551 0505	165	.035 735 8376
46	.044 522 3812	106	.036 518 3959	166	.035 732 0134
47	.044 143 1336	107	.036 486 9200	167	.035 728 3215
48	.043 783 0134	108	.036 456 5782	168	.035 724 7574
49	.043 440 8135	109	.036 427 3281	169	.035 721 3165
50	.043 115 4234	110	.036 399 1287	170	.035 717 9946
51	.042 805 8193	111	.036 371 9407	171	.035 714 7876
52	.042 511 0561	112	.036 345 7265	172	.035 711 6914
53	.042 230 2595	113	.036 320 4498	173	.035 708 7022
54	.041 962 6202	114	.036 296 0760	174	.035 705 8164
55	.041 707 3873	115	.036 272 5717	175	.035 703 0303
56	.041 463 8635	116	.036 249 9048	176	.035 700 3404
57	.041 231 4005	117	.036 228 0445	177	.035 697 7434
58	.041 009 3944	118	.036 206 9612	178	.035 695 2361
59	.040 797 2822	119	.036 186 6264	179	.035 692 8155
60	.040 594 5385	120	.036 167 0128	180	.035 690 4784

Repayment of a Loan by way of an Annuity

NOMINAL INTEREST RATE COMPOUNDED

YEARLY @ $3\frac{5}{8}\%$ 3.6250% PER ANNUM		HALF-YEARLY @ $7\frac{1}{4}\%$ 7.2500% PER ANNUM		QUARTERLY @ $14\frac{1}{2}\%$ 14.5000% PER ANNUM	
Periods	Loan of 1	Periods	Loan of 1	Periods	Loan of 1
1	1.036 250 0000	61	.040 911 2887	121	.036 744 2880
2	.527 348 8336	62	.040 728 0845	122	.036 726 7694
3	.357 786 7851	63	.040 552 8381	123	.036 709 8796
4	.273 059 4819	64	.040 385 1462	124	.036 693 5952
5	.222 266 0387	65	.040 224 6302	125	.036 677 8942
6	.188 439 4848	66	.040 070 9345	126	.036 662 7553
7	.164 308 2535	67	.039 923 7249	127	.036 648 1577
8	.146 236 5548	68	.039 782 6869	128	.036 634 0818
9	.132 204 4994	69	.039 647 5243	129	.036 620 5086
10	.121 000 1484	70	.039 517 9578	130	.036 607 4197
11	.111 852 2633	71	.039 393 7243	131	.036 594 7975
12	.104 246 6807	72	.039 274 5750	132	.036 582 6252
13	.097 827 4373	73	.039 160 2752	133	.036 570 8863
14	.092 340 2699	74	.039 050 6028	134	.036 559 5652
15	.087 598 7156	75	.038 945 3478	135	.036 548 6468
16	.083 462 9241	76	.038 844 3115	136	.036 538 1166
17	.079 825 9481	77	.038 747 3054	137	.036 527 9604
18	.076 604 6036	78	.038 654 1510	138	.036 518 1649
19	.073 733 2166	79	.038 564 6790	139	.036 508 7170
20	.071 159 2457	80	.038 478 7288	140	.036 499 6043
21	.068 840 1548	81	.038 396 1478	141	.036 490 8147
22	.066 741 1400	82	.038 316 7910	142	.036 482 3365
23	.064 833 4481	83	.038 240 5206	143	.036 474 1587
24	.063 093 1163	84	.038 167 2057	144	.036 466 2704
25	.061 500 0142	85	.038 096 7215	145	.036 458 6613
26	.060 037 1068	86	.038 028 9493	146	.036 451 3214
27	.058 689 8813	87	.037 963 7762	147	.036 444 2410
28	.057 445 8966	88	.037 901 0945	148	.036 437 4110
29	.056 294 4266	89	.037 840 8013	149	.036 430 8223
30	.055 226 1737	90	.037 782 7990	150	.036 424 4663
31	.054 233 0393	91	.037 726 9940	151	.036 418 3348
32	.053 307 9356	92	.037 673 2973	152	.036 412 4198
33	.052 444 6331	93	.037 621 6237	153	.036 406 7135
34	.051 637 6343	94	.037 571 8920	154	.036 401 2085
35	.050 882 0689	95	.037 524 0245	155	.036 395 8976
36	.050 173 6070	96	.037 477 9470	156	.036 390 7740
37	.049 508 3859	97	.037 433 5885	157	.036 385 8310
38	.048 882 9490	98	.037 390 8812	158	.036 381 0622
39	.048 294 1933	99	.037 349 7602	159	.036 376 4614
40	.047 739 3256	100	.037 310 1634	160	.036 372 0227
41	.047 215 8245	101	.037 272 0312	161	.036 367 7402
42	.046 721 4084	102	.037 235 3068	162	.036 363 6085
43	.046 254 0071	103	.037 199 9357	163	.036 359 6223
44	.045 811 7383	104	.037 165 8655	164	.036 355 7763
45	.045 392 8868	105	.037 133 0464	165	.036 352 0656
46	.044 995 8858	106	.037 101 4302	166	.036 348 4855
47	.044 619 3017	107	.037 070 9710	167	.036 345 0312
48	.044 261 8199	108	.037 041 6247	168	.036 341 6984
49	.043 922 2329	109	.037 013 3490	169	.036 338 4828
50	.043 599 4295	110	.036 986 1033	170	.036 335 3802
51	.043 292 3855	111	.036 959 8488	171	.036 332 3867
52	.043 000 1552	112	.036 934 5480	172	.036 329 4983
53	.042 721 8640	113	.036 910 1651	173	.036 326 7114
54	.042 456 7022	114	.036 886 6657	174	.036 324 0224
55	.042 203 9184	115	.036 864 0166	175	.036 321 4279
56	.041 962 8152	116	.036 842 1863	176	.036 318 9245
57	.041 732 7439	117	.036 821 1441	177	.036 316 5089
58	.041 513 1002	118	.036 800 8608	178	.036 314 1782
59	.041 303 3212	119	.036 781 3082	179	.036 311 9293
60	.041 102 8811	120	.036 762 4592	180	.036 309 7593

Repayment of a Loan by way of an Annuity

NOMINAL INTEREST RATE COMPOUNDED

	YEARLY		HALF-YEARLY		QUARTERLY
	@		@		@
	$3\frac{11}{16}\%$		$7\frac{3}{8}\%$		$14\frac{3}{4}\%$
	3.6875%		7.3750%		14.7500%
	PER ANNUM		PER ANNUM		PER ANNUM

Periods	Loan of 1	Periods	Loan of 1	Periods	Loan of 1
1	1,036 875 0000	61	,041 424 3000	121	,037 341 9846
2	,527 823 1436	62	,041 243 3443	122	,037 325 1742
3	,358 213 3340	63	,041 070 3155	123	,037 308 9760
4	,273 463 9996	64	,040 904 8099	124	,037 293 3672
5	,222 658 8146	65	,040 746 4490	125	,037 278 3258
6	,188 825 6606	66	,040 594 8773	126	,037 263 8308
7	,164 690 7645	67	,040 449 7603	127	,037 249 8620
8	,146 617 2323	68	,040 310 7837	128	,037 236 3999
9	,132 584 5613	69	,040 177 6512	129	,037 223 4258
10	,121 380 4441	70	,040 050 0838	130	,037 210 9216
11	,112 233 4072	71	,039 927 8182	131	,037 198 8701
12	,104 629 1303	72	,039 810 6058	132	,037 187 2546
13	,098 211 5413	73	,039 698 2121	133	,037 176 0591
14	,092 726 2991	74	,039 590 4149	134	,037 165 2680
15	,087 986 8834	75	,039 487 0046	135	,037 154 8667
16	,083 853 4003	76	,039 387 7824	136	,037 144 8408
17	,080 218 8695	77	,039 292 5600	137	,037 135 1766
18	,077 000 0809	78	,039 201 1593	138	,037 125 8608
19	,074 131 3397	79	,039 113 4110	139	,037 116 8808
20	,071 560 0877	80	,039 029 1546	140	,037 108 2242
21	,069 243 7753	81	,038 948 2379	141	,037 099 8794
22	,067 147 5871	82	,038 870 5161	142	,037 091 8348
23	,065 242 7604	83	,038 795 8516	143	,037 084 0797
24	,063 505 3245	84	,038 724 1136	144	,037 076 6034
25	,061 915 1422	85	,038 655 1778	145	,037 069 3959
26	,060 455 1724	86	,038 588 9257	146	,037 062 4473
27	,059 110 8974	87	,038 525 2446	147	,037 055 7483
28	,057 869 8717	88	,038 464 0269	148	,037 049 2899
29	,056 721 3651	89	,038 405 1704	149	,037 043 0633
30	,055 656 0768	90	,038 348 5774	150	,037 037 0601
31	,054 665 9048	91	,038 294 1548	151	,037 031 2722
32	,053 743 7589	92	,038 241 8139	152	,037 025 6919
33	,052 883 4069	93	,038 191 4697	153	,037 020 3116
34	,052 079 3491	94	,038 143 0413	154	,037 015 1242
35	,051 326 7133	95	,038 096 4514	155	,037 010 1226
36	,050 621 1677	96	,038 051 6262	156	,037 005 3002
37	,049 958 8480	97	,038 008 4948	157	,037 000 6504
38	,049 336 2960	98	,037 966 9899	158	,036 996 1672
39	,048 750 4074	99	,037 927 0469	159	,036 991 8444
40	,048 198 3877	100	,037 888 6039	160	,036 987 6763
41	,047 677 7142	101	,037 851 6018	161	,036 983 6573
42	,047 186 1044	102	,037 815 9841	162	,036 979 7821
43	,046 721 4870	103	,037 781 6964	163	,036 976 0454
44	,046 281 9790	104	,037 748 6871	164	,036 972 4424
45	,045 865 8640	105	,037 716 9062	165	,036 968 9682
46	,045 471 5747	106	,037 686 3062	166	,036 965 6181
47	,045 097 6766	107	,037 656 8415	167	,036 962 3878
48	,044 742 8546	108	,037 628 4683	168	,036 959 2728
49	,044 405 9006	109	,037 601 1446	169	,036 956 2692
50	,044 085 7029	110	,037 574 8302	170	,036 953 3728
51	,043 781 2366	111	,037 549 4864	171	,036 950 5799
52	,043 491 5556	112	,037 525 0764	172	,036 947 8867
53	,043 215 7850	113	,037 501 5645	173	,036 945 2896
54	,042 953 1145	114	,037 478 9167	174	,036 942 7853
55	,042 702 7927	115	,037 457 1002	175	,036 940 3703
56	,042 464 1216	116	,037 436 0837	176	,036 938 0415
57	,042 236 4522	117	,037 415 8368	177	,036 935 7959
58	,042 019 1803	118	,037 396 3308	178	,036 933 6303
59	,041 811 7424	119	,037 377 5377	179	,036 931 5420
60	,041 613 6128	120	,037 359 4309	180	,036 929 5282

Repayment of a Loan by way of an Annuity

NOMINAL INTEREST RATE COMPOUNDED

YEARLY	HALF-YEARLY	QUARTERLY
@	@	@
$3\frac{3}{4}\%$	$7\frac{1}{2}\%$	15%
3.7500%	7.5000%	15.0000%
PER ANNUM	PER ANNUM	PER ANNUM

Periods	Loan of 1	Periods	Loan of 1	Periods	Loan of 1
1	1.037 500 0000	61	.041 939 6687	121	.037 941 1124
2	.528 297 5460	62	.041 760 9653	122	.037 924 9879
3	.358 640 0472	63	.041 590 1564	123	.037 909 4592
4	.273 868 7482	64	.041 426 8386	124	.037 894 5038
5	.223 051 8856	65	.041 270 6332	125	.037 880 1001
6	.189 212 1945	66	.041 121 1846	126	.037 866 2273
7	.165 073 6956	67	.040 978 1586	127	.037 852 8656
8	.146 998 3915	68	.040 841 2407	128	.037 839 9958
9	.132 965 1657	69	.040 710 1348	129	.037 827 5995
10	.121 761 3423	70	.040 584 5619	130	.037 815 6589
11	.112 615 2131	71	.040 464 2587	131	.037 804 1570
12	.105 012 3010	72	.040 348 9770	132	.037 793 0774
13	.098 596 4248	73	.040 238 4820	133	.037 782 4045
14	.093 113 1655	74	.040 132 5521	134	.037 772 1230
15	.088 375 9452	75	.040 030 9775	135	.037 762 2185
16	.084 244 8270	76	.039 933 5598	136	.037 752 6768
17	.080 612 7968	77	.039 840 1108	137	.037 743 4846
18	.077 396 6188	78	.039 750 4525	138	.037 734 6289
19	.074 530 5773	79	.039 664 4160	139	.037 726 0972
20	.071 962 0973	80	.039 581 8410	140	.037 717 8776
21	.069 648 6155	81	.039 502 5754	141	.037 709 9584
22	.067 555 3051	82	.039 426 4747	142	.037 702 3286
23	.065 653 3940	83	.039 353 4016	143	.037 694 9775
24	.063 918 9033	84	.039 283 2256	144	.037 687 8948
25	.062 331 6890	85	.039 215 8225	145	.037 681 0706
26	.060 874 7042	86	.039 151 0743	146	.037 674 4954
27	.059 533 4259	87	.039 088 8684	147	.037 668 1601
28	.058 295 4043	88	.039 029 0977	148	.037 662 0557
29	.057 149 9051	89	.038 971 6601	149	.037 656 1739
30	.056 087 6242	90	.038 916 4584	150	.037 650 5064
31	.055 100 4564	91	.038 863 3997	151	.037 645 0454
32	.054 181 3087	92	.038 812 3956	152	.037 639 7832
33	.053 323 9465	93	.038 763 3615	153	.037 634 7127
34	.052 522 8679	94	.038 716 2168	154	.037 629 8267
35	.051 773 1986	95	.038 670 8846	155	.037 625 1185
36	.051 070 6050	96	.038 627 2913	156	.037 620 5816
37	.050 411 2211	97	.038 585 3665	157	.037 616 2097
38	.049 791 5872	98	.038 545 0431	158	.037 611 9968
39	.049 208 5975	99	.038 506 2569	159	.037 607 9371
40	.048 659 4563	100	.038 468 9464	160	.037 604 0249
41	.048 141 6399	101	.038 433 0528	161	.037 600 2549
42	.047 652 8644	102	.038 398 5200	162	.037 596 6219
43	.047 191 0577	103	.038 365 2940	163	.037 593 1209
44	.046 754 3358	104	.038 333 3233	164	.037 589 7470
45	.046 340 9816	105	.038 302 5585	165	.037 586 4957
46	.045 949 4269	106	.038 272 9525	166	.037 583 3624
47	.045 578 2365	107	.038 244 4598	167	.037 580 3428
48	.045 226 0947	108	.038 217 0371	168	.037 577 4329
49	.044 891 7928	109	.038 190 6428	169	.037 574 6285
50	.044 574 2185	110	.038 165 2370	170	.037 571 9259
51	.044 272 3464	111	.038 140 7814	171	.037 569 3214
52	.043 985 2301	112	.038 117 2394	172	.037 566 8113
53	.043 711 9941	113	.038 094 5758	173	.037 564 3923
54	.043 451 8278	114	.038 072 7569	174	.037 562 0610
55	.043 203 9795	115	.038 051 7502	175	.037 559 8143
56	.042 967 7509	116	.038 031 5248	176	.037 557 6490
57	.042 742 4928	117	.038 012 0507	177	.037 555 5622
58	.042 527 6006	118	.037 993 2994	178	.037 553 5511
59	.042 322 5108	119	.037 975 2433	179	.037 551 6128
60	.042 126 6973	120	.037 957 8561	180	.037 549 7448

Repayment of a Loan by way of an Annuity

NOMINAL INTEREST RATE COMPOUNDED

YEARLY @ $3\frac{13}{16}\%$ 3.8125% PER ANNUM		HALF-YEARLY @ $7\frac{5}{8}\%$ 7.6250% PER ANNUM		QUARTERLY @ $15\frac{1}{4}\%$ 15.2500% PER ANNUM	
Periods	Loan of 1	Periods	Loan of 1	Periods	Loan of 1
1	1.038 125 0000	61	.042 457 3579	121	.038 541 6028
2	.528 772 0408	62	.042 280 9090	122	.038 526 1421
3	.359 066 9244	63	.042 112 3214	123	.038 511 2610
4	.274 273 7272	64	.041 951 1916	124	.038 496 9372
5	.223 445 2512	65	.041 797 1409	125	.038 483 1495
6	.189 599 0860	66	.041 649 8138	126	.038 469 8776
7	.165 457 0464	67	.041 508 8760	127	.038 457 1016
8	.147 380 0316	68	.041 374 0131	128	.038 444 8029
9	.133 346 3116	69	.041 244 9291	129	.038 432 9634
10	.122 142 8423	70	.041 121 3451	130	.038 421 5655
11	.112 997 6803	71	.041 002 9979	131	.038 410 5926
12	.105 396 1917	72	.040 889 6394	132	.038 400 0285
13	.098 982 0865	73	.040 781 0351	133	.038 389 8580
14	.093 500 8676	74	.040 676 9634	134	.038 380 0660
15	.088 765 8996	75	.040 577 2147	135	.038 370 6384
16	.084 637 2021	76	.040 481 5908	136	.038 361 5614
17	.081 007 7280	77	.040 389 9039	137	.038 352 8218
18	.077 794 2150	78	.040 301 9761	138	.038 344 4069
19	.074 930 9268	79	.040 217 6386	139	.038 336 3046
20	.072 365 2715	80	.040 136 7315	140	.038 328 5030
21	.070 054 6721	81	.040 059 1029	141	.038 320 9910
22	.067 964 2904	82	.039 984 6087	142	.038 313 7576
23	.066 065 3447	83	.039 913 1117	143	.038 306 7925
24	.064 333 8481	84	.039 844 4819	144	.038 300 0855
25	.062 749 6497	85	.039 778 5952	145	.038 293 6271
26	.061 295 6966	86	.039 715 3340	146	.038 287 4079
27	.059 957 4607	87	.039 654 5860	147	.038 281 4190
28	.058 722 4876	88	.039 596 2444	148	.038 275 6518
29	.057 580 0393	89	.039 540 2075	149	.038 270 0981
30	.056 520 8080	90	.039 486 3783	150	.038 264 7499
31	.055 536 6855	91	.039 434 6644	151	.038 259 5995
32	.054 620 5758	92	.039 384 9776	152	.038 254 6395
33	.053 766 2422	93	.039 337 2338	153	.038 249 8629
34	.052 968 1802	94	.039 291 3527	154	.038 245 2629
35	.052 221 5135	95	.039 247 2577	155	.038 240 8328
36	.051 521 9068	96	.039 204 8755	156	.038 236 5664
37	.050 865 4923	97	.039 164 1363	157	.038 232 4576
38	.050 248 8088	98	.039 124 9732	158	.038 228 5005
39	.049 668 7492	99	.039 087 3224	159	.038 224 6896
40	.049 122 5163	100	.039 051 1227	160	.038 221 0192
41	.048 607 5853	101	.039 016 3158	161	.038 217 4844
42	.048 121 6713	102	.038 982 8459	162	.038 214 0800
43	.047 662 7011	103	.038 950 6593	163	.038 210 8012
44	.047 228 7899	104	.038 919 7050	164	.038 207 6433
45	.046 818 2197	105	.038 889 9340	165	.038 204 6019
46	.046 429 4214	106	.038 861 2994	166	.038 201 6727
47	.046 060 9594	107	.038 833 7562	167	.038 198 8514
48	.045 711 5172	108	.038 807 2614	168	.038 196 1342
49	.045 379 8854	109	.038 781 7738	169	.038 193 5171
50	.045 064 9512	110	.038 757 2539	170	.038 190 9964
51	.044 765 6889	111	.038 733 6638	171	.038 188 5687
52	.044 481 1514	112	.038 710 9671	172	.038 186 2304
53	.044 210 4630	113	.038 689 1291	173	.038 183 9782
54	.043 952 8127	114	.038 668 1164	174	.038 181 8090
55	.043 707 4484	115	.038 647 8970	175	.038 179 7197
56	.043 473 6716	116	.038 628 4401	176	.038 177 7074
57	.043 250 8328	117	.038 609 7163	177	.038 175 7691
58	.043 038 3273	118	.038 591 6972	178	.038 173 9023
59	.042 835 5913	119	.038 574 3558	179	.038 172 1041
60	.042 642 0987	120	.038 557 6660	180	.038 170 3722

Repayment of a Loan by way of an Annuity

NOMINAL INTEREST RATE COMPOUNDED

YEARLY	HALF-YEARLY	QUARTERLY
@	@	@
$3\frac{7}{8}\%$	$7\frac{3}{4}\%$	$15\frac{1}{2}\%$
3.8750%	7.7500%	15.5000%
PER ANNUM	PER ANNUM	PER ANNUM

Periods	Loan of 1	Periods	Loan of 1	Periods	Loan of 1
1	1.038 750 0000	61	.042 977 3304	121	.039 143 3897
2	.529 246 6278	62	.042 803 1374	122	.039 128 5711
3	.359 493 9656	63	.042 636 7713	123	.039 114 3160
4	.274 678 9366	64	.042 477 8288	124	.039 100 6024
5	.223 838 9113	65	.042 325 9310	125	.039 087 4095
6	.189 986 3348	66	.042 180 7225	126	.039 074 7171
7	.165 840 8164	67	.042 041 8690	127	.039 062 5060
8	.147 762 1521	68	.041 909 0564	128	.039 050 7577
9	.133 727 9986	69	.041 781 9886	129	.039 039 4543
10	.122 524 9431	70	.041 660 3869	130	.039 028 5787
11	.113 380 8077	71	.041 543 9882	131	.039 018 1146
12	.105 780 8013	72	.041 432 5446	132	.039 008 0461
13	.099 368 5251	73	.041 325 8218	133	.038 998 3582
14	.093 889 4039	74	.041 223 5983	134	.038 989 0361
15	.089 156 7447	75	.041 125 6649	135	.038 980 0661
16	.085 030 5238	76	.041 031 8234	136	.038 971 4346
17	.081 403 6607	77	.040 941 8863	137	.038 963 1286
18	.078 192 8670	78	.040 855 6759	138	.038 955 1359
19	.075 332 3854	79	.040 773 0239	139	.038 947 4444
20	.072 769 6072	80	.040 693 7705	140	.038 940 0427
21	.070 461 9417	81	.040 617 7641	141	.038 932 9198
22	.068 374 5391	82	.040 544 8609	142	.038 926 0651
23	.066 478 6083	83	.040 474 9241	143	.038 919 4684
24	.064 750 1542	84	.040 407 8238	144	.038 913 1198
25	.063 169 0190	85	.040 343 4365	145	.038 907 0101
26	.061 718 1439	86	.040 281 6447	146	.038 901 1301
27	.060 382 9955	87	.040 222 3366	147	.038 895 4711
28	.059 151 1151	88	.040 165 4056	148	.038 890 0247
29	.058 011 7605	89	.040 110 7505	149	.038 884 7830
30	.056 955 6204	90	.040 058 2747	150	.038 879 7382
31	.055 974 5836	91	.040 007 8859	151	.038 874 8828
32	.055 061 5513	92	.039 959 4965	152	.038 870 2096
33	.054 210 2840	93	.039 913 0227	153	.038 865 7119
34	.053 415 2753	94	.039 868 3846	154	.038 861 3829
35	.052 671 6467	95	.039 825 5059	155	.038 857 2163
36	.051 975 0610	96	.039 784 3139	156	.038 853 2060
37	.051 321 6488	97	.039 744 7388	157	.038 849 3461
38	.050 707 9472	98	.039 706 7145	158	.038 845 6309
39	.050 130 8478	99	.039 670 1773	159	.038 842 0550
40	.049 587 5521	100	.039 635 0665	160	.038 838 6131
41	.049 075 5341	101	.039 601 3242	161	.038 835 3001
42	.048 592 5078	102	.039 568 8949	162	.038 832 1113
43	.048 136 3991	103	.039 537 7255	163	.038 829 0420
44	.047 705 3222	104	.039 507 7652	164	.038 826 0875
45	.047 297 5582	105	.039 478 9654	165	.038 823 2438
46	.046 911 5374	106	.039 451 2796	166	.038 820 5065
47	.046 545 8233	107	.039 424 6633	167	.038 817 8717
48	.046 199 0989	108	.039 399 0737	168	.038 815 3355
49	.045 870 1542	109	.039 374 4702	169	.038 812 8942
50	.045 557 8758	110	.039 350 8135	170	.038 810 5443
51	.045 261 2377	111	.039 328 0661	171	.038 808 2824
52	.044 979 2922	112	.039 306 1921	172	.038 806 1050
53	.044 711 1633	113	.039 285 1572	173	.038 804 0091
54	.044 456 0396	114	.039 264 9281	174	.038 801 9917
55	.044 213 1688	115	.039 245 4734	175	.038 800 0496
56	.043 981 8520	116	.039 226 7626	176	.038 798 1802
57	.043 761 4396	117	.039 208 7667	177	.038 796 3807
58	.043 551 3267	118	.039 191 4577	178	.038 794 6485
59	.043 350 9492	119	.039 174 8088	179	.038 792 9811
60	.043 159 7810	120	.039 158 7944	180	.038 791 3760

Repayment of a Loan by way of an Annuity

NOMINAL INTEREST RATE COMPOUNDED

YEARLY	HALF-YEARLY	QUARTERLY
@	@	@
$3\frac{15}{16}\%$	$7\frac{7}{8}\%$	$15\frac{3}{4}\%$
3.9375%	7.8750%	15.7500%
PER ANNUM	PER ANNUM	PER ANNUM

Periods	Loan of 1	Periods	Loan of 1	Periods	Loan of 1
1	1.039 375 0000	61	.043 499 5493	121	.039 746 4101
2	.529 721 3071	62	.043 327 6124	122	.039 732 2122
3	.359 921 1706	63	.043 163 4672	123	.039 718 5617
4	.275 084 3761	64	.043 006 7100	124	.039 705 4372
5	.224 232 8655	65	.042 856 9622	125	.039 692 8181
6	.190 373 9404	66	.042 713 8685	126	.039 680 6846
7	.166 225 0051	67	.042 577 0946	127	.039 669 0178
8	.148 144 7524	68	.042 446 3265	128	.039 657 7994
9	.134 110 2259	69	.042 321 2682	129	.039 647 0120
10	.122 907 6441	70	.042 201 6412	130	.039 636 6388
11	.113 764 5943	71	.042 087 1826	131	.039 626 6637
12	.106 166 1287	72	.041 977 6446	132	.039 617 0712
13	.099 755 7393	73	.041 872 7932	133	.039 607 8465
14	.094 278 7729	74	.041 772 4070	134	.039 598 9754
15	.089 548 4788	75	.041 676 2771	135	.039 590 4440
16	.085 424 7902	76	.041 584 2057	136	.039 582 2393
17	.081 800 5928	77	.041 496 0054	137	.039 574 3486
18	.078 592 5722	78	.041 411 4988	138	.039 566 7599
19	.075 734 9502	79	.041 330 5179	139	.039 559 4613
20	.073 175 1012	80	.041 252 9032	140	.039 552 4418
21	.070 870 4206	81	.041 178 5034	141	.039 545 6906
22	.068 786 0473	82	.041 107 1750	142	.039 539 1973
23	.066 893 1804	83	.041 038 7817	143	.039 532 9520
24	.065 167 8169	84	.040 973 1937	144	.039 526 9452
25	.063 589 7918	85	.040 910 2881	145	.039 521 1676
26	.062 142 0404	86	.040 849 9476	146	.039 515 6105
27	.060 810 0243	87	.040 792 0607	147	.039 510 2654
28	.059 581 2799	88	.040 736 5214	148	.039 505 1242
29	.058 445 0612	89	.040 683 2287	149	.039 500 1790
30	.057 392 0534	90	.040 632 0864	150	.039 495 4223
31	.056 414 1421	91	.040 583 0027	151	.039 490 8468
32	.055 504 2257	92	.040 535 8903	152	.039 486 4458
33	.054 656 0621	93	.040 490 6658	153	.039 482 2123
34	.053 864 1427	94	.040 447 2497	154	.039 478 1401
35	.053 123 5868	95	.040 405 5661	155	.039 474 2230
36	.052 430 0554	96	.040 365 5427	156	.039 470 4550
37	.051 779 6775	97	.040 327 1103	157	.039 466 8304
38	.051 168 9886	98	.040 290 2028	158	.039 463 3437
39	.050 594 8787	99	.040 254 7572	159	.039 459 9898
40	.050 054 5483	100	.040 220 7132	160	.039 456 7634
41	.049 545 4700	101	.040 188 0132	161	.039 453 6597
42	.049 065 3567	102	.040 156 6022	162	.039 450 6741
43	.048 612 1335	103	.040 126 4274	163	.039 447 8020
44	.048 183 9134	104	.040 097 4385	164	.039 445 0391
45	.047 778 9769	105	.040 069 5874	165	.039 442 3813
46	.047 395 7535	106	.040 042 8278	166	.039 439 8244
47	.047 032 8060	107	.040 017 1157	167	.039 437 3648
48	.046 688 8167	108	.039 992 4087	168	.039 434 9986
49	.046 362 5751	109	.039 968 6666	169	.039 432 7223
50	.046 052 9673	110	.039 945 8505	170	.039 430 5325
51	.045 758 9667	111	.039 923 9232	171	.039 428 4259
52	.045 479 6254	112	.039 902 8494	172	.039 426 3993
53	.045 214 0668	113	.039 882 5949	173	.039 424 4497
54	.044 961 4794	114	.039 863 1272	174	.039 422 5741
55	.044 721 1103	115	.039 844 4148	175	.039 420 7697
56	.044 492 2607	116	.039 826 4279	176	.039 419 0339
57	.044 274 2807	117	.039 809 1378	177	.039 417 3639
58	.044 066 5650	118	.039 792 5168	178	.039 415 7574
59	.043 868 5497	119	.039 776 5386	179	.039 414 2118
60	.043 679 7084	120	.039 761 1778	180	.039 412 7249

Repayment of a Loan by way of an Annuity

NOMINAL INTEREST RATE COMPOUNDED

YEARLY	HALF-YEARLY	QUARTERLY
@	@	@
4%	8%	16%
4.0000%	8.0000%	16.0000%
PER ANNUM	PER ANNUM	PER ANNUM

Periods	Loan of 1	Periods	Loan of 1	Periods	Loan of 1
1	1.040 000 0000	61	.044 023 9779	121	.040 350 6033
2	.530 196 0784	62	.043 854 2964	122	.040 337 0049
3	.360 348 5392	63	.043 692 3701	123	.040 323 9382
4	.275 490 0454	64	.043 537 7955	124	.040 311 3821
5	.224 627 1135	65	.043 390 1939	125	.040 299 3162
6	.190 761 9025	66	.043 249 2100	126	.040 287 7213
7	.166 609 6120	67	.043 114 5099	127	.040 276 5785
8	.148 527 8320	68	.042 985 7795	128	.040 265 8702
9	.134 492 9927	69	.042 862 7231	129	.040 255 5791
10	.123 290 9443	70	.042 745 0623	130	.040 245 6887
11	.114 149 0393	71	.042 632 5344	131	.040 236 1834
12	.106 552 1727	72	.042 524 8919	132	.040 227 0478
13	.100 143 7278	73	.042 421 9008	133	.040 218 2676
14	.094 668 9731	74	.042 323 3403	134	.040 209 8286
15	.089 941 1004	75	.042 229 0015	135	.040 201 7176
16	.085 819 9992	76	.042 138 6869	136	.040 193 9216
17	.082 198 5221	77	.042 052 2095	137	.040 186 4283
18	.078 993 3281	78	.041 969 3922	138	.040 179 2259
19	.076 138 6184	79	.041 890 0672	139	.040 172 3029
20	.073 581 7503	80	.041 814 0755	140	.040 165 6484
21	.071 280 1054	81	.041 741 2661	141	.040 159 2520
22	.069 198 8111	82	.041 671 4957	142	.040 153 1034
23	.067 309 0568	83	.041 604 6284	143	.040 147 1932
24	.065 586 8313	84	.041 540 5351	144	.040 141 5119
25	.064 011 9628	85	.041 479 0928	145	.040 136 0506
26	.062 567 3805	86	.041 420 1848	146	.040 130 8008
27	.061 238 5406	87	.041 363 7001	147	.040 125 7542
28	.060 012 9752	88	.041 309 5329	148	.040 120 9028
29	.058 879 9342	89	.041 257 5828	149	.040 116 2392
30	.057 830 0991	90	.041 207 7538	150	.040 111 7560
31	.056 855 3524	91	.041 159 9547	151	.040 107 4461
32	.055 948 5897	92	.041 114 0984	152	.040 103 3029
33	.055 103 5665	93	.041 070 1021	153	.040 099 3199
34	.054 314 7715	94	.041 027 8867	154	.040 095 4907
35	.053 577 3224	95	.040 987 3767	155	.040 091 8096
36	.052 886 8780	96	.040 948 5002	156	.040 088 2707
37	.052 239 5655	97	.040 911 1884	157	.040 084 8684
38	.051 631 9191	98	.040 875 3757	158	.040 081 5976
39	.051 060 8274	99	.040 840 9996	159	.040 078 4531
40	.050 523 4893	100	.040 808 0000	160	.040 075 4300
41	.050 017 3765	101	.040 776 3200	161	.040 072 5236
42	.049 540 2007	102	.040 745 9047	162	.040 069 7293
43	.049 089 8859	103	.040 716 7020	163	.040 067 0429
44	.048 664 5444	104	.040 688 6620	164	.040 064 4602
45	.048 262 4558	105	.040 661 7368	165	.040 061 9771
46	.047 882 0488	106	.040 635 8808	166	.040 059 5898
47	.047 521 8855	107	.040 611 0502	167	.040 057 2946
48	.047 180 6476	108	.040 587 2033	168	.040 055 0880
49	.046 857 1240	109	.040 564 2999	169	.040 052 9664
50	.046 550 2004	110	.040 542 3018	170	.040 050 9266
51	.046 258 8497	111	.040 521 1723	171	.040 048 9655
52	.045 982 1236	112	.040 500 8762	172	.040 047 0800
53	.045 719 1451	113	.040 481 3799	173	.040 045 2672
54	.045 469 1025	114	.040 462 6512	174	.040 043 5242
55	.045 231 2426	115	.040 444 6591	175	.040 041 8485
56	.045 004 8662	116	.040 427 3741	176	.040 040 2373
57	.044 789 3234	117	.040 410 7678	177	.040 038 6882
58	.044 584 0087	118	.040 394 8131	178	.040 037 1988
59	.044 388 3581	119	.040 379 4839	179	.040 035 7668
60	.044 201 8451	120	.040 364 7553	180	.040 034 3900

Repayment of a Loan by way of an Annuity

NOMINAL INTEREST RATE COMPOUNDED

YEARLY	HALF-YEARLY	QUARTERLY
@	@	@
$4\frac{1}{16}\%$	$8\frac{1}{8}\%$	$16\frac{1}{4}\%$
4.0625%	8.1250%	16.2500%
PER ANNUM	PER ANNUM	PER ANNUM

Periods	Loan of 1	Periods	Loan of 1	Periods	Loan of 1
1	1,040 625 0000	61	,044 550 5796	121	,040 955 9114
2	,530 670 9418	62	,044 383 1518	122	,040 942 8918
3	,360 776 0713	63	,044 223 4416	123	,040 930 3884
4	,275 895 9443	64	,044 071 0456	124	,040 918 3802
5	,225 021 6550	65	,043 925 5854	125	,040 906 8475
6	,191 150 2207	66	,043 786 7056	126	,040 895 7711
7	,166 994 6368	67	,043 654 0725	127	,040 885 1327
8	,148 911 3904	68	,043 527 3721	128	,040 874 9149
9	,134 876 2985	69	,043 406 3091	129	,040 865 1008
10	,123 674 8430	70	,043 290 6050	130	,040 855 6743
11	,114 534 1416	71	,043 179 9976	131	,040 846 6199
12	,106 938 9323	72	,043 074 2394	132	,040 837 9227
13	,100 532 4893	73	,042 973 0970	133	,040 829 5685
14	,095 060 0030	74	,042 876 3495	134	,040 821 5437
15	,090 334 6075	75	,042 783 7885	135	,040 813 8352
16	,086 216 1490	76	,042 695 2168	136	,040 806 4303
17	,082 597 4463	77	,042 610 4477	137	,040 799 3171
18	,079 395 1324	78	,042 529 3044	138	,040 792 4838
19	,076 543 3873	79	,042 451 6196	139	,040 785 9195
20	,073 989 5515	80	,042 377 2344	140	,040 779 6135
21	,071 690 9926	81	,042 305 9983	141	,040 773 5555
22	,069 612 8266	82	,042 237 7685	142	,040 767 7356
23	,067 726 2331	83	,042 172 4094	143	,040 762 1445
24	,066 007 1928	84	,042 109 7921	144	,040 756 7732
25	,064 435 5268	85	,042 049 7944	145	,040 751 6129
26	,062 994 1583	86	,041 992 2997	146	,040 746 6552
27	,061 668 5383	87	,041 937 1975	147	,040 741 8922
28	,060 446 1942	88	,041 884 3825	148	,040 737 3163
29	,059 316 3719	89	,041 833 7546	149	,040 732 9199
30	,058 269 7494	90	,041 785 2183	150	,040 728 6961
31	,057 298 2059	91	,041 738 6828	151	,040 724 6379
32	,056 394 6341	92	,041 694 0616	152	,040 720 7390
33	,055 552 7870	93	,041 651 2721	153	,040 716 9930
34	,054 767 1511	94	,041 610 2358	154	,040 713 3938
35	,054 032 8418	95	,041 570 8776	155	,040 709 9358
36	,053 345 5162	96	,041 533 1260	156	,040 706 6133
37	,052 701 2998	97	,041 496 9128	157	,040 703 4211
38	,052 096 7249	98	,041 462 1727	158	,040 700 3539
39	,051 528 6790	99	,041 428 8436	159	,040 697 4069
40	,050 994 3596	100	,041 396 8661	160	,040 694 5754
41	,050 491 2371	101	,041 366 1834	161	,040 691 8548
42	,050 017 0223	102	,041 336 7414	162	,040 689 2407
43	,049 569 6381	103	,041 308 4882	163	,040 686 7290
44	,049 147 1960	104	,041 281 3744	164	,040 684 3156
45	,048 747 9745	105	,041 255 3525	165	,040 681 9968
46	,048 370 4019	106	,041 230 3775	166	,040 679 7687
47	,048 013 0395	107	,041 206 4059	167	,040 677 6278
48	,047 674 5683	108	,041 183 3964	168	,040 675 5707
49	,047 353 7767	109	,041 161 3093	169	,040 673 5941
50	,047 049 5500	110	,041 140 1069	170	,040 671 6948
51	,046 760 8605	111	,041 119 7527	171	,040 669 8699
52	,046 486 7596	112	,041 100 2121	172	,040 668 1164
53	,046 226 3701	113	,041 081 4518	173	,040 666 4314
54	,045 978 8797	114	,041 063 4401	174	,040 664 8124
55	,045 743 5351	115	,041 046 1464	175	,040 663 2567
56	,045 519 6371	116	,041 029 5415	176	,040 661 7618
57	,045 306 5353	117	,041 013 5975	177	,040 660 3254
58	,045 103 6244	118	,040 998 2876	178	,040 658 9452
59	,044 910 3400	119	,040 983 5862	179	,040 657 6190
60	,044 726 1557	120	,040 969 4687	180	,040 656 3446

NOMINAL INTEREST RATE COMPOUNDED

YEARLY	HALF-YEARLY	QUARTERLY
@	@	@
$4\frac{1}{8}\%$	$8\frac{1}{4}\%$	$16\frac{1}{2}\%$
4.1250%	8.2500%	16.5000%
PER ANNUM	PER ANNUM	PER ANNUM

Periods	Loan of 1	Periods	Loan of 1	Periods	Loan of 1
1	1,041 250 0000	61	,045 079 3182	121	,041 562 2789
2	,531 145 8971	62	,044 914 1412	122	,041 549 8178
3	,361 203 7667	63	,044 756 6434	123	,041 537 8573
4	,276 302 0727	64	,044 606 4212	124	,041 526 3772
5	,225 416 4898	65	,044 463 0965	125	,041 515 3579
6	,191 538 8947	66	,044 326 3140	126	,041 504 7806
7	,167 380 0788	67	,044 195 7402	127	,041 494 6274
8	,149 295 4268	68	,044 071 0613	128	,041 484 8811
9	,135 260 1424	69	,043 951 9821	129	,041 475 5252
10	,124 059 3394	70	,043 838 2245	130	,041 466 5439
11	,114 919 9002	71	,043 729 5265	131	,041 457 9221
12	,107 326 4062	72	,043 625 6408	132	,041 449 6452
13	,100 922 0225	73	,043 526 3343	133	,041 441 6993
14	,095 451 8611	74	,043 431 3865	134	,041 434 0711
15	,090 728 9986	75	,043 340 5893	135	,041 426 7477
16	,086 613 2375	76	,043 253 7458	136	,041 419 7169
17	,082 997 3632	77	,043 170 6697	137	,041 412 9669
18	,079 797 9823	78	,043 091 1845	138	,041 406 4863
19	,076 949 2539	79	,043 015 1232	139	,041 400 2644
20	,074 398 5014	80	,042 942 3276	140	,041 394 2907
21	,072 103 0786	81	,042 872 6473	141	,041 388 5553
22	,070 028 0897	82	,042 805 9400	142	,041 383 0486
23	,068 144 7049	83	,042 742 0706	143	,041 377 7615
24	,066 428 8965	84	,042 680 9105	144	,041 372 6850
25	,064 860 4784	85	,042 622 3379	145	,041 367 8109
26	,063 422 3680	86	,042 566 2368	146	,041 363 1309
27	,062 100 0110	87	,042 512 4970	147	,041 358 6373
28	,060 880 9300	88	,042 461 0138	148	,041 354 3227
29	,059 754 3669	89	,042 411 6874	149	,041 350 1798
30	,058 710 9962	90	,042 364 4228	150	,041 346 2019
31	,057 742 6937	91	,042 319 1298	151	,041 342 3822
32	,056 842 3494	92	,042 275 7221	152	,041 338 7145
33	,056 003 7137	93	,042 234 1178	153	,041 335 1928
34	,055 221 2706	94	,042 194 2387	154	,041 331 8111
35	,054 490 1336	95	,042 156 0103	155	,041 328 5639
36	,053 805 9578	96	,042 119 3615	156	,041 325 4458
37	,053 164 8670	97	,042 084 2245	157	,041 322 4517
38	,052 563 3920	98	,042 050 5346	158	,041 319 5767
39	,051 998 4187	99	,042 018 2301	159	,041 316 8159
40	,051 467 1434	100	,041 987 2521	160	,041 314 1648
41	,050 967 0353	101	,041 957 5442	161	,041 311 6190
42	,050 495 8041	102	,041 929 0529	162	,041 309 1744
43	,050 051 3717	103	,041 901 7266	163	,041 306 8270
44	,049 631 8487	104	,041 875 5164	164	,041 304 5727
45	,049 235 5129	105	,041 850 3753	165	,041 302 4080
46	,048 860 7917	106	,041 826 2587	166	,041 300 3293
47	,048 506 2458	107	,041 803 1236	167	,041 298 3332
48	,048 170 5556	108	,041 780 9291	168	,041 296 4162
49	,047 852 5091	109	,041 759 6360	169	,041 294 5754
50	,047 550 9909	110	,041 739 2069	170	,041 292 8077
51	,047 264 9729	111	,041 719 6060	171	,041 291 1102
52	,046 993 5063	112	,041 700 7988	172	,041 289 4800
53	,046 735 7134	113	,041 682 7527	173	,041 287 9145
54	,046 490 7817	114	,041 665 4362	174	,041 286 4112
55	,046 257 9578	115	,041 648 8192	175	,041 284 9675
56	,046 036 5422	116	,041 632 8730	176	,041 283 5811
57	,045 825 8843	117	,041 617 5700	177	,041 282 2497
58	,045 625 3787	118	,041 602 8838	178	,041 280 9712
59	,045 434 4611	119	,041 588 7892	179	,041 279 7433
60	,045 252 6049	120	,041 575 2620	180	,041 278 5642

Repayment of a Loan by way of an Annuity

NOMINAL INTEREST RATE COMPOUNDED

YEARLY	HALF-YEARLY	QUARTERLY
@	@	@
$4\frac{3}{16}\%$	$8\frac{3}{8}\%$	$16\frac{3}{4}\%$
4.1875%	8.3750%	16.7500%
PER ANNUM	PER ANNUM	PER ANNUM

Periods	Loan of 1	Periods	Loan of 1	Periods	Loan of 1
1	1.041 875 0000	61	.045 610 1575	121	.042 169 6526
2	.531 620 9443	62	.045 447 2277	122	.042 157 7300
3	.361 631 6252	63	.045 291 9374	123	.042 146 2929
4	.276 708 4302	64	.045 143 8833	124	.042 135 3213
5	.225 811 6175	65	.045 002 6873	125	.042 124 7961
6	.191 927 9240	66	.044 867 9945	126	.042 114 6988
7	.167 765 9377	67	.044 739 4715	127	.042 105 0120
8	.149 679 9407	68	.044 616 8046	128	.042 095 7186
9	.135 644 5239	69	.044 499 6989	129	.042 086 8026
10	.124 444 4326	70	.044 387 8766	130	.042 078 2485
11	.115 306 3143	71	.044 281 0760	131	.042 070 0415
12	.107 714 5935	72	.044 179 0502	132	.042 062 1674
13	.101 312 3261	73	.044 081 5662	133	.042 054 6125
14	.095 844 5458	74	.043 988 4040	134	.042 047 3638
15	.091 124 2717	75	.043 899 3559	135	.042 040 4088
16	.087 011 2627	76	.043 814 2251	136	.042 033 7355
17	.083 398 2705	77	.043 732 8259	137	.042 027 3324
18	.080 201 8754	78	.043 654 9823	138	.042 021 1885
19	.077 356 2154	79	.043 580 5275	139	.042 015 2932
20	.074 808 5969	80	.043 509 3037	140	.042 009 6364
21	.072 516 3598	81	.043 441 1611	141	.042 004 2084
22	.070 444 5967	82	.043 375 9578	142	.041 998 9999
23	.068 564 4679	83	.043 313 5589	143	.041 994 0019
24	.066 851 9374	84	.043 253 8366	144	.041 989 2060
25	.065 286 8124	85	.043 196 6693	145	.041 984 6038
26	.063 852 0039	86	.043 141 9416	146	.041 980 1875
27	.062 532 9522	87	.043 089 5439	147	.041 975 9496
28	.061 317 1756	88	.043 039 3716	148	.041 971 8829
29	.060 193 9117	89	.042 991 3257	149	.041 967 9803
30	.059 153 8312	90	.042 945 3116	150	.041 964 2353
31	.058 188 8070	91	.042 901 2394	151	.041 960 6414
32	.057 291 7261	92	.042 859 0236	152	.041 957 1926
33	.056 456 3362	93	.042 818 5825	153	.041 953 8829
34	.055 677 1191	94	.042 779 8386	154	.041 950 7067
35	.054 949 1861	95	.042 742 7178	155	.041 947 6586
36	.054 268 1904	96	.042 707 1495	156	.041 944 7335
37	.053 630 2540	97	.042 673 0663	157	.041 941 9262
38	.053 031 9063	98	.042 640 4042	158	.041 939 2322
39	.052 470 0316	99	.042 609 1018	159	.041 936 6468
40	.051 941 8250	100	.042 579 1007	160	.041 934 1656
41	.051 444 7545	101	.042 550 3451	161	.041 931 7844
42	.050 976 5286	102	.042 522 7818	162	.041 929 4991
43	.050 535 0683	103	.042 496 3598	163	.041 927 3060
44	.050 118 4833	104	.042 471 0307	164	.041 925 2012
45	.049 725 0507	105	.042 446 7480	165	.041 923 1812
46	.049 353 1970	106	.042 423 4673	166	.041 921 2425
47	.049 001 4823	107	.042 401 1463	167	.041 919 3820
48	.048 668 5865	108	.042 379 7446	168	.041 917 5964
49	.048 353 2969	109	.042 359 2233	169	.041 915 8827
50	.048 054 4978	110	.042 339 5455	170	.041 914 2380
51	.047 771 1608	111	.042 320 6758	171	.041 912 6595
52	.047 502 3364	112	.042 302 5803	172	.041 911 1446
53	.047 247 1469	113	.042 285 2267	173	.041 909 6907
54	.047 004 7794	114	.042 268 5839	174	.041 908 2953
55	.046 774 4804	115	.042 252 6224	175	.041 906 9561
56	.046 555 5501	116	.042 237 3137	176	.041 905 6707
57	.046 347 3380	117	.042 222 6307	177	.041 904 4372
58	.046 149 2384	118	.042 208 5474	178	.041 903 2532
59	.045 960 6871	119	.042 195 0390	179	.041 902 1169
60	.045 781 1574	120	.042 182 0817	180	.041 901 0264

Repayment of a Loan by way of an Annuity

NOMINAL INTEREST RATE COMPOUNDED

YEARLY	HALF-YEARLY	QUARTERLY
@	@	@
4¼%	8½%	17%
4.2500%	8.5000%	17.0000%
PER ANNUM	PER ANNUM	PER ANNUM

Periods	Loan of 1	Periods	Loan of 1	Periods	Loan of 1
1	1.042 500 0000	61	.046 143 0617	121	.042 777 9819
2	.532 096 0832	62	.045 982 3743	122	.042 766 5783
3	.362 059 6468	63	.045 829 2858	123	.042 755 6452
4	.277 115 0167	64	.045 683 3932	124	.042 745 1631
5	.226 207 0379	65	.045 544 3184	125	.042 735 1131
6	.192 317 3083	66	.045 411 7067	126	.042 725 4773
7	.168 152 2129	67	.045 285 2249	127	.042 716 2384
8	.150 064 9316	68	.045 164 5597	128	.042 707 3800
9	.136 029 4423	69	.045 049 4164	129	.042 698 8861
10	.124 830 1217	70	.044 939 5176	130	.042 690 7416
11	.115 693 3829	71	.044 834 6017	131	.042 682 9321
12	.108 103 4928	72	.044 734 4223	132	.042 675 4436
13	.101 703 3987	73	.044 638 7467	133	.042 668 2629
14	.096 238 0557	74	.044 547 3553	134	.042 661 3773
15	.091 520 4253	75	.044 460 0407	135	.042 654 7744
16	.087 410 2226	76	.044 376 6067	136	.042 648 4426
17	.083 800 1659	77	.044 296 8678	137	.042 642 3707
18	.080 606 8090	78	.044 220 6484	138	.042 636 5480
19	.077 764 2688	79	.044 147 7824	139	.042 630 9641
20	.075 219 8348	80	.044 078 1123	140	.042 625 6093
21	.072 930 8326	81	.044 011 4887	141	.042 620 4740
22	.070 862 3433	82	.043 947 7702	142	.042 615 5492
23	.068 985 5175	83	.043 886 8224	143	.042 610 8263
24	.067 276 3108	84	.043 828 5180	144	.042 606 2969
25	.065 714 5234	85	.043 772 7359	145	.042 601 9531
26	.064 283 0600	86	.043 719 3611	146	.042 597 7871
27	.062 967 3557	87	.043 668 2844	147	.042 593 7918
28	.061 754 9240	88	.043 619 4021	148	.042 589 9601
29	.060 634 9986	89	.043 572 6152	149	.042 586 2852
30	.059 598 2464	90	.043 527 8300	150	.042 582 7607
31	.058 636 5371	91	.043 484 9570	151	.042 579 3805
32	.057 742 7548	92	.043 443 9110	152	.042 576 1385
33	.056 910 6445	93	.043 404 6112	153	.042 573 0292
34	.056 134 6857	94	.043 366 9802	154	.042 570 0471
35	.055 409 9876	95	.043 330 9447	155	.042 567 1870
36	.054 732 2015	96	.043 296 4344	156	.042 564 4438
37	.054 097 4476	97	.043 263 3827	157	.042 561 8128
38	.053 502 2538	98	.043 231 7257	158	.042 559 2893
39	.052 943 5028	99	.043 201 4029	159	.042 556 8690
40	.052 418 3886	100	.043 172 3562	160	.042 554 5476
41	.051 924 3779	101	.043 144 5303	161	.042 552 3211
42	.051 459 1782	102	.043 117 8725	162	.042 550 1856
43	.051 020 7095	103	.043 092 3323	163	.042 548 1373
44	.050 607 0805	104	.043 067 8618	164	.042 546 1728
45	.050 216 5675	105	.043 044 4151	165	.042 544 2885
46	.049 847 5964	106	.043 021 9481	166	.042 542 4811
47	.049 498 7267	107	.043 000 4191	167	.042 540 7476
48	.049 168 6377	108	.042 979 7880	168	.042 539 0849
49	.048 856 1161	109	.042 960 0166	169	.042 537 4901
50	.048 560 0458	110	.042 941 0683	170	.042 535 9605
51	.048 279 3980	111	.042 922 9082	171	.042 534 4933
52	.048 013 2229	112	.042 905 5028	172	.042 533 0860
53	.047 760 6425	113	.042 888 8203	173	.042 531 7361
54	.047 520 8438	114	.042 872 8300	174	.042 530 4414
55	.047 293 0729	115	.042 857 5029	175	.042 529 1995
56	.047 076 6300	116	.042 842 8109	176	.042 528 0084
57	.046 870 8644	117	.042 828 7273	177	.042 526 8658
58	.046 675 1706	118	.042 815 2265	178	.042 525 7699
59	.046 488 9841	119	.042 802 2841	179	.042 524 7187
60	.046 311 7784	120	.042 789 8768	180	.042 523 7104

Repayment of a Loan by way of an Annuity

NOMINAL INTEREST RATE COMPOUNDED

YEARLY	HALF-YEARLY	QUARTERLY
@	@	@
$4\frac{5}{16}\%$	$8\frac{5}{8}\%$	$17\frac{1}{4}\%$
4.3125%	8.6250%	17.2500%
PER ANNUM	PER ANNUM	PER ANNUM

Periods	Loan of 1	Periods	Loan of 1	Periods	Loan of 1
1	1.043 125 0000	61	.046 677 9950	121	.043 387 2183
2	.532 571 3139	62	.046 519 5445	122	.043 376 3144
3	.362 487 8312	63	.046 368 6513	123	.043 365 8665
4	.277 521 8320	64	.046 224 9125	124	.043 355 8553
5	.226 602 7505	65	.046 087 9504	125	.043 346 2623
6	.192 707 0472	66	.045 957 4104	126	.043 337 0699
7	.168 538 9041	67	.045 832 9596	127	.043 328 2611
8	.150 450 3989	68	.045 714 2850	128	.043 319 8199
9	.136 414 8968	69	.045 601 0922	129	.043 311 7308
10	.125 216 4061	70	.045 493 1041	130	.043 303 9789
11	.116 081 1048	71	.045 390 0595	131	.043 296 5501
12	.108 493 1032	72	.045 291 7123	132	.043 289 4308
13	.102 095 2390	73	.045 197 8303	133	.043 282 6080
14	.096 632 3893	74	.045 108 1942	134	.043 276 0694
15	.091 917 4575	75	.045 022 5970	135	.043 269 8029
16	.087 810 1153	76	.044 940 8431	136	.043 263 7971
17	.084 203 0473	77	.044 862 7472	137	.043 258 0413
18	.081 012 7807	78	.044 788 1344	138	.043 252 5248
19	.078 173 4114	79	.044 716 8390	139	.043 247 2377
20	.075 632 2118	80	.044 648 7037	140	.043 242 1704
21	.073 346 4934	81	.044 583 5800	141	.043 237 3137
22	.071 281 3256	82	.044 521 3268	142	.043 232 6588
23	.069 407 8493	83	.044 461 8102	143	.043 228 1973
24	.067 702 0118	84	.044 404 9034	144	.043 223 9212
25	.066 143 6058	85	.044 350 4858	145	.043 219 8226
26	.064 715 5303	86	.044 298 4430	146	.043 215 8941
27	.063 403 2149	87	.044 248 6664	147	.043 212 1288
28	.062 194 1683	88	.044 201 0525	148	.043 208 5197
29	.061 077 6200	89	.044 155 5032	149	.043 205 0604
30	.060 044 2335	90	.044 111 9250	150	.043 201 7447
31	.059 085 8750	91	.044 070 2291	151	.043 198 5665
32	.058 195 4257	92	.044 030 3310	152	.043 195 5201
33	.057 366 6281	93	.043 992 1501	153	.043 192 6001
34	.056 593 9593	94	.043 955 6098	154	.043 189 8011
35	.055 872 5263	95	.043 920 6371	155	.043 187 1183
36	.055 197 9785	96	.043 887 1624	156	.043 184 5466
37	.054 566 4345	97	.043 855 1195	157	.043 182 0816
38	.053 974 4203	98	.043 824 4453	158	.043 179 7187
39	.053 418 8175	99	.043 795 0794	159	.043 177 4538
40	.052 896 8185	100	.043 766 9645	160	.043 175 2827
41	.052 405 8890	101	.043 740 0458	161	.043 173 2016
42	.051 943 7353	102	.043 714 2711	162	.043 171 2067
43	.051 508 2766	103	.043 689 5904	163	.043 169 2944
44	.051 097 6207	104	.043 665 9563	164	.043 167 4614
45	.050 710 0430	105	.043 643 3232	165	.043 165 7043
46	.050 343 9688	106	.043 621 6478	166	.043 164 0200
47	.049 997 9569	107	.043 600 8888	167	.043 162 4054
48	.049 670 6859	108	.043 581 0065	168	.043 160 8577
49	.049 360 9424	109	.043 561 9632	169	.043 159 3741
50	.049 067 6096	110	.043 543 7228	170	.043 157 9519
51	.048 789 6584	111	.043 526 2508	171	.043 156 5886
52	.048 526 1386	112	.043 509 5144	172	.043 155 2818
53	.048 276 1721	113	.043 493 4819	173	.043 154 0290
54	.048 038 9457	114	.043 478 1233	174	.043 152 8281
55	.047 813 7052	115	.043 463 4099	175	.043 151 6769
56	.047 599 7508	116	.043 449 3141	176	.043 150 5734
57	.047 396 4317	117	.043 435 8097	177	.043 149 5155
58	.047 203 1423	118	.043 422 8714	178	.043 148 5015
59	.047 019 3183	119	.043 410 4752	179	.043 147 5293
60	.046 844 4330	120	.043 398 5982	180	.043 146 5975

Repayment of a Loan by way of an Annuity

NOMINAL INTEREST RATE COMPOUNDED

YEARLY	HALF-YEARLY	QUARTERLY
@	@	@
$4\frac{3}{8}\%$	$8\frac{3}{4}\%$	$17\frac{1}{2}\%$
4.3750%	8.7500%	17.5000%
PER ANNUM	PER ANNUM	PER ANNUM

Periods	Loan of 1	Periods	Loan of 1	Periods	Loan of 1
1	1.043 750 0000	61	.047 214 9221	121	.043 997 3153
2	.533 046 6361	62	.047 058 7020	122	.043 986 8927
3	.362 916 1784	63	.046 909 9967	123	.043 976 9116
4	.277 928 8757	64	.046 768 4034	124	.043 967 3531
5	.226 998 7552	65	.046 633 5446	125	.043 958 1991
6	.193 097 1403	66	.046 505 0661	126	.043 949 4324
7	.168 926 0106	67	.046 382 6352	127	.043 941 0365
8	.150 836 3420	68	.046 265 9393	128	.043 932 9954
9	.136 800 8867	69	.046 154 6844	129	.043 925 2942
10	.125 603 2847	70	.046 048 5935	130	.043 917 9184
11	.116 469 4793	71	.045 947 4060	131	.043 910 8540
12	.108 883 4234	72	.045 850 8762	132	.043 904 0879
13	.102 487 8457	73	.045 758 7723	133	.043 897 6073
14	.097 027 5449	74	.045 670 8754	134	.043 891 4002
15	.092 315 3666	75	.045 586 9789	135	.043 885 4549
16	.088 210 9387	76	.045 506 8877	136	.043 879 7603
17	.084 606 9121	77	.045 430 4172	137	.043 874 3058
18	.081 419 7877	78	.045 357 3927	138	.043 869 0812
19	.078 583 6401	79	.045 287 6489	139	.043 864 0767
20	.076 045 7245	80	.045 221 0294	140	.043 859 2831
21	.073 763 3385	81	.045 157 3860	141	.043 854 6914
22	.071 701 5396	82	.045 096 5781	142	.043 850 2931
23	.069 831 4588	83	.045 038 4724	143	.043 846 0800
24	.068 129 0352	84	.044 982 9425	144	.043 842 0442
25	.066 574 0544	85	.044 929 8686	145	.043 838 1783
26	.065 149 4090	86	.044 879 1366	146	.043 834 4751
27	.063 840 5233	87	.044 830 6385	147	.043 830 9276
28	.062 634 9013	88	.044 784 2714	148	.043 827 5294
29	.061 521 7684	89	.044 739 9378	149	.043 824 2742
30	.060 491 7842	90	.044 697 5447	150	.043 821 1558
31	.059 536 8118	91	.044 657 0038	151	.043 818 1686
32	.058 649 7294	92	.044 618 2312	152	.043 815 3070
33	.057 824 2769	93	.044 581 1469	153	.043 812 5656
34	.057 054 9290	94	.044 545 6748	154	.043 809 9395
35	.056 336 7905	95	.044 511 7425	155	.043 807 4238
36	.055 665 5090	96	.044 479 2809	156	.043 805 0138
37	.055 037 2012	97	.044 448 2244	157	.043 802 7051
38	.054 448 3917	98	.044 418 5103	158	.043 800 4933
39	.053 895 9604	99	.044 390 0790	159	.043 798 3745
40	.053 377 0987	100	.044 362 8735	160	.043 796 3447
41	.052 889 2709	101	.044 336 8396	161	.043 794 4001
42	.052 430 1824	102	.044 311 9256	162	.043 792 5372
43	.051 997 7513	103	.044 288 0821	163	.043 790 7525
44	.051 590 0845	104	.044 265 2621	164	.043 789 0428
45	.051 205 4569	105	.044 243 4207	165	.043 787 4049
46	.050 842 2928	106	.044 222 5151	166	.043 785 8358
47	.050 499 1505	107	.044 202 5042	167	.043 784 3325
48	.050 174 7082	108	.044 183 3491	168	.043 782 8923
49	.049 867 7518	109	.044 165 0124	169	.043 781 5126
50	.049 577 1642	110	.044 147 4587	170	.043 780 1908
51	.049 301 9160	111	.044 130 6538	171	.043 778 9245
52	.049 041 0567	112	.044 114 5653	172	.043 777 7113
53	.048 793 7080	113	.044 099 1621	173	.043 776 5491
54	.048 559 0563	114	.044 084 4147	174	.043 775 4356
55	.048 336 3476	115	.044 070 2947	175	.043 774 3688
56	.048 124 8818	116	.044 056 7751	176	.043 773 3468
57	.047 924 0081	117	.044 043 8299	177	.043 772 3677
58	.047 733 1210	118	.044 031 4344	178	.043 771 4297
59	.047 551 6561	119	.044 019 5651	179	.043 770 5310
60	.047 379 0870	120	.044 008 1993	180	.043 769 6700

Repayment of a Loan by way of an Annuity

	NOMINAL INTEREST RATE COMPOUNDED				
	YEARLY @ $4\frac{7}{16}\%$ 4.4375% PER ANNUM		HALF-YEARLY @ $8\frac{7}{8}\%$ 8.8750% PER ANNUM		QUARTERLY @ $17\frac{3}{4}\%$ 17.7500% PER ANNUM
Periods	Loan of 1	Periods	Loan of 1	Periods	Loan of 1
1	1.044 375 0000	61	.047 753 8079	121	.044 608 2289
2	.533 522 0498	62	.047 599 8109	122	.044 598 2693
3	.363 344 6880	63	.047 453 2852	123	.044 588 7370
4	.278 336 1478	64	.047 313 8281	124	.044 579 6135
5	.227 395 0516	65	.047 181 0625	125	.044 570 8812
6	.193 487 5872	66	.047 054 6345	126	.044 562 5232
7	.169 313 5321	67	.046 934 2118	127	.044 554 5232
8	.151 222 7604	68	.046 819 4819	128	.044 546 8658
9	.137 187 4113	69	.046 710 1514	129	.044 539 5362
10	.125 990 7569	70	.046 605 9436	130	.044 532 5203
11	.116 858 5052	71	.046 506 5985	131	.044 525 8046
12	.109 274 4522	72	.046 411 8706	132	.044 519 3761
13	.102 881 2174	73	.046 321 5285	133	.044 513 2225
14	.097 423 5210	74	.046 235 3541	134	.044 507 3320
15	.092 714 1507	75	.046 153 1411	135	.044 501 6932
16	.088 612 6908	76	.046 074 6948	136	.044 496 2954
17	.085 011 7583	77	.045 999 8312	137	.044 491 1281
18	.081 827 8276	78	.045 928 3762	138	.044 486 1815
19	.078 994 9521	79	.045 860 1650	139	.044 481 4461
20	.076 460 3698	80	.045 795 0416	140	.044 476 9129
21	.074 181 3642	81	.045 732 8585	141	.044 472 5732
22	.072 122 9811	82	.045 673 4755	142	.044 468 4186
23	.070 256 3416	83	.045 616 7600	143	.044 464 4413
24	.068 557 3763	84	.045 562 5861	144	.044 460 6336
25	.067 005 8637	85	.045 510 8346	145	.044 456 9884
26	.065 584 6901	86	.045 461 3920	146	.044 453 4986
27	.064 279 2744	87	.045 414 1507	147	.044 450 1576
28	.063 077 1160	88	.045 369 0087	148	.044 446 9590
29	.061 967 4358	89	.045 325 8687	149	.044 443 8967
30	.060 940 8901	90	.045 284 6385	150	.044 440 9650
31	.059 989 3384	91	.045 245 2305	151	.044 438 1582
32	.059 105 6561	92	.045 207 5611	152	.044 435 4709
33	.058 283 5803	93	.045 171 5509	153	.044 432 8982
34	.057 517 5835	94	.045 137 1246	154	.044 430 4351
35	.056 802 7683	95	.045 104 2101	155	.044 428 0768
36	.056 134 7802	96	.045 072 7392	156	.044 425 8191
37	.055 509 7344	97	.045 042 6465	157	.044 423 6574
38	.054 924 1537	98	.045 013 8701	158	.044 421 5878
39	.054 374 9167	99	.044 986 3508	159	.044 419 6063
40	.053 859 2134	100	.044 960 0324	160	.044 417 7092
41	.053 374 5070	101	.044 934 8610	161	.044 415 8928
42	.052 918 5018	102	.044 910 7855	162	.044 414 1538
43	.052 489 1150	103	.044 887 7572	163	.044 412 4887
44	.052 084 4527	104	.044 865 7295	164	.044 410 8946
45	.051 702 7888	105	.044 844 6579	165	.044 409 3683
46	.051 342 5472	106	.044 824 5002	166	.044 407 9069
47	.051 002 2855	107	.044 805 2160	167	.044 406 5077
48	.050 680 6813	108	.044 786 7667	168	.044 405 1680
49	.050 376 5202	109	.044 769 1156	169	.044 403 8854
50	.050 088 6846	110	.044 752 2274	170	.044 402 6573
51	.049 816 1448	111	.044 736 0688	171	.044 401 4814
52	.049 557 9502	112	.044 720 6077	172	.044 400 3556
53	.049 313 2221	113	.044 705 8135	173	.044 399 2777
54	.049 081 1468	114	.044 691 6571	174	.044 398 2456
55	.048 860 9702	115	.044 678 1106	175	.044 397 2574
56	.048 651 9923	116	.044 665 1473	176	.044 396 3112
57	.048 453 5621	117	.044 652 7419	177	.044 395 4053
58	.048 265 0741	118	.044 640 8701	178	.044 394 5379
59	.048 085 9642	119	.044 629 5086	179	.044 393 7074
60	.047 915 7059	120	.044 618 6353	180	.044 392 9122

Repayment of a Loan by way of an Annuity

NOMINAL INTEREST RATE COMPOUNDED

YEARLY	HALF-YEARLY	QUARTERLY
@	@	@
4½%	**9%**	**18%**
4.5000%	9.0000%	18.0000%
PER ANNUM	PER ANNUM	PER ANNUM

Periods	Loan of 1	Periods	Loan of 1	Periods	Loan of 1
1	1.045 000 0000	61	.048 294 6176	121	.045 219 9169
2	.533 997 5550	62	.048 142 8356	122	.045 210 4025
3	.363 773 3601	63	.047 998 4802	123	.045 201 3016
4	.278 743 6479	64	.047 861 1494	124	.045 192 5960
5	.227 791 6395	65	.047 730 4661	125	.045 184 2684
6	.193 878 3875	66	.047 606 0769	126	.045 176 3023
7	.169 701 4680	67	.047 487 6496	127	.045 168 6819
8	.151 609 6533	68	.047 374 8725	128	.045 161 3921
9	.137 574 4700	69	.047 267 4523	129	.045 154 4183
10	.126 378 8217	70	.047 165 1129	130	.045 147 7469
11	.117 248 1817	71	.047 067 5946	131	.045 141 3646
12	.109 666 1886	72	.046 974 6524	132	.045 135 2588
13	.103 275 3528	73	.046 886 0556	133	.045 129 4175
14	.097 820 3160	74	.046 801 5863	134	.045 123 8292
15	.093 113 8081	75	.046 721 0390	135	.045 118 4828
16	.089 015 3694	76	.046 644 2194	136	.045 113 3678
17	.085 417 5833	77	.046 570 9439	137	.045 108 4742
18	.082 236 8975	78	.046 501 0391	138	.045 103 7923
19	.079 407 3443	79	.046 434 3408	139	.045 099 3129
20	.076 876 1443	80	.046 370 6935	140	.045 095 0272
21	.074 600 5669	81	.046 309 9502	141	.045 090 9269
22	.072 545 6461	82	.046 251 9715	142	.045 087 0038
23	.070 682 4930	83	.046 196 6252	143	.045 083 2503
24	.068 987 0299	84	.046 143 7861	144	.045 079 6590
25	.067 439 0280	85	.046 093 3355	145	.045 076 2229
26	.066 021 3674	86	.046 045 1606	146	.045 072 9352
27	.064 719 4616	87	.045 999 1543	147	.045 069 7896
28	.063 520 8051	88	.045 955 2152	148	.045 066 7799
29	.062 414 6147	89	.045 913 2468	149	.045 063 9001
30	.061 391 5429	90	.045 873 1573	150	.045 061 1447
31	.060 443 4459	91	.045 834 8597	151	.045 058 5082
32	.059 563 1962	92	.045 798 2710	152	.045 055 9856
33	.058 744 5281	93	.045 763 3126	153	.045 053 5719
34	.057 981 9119	94	.045 729 9095	154	.045 051 2623
35	.057 270 4478	95	.045 697 9905	155	.045 049 0524
36	.056 605 7796	96	.045 667 4877	156	.045 046 9379
37	.055 984 0206	97	.045 638 3364	157	.045 044 9147
38	.055 401 6920	98	.045 610 4754	158	.045 042 9787
39	.054 855 6712	99	.045 583 8459	159	.045 041 1262
40	.054 343 1466	100	.045 558 3922	160	.045 039 3537
41	.053 861 5804	101	.045 534 0612	161	.045 037 6576
42	.053 408 6759	102	.045 510 8023	162	.045 036 0347
43	.052 982 3492	103	.045 488 5672	163	.045 034 4818
44	.052 580 7056	104	.045 467 3100	164	.045 032 9958
45	.052 202 0184	105	.045 446 9867	165	.045 031 5740
46	.051 844 7107	106	.045 427 5556	166	.045 030 2134
47	.051 507 3395	107	.045 408 9768	167	.045 028 9115
48	.051 188 5821	108	.045 391 2122	168	.045 027 6658
49	.050 887 2235	109	.045 374 2257	169	.045 026 4737
50	.050 602 1459	110	.045 357 9825	170	.045 025 3331
51	.050 332 3191	111	.045 342 4497	171	.045 024 2416
52	.050 076 7923	112	.045 327 5957	172	.045 023 1971
53	.049 834 6867	113	.045 313 3904	173	.045 022 1977
54	.049 605 1886	114	.045 299 8052	174	.045 021 2414
55	.049 387 5437	115	.045 286 8127	175	.045 020 3263
56	.049 181 0518	116	.045 274 3866	176	.045 019 4506
57	.048 985 0622	117	.045 262 5020	177	.045 018 6127
58	.048 798 9695	118	.045 251 1350	178	.045 017 8109
59	.048 622 2094	119	.045 240 2628	179	.045 017 0436
60	.048 454 2558	120	.045 229 8637	180	.045 016 3094

NOMINAL INTEREST RATE COMPOUNDED

	YEARLY @ $4\frac{9}{16}\%$ 4.5625% PER ANNUM		HALF-YEARLY @ $9\frac{1}{8}\%$ 9.1250% PER ANNUM		QUARTERLY @ $18\frac{1}{4}\%$ 18.2500% PER ANNUM
Periods	Loan of 1	Periods	Loan of 1	Periods	Loan of 1
1	1.045 625 0000	61	.048 837 3166	121	.045 832 3390
2	.534 473 1515	62	.048 687 7405	122	.045 823 2526
3	.364 202 1944	63	.048 545 5458	123	.045 814 5661
4	.279 151 3759	64	.048 410 3304	124	.045 806 2617
5	.228 188 5185	65	.048 281 7178	125	.045 798 3224
6	.194 269 5409	66	.048 159 3548	126	.045 790 7322
7	.170 089 8179	67	.048 042 9098	127	.045 783 4755
8	.151 997 0203	68	.047 932 0714	128	.045 776 5376
9	.137 962 0620	69	.047 826 5467	129	.045 769 9043
10	.126 767 4784	70	.047 726 0602	130	.045 763 5624
11	.117 638 5076	71	.047 630 3527	131	.045 757 4987
12	.110 058 6314	72	.047 539 1796	132	.045 751 7012
13	.103 670 2506	73	.047 452 3108	133	.045 746 1580
14	.098 217 9285	74	.047 369 5288	134	.045 740 8580
15	.093 514 3370	75	.047 290 6288	135	.045 735 7903
16	.089 418 9727	76	.047 215 4170	136	.045 730 9448
17	.085 824 3850	77	.047 143 7104	137	.045 726 3118
18	.082 646 9950	78	.047 075 3362	138	.045 721 8817
19	.079 820 8138	79	.047 010 1307	139	.045 717 6458
20	.077 293 0447	80	.046 947 9391	140	.045 713 5954
21	.075 020 9428	81	.046 888 6150	141	.045 709 7224
22	.072 969 5303	82	.046 832 0196	142	.045 706 0191
23	.071 109 9085	83	.046 778 0212	143	.045 702 4779
24	.069 417 9911	84	.046 726 4955	144	.045 699 0917
25	.067 873 5420	85	.046 677 3240	145	.045 695 8538
26	.066 459 4351	86	.046 630 3949	146	.045 692 7575
27	.065 161 0784	87	.046 585 6017	147	.045 689 7968
28	.063 965 9615	88	.046 542 8434	148	.045 686 9656
29	.062 863 2973	89	.046 502 0242	149	.045 684 2582
30	.061 843 7342	90	.046 463 0530	150	.045 681 6693
31	.060 899 1252	91	.046 425 8434	151	.045 679 1937
32	.060 022 3398	92	.046 390 3131	152	.045 676 8263
33	.059 207 1098	93	.046 356 3840	153	.045 674 5625
34	.058 447 9028	94	.046 323 9817	154	.045 672 3976
35	.057 739 8171	95	.046 293 0356	155	.045 670 3274
36	.057 078 4945	96	.046 263 4785	156	.045 668 3477
37	.056 460 0463	97	.046 235 2464	157	.045 666 4545
38	.055 880 9925	98	.046 208 2784	158	.045 664 6441
39	.055 338 2088	99	.046 182 5165	159	.045 662 9128
40	.054 828 8824	100	.046 157 9056	160	.045 661 2572
41	.054 350 4744	101	.046 134 3931	161	.045 659 6740
42	.053 900 6869	102	.046 111 9289	162	.045 658 1599
43	.053 477 4352	103	.046 090 4654	163	.045 656 7120
44	.053 078 8239	104	.046 069 9571	164	.045 655 3273
45	.052 703 1253	105	.046 050 3608	165	.045 654 0032
46	.052 348 7620	106	.046 031 6351	166	.045 652 7369
47	.052 014 2906	107	.046 013 7407	167	.045 651 5259
48	.051 698 3876	108	.045 996 6401	168	.045 650 3678
49	.051 399 8378	109	.045 980 2976	169	.045 649 2603
50	.051 117 5230	110	.045 964 6791	170	.045 648 2012
51	.050 850 4129	111	.045 949 7520	171	.045 647 1884
52	.050 597 5563	112	.045 935 4853	172	.045 646 2197
53	.050 358 0743	113	.045 921 8493	173	.045 645 2934
54	.050 131 1531	114	.045 908 8160	174	.045 644 4076
55	.049 916 0384	115	.045 896 3582	175	.045 643 5604
56	.049 712 0301	116	.045 884 4504	176	.045 642 7502
57	.049 518 4774	117	.045 873 0680	177	.045 641 9754
58	.049 334 7750	118	.045 862 1874	178	.045 641 2344
59	.049 160 3589	119	.045 851 7865	179	.045 640 5258
60	.048 994 7031	120	.045 841 8438	180	.045 639 8481

Repayment of a Loan by way of an Annuity

NOMINAL INTEREST RATE COMPOUNDED

YEARLY	HALF-YEARLY	QUARTERLY
@	@	@
$4\frac{5}{8}\%$	$9\frac{1}{4}\%$	$18\frac{1}{2}\%$
4.6250%	9.2500%	18.5000%
PER ANNUM	PER ANNUM	PER ANNUM

Periods	Loan of 1	Periods	Loan of 1	Periods	Loan of 1
1	1.046 250 0000	61	.049 381 8706	121	.046 445 4570
2	.534 948 8393	62	.049 234 4908	122	.046 436 7818
3	.364 631 1908	63	.049 094 4460	123	.046 428 4932
4	.279 559 3315	64	.048 961 3345	124	.046 420 5737
5	.228 585 6883	65	.048 834 7802	125	.046 413 0068
6	.194 661 0470	66	.048 714 4303	126	.046 405 7768
7	.170 478 5813	67	.048 599 9537	127	.046 398 8684
8	.152 384 8608	68	.048 491 0393	128	.046 392 2674
9	.138 350 1867	69	.048 387 3948	129	.046 385 9599
10	.127 156 7260	70	.048 288 7452	130	.046 379 9328
11	.118 029 4821	71	.048 194 8317	131	.046 374 1737
12	.110 451 7793	72	.048 105 4105	132	.046 368 6704
13	.104 065 9093	73	.048 020 2518	133	.046 363 4117
14	.098 616 3567	74	.047 939 1389	134	.046 358 3865
15	.093 915 7356	75	.047 861 8674	135	.046 353 5845
16	.089 823 4984	76	.047 788 2442	136	.046 348 9957
17	.086 232 1608	77	.047 718 0869	137	.046 344 6106
18	.083 058 1173	78	.047 651 2232	138	.046 340 4201
19	.080 235 3575	79	.047 587 4901	139	.046 336 4156
20	.077 711 0675	80	.047 526 7336	140	.046 332 5887
21	.075 442 4881	81	.047 468 8077	141	.046 328 9316
22	.073 394 6297	82	.047 413 5742	142	.046 325 4367
23	.071 538 5835	83	.047 360 9023	143	.046 322 0968
24	.069 850 2547	84	.047 310 6681	144	.046 318 9050
25	.068 309 4000	85	.047 262 7541	145	.046 315 8546
26	.066 898 8869	86	.047 217 0487	146	.046 312 9395
27	.065 604 1180	87	.047 173 4463	147	.046 310 1537
28	.064 412 5781	88	.047 131 8465	148	.046 307 4912
29	.063 313 4756	89	.047 092 1542	149	.046 304 9468
30	.062 297 4554	90	.047 054 2790	150	.046 302 5151
31	.061 356 3672	91	.047 018 1350	151	.046 300 1911
32	.060 483 0773	92	.046 983 6406	152	.046 297 9701
33	.059 671 3148	93	.046 950 7183	153	.046 295 8474
34	.058 915 5451	94	.046 919 2944	154	.046 293 8188
35	.058 210 8643	95	.046 889 2990	155	.046 291 8800
36	.057 552 9120	96	.046 860 6653	156	.046 290 0271
37	.056 937 7981	97	.046 833 3301	157	.046 288 2562
38	.056 362 0408	98	.046 807 2330	158	.046 286 5637
39	.055 822 5143	99	.046 782 3167	159	.046 284 9462
40	.055 316 4048	100	.046 758 5267	160	.046 283 4003
41	.054 841 1721	101	.046 735 8109	161	.046 281 9228
42	.054 394 5172	102	.046 714 1198	162	.046 280 5107
43	.053 974 3546	103	.046 693 4065	163	.046 279 1611
44	.053 578 7880	104	.046 673 6260	164	.046 277 8712
45	.053 206 0892	105	.046 654 7355	165	.046 276 6385
46	.052 854 6800	106	.046 636 6944	166	.046 275 4602
47	.052 523 1165	107	.046 619 4638	167	.046 274 3342
48	.052 210 0748	108	.046 603 0068	168	.046 273 2579
49	.051 914 3392	109	.046 587 2882	169	.046 272 2293
50	.051 634 7913	110	.046 572 2743	170	.046 271 2462
51	.051 370 4005	111	.046 557 9331	171	.046 270 3066
52	.051 120 2156	112	.046 544 2342	172	.046 269 4085
53	.050 883 3573	113	.046 531 1484	173	.046 268 5502
54	.050 659 0120	114	.046 518 6479	174	.046 267 7299
55	.050 446 4252	115	.046 506 7062	175	.046 266 9459
56	.050 244 8970	116	.046 495 2982	176	.046 266 1965
57	.050 053 7766	117	.046 484 3997	177	.046 265 4803
58	.049 872 4589	118	.046 473 9878	178	.046 264 7957
59	.049 700 3799	119	.046 464 0405	179	.046 264 1415
60	.049 537 0141	120	.046 454 5369	180	.046 263 5162

Repayment of a Loan by way of an Annuity

NOMINAL INTEREST RATE COMPOUNDED

YEARLY	HALF-YEARLY	QUARTERLY
@	@	@
$4\frac{11}{16}\%$	$9\frac{3}{8}\%$	$18\frac{3}{4}\%$
4.6875%	9.3750%	18.7500%
PER ANNUM	PER ANNUM	PER ANNUM

Periods	Loan of 1	Periods	Loan of 1	Periods	Loan of 1
1	1.046 875 0000	61	.049 928 2457	121	.047 059 2343
2	.535 424 6183	62	.049 783 0518	122	.047 050 9541
3	.365 060 3492	63	.049 645 1455	123	.047 043 0473
4	.279 967 5145	64	.049 514 1257	124	.047 035 4970
5	.228 983 1487	65	.049 389 6167	125	.047 028 2871
6	.195 052 9054	66	.049 271 2660	126	.047 021 4020
7	.170 867 7577	67	.049 158 7431	127	.047 014 8272
8	.152 773 1742	68	.049 051 7374	128	.047 008 5484
9	.138 738 8432	69	.048 949 9572	129	.047 002 5524
10	.127 546 5638	70	.048 853 1279	130	.046 996 8262
11	.118 421 1041	71	.048 760 9913	131	.046 991 3578
12	.110 845 6313	72	.048 673 3042	132	.046 986 1354
13	.104 462 3276	73	.048 589 8374	133	.046 981 1479
14	.099 015 5992	74	.048 510 3748	134	.046 976 3847
15	.094 318 0020	75	.048 434 7126	135	.046 971 8357
16	.090 228 9445	76	.048 362 6583	136	.046 967 4913
17	.086 640 9086	77	.048 294 0302	137	.046 963 3420
18	.083 470 2618	78	.048 228 6567	138	.046 959 3793
19	.080 650 9726	79	.048 166 3754	139	.046 955 5946
20	.078 130 2095	80	.048 107 0328	140	.046 951 9800
21	.075 865 1992	81	.048 050 4838	141	.046 948 5277
22	.073 820 9401	82	.047 996 5908	142	.046 945 2305
23	.071 968 5133	83	.047 945 2237	143	.046 942 0814
24	.070 283 8157	84	.047 896 2592	144	.046 939 0736
25	.068 746 5964	85	.047 849 5804	145	.046 936 2009
26	.067 339 7168	86	.047 805 0767	146	.046 933 4571
27	.066 048 5738	87	.047 762 6428	147	.046 930 8365
28	.064 860 6474	88	.047 722 1793	148	.046 928 3335
29	.063 765 1419	89	.047 683 5916	149	.046 925 9429
30	.062 752 6982	90	.047 646 7898	150	.046 923 6595
31	.061 815 1627	91	.047 611 6890	151	.046 921 4785
32	.060 945 3987	92	.047 578 2081	152	.046 919 3954
33	.060 137 1327	93	.047 546 2702	153	.046 917 4058
34	.059 384 8276	94	.047 515 8025	154	.046 915 5054
35	.058 683 5772	95	.047 486 7354	155	.046 913 6902
36	.058 029 0195	96	.047 459 0030	156	.046 911 9565
37	.057 417 2623	97	.047 432 5426	157	.046 910 3004
38	.056 844 8224	98	.047 407 2945	158	.046 908 7187
39	.056 308 5727	99	.047 383 2020	159	.046 907 2079
40	.055 805 6978	100	.047 360 2111	160	.046 905 7648
41	.055 333 6566	101	.047 338 2705	161	.046 904 3864
42	.054 890 1491	102	.047 317 3313	162	.046 903 0698
43	.054 473 0888	103	.047 297 3470	163	.046 901 8122
44	.054 080 5787	104	.047 278 2733	164	.046 900 6110
45	.053 710 8898	105	.047 260 0679	165	.046 899 4636
46	.053 362 4435	106	.047 242 6908	166	.046 898 3677
47	.053 033 7951	107	.047 226 1037	167	.046 897 3209
48	.052 723 6206	108	.047 210 2702	168	.046 896 3210
49	.052 430 7038	109	.047 195 1556	169	.046 895 3659
50	.052 153 9260	110	.047 180 7268	170	.046 894 4536
51	.051 892 2563	111	.047 166 9523	171	.046 893 5822
52	.051 644 7436	112	.047 153 8020	172	.046 892 7499
53	.051 410 5084	113	.047 141 2474	173	.046 891 9548
54	.051 188 7370	114	.047 129 2612	174	.046 891 1954
55	.050 978 6751	115	.047 117 8174	175	.046 890 4700
56	.050 779 6226	116	.047 106 8912	176	.046 889 7771
57	.050 590 9291	117	.047 096 4590	177	.046 889 1152
58	.050 411 9895	118	.047 086 4982	178	.046 888 4830
59	.050 242 2402	119	.047 076 9873	179	.046 887 8791
60	.050 081 1558	120	.047 067 9059	180	.046 887 3023

Repayment of a Loan by way of an Annuity

NOMINAL INTEREST RATE COMPOUNDED

	YEARLY	HALF-YEARLY	QUARTERLY
	@	@	@
	$4\frac{3}{4}\%$	$9\frac{1}{2}\%$	19%
	4.7500%	9.5000%	19.0000%
	PER ANNUM	PER ANNUM	PER ANNUM

Periods	Loan of 1	Periods	Loan of 1	Periods	Loan of 1
1	1.047 500 0000	61	.050 476 4084	121	.047 673 6363
2	.535 900 4884	62	.050 333 3891	122	.047 665 7351
3	.365 489 6693	63	.050 197 6092	123	.047 658 1946
4	.280 375 9246	64	.050 068 6682	124	.047 650 9983
5	.229 380 8993	65	.049 946 1907	125	.047 644 1304
6	.195 445 1156	66	.049 829 8248	126	.047 637 5757
7	.171 257 3467	67	.049 719 2405	127	.047 631 3199
8	.153 161 9598	68	.049 614 1277	128	.047 625 3494
9	.139 128 0310	69	.049 514 1951	129	.047 619 6509
10	.127 936 9909	70	.049 419 1690	130	.047 614 2122
11	.118 813 3726	71	.049 328 7917	131	.047 609 0212
12	.111 240 1861	72	.049 242 8204	132	.047 604 0667
13	.104 859 5042	73	.049 161 0268	133	.047 599 3378
14	.099 415 6544	74	.049 083 1953	134	.047 594 8243
15	.094 721 1344	75	.049 009 1227	135	.047 590 5162
16	.090 635 3090	76	.048 938 6173	136	.047 586 4041
17	.087 050 6258	77	.048 871 4981	137	.047 582 4793
18	.083 883 4258	78	.048 807 5940	138	.047 578 7329
19	.081 067 6559	79	.048 746 7435	139	.047 575 1571
20	.078 550 4673	80	.048 688 7937	140	.047 571 7438
21	.076 289 0722	81	.048 633 6000	141	.047 568 4859
22	.074 248 4572	82	.048 581 0259	142	.047 565 3760
23	.072 399 6934	83	.048 530 9417	143	.047 562 4076
24	.070 718 6689	84	.048 483 2248	144	.047 559 5741
25	.069 185 1257	85	.048 437 7592	145	.047 556 8694
26	.067 781 9186	86	.048 394 4348	146	.047 554 2877
27	.066 494 4391	87	.048 353 1472	147	.047 551 8232
28	.065 310 1623	88	.048 313 7976	148	.047 549 4708
29	.064 218 2882	89	.048 276 2920	149	.047 547 2253
30	.063 209 4539	90	.048 240 5414	150	.047 545 0818
31	.062 275 5025	91	.048 206 4613	151	.047 543 0356
32	.061 409 2942	92	.048 173 9715	152	.047 541 0824
33	.060 604 5529	93	.048 142 9958	153	.047 539 2180
34	.059 855 7388	94	.048 113 4620	154	.047 537 4382
35	.059 157 9440	95	.048 085 3011	155	.047 535 7392
36	.058 506 8041	96	.048 058 4480	156	.047 534 1174
37	.057 898 4255	97	.048 032 8405	157	.047 532 5693
38	.057 329 3231	98	.048 008 4196	158	.047 531 0914
39	.056 796 3686	99	.047 985 1293	159	.047 529 6807
40	.056 296 7454	100	.047 962 9162	160	.047 528 3340
41	.055 827 9111	101	.047 941 7296	161	.047 527 0484
42	.055 387 5648	102	.047 921 5211	162	.047 525 8212
43	.054 973 6193	103	.047 902 2450	163	.047 524 6497
44	.054 584 1765	104	.047 883 8573	164	.047 523 5314
45	.054 217 5069	105	.047 866 3167	165	.047 522 4638
46	.053 872 0312	106	.047 849 5834	166	.047 521 4447
47	.053 546 3045	107	.047 833 6198	167	.047 520 4719
48	.053 239 0022	108	.047 818 3901	168	.047 519 5432
49	.052 948 9078	109	.047 803 8600	169	.047 518 6566
50	.052 674 9023	110	.047 789 9970	170	.047 517 8103
51	.052 415 9549	111	.047 776 7702	171	.047 517 0024
52	.052 171 1140	112	.047 764 1499	172	.047 516 2311
53	.051 939 5003	113	.047 752 1082	173	.047 515 4949
54	.051 720 3000	114	.047 740 6182	174	.047 514 7920
55	.051 512 7589	115	.047 729 6543	175	.047 514 1211
56	.051 316 1771	116	.047 719 1924	176	.047 513 4805
57	.051 129 9043	117	.047 709 2091	177	.047 512 8691
58	.050 953 3356	118	.047 699 6824	178	.047 512 2854
59	.050 785 9076	119	.047 690 5912	179	.047 511 7281
60	.050 627 0953	120	.047 681 9156	180	.047 511 1962

Repayment of a Loan by way of an Annuity

NOMINAL INTEREST RATE COMPOUNDED

YEARLY	HALF-YEARLY	QUARTERLY
@	@	@
$4\frac{13}{16}\%$	$9\frac{5}{8}\%$	$19\frac{1}{4}\%$
4.8125%	9.6250%	19.2500%
PER ANNUM	PER ANNUM	PER ANNUM

Periods	Loan of 1	Periods	Loan of 1	Periods	Loan of 1
1	1,048 125 0000	61	,051 026 3252	121	,048 288 6297
2	,536 376 4495	62	,050 885 4687	122	,048 281 0922
3	,365 919 1511	63	,050 751 8026	123	,048 273 9030
4	,280 784 5617	64	,050 624 9268	124	,048 267 0459
5	,229 778 9399	65	,050 504 4665	125	,048 260 5055
6	,195 837 6774	66	,050 390 0703	126	,048 254 2670
7	,171 647 3477	67	,050 281 4087	127	,048 248 3164
8	,153 551 2172	68	,050 178 1723	128	,048 242 6405
9	,139 517 7493	69	,050 080 0705	129	,048 237 2264
10	,128 328 0064	70	,049 986 8299	130	,048 232 0620
11	,119 206 2866	71	,049 898 1936	131	,048 227 1358
12	,111 635 4425	72	,049 813 9195	132	,048 222 4367
13	,105 257 4376	73	,049 733 7799	133	,048 217 9542
14	,099 816 5206	74	,049 657 5599	134	,048 213 6783
15	,095 125 1310	75	,049 585 0570	135	,048 209 5995
16	,091 042 5897	76	,049 516 0802	136	,048 205 7086
17	,087 461 3102	77	,049 450 4492	137	,048 201 9969
18	,084 297 6066	78	,049 387 9936	138	,048 198 4561
19	,081 485 4043	79	,049 328 5525	139	,048 195 0785
20	,078 971 8373	80	,049 271 9740	140	,048 191 8563
21	,076 714 1033	81	,049 218 1141	141	,048 188 7825
22	,074 677 1769	82	,049 166 8368	142	,048 185 8502
23	,072 832 1190	83	,049 118 0135	143	,048 183 0529
24	,071 154 8092	84	,049 071 5222	144	,048 180 3843
25	,069 624 9821	85	,049 027 2476	145	,048 177 8385
26	,068 225 4861	86	,048 985 0802	146	,048 175 4099
27	,066 941 7071	87	,048 944 9165	147	,048 173 0930
28	,065 761 1154	88	,048 906 6583	148	,048 170 8827
29	,064 672 9066	89	,048 870 2125	149	,048 168 7740
30	,063 667 7141	90	,048 835 4906	150	,048 166 7624
31	,062 737 3775	91	,048 802 4090	151	,048 164 8433
32	,061 874 7539	92	,048 770 8881	152	,048 163 0124
33	,061 073 5647	93	,048 740 8525	153	,048 161 2657
34	,060 328 2676	94	,048 712 2304	154	,048 159 5994
35	,059 633 9525	95	,048 684 9538	155	,048 158 0097
36	,058 986 2530	96	,048 658 9580	156	,048 156 4930
37	,058 381 2739	97	,048 634 1818	157	,048 155 0461
38	,057 815 5285	98	,048 610 5666	158	,048 153 6657
39	,057 285 8869	99	,048 588 0572	159	,048 152 3488
40	,056 789 5316	100	,048 566 6007	160	,048 151 0924
41	,056 323 9188	101	,048 546 1470	161	,048 149 8937
42	,055 886 7468	102	,048 526 6485	162	,048 148 7501
43	,055 475 9274	103	,048 508 0599	163	,048 147 6591
44	,055 089 5619	104	,048 490 3380	164	,048 146 6183
45	,054 725 9201	105	,048 473 4420	165	,048 145 6252
46	,054 383 4222	106	,048 457 3327	166	,048 144 6778
47	,054 060 6227	107	,048 441 9730	167	,048 143 7740
48	,053 756 1967	108	,048 427 3277	168	,048 142 9116
49	,053 468 9275	109	,048 413 3630	169	,048 142 0889
50	,053 197 6959	110	,048 400 0470	170	,048 141 3040
51	,052 941 4707	111	,048 387 3493	171	,048 140 5552
52	,052 699 3005	112	,048 375 2408	172	,048 139 8407
53	,052 470 3059	113	,048 363 6940	173	,048 139 1591
54	,052 253 6732	114	,048 352 6824	174	,048 138 5088
55	,052 048 6482	115	,048 342 1811	175	,048 137 8884
56	,051 854 5311	116	,048 332 1662	176	,048 137 2964
57	,051 670 6720	117	,048 322 6151	177	,048 136 7317
58	,051 496 4660	118	,048 313 5060	178	,048 136 1929
59	,051 331 3503	119	,048 304 8183	179	,048 135 6789
60	,051 174 8000	120	,048 296 5325	180	,048 135 1885

Repayment of a Loan by way of an Annuity

NOMINAL INTEREST RATE COMPOUNDED

YEARLY	HALF-YEARLY	QUARTERLY
@	@	@
$4\frac{7}{8}\%$	$9\frac{3}{4}\%$	$19\frac{1}{2}\%$
4.8750%	9.7500%	19.5000%
PER ANNUM	PER ANNUM	PER ANNUM

Periods	Loan of 1	Periods	Loan of 1	Periods	Loan of 1
1	1.048 750 0000	61	.051 577 9634	121	.048 904 1832
2	.536 852 5015	62	.051 439 2570	122	.048 896 9946
3	.366 348 7943	63	.051 307 6913	123	.048 890 1421
4	.281 193 4256	64	.051 182 8665	124	.048 883 6099
5	.230 177 2700	65	.051 064 4084	125	.048 877 3829
6	.196 230 5904	66	.050 951 9663	126	.048 871 4469
7	.172 037 7604	67	.050 845 2112	127	.048 865 7882
8	.153 940 9457	68	.050 743 8343	128	.048 860 3937
9	.139 907 9973	69	.050 647 5455	129	.048 855 2511
10	.128 719 6094	70	.050 556 0724	130	.048 850 3485
11	.119 599 8451	71	.050 469 1585	131	.048 845 6748
12	.112 031 3995	72	.050 386 5626	132	.048 841 2191
13	.105 656 1265	73	.050 308 0574	133	.048 836 9713
14	.100 218 1962	74	.050 233 4290	134	.048 832 9217
15	.095 529 9900	75	.050 162 4755	135	.048 829 0609
16	.091 450 7845	76	.050 095 0066	136	.048 825 3802
17	.087 872 9592	77	.050 030 8428	137	.048 821 8711
18	.084 712 8014	78	.049 969 8145	138	.048 818 5255
19	.081 904 2150	79	.049 911 7615	139	.048 815 3359
20	.079 394 3163	80	.049 856 5325	140	.048 812 2950
21	.077 140 2887	81	.049 803 9845	141	.048 809 3957
22	.075 107 0948	82	.049 753 9821	142	.048 806 6316
23	.073 265 7854	83	.049 706 3976	143	.048 803 9962
24	.071 592 2314	84	.049 661 1096	144	.048 801 4836
25	.070 066 1599	85	.049 618 0036	145	.048 799 0880
26	.068 670 4131	86	.049 576 9709	146	.048 796 8040
27	.067 390 3711	87	.049 537 9088	147	.048 794 6264
28	.066 213 4994	88	.049 500 7197	148	.048 792 5502
29	.065 128 9892	89	.049 465 3113	149	.048 790 5706
30	.064 127 4701	90	.049 431 5959	150	.048 788 6833
31	.063 200 7783	91	.049 399 4906	151	.048 786 8837
32	.062 341 7680	92	.049 368 9164	152	.048 785 1680
33	.061 544 1576	93	.049 339 7987	153	.048 783 5321
34	.060 802 4026	94	.049 312 0664	154	.048 781 9724
35	.060 111 5906	95	.049 285 6523	155	.048 780 4853
36	.059 467 3534	96	.049 260 4924	156	.048 779 0674
37	.058 865 7939	97	.049 236 5259	157	.048 777 7154
38	.058 303 4240	98	.049 213 6951	158	.048 776 4264
39	.057 777 1125	99	.049 191 9454	159	.048 775 1974
40	.057 284 0403	100	.049 171 2245	160	.048 774 0255
41	.056 821 6628	101	.049 151 4831	161	.048 772 9082
42	.056 387 6773	102	.049 132 6741	162	.048 771 8429
43	.055 979 9947	103	.049 114 7528	163	.048 770 8271
44	.055 596 7156	104	.049 097 6768	164	.048 769 8586
45	.055 236 1092	105	.049 081 4055	165	.048 768 9351
46	.054 896 5952	106	.049 065 9007	166	.048 768 0546
47	.054 576 7277	107	.049 051 1257	167	.048 767 2151
48	.054 275 1814	108	.049 037 0458	168	.048 766 4146
49	.053 990 7393	109	.049 023 6279	169	.048 765 6513
50	.053 722 2821	110	.049 010 8405	170	.048 764 9235
51	.053 468 7786	111	.048 998 6538	171	.048 764 2296
52	.053 229 2771	112	.048 987 0392	172	.048 763 5680
53	.053 002 8984	113	.048 975 9696	173	.048 762 9371
54	.052 788 8287	114	.048 965 4192	174	.048 762 3356
55	.052 586 3142	115	.048 955 3635	175	.048 761 7621
56	.052 394 6552	116	.048 945 7791	176	.048 761 2152
57	.052 213 2020	117	.048 936 6437	177	.048 760 6938
58	.052 041 3500	118	.048 927 9361	178	.048 760 1966
59	.051 878 5368	119	.048 919 6361	179	.048 759 7225
60	.051 724 2377	120	.048 911 7246	180	.048 759 2705

Repayment of a Loan by way of an Annuity

NOMINAL INTEREST RATE COMPOUNDED

YEARLY	HALF-YEARLY	QUARTERLY
@	@	@
$4\frac{15}{16}\%$	$9\frac{7}{8}\%$	$19\frac{3}{4}\%$
4.9375%	9.8750%	19.7500%
PER ANNUM	PER ANNUM	PER ANNUM

Periods	Loan of 1	Periods	Loan of 1	Periods	Loan of 1
1	1.049 375 0000	61	.052 131 2903	121	.049 520 2669
2	.537 328 6444	62	.051 994 7208	122	.049 513 4127
3	.366 778 5989	63	.051 865 2414	123	.049 506 8827
4	.281 602 5160	64	.051 742 4529	124	.049 500 6616
5	.230 575 8896	65	.051 625 9816	125	.049 494 7346
6	.196 623 8541	66	.051 515 4774	126	.049 489 0879
7	.172 428 5841	67	.051 410 6118	127	.049 483 7080
8	.154 331 1447	68	.051 311 0769	128	.049 478 5824
9	.140 298 7745	69	.051 216 5833	129	.049 473 6989
10	.129 111 7993	70	.051 126 8591	130	.049 469 0461
11	.119 994 0470	71	.051 041 6486	131	.049 464 6130
12	.112 428 0557	72	.050 960 7113	132	.049 460 3893
13	.106 055 5695	73	.050 883 8207	133	.049 456 3649
14	.100 620 6797	74	.050 810 7635	134	.049 452 5306
15	.095 935 7095	75	.050 741 3388	135	.049 448 8771
16	.091 859 8913	76	.050 675 3570	136	.049 445 3961
17	.088 285 5705	77	.050 612 6392	137	.049 442 0794
18	.085 129 0076	78	.050 553 0166	138	.049 438 9191
19	.082 324 0847	79	.050 496 3300	139	.049 435 9079
20	.079 817 9008	80	.050 442 4288	140	.049 433 0387
21	.077 567 6246	81	.050 391 1707	141	.049 430 3048
22	.075 538 2068	82	.050 342 4212	142	.049 427 6998
23	.073 700 6880	83	.050 296 0531	143	.049 425 2177
24	.072 030 9303	84	.050 251 9462	144	.049 422 8525
25	.070 508 6536	85	.050 209 9865	145	.049 420 5989
26	.069 116 6934	86	.050 170 0662	146	.049 418 4515
27	.067 840 4243	87	.050 132 0833	147	.049 416 4053
28	.066 667 3069	88	.050 095 9410	148	.049 414 4556
29	.065 586 5280	89	.050 061 5478	149	.049 412 5977
30	.064 588 7133	90	.050 028 8167	150	.049 410 8274
31	.063 665 6957	91	.049 997 6655	151	.049 409 1405
32	.062 810 3263	92	.049 968 0161	152	.049 407 5330
33	.062 016 3208	93	.049 939 7944	153	.049 406 0013
34	.061 278 1323	94	.049 912 9303	154	.049 404 5418
35	.060 590 8462	95	.049 887 3570	155	.049 403 1510
36	.059 950 0924	96	.049 863 0114	156	.049 401 8257
37	.059 351 9720	97	.049 839 8335	157	.049 400 5629
38	.058 792 9954	98	.049 817 7661	158	.049 399 3595
39	.058 270 0300	99	.049 796 7552	159	.049 398 2128
40	.057 780 2555	100	.049 776 7494	160	.049 397 1201
41	.057 321 1263	101	.049 757 6998	161	.049 396 0789
42	.056 890 3386	102	.049 739 5601	162	.049 395 0867
43	.056 485 8026	103	.049 722 2863	163	.049 394 1412
44	.056 105 6183	104	.049 705 8363	164	.049 393 2402
45	.055 748 0541	105	.049 690 1705	165	.049 392 3817
46	.055 411 5294	106	.049 675 2510	166	.049 391 5636
47	.055 094 5977	107	.049 661 0418	167	.049 390 7840
48	.054 795 9335	108	.049 647 5087	168	.049 390 0411
49	.054 514 3197	109	.049 634 6193	169	.049 389 3332
50	.054 248 6367	110	.049 622 3425	170	.049 388 6586
51	.053 997 8532	111	.049 610 6491	171	.049 388 0158
52	.053 761 0177	112	.049 599 5109	172	.049 387 4032
53	.053 537 2509	113	.049 588 9015	173	.049 386 8195
54	.053 325 7391	114	.049 578 7955	174	.049 386 2632
55	.053 125 7288	115	.049 569 1689	175	.049 385 7331
56	.052 936 5204	116	.049 559 9986	176	.049 385 2280
57	.052 757 4645	117	.049 551 2630	177	.049 384 7467
58	.052 587 9570	118	.049 542 9413	178	.049 384 2880
59	.052 427 4357	119	.049 535 0138	179	.049 383 8509
60	.052 275 3764	120	.049 527 4616	180	.049 383 4344

Repayment of a Loan by way of an Annuity

NOMINAL INTEREST RATE COMPOUNDED

YEARLY	HALF-YEARLY	QUARTERLY
@	@	@
5%	10%	20%
5.0000%	10.0000%	20.0000%
PER ANNUM	PER ANNUM	PER ANNUM

Periods	Loan of 1	Periods	Loan of 1	Periods	Loan of 1
1	1.050 000 0000	61	.052 686 2736	121	.050 136 8522
2	.537 804 8780	62	.052 551 8273	122	.050 130 3185
3	.367 208 5646	63	.052 424 4196	123	.050 124 0974
4	.282 011 8326	64	.052 303 6520	124	.050 118 1741
5	.230 974 7981	65	.052 189 1514	125	.050 112 5341
6	.197 017 4681	66	.052 080 5683	126	.050 107 1638
7	.172 819 8184	67	.051 977 5751	127	.050 102 0504
8	.154 721 8136	68	.051 879 8643	128	.050 097 1814
9	.140 690 0800	69	.051 787 1473	129	.050 092 5451
10	.129 504 5750	70	.051 699 1530	130	.050 088 1304
11	.120 388 8915	71	.051 615 6265	131	.050 083 9267
12	.112 825 4100	72	.051 536 3280	132	.050 079 9238
13	.106 455 7652	73	.051 461 0318	133	.050 076 1121
14	.101 023 9695	74	.051 389 5254	134	.050 072 4825
15	.096 342 2876	75	.051 321 6085	135	.050 069 0262
16	.092 269 9080	76	.051 257 0925	136	.050 065 7349
17	.088 699 1417	77	.051 195 7993	137	.050 062 6007
18	.085 546 2223	78	.051 137 5610	138	.050 059 6162
19	.082 745 0104	79	.051 082 2189	139	.050 056 7741
20	.080 242 5872	80	.051 029 6235	140	.050 054 0677
21	.077 996 1071	81	.050 979 6332	141	.050 051 4904
22	.075 970 5086	82	.050 932 1143	142	.050 049 0360
23	.074 136 8219	83	.050 886 9406	143	.050 046 6988
24	.072 470 9008	84	.050 843 9924	144	.050 044 4731
25	.070 952 4573	85	.050 803 1567	145	.050 042 3535
26	.069 564 3207	86	.050 764 3265	146	.050 040 3350
27	.068 291 8599	87	.050 727 4005	147	.050 038 4129
28	.067 122 5304	88	.050 692 2828	148	.050 036 5823
29	.066 045 5149	89	.050 658 8825	149	.050 034 8391
30	.065 051 4351	90	.050 627 1136	150	.050 033 1790
31	.064 132 1204	91	.050 596 8946	151	.050 031 5980
32	.063 280 4189	92	.050 568 1481	152	.050 030 0925
33	.062 490 0437	93	.050 540 8008	153	.050 028 6587
34	.061 755 4454	94	.050 514 7832	154	.050 027 2932
35	.061 071 7072	95	.050 490 0295	155	.050 025 9929
36	.060 434 4571	96	.050 466 4770	156	.050 024 7545
37	.059 839 7945	97	.050 444 0666	157	.050 023 5752
38	.059 284 2282	98	.050 422 7418	158	.050 022 4520
39	.058 764 6242	99	.050 402 4492	159	.050 021 3824
40	.058 278 1612	100	.050 383 1381	160	.050 020 3638
41	.057 822 2924	101	.050 364 7603	161	.050 019 3937
42	.057 394 7131	102	.050 347 2701	162	.050 018 4699
43	.056 993 3328	103	.050 330 6241	163	.050 017 5900
44	.056 616 2506	104	.050 314 7810	164	.050 016 7521
45	.056 261 7347	105	.050 299 7016	165	.050 015 9542
46	.055 928 2036	106	.050 285 3486	166	.050 015 1942
47	.055 614 2109	107	.050 271 6867	167	.050 014 4705
48	.055 318 4306	108	.050 258 6824	168	.050 013 7812
49	.055 039 6453	109	.050 246 3035	169	.050 013 1248
50	.054 776 7355	110	.050 234 5197	170	.050 012 4996
51	.054 528 6697	111	.050 223 3022	171	.050 011 9043
52	.054 294 4966	112	.050 212 6236	172	.050 011 3373
53	.054 073 3368	113	.050 202 4576	173	.050 010 7973
54	.053 864 3770	114	.050 192 7796	174	.050 010 2830
55	.053 666 8637	115	.050 183 5659	175	.050 009 7933
56	.053 480 0978	116	.050 174 7942	176	.050 009 3268
57	.053 303 4300	117	.050 166 4429	177	.050 008 8826
58	.053 136 2568	118	.050 158 4919	178	.050 008 4596
59	.052 978 0161	119	.050 150 9219	179	.050 008 0567
60	.052 828 1845	120	.050 143 7145	180	.050 007 6730

Repayment of a Loan by way of an Annuity

NOMINAL INTEREST RATE COMPOUNDED

	YEARLY @ $5\frac{1}{16}\%$ 5.0625% PER ANNUM		HALF-YEARLY @ $10\frac{1}{8}\%$ 10.1250% PER ANNUM		QUARTERLY @ $20\frac{1}{4}\%$ 20.2500% PER ANNUM
Periods	Loan of 1	Periods	Loan of 1	Periods	Loan of 1
1	1,050 625 0000	61	,053 242 8814	121	,050 753 9122
2	,538 281 2024	62	,053 110 5439	122	,050 747 6855
3	,367 638 6914	63	,052 985 1928	123	,050 741 7601
4	,282 421 3753	64	,052 866 4302	124	,050 736 1216
5	,231 373 9954	65	,052 753 8837	125	,050 730 7560
6	,197 411 4322	66	,052 647 2046	126	,050 725 6499
7	,173 211 4629	67	,052 546 0658	127	,050 720 7909
8	,155 112 9519	68	,052 450 1608	128	,050 716 1668
9	,141 081 9131	69	,052 359 2016	129	,050 711 7664
10	,129 897 9357	70	,052 272 9180	130	,050 707 5787
11	,120 784 3774	71	,052 191 0557	131	,050 703 5934
12	,113 223 4612	72	,052 113 3758	132	,050 699 8007
13	,106 856 7121	73	,052 039 6534	133	,050 696 1913
14	,101 428 0638	74	,051 969 6769	134	,050 692 7563
15	,096 749 7225	75	,051 903 2468	135	,050 689 4873
16	,092 680 8324	76	,051 840 1753	136	,050 686 3762
17	,089 113 6704	77	,051 780 2851	137	,050 683 4153
18	,085 964 4429	78	,051 723 4091	138	,050 680 5975
19	,083 166 9890	79	,051 669 3897	139	,050 677 9157
20	,080 668 3722	80	,051 618 0780	140	,050 675 3633
21	,078 425 7323	81	,051 569 3333	141	,050 672 9343
22	,076 403 9957	82	,051 523 0229	142	,050 670 6224
23	,074 574 1825	83	,051 479 0211	143	,050 668 4222
24	,072 912 1374	84	,051 437 2094	144	,050 666 3282
25	,071 397 5653	85	,051 397 4754	145	,050 664 3352
26	,070 013 2887	86	,051 359 7130	146	,050 662 4384
27	,068 744 6709	87	,051 323 8217	147	,050 660 6331
28	,067 579 1626	88	,051 289 7065	148	,050 658 9150
29	,066 505 9419	89	,051 257 2772	149	,050 657 2797
30	,065 515 6267	90	,051 226 4485	150	,050 655 7234
31	,064 600 0430	91	,051 197 1399	151	,050 654 2421
32	,063 752 0359	92	,051 169 2746	152	,050 652 8323
33	,062 965 3157	93	,051 142 7801	153	,050 651 4905
34	,062 234 3305	94	,051 117 5878	154	,050 650 2134
35	,061 554 1615	95	,051 093 6324	155	,050 648 9979
36	,060 920 4346	96	,051 070 8522	156	,050 647 8410
37	,060 329 2476	97	,051 049 1866	157	,050 646 7399
38	,059 777 1079	98	,051 028 5858	158	,050 645 6919
39	,059 260 8799	99	,051 008 9913	159	,050 644 6945
40	,058 777 7413	100	,050 990 3549	160	,050 643 7451
41	,058 325 1442	101	,050 972 6292	161	,050 642 8416
42	,057 900 7831	102	,050 955 7690	162	,050 641 9816
43	,057 502 5666	103	,050 939 7316	163	,050 641 1631
44	,057 128 5933	104	,050 924 4764	164	,050 640 3840
45	,056 777 1307	105	,050 909 9647	165	,050 639 6425
46	,056 446 5972	106	,050 896 1600	166	,050 638 9367
47	,056 135 5456	107	,050 883 0274	167	,050 638 2650
48	,055 842 6500	108	,050 870 5338	168	,050 637 6257
49	,055 566 6928	109	,050 858 6480	169	,050 637 0172
50	,055 306 5543	110	,050 847 3401	170	,050 636 4380
51	,055 061 2032	111	,050 836 5818	171	,050 635 8867
52	,054 829 6880	112	,050 826 3460	172	,050 635 3620
53	,054 611 1297	113	,050 816 6073	173	,050 634 8626
54	,054 404 7152	114	,050 807 3413	174	,050 634 3873
55	,054 209 6911	115	,050 798 5250	175	,050 633 9349
56	,054 025 3587	116	,050 790 1363	176	,050 633 5043
57	,053 851 0692	117	,050 782 1544	177	,050 633 0944
58	,053 686 2192	118	,050 774 5595	178	,050 632 7043
59	,053 530 2475	119	,050 767 3326	179	,050 632 3330
60	,053 382 6308	120	,050 760 4559	180	,050 631 9796

Repayment of a Loan by way of an Annuity

NOMINAL INTEREST RATE COMPOUNDED

YEARLY	HALF-YEARLY	QUARTERLY
@	@	@
5⅛%	10¼%	20½%
5.1250%	10.2500%	20.5000%
PER ANNUM	PER ANNUM	PER ANNUM

Periods	Loan of 1	Periods	Loan of 1	Periods	Loan of 1
1	1.051 250 0000	61	.053 801 0823	121	.051 371 4212
2	.538 757 6173	62	.053 670 8386	122	.051 365 4884
3	.368 068 9790	63	.053 547 5283	123	.051 359 8461
4	.282 831 1439	64	.053 430 7543	124	.051 354 4800
5	.231 773 4812	65	.053 320 1449	125	.051 349 3766
6	.197 805 7458	66	.053 215 3521	126	.051 344 5229
7	.173 603 5171	67	.053 116 0496	127	.051 339 9067
8	.155 504 5590	68	.053 021 9316	128	.051 335 5163
9	.141 474 2732	69	.052 932 7110	129	.051 331 3406
10	.130 291 8806	70	.052 848 1183	130	.051 327 3692
11	.121 180 5037	71	.052 767 9001	131	.051 323 5919
12	.113 622 2081	72	.052 691 8184	132	.051 319 9993
13	.107 258 4090	73	.052 619 6491	133	.051 316 5823
14	.101 832 9611	74	.052 551 1814	134	.051 313 3323
15	.097 158 0123	75	.052 486 2167	135	.051 310 2411
16	.093 092 6624	76	.052 424 5681	136	.051 307 3010
17	.089 529 1540	77	.052 366 0592	137	.051 304 5045
18	.086 383 6666	78	.052 310 5237	138	.051 301 8446
19	.083 590 0173	79	.052 257 8049	139	.051 299 3147
20	.081 095 2521	80	.052 207 7547	140	.051 296 9083
21	.078 856 4964	81	.052 160 2335	141	.051 294 6195
22	.076 838 6640	82	.052 115 1092	142	.051 292 4424
23	.075 012 7649	83	.052 072 2572	143	.051 290 3717
24	.073 354 6351	84	.052 031 5596	144	.051 288 4020
25	.071 843 9718	85	.051 992 9051	145	.051 286 5285
26	.070 463 5911	86	.051 956 1883	146	.051 284 7465
27	.069 198 8506	87	.051 921 3096	147	.051 283 0515
28	.068 037 1960	88	.051 888 1748	148	.051 281 4392
29	.066 967 8009	89	.051 856 6945	149	.051 279 9056
30	.065 981 2795	90	.051 826 7844	150	.051 278 4468
31	.065 069 4542	91	.051 798 3644	151	.051 277 0593
32	.064 225 1672	92	.051 771 3589	152	.051 275 7394
33	.063 442 1258	93	.051 745 6960	153	.051 274 4840
34	.062 714 7761	94	.051 721 3078	154	.051 273 2898
35	.062 038 1967	95	.051 698 1300	155	.051 272 1539
36	.061 408 0120	96	.051 676 1013	156	.051 271 0734
37	.060 820 3178	97	.051 655 1640	157	.051 270 0457
38	.060 271 6200	98	.051 635 2632	158	.051 269 0680
39	.059 758 7819	99	.051 616 3468	159	.051 268 1381
40	.059 278 9799	100	.051 598 3654	160	.051 267 2536
41	.058 829 6651	101	.051 581 2723	161	.051 266 4122
42	.058 408 5311	102	.051 565 0230	162	.051 265 6118
43	.058 013 4858	103	.051 549 5754	163	.051 264 8505
44	.057 642 6272	104	.051 534 8895	164	.051 264 1263
45	.057 294 2224	105	.051 520 9273	165	.051 263 4374
46	.056 966 6891	106	.051 507 6528	166	.051 262 7822
47	.056 658 5802	107	.051 495 0318	167	.051 262 1589
48	.056 368 5693	108	.051 483 0318	168	.051 261 5660
49	.056 095 4389	109	.051 471 6220	169	.051 261 0020
50	.055 838 0691	110	.051 460 7732	170	.051 260 4655
51	.055 595 4288	111	.051 450 4575	171	.051 259 9552
52	.055 366 5665	112	.051 440 6485	172	.051 259 4698
53	.055 150 6035	113	.051 431 3212	173	.051 259 0080
54	.054 946 7268	114	.051 422 4518	174	.051 258 5688
55	.054 754 1833	115	.051 414 0176	175	.051 258 1510
56	.054 572 2749	116	.051 405 9972	176	.051 257 7536
57	.054 400 3530	117	.051 398 3701	177	.051 257 3755
58	.054 237 8148	118	.051 391 1169	178	.051 257 0159
59	.054 084 0994	119	.051 384 2192	179	.051 256 6738
60	.053 938 6844	120	.051 377 6595	180	.051 256 3484

Repayment of a Loan by way of an Annuity

NOMINAL INTEREST RATE COMPOUNDED

YEARLY	HALF-YEARLY	QUARTERLY
@	@	@
$5\frac{3}{16}\%$	$10\frac{3}{8}\%$	$20\frac{3}{4}\%$
5.1875%	10.3750%	20.7500%
PER ANNUM	PER ANNUM	PER ANNUM

Periods	Loan of 1	Periods	Loan of 1	Periods	Loan of 1
1	1,051 875 0000	61	,054 360 8451	121	,051 989 3548
2	,539 234 1228	62	,054 232 6797	122	,051 983 7034
3	,368 499 4274	63	,054 111 3940	123	,051 978 3318
4	,283 241 1380	64	,053 996 5917	124	,051 973 2262
5	,232 173 2551	65	,053 887 9019	125	,051 968 3732
6	,198 200 4086	66	,053 784 9772	126	,051 963 7605
7	,173 995 9804	67	,053 687 4924	127	,051 959 3760
8	,155 896 6342	68	,053 595 1422	128	,051 955 2084
9	,141 867 1594	69	,053 507 6406	129	,051 951 2470
10	,130 686 4087	70	,053 424 7188	130	,051 947 4815
11	,121 577 2695	71	,053 346 1244	131	,051 943 9022
12	,114 021 6495	72	,053 271 6202	132	,051 940 4999
13	,107 660 8544	73	,053 200 9829	133	,051 937 2658
14	,102 238 6597	74	,053 134 0027	134	,051 934 1915
15	,097 567 1550	75	,053 070 4820	135	,051 931 2692
16	,093 505 3958	76	,053 010 2345	136	,051 928 4914
17	,089 945 5902	77	,052 953 0850	137	,051 925 8507
18	,086 803 8905	78	,052 898 8680	138	,051 923 3406
19	,084 014 0923	79	,052 847 4277	139	,051 920 9545
20	,081 523 2237	80	,052 798 6169	140	,051 918 6863
21	,079 288 3953	81	,052 752 2969	141	,051 916 5301
22	,077 274 5090	82	,052 708 3364	142	,051 914 4804
23	,075 452 5643	83	,052 666 6119	143	,051 912 5320
24	,073 798 3884	84	,052 627 0063	144	,051 910 6797
25	,072 291 6710	85	,052 589 4091	145	,051 908 9190
26	,070 915 2216	86	,052 553 7158	146	,051 907 2452
27	,069 654 3920	87	,052 519 8277	147	,051 905 6540
28	,068 496 6230	88	,052 487 6514	148	,051 904 1414
29	,067 431 0838	89	,052 457 0984	149	,051 902 7035
30	,066 448 3847	90	,052 428 0851	150	,051 901 3365
31	,065 540 3446	91	,052 400 5325	151	,051 900 0371
32	,064 699 8026	92	,052 374 3655	152	,051 898 8018
33	,063 920 4635	93	,052 349 5131	153	,051 897 6274
34	,063 196 7707	94	,052 325 9083	154	,051 896 5111
35	,062 523 8008	95	,052 303 4873	155	,051 895 4498
36	,061 897 1763	96	,052 282 1899	156	,051 894 4409
37	,061 312 9913	97	,052 261 9588	157	,051 893 4818
38	,060 767 7502	98	,052 242 7400	158	,051 892 5700
39	,060 258 3150	99	,052 224 4821	159	,051 891 7032
40	,059 781 8609	100	,052 207 1365	160	,051 890 8792
41	,059 335 8381	101	,052 190 6569	161	,051 890 0959
42	,058 917 9394	102	,052 174 9997	162	,051 889 3512
43	,058 526 0719	103	,052 160 1234	163	,051 888 6433
44	,058 158 3331	104	,052 145 9886	164	,051 887 9703
45	,057 812 9895	105	,052 132 5580	165	,051 887 3305
46	,057 488 4587	106	,052 119 7961	166	,051 886 7222
47	,057 183 2931	107	,052 107 6695	167	,051 886 1440
48	,056 896 1663	108	,052 096 1461	168	,051 885 5943
49	,056 625 8605	109	,052 085 1957	169	,051 885 0717
50	,056 371 2562	110	,052 074 7896	170	,051 884 5749
51	,056 131 3220	111	,052 064 9006	171	,051 884 1026
52	,055 905 1067	112	,052 055 5027	172	,051 883 6537
53	,055 691 7319	113	,052 046 5715	173	,051 883 2268
54	,055 490 3849	114	,052 038 0835	174	,051 882 8210
55	,055 300 3129	115	,052 030 0168	175	,051 882 4353
56	,055 120 8182	116	,052 022 3501	176	,051 882 0685
57	,054 951 2526	117	,052 015 0637	177	,051 881 7199
58	,054 791 0140	118	,052 008 1385	178	,051 881 3885
59	,054 639 5419	119	,052 001 5565	179	,051 881 0734
60	,054 496 3145	120	,051 995 3007	180	,051 880 7738

Repayment of a Loan by way of an Annuity

NOMINAL INTEREST RATE COMPOUNDED

YEARLY	HALF-YEARLY	QUARTERLY
@	@	@
$5\frac{1}{4}\%$	$10\frac{1}{2}\%$	21 %
5.2500%	10.5000%	21.0000%
PER ANNUM	PER ANNUM	PER ANNUM

Periods	Loan of 1	Periods	Loan of 1	Periods	Loan of 1
1	1.052 500 0000	61	.054 922 1390	121	.052 607 6898
2	.539 710 7186	62	.054 796 0358	122	.052 602 3076
3	.368 930 0363	63	.054 676 7581	123	.052 597 1950
4	.283 651 3576	64	.054 563 9102	124	.052 592 3382
5	.232 573 3168	65	.054 457 1220	125	.052 587 7246
6	.198 595 4203	66	.054 356 0470	126	.052 583 3418
7	.174 388 8524	67	.054 260 3607	127	.052 579 1784
8	.156 289 1770	68	.054 169 7590	128	.052 575 2232
9	.142 260 5712	69	.054 083 9565	129	.052 571 4659
10	.131 081 5194	70	.054 002 6853	130	.052 567 8964
11	.121 974 6736	71	.053 925 6940	131	.052 564 5055
12	.114 421 7842	72	.053 852 7462	132	.052 561 2842
13	.108 064 0468	73	.053 783 6198	133	.052 558 2238
14	.102 645 1581	74	.053 718 1056	134	.052 555 3165
15	.097 977 1489	75	.053 656 0071	135	.052 552 5545
16	.093 919 0304	76	.053 597 1390	136	.052 549 9305
17	.090 362 9764	77	.053 541 3269	137	.052 547 4377
18	.087 225 1119	78	.053 488 4063	138	.052 545 0694
19	.084 439 2107	79	.053 438 2223	139	.052 542 8194
20	.081 952 2832	80	.053 390 6287	140	.052 540 6819
21	.079 721 4252	81	.053 345 4876	141	.052 538 6511
22	.077 711 5264	82	.053 302 6688	142	.052 536 7218
23	.075 893 5759	83	.053 262 0495	143	.052 534 8889
24	.074 243 3921	84	.053 223 5137	144	.052 533 1475
25	.072 740 6571	85	.053 186 9517	145	.052 531 4930
26	.071 368 1737	86	.053 152 2600	146	.052 529 9212
27	.070 111 2882	87	.053 119 3406	147	.052 528 4279
28	.068 957 4362	88	.053 088 1011	148	.052 527 0092
29	.067 895 7825	89	.053 058 4538	149	.052 525 6613
30	.066 916 9335	90	.053 030 3161	150	.052 524 3806
31	.066 012 7048	91	.053 003 6095	151	.052 523 1640
32	.065 175 9322	92	.052 978 2600	152	.052 522 0080
33	.064 400 3179	93	.052 954 1974	153	.052 520 9098
34	.063 680 3028	94	.052 931 3554	154	.052 519 8664
35	.063 010 9616	95	.052 909 6709	155	.052 518 8751
36	.062 387 9146	96	.052 889 0846	156	.052 517 9333
37	.061 807 2544	97	.052 869 5399	157	.052 517 0384
38	.061 265 4839	98	.052 850 9836	158	.052 516 1883
39	.060 759 4639	99	.052 833 3649	159	.052 515 3806
40	.060 286 3683	100	.052 816 6360	160	.052 514 6131
41	.059 843 6465	101	.052 800 7513	161	.052 513 8840
42	.059 428 9905	102	.052 785 6678	162	.052 513 1913
43	.059 040 3066	103	.052 771 3447	163	.052 512 5331
44	.058 675 6919	104	.052 757 7433	164	.052 511 9078
45	.058 333 4124	105	.052 744 8268	165	.052 511 3137
46	.058 011 8853	106	.052 732 5604	166	.052 510 7493
47	.057 709 6629	107	.052 720 9112	167	.052 510 2130
48	.057 425 4187	108	.052 709 8478	168	.052 509 7034
49	.057 157 9348	109	.052 699 3406	169	.052 509 2193
50	.056 906 0917	110	.052 689 3614	170	.052 508 7594
51	.056 668 8583	111	.052 679 8834	171	.052 508 3224
52	.056 445 2836	112	.052 670 8814	172	.052 507 9072
53	.056 234 4893	113	.052 662 3313	173	.052 507 5127
54	.056 035 6631	114	.052 654 2102	174	.052 507 1379
55	.055 848 0527	115	.052 646 4966	175	.052 506 7818
56	.055 670 9607	116	.052 639 1698	176	.052 506 4435
57	.055 503 7397	117	.052 632 2103	177	.052 506 1221
58	.055 345 7878	118	.052 625 5997	178	.052 505 8166
59	.055 196 5454	119	.052 619 3204	179	.052 505 5265
60	.055 055 4911	120	.052 613 3557	180	.052 505 2508

Repayment of a Loan by way of an Annuity

NOMINAL INTEREST RATE COMPOUNDED

YEARLY @ $5\frac{5}{16}\%$ 5.3125% PER ANNUM		HALF-YEARLY @ $10\frac{5}{8}\%$ 10.6250% PER ANNUM		QUARTERLY @ $21\frac{1}{4}\%$ 21.2500% PER ANNUM	
Periods	Loan of 1	Periods	Loan of 1	Periods	Loan of 1
1	1.053 125 0000	61	.055 484 9337	121	.053 226 4043
2	.540 187 4049	62	.055 360 8762	122	.053 221 2797
3	.369 360 8057	63	.055 243 5893	123	.053 216 4145
4	.284 061 8023	64	.055 132 6779	124	.053 211 7956
5	.232 973 6661	65	.055 027 7730	125	.053 207 4104
6	.198 990 7805	66	.054 928 5288	126	.053 203 2470
7	.174 782 1327	67	.054 834 6218	127	.053 199 2943
8	.156 682 1867	68	.054 745 7486	128	.053 195 5416
9	.142 654 5077	69	.054 661 6250	129	.053 191 9786
10	.131 477 2115	70	.054 581 9839	130	.053 188 5958
11	.122 372 7150	71	.054 506 5748	131	.053 185 3841
12	.114 822 6109	72	.054 435 1623	132	.053 182 3347
13	.108 467 9849	73	.054 367 5252	133	.053 179 4395
14	.103 052 4545	74	.054 303 4555	134	.053 176 6906
15	.098 387 9921	75	.054 242 7574	135	.053 174 0807
16	.094 333 5642	76	.054 185 2467	136	.053 171 6026
17	.090 781 3102	77	.054 130 7499	137	.053 169 2498
18	.087 647 3280	78	.054 079 1036	138	.053 167 0158
19	.084 865 3695	79	.054 030 1537	139	.053 164 8947
20	.082 382 4271	80	.053 983 7550	140	.053 162 8808
21	.080 155 5821	81	.053 939 7706	141	.053 160 9686
22	.078 149 7118	82	.053 898 0713	142	.053 159 1530
23	.076 335 7949	83	.053 858 5352	143	.053 157 4291
24	.074 689 6409	84	.053 821 0471	144	.053 155 7923
25	.073 190 9242	85	.053 785 4984	145	.053 154 2381
26	.071 822 4412	86	.053 751 7864	146	.053 152 7624
27	.070 569 5323	87	.053 719 8141	147	.053 151 3612
28	.069 419 6280	88	.053 689 4898	148	.053 150 0308
29	.068 361 8889	89	.053 660 7269	149	.053 148 7676
30	.067 386 9173	90	.053 633 4434	150	.053 147 5681
31	.066 486 5253	91	.053 607 5620	151	.053 146 4292
32	.065 653 5458	92	.053 583 0092	152	.053 145 3478
33	.064 881 6782	93	.053 559 7158	153	.053 144 3210
34	.064 165 3610	94	.053 537 6162	154	.053 143 3460
35	.063 499 6668	95	.053 516 6483	155	.053 142 4202
36	.062 880 2140	96	.053 496 7533	156	.053 141 5412
37	.062 303 0935	97	.053 477 8756	157	.053 140 7065
38	.061 764 8068	98	.053 459 9625	158	.053 139 9140
39	.061 262 2134	99	.053 442 9642	159	.053 139 1614
40	.060 792 4862	100	.053 426 8333	160	.053 138 4469
41	.060 353 0736	101	.053 411 5252	161	.053 137 7684
42	.059 941 6668	102	.053 396 9974	162	.053 137 1241
43	.059 556 1717	103	.053 383 2098	163	.053 136 5124
44	.059 194 6845	104	.053 370 1242	164	.053 135 9315
45	.058 855 4711	105	.053 357 7048	165	.053 135 3800
46	.058 536 9483	106	.053 345 9171	166	.053 134 8563
47	.058 237 6683	107	.053 334 7289	167	.053 134 3590
48	.057 956 3044	108	.053 324 1095	168	.053 133 8868
49	.057 691 6389	109	.053 314 0297	169	.053 133 4384
50	.057 442 5522	110	.053 304 4618	170	.053 133 0127
51	.057 208 0135	111	.053 295 3798	171	.053 132 6084
52	.056 987 0720	112	.053 286 7588	172	.053 132 2246
53	.056 778 8498	113	.053 278 5753	173	.053 131 8601
54	.056 582 5350	114	.053 270 8069	174	.053 131 5140
55	.056 397 3757	115	.053 263 4325	175	.053 131 1853
56	.056 222 6749	116	.053 256 4320	176	.053 130 8733
57	.056 057 7859	117	.053 249 7863	177	.053 130 5770
58	.055 902 1074	118	.053 243 4774	178	.053 130 2956
59	.055 755 0803	119	.053 237 4881	179	.053 130 0284
60	.055 616 1842	120	.053 231 8023	180	.053 129 7748

Repayment of a Loan by way of an Annuity

NOMINAL INTEREST RATE COMPOUNDED

YEARLY	HALF-YEARLY	QUARTERLY
@	@	@
$5\frac{3}{8}\%$	$10\frac{3}{4}\%$	$21\frac{1}{2}\%$
5.3750%	10.7500%	21.5000%
PER ANNUM	PER ANNUM	PER ANNUM

Periods	Loan of 1	Periods	Loan of 1	Periods	Loan of 1
1	1.053 750 0000	61	.056 049 1990	121	.053 845 4775
2	.540 664 1814	62	.055 927 1704	122	.053 840 5992
3	.369 791 7353	63	.055 811 8566	123	.053 835 9705
4	.284 472 4720	64	.055 702 8636	124	.053 831 5786
5	.233 374 3026	65	.055 599 8232	125	.053 827 4114
6	.199 386 4886	66	.055 502 3906	126	.053 823 4574
7	.175 175 8206	67	.055 410 2431	127	.053 819 7056
8	.157 075 6628	68	.055 323 0784	128	.053 816 1457
9	.143 048 9682	69	.055 240 6131	129	.053 812 7677
10	.131 873 4844	70	.055 162 5813	130	.053 809 5625
11	.122 771 3928	71	.055 088 7333	131	.053 806 5211
12	.115 224 1284	72	.055 018 8348	132	.053 803 6352
13	.108 872 6672	73	.054 952 6655	133	.053 800 8968
14	.103 460 5473	74	.054 890 0185	134	.053 798 2983
15	.098 799 6825	75	.054 830 6989	135	.053 795 8326
16	.094 748 9948	76	.054 774 5236	136	.053 793 4928
17	.091 200 5891	77	.054 721 3200	137	.053 791 2726
18	.088 070 5360	78	.054 670 9257	138	.053 789 1659
19	.085 292 5654	79	.054 623 1877	139	.053 787 1667
20	.082 813 6520	80	.054 577 9618	140	.053 785 2696
21	.080 590 8621	81	.054 535 1120	141	.053 783 4695
22	.078 589 0608	82	.054 494 5101	142	.053 781 7612
23	.076 779 2163	83	.054 456 0350	143	.053 780 1403
24	.075 137 1293	84	.054 419 5727	144	.053 778 6020
25	.073 642 4665	85	.054 385 0155	145	.053 777 1424
26	.072 278 0176	86	.054 352 2615	146	.053 775 7572
27	.071 029 1172	87	.054 321 2147	147	.053 774 4428
28	.069 883 1909	88	.054 291 7843	148	.053 773 1955
29	.068 829 3947	89	.054 263 8846	149	.053 772 0118
30	.067 858 3271	90	.054 237 4345	150	.053 770 8886
31	.066 961 7967	91	.054 212 3574	151	.053 769 8227
32	.066 132 6333	92	.054 188 5809	152	.053 768 8112
33	.065 364 5336	93	.054 166 0365	153	.053 767 8514
34	.064 651 9338	94	.054 144 6593	154	.053 766 9405
35	.063 989 9042	95	.054 124 3882	155	.053 766 0762
36	.063 374 0614	96	.054 105 1651	156	.053 765 2559
37	.062 800 4948	97	.054 086 9352	157	.053 764 4775
38	.062 265 7044	98	.054 069 6465	158	.053 763 7389
39	.061 766 5483	99	.054 053 2499	159	.053 763 0379
40	.061 300 1986	100	.054 037 6988	160	.053 762 3727
41	.060 864 1027	101	.054 022 9493	161	.053 761 7414
42	.060 455 9510	102	.054 008 9595	162	.053 761 1424
43	.060 073 6488	103	.053 995 6901	163	.053 760 5739
44	.059 715 2920	104	.053 983 1035	164	.053 760 0345
45	.059 379 1459	105	.053 971 1643	165	.053 759 5226
46	.059 063 6272	106	.053 959 8391	166	.053 759 0367
47	.058 767 2880	107	.053 949 0959	167	.053 758 5757
48	.058 488 8015	108	.053 938 9047	168	.053 758 1382
49	.058 226 9500	109	.053 929 2368	169	.053 757 7230
50	.057 980 6143	110	.053 920 0653	170	.053 757 3291
51	.057 748 7635	111	.053 911 3645	171	.053 756 9552
52	.057 530 4474	112	.053 903 1102	172	.053 756 6003
53	.057 324 7882	113	.053 895 2792	173	.053 756 2636
54	.057 130 9745	114	.053 887 8497	174	.053 755 9441
55	.056 948 2551	115	.053 880 8011	175	.053 755 6409
56	.056 775 9335	116	.053 874 1138	176	.053 755 3531
57	.056 613 3633	117	.053 867 7691	177	.053 755 0800
58	.056 459 9443	118	.053 861 7494	178	.053 754 8209
59	.056 315 1179	119	.053 856 0380	179	.053 754 5750
60	.056 178 3643	120	.053 850 6190	180	.053 754 3416

Repayment of a Loan by way of an Annuity

NOMINAL INTEREST RATE COMPOUNDED

YEARLY	HALF-YEARLY	QUARTERLY
@	@	@
$5\frac{7}{16}\%$	$10\frac{7}{8}\%$	$21\frac{3}{4}\%$
7.4375%	10.8750%	21.7500%
PER ANNUM	PER ANNUM	PER ANNUM

Periods	Loan of 1	Periods	Loan of 1	Periods	Loan of 1
1	1.054 375 0000	61	.056 614 9055	121	.054 464 8896
2	.541 141 0481	62	.056 494 8882	122	.054 460 2467
3	.370 222 8250	63	.056 381 5295	123	.054 455 8439
4	.284 883 3664	64	.056 274 4364	124	.054 451 6688
5	.233 775 2261	65	.056 173 2414	125	.054 447 7097
6	.199 782 5445	66	.056 077 6008	126	.054 443 9552
7	.175 569 9158	67	.055 987 1929	127	.054 440 3949
8	.157 469 6047	68	.055 901 7163	128	.054 437 0185
9	.143 443 9521	69	.055 820 8887	129	.054 433 8167
10	.132 270 3371	70	.055 744 4450	130	.054 430 7804
11	.123 170 7059	71	.055 672 1368	131	.054 427 9010
12	.115 626 3356	72	.055 603 7308	132	.054 425 1703
13	.109 278 0923	73	.055 539 0076	133	.054 422 5807
14	.103 869 4348	74	.055 477 7613	134	.054 420 1249
15	.099 212 2183	75	.055 419 7983	135	.054 417 7959
16	.095 165 3202	76	.055 364 9362	136	.054 415 5873
17	.091 620 8107	77	.055 313 0037	137	.054 413 4927
18	.088 494 7331	78	.055 263 8393	138	.054 411 5062
19	.085 720 7953	79	.055 217 2911	139	.054 409 6224
20	.083 245 9541	80	.055 173 2158	140	.054 407 8358
21	.081 027 2612	81	.055 131 4784	141	.054 406 1415
22	.079 029 5690	82	.055 091 9518	142	.054 404 5346
23	.077 223 8354	83	.055 054 5159	143	.054 403 0107
24	.075 585 8520	84	.055 019 0577	144	.054 401 5654
25	.074 095 2780	85	.054 985 4702	145	.054 400 1948
26	.072 734 8964	86	.054 953 6527	146	.054 398 8949
27	.071 490 0360	87	.054 923 5101	147	.054 397 6621
28	.070 348 1173	88	.054 894 9524	148	.054 396 4930
29	.069 298 2918	89	.054 867 8950	149	.054 395 3841
30	.068 331 1542	90	.054 842 2576	150	.054 394 3325
31	.067 438 5095	91	.054 817 9644	151	.054 393 3352
32	.066 613 1846	92	.054 794 9439	152	.054 392 3893
33	.065 848 8733	93	.054 773 1285	153	.054 391 4923
34	.065 140 0096	94	.054 752 4541	154	.054 390 6415
35	.064 481 6615	95	.054 732 8604	155	.054 389 8346
36	.063 869 4440	96	.054 714 2901	156	.054 389 0694
37	.063 299 4447	97	.054 696 6891	157	.054 388 3437
38	.062 768 1622	98	.054 680 0063	158	.054 387 6554
39	.062 272 4535	99	.054 664 1932	159	.054 387 0026
40	.061 809 4896	100	.054 649 2040	160	.054 386 3835
41	.061 376 7171	101	.054 634 9955	161	.054 385 7963
42	.060 971 8256	102	.054 621 5265	162	.054 385 2394
43	.060 592 7198	103	.054 608 7583	163	.054 384 7113
44	.060 237 4953	104	.054 596 6540	164	.054 384 2104
45	.059 904 4171	105	.054 585 1790	165	.054 383 7353
46	.059 591 9016	106	.054 574 3001	166	.054 383 2847
47	.059 298 5008	107	.054 563 9863	167	.054 382 8574
48	.059 022 8881	108	.054 554 2080	168	.054 382 4522
49	.058 763 8457	109	.054 544 9372	169	.054 382 0678
50	.058 520 2546	110	.054 536 1475	170	.054 381 7033
51	.058 291 0844	111	.054 527 8136	171	.054 381 3575
52	.058 075 3849	112	.054 519 9119	172	.054 381 0296
53	.057 872 2791	113	.054 512 4198	173	.054 380 7186
54	.057 680 9559	114	.054 505 3159	174	.054 380 4237
55	.057 500 6646	115	.054 498 5801	175	.054 380 1440
56	.057 330 7093	116	.054 492 1933	176	.054 379 8787
57	.057 170 4445	117	.054 486 1372	177	.054 379 6270
58	.057 019 2704	118	.054 480 3946	178	.054 379 3884
59	.056 876 6293	119	.054 474 9493	179	.054 379 1621
60	.056 742 0022	120	.054 469 7859	180	.054 378 9474

Repayment of a Loan by way of an Annuity

NOMINAL INTEREST RATE COMPOUNDED

YEARLY	HALF-YEARLY	QUARTERLY
@	@	@
$5\frac{1}{2}\%$	11%	22%
5.5000%	11.0000%	22.0000%
PER ANNUM	PER ANNUM	PER ANNUM

Periods	Loan of 1	Periods	Loan of 1	Periods	Loan of 1
1	1.055 000 0000	61	.057 182 0238	121	.055 084 6219
2	.541 618 0049	62	.057 064 0001	122	.055 080 2039
3	.370 654 0747	63	.056 952 5782	123	.055 076 0169
4	.285 294 4853	64	.056 847 3659	124	.055 072 0487
5	.234 176 4362	65	.056 747 9969	125	.055 068 2880
6	.200 178 9476	66	.056 654 1284	126	.055 064 7237
7	.175 964 4178	67	.056 565 4398	127	.055 061 3457
8	.157 864 0118	68	.056 481 6307	128	.055 058 1442
9	.143 839 4585	69	.056 402 4198	129	.055 055 1100
10	.132 667 7687	70	.056 327 5431	130	.055 052 2342
11	.123 570 6532	71	.056 256 7533	131	.055 049 5087
12	.116 029 2312	72	.056 189 8180	132	.055 046 9254
13	.109 684 2587	73	.056 126 5191	133	.055 044 4771
14	.104 279 1154	74	.056 066 6516	134	.055 042 1566
15	.099 625 5976	75	.056 010 0230	135	.055 039 9573
16	.095 582 5380	76	.055 956 4521	136	.055 037 8728
17	.092 041 9723	77	.055 905 7685	137	.055 035 8971
18	.088 919 9163	78	.055 857 8119	138	.055 034 0245
19	.086 150 0559	79	.055 812 4313	139	.055 032 2497
20	.083 679 3300	80	.055 769 4845	140	.055 030 5675
21	.081 464 7754	81	.055 728 8376	141	.055 028 9731
22	.079 471 2319	82	.055 690 3644	142	.055 027 4619
23	.077 669 6472	83	.055 653 9459	143	.055 026 0295
24	.076 035 8037	84	.055 619 4699	144	.055 024 6719
25	.074 549 3529	85	.055 586 8307	145	.055 023 3852
26	.073 193 0713	86	.055 555 9284	146	.055 022 1656
27	.071 952 2817	87	.055 526 6688	147	.055 021 0096
28	.070 814 3996	88	.055 498 9631	148	.055 019 9139
29	.069 768 5720	89	.055 472 7272	149	.055 018 8754
30	.068 805 3897	90	.055 447 8820	150	.055 017 8910
31	.067 916 6543	91	.055 424 3525	151	.055 016 9580
32	.067 095 1895	92	.055 402 0682	152	.055 016 0737
33	.066 334 6865	93	.055 380 9621	153	.055 015 2355
34	.065 629 5769	94	.055 360 9712	154	.055 014 4410
35	.064 974 9266	95	.055 342 0357	155	.055 013 6880
36	.064 366 3488	96	.055 324 0994	156	.055 012 9742
37	.063 799 9295	97	.055 307 1089	157	.055 012 2977
38	.063 272 1659	98	.055 291 0137	158	.055 011 6564
39	.062 779 9139	99	.055 275 7663	159	.055 011 0486
40	.062 320 3434	100	.055 261 3216	160	.055 010 4725
41	.061 890 9001	101	.055 247 6369	161	.055 009 9265
42	.061 489 2731	102	.055 234 6718	162	.055 009 4089
43	.061 113 3667	103	.055 222 3883	163	.055 008 9183
44	.060 761 2757	104	.055 210 7501	164	.055 008 4533
45	.060 431 2651	105	.055 199 7233	165	.055 008 0125
46	.060 121 7512	106	.055 189 2753	166	.055 007 5948
47	.059 831 2858	107	.055 179 3757	167	.055 007 1988
48	.059 558 5424	108	.055 169 9955	168	.055 006 8234
49	.059 302 3035	109	.055 161 1072	169	.055 006 4677
50	.059 061 4501	110	.055 152 6849	170	.055 006 1305
51	.058 834 9523	111	.055 144 7041	171	.055 005 8108
52	.058 621 8603	112	.055 137 1415	172	.055 005 5079
53	.058 421 2975	113	.055 129 9750	173	.055 005 2207
54	.058 232 4534	114	.055 123 1839	174	.055 004 9485
55	.058 054 5778	115	.055 116 7483	175	.055 004 6905
56	.057 886 9756	116	.055 110 6497	176	.055 004 4460
57	.057 729 0020	117	.055 104 8702	177	.055 004 2142
58	.057 580 0578	118	.055 099 3932	178	.055 003 9944
59	.057 439 5863	119	.055 094 2027	179	.055 003 7862
60	.057 307 0692	120	.055 089 2837	180	.055 003 5888

Repayment of a Loan by way of an Annuity

NOMINAL INTEREST RATE COMPOUNDED

	YEARLY @ $5\frac{9}{16}\%$ 5.5625% PER ANNUM		HALF-YEARLY @ $11\frac{1}{8}\%$ 11.1250% PER ANNUM		QUARTERLY @ $22\frac{1}{4}\%$ 22.2500% PER ANNUM
Periods	Loan of 1	Periods	Loan of 1	Periods	Loan of 1
1	1.055 625 0000	61	.057 750 5252	121	.055 704 6566
2	.542 095 0517	62	.057 634 4768	122	.055 700 4535
3	.371 085 4842	63	.057 524 9729	123	.055 696 4724
4	.285 705 8285	64	.057 421 6223	124	.055 692 7017
5	.234 577 9326	65	.057 324 0595	125	.055 689 1301
6	.200 575 6977	66	.057 231 9430	126	.055 685 7472
7	.176 359 3260	67	.057 144 9531	127	.055 682 5428
8	.158 258 8835	68	.057 062 7907	128	.055 679 5077
9	.144 235 4868	69	.056 985 1753	129	.055 676 6328
10	.133 065 7784	70	.056 911 8442	130	.055 673 9097
11	.123 971 2336	71	.056 842 5511	131	.055 671 3303
12	.116 432 8139	72	.056 777 0648	132	.055 668 8871
13	.110 091 1651	73	.056 715 1683	133	.055 666 5728
14	.104 689 5875	74	.056 656 6576	134	.055 664 3806
15	.100 039 8184	75	.056 601 3414	135	.055 662 3041
16	.096 000 6461	76	.056 549 0395	136	.055 660 3371
17	.092 464 0715	77	.056 499 5827	137	.055 658 4739
18	.089 346 0829	78	.056 452 8117	138	.055 656 7091
19	.086 580 3441	79	.056 408 5766	139	.055 655 0373
20	.084 113 7761	80	.056 366 7363	140	.055 653 4537
21	.081 903 4006	81	.056 327 1580	141	.055 651 9536
22	.079 914 0452	82	.056 289 7164	142	.055 650 5327
23	.078 116 6467	83	.056 254 2936	143	.055 649 1867
24	.076 486 9789	84	.056 220 7785	144	.055 647 9117
25	.075 004 6853	85	.056 189 0663	145	.055 646 7039
26	.073 652 5357	86	.056 159 0580	146	.055 645 5598
27	.072 415 8472	87	.056 130 6606	147	.055 644 4761
28	.071 282 0301	88	.056 103 7860	148	.055 643 4494
29	.070 240 2270	89	.056 078 3513	149	.055 642 4770
30	.069 281 0248	90	.056 054 2781	150	.055 641 5558
31	.068 396 2214	91	.056 031 4925	151	.055 640 6831
32	.067 578 6378	92	.056 009 9246	152	.055 639 8565
33	.066 821 9623	93	.055 989 5085	153	.055 639 0735
34	.066 120 6241	94	.055 970 1819	154	.055 638 3317
35	.065 469 6873	95	.055 951 8860	155	.055 637 6290
36	.064 864 7629	96	.055 934 5653	156	.055 636 9634
37	.064 301 9355	97	.055 918 1671	157	.055 636 3329
38	.063 777 7011	98	.055 902 6419	158	.055 635 7356
39	.063 288 9142	99	.055 887 9427	159	.055 635 1698
40	.062 832 7439	100	.055 874 0252	160	.055 634 6338
41	.062 406 6352	101	.055 860 8474	161	.055 634 1261
42	.062 008 2764	102	.055 848 3698	162	.055 633 6451
43	.061 635 5712	103	.055 836 5548	163	.055 633 1895
44	.061 286 6144	104	.055 825 3670	164	.055 632 7579
45	.060 959 6705	105	.055 814 7729	165	.055 632 3491
46	.060 653 1558	106	.055 804 7407	166	.055 631 9618
47	.060 365 6221	107	.055 795 2405	167	.055 631 5949
48	.060 095 7429	108	.055 786 2438	168	.055 631 2473
49	.059 842 3011	109	.055 777 7239	169	.055 630 9181
50	.059 604 1779	110	.055 769 6554	170	.055 630 6062
51	.059 380 3437	111	.055 762 0142	171	.055 630 3108
52	.059 169 8494	112	.055 754 7775	172	.055 630 0309
53	.058 971 8186	113	.055 747 9239	173	.055 629 7658
54	.058 785 4416	114	.055 741 4330	174	.055 629 5146
55	.058 609 9689	115	.055 735 2855	175	.055 629 2767
56	.058 444 7060	116	.055 729 4632	176	.055 629 0514
57	.058 289 0088	117	.055 723 9489	177	.055 628 8379
58	.058 142 2791	118	.055 718 7261	178	.055 628 6356
59	.058 003 9609	119	.055 713 7794	179	.055 628 4440
60	.057 873 5369	120	.055 709 0942	180	.055 628 2625

Repayment of a Loan by way of an Annuity

NOMINAL INTEREST RATE COMPOUNDED

	YEARLY @ $5\frac{5}{8}\%$ 5.6250% PER ANNUM		HALF-YEARLY @ $11\frac{1}{4}\%$ 11.2500% PER ANNUM		QUARTERLY @ $22\frac{1}{2}\%$ 22.5000% PER ANNUM
Periods	Loan of 1	Periods	Loan of 1	Periods	Loan of 1
1	1.056 250 0000	61	.058 320 3812	121	.056 324 9769
2	.542 572 1884	62	.058 206 2896	122	.056 320 9790
3	.371 517 0534	63	.058 098 6846	123	.056 317 1946
4	.286 117 3958	64	.057 997 1759	124	.056 313 6121
5	.234 979 7152	65	.057 901 3994	125	.056 310 2209
6	.200 972 7942	66	.057 811 0145	126	.056 307 0106
7	.176 754 6400	67	.057 725 7026	127	.056 303 9716
8	.158 654 2191	68	.057 645 1657	128	.056 301 0948
9	.144 632 0362	69	.057 569 1246	129	.056 298 3714
10	.133 464 3653	70	.057 497 3176	130	.056 295 7933
11	.124 372 4462	71	.057 429 4995	131	.056 293 3527
12	.116 837 0826	72	.057 365 4404	132	.056 291 0423
13	.110 498 8099	73	.057 304 9242	133	.056 288 8551
14	.105 100 8492	74	.057 247 7483	134	.056 286 7846
15	.100 454 8789	75	.057 193 7223	135	.056 284 8244
16	.096 419 6423	76	.057 142 6673	136	.056 282 9688
17	.092 887 1057	77	.057 094 4152	137	.056 281 2121
18	.089 773 2299	78	.057 048 8077	138	.056 279 5490
19	.087 011 6566	79	.057 005 6962	139	.056 277 9746
20	.084 549 2886	80	.056 964 9405	140	.056 276 4841
21	.082 343 1328	81	.056 926 4089	141	.056 275 0731
22	.080 358 0042	82	.056 889 9773	142	.056 273 7373
23	.078 564 8291	83	.056 855 5288	143	.056 272 4727
24	.076 939 3721	84	.056 822 9532	144	.056 271 2755
25	.075 461 2691	85	.056 792 1468	145	.056 270 1420
26	.074 113 2831	86	.056 763 0118	146	.056 269 0690
27	.072 880 7255	87	.056 735 4558	147	.056 268 0532
28	.071 751 0012	88	.056 709 3920	148	.056 267 0915
29	.070 713 2487	89	.056 684 7383	149	.056 266 1810
30	.069 758 0505	90	.056 661 4172	150	.056 265 3191
31	.068 877 2016	91	.056 639 3558	151	.056 264 5031
32	.068 063 5194	92	.056 618 4850	152	.056 263 7305
33	.067 310 6899	93	.056 598 7399	153	.056 262 9991
34	.066 613 1398	94	.056 580 0590	154	.056 262 3067
35	.065 965 9312	95	.056 562 3842	155	.056 261 6512
36	.065 364 6732	96	.056 545 6610	156	.056 261 0306
37	.064 805 4491	97	.056 529 8374	157	.056 260 4431
38	.064 284 7533	98	.056 514 8646	158	.056 259 8868
39	.063 799 4395	99	.056 500 6965	159	.056 259 3602
40	.063 346 6755	100	.056 487 2895	160	.056 258 8617
41	.062 923 9058	101	.056 474 6023	161	.056 258 3897
42	.062 528 8180	102	.056 462 5961	162	.056 257 9428
43	.062 159 3155	103	.056 451 2339	163	.056 257 5198
44	.061 813 4926	104	.056 440 4810	164	.056 257 1193
45	.061 489 6138	105	.056 430 3045	165	.056 256 7401
46	.061 186 0952	106	.056 420 6734	166	.056 256 3811
47	.060 901 4888	107	.056 411 5581	167	.056 256 0412
48	.060 634 4681	108	.056 402 9311	168	.056 255 7195
49	.060 383 8164	109	.056 394 7658	169	.056 255 4149
50	.060 148 4152	110	.056 387 0376	170	.056 255 1265
51	.059 927 2353	111	.056 379 7229	171	.056 254 8534
52	.059 719 3281	112	.056 372 7995	172	.056 254 5950
53	.059 523 8179	113	.056 366 2464	173	.056 254 3502
54	.059 339 8955	114	.056 360 0437	174	.056 254 1186
55	.059 166 8122	115	.056 354 1725	175	.056 253 8992
56	.059 003 8742	116	.056 348 6151	176	.056 253 6915
57	.058 850 4383	117	.056 343 3547	177	.056 253 4949
58	.058 705 9071	118	.056 338 3753	178	.056 253 3088
59	.058 569 7255	119	.056 333 6620	179	.056 253 1326
60	.058 441 3771	120	.056 329 2003	180	.056 252 9658

Repayment of a Loan by way of an Annuity

NOMINAL INTEREST RATE COMPOUNDED

	YEARLY @ $5\frac{11}{16}\%$ 5.6875% PER ANNUM		HALF-YEARLY @ $11\frac{3}{8}\%$ 11.3750% PER ANNUM		QUARTERLY @ $22\frac{3}{4}\%$ 22.7500% PER ANNUM
Periods	**Loan of 1**	**Periods**	**Loan of 1**	**Periods**	**Loan of 1**
1	1.056 875 0000	61	.058 891 5638	121	.056 945 5669
2	.543 049 4151	62	.058 779 4101	122	.056 941 7650
3	.371 948 7820	63	.058 673 6845	123	.056 938 1681
4	.286 529 1869	64	.058 573 9980	124	.056 934 7652
5	.235 381 7834	65	.058 479 9875	125	.056 931 5457
6	.201 370 2369	66	.058 391 3135	126	.056 928 4999
7	.177 150 3593	67	.058 307 6587	127	.056 925 6183
8	.159 050 0181	68	.058 228 7261	128	.056 922 8920
9	.145 029 1060	69	.058 154 2377	129	.056 920 3127
10	.133 863 5285	70	.058 083 9331	130	.056 917 8724
11	.124 774 2900	71	.058 017 5682	131	.056 915 5636
12	.117 242 0359	72	.057 954 9142	132	.056 913 3792
13	.110 907 1918	73	.057 895 7564	133	.056 911 3125
14	.105 512 8990	74	.057 839 8932	134	.056 909 3572
15	.100 870 7770	75	.057 787 1354	135	.056 907 5072
16	.096 839 5244	76	.057 737 3052	136	.056 905 7569
17	.093 311 0724	77	.057 690 2357	137	.056 904 1009
18	.090 201 3546	78	.057 645 7698	138	.056 902 5341
19	.087 443 9902	79	.057 603 7599	139	.056 901 0517
20	.084 985 8641	80	.057 564 0670	140	.056 899 6492
21	.082 783 9681	81	.057 526 5606	141	.056 898 3221
22	.080 803 1046	82	.057 491 1174	142	.056 897 0666
23	.079 014 1894	83	.057 457 6219	143	.056 895 8787
24	.077 392 9780	84	.057 425 9647	144	.056 894 7547
25	.075 919 0985	85	.057 396 0433	145	.056 893 6913
26	.074 575 3071	86	.057 367 7608	146	.056 892 6851
27	.073 346 9094	87	.057 341 0259	147	.056 891 7331
28	.072 221 3054	88	.057 315 7527	148	.056 890 8324
29	.071 187 6286	89	.057 291 8601	149	.056 889 9801
30	.070 236 4581	90	.057 269 2715	150	.056 889 1738
31	.069 359 5851	91	.057 247 9150	151	.056 888 4109
32	.068 549 8241	92	.057 227 7223	152	.056 887 6890
33	.067 800 8584	93	.057 208 6295	153	.056 887 0060
34	.067 107 1124	94	.057 190 5758	154	.056 886 3598
35	.066 463 6461	95	.057 173 5042	155	.056 885 7483
36	.065 866 0670	96	.057 157 3606	156	.056 885 1698
37	.065 310 4566	97	.057 142 0942	157	.056 884 6225
38	.064 793 3083	98	.057 127 6569	158	.056 884 1045
39	.064 311 4745	99	.057 114 0032	159	.056 883 6145
40	.063 862 1224	100	.057 101 0903	160	.056 883 1509
41	.063 442 6954	101	.057 088 8776	161	.056 882 7122
42	.063 050 8809	102	.057 077 3270	162	.056 882 2971
43	.062 684 5816	103	.057 066 4023	163	.056 881 9044
44	.062 341 8918	104	.057 056 0693	164	.056 881 5328
45	.062 021 0757	105	.057 046 2958	165	.056 881 1812
46	.061 720 5495	106	.057 037 0514	166	.056 880 8485
47	.061 438 8653	107	.057 028 3072	167	.056 880 5337
48	.061 174 6968	108	.057 020 0361	168	.056 880 2359
49	.060 926 8274	109	.057 012 2122	169	.056 879 9541
50	.060 694 1394	110	.057 004 8114	170	.056 879 6875
51	.060 475 6038	111	.056 997 8106	171	.056 879 4352
52	.060 270 2727	112	.056 991 1881	172	.056 879 1965
53	.060 077 2709	113	.056 984 9235	173	.056 878 9707
54	.059 895 7901	114	.056 978 9972	174	.056 878 7570
55	.059 725 0822	115	.056 973 3910	175	.056 878 5548
56	.059 564 4543	116	.056 968 0875	176	.056 878 3635
57	.059 413 2640	117	.056 963 0703	177	.056 878 1825
58	.059 270 9149	118	.056 958 3239	178	.056 878 0112
59	.059 136 8528	119	.056 953 8336	179	.056 877 8491
60	.059 010 5624	120	.056 949 5857	180	.056 877 6958

Repayment of a Loan by way of an Annuity

NOMINAL INTEREST RATE COMPOUNDED

	YEARLY @ 5¾% 5.7500% PER ANNUM		HALF-YEARLY @ 11½% 11.5000% PER ANNUM		QUARTERLY @ 23% 23.0000% PER ANNUM
Periods	Loan of 1	Periods	Loan of 1	Periods	Loan of 1
1	1.057 500 0000	61	.059 464 0454	121	.057 566 4116
2	.543 526 7315	62	.059 353 8103	122	.057 562 7966
3	.372 380 6701	63	.059 249 9444	123	.057 559 3786
4	.286 941 2017	64	.059 152 0600	124	.057 556 1468
5	.235 784 1371	65	.059 059 7949	125	.057 553 0911
6	.201 768 0253	66	.058 972 8110	126	.057 550 2018
7	.177 546 4834	67	.058 890 7921	127	.057 547 4699
8	.159 446 2799	68	.058 813 4424	128	.057 544 8868
9	.145 426 6954	69	.058 740 4852	129	.057 542 4443
10	.134 263 2671	70	.058 671 6612	130	.057 540 1349
11	.125 176 7637	71	.058 606 7277	131	.057 537 9512
12	.117 647 6727	72	.058 545 4569	132	.057 535 8863
13	.111 316 3092	73	.058 487 6353	133	.057 533 9339
14	.105 925 7351	74	.058 433 0627	134	.057 532 0878
15	.101 287 5108	75	.058 381 5510	135	.057 530 3421
16	.097 260 2900	76	.058 332 9236	136	.057 528 6915
17	.093 735 9691	77	.058 287 0147	137	.057 527 1307
18	.090 630 4539	78	.058 243 6685	138	.057 525 6549
19	.087 877 3417	79	.058 202 7384	139	.057 524 2593
20	.085 423 4988	80	.058 164 0868	140	.057 522 9397
21	.083 225 9022	81	.058 127 5839	141	.057 521 6920
22	.081 249 3418	82	.058 093 1080	142	.057 520 5121
23	.079 464 7226	83	.058 060 5442	143	.057 519 3964
24	.077 847 7910	84	.058 029 7847	144	.057 518 3414
25	.076 378 1674	85	.058 000 7275	145	.057 517 3438
26	.075 038 6012	86	.057 973 2771	146	.057 516 4005
27	.073 814 3920	87	.057 947 3432	147	.057 515 5085
28	.072 692 9348	88	.057 922 8407	148	.057 514 6650
29	.071 663 3587	89	.057 899 6895	149	.057 513 8674
30	.070 716 2386	90	.057 877 8142	150	.057 513 1133
31	.069 843 3625	91	.057 857 1435	151	.057 512 4001
32	.069 037 5417	92	.057 837 6103	152	.057 511 7257
33	.068 292 4570	93	.057 819 1514	153	.057 511 0880
34	.067 602 5304	94	.057 801 7070	154	.057 510 4850
35	.066 962 8198	95	.057 785 2207	155	.057 509 9148
36	.066 368 9312	96	.057 769 6395	156	.057 509 3756
37	.065 816 9445	97	.057 754 9133	157	.057 508 8658
38	.065 303 3517	98	.057 740 9947	158	.057 508 3836
39	.064 825 0044	99	.057 727 8390	159	.057 507 9277
40	.064 379 0687	100	.057 715 4042	160	.057 507 4966
41	.063 962 9876	101	.057 703 6504	161	.057 507 0889
42	.063 574 4478	102	.057 692 5401	162	.057 506 7034
43	.063 211 3517	103	.057 682 0379	163	.057 506 3389
44	.062 871 7934	104	.057 672 1102	164	.057 505 9942
45	.062 554 0370	105	.057 662 7255	165	.057 505 6682
46	.062 256 4988	106	.057 653 8539	166	.057 505 3600
47	.061 977 7310	107	.057 645 4671	167	.057 505 0685
48	.061 716 4076	108	.057 637 5387	168	.057 504 7929
49	.061 471 3125	109	.057 630 0433	169	.057 504 5323
50	.061 241 3281	110	.057 622 9573	170	.057 504 2858
51	.061 025 4263	111	.057 616 2581	171	.057 504 0528
52	.060 822 6596	112	.057 609 9247	172	.057 503 8324
53	.060 632 1537	113	.057 603 9369	173	.057 503 6240
54	.060 453 1008	114	.057 598 2758	174	.057 503 4270
55	.060 284 7538	115	.057 592 9236	175	.057 503 2406
56	.060 126 4207	116	.057 587 8633	176	.057 503 0644
57	.059 977 4599	117	.057 583 0789	177	.057 502 8978
58	.059 837 2760	118	.057 578 5555	178	.057 502 7402
59	.059 705 3159	119	.057 574 2786	179	.057 502 5912
60	.059 581 0653	120	.057 570 2349	180	.057 502 4503

Repayment of a Loan by way of an Annuity

NOMINAL INTEREST RATE COMPOUNDED

YEARLY @ $5\frac{13}{16}\%$ 5.8125% PER ANNUM		HALF-YEARLY @ $11\frac{5}{8}\%$ 11.6250% PER ANNUM		QUARTERLY @ $23\frac{1}{4}\%$ 23.2500% PER ANNUM	
Periods	Loan of 1	Periods	Loan of 1	Periods	Loan of 1
1	1.058 125 0000	61	.060 037 7987	121	.058 187 4965
2	.544 004 1376	62	.059 929 4627	122	.058 184 0599
3	.372 812 7173	63	.059 827 4366	123	.058 180 8125
4	.287 353 4398	64	.059 731 3337	124	.058 177 7439
5	.236 186 7760	65	.059 640 7934	125	.058 174 8440
6	.202 166 1590	66	.059 555 4785	126	.058 172 1038
7	.177 943 0118	67	.059 475 0742	127	.058 169 5143
8	.159 843 0038	68	.059 399 2859	128	.058 167 0673
9	.145 824 8038	69	.059 327 8382	129	.058 164 7548
10	.134 663 5803	70	.059 260 4731	130	.058 162 5696
11	.125 579 8665	71	.059 196 9489	131	.058 160 5046
12	.118 053 9917	72	.059 137 0392	132	.058 158 5531
13	.111 726 1607	73	.059 080 5319	133	.058 156 7090
14	.106 339 3559	74	.059 027 2278	134	.058 154 9662
15	.101 705 0784	75	.058 976 9401	135	.058 153 3193
16	.097 681 9370	76	.058 929 4936	136	.058 151 7630
17	.094 161 7932	77	.058 884 7234	137	.058 150 2922
18	.091 060 5251	78	.058 842 4751	138	.058 148 9023
19	.088 311 7077	79	.058 802 6033	139	.058 147 5887
20	.085 862 1891	80	.058 764 9713	140	.058 146 3474
21	.083 668 9313	81	.058 729 4508	141	.058 145 1744
22	.081 696 7114	82	.058 695 9209	142	.058 144 0658
23	.079 916 4237	83	.058 664 2681	143	.058 143 0181
24	.078 303 8057	84	.058 634 3853	144	.058 142 0281
25	.076 838 4698	85	.058 606 1721	145	.058 141 0924
26	.075 503 1587	86	.058 579 5336	146	.058 140 2082
27	.074 283 1661	87	.058 554 3807	147	.058 139 3726
28	.073 165 8818	88	.058 530 6293	148	.058 138 5829
29	.072 140 4305	89	.058 508 2004	149	.058 137 8366
30	.071 197 3831	90	.058 487 0193	150	.058 137 1313
31	.070 328 5241	91	.058 467 0158	151	.058 136 4648
32	.069 526 6621	92	.058 448 1237	152	.058 135 8349
33	.068 785 4748	93	.058 430 2806	153	.058 135 2396
34	.068 099 3822	94	.058 413 4277	154	.058 134 6770
35	.067 463 4402	95	.058 397 5095	155	.058 134 1453
36	.066 873 2530	96	.058 382 4737	156	.058 133 6429
37	.066 324 8991	97	.058 368 2709	157	.058 133 1681
38	.065 814 8693	98	.058 354 8547	158	.058 132 7193
39	.065 340 0140	99	.058 342 1811	159	.058 132 2952
40	.064 897 4989	100	.058 330 2088	160	.058 131 8944
41	.064 484 7660	101	.058 318 8987	161	.058 131 5157
42	.064 099 5016	102	.058 308 2138	162	.058 131 1577
43	.063 739 6081	103	.058 298 1195	163	.058 130 8194
44	.063 403 1790	104	.058 288 5830	164	.058 130 4997
45	.063 088 4787	105	.058 279 5731	165	.058 130 1976
46	.062 793 9234	106	.058 271 0607	166	.058 129 9120
47	.062 518 0656	107	.058 263 0183	167	.058 129 6422
48	.062 259 5796	108	.058 255 4196	168	.058 129 3872
49	.062 017 2498	109	.058 248 2402	169	.058 129 1462
50	.061 789 9591	110	.058 241 4568	170	.058 128 9184
51	.061 576 6800	111	.058 235 0475	171	.058 128 7031
52	.061 376 4655	112	.058 228 9915	172	.058 128 4997
53	.061 188 4423	113	.058 223 2694	173	.058 128 3074
54	.061 011 8033	114	.058 217 8626	174	.058 128 1257
55	.060 845 8022	115	.058 212 7538	175	.058 127 9540
56	.060 689 7481	116	.058 207 9264	176	.058 127 7917
57	.060 543 0002	117	.058 203 3650	177	.058 127 6384
58	.060 404 9643	118	.058 199 0547	178	.058 127 4934
59	.060 275 0883	119	.058 194 9819	179	.058 127 3565
60	.060 152 8590	120	.058 191 1332	180	.058 127 2270

Repayment of a Loan by way of an Annuity

NOMINAL INTEREST RATE COMPOUNDED

YEARLY	HALF-YEARLY	QUARTERLY
@	@	@
$5\frac{7}{8}\%$	$11\frac{3}{4}\%$	$23\frac{1}{2}\%$
5.8750%	11.7500%	23.5000%
PER ANNUM	PER ANNUM	PER ANNUM

Periods	Loan of 1	Periods	Loan of 1	Periods	Loan of 1
1	1.058 750 0000	61	.060 612 7969	121	.058 808 8082
2	.544 481 6333	62	.060 506 3402	122	.058 805 5419
3	.373 244 9236	63	.060 406 1336	123	.058 802 4571
4	.287 765 9011	64	.060 311 7918	124	.058 799 5438
5	.236 589 6997	65	.060 222 9552	125	.058 796 7924
6	.202 564 6377	66	.060 139 2882	126	.058 794 1940
7	.178 339 9440	67	.060 060 4770	127	.058 791 7399
8	.160 240 1893	68	.059 986 2286	128	.058 789 4222
9	.146 223 4303	69	.059 916 2685	129	.058 787 2333
10	.135 064 4671	70	.059 850 3402	130	.058 785 1660
11	.125 983 5972	71	.059 788 2034	131	.058 783 2135
12	.118 460 9916	72	.059 729 6329	132	.058 781 3695
13	.112 136 7449	73	.059 674 4178	133	.058 779 6279
14	.106 753 7596	74	.059 622 3602	134	.058 777 9831
15	.102 123 4778	75	.059 573 2746	135	.058 776 4296
16	.098 104 4631	76	.059 526 9870	136	.058 774 9624
17	.094 588 5422	77	.059 483 3338	137	.058 773 5767
18	.091 491 5652	78	.059 442 1617	138	.058 772 2679
19	.088 747 0850	79	.059 403 3266	139	.058 771 0318
20	.086 301 9314	80	.059 366 6930	140	.058 769 8644
21	.084 113 0511	81	.059 332 1336	141	.058 768 7618
22	.082 145 2087	82	.059 299 5289	142	.058 767 7204
23	.080 369 2878	83	.059 268 7663	143	.058 766 7368
24	.078 761 0166	84	.059 239 7400	144	.058 765 8078
25	.077 299 9998	85	.059 212 3505	145	.058 764 9304
26	.075 968 9732	86	.059 186 5041	146	.058 764 1017
27	.074 753 2246	87	.059 162 1126	147	.058 763 3190
28	.073 640 1387	88	.059 139 0930	148	.058 762 5798
29	.072 618 8358	89	.059 117 3672	149	.058 761 8816
30	.071 679 8827	90	.059 096 8617	150	.058 761 2222
31	.070 815 0606	91	.059 077 5070	151	.058 760 5994
32	.070 017 1749	92	.059 059 2380	152	.058 760 0111
33	.069 279 9010	93	.059 041 9931	153	.058 759 4555
34	.068 597 6563	94	.059 025 7144	154	.058 758 9307
35	.067 965 4950	95	.059 010 3472	155	.058 758 4351
36	.067 379 0194	96	.058 995 8401	156	.058 757 9670
37	.066 834 3068	97	.058 982 1446	157	.058 757 5248
38	.066 327 8466	98	.058 969 2148	158	.058 757 1072
39	.065 856 4885	99	.058 957 0077	159	.058 756 7128
40	.065 417 3972	100	.058 945 4826	160	.058 756 3403
41	.065 008 0142	101	.058 934 6012	161	.058 755 9884
42	.064 626 0254	102	.058 924 3273	162	.058 755 6561
43	.064 269 3329	103	.058 914 6268	163	.058 755 3422
44	.063 936 0302	104	.058 905 4675	164	.058 755 0457
45	.063 624 3816	105	.058 896 8190	165	.058 754 7657
46	.063 332 8035	106	.058 888 6528	166	.058 754 5012
47	.063 059 8487	107	.058 880 9418	167	.058 754 2515
48	.062 804 1920	108	.058 873 6606	168	.058 754 0155
49	.062 564 6180	109	.058 866 7850	169	.058 753 7927
50	.062 340 0104	110	.058 860 2925	170	.058 753 5822
51	.062 129 3421	111	.058 854 1615	171	.058 753 3834
52	.061 931 6673	112	.058 848 3719	172	.058 753 1957
53	.061 746 1130	113	.058 842 9046	173	.058 753 0183
54	.061 571 8733	114	.058 837 7416	174	.058 752 8508
55	.061 408 2028	115	.058 832 8660	175	.058 752 6926
56	.061 254 4114	116	.058 828 2616	176	.058 752 5432
57	.061 109 8595	117	.058 823 9134	177	.058 752 4021
58	.060 973 9540	118	.058 819 8071	178	.058 752 2688
59	.060 846 1438	119	.058 815 9292	179	.058 752 1429
60	.060 725 9169	120	.058 812 2669	180	.058 752 0240

Repayment of a Loan by way of an Annuity

NOMINAL INTEREST RATE COMPOUNDED

YEARLY	HALF-YEARLY	QUARTERLY
@	@	@
$5\frac{15}{16}\%$	$11\frac{7}{8}\%$	$23\frac{3}{4}\%$
5.9375%	11.8750%	23.7500%
PER ANNUM	PER ANNUM	PER ANNUM

Periods	Loan of 1	Periods	Loan of 1	Periods	Loan of 1
1	1.059 375 0000	61	.061 189 0136	121	.059 430 3340
2	.544 959 2185	62	.061 084 4161	122	.059 427 2300
3	.373 677 2888	63	.060 986 0086	123	.059 424 3002
4	.288 178 5854	64	.060 893 4070	124	.059 421 5349
5	.236 992 9079	65	.060 806 2531	125	.059 418 9248
6	.202 963 4610	66	.060 724 2126	126	.059 416 4612
7	.178 737 2796	67	.060 646 9730	127	.059 414 1359
8	.160 637 8358	68	.060 574 2426	128	.059 411 9411
9	.146 622 5743	69	.060 505 7484	129	.059 409 8694
10	.135 465 9267	70	.060 441 2350	130	.059 407 9140
11	.126 387 9547	71	.060 380 4635	131	.059 406 0683
12	.118 868 6713	72	.060 323 2102	132	.059 404 3261
13	.112 548 0603	73	.060 269 2652	133	.059 402 6817
14	.107 168 9445	74	.060 218 4322	134	.059 401 1296
15	.102 542 7069	75	.060 170 5268	135	.059 399 6645
16	.098 527 8661	76	.060 125 3763	136	.059 398 2816
17	.095 016 2134	77	.060 082 8184	137	.059 396 9762
18	.091 923 5714	78	.060 042 7011	138	.059 395 7441
19	.089 183 4703	79	.060 004 8813	139	.059 394 5810
20	.086 742 7219	80	.059 969 2249	140	.059 393 4832
21	.084 558 2576	81	.059 935 6058	141	.059 392 4470
22	.082 594 8293	82	.059 903 9055	142	.059 391 4689
23	.080 823 3098	83	.059 874 0127	143	.059 390 5456
24	.079 219 4182	84	.059 845 8227	144	.059 389 6741
25	.077 762 7513	85	.059 819 2370	145	.059 388 8515
26	.076 436 0380	86	.059 794 1629	146	.059 388 0750
27	.075 224 5604	87	.059 770 5135	147	.059 387 3420
28	.074 115 6979	88	.059 748 2068	148	.059 386 6501
29	.073 098 5662	89	.059 727 1655	149	.059 385 9970
30	.072 163 7285	90	.059 707 3172	150	.059 385 3806
31	.071 302 9623	91	.059 688 5933	151	.059 384 7987
32	.070 509 0701	92	.059 670 9297	152	.059 384 2494
33	.069 775 7247	93	.059 654 2657	153	.059 383 7309
34	.069 097 3413	94	.059 638 5441	154	.059 383 2415
35	.068 468 9720	95	.059 623 7114	155	.059 382 7795
36	.067 886 2176	96	.059 609 7167	156	.059 382 3435
37	.067 345 1540	97	.059 596 5124	157	.059 381 9318
38	.066 842 2696	98	.059 584 0535	158	.059 381 5433
39	.066 374 4130	99	.059 572 2977	159	.059 381 1765
40	.065 938 7480	100	.059 561 2051	160	.059 380 8303
41	.065 532 7160	101	.059 550 7379	161	.059 380 5035
42	.065 154 0022	102	.059 540 8608	162	.059 380 1950
43	.064 800 5086	103	.059 531 5402	163	.059 379 9038
44	.064 470 3288	104	.059 522 7448	164	.059 379 6290
45	.064 161 7269	105	.059 514 4446	165	.059 379 3695
46	.063 873 1198	106	.059 506 6118	166	.059 379 1246
47	.063 603 0604	107	.059 499 2199	167	.059 378 8934
48	.063 350 2239	108	.059 492 2440	168	.059 378 6752
49	.063 113 3957	109	.059 485 6605	169	.059 378 4692
50	.062 891 4600	110	.059 479 4474	170	.059 378 2747
51	.062 683 3905	111	.059 473 5837	171	.059 378 0912
52	.062 488 2419	112	.059 468 0497	172	.059 377 9179
53	.062 305 1425	113	.059 462 8268	173	.059 377 7544
54	.062 133 2870	114	.059 457 8975	174	.059 377 6000
55	.061 971 9312	115	.059 453 2452	175	.059 377 4543
56	.061 820 3859	116	.059 448 8543	176	.059 377 3167
57	.061 678 0127	117	.059 444 7101	177	.059 377 1869
58	.061 544 2196	118	.059 440 7988	178	.059 377 0643
59	.061 418 4566	119	.059 437 1071	179	.059 376 9486
60	.061 300 2130	120	.059 433 6227	180	.059 376 8394

Repayment of a Loan by way of an Annuity

NOMINAL INTEREST RATE COMPOUNDED

YEARLY	HALF-YEARLY	QUARTERLY
@	@	@
6%	12%	24%
6.0000%	12.0000%	24.0000%
PER ANNUM	PER ANNUM	PER ANNUM

Periods	Loan of 1	Periods	Loan of 1	Periods	Loan of 1
1	1,060 000 0000	61	,061 766 4228	121	,060 052 0617
2	,545 436 8932	62	,061 663 6642	122	,060 049 1124
3	,374 109 8128	63	,061 567 0351	123	,060 046 3303
4	,288 591 4924	64	,061 476 1528	124	,060 043 7059
5	,237 396 4004	65	,061 390 6603	125	,060 041 2303
6	,203 362 6285	66	,061 310 2248	126	,060 038 8950
7	,179 135 0181	67	,061 234 5351	127	,060 036 6920
8	,161 035 9426	68	,061 163 3009	128	,060 034 6139
9	,147 022 2350	69	,061 096 2506	129	,060 032 6536
10	,135 867 9582	70	,061 033 1302	130	,060 030 8043
11	,126 792 9381	71	,060 973 7022	131	,060 029 0598
12	,119 277 0294	72	,060 917 7439	132	,060 027 4142
13	,112 960 1053	73	,060 865 0472	133	,060 025 8618
14	,107 584 9090	74	,060 815 4168	134	,060 024 3973
15	,102 962 7640	75	,060 768 6698	135	,060 023 0158
16	,098 952 1436	76	,060 724 6347	136	,060 021 7125
17	,095 444 8042	77	,060 683 1507	137	,060 020 4831
18	,092 356 5406	78	,060 644 0667	138	,060 019 3233
19	,089 620 8604	79	,060 607 2411	139	,060 018 2292
20	,087 184 5570	80	,060 572 5410	140	,060 017 1971
21	,085 004 5467	81	,060 539 8414	141	,060 016 2234
22	,083 045 5685	82	,060 509 0251	142	,060 015 3049
23	,081 278 4847	83	,060 479 9819	143	,060 014 4383
24	,079 679 0050	84	,060 452 6081	144	,060 013 6209
25	,078 226 7182	85	,060 426 8066	145	,060 012 8497
26	,076 904 3467	86	,060 402 4856	146	,060 012 1222
27	,075 697 1663	87	,060 379 5593	147	,060 011 4359
28	,074 592 5515	88	,060 357 9467	148	,060 010 7885
29	,073 579 6135	89	,060 337 5715	149	,060 010 1777
30	,072 648 9115	90	,060 318 3623	150	,060 009 6015
31	,071 792 2196	91	,060 300 2516	151	,060 009 0580
32	,071 002 3374	92	,060 283 1761	152	,060 008 5452
33	,070 272 9350	93	,060 267 0759	153	,060 008 0614
34	,069 598 4254	94	,060 251 8949	154	,060 007 6051
35	,068 973 8590	95	,060 237 5802	155	,060 007 1745
36	,068 394 8348	96	,060 224 0821	156	,060 006 7684
37	,067 857 4274	97	,060 211 3535	157	,060 006 3852
38	,067 358 1240	98	,060 199 3504	158	,060 006 0238
39	,066 893 7724	99	,060 188 0310	159	,060 005 6828
40	,066 461 5359	100	,060 177 3563	160	,060 005 3611
41	,066 058 8551	101	,060 167 2893	161	,060 005 0576
42	,065 683 4152	102	,060 157 7952	162	,060 004 7713
43	,065 333 1178	103	,060 148 8412	163	,060 004 5012
44	,065 006 0565	104	,060 140 3965	164	,060 004 2464
45	,064 700 4958	105	,060 132 4320	165	,060 004 0060
46	,064 414 8527	106	,060 124 9202	166	,060 003 7792
47	,064 147 6805	107	,060 117 8354	167	,060 003 5653
48	,063 897 6549	108	,060 111 1531	168	,060 003 3635
49	,063 663 5619	109	,060 104 8504	169	,060 003 1731
50	,063 444 2864	110	,060 098 9057	170	,060 002 9935
51	,063 238 8028	111	,060 093 2986	171	,060 002 8240
52	,063 046 1669	112	,060 088 0098	172	,060 002 6642
53	,062 865 5076	113	,060 083 0212	173	,060 002 5134
54	,062 696 0209	114	,060 078 3157	174	,060 002 3711
55	,062 536 9634	115	,060 073 8773	175	,060 002 2369
56	,062 387 6472	116	,060 069 6907	176	,060 002 1103
57	,062 247 4350	117	,060 065 7417	177	,060 001 9908
58	,062 115 7359	118	,060 062 0166	178	,060 001 8781
59	,061 992 0012	119	,060 058 5028	179	,060 001 7718
60	,061 875 7215	120	,060 055 1883	180	,060 001 6715

Sinking Fund

The periodical sum which, accumulated at compound interest, will amount to 1 at the end of a period

$$\frac{1}{s_{\overline{n}|}} = \frac{i}{(1+i)^n - 1}$$

Effective Rates	*Number of periods*
3% increasing by $\frac{1}{16}$% to 6%	180

NOTE

Nominal annual rates at these effective rates, compounded half yearly and quarterly, are shown in the heading to each table.

NOMINAL INTEREST RATE COMPOUNDED

	YEARLY	HALF-YEARLY	QUARTERLY
	@	@	@
	3%	**6%**	**12%**
	3.0000%	6.0000%	12.0000%
	PER ANNUM	PER ANNUM	PER ANNUM

Periods	Sinking Fund	Periods	Sinking Fund	Periods	Sinking Fund
1	1.000 000 0000	61	.005 919 0847	121	.000 863 2518
2	.492 610 8374	62	.005 713 8485	122	.000 837 4067
3	.323 530 3633	63	.005 516 8216	123	.000 812 3558
4	.239 027 0452	64	.005 327 6021	124	.000 788 0734
5	.188 354 5714	65	.005 145 8128	125	.000 764 5348
6	.154 597 5005	66	.004 971 0995	126	.000 741 7163
7	.130 506 3538	67	.004 803 1288	127	.000 719 5947
8	.112 456 3888	68	.004 641 5871	128	.000 698 1479
9	.098 433 8570	69	.004 486 1787	129	.000 677 3543
10	.087 230 5066	70	.004 336 6251	130	.000 657 1934
11	.078 077 4478	71	.004 192 6632	131	.000 637 6450
12	.070 462 0855	72	.004 054 0446	132	.000 618 6898
13	.064 029 5440	73	.003 920 5345	133	.000 600 3091
14	.058 526 3390	74	.003 791 9109	134	.000 582 4849
15	.053 766 5805	75	.003 667 9634	135	.000 565 1997
16	.049 610 8493	76	.003 548 4929	136	.000 548 4366
17	.045 952 5294	77	.003 433 3105	137	.000 532 1794
18	.042 708 6959	78	.003 322 2371	138	.000 516 4122
19	.039 813 8806	79	.003 215 1027	139	.000 501 1198
20	.037 215 7076	80	.003 111 7457	140	.000 486 2875
21	.034 871 7765	81	.003 012 0127	141	.000 471 9010
22	.032 747 3948	82	.002 915 7577	142	.000 457 9465
23	.030 813 9027	83	.002 822 8417	143	.000 444 4106
24	.029 047 4159	84	.002 733 1325	144	.000 431 2805
25	.027 427 8710	85	.002 646 5042	145	.000 418 5437
26	.025 938 2903	86	.002 562 8365	146	.000 406 1881
27	.024 564 2103	87	.002 482 0151	147	.000 394 2019
28	.023 293 2334	88	.002 403 9306	148	.000 382 5739
29	.022 114 6711	89	.002 328 4787	149	.000 371 2930
30	.021 019 2593	90	.002 255 5599	150	.000 360 3488
31	.019 998 9288	91	.002 185 0789	151	.000 349 7308
32	.019 046 6183	92	.002 116 9449	152	.000 339 4292
33	.018 156 1219	93	.002 051 0708	153	.000 329 4344
34	.017 321 9633	94	.001 987 3733	154	.000 319 7369
35	.016 539 2916	95	.001 925 7729	155	.000 310 3279
36	.015 803 7942	96	.001 866 1932	156	.000 301 1985
37	.015 111 6244	97	.001 808 5613	157	.000 292 3402
38	.014 459 3401	98	.001 752 8070	158	.000 283 7449
39	.013 843 8516	99	.001 698 8633	159	.000 275 4046
40	.013 262 3779	100	.001 646 6659	160	.000 267 3117
41	.012 712 4089	101	.001 596 1530	161	.000 259 4585
42	.012 191 6731	102	.001 547 2653	162	.000 251 8381
43	.011 698 1103	103	.001 499 9461	163	.000 244 4432
44	.011 229 8469	104	.001 454 1408	164	.000 237 2672
45	.010 785 1757	105	.001 409 7968	165	.000 230 3034
46	.010 362 5378	106	.001 366 8639	166	.000 223 5456
47	.009 960 5065	107	.001 325 2936	167	.000 216 9875
48	.009 577 7738	108	.001 285 0394	168	.000 210 6231
49	.009 213 1383	109	.001 246 0565	169	.000 204 4466
50	.008 865 4944	110	.001 208 3018	170	.000 198 4525
51	.008 533 8232	111	.001 171 7340	171	.000 192 6352
52	.008 217 1837	112	.001 136 3131	172	.000 186 9895
53	.007 914 7059	113	.001 102 0009	173	.000 181 5102
54	.007 625 5841	114	.001 068 7603	174	.000 176 1925
55	.007 349 0710	115	.001 036 5558	175	.000 171 0314
56	.007 084 4726	116	.001 005 3531	176	.000 166 0223
57	.006 831 1432	117	.000 975 1192	177	.000 161 1607
58	.006 588 4819	118	.000 945 8222	178	.000 156 4423
59	.006 355 9281	119	.000 917 4315	179	.000 151 8626
60	.006 132 9587	120	.000 889 9176	180	.000 147 4177

Sinking Fund

NOMINAL INTEREST RATE COMPOUNDED

YEARLY	HALF-YEARLY	QUARTERLY
@	@	@
$3\frac{1}{16}\%$	$6\frac{1}{8}\%$	$12\frac{1}{4}\%$
3.0625%	6.1250%	12.2500%
PER ANNUM	PER ANNUM	PER ANNUM

Periods	Sinking Fund	Periods	Sinking Fund	Periods	Sinking Fund
1	1.000 000 0000	61	.005 781 4580	121	.000 817 2061
2	.492 459 2182	62	.005 578 3693	122	.000 792 2946
3	.323 330 2613	63	.005 383 4696	123	.000 768 1610
4	.238 804 2430	64	.005 196 3568	124	.000 744 7800
5	.188 119 3807	65	.005 016 6534	125	.000 722 1271
6	.154 355 0753	66	.004 844 0051	126	.000 700 1785
7	.130 259 6377	67	.004 678 0783	127	.000 678 9115
8	.112 207 2198	68	.004 518 5592	128	.000 658 3040
9	.098 183 4585	69	.004 365 1523	129	.000 638 3347
10	.086 979 7331	70	.004 217 5785	130	.000 618 9833
11	.077 826 9191	71	.004 075 5750	131	.000 600 2297
12	.070 212 2643	72	.003 938 8931	132	.000 582 0549
13	.063 780 7845	73	.003 807 2981	133	.000 564 4404
14	.058 278 9175	74	.003 680 5677	134	.000 547 3683
15	.053 520 7162	75	.003 558 4916	135	.000 530 8213
16	.049 366 7183	76	.003 440 8706	136	.000 514 7828
17	.045 710 2749	77	.003 327 5159	137	.000 499 2367
18	.042 468 4352	78	.003 218 2483	138	.000 484 1674
19	.039 575 7106	79	.003 112 8977	139	.000 469 5598
20	.036 979 7088	80	.003 011 3027	140	.000 455 3993
21	.034 638 0158	81	.002 913 3097	141	.000 441 6720
22	.032 515 9282	82	.002 818 7729	142	.000 428 3641
23	.030 584 7770	83	.002 727 5532	143	.000 415 4626
24	.028 820 6702	84	.002 639 5185	144	.000 402 9547
25	.027 203 5377	85	.002 554 5429	145	.000 390 8281
26	.025 716 3961	86	.002 472 5062	146	.000 379 0709
27	.024 344 7774	87	.002 393 2942	147	.000 367 6716
28	.023 076 2794	88	.002 316 7975	148	.000 356 6190
29	.021 900 2101	89	.002 242 9119	149	.000 345 9024
30	.020 807 3022	90	.002 171 5380	150	.000 335 5113
31	.019 789 4835	91	.002 102 5806	151	.000 325 4357
32	.018 839 6903	92	.002 035 9489	152	.000 315 6657
33	.017 951 7143	93	.001 971 5561	153	.000 306 1919
34	.017 120 0772	94	.001 909 3188	154	.000 297 0052
35	.016 339 9261	95	.001 849 1578	155	.000 288 0966
36	.015 606 9470	96	.001 790 9966	156	.000 279 4577
37	.014 917 2916	97	.001 734 7626	157	.000 271 0802
38	.014 267 5162	98	.001 680 3857	158	.000 262 9558
39	.013 654 5300	99	.001 627 7990	159	.000 255 0770
40	.013 075 5508	100	.001 576 9384	160	.000 247 4362
41	.012 528 0673	101	.001 527 7421	161	.000 240 0260
42	.012 009 8073	102	.001 480 1512	162	.000 232 8394
43	.011 518 7093	103	.001 434 1089	163	.000 225 8696
44	.011 052 8992	104	.001 389 5608	164	.000 219 1098
45	.010 610 6688	105	.001 346 4547	165	.000 212 5538
46	.010 190 4584	106	.001 304 7402	166	.000 206 1952
47	.009 790 8408	107	.001 264 3692	167	.000 200 0281
48	.009 410 5072	108	.001 225 2953	168	.000 194 0466
49	.009 048 2557	109	.001 187 4739	169	.000 188 2451
50	.008 702 9801	110	.001 150 8622	170	.000 182 6181
51	.008 373 6610	111	.001 115 4188	171	.000 177 1602
52	.008 059 3568	112	.001 081 1041	172	.000 171 8663
53	.007 759 1973	113	.001 047 8799	173	.000 166 7315
54	.007 472 3761	114	.001 015 7094	174	.000 161 7509
55	.007 198 1457	115	.000 984 5574	175	.000 156 9199
56	.006 935 8115	116	.000 954 3895	176	.000 152 2338
57	.006 684 7277	117	.000 925 1731	177	.000 147 6884
58	.006 444 2929	118	.000 896 8765	178	.000 143 2793
59	.006 213 9463	119	.000 869 4692	179	.000 139 0024
60	.005 993 1644	120	.000 842 9218	180	.000 134 8538

Sinking Fund

	NOMINAL INTEREST RATE COMPOUNDED		
	YEARLY @ $3\frac{1}{8}\%$ 3.1250% PER ANNUM	HALF-YEARLY @ $6\frac{1}{4}\%$ 6.2500% PER ANNUM	QUARTERLY @ $12\frac{1}{2}\%$ 12.5000% PER ANNUM

Periods	Sinking Fund	Periods	Sinking Fund	Periods	Sinking Fund
1	1.000 000 0000	61	.005 646 5642	121	.000 773 4437
2	.492 307 6923	62	.005 445 6389	122	.000 749 4439
3	.323 130 3250	63	.005 252 8810	123	.000 726 2057
4	.238 581 6739	64	.005 067 8885	124	.000 703 7039
5	.187 884 4880	65	.004 890 2837	125	.000 681 9142
6	.154 113 0120	66	.004 719 7120	126	.000 660 8132
7	.130 013 3465	67	.004 555 8397	127	.000 640 3782
8	.111 958 5380	68	.004 398 3530	128	.000 620 5875
9	.097 933 6090	69	.004 246 9560	129	.000 601 4198
10	.086 729 5701	70	.004 101 3699	130	.000 582 8551
11	.077 577 0617	71	.003 961 3314	131	.000 564 8735
12	.069 963 1750	72	.003 826 5920	132	.000 547 4563
13	.063 532 8169	73	.003 696 9168	133	.000 530 5850
14	.058 032 3475	74	.003 572 0835	134	.000 514 2421
15	.053 275 7624	75	.003 451 8817	135	.000 498 4105
16	.049 123 5563	76	.003 336 1124	136	.000 483 0737
17	.045 469 0473	77	.003 224 5865	137	.000 468 2157
18	.042 229 2588	78	.003 117 1249	138	.000 453 8213
19	.039 338 6816	79	.003 013 5576	139	.000 439 8756
20	.036 744 9071	80	.002 913 7230	140	.000 426 3642
21	.034 405 5078	81	.002 817 4678	141	.000 413 2732
22	.032 285 7692	82	.002 724 6461	142	.000 400 5892
23	.030 357 0130	83	.002 635 1188	143	.000 388 2993
24	.028 595 3396	84	.002 548 7540	144	.000 376 3909
25	.026 980 6721	85	.002 465 4257	145	.000 364 8520
26	.025 496 0216	86	.002 385 0139	146	.000 353 6707
27	.024 126 9152	87	.002 307 4043	147	.000 342 8359
28	.022 860 9465	88	.002 232 4878	148	.000 332 3364
29	.021 687 4197	89	.002 160 1603	149	.000 322 1618
30	.020 597 0642	90	.002 090 3223	150	.000 312 3018
31	.019 581 8051	91	.002 022 8789	151	.000 302 7464
32	.018 634 5760	92	.001 957 7392	152	.000 293 4861
33	.017 749 1664	93	.001 894 8167	153	.000 284 5116
34	.016 920 0958	94	.001 834 0281	154	.000 275 8140
35	.016 142 5095	95	.001 775 2943	155	.000 267 3844
36	.015 412 0918	96	.001 718 5390	156	.000 259 2147
37	.014 724 9929	97	.001 663 6896	157	.000 251 2965
38	.014 077 7676	98	.001 610 6763	158	.000 243 6221
39	.013 467 3239	99	.001 559 4323	159	.000 236 1838
40	.012 890 8783	100	.001 509 8935	160	.000 228 9743
41	.012 345 9186	101	.001 461 9986	161	.000 221 9864
42	.011 830 1714	102	.001 415 6886	162	.000 215 2132
43	.011 341 5744	103	.001 370 9070	163	.000 208 6480
44	.010 878 2525	104	.001 327 5995	164	.000 202 2845
45	.010 438 4969	105	.001 285 7140	165	.000 196 1161
46	.010 020 7470	106	.001 245 2005	166	.000 190 1371
47	.009 623 5749	107	.001 206 0110	167	.000 184 3414
48	.009 245 6713	108	.001 168 0991	168	.000 178 7233
49	.008 885 8335	109	.001 131 4206	169	.000 173 2774
50	.008 542 9549	110	.001 095 9328	170	.000 167 9984
51	.008 216 0153	111	.001 061 5945	171	.000 162 8810
52	.007 904 0731	112	.001 028 3663	172	.000 157 9202
53	.007 606 2571	113	.000 996 2103	173	.000 153 1113
54	.007 321 7609	114	.000 965 0898	174	.000 148 4496
55	.007 049 8363	115	.000 934 9697	175	.000 143 9304
56	.006 789 7885	116	.000 905 8160	176	.000 139 5494
57	.006 540 9713	117	.000 877 5962	177	.000 135 3023
58	.006 302 7830	118	.000 850 2788	178	.000 131 1850
59	.006 074 6626	119	.000 823 8335	179	.000 127 1935
60	.005 856 0861	120	.000 798 2312	180	.000 123 3240

Sinking Fund

NOMINAL INTEREST RATE COMPOUNDED

	YEARLY @ $3\frac{3}{16}\%$ 3.1875% PER ANNUM		HALF-YEARLY @ $6\frac{3}{8}\%$ 6.3750% PER ANNUM		QUARTERLY @ $12\frac{3}{4}\%$ 12.7500% PER ANNUM
Periods	Sinking Fund	Periods	Sinking Fund	Periods	Sinking Fund
1	1.000 000 0000	61	.005 514 3658	121	.000 731 8652
2	.492 156 2596	62	.005 315 6182	122	.000 708 7549
3	.322 930 5544	63	.005 125 0157	123	.000 686 3897
4	.238 359 3375	64	.004 942 1559	124	.000 664 7447
5	.187 649 8930	65	.004 766 6610	125	.000 643 7958
6	.153 871 3101	66	.004 598 1761	126	.000 623 5197
7	.129 767 4796	67	.004 436 3677	127	.000 603 8940
8	.111 710 3428	68	.004 280 9216	128	.000 584 8972
9	.097 684 3080	69	.004 131 5419	129	.000 566 5084
10	.086 480 0168	70	.003 987 9496	130	.000 548 7075
11	.077 327 8749	71	.003 849 8815	131	.000 531 4751
12	.069 714 8165	72	.003 717 0890	132	.000 514 7925
13	.063 285 6400	73	.003 589 3370	133	.000 498 6416
14	.057 786 6275	74	.003 466 4033	134	.000 483 0050
15	.053 031 7174	75	.003 348 0775	135	.000 467 8658
16	.048 881 3615	76	.003 234 1604	136	.000 453 2077
17	.045 228 8445	77	.003 124 4631	137	.000 439 0152
18	.041 991 1643	78	.003 018 8065	138	.000 425 2729
19	.039 102 7911	79	.002 917 0206	139	.000 411 9663
20	.036 511 2997	80	.002 818 9438	140	.000 399 0811
21	.034 174 2493	81	.002 724 4229	141	.000 386 6039
22	.032 056 9142	82	.002 633 3118	142	.000 374 5212
23	.030 130 6068	83	.002 545 4719	143	.000 362 8204
24	.028 371 4197	84	.002 460 7710	144	.000 351 4892
25	.026 759 2695	85	.002 379 0833	145	.000 340 5155
26	.025 277 1616	86	.002 300 2890	146	.000 329 8880
27	.023 910 6181	87	.002 224 2738	147	.000 319 5955
28	.022 647 2285	88	.002 150 9287	148	.000 309 6272
29	.021 476 2931	89	.002 080 1497	149	.000 299 9727
30	.020 388 5382	90	.002 011 8374	150	.000 290 6219
31	.019 375 8859	91	.001 945 8971	151	.000 281 5652
32	.018 431 2671	92	.001 882 2382	152	.000 272 7931
33	.017 548 4691	93	.001 820 7739	153	.000 264 2966
34	.016 722 0094	94	.001 761 4214	154	.000 256 0668
35	.015 947 0314	95	.001 704 1015	155	.000 248 0952
36	.015 219 2175	96	.001 648 7384	156	.000 240 3736
37	.014 534 7164	97	.001 595 2593	157	.000 232 8942
38	.013 890 0816	98	.001 543 5948	158	.000 225 6490
39	.013 282 2198	99	.001 493 6782	159	.000 218 6309
40	.012 708 3462	100	.001 445 4456	160	.000 211 8324
41	.012 165 9475	101	.001 398 8357	161	.000 205 2467
42	.011 652 7494	102	.001 353 7899	162	.000 198 8670
43	.011 166 6886	103	.001 310 2519	163	.000 192 6868
44	.010 705 8890	104	.001 268 1674	164	.000 186 6997
45	.010 268 6412	105	.001 227 4847	165	.000 180 8998
46	.009 853 3837	106	.001 188 1538	166	.000 175 2810
47	.009 458 6879	107	.001 150 1270	167	.000 169 8376
48	.009 083 2440	108	.001 113 3582	168	.000 164 5642
49	.008 725 8485	109	.001 077 8033	169	.000 159 4553
50	.008 385 3944	110	.001 043 4196	170	.000 154 5058
51	.008 060 8610	111	.001 010 1666	171	.000 149 7107
52	.007 751 3059	112	.000 978 0047	172	.000 145 0650
53	.007 455 8578	113	.000 946 8963	173	.000 140 5641
54	.007 173 7096	114	.000 916 8050	174	.000 136 2035
55	.006 904 1129	115	.000 887 6959	175	.000 131 9787
56	.006 646 3725	116	.000 859 5352	176	.000 127 8855
57	.006 399 8418	117	.000 832 2906	177	.000 123 9197
58	.006 163 9188	118	.000 805 9307	178	.000 120 0773
59	.005 938 0421	119	.000 780 4257	179	.000 116 3546
60	.005 721 6877	120	.000 755 7465	180	.000 112 7476

Sinking Fund

NOMINAL INTEREST RATE COMPOUNDED

YEARLY	HALF-YEARLY	QUARTERLY
@	@	@
$3\frac{1}{4}\%$	$6\frac{1}{2}\%$	13%
3.2500%	6.5000%	13.0000%
PER ANNUM	PER ANNUM	PER ANNUM

Periods	Sinking Fund	Periods	Sinking Fund	Periods	Sinking Fund
1	1.000 000 0000	61	.005 384 8252	121	.000 692 3744
2	.492 004 9200	62	.005 188 2685	122	.000 670 1312
3	.322 730 9493	63	.004 999 8335	123	.000 648 6165
4	.238 137 2337	64	.004 819 1174	124	.000 627 8056
5	.187 415 5954	65	.004 645 7424	125	.000 607 6747
6	.153 629 9692	66	.004 479 3534	126	.000 588 2007
7	.129 522 0366	67	.004 319 6168	127	.000 569 3616
8	.111 462 6337	68	.004 166 2182	128	.000 551 1359
9	.097 435 5546	69	.004 018 8618	129	.000 533 5030
10	.086 231 0724	70	.003 877 2684	130	.000 516 4431
11	.077 079 3576	71	.003 741 1746	131	.000 499 9369
12	.069 467 1878	72	.003 610 3320	132	.000 483 9661
13	.063 039 2525	73	.003 484 5053	133	.000 468 5127
14	.057 541 7561	74	.003 363 4724	134	.000 453 5595
15	.052 788 5797	75	.003 247 0229	135	.000 439 0899
16	.048 640 1319	76	.003 134 9575	136	.000 425 0879
17	.044 989 6646	77	.003 027 0874	137	.000 411 5380
18	.041 754 1496	78	.002 923 2334	138	.000 398 4252
19	.038 868 0366	79	.002 823 2256	139	.000 385 7351
20	.036 278 8839	80	.002 726 9026	140	.000 373 4538
21	.033 944 2371	81	.002 634 1111	141	.000 361 5678
22	.031 829 3596	82	.002 544 7051	142	.000 350 0642
23	.029 905 5544	83	.002 458 5461	143	.000 338 9303
24	.028 148 9063	84	.002 375 5020	144	.000 328 1541
25	.026 539 3253	85	.002 295 4471	145	.000 317 7238
26	.025 059 8109	86	.002 218 2617	146	.000 307 6281
27	.023 695 8805	87	.002 143 8316	147	.000 297 8562
28	.022 435 1193	88	.002 072 0479	148	.000 288 3973
29	.021 266 8238	89	.002 002 8068	149	.000 279 2415
30	.020 181 7169	90	.001 936 0091	150	.000 270 3787
31	.019 171 7179	91	.001 871 5600	151	.000 261 7994
32	.018 229 7552	92	.001 809 3692	152	.000 253 4945
33	.017 349 6135	93	.001 749 3501	153	.000 245 4550
34	.016 525 8084	94	.001 691 4200	154	.000 237 6723
35	.015 753 4812	95	.001 635 5000	155	.000 230 1381
36	.015 028 3128	96	.001 581 5142	156	.000 222 8444
37	.014 346 4502	97	.001 529 3902	157	.000 215 7833
38	.013 704 4456	98	.001 479 0588	158	.000 208 9474
39	.013 099 2041	99	.001 430 4533	159	.000 202 3294
40	.012 527 9400	100	.001 383 5102	160	.000 195 9223
41	.011 988 1388	101	.001 338 1683	161	.000 189 7193
42	.011 477 5251	102	.001 294 3693	162	.000 183 7137
43	.010 994 0347	103	.001 252 0568	163	.000 177 8993
44	.010 535 7906	104	.001 211 1771	164	.000 172 2699
45	.010 101 0826	105	.001 171 6784	165	.000 166 8195
46	.009 688 3484	106	.001 133 5112	166	.000 161 5425
47	.009 296 1588	107	.001 096 6278	167	.000 156 4331
48	.008 923 2032	108	.001 060 9823	168	.000 151 4861
49	.008 568 2777	109	.001 026 5309	169	.000 146 6963
50	.008 230 2745	110	.000 993 2313	170	.000 142 0585
51	.007 908 1725	111	.000 961 0429	171	.000 137 5680
52	.007 601 0288	112	.000 929 9266	172	.000 133 2200
53	.007 307 9716	113	.000 899 8448	173	.000 129 0100
54	.007 028 1935	114	.000 870 7615	174	.000 124 9336
55	.006 760 9455	115	.000 842 6419	175	.000 120 9864
56	.006 505 5322	116	.000 815 4526	176	.000 117 1644
57	.006 261 3066	117	.000 789 1613	177	.000 113 4635
58	.006 027 6664	118	.000 763 7372	178	.000 109 8800
59	.005 804 0499	119	.000 739 1503	179	.000 106 4099
60	.005 589 9328	120	.000 715 3719	180	.000 103 0499

Sinking Fund

NOMINAL INTEREST RATE COMPOUNDED

YEARLY	HALF-YEARLY	QUARTERLY
@	@	@
$3\frac{5}{16}\%$	$6\frac{5}{8}\%$	$13\frac{1}{4}\%$
3.3125%	6.6250%	12.2500%
PER ANNUM	PER ANNUM	PER ANNUM

Periods	Sinking Fund	Periods	Sinking Fund	Periods	Sinking Fund
1	1.000 000 0000	61	.005 257 9047	121	.000 654 8785
2	.491 853 6735	62	.005 063 5509	122	.000 633 4796
3	.322 531 5095	63	.004 877 2941	123	.000 612 7926
4	.237 915 3622	64	.004 698 7316	124	.000 592 7931
5	.187 181 5949	65	.004 527 4852	125	.000 573 4574
6	.153 388 9891	66	.004 363 1999	126	.000 554 7627
7	.129 277 0169	67	.004 205 5417	127	.000 536 6872
8	.111 215 4100	68	.004 054 1963	128	.000 519 2098
9	.097 187 3483	69	.003 908 8678	129	.000 502 3099
10	.085 982 7361	70	.003 769 2769	130	.000 485 9681
11	.076 831 5090	71	.003 635 1603	131	.000 470 1654
12	.069 220 2878	72	.003 506 2692	132	.000 454 8835
13	.062 793 6533	73	.003 382 3688	133	.000 440 1049
14	.057 297 7320	74	.003 263 2366	134	.000 425 8124
15	.052 546 3477	75	.003 148 6623	135	.000 411 9898
16	.048 399 8659	76	.003 038 4467	136	.000 398 6213
17	.044 751 5054	77	.002 932 4010	137	.000 385 6915
18	.041 518 2122	78	.002 830 3461	138	.000 373 1858
19	.038 634 4153	79	.002 732 1120	139	.000 361 0899
20	.036 047 6566	80	.002 637 5376	140	.000 349 3902
21	.033 715 4681	81	.002 546 4694	141	.000 338 0734
22	.031 603 1019	82	.002 458 7617	142	.000 327 1268
23	.029 681 8520	83	.002 374 2760	143	.000 316 5379
24	.027 927 7951	84	.002 292 8804	144	.000 306 2949
25	.026 320 8346	85	.002 214 4493	145	.000 296 3863
26	.024 843 9644	86	.002 138 8631	146	.000 286 8010
27	.023 482 6968	87	.002 066 0077	147	.000 277 5283
28	.022 224 6126	88	.001 995 7744	148	.000 268 5578
29	.021 059 0049	89	.001 928 0594	149	.000 259 8795
30	.019 976 5931	90	.001 862 7639	150	.000 251 4838
31	.018 969 2934	91	.001 799 7931	151	.000 243 3612
32	.018 030 0316	92	.001 739 0569	152	.000 235 5029
33	.017 152 5903	93	.001 680 4690	153	.000 227 9000
34	.016 331 4827	94	.001 623 9467	154	.000 220 5442
35	.015 561 8484	95	.001 569 4113	155	.000 213 4274
36	.014 839 3664	96	.001 516 7873	156	.000 206 5416
37	.014 160 1823	97	.001 466 0024	157	.000 199 8793
38	.013 520 8466	98	.001 416 9873	158	.000 193 4332
39	.012 918 2632	99	.001 369 6760	159	.000 187 1961
40	.012 349 6453	100	.001 324 0049	160	.000 181 1612
41	.011 812 4771	101	.001 279 9132	161	.000 175 3219
42	.011 304 4822	102	.001 237 3425	162	.000 169 6718
43	.010 823 5954	103	.001 196 2370	163	.000 164 2047
44	.010 367 9391	104	.001 156 5430	164	.000 158 9145
45	.009 935 8018	105	.001 118 2091	165	.000 153 7956
46	.009 525 6210	106	.001 081 1858	166	.000 148 8423
47	.009 135 9663	107	.001 045 4258	167	.000 144 0492
48	.008 765 5267	108	.001 010 8835	168	.000 139 4112
49	.008 413 0976	109	.000 977 5151	169	.000 134 9230
50	.008 077 5707	110	.000 945 2787	170	.000 130 5799
51	.007 757 9243	111	.000 914 1339	171	.000 126 3772
52	.007 453 2150	112	.000 884 0419	172	.000 122 3102
53	.007 162 5707	113	.000 854 9654	173	.000 118 3746
54	.006 885 1834	114	.000 826 8684	174	.000 114 5660
55	.006 620 3038	115	.000 799 7165	175	.000 110 8804
56	.006 367 2361	116	.000 773 4766	176	.000 107 3137
57	.006 125 3330	117	.000 748 1165	177	.000 103 8622
58	.005 893 9919	118	.000 723 6058	178	.000 100 5219
59	.005 672 6507	119	.000 699 9146	179	.000 097 2894
60	.005 460 7851	120	.000 677 0147	180	.000 094 1612

NOMINAL INTEREST RATE COMPOUNDED

YEARLY	HALF-YEARLY	QUARTERLY
@	@	@
$3\frac{3}{8}\%$	$6\frac{3}{4}\%$	$13\frac{1}{2}\%$
3.3750%	6.7500%	13.5000%
PER ANNUM	PER ANNUM	PER ANNUM

Periods	Sinking Fund	Periods	Sinking Fund	Periods	Sinking Fund
1	1.000 000 0000	61	.005 133 5668	121	.000 619 2875
2	.491 702 5200	62	.004 941 4265	122	.000 598 7102
3	.322 332 2349	63	.004 757 3576	123	.000 578 8282
4	.237 693 7228	64	.004 580 9570	124	.000 559 6172
5	.186 947 8913	65	.004 411 8467	125	.000 541 0539
6	.153 148 3691	66	.004 249 6714	126	.000 523 1157
7	.129 032 4202	67	.004 094 0971	127	.000 505 7810
8	.110 968 6713	68	.003 944 8093	128	.000 489 0289
9	.096 939 6884	69	.003 801 5121	129	.000 472 8394
10	.085 735 0071	70	.003 663 9261	130	.000 457 1929
11	.076 584 3281	71	.003 531 7880	131	.000 442 0709
12	.068 974 1154	72	.003 404 8492	132	.000 427 4553
13	.062 548 8410	73	.003 282 8745	133	.000 413 3288
14	.057 054 5536	74	.003 165 6417	134	.000 399 6746
15	.052 305 0197	75	.003 052 9404	135	.000 386 4765
16	.048 160 5616	76	.002 944 5715	136	.000 373 7191
17	.044 514 3650	77	.002 840 3462	137	.000 361 3872
18	.041 283 3498	78	.002 740 0855	138	.000 349 4664
19	.038 401 9248	79	.002 643 6196	139	.000 337 9428
20	.035 817 6149	80	.002 550 7873	140	.000 326 8027
21	.033 487 9389	81	.002 461 4352	141	.000 316 0333
22	.031 378 1376	82	.002 375 4179	142	.000 305 6220
23	.029 459 4955	83	.002 292 5969	143	.000 295 5566
24	.027 708 0816	84	.002 212 8404	144	.000 285 8255
25	.026 103 7926	85	.002 136 0229	145	.000 276 4174
26	.024 629 6167	86	.002 062 0251	146	.000 267 3215
27	.023 271 0610	87	.001 990 7329	147	.000 258 5271
28	.022 015 7023	88	.001 922 0378	148	.000 250 0241
29	.020 852 8296	89	.001 855 8364	149	.000 241 8028
30	.019 773 1592	90	.001 792 0297	150	.000 233 8537
31	.018 768 6042	91	.001 730 5234	151	.000 226 1676
32	.017 832 0878	92	.001 671 2273	152	.000 218 7358
33	.016 957 3902	93	.001 614 0555	153	.000 211 5498
34	.016 139 0225	94	.001 558 9256	154	.000 204 6012
35	.015 372 1224	95	.001 505 7588	155	.000 197 8822
36	.014 652 3670	96	.001 454 4800	156	.000 191 3851
37	.013 975 9003	97	.001 405 0172	157	.000 185 1024
38	.013 339 2716	98	.001 357 3012	158	.000 179 0271
39	.012 739 3833	99	.001 311 2662	159	.000 173 1522
40	.012 173 4473	100	.001 266 8489	160	.000 167 4711
41	.011 638 9467	101	.001 223 9886	161	.000 161 9772
42	.011 133 6041	102	.001 182 6274	162	.000 156 6644
43	.010 655 3535	103	.001 142 7096	163	.000 151 5267
44	.010 202 3160	104	.001 104 1817	164	.000 146 5581
45	.009 772 7797	105	.001 066 9925	165	.000 141 7532
46	.009 365 1810	106	.001 031 0930	166	.000 137 1064
47	.008 978 0891	107	.000 996 4359	167	.000 132 6125
48	.008 610 1920	108	.000 962 9759	168	.000 128 2665
49	.008 260 2848	109	.000 930 6696	169	.000 124 0635
50	.007 927 2584	110	.000 899 4752	170	.000 119 9986
51	.007 610 0907	111	.000 869 3526	171	.000 116 0674
52	.007 307 8378	112	.000 840 2632	172	.000 112 2655
53	.007 019 6271	113	.000 812 1700	173	.000 108 5884
54	.006 744 6503	114	.000 785 0374	174	.000 105 0322
55	.006 482 1576	115	.000 758 8312	175	.000 101 5927
56	.006 231 4528	116	.000 733 5183	176	.000 098 2663
57	.005 991 8884	117	.000 709 0672	177	.000 095 0490
58	.005 762 8614	118	.000 685 4473	178	.000 091 9374
59	.005 543 8096	119	.000 662 6294	179	.000 088 9279
60	.005 334 2082	120	.000 640 5851	180	.000 086 0172

Sinking Fund

NOMINAL INTEREST RATE COMPOUNDED

YEARLY	HALF-YEARLY	QUARTERLY
@	@	@
$3\frac{7}{16}\%$	$6\frac{7}{8}\%$	$13\frac{3}{4}\%$
3.4375%	6.8750%	13.7500%
PER ANNUM	PER ANNUM	PER ANNUM

Periods	Sinking Fund	Periods	Sinking Fund	Periods	Sinking Fund
1	1.000 000 0000	61	.005 011 7739	121	.000 585 5149
2	.491 551 4593	62	.004 821 8565	122	.000 565 7365
3	.322 133 1253	63	.004 639 9837	123	.000 546 6366
4	.237 472 3153	64	.004 465 7525	124	.000 528 1913
5	.186 714 4841	65	.004 298 7844	125	.000 510 3775
6	.152 908 1091	66	.004 138 7243	126	.000 493 1729
7	.128 788 2460	67	.003 985 2379	127	.000 476 5563
8	.110 722 4170	68	.003 838 0109	128	.000 460 5069
9	.096 692 5743	69	.003 696 7471	129	.000 445 0049
10	.085 487 8846	70	.003 561 1672	130	.000 430 0313
11	.076 337 8140	71	.003 431 0079	131	.000 415 5674
12	.068 728 6696	72	.003 306 0205	132	.000 401 5957
13	.062 304 8146	73	.003 185 9699	133	.000 388 0989
14	.056 812 2197	74	.003 070 6339	134	.000 375 0606
15	.052 064 5941	75	.002 959 8023	135	.000 362 4650
16	.047 922 2171	76	.002 853 2758	136	.000 350 2966
17	.044 278 2411	77	.002 750 8658	137	.000 338 5406
18	.041 049 5602	78	.002 652 3934	138	.000 327 1829
19	.038 170 5623	79	.002 557 6888	139	.000 316 2098
20	.035 588 7560	80	.002 466 5910	140	.000 305 6079
21	.033 261 6463	81	.002 378 9468	141	.000 295 3645
22	.031 154 4629	82	.002 294 6108	142	.000 285 4672
23	.029 238 4809	83	.002 213 4446	143	.000 275 9042
24	.027 489 7615	84	.002 135 3167	144	.000 266 6641
25	.025 888 1945	85	.002 060 1018	145	.000 257 7357
26	.024 416 7624	86	.001 987 6804	146	.000 249 1084
27	.023 060 9675	87	.001 917 9390	147	.000 240 7719
28	.021 808 3820	88	.001 850 7692	148	.000 232 7162
29	.020 648 2912	89	.001 786 0675	149	.000 224 9318
30	.019 571 4079	90	.001 723 7354	150	.000 217 4095
31	.018 569 6424	91	.001 663 6787	151	.000 210 1402
32	.017 635 9152	92	.001 605 8075	152	.000 203 1155
33	.016 764 0040	93	.001 550 0360	153	.000 196 3268
34	.015 948 4178	94	.001 496 2820	154	.000 189 7664
35	.015 184 2923	95	.001 444 4671	155	.000 183 4263
36	.014 467 3030	96	.001 394 5163	156	.000 177 2991
37	.013 793 5922	97	.001 346 3577	157	.000 171 3776
38	.013 159 7076	98	.001 299 9227	158	.000 165 6548
39	.012 562 5504	99	.001 255 1455	159	.000 160 1240
40	.011 999 3312	100	.001 211 9631	160	.000 154 7787
41	.011 467 5321	101	.001 170 3151	161	.000 149 6127
42	.010 964 8745	102	.001 130 1438	162	.000 144 6197
43	.010 489 2913	103	.001 091 3937	163	.000 139 7941
44	.010 038 9031	104	.001 054 0117	164	.000 135 1301
45	.009 611 9968	105	.001 017 9468	165	.000 130 6223
46	.009 207 0081	106	.000 983 1503	166	.000 126 2654
47	.008 822 5056	107	.000 949 5750	167	.000 122 0544
48	.008 457 1767	108	.000 917 1762	168	.000 117 9843
49	.008 109 8156	109	.000 885 9105	169	.000 114 0504
50	.007 779 3129	110	.000 855 7364	170	.000 110 2480
51	.007 464 6459	111	.000 826 6142	171	.000 106 5728
52	.007 164 8703	112	.000 798 5055	172	.000 103 0205
53	.006 879 1128	113	.000 771 3736	173	.000 099 5869
54	.006 606 5649	114	.000 745 1831	174	.000 096 2681
55	.006 346 4763	115	.000 719 9001	175	.000 093 0602
56	.006 098 1506	116	.000 695 4919	176	.000 089 9595
57	.005 860 9399	117	.000 671 9271	177	.000 086 9624
58	.005 634 2409	118	.000 649 1755	178	.000 084 0653
59	.005 417 4912	119	.000 627 2080	179	.000 081 2650
60	.005 210 1658	120	.000 605 9968	180	.000 078 5582

NOMINAL INTEREST RATE COMPOUNDED

YEARLY	HALF-YEARLY	QUARTERLY
@	@	@
$3\frac{1}{2}\%$	7%	14%
3.5000%	7.0000%	14.0000%
PER ANNUM	PER ANNUM	PER ANNUM

Periods	Sinking Fund	Periods	Sinking Fund	Periods	Sinking Fund
1	1.000 000 0000	61	.004 892 4882	121	.000 553 4772
2	.491 400 4914	62	.004 704 8020	122	.000 534 4748
3	.321 934 1806	63	.004 525 1325	123	.000 516 1342
4	.237 251 1395	64	.004 353 0765	124	.000 498 4319
5	.186 481 3732	65	.004 188 2558	125	.000 481 3449
6	.152 668 2087	66	.004 030 3148	126	.000 464 8513
7	.128 544 4938	67	.003 878 9193	127	.000 448 9301
8	.110 476 6465	68	.003 733 7550	128	.000 433 5608
9	.096 446 0051	69	.003 594 5255	129	.000 418 7239
10	.085 241 3679	70	.003 460 9517	130	.000 404 4006
11	.076 091 9658	71	.003 332 7702	131	.000 390 5726
12	.068 483 9493	72	.003 209 7323	132	.000 377 2225
13	.062 061 5726	73	.003 091 6030	133	.000 364 3334
14	.056 570 7287	74	.002 978 1601	134	.000 351 8891
15	.051 825 0694	75	.002 869 1934	135	.000 339 8739
16	.047 684 8306	76	.002 764 5038	136	.000 328 2727
17	.044 043 1317	77	.002 663 9029	137	.000 317 0712
18	.040 816 8408	78	.002 567 2117	138	.000 306 2551
19	.037 940 3252	79	.002 474 2606	139	.000 295 8112
20	.035 361 0768	80	.002 384 8887	140	.000 285 7262
21	.033 036 5870	81	.002 298 9429	141	.000 275 9878
22	.030 932 0742	82	.002 216 2781	142	.000 266 5838
23	.029 018 8042	83	.002 136 7560	143	.000 257 5025
24	.027 272 8303	84	.002 060 2452	144	.000 248 7328
25	.025 674 0354	85	.001 986 6205	145	.000 240 2638
26	.024 205 3963	86	.001 915 7629	146	.000 232 0851
27	.022 852 4103	87	.001 847 5589	147	.000 224 1865
28	.021 602 6452	88	.001 781 9002	148	.000 216 5585
29	.020 445 3825	89	.001 718 6838	149	.000 209 1915
30	.019 371 3316	90	.001 657 8111	150	.000 202 0765
31	.018 372 3998	91	.001 599 1884	151	.000 195 2049
32	.017 441 5048	92	.001 542 7259	152	.000 188 5682
33	.016 572 4221	93	.001 488 3379	153	.000 182 1583
34	.015 759 6583	94	.001 435 9428	154	.000 175 9674
35	.014 998 3473	95	.001 385 4621	155	.000 169 9879
36	.014 284 1628	96	.001 336 8213	156	.000 164 2125
37	.013 613 2454	97	.001 289 9487	157	.000 158 6343
38	.012 982 1414	98	.001 244 7758	158	.000 153 2464
39	.012 387 7506	99	.001 201 2372	159	.000 148 0422
40	.011 827 2823	100	.001 159 2702	160	.000 143 0155
41	.011 298 2174	101	.001 118 8147	161	.000 138 1601
42	.010 798 2765	102	.001 079 8131	162	.000 133 4702
43	.010 325 3914	103	.001 042 2104	163	.000 128 9401
44	.009 877 6816	104	.001 005 9536	164	.000 124 5643
45	.009 453 4334	105	.000 970 9921	165	.000 120 3375
46	.009 051 0817	106	.000 937 2773	166	.000 116 2546
47	.008 669 1944	107	.000 904 7626	167	.000 112 3107
48	.008 306 4580	108	.000 873 4032	168	.000 108 5009
49	.007 961 6665	109	.000 843 1564	169	.000 104 8208
50	.007 633 7096	110	.000 813 9807	170	.000 101 2659
51	.007 321 5641	111	.000 785 8368	171	.000 097 8319
52	.007 024 2854	112	.000 758 6865	172	.000 094 5146
53	.006 740 9997	113	.000 732 4935	173	.000 091 3102
54	.006 470 8979	114	.000 707 2227	174	.000 088 2146
55	.006 213 2297	115	.000 682 8404	175	.000 085 2242
56	.005 967 2981	116	.000 659 3142	176	.000 082 3355
57	.005 732 4549	117	.000 636 6130	177	.000 079 5448
58	.005 508 0966	118	.000 614 7069	178	.000 076 8490
59	.005 293 6605	119	.000 593 5672	179	.000 074 2447
60	.005 088 6213	120	.000 573 1662	180	.000 071 7289

NOMINAL INTEREST RATE COMPOUNDED

YEARLY	HALF-YEARLY	QUARTERLY
@	@	@
$3\frac{9}{16}\%$	$7\frac{1}{8}\%$	$14\frac{1}{4}\%$
3.5625%	7.1250%	14.2500%
PER ANNUM	PER ANNUM	PER ANNUM

Periods	Sinking Fund	Periods	Sinking Fund	Periods	Sinking Fund
1	1.000 000 0000	61	.004 775 6723	121	.000 523 0941
2	.491 249 6162	62	.004 590 2242	122	.000 504 8449
3	.321 735 4005	63	.004 412 7639	123	.000 487 2409
4	.237 030 1951	64	.004 242 8881	124	.000 470 2588
5	.186 248 5581	65	.004 080 2184	125	.000 453 8761
6	.152 428 6673	66	.003 924 3993	126	.000 438 0710
7	.128 301 1631	67	.003 775 0965	127	.000 422 8227
8	.110 231 3593	68	.003 631 9955	128	.000 408 1112
9	.096 199 9804	69	.003 494 8002	129	.000 393 9171
10	.084 995 4561	70	.003 363 2313	130	.000 380 2219
11	.075 846 7826	71	.003 237 0254	131	.000 367 0077
12	.068 239 9533	72	.003 115 9339	132	.000 354 2573
13	.061 819 1139	73	.002 999 7218	133	.000 341 9540
14	.056 330 0793	74	.002 888 1672	134	.000 330 0820
15	.051 586 4438	75	.002 781 0598	135	.000 318 6258
16	.047 448 4003	76	.002 678 2006	136	.000 307 5706
17	.043 809 0348	77	.002 579 4013	137	.000 296 9021
18	.040 585 1894	78	.002 484 4831	138	.000 286 6067
19	.037 711 2109	79	.002 393 2766	139	.000 276 6710
20	.035 134 5744	80	.002 305 6208	140	.000 267 0823
21	.032 812 7576	81	.002 221 3632	141	.000 257 8283
22	.030 710 9678	82	.002 140 3584	142	.000 248 8971
23	.028 800 4613	83	.002 062 4685	143	.000 240 2774
24	.027 057 2834	84	.001 987 5623	144	.000 231 9582
25	.025 461 3103	85	.001 915 5149	145	.000 223 9288
26	.023 995 5130	86	.001 846 2073	146	.000 216 1790
27	.022 645 3836	87	.001 779 5263	147	.000 208 6990
28	.021 398 4856	88	.001 715 3640	148	.000 201 4792
29	.020 244 0967	89	.001 653 6173	149	.000 194 5106
30	.019 172 9228	90	.001 594 1882	150	.000 187 7843
31	.018 176 8682	91	.001 536 9829	151	.000 181 2917
32	.017 248 8479	92	.001 481 9121	152	.000 175 0247
33	.016 382 6350	93	.001 428 8904	153	.000 168 9754
34	.015 572 7339	94	.001 377 8362	154	.000 163 1361
35	.014 814 2765	95	.001 328 6716	155	.000 157 4995
36	.014 102 9347	96	.001 281 3220	156	.000 152 0585
37	.013 434 8475	97	.001 235 7163	157	.000 146 8062
38	.012 806 5596	98	.001 191 7862	158	.000 141 7360
39	.012 214 9696	99	.001 149 4665	159	.000 136 8416
40	.011 657 2854	100	.001 108 6949	160	.000 132 1169
41	.011 130 9869	101	.001 069 4114	161	.000 127 5559
42	.010 633 7934	102	.001 031 5590	162	.000 123 1528
43	.010 163 6359	103	.000 995 0827	163	.000 118 9023
44	.009 718 6329	104	.000 959 9300	164	.000 114 7989
45	.009 297 0700	105	.000 926 0505	165	.000 110 8376
46	.008 897 3812	106	.000 893 3959	166	.000 107 0134
47	.008 518 1336	107	.000 861 9200	167	.000 103 3215
48	.008 158 0134	108	.000 831 5782	168	.000 099 7574
49	.007 815 8135	109	.000 802 3281	169	.000 096 3165
50	.007 490 4234	110	.000 774 1287	170	.000 092 9946
51	.007 180 8193	111	.000 746 9407	171	.000 089 7876
52	.006 886 0561	112	.000 720 7265	172	.000 086 6914
53	.006 605 2595	113	.000 695 4498	173	.000 083 7022
54	.006 337 6202	114	.000 671 0760	174	.000 080 8164
55	.006 082 3873	115	.000 647 5717	175	.000 078 0303
56	.005 838 8635	116	.000 624 9048	176	.000 075 3404
57	.005 606 4005	117	.000 603 0445	177	.000 072 7434
58	.005 384 3944	118	.000 581 9612	178	.000 070 2361
59	.005 172 2822	119	.000 561 6264	179	.000 067 8155
60	.004 969 5385	120	.000 542 0128	180	.000 065 4784

Sinking Fund

NOMINAL INTEREST RATE COMPOUNDED

YEARLY	HALF-YEARLY	QUARTERLY
@	@	@
$3\frac{5}{8}\%$	$7\frac{1}{4}\%$	$14\frac{1}{2}\%$
3.6250%	7.2500%	14.5000%
PER ANNUM	PER ANNUM	PER ANNUM

Periods	Sinking Fund	Periods	Sinking Fund	Periods	Sinking Fund
1	1.000 000 0000	61	.004 661 2887	121	.000 494 2880
2	.491 098 8336	62	.004 478 0845	122	.000 476 7694
3	.321 536 7851	63	.004 302 8381	123	.000 459 8796
4	.236 809 4819	64	.004 135 1462	124	.000 443 5952
5	.186 016 0387	65	.003 974 6302	125	.000 427 8942
6	.152 189 4848	66	.003 820 9345	126	.000 412 7553
7	.128 058 2535	67	.003 673 7249	127	.000 398 1577
8	.109 986 5548	68	.003 532 6869	128	.000 384 0818
9	.095 954 4994	69	.003 397 5243	129	.000 370 5086
10	.084 750 1484	70	.003 267 9578	130	.000 357 4197
11	.075 602 2633	71	.003 143 7243	131	.000 344 7975
12	.067 996 6807	72	.003 024 5750	132	.000 332 6252
13	.061 577 4373	73	.002 910 2752	133	.000 320 8863
14	.056 090 2699	74	.002 800 6028	134	.000 309 5652
15	.051 348 7156	75	.002 695 3478	135	.000 298 6468
16	.047 212 9241	76	.002 594 3115	136	.000 288 1166
17	.043 575 9481	77	.002 497 3054	137	.000 277 9604
18	.040 354 6036	78	.002 404 1510	138	.000 268 1649
19	.037 483 2166	79	.002 314 6790	139	.000 258 7170
20	.034 909 2457	80	.002 228 7288	140	.000 249 6043
21	.032 590 1548	81	.002 146 1478	141	.000 240 8147
22	.030 491 1400	82	.002 066 7910	142	.000 232 3365
23	.028 583 4481	83	.001 990 5206	143	.000 224 1587
24	.026 843 1163	84	.001 917 2057	144	.000 216 2704
25	.025 250 0142	85	.001 846 7215	145	.000 208 6613
26	.023 787 1068	86	.001 778 9493	146	.000 201 3214
27	.022 439 8813	87	.001 713 7762	147	.000 194 2410
28	.021 195 8966	88	.001 651 0945	148	.000 187 4110
29	.020 044 4266	89	.001 590 8013	149	.000 180 8223
30	.018 976 1737	90	.001 532 7990	150	.000 174 4663
31	.017 983 0393	91	.001 476 9940	151	.000 168 3348
32	.017 057 9356	92	.001 423 2973	152	.000 162 4198
33	.016 194 6331	93	.001 371 6237	153	.000 156 7135
34	.015 387 6343	94	.001 321 8920	154	.000 151 2085
35	.014 632 0689	95	.001 274 0245	155	.000 145 8976
36	.013 923 6070	96	.001 227 9470	156	.000 140 7740
37	.013 258 3859	97	.001 183 5885	157	.000 135 8310
38	.012 632 9490	98	.001 140 8812	158	.000 131 0622
39	.012 044 1933	99	.001 099 7602	159	.000 126 4614
40	.011 489 3256	100	.001 060 1634	160	.000 122 0227
41	.010 965 8245	101	.001 022 0312	161	.000 117 7402
42	.010 471 4084	102	.000 985 3068	162	.000 113 6085
43	.010 004 0071	103	.000 949 9357	163	.000 109 6223
44	.009 561 7383	104	.000 915 8655	164	.000 105 7763
45	.009 142 8868	105	.000 883 0464	165	.000 102 0656
46	.008 745 8858	106	.000 851 4302	166	.000 098 4855
47	.008 369 3017	107	.000 820 9710	167	.000 095 0312
48	.008 011 8199	108	.000 791 6247	168	.000 091 6984
49	.007 672 2329	109	.000 763 3490	169	.000 088 4828
50	.007 349 4295	110	.000 736 1033	170	.000 085 3802
51	.007 042 3855	111	.000 709 8488	171	.000 082 3867
52	.006 750 1552	112	.000 684 5480	172	.000 079 4983
53	.006 471 8640	113	.000 660 1651	173	.000 076 7114
54	.006 206 7022	114	.000 636 6657	174	.000 074 0224
55	.005 953 9184	115	.000 614 0166	175	.000 071 4279
56	.005 712 8152	116	.000 592 1863	176	.000 068 9245
57	.005 482 7439	117	.000 571 1441	177	.000 066 5089
58	.005 263 1002	118	.000 550 8608	178	.000 064 1782
59	.005 053 3212	119	.000 531 3082	179	.000 061 9293
60	.004 852 8811	120	.000 512 4592	180	.000 059 7593

Sinking Fund

NOMINAL INTEREST RATE COMPOUNDED

YEARLY	HALF-YEARLY	QUARTERLY
@	@	@
$3\frac{11}{16}\%$	$7\frac{3}{8}\%$	$14\frac{3}{4}\%$
3.6875%	7.3750%	14.7500%
PER ANNUM	PER ANNUM	PER ANNUM

Periods	Sinking Fund	Periods	Sinking Fund	Periods	Sinking Fund
1	1.000 000 0000	61	.004 549 3000	121	.000 466 9846
2	.490 948 1436	62	.004 368 3443	122	.000 450 1742
3	.321 338 3340	63	.004 195 3155	123	.000 433 9760
4	.236 588 9996	64	.004 029 8099	124	.000 418 3672
5	.185 783 8146	65	.003 871 4490	125	.000 403 3258
6	.151 950 6606	66	.003 719 8773	126	.000 388 8308
7	.127 815 7645	67	.003 574 7603	127	.000 374 8620
8	.109 742 2323	68	.003 435 7837	128	.000 361 3999
9	.095 709 5613	69	.003 302 6512	129	.000 348 4258
10	.084 505 4441	70	.003 175 0838	130	.000 335 9216
11	.075 358 4072	71	.003 052 8182	131	.000 323 8701
12	.067 754 1303	72	.002 935 6058	132	.000 312 2546
13	.061 336 5413	73	.002 823 2121	133	.000 301 0591
14	.055 851 2991	74	.002 715 4149	134	.000 290 2680
15	.051 111 8834	75	.002 612 0046	135	.000 279 8667
16	.046 978 4003	76	.002 512 7824	136	.000 269 8408
17	.043 343 8695	77	.002 417 5600	137	.000 260 1766
18	.040 125 0809	78	.002 326 1593	138	.000 250 8608
19	.037 256 3397	79	.002 238 4110	139	.000 241 8808
20	.034 685 0877	80	.002 154 1546	140	.000 233 2242
21	.032 368 7753	81	.002 073 2379	141	.000 224 8794
22	.030 272 5871	82	.001 995 5161	142	.000 216 8348
23	.028 367 7604	83	.001 920 8516	143	.000 209 0797
24	.026 630 3245	84	.001 849 1136	144	.000 201 6034
25	.025 040 1422	85	.001 780 1778	145	.000 194 3959
26	.023 580 1724	86	.001 713 9257	146	.000 187 4473
27	.022 235 8974	87	.001 650 2446	147	.000 180 7483
28	.020 994 8717	88	.001 589 0269	148	.000 174 2899
29	.019 846 3651	89	.001 530 1704	149	.000 168 0633
30	.018 781 0768	90	.001 473 5774	150	.000 162 0601
31	.017 790 9048	91	.001 419 1548	151	.000 156 2722
32	.016 868 7589	92	.001 366 8139	152	.000 150 6919
33	.016 008 4069	93	.001 316 4697	153	.000 145 3116
34	.015 204 3491	94	.001 268 0413	154	.000 140 1242
35	.014 451 7133	95	.001 221 4514	155	.000 135 1226
36	.013 746 1677	96	.001 176 6262	156	.000 130 3002
37	.013 083 8480	97	.001 133 4948	157	.000 125 6504
38	.012 461 2960	98	.001 091 9899	158	.000 121 1672
39	.011 875 4074	99	.001 052 0469	159	.000 116 8444
40	.011 323 3877	100	.001 013 6039	160	.000 112 6763
41	.010 802 7142	101	.000 976 6018	161	.000 108 6573
42	.010 311 1044	102	.000 940 9841	162	.000 104 7821
43	.009 846 4870	103	.000 906 6964	163	.000 101 0454
44	.009 406 9790	104	.000 873 6871	164	.000 097 4424
45	.008 990 8640	105	.000 841 9062	165	.000 093 9682
46	.008 596 5747	106	.000 811 3062	166	.000 090 6181
47	.008 222 6766	107	.000 781 8415	167	.000 087 3878
48	.007 867 8546	108	.000 753 4683	168	.000 084 2728
49	.007 530 9006	109	.000 726 1446	169	.000 081 2692
50	.007 210 7029	110	.000 699 8302	170	.000 078 3728
51	.006 906 2366	111	.000 674 4864	171	.000 075 5799
52	.006 616 5556	112	.000 650 0764	172	.000 072 8867
53	.006 340 7850	113	.000 626 5645	173	.000 070 2896
54	.006 078 1145	114	.000 603 9167	174	.000 067 7853
55	.005 827 7927	115	.000 582 1002	175	.000 065 3703
56	.005 589 1216	116	.000 561 0837	176	.000 063 0415
57	.005 361 4522	117	.000 540 8368	177	.000 060 7959
58	.005 144 1803	118	.000 521 3308	178	.000 058 6303
59	.004 936 7424	119	.000 502 5377	179	.000 056 5420
60	.004 738 6128	120	.000 484 4309	180	.000 054 5282

NOMINAL INTEREST RATE COMPOUNDED

YEARLY	HALF-YEARLY	QUARTERLY
@	@	@
$3\frac{3}{4}\%$	$7\frac{1}{2}\%$	15%
3.7500%	7.5000%	15.0000%
PER ANNUM	PER ANNUM	PER ANNUM

Periods	Sinking Fund	Periods	Sinking Fund	Periods	Sinking Fund
1	1.000 000 0000	61	.004 439 6687	121	.000 441 1124
2	.490 797 5460	62	.004 260 9653	122	.000 424 9879
3	.321 140 0472	63	.004 090 1564	123	.000 409 4592
4	.236 368 7482	64	.003 926 8386	124	.000 394 5038
5	.185 551 8856	65	.003 770 6332	125	.000 380 1001
6	.151 712 1945	66	.003 621 1846	126	.000 366 2273
7	.127 573 6956	67	.003 478 1586	127	.000 352 8656
8	.109 498 3915	68	.003 341 2407	128	.000 339 9958
9	.095 465 1657	69	.003 210 1348	129	.000 327 5995
10	.084 261 3423	70	.003 084 5619	130	.000 315 6589
11	.075 115 2131	71	.002 964 2587	131	.000 304 1570
12	.067 512 3010	72	.002 848 9770	132	.000 293 0774
13	.061 096 4248	73	.002 738 4820	133	.000 282 4045
14	.055 613 1655	74	.002 632 5521	134	.000 272 1230
15	.050 875 9452	75	.002 530 9775	135	.000 262 2185
16	.046 744 8270	76	.002 433 5598	136	.000 252 6768
17	.043 112 7968	77	.002 340 1108	137	.000 243 4846
18	.039 896 6188	78	.002 250 4525	138	.000 234 6289
19	.037 030 5773	79	.002 164 4160	139	.000 226 0972
20	.034 462 0973	80	.002 081 8410	140	.000 217 8776
21	.032 148 6155	81	.002 002 5754	141	.000 209 9584
22	.030 055 3051	82	.001 926 4747	142	.000 202 3286
23	.028 153 3940	83	.001 853 4016	143	.000 194 9775
24	.026 418 9033	84	.001 783 2256	144	.000 187 8948
25	.024 831 6890	85	.001 715 8225	145	.000 181 0706
26	.023 374 7042	86	.001 651 0743	146	.000 174 4954
27	.022 033 4259	87	.001 588 8684	147	.000 168 1601
28	.020 795 4043	88	.001 529 0977	148	.000 162 0557
29	.019 649 9051	89	.001 471 6601	149	.000 156 1739
30	.018 587 6242	90	.001 416 4584	150	.000 150 5064
31	.017 600 4564	91	.001 363 3997	151	.000 145 0454
32	.016 681 3087	92	.001 312 3956	152	.000 139 7832
33	.015 823 9465	93	.001 263 3615	153	.000 134 7127
34	.015 022 8679	94	.001 216 2168	154	.000 129 8267
35	.014 273 1986	95	.001 170 8846	155	.000 125 1185
36	.013 570 6050	96	.001 127 2913	156	.000 120 5816
37	.012 911 2211	97	.001 085 3665	157	.000 116 2097
38	.012 291 5872	98	.001 045 0431	158	.000 111 9968
39	.011 708 5975	99	.001 006 2569	159	.000 107 9371
40	.011 159 4563	100	.000 968 9464	160	.000 104 0249
41	.010 641 6399	101	.000 933 0528	161	.000 100 2549
42	.010 152 8644	102	.000 898 5200	162	.000 096 6219
43	.009 691 0577	103	.000 865 2940	163	.000 093 1209
44	.009 254 3358	104	.000 833 3233	164	.000 089 7470
45	.008 840 9816	105	.000 802 5585	165	.000 086 4957
46	.008 449 4269	106	.000 772 9525	166	.000 083 3624
47	.008 078 2365	107	.000 744 4598	167	.000 080 3428
48	.007 726 0947	108	.000 717 0371	168	.000 077 4329
49	.007 391 7928	109	.000 690 6428	169	.000 074 6285
50	.007 074 2185	110	.000 665 2370	170	.000 071 9259
51	.006 772 3464	111	.000 640 7814	171	.000 069 3214
52	.006 485 2301	112	.000 617 2394	172	.000 066 8113
53	.006 211 9941	113	.000 594 5758	173	.000 064 3923
54	.005 951 8278	114	.000 572 7569	174	.000 062 0610
55	.005 703 9795	115	.000 551 7502	175	.000 059 8143
56	.005 467 7509	116	.000 531 5248	176	.000 057 6490
57	.005 242 4928	117	.000 512 0507	177	.000 055 5622
58	.005 027 6006	118	.000 493 2994	178	.000 053 5511
59	.004 822 5108	119	.000 475 2433	179	.000 051 6128
60	.004 626 6973	120	.000 457 8561	180	.000 049 7448

NOMINAL INTEREST RATE COMPOUNDED

YEARLY @	HALF-YEARLY @	QUARTERLY @
$3\frac{13}{16}\%$ 3.8125% PER ANNUM	$7\frac{5}{8}\%$ 7.6250% PER ANNUM	$15\frac{1}{4}\%$ 15.2500% PER ANNUM

Periods	Sinking Fund	Periods	Sinking Fund	Periods	Sinking Fund
1	1.000 000 0000	61	.004 332 3579	121	.000 416 6028
2	.490 647 0408	62	.004 155 9090	122	.000 401 1421
3	.320 941 9244	63	.003 987 3214	123	.000 386 2610
4	.236 148 7272	64	.003 826 1916	124	.000 371 9372
5	.185 320 2512	65	.003 672 1409	125	.000 358 1495
6	.151 474 0860	66	.003 524 8138	126	.000 344 8776
7	.127 332 0464	67	.003 383 8760	127	.000 332 1016
8	.109 255 0316	68	.003 249 0131	128	.000 319 8029
9	.095 221 3116	69	.003 119 9291	129	.000 307 9634
10	.084 017 8423	70	.002 996 3451	130	.000 296 5655
11	.074 872 6803	71	.002 877 9979	131	.000 285 5926
12	.067 271 1917	72	.002 764 6394	132	.000 275 0285
13	.060 857 0865	73	.002 656 0351	133	.000 264 8580
14	.055 375 8676	74	.002 551 9634	134	.000 255 0660
15	.050 640 8996	75	.002 452 2147	135	.000 245 6384
16	.046 512 2021	76	.002 356 5908	136	.000 236 5614
17	.042 882 7280	77	.002 264 9039	137	.000 227 8218
18	.039 669 2150	78	.002 176 9761	138	.000 219 4069
19	.036 805 9268	79	.002 092 6386	139	.000 211 3046
20	.034 240 2715	80	.002 011 7315	140	.000 203 5030
21	.031 929 6721	81	.001 934 1029	141	.000 195 9910
22	.029 839 2904	82	.001 859 6087	142	.000 188 7576
23	.027 940 3447	83	.001 788 1117	143	.000 181 7925
24	.026 208 8481	84	.001 719 4819	144	.000 175 0855
25	.024 624 6497	85	.001 653 5952	145	.000 168 6271
26	.023 170 6966	86	.001 590 3340	146	.000 162 4079
27	.021 832 4607	87	.001 529 5860	147	.000 156 4190
28	.020 597 4876	88	.001 471 2444	148	.000 150 6518
29	.019 455 0393	89	.001 415 2075	149	.000 145 0981
30	.018 395 8080	90	.001 361 3783	150	.000 139 7499
31	.017 411 6855	91	.001 309 6644	151	.000 134 5995
32	.016 495 5758	92	.001 259 9776	152	.000 129 6395
33	.015 641 2422	93	.001 212 2338	153	.000 124 8629
34	.014 843 1802	94	.001 166 3527	154	.000 120 2629
35	.014 096 5135	95	.001 122 2577	155	.000 115 8328
36	.013 396 9068	96	.001 079 8755	156	.000 111 5664
37	.012 740 4923	97	.001 039 1363	157	.000 107 4576
38	.012 123 8088	98	.000 999 9732	158	.000 103 5005
39	.011 543 7492	99	.000 962 3224	159	.000 099 6896
40	.010 997 5163	100	.000 926 1227	160	.000 096 0192
41	.010 482 5853	101	.000 891 3158	161	.000 092 4844
42	.009 996 6713	102	.000 857 8459	162	.000 089 0800
43	.009 537 7011	103	.000 825 6593	163	.000 085 8012
44	.009 103 7899	104	.000 794 7050	164	.000 082 6433
45	.008 693 2197	105	.000 764 9340	165	.000 079 6019
46	.008 304 4214	106	.000 736 2994	166	.000 076 6727
47	.007 935 9594	107	.000 708 7562	167	.000 073 8514
48	.007 586 5172	108	.000 682 2614	168	.000 071 1342
49	.007 254 8854	109	.000 656 7738	169	.000 068 5171
50	.006 939 9512	110	.000 632 2539	170	.000 065 9964
51	.006 640 6889	111	.000 608 6638	171	.000 063 5687
52	.006 356 1514	112	.000 585 9671	172	.000 061 2304
53	.006 085 4630	113	.000 564 1291	173	.000 058 9782
54	.005 827 8127	114	.000 543 1164	174	.000 056 8090
55	.005 582 4484	115	.000 522 8970	175	.000 054 7197
56	.005 348 6716	116	.000 503 4401	176	.000 052 7074
57	.005 125 8328	117	.000 484 7163	177	.000 050 7691
58	.004 913 3273	118	.000 466 6972	178	.000 048 9023
59	.004 710 5913	119	.000 449 3558	179	.000 047 1041
60	.004 517 0987	120	.000 432 6660	180	.000 045 3722

NOMINAL INTEREST RATE COMPOUNDED

YEARLY	HALF-YEARLY	QUARTERLY
@	@	@
$3\frac{7}{8}\%$	$7\frac{3}{4}\%$	$15\frac{1}{2}\%$
3.8750%	7.7500%	15.5000%
PER ANNUM	PER ANNUM	PER ANNUM

Periods	Sinking Fund	Periods	Sinking Fund	Periods	Sinking Fund
1	1.000 000 0000	61	.004 227 3304	121	.000 393 3897
2	.490 496 6278	62	.004 053 1374	122	.000 378 5711
3	.320 743 9656	63	.003 886 7713	123	.000 364 3160
4	.235 928 9366	64	.003 727 8288	124	.000 350 6024
5	.185 088 9113	65	.003 575 9310	125	.000 337 4095
6	.151 236 3348	66	.003 430 7225	126	.000 324 7171
7	.127 090 8164	67	.003 291 8690	127	.000 312 5060
8	.109 012 1521	68	.003 159 0564	128	.000 300 7577
9	.094 977 9986	69	.003 031 9886	129	.000 289 4543
10	.083 774 9431	70	.002 910 3869	130	.000 278 5787
11	.074 630 8077	71	.002 793 9882	131	.000 268 1146
12	.067 030 8013	72	.002 682 5446	132	.000 258 0461
13	.060 618 5251	73	.002 575 8218	133	.000 248 3582
14	.055 139 4039	74	.002 473 5983	134	.000 239 0361
15	.050 406 7447	75	.002 375 6649	135	.000 230 0661
16	.046 280 5238	76	.002 281 8234	136	.000 221 4346
17	.042 653 6607	77	.002 191 8863	137	.000 213 1286
18	.039 442 8670	78	.002 105 6759	138	.000 205 1359
19	.036 582 3854	79	.002 023 0239	139	.000 197 4444
20	.034 019 6072	80	.001 943 7705	140	.000 190 0427
21	.031 711 9417	81	.001 867 7641	141	.000 182 9198
22	.029 624 5391	82	.001 794 8609	142	.000 176 0651
23	.027 728 6083	83	.001 724 9241	143	.000 169 4684
24	.026 000 1542	84	.001 657 8238	144	.000 163 1198
25	.024 419 0190	85	.001 593 4365	145	.000 157 0101
26	.022 968 1439	86	.001 531 6447	146	.000 151 1301
27	.021 632 9955	87	.001 472 3366	147	.000 145 4711
28	.020 401 1151	88	.001 415 4056	148	.000 140 0247
29	.019 261 7605	89	.001 360 7505	149	.000 134 7830
30	.018 205 6204	90	.001 308 2747	150	.000 129 7382
31	.017 224 5836	91	.001 257 8859	151	.000 124 8828
32	.016 311 5513	92	.001 209 4965	152	.000 120 2096
33	.015 460 2840	93	.001 163 0227	153	.000 115 7119
34	.014 665 2753	94	.001 118 3846	154	.000 111 3829
35	.013 921 6467	95	.001 075 5059	155	.000 107 2163
36	.013 225 0610	96	.001 034 3139	156	.000 103 2060
37	.012 571 6488	97	.000 994 7388	157	.000 099 3461
38	.011 957 9472	98	.000 956 7145	158	.000 095 6309
39	.011 380 8478	99	.000 920 1773	159	.000 092 0550
40	.010 837 5521	100	.000 885 0665	160	.000 088 6131
41	.010 325 5341	101	.000 851 3242	161	.000 085 3001
42	.009 842 5078	102	.000 818 8949	162	.000 082 1113
43	.009 386 3991	103	.000 787 7255	163	.000 079 0420
44	.008 955 3222	104	.000 757 7652	164	.000 076 0875
45	.008 547 5582	105	.000 728 9654	165	.000 073 2438
46	.008 161 5374	106	.000 701 2796	166	.000 070 5065
47	.007 795 8233	107	.000 674 6633	167	.000 067 8717
48	.007 449 0989	108	.000 649 0737	168	.000 065 3355
49	.007 120 1542	109	.000 624 4702	169	.000 062 8942
50	.006 807 8758	110	.000 600 8135	170	.000 060 5443
51	.006 511 2377	111	.000 578 0661	171	.000 058 2824
52	.006 229 2922	112	.000 556 1921	172	.000 056 1050
53	.005 961 1633	113	.000 535 1572	173	.000 054 0091
54	.005 706 0396	114	.000 514 9281	174	.000 051 9917
55	.005 463 1688	115	.000 495 4734	175	.000 050 0496
56	.005 231 8520	116	.000 476 7626	176	.000 048 1802
57	.005 011 4396	117	.000 458 7667	177	.000 046 3807
58	.004 801 3267	118	.000 441 4577	178	.000 044 6485
59	.004 600 9492	119	.000 424 8088	179	.000 042 9811
60	.004 409 7810	120	.000 408 7944	180	.000 041 3760

NOMINAL INTEREST RATE COMPOUNDED		
YEARLY @ $3\frac{15}{16}\%$ 3.9375% PER ANNUM	HALF-YEARLY @ $7\frac{7}{8}\%$ 7.8750% PER ANNUM	QUARTERLY @ $15\frac{3}{4}\%$ 15.7500% PER ANNUM

Periods	Sinking Fund	Periods	Sinking Fund	Periods	Sinking Fund
1	1.000 000 0000	61	.004 124 5493	121	.000 371 4101
2	.490 346 3071	62	.003 952 6124	122	.000 357 2122
3	.320 546 1706	63	.003 788 4672	123	.000 343 5617
4	.235 709 3761	64	.003 631 7100	124	.000 330 4372
5	.184 857 8655	65	.003 481 9622	125	.000 317 8181
6	.150 998 9404	66	.003 338 8685	126	.000 305 6846
7	.126 850 0051	67	.003 202 0946	127	.000 294 0178
8	.108 769 7524	68	.003 071 3265	128	.000 282 7994
9	.094 735 2259	69	.002 946 2682	129	.000 272 0120
10	.083 532 6441	70	.002 826 6412	130	.000 261 6388
11	.074 389 5943	71	.002 712 1826	131	.000 251 6637
12	.066 791 1287	72	.002 602 6446	132	.000 242 0712
13	.060 380 7393	73	.002 497 7932	133	.000 232 8465
14	.054 903 7729	74	.002 397 4070	134	.000 223 9754
15	.050 173 4788	75	.002 301 2771	135	.000 215 4440
16	.046 049 7902	76	.002 209 2057	136	.000 207 2393
17	.042 425 5928	77	.002 121 0054	137	.000 199 3486
18	.039 217 5722	78	.002 036 4988	138	.000 191 7599
19	.036 359 9502	79	.001 955 5179	139	.000 184 4613
20	.033 800 1012	80	.001 877 9032	140	.000 177 4418
21	.031 495 4206	81	.001 803 5034	141	.000 170 6906
22	.029 411 0473	82	.001 732 1750	142	.000 164 1973
23	.027 518 1804	83	.001 663 7817	143	.000 157 9520
24	.025 792 8169	84	.001 598 1937	144	.000 151 9452
25	.024 214 7918	85	.001 535 2881	145	.000 146 1676
26	.022 767 0404	86	.001 474 9476	146	.000 140 6105
27	.021 435 0243	87	.001 417 0607	147	.000 135 2654
28	.020 206 2799	88	.001 361 5214	148	.000 130 1242
29	.019 070 0612	89	.001 308 2287	149	.000 125 1790
30	.018 017 0534	90	.001 257 0864	150	.000 120 4223
31	.017 039 1421	91	.001 208 0027	151	.000 115 8468
32	.016 129 2257	92	.001 160 8903	152	.000 111 4458
33	.015 281 0621	93	.001 115 6658	153	.000 107 2123
34	.014 489 1427	94	.001 072 2497	154	.000 103 1401
35	.013 748 5868	95	.001 030 5661	155	.000 099 2230
36	.013 055 0554	96	.000 990 5427	156	.000 095 4550
37	.012 404 6775	97	.000 952 1103	157	.000 091 8304
38	.011 793 9886	98	.000 915 2028	158	.000 088 3437
39	.011 219 8787	99	.000 879 7572	159	.000 084 9898
40	.010 679 5483	100	.000 845 7132	160	.000 081 7634
41	.010 170 4700	101	.000 813 0132	161	.000 078 6597
42	.009 690 3567	102	.000 781 6022	162	.000 075 6741
43	.009 237 1335	103	.000 751 4274	163	.000 072 8020
44	.008 808 9134	104	.000 722 4385	164	.000 070 0391
45	.008 403 9769	105	.000 694 5874	165	.000 067 3813
46	.008 020 7535	106	.000 667 8278	166	.000 064 8244
47	.007 657 8060	107	.000 642 1157	167	.000 062 3648
48	.007 313 8167	108	.000 617 4087	168	.000 059 9986
49	.006 987 5751	109	.000 593 6666	169	.000 057 7223
50	.006 677 9673	110	.000 570 8505	170	.000 055 5325
51	.006 383 9667	111	.000 548 9232	171	.000 053 4259
52	.006 104 6254	112	.000 527 8494	172	.000 051 3993
53	.005 839 0668	113	.000 507 5949	173	.000 049 4497
54	.005 586 4794	114	.000 488 1272	174	.000 047 5741
55	.005 346 1103	115	.000 469 4148	175	.000 045 7697
56	.005 117 2607	116	.000 451 4279	176	.000 044 0339
57	.004 899 2807	117	.000 434 1378	177	.000 042 3639
58	.004 691 5650	118	.000 417 5168	178	.000 040 7574
59	.004 493 5497	119	.000 401 5386	179	.000 039 2118
60	.004 304 7084	120	.000 386 1778	180	.000 037 7249

Sinking Fund

NOMINAL INTEREST RATE COMPOUNDED

YEARLY	HALF-YEARLY	QUARTERLY
@	@	@
4%	**8%**	**16%**
4.0000%	8.0000%	16.0000%
PER ANNUM	PER ANNUM	PER ANNUM

Periods	Sinking Fund	Periods	Sinking Fund	Periods	Sinking Fund
1	1.000 000 0000	61	.004 023 9779	121	.000 350 6033
2	.490 196 0784	62	.003 854 2964	122	.000 337 0049
3	.320 348 5392	63	.003 692 3701	123	.000 323 9382
4	.235 490 0454	64	.003 537 7955	124	.000 311 3821
5	.184 627 1135	65	.003 390 1939	125	.000 299 3162
6	.150 761 9025	66	.003 249 2100	126	.000 287 7213
7	.126 609 6120	67	.003 114 5099	127	.000 276 5785
8	.108 527 8320	68	.002 985 7795	128	.000 265 8702
9	.094 492 9927	69	.002 862 7231	129	.000 255 5791
10	.083 290 9443	70	.002 745 0623	130	.000 245 6887
11	.074 149 0393	71	.002 632 5344	131	.000 236 1834
12	.066 552 1727	72	.002 524 8919	132	.000 227 0478
13	.060 143 7278	73	.002 421 9008	133	.000 218 2676
14	.054 668 9731	74	.002 323 3403	134	.000 209 8286
15	.049 941 1004	75	.002 229 0015	135	.000 201 7176
16	.045 819 9992	76	.002 138 6869	136	.000 193 9216
17	.042 198 5221	77	.002 052 2095	137	.000 186 4283
18	.038 993 3281	78	.001 969 3922	138	.000 179 2259
19	.036 138 6184	79	.001 890 0672	139	.000 172 3029
20	.033 581 7503	80	.001 814 0755	140	.000 165 6484
21	.031 280 1054	81	.001 741 2661	141	.000 159 2520
22	.029 198 8111	82	.001 671 4957	142	.000 153 1034
23	.027 309 0568	83	.001 604 6284	143	.000 147 1932
24	.025 586 8313	84	.001 540 5351	144	.000 141 5119
25	.024 011 9628	85	.001 479 0928	145	.000 136 0506
26	.022 567 3805	86	.001 420 1848	146	.000 130 8008
27	.021 238 5406	87	.001 363 7001	147	.000 125 7542
28	.020 012 9752	88	.001 309 5329	148	.000 120 9028
29	.018 879 9342	89	.001 257 5828	149	.000 116 2392
30	.017 830 0991	90	.001 207 7538	150	.000 111 7560
31	.016 855 3524	91	.001 159 9547	151	.000 107 4461
32	.015 948 5897	92	.001 114 0984	152	.000 103 3029
33	.015 103 5665	93	.001 070 1021	153	.000 099 3199
34	.014 314 7715	94	.001 027 8867	154	.000 095 4907
35	.013 577 3224	95	.000 987 3767	155	.000 091 8096
36	.012 886 8780	96	.000 948 5002	156	.000 088 2707
37	.012 239 5655	97	.000 911 1884	157	.000 084 8684
38	.011 631 9191	98	.000 875 3757	158	.000 081 5976
39	.011 060 8274	99	.000 840 9996	159	.000 078 4531
40	.010 523 4893	100	.000 808 0000	160	.000 075 4300
41	.010 017 3765	101	.000 776 3200	161	.000 072 5236
42	.009 540 2007	102	.000 745 9047	162	.000 069 7293
43	.009 089 8859	103	.000 716 7020	163	.000 067 0429
44	.008 664 5444	104	.000 688 6620	164	.000 064 4602
45	.008 262 4558	105	.000 661 7368	165	.000 061 9771
46	.007 882 0488	106	.000 635 8808	166	.000 059 5898
47	.007 521 8855	107	.000 611 0502	167	.000 057 2946
48	.007 180 6476	108	.000 587 2033	168	.000 055 0880
49	.006 857 1240	109	.000 564 2999	169	.000 052 9664
50	.006 550 2004	110	.000 542 3018	170	.000 050 9266
51	.006 258 8497	111	.000 521 1723	171	.000 048 9655
52	.005 982 1236	112	.000 500 8762	172	.000 047 0800
53	.005 719 1451	113	.000 481 3799	173	.000 045 2672
54	.005 469 1025	114	.000 462 6512	174	.000 043 5242
55	.005 231 2426	115	.000 444 6591	175	.000 041 8485
56	.005 004 8662	116	.000 427 3741	176	.000 040 2373
57	.004 789 3234	117	.000 410 7678	177	.000 038 6882
58	.004 584 0087	118	.000 394 8131	178	.000 037 1988
59	.004 388 3581	119	.000 379 4839	179	.000 035 7668
60	.004 201 8451	120	.000 364 7553	180	.000 034 3900

Sinking Fund

NOMINAL INTEREST RATE COMPOUNDED

	YEARLY	HALF-YEARLY	QUARTERLY
	@	@	@
	$4\frac{1}{16}\%$	$8\frac{1}{8}\%$	$16\frac{1}{4}\%$
	4.0625%	8.1250%	16.2500%
	PER ANNUM	PER ANNUM	PER ANNUM

Periods	Sinking Fund	Periods	Sinking Fund	Periods	Sinking Fund
1	1.000 000 0000	61	.003 925 5796	121	.000 330 9114
2	.490 045 9418	62	.003 758 1518	122	.000 317 8918
3	.320 151 0713	63	.003 598 4416	123	.000 305 3884
4	.235 270 9443	64	.003 446 0456	124	.000 293 3802
5	.184 396 6550	65	.003 300 5854	125	.000 281 8475
6	.150 525 2207	66	.003 161 7056	126	.000 270 7711
7	.126 369 6368	67	.003 029 0725	127	.000 260 1327
8	.108 286 3904	68	.002 902 3721	128	.000 249 9149
9	.094 251 2985	69	.002 781 3091	129	.000 240 1008
10	.083 049 8430	70	.002 665 6050	130	.000 230 6743
11	.073 909 1416	71	.002 554 9976	131	.000 221 6199
12	.066 313 9323	72	.002 449 2394	132	.000 212 9227
13	.059 907 4893	73	.002 348 0970	133	.000 204 5685
14	.054 435 0030	74	.002 251 3495	134	.000 196 5437
15	.049 709 6075	75	.002 158 7885	135	.000 188 8352
16	.045 591 1490	76	.002 070 2168	136	.000 181 4303
17	.041 972 4463	77	.001 985 4477	137	.000 174 3171
18	.038 770 1324	78	.001 904 3044	138	.000 167 4838
19	.035 918 3873	79	.001 826 6196	139	.000 160 9195
20	.033 364 5515	80	.001 752 2344	140	.000 154 6135
21	.031 065 9926	81	.001 680 9983	141	.000 148 5555
22	.028 987 8266	82	.001 612 7685	142	.000 142 7356
23	.027 101 2331	83	.001 547 4094	143	.000 137 1445
24	.025 382 1928	84	.001 484 7921	144	.000 131 7732
25	.023 810 5268	85	.001 424 7944	145	.000 126 6129
26	.022 369 1583	86	.001 367 2997	146	.000 121 6552
27	.021 043 5383	87	.001 312 1975	147	.000 116 8922
28	.019 821 1942	88	.001 259 3825	148	.000 112 3163
29	.018 691 3719	89	.001 208 7546	149	.000 107 9199
30	.017 644 7494	90	.001 160 2183	150	.000 103 6961
31	.016 673 2059	91	.001 113 6828	151	.000 099 6379
32	.015 769 6341	92	.001 069 0616	152	.000 095 7390
33	.014 927 7870	93	.001 026 2721	153	.000 091 9930
34	.014 142 1511	94	.000 985 2358	154	.000 088 3938
35	.013 407 8418	95	.000 945 8776	155	.000 084 9358
36	.012 720 5162	96	.000 908 1260	156	.000 081 6133
37	.012 076 2998	97	.000 871 9128	157	.000 078 4211
38	.011 471 7249	98	.000 837 1727	158	.000 075 3539
39	.010 903 6790	99	.000 803 8436	159	.000 072 4069
40	.010 369 3596	100	.000 771 8661	160	.000 069 5754
41	.009 866 2371	101	.000 741 1834	161	.000 066 8548
42	.009 392 0223	102	.000 711 7414	162	.000 064 2407
43	.008 944 6381	103	.000 683 4882	163	.000 061 7290
44	.008 522 1960	104	.000 656 3744	164	.000 059 3156
45	.008 122 9745	105	.000 630 3525	165	.000 056 9968
46	.007 745 4019	106	.000 605 3775	166	.000 054 7687
47	.007 388 0395	107	.000 581 4059	167	.000 052 6278
48	.007 049 5683	108	.000 558 3964	168	.000 050 5707
49	.006 728 7767	109	.000 536 3093	169	.000 048 5941
50	.006 424 5500	110	.000 515 1069	170	.000 046 6948
51	.006 135 8605	111	.000 494 7527	171	.000 044 8699
52	.005 861 7596	112	.000 475 2121	172	.000 043 1164
53	.005 601 3701	113	.000 456 4518	173	.000 041 4314
54	.005 353 8797	114	.000 438 4401	174	.000 039 8124
55	.005 118 5351	115	.000 421 1464	175	.000 038 2567
56	.004 894 6371	116	.000 404 5415	176	.000 036 7618
57	.004 681 5353	117	.000 388 5975	177	.000 035 3254
58	.004 478 6244	118	.000 373 2876	178	.000 033 9452
59	.004 285 3400	119	.000 358 5862	179	.000 032 6190
60	.004 101 1557	120	.000 344 4687	180	.000 031 3446

NOMINAL INTEREST RATE COMPOUNDED

	YEARLY	HALF-YEARLY	QUARTERLY
	@	@	@
	$4\frac{1}{8}\%$	$8\frac{1}{4}\%$	$16\frac{1}{2}\%$
	4.1250%	8.2500%	16.5000%
	PER ANNUM	PER ANNUM	PER ANNUM

Periods	Sinking Fund	Periods	Sinking Fund	Periods	Sinking Fund
1	1.000 000 0000	61	.003 829 3182	121	.000 312 2789
2	.489 895 8971	62	.003 664 1412	122	.000 299 8178
3	.319 953 7667	63	.003 506 6434	123	.000 287 8573
4	.235 052 0727	64	.003 356 4212	124	.000 276 3772
5	.184 166 4898	65	.003 213 0965	125	.000 265 3579
6	.150 288 8947	66	.003 076 3140	126	.000 254 7806
7	.126 130 0788	67	.002 945 7402	127	.000 244 6274
8	.108 045 4268	68	.002 821 0613	128	.000 234 8811
9	.094 010 1424	69	.002 701 9821	129	.000 225 5252
10	.082 809 3394	70	.002 588 2245	130	.000 216 5439
11	.073 669 9002	71	.002 479 5265	131	.000 207 9221
12	.066 076 4062	72	.002 375 6408	132	.000 199 6452
13	.059 672 0225	73	.002 276 3343	133	.000 191 6993
14	.054 201 8611	74	.002 181 3865	134	.000 184 0711
15	.049 478 9986	75	.002 090 5893	135	.000 176 7477
16	.045 363 2375	76	.002 003 7458	136	.000 169 7169
17	.041 747 3632	77	.001 920 6697	137	.000 162 9669
18	.038 547 9823	78	.001 841 1845	138	.000 156 4863
19	.035 699 2539	79	.001 765 1232	139	.000 150 2644
20	.033 148 5014	80	.001 692 3276	140	.000 144 2907
21	.030 853 0786	81	.001 622 6473	141	.000 138 5553
22	.028 778 0897	82	.001 555 9400	142	.000 133 0486
23	.026 894 7049	83	.001 492 0706	143	.000 127 7615
24	.025 178 8965	84	.001 430 9105	144	.000 122 6850
25	.023 610 4784	85	.001 372 3379	145	.000 117 8109
26	.022 172 3680	86	.001 316 2368	146	.000 113 1309
27	.020 850 0110	87	.001 262 4970	147	.000 108 6373
28	.019 630 9300	88	.001 211 0138	148	.000 104 3227
29	.018 504 3669	89	.001 161 6874	149	.000 100 1798
30	.017 460 9962	90	.001 114 4228	150	.000 096 2019
31	.016 492 6937	91	.001 069 1298	151	.000 092 3822
32	.015 592 3494	92	.001 025 7221	152	.000 088 7145
33	.014 753 7137	93	.000 984 1178	153	.000 085 1928
34	.013 971 2706	94	.000 944 2387	154	.000 081 8111
35	.013 240 1336	95	.000 906 0103	155	.000 078 5639
36	.012 555 9578	96	.000 869 3615	156	.000 075 4458
37	.011 914 8670	97	.000 834 2245	157	.000 072 4517
38	.011 313 3920	98	.000 800 5346	158	.000 069 5767
39	.010 748 4187	99	.000 768 2301	159	.000 066 8159
40	.010 217 1434	100	.000 737 2521	160	.000 064 1648
41	.009 717 0353	101	.000 707 5442	161	.000 061 6190
42	.009 245 8041	102	.000 679 0529	162	.000 059 1744
43	.008 801 3717	103	.000 651 7266	163	.000 056 8270
44	.008 381 8487	104	.000 625 5164	164	.000 054 5727
45	.007 985 5129	105	.000 600 3753	165	.000 052 4080
46	.007 610 7917	106	.000 576 2587	166	.000 050 3293
47	.007 256 2458	107	.000 553 1236	167	.000 048 3332
48	.006 920 5556	108	.000 530 9291	168	.000 046 4162
49	.006 602 5091	109	.000 509 6360	169	.000 044 5754
50	.006 300 9909	110	.000 489 2069	170	.000 042 8077
51	.006 014 9729	111	.000 469 6060	171	.000 041 1102
52	.005 743 5063	112	.000 450 7988	172	.000 039 4800
53	.005 485 7134	113	.000 432 7527	173	.000 037 9145
54	.005 240 7817	114	.000 415 4362	174	.000 036 4112
55	.005 007 9578	115	.000 398 8192	175	.000 034 9675
56	.004 786 5422	116	.000 382 8730	176	.000 033 5811
57	.004 575 8843	117	.000 367 5700	177	.000 032 2497
58	.004 375 3787	118	.000 352 8838	178	.000 030 9712
59	.004 184 4611	119	.000 338 7892	179	.000 029 7433
60	.004 002 6049	120	.000 325 2620	180	.000 028 5642

NOMINAL INTEREST RATE COMPOUNDED

YEARLY	HALF-YEARLY	QUARTERLY
@	@	@
$4\frac{3}{16}\%$	$8\frac{3}{8}\%$	$16\frac{3}{4}\%$
4.1875%	8.3750%	16.7500%
PER ANNUM	PER ANNUM	PER ANNUM

Periods	Sinking Fund	Periods	Sinking Fund	Periods	Sinking Fund
1	1.000 000 0000	61	.003 735 1575	121	.000 294 6526
2	.489 745 9443	62	.003 572 2277	122	.000 282 7300
3	.319 756 6252	63	.003 416 9374	123	.000 271 2929
4	.234 833 4302	64	.003 268 8833	124	.000 260 3213
5	.183 936 6175	65	.003 127 6873	125	.000 249 7961
6	.150 052 9240	66	.002 992 9945	126	.000 239 6988
7	.125 890 9377	67	.002 864 4715	127	.000 230 0120
8	.107 804 9407	68	.002 741 8046	128	.000 220 7186
9	.093 769 5239	69	.002 624 6989	129	.000 211 8026
10	.082 569 4326	70	.002 512 8766	130	.000 203 2485
11	.073 431 3143	71	.002 406 0760	131	.000 195 0415
12	.065 839 5935	72	.002 304 0502	132	.000 187 1674
13	.059 437 3261	73	.002 206 5662	133	.000 179 6125
14	.053 969 5458	74	.002 113 4040	134	.000 172 3638
15	.049 249 2717	75	.002 024 3559	135	.000 165 4088
16	.045 136 2627	76	.001 939 2251	136	.000 158 7355
17	.041 523 2705	77	.001 857 8259	137	.000 152 3324
18	.038 326 8754	78	.001 779 9823	138	.000 146 1885
19	.035 481 2154	79	.001 705 5275	139	.000 140 2932
20	.032 933 5969	80	.001 634 3037	140	.000 134 6364
21	.030 641 3598	81	.001 566 1611	141	.000 129 2084
22	.028 569 5967	82	.001 500 9578	142	.000 123 9999
23	.026 689 4679	83	.001 438 5589	143	.000 119 0019
24	.024 976 9374	84	.001 378 8366	144	.000 114 2060
25	.023 411 8124	85	.001 321 6693	145	.000 109 6038
26	.021 977 0039	86	.001 266 9416	146	.000 105 1875
27	.020 657 9522	87	.001 214 5439	147	.000 100 9496
28	.019 442 1756	88	.001 164 3716	148	.000 096 8829
29	.018 318 9117	89	.001 116 3257	149	.000 092 9803
30	.017 278 8312	90	.001 070 3116	150	.000 089 2353
31	.016 313 8070	91	.001 026 2394	151	.000 085 6414
32	.015 416 7261	92	.000 984 0236	152	.000 082 1926
33	.014 581 3362	93	.000 943 5825	153	.000 078 8829
34	.013 802 1191	94	.000 904 8386	154	.000 075 7067
35	.013 074 1861	95	.000 867 7178	155	.000 072 6586
36	.012 393 1904	96	.000 832 1495	156	.000 069 7335
37	.011 755 2540	97	.000 798 0663	157	.000 066 9262
38	.011 156 9063	98	.000 765 4042	158	.000 064 2322
39	.010 595 0316	99	.000 734 1018	159	.000 061 6468
40	.010 066 8250	100	.000 704 1007	160	.000 059 1656
41	.009 569 7545	101	.000 675 3451	161	.000 056 7844
42	.009 101 5286	102	.000 647 7818	162	.000 054 4991
43	.008 660 0683	103	.000 621 3598	163	.000 052 3060
44	.008 243 4833	104	.000 596 0307	164	.000 050 2012
45	.007 850 0507	105	.000 571 7480	165	.000 048 1812
46	.007 478 1970	106	.000 548 4673	166	.000 046 2425
47	.007 126 4823	107	.000 526 1463	167	.000 044 3820
48	.006 793 5865	108	.000 504 7446	168	.000 042 5964
49	.006 478 2969	109	.000 484 2233	169	.000 040 8827
50	.006 179 4978	110	.000 464 5455	170	.000 039 2380
51	.005 896 1608	111	.000 445 6758	171	.000 037 6595
52	.005 627 3364	112	.000 427 5803	172	.000 036 1446
53	.005 372 1469	113	.000 410 2267	173	.000 034 6907
54	.005 129 7794	114	.000 393 5839	174	.000 033 2953
55	.004 899 4804	115	.000 377 6224	175	.000 031 9561
56	.004 680 5501	116	.000 362 3137	176	.000 030 6707
57	.004 472 3380	117	.000 347 6307	177	.000 029 4372
58	.004 274 2384	118	.000 333 5474	178	.000 028 2532
59	.004 085 6871	119	.000 320 0390	179	.000 027 1169
60	.003 906 1574	120	.000 307 0817	180	.000 026 0264

NOMINAL INTEREST RATE COMPOUNDED

YEARLY	HALF-YEARLY	QUARTERLY
@	@	@
$4\frac{1}{4}\%$	$8\frac{1}{2}\%$	17%
4.2500%	8.5000%	17.0000%
PER ANNUM	PER ANNUM	PER ANNUM

Periods	Sinking Fund	Periods	Sinking Fund	Periods	Sinking Fund
1	1.000 000 0000	61	.003 643 0617	121	.000 277 9819
2	.489 596 0832	62	.003 482 3743	122	.000 266 5783
3	.319 559 6468	63	.003 329 2858	123	.000 255 6452
4	.234 615 0167	64	.003 183 3932	124	.000 245 1631
5	.183 707 0379	65	.003 044 3184	125	.000 235 1131
6	.149 817 3083	66	.002 911 7067	126	.000 225 4773
7	.125 652 2129	67	.002 785 2249	127	.000 216 2384
8	.107 564 9316	68	.002 664 5597	128	.000 207 3800
9	.093 529 4423	69	.002 549 4164	129	.000 198 8861
10	.082 330 1217	70	.002 439 5176	130	.000 190 7416
11	.073 193 3829	71	.002 334 6017	131	.000 182 9321
12	.065 603 4928	72	.002 234 4223	132	.000 175 4436
13	.059 203 3987	73	.002 138 7467	133	.000 168 2629
14	.053 738 0557	74	.002 047 3553	134	.000 161 3773
15	.049 020 4253	75	.001 960 0407	135	.000 154 7744
16	.044 910 2226	76	.001 876 6067	136	.000 148 4426
17	.041 300 1659	77	.001 796 8678	137	.000 142 3707
18	.038 106 8090	78	.001 720 6484	138	.000 136 5480
19	.035 264 2688	79	.001 647 7824	139	.000 130 9641
20	.032 719 8348	80	.001 578 1123	140	.000 125 6093
21	.030 430 8326	81	.001 511 4887	141	.000 120 4740
22	.028 362 3433	82	.001 447 7702	142	.000 115 5492
23	.026 485 5175	83	.001 386 8224	143	.000 110 8263
24	.024 776 3108	84	.001 328 5180	144	.000 106 2969
25	.023 214 5234	85	.001 272 7359	145	.000 101 9531
26	.021 783 0600	86	.001 219 3611	146	.000 097 7871
27	.020 467 3557	87	.001 168 2844	147	.000 093 7918
28	.019 254 9240	88	.001 119 4021	148	.000 089 9601
29	.018 134 9986	89	.001 072 6152	149	.000 086 2852
30	.017 098 2464	90	.001 027 8300	150	.000 082 7607
31	.016 136 5371	91	.000 984 9570	151	.000 079 3805
32	.015 242 7548	92	.000 943 9110	152	.000 076 1385
33	.014 410 6445	93	.000 904 6112	153	.000 073 0292
34	.013 634 6857	94	.000 866 9802	154	.000 070 0471
35	.012 909 9876	95	.000 830 9447	155	.000 067 1870
36	.012 232 2015	96	.000 796 4344	156	.000 064 4438
37	.011 597 4476	97	.000 763 3827	157	.000 061 8128
38	.011 002 2538	98	.000 731 7257	158	.000 059 2893
39	.010 443 5028	99	.000 701 4029	159	.000 056 8690
40	.009 918 3886	100	.000 672 3562	160	.000 054 5476
41	.009 424 3779	101	.000 644 5303	161	.000 052 3211
42	.008 959 1782	102	.000 617 8725	162	.000 050 1856
43	.008 520 7095	103	.000 592 3323	163	.000 048 1373
44	.008 107 0805	104	.000 567 8618	164	.000 046 1728
45	.007 716 5675	105	.000 544 4151	165	.000 044 2885
46	.007 347 5964	106	.000 521 9481	166	.000 042 4811
47	.006 998 7267	107	.000 500 4191	167	.000 040 7476
48	.006 668 6377	108	.000 479 7880	168	.000 039 0849
49	.006 356 1161	109	.000 460 0166	169	.000 037 4901
50	.006 060 0458	110	.000 441 0683	170	.000 035 9605
51	.005 779 3980	111	.000 422 9082	171	.000 034 4933
52	.005 513 2229	112	.000 405 5028	172	.000 033 0860
53	.005 260 6425	113	.000 388 8203	173	.000 031 7361
54	.005 020 8438	114	.000 372 8300	174	.000 030 4414
55	.004 793 0729	115	.000 357 5029	175	.000 029 1995
56	.004 576 6300	116	.000 342 8109	176	.000 028 0084
57	.004 370 8644	117	.000 328 7273	177	.000 026 8658
58	.004 175 1706	118	.000 315 2265	178	.000 025 7699
59	.003 988 9841	119	.000 302 2841	179	.000 024 7187
60	.003 811 7784	120	.000 289 8768	180	.000 023 7104

NOMINAL INTEREST RATE COMPOUNDED

YEARLY	HALF-YEARLY	QUARTERLY
@	@	@
$4\frac{5}{16}\%$	$8\frac{5}{8}\%$	$17\frac{1}{4}\%$
4.3125%	8.6250%	17.2500%
PER ANNUM	PER ANNUM	PER ANNUM

Periods	Sinking Fund	Periods	Sinking Fund	Periods	Sinking Fund
1	1.000 000 0000	61	.003 552 9950	121	.000 262 2183
2	.489 446 3139	62	.003 394 5445	122	.000 251 3144
3	.319 362 8312	63	.003 243 6513	123	.000 240 8665
4	.234 396 8320	64	.003 099 9125	124	.000 230 8553
5	.183 477 7505	65	.002 962 9504	125	.000 221 2623
6	.149 582 0472	66	.002 832 4104	126	.000 212 0699
7	.125 413 9041	67	.002 707 9596	127	.000 203 2611
8	.107 325 3989	68	.002 589 2850	128	.000 194 8199
9	.093 289 8968	69	.002 476 0922	129	.000 186 7308
10	.082 091 4061	70	.002 368 1041	130	.000 178 9789
11	.072 956 1048	71	.002 265 0595	131	.000 171 5501
12	.065 368 1032	72	.002 166 7123	132	.000 164 4308
13	.058 970 2390	73	.002 072 8303	133	.000 157 6080
14	.053 507 3893	74	.001 983 1942	134	.000 151 0694
15	.048 792 4575	75	.001 897 5970	135	.000 144 8029
16	.044 685 1153	76	.001 815 8431	136	.000 138 7971
17	.041 078 0473	77	.001 737 7472	137	.000 133 0413
18	.037 887 7807	78	.001 663 1344	138	.000 127 5248
19	.035 048 4114	79	.001 591 8390	139	.000 122 2377
20	.032 507 2118	80	.001 523 7037	140	.000 117 1704
21	.030 221 4934	81	.001 458 5800	141	.000 112 3137
22	.028 156 3256	82	.001 396 3268	142	.000 107 6588
23	.026 282 8493	83	.001 336 8102	143	.000 103 1973
24	.024 577 0118	84	.001 279 9034	144	.000 098 9212
25	.023 018 6058	85	.001 225 4858	145	.000 094 8226
26	.021 590 5303	86	.001 173 4430	146	.000 090 8941
27	.020 278 2149	87	.001 123 6664	147	.000 087 1288
28	.019 069 1683	88	.001 076 0525	148	.000 083 5197
29	.017 952 6200	89	.001 030 5032	149	.000 080 0604
30	.016 919 2335	90	.000 986 9250	150	.000 076 7447
31	.015 960 8750	91	.000 945 2291	151	.000 073 5665
32	.015 070 4257	92	.000 905 3310	152	.000 070 5201
33	.014 241 6281	93	.000 867 1501	153	.000 067 6001
34	.013 468 9593	94	.000 830 6098	154	.000 064 8011
35	.012 747 5263	95	.000 795 6371	155	.000 062 1183
36	.012 072 9785	96	.000 762 1624	156	.000 059 5466
37	.011 441 4345	97	.000 730 1195	157	.000 057 0816
38	.010 849 4203	98	.000 699 4453	158	.000 054 7187
39	.010 293 8175	99	.000 670 0794	159	.000 052 4538
40	.009 771 8185	100	.000 641 9645	160	.000 050 2827
41	.009 280 8890	101	.000 615 0458	161	.000 048 2016
42	.008 818 7353	102	.000 589 2711	162	.000 046 2067
43	.008 383 2766	103	.000 564 5904	163	.000 044 2944
44	.007 972 6207	104	.000 540 9563	164	.000 042 4614
45	.007 585 0430	105	.000 518 3232	165	.000 040 7043
46	.007 218 9688	106	.000 496 6478	166	.000 039 0200
47	.006 872 9569	107	.000 475 8888	167	.000 037 4054
48	.006 545 6859	108	.000 456 0065	168	.000 035 8577
49	.006 235 9424	109	.000 436 9632	169	.000 034 3741
50	.005 942 6096	110	.000 418 7228	170	.000 032 9519
51	.005 664 6584	111	.000 401 2508	171	.000 031 5886
52	.005 401 1386	112	.000 384 5144	172	.000 030 2818
53	.005 151 1721	113	.000 368 4819	173	.000 029 0290
54	.004 913 9457	114	.000 353 1233	174	.000 027 8281
55	.004 688 7052	115	.000 338 4099	175	.000 026 6769
56	.004 474 7508	116	.000 324 3141	176	.000 025 5734
57	.004 271 4317	117	.000 310 8097	177	.000 024 5155
58	.004 078 1423	118	.000 297 8714	178	.000 023 5015
59	.003 894 3183	119	.000 285 4752	179	.000 022 5293
60	.003 719 4330	120	.000 273 5982	180	.000 021 5975

Sinking Fund

NOMINAL INTEREST RATE COMPOUNDED

YEARLY	HALF-YEARLY	QUARTERLY
@	@	@
$4\frac{3}{8}\%$	$8\frac{3}{4}\%$	$17\frac{1}{2}\%$
4.3750%	8.7500%	17.5000%
PER ANNUM	PER ANNUM	PER ANNUM

Periods	Sinking Fund	Periods	Sinking Fund	Periods	Sinking Fund
1	1.000 000 0000	61	.003 464 9221	121	.000 247 3153
2	.489 296 6361	62	.003 308 7020	122	.000 236 8927
3	.319 166 1784	63	.003 159 9967	123	.000 226 9116
4	.234 178 8757	64	.003 018 4034	124	.000 217 3531
5	.183 248 7552	65	.002 883 5446	125	.000 208 1991
6	.149 347 1403	66	.002 755 0661	126	.000 199 4324
7	.125 176 0106	67	.002 632 6352	127	.000 191 0365
8	.107 086 3420	68	.002 515 9393	128	.000 182 9954
9	.093 050 8867	69	.002 404 6844	129	.000 175 2942
10	.081 853 2847	70	.002 298 5935	130	.000 167 9184
11	.072 719 4793	71	.002 197 4060	131	.000 160 8540
12	.065 133 4234	72	.002 100 8762	132	.000 154 0879
13	.058 737 8457	73	.002 008 7723	133	.000 147 6073
14	.053 277 5449	74	.001 920 8754	134	.000 141 4002
15	.048 565 3666	75	.001 836 9789	135	.000 135 4549
16	.044 460 9387	76	.001 756 8877	136	.000 129 7603
17	.040 856 9121	77	.001 680 4172	137	.000 124 3058
18	.037 669 7877	78	.001 607 3927	138	.000 119 0812
19	.034 833 6401	79	.001 537 6489	139	.000 114 0767
20	.032 295 7245	80	.001 471 0294	140	.000 109 2831
21	.030 013 3385	81	.001 407 3860	141	.000 104 6914
22	.027 951 5396	82	.001 346 5781	142	.000 100 2931
23	.026 081 4588	83	.001 288 4724	143	.000 096 0800
24	.024 379 0352	84	.001 232 9425	144	.000 092 0442
25	.022 824 0544	85	.001 179 8686	145	.000 088 1783
26	.021 399 4090	86	.001 129 1366	146	.000 084 4751
27	.020 090 5233	87	.001 080 6385	147	.000 080 9276
28	.018 884 9013	88	.001 034 2714	148	.000 077 5294
29	.017 771 7684	89	.000 989 9378	149	.000 074 2742
30	.016 741 7842	90	.000 947 5447	150	.000 071 1558
31	.015 786 8118	91	.000 907 0038	151	.000 068 1686
32	.014 899 7294	92	.000 868 2312	152	.000 065 3070
33	.014 074 2769	93	.000 831 1469	153	.000 062 5656
34	.013 304 9290	94	.000 795 6748	154	.000 059 9395
35	.012 586 7905	95	.000 761 7425	155	.000 057 4238
36	.011 915 5090	96	.000 729 2809	156	.000 055 0138
37	.011 287 2012	97	.000 698 2244	157	.000 052 7051
38	.010 698 3917	98	.000 668 5103	158	.000 050 4933
39	.010 145 9604	99	.000 640 0790	159	.000 048 3745
40	.009 627 0987	100	.000 612 8735	160	.000 046 3447
41	.009 139 2709	101	.000 586 8396	161	.000 044 4001
42	.008 680 1824	102	.000 561 9256	162	.000 042 5372
43	.008 247 7513	103	.000 538 0821	163	.000 040 7525
44	.007 840 0845	104	.000 515 2621	164	.000 039 0428
45	.007 455 4569	105	.000 493 4207	165	.000 037 4049
46	.007 092 2928	106	.000 472 5151	166	.000 035 8358
47	.006 749 1505	107	.000 452 5042	167	.000 034 3325
48	.006 424 7082	108	.000 433 3491	168	.000 032 8923
49	.006 117 7518	109	.000 415 0124	169	.000 031 5126
50	.005 827 1642	110	.000 397 4587	170	.000 030 1908
51	.005 551 9160	111	.000 380 6538	171	.000 028 9245
52	.005 291 0567	112	.000 364 5653	172	.000 027 7113
53	.005 043 7080	113	.000 349 1621	173	.000 026 5491
54	.004 809 0563	114	.000 334 4147	174	.000 025 4356
55	.004 586 3476	115	.000 320 2947	175	.000 024 3688
56	.004 374 8818	116	.000 306 7751	176	.000 023 3468
57	.004 174 0081	117	.000 293 8299	177	.000 022 3677
58	.003 983 1210	118	.000 281 4344	178	.000 021 4297
59	.003 801 6561	119	.000 269 5651	179	.000 020 5310
60	.003 629 0870	120	.000 258 1993	180	.000 019 6700

Sinking Fund

	NOMINAL INTEREST RATE COMPOUNDED		
	YEARLY @ $4\frac{7}{16}\%$ 4.4375% PER ANNUM	HALF-YEARLY @ $8\frac{7}{8}\%$ 8.8750% PER ANNUM	QUARTERLY @ $17\frac{3}{4}\%$ 17.7500% PER ANNUM

Periods	Sinking Fund	Periods	Sinking Fund	Periods	Sinking Fund
1	1.000 000 0000	61	.003 378 8079	121	.000 233 2289
2	.489 147 0498	62	.003 224 8109	122	.000 223 2693
3	.318 969 6880	63	.003 078 2852	123	.000 213 7370
4	.233 961 1478	64	.002 938 8281	124	.000 204 6135
5	.183 020 0516	65	.002 806 0625	125	.000 195 8812
6	.149 112 5872	66	.002 679 6345	126	.000 187 5232
7	.124 938 5321	67	.002 559 2118	127	.000 179 5232
8	.106 847 7604	68	.002 444 4819	128	.000 171 8658
9	.092 812 4113	69	.002 335 1514	129	.000 164 5362
10	.081 615 7569	70	.002 230 9436	130	.000 157 5203
11	.072 483 5052	71	.002 131 5985	131	.000 150 8046
12	.064 899 4522	72	.002 036 8706	132	.000 144 3761
13	.058 506 2174	73	.001 946 5285	133	.000 138 2225
14	.053 048 5210	74	.001 860 3541	134	.000 132 3320
15	.048 339 1507	75	.001 778 1411	135	.000 126 6932
16	.044 237 6908	76	.001 699 6948	136	.000 121 2954
17	.040 636 7583	77	.001 624 8312	137	.000 116 1281
18	.037 452 8276	78	.001 553 3762	138	.000 111 1815
19	.034 619 9521	79	.001 485 1650	139	.000 106 4461
20	.032 085 3698	80	.001 420 0416	140	.000 101 9129
21	.029 806 3642	81	.001 357 8585	141	.000 097 5732
22	.027 747 9811	82	.001 298 4755	142	.000 093 4186
23	.025 881 3416	83	.001 241 7600	143	.000 089 4413
24	.024 182 3763	84	.001 187 5861	144	.000 085 6336
25	.022 630 8637	85	.001 135 8346	145	.000 081 9884
26	.021 209 6901	86	.001 086 3920	146	.000 078 4986
27	.019 904 2744	87	.001 039 1507	147	.000 075 1576
28	.018 702 1160	88	.000 994 0087	148	.000 071 9590
29	.017 592 4358	89	.000 950 8687	149	.000 068 8967
30	.016 565 8901	90	.000 909 6385	150	.000 065 9650
31	.015 614 3384	91	.000 870 2305	151	.000 063 1582
32	.014 730 6561	92	.000 832 5611	152	.000 060 4709
33	.013 908 5803	93	.000 796 5509	153	.000 057 8982
34	.013 142 5835	94	.000 762 1246	154	.000 055 4351
35	.012 427 7683	95	.000 729 2101	155	.000 053 0768
36	.011 759 7802	96	.000 697 7392	156	.000 050 8191
37	.011 134 7344	97	.000 667 6465	157	.000 048 6574
38	.010 549 1537	98	.000 638 8701	158	.000 046 5878
39	.009 999 9167	99	.000 611 3508	159	.000 044 6063
40	.009 484 2134	100	.000 585 0324	160	.000 042 7092
41	.008 999 5070	101	.000 559 8610	161	.000 040 8928
42	.008 543 5018	102	.000 535 7855	162	.000 039 1538
43	.008 114 1150	103	.000 512 7572	163	.000 037 4887
44	.007 709 4527	104	.000 490 7295	164	.000 035 8946
45	.007 327 7888	105	.000 469 6579	165	.000 034 3683
46	.006 967 5472	106	.000 449 5002	166	.000 032 9069
47	.006 627 2855	107	.000 430 2160	167	.000 031 5077
48	.006 305 6813	108	.000 411 7667	168	.000 030 1680
49	.006 001 5202	109	.000 394 1156	169	.000 028 8854
50	.005 713 6846	110	.000 377 2274	170	.000 027 6573
51	.005 441 1448	111	.000 361 0688	171	.000 026 4814
52	.005 182 9502	112	.000 345 6077	172	.000 025 3556
53	.004 938 2221	113	.000 330 8135	173	.000 024 2777
54	.004 706 1468	114	.000 316 6571	174	.000 023 2456
55	.004 485 9702	115	.000 303 1106	175	.000 022 2574
56	.004 276 9923	116	.000 290 1473	176	.000 021 3112
57	.004 078 5621	117	.000 277 7419	177	.000 020 4053
58	.003 890 0741	118	.000 265 8701	178	.000 019 5379
59	.003 710 9642	119	.000 254 5086	179	.000 018 7074
60	.003 540 7059	120	.000 243 6353	180	.000 017 9122

NOMINAL INTEREST RATE COMPOUNDED

YEARLY @ 4½% 4.5000% PER ANNUM	HALF-YEARLY @ 9% 9.0000% PER ANNUM	QUARTERLY @ 18% 18.0000% PER ANNUM

Periods	Sinking Fund	Periods	Sinking Fund	Periods	Sinking Fund
1	1.000 000 0000	61	.003 294 6176	121	.000 219 9169
2	.488 997 5550	62	.003 142 8356	122	.000 210 4025
3	.318 773 3601	63	.002 998 4802	123	.000 201 3016
4	.233 743 6479	64	.002 861 1494	124	.000 192 5960
5	.182 791 6395	65	.002 730 4661	125	.000 184 2684
6	.148 878 3875	66	.002 606 0769	126	.000 176 3023
7	.124 701 4680	67	.002 487 6496	127	.000 168 6819
8	.106 609 6533	68	.002 374 8725	128	.000 161 3921
9	.092 574 4700	69	.002 267 4523	129	.000 154 4183
10	.081 378 8217	70	.002 165 1129	130	.000 147 7469
11	.072 248 1817	71	.002 067 5946	131	.000 141 3646
12	.064 666 1886	72	.001 974 6524	132	.000 135 2588
13	.058 275 3528	73	.001 886 0556	133	.000 129 4175
14	.052 820 3160	74	.001 801 5863	134	.000 123 8292
15	.048 113 8081	75	.001 721 0390	135	.000 118 4828
16	.044 015 3694	76	.001 644 2194	136	.000 113 3678
17	.040 417 5833	77	.001 570 9439	137	.000 108 4742
18	.037 236 8975	78	.001 501 0391	138	.000 103 7923
19	.034 407 3443	79	.001 434 3408	139	.000 099 3129
20	.031 876 1443	80	.001 370 6935	140	.000 095 0272
21	.029 600 5669	81	.001 309 9502	141	.000 090 9269
22	.027 545 6461	82	.001 251 9715	142	.000 087 0038
23	.025 682 4930	83	.001 196 6252	143	.000 083 2503
24	.023 987 0299	84	.001 143 7861	144	.000 079 6590
25	.022 439 0280	85	.001 093 3355	145	.000 076 2229
26	.021 021 3674	86	.001 045 1606	146	.000 072 9352
27	.019 719 4616	87	.000 999 1543	147	.000 069 7896
28	.018 520 8051	88	.000 955 2152	148	.000 066 7799
29	.017 414 6147	89	.000 913 2468	149	.000 063 9001
30	.016 391 5429	90	.000 873 1573	150	.000 061 1447
31	.015 443 4459	91	.000 834 8597	151	.000 058 5082
32	.014 563 1962	92	.000 798 2710	152	.000 055 9856
33	.013 744 5281	93	.000 763 3126	153	.000 053 5719
34	.012 981 9119	94	.000 729 9095	154	.000 051 2623
35	.012 270 4478	95	.000 697 9905	155	.000 049 0524
36	.011 605 7796	96	.000 667 4877	156	.000 046 9379
37	.010 984 0206	97	.000 638 3364	157	.000 044 9147
38	.010 401 6920	98	.000 610 4754	158	.000 042 9787
39	.009 855 6712	99	.000 583 8459	159	.000 041 1262
40	.009 343 1466	100	.000 558 3922	160	.000 039 3537
41	.008 861 5804	101	.000 534 0612	161	.000 037 6576
42	.008 408 6759	102	.000 510 8023	162	.000 036 0347
43	.007 982 3492	103	.000 488 5672	163	.000 034 4818
44	.007 580 7056	104	.000 467 3100	164	.000 032 9958
45	.007 202 0184	105	.000 446 9867	165	.000 031 5740
46	.006 844 7107	106	.000 427 5556	166	.000 030 2134
47	.006 507 3395	107	.000 408 9768	167	.000 028 9115
48	.006 188 5821	108	.000 391 2122	168	.000 027 6658
49	.005 887 2235	109	.000 374 2257	169	.000 026 4737
50	.005 602 1459	110	.000 357 9825	170	.000 025 3331
51	.005 332 3191	111	.000 342 4497	171	.000 024 2416
52	.005 076 7923	112	.000 327 5957	172	.000 023 1971
53	.004 834 6867	113	.000 313 3904	173	.000 022 1977
54	.004 605 1886	114	.000 299 8052	174	.000 021 2414
55	.004 387 5437	115	.000 286 8127	175	.000 020 3263
56	.004 181 0518	116	.000 274 3866	176	.000 019 4506
57	.003 985 0622	117	.000 262 5020	177	.000 018 6127
58	.003 798 9695	118	.000 251 1350	178	.000 017 8109
59	.003 622 2094	119	.000 240 2628	179	.000 017 0436
60	.003 454 2558	120	.000 229 8637	180	.000 016 3094

NOMINAL INTEREST RATE COMPOUNDED

YEARLY	HALF-YEARLY	QUARTERLY
@	@	@
$4\frac{9}{16}\%$	$9\frac{1}{8}\%$	$18\frac{1}{4}\%$
4.5625%	9.1250%	18.2500%
PER ANNUM	PER ANNUM	PER ANNUM

Periods	Sinking Fund	Periods	Sinking Fund	Periods	Sinking Fund
1	1.000 000 0000	61	.003 212 3166	121	.000 207 3390
2	.488 848 1515	62	.003 062 7405	122	.000 198 2526
3	.318 577 1944	63	.002 920 5458	123	.000 189 5661
4	.233 526 3759	64	.002 785 3304	124	.000 181 2617
5	.182 563 5185	65	.002 656 7178	125	.000 173 3224
6	.148 644 5409	66	.002 534 3548	126	.000 165 7322
7	.124 464 8179	67	.002 417 9098	127	.000 158 4755
8	.106 372 0203	68	.002 307 0714	128	.000 151 5376
9	.092 337 0620	69	.002 201 5467	129	.000 144 9043
10	.081 142 4784	70	.002 101 0602	130	.000 138 5624
11	.072 013 5076	71	.002 005 3527	131	.000 132 4987
12	.064 433 6314	72	.001 914 1796	132	.000 126 7012
13	.058 045 2506	73	.001 827 3108	133	.000 121 1580
14	.052 592 9285	74	.001 744 5288	134	.000 115 8580
15	.047 889 3370	75	.001 665 6288	135	.000 110 7903
16	.043 793 9727	76	.001 590 4170	136	.000 105 9448
17	.040 199 3850	77	.001 518 7104	137	.000 101 3118
18	.037 021 9950	78	.001 450 3362	138	.000 096 8817
19	.034 195 8138	79	.001 385 1307	139	.000 092 6458
20	.031 668 0447	80	.001 322 9391	140	.000 088 5954
21	.029 395 9428	81	.001 263 6150	141	.000 084 7224
22	.027 344 5303	82	.001 207 0196	142	.000 081 0191
23	.025 484 9085	83	.001 153 0212	143	.000 077 4779
24	.023 792 9911	84	.001 101 4955	144	.000 074 0917
25	.022 248 5420	85	.001 052 3240	145	.000 070 8538
26	.020 834 4351	86	.001 005 3949	146	.000 067 7575
27	.019 536 0784	87	.000 960 6017	147	.000 064 7968
28	.018 340 9615	88	.000 917 8434	148	.000 061 9656
29	.017 238 2973	89	.000 877 0242	149	.000 059 2582
30	.016 218 7342	90	.000 838 0530	150	.000 056 6693
31	.015 274 1252	91	.000 800 8434	151	.000 054 1937
32	.014 397 3398	92	.000 765 3131	152	.000 051 8263
33	.013 582 1098	93	.000 731 3840	153	.000 049 5625
34	.012 822 9028	94	.000 698 9817	154	.000 047 3976
35	.012 114 8171	95	.000 668 0356	155	.000 045 3274
36	.011 453 4945	96	.000 638 4785	156	.000 043 3477
37	.010 835 0463	97	.000 610 2464	157	.000 041 4545
38	.010 255 9925	98	.000 583 2784	158	.000 039 6441
39	.009 713 2088	99	.000 557 5165	159	.000 037 9128
40	.009 203 8824	100	.000 532 9056	160	.000 036 2572
41	.008 725 4744	101	.000 509 3931	161	.000 034 6740
42	.008 275 6869	102	.000 486 9289	162	.000 033 1599
43	.007 852 4352	103	.000 465 4654	163	.000 031 7120
44	.007 453 8239	104	.000 444 9571	164	.000 030 3273
45	.007 078 1253	105	.000 425 3608	165	.000 029 0032
46	.006 723 7620	106	.000 406 6351	166	.000 027 7369
47	.006 389 2906	107	.000 388 7407	167	.000 026 5259
48	.006 073 3876	108	.000 371 6401	168	.000 025 3678
49	.005 774 8378	109	.000 355 2976	169	.000 024 2603
50	.005 492 5230	110	.000 339 6791	170	.000 023 2012
51	.005 225 4129	111	.000 324 7520	171	.000 022 1884
52	.004 972 5563	112	.000 310 4853	172	.000 021 2197
53	.004 733 0743	113	.000 296 8493	173	.000 020 2934
54	.004 506 1531	114	.000 283 8160	174	.000 019 4076
55	.004 291 0384	115	.000 271 3582	175	.000 018 5604
56	.004 087 0301	116	.000 259 4504	176	.000 017 7502
57	.003 893 4774	117	.000 248 0680	177	.000 016 9754
58	.003 709 7750	118	.000 237 1874	178	.000 016 2344
59	.003 535 3589	119	.000 226 7865	179	.000 015 5258
60	.003 369 7031	120	.000 216 8438	180	.000 014 8481

NOMINAL INTEREST RATE COMPOUNDED		
YEARLY @ $4\frac{5}{8}\%$ 4.6250% PER ANNUM	HALF-YEARLY @ $9\frac{1}{4}\%$ 9.2500% PER ANNUM	QUARTERLY @ $18\frac{1}{2}\%$ 18.5000% PER ANNUM

Periods	Sinking Fund	Periods	Sinking Fund	Periods	Sinking Fund
1	1.000 000 0000	61	.003 131 8706	121	.000 195 4570
2	.488 698 8393	62	.002 984 4908	122	.000 186 7818
3	.318 381 1908	63	.002 844 4460	123	.000 178 4932
4	.233 309 3315	64	.002 711 3345	124	.000 170 5737
5	.182 335 6883	65	.002 584 7802	125	.000 163 0068
6	.148 411 0470	66	.002 464 4303	126	.000 155 7768
7	.124 228 5813	67	.002 349 9537	127	.000 148 8684
8	.106 134 8608	68	.002 241 0393	128	.000 142 2674
9	.092 100 1867	69	.002 137 3948	129	.000 135 9599
10	.080 906 7260	70	.002 038 7452	130	.000 129 9328
11	.071 779 4821	71	.001 944 8317	131	.000 124 1737
12	.064 201 7793	72	.001 855 4105	132	.000 118 6704
13	.057 815 9093	73	.001 770 2518	133	.000 113 4117
14	.052 366 3567	74	.001 689 1389	134	.000 108 3865
15	.047 665 7356	75	.001 611 8674	135	.000 103 5845
16	.043 573 4984	76	.001 538 2442	136	.000 098 9957
17	.039 982 1608	77	.001 468 0869	137	.000 094 6106
18	.036 808 1173	78	.001 401 2232	138	.000 090 4201
19	.033 985 3575	79	.001 337 4901	139	.000 086 4156
20	.031 461 0675	80	.001 276 7336	140	.000 082 5887
21	.029 192 4881	81	.001 218 8077	141	.000 078 9316
22	.027 144 6297	82	.001 163 5742	142	.000 075 4367
23	.025 288 5835	83	.001 110 9023	143	.000 072 0968
24	.023 600 2547	84	.001 060 6681	144	.000 068 9050
25	.022 059 4000	85	.001 012 7541	145	.000 065 8546
26	.020 648 8869	86	.000 967 0487	146	.000 062 9395
27	.019 354 1180	87	.000 923 4463	147	.000 060 1537
28	.018 162 5781	88	.000 881 8465	148	.000 057 4912
29	.017 063 4756	89	.000 842 1542	149	.000 054 9468
30	.016 047 4554	90	.000 804 2790	150	.000 052 5151
31	.015 106 3672	91	.000 768 1350	151	.000 050 1911
32	.014 233 0773	92	.000 733 6406	152	.000 047 9701
33	.013 421 3148	93	.000 700 7183	153	.000 045 8474
34	.012 665 5451	94	.000 669 2944	154	.000 043 8188
35	.011 960 8643	95	.000 639 2990	155	.000 041 8800
36	.011 302 9120	96	.000 610 6653	156	.000 040 0271
37	.010 687 7981	97	.000 583 3301	157	.000 038 2562
38	.010 112 0408	98	.000 557 2330	158	.000 036 5637
39	.009 572 5143	99	.000 532 3167	159	.000 034 9462
40	.009 066 4048	100	.000 508 5267	160	.000 033 4003
41	.008 591 1721	101	.000 485 8109	161	.000 031 9228
42	.008 144 5172	102	.000 464 1198	162	.000 030 5107
43	.007 724 3546	103	.000 443 4065	163	.000 029 1611
44	.007 328 7880	104	.000 423 6260	164	.000 027 8712
45	.006 956 0892	105	.000 404 7355	165	.000 026 6385
46	.006 604 6800	106	.000 386 6944	166	.000 025 4602
47	.006 273 1165	107	.000 369 4638	167	.000 024 3342
48	.005 960 0748	108	.000 353 0068	168	.000 023 2579
49	.005 664 3392	109	.000 337 2882	169	.000 022 2293
50	.005 384 7913	110	.000 322 2743	170	.000 021 2462
51	.005 120 4005	111	.000 307 9331	171	.000 020 3066
52	.004 870 2156	112	.000 294 2342	172	.000 019 4085
53	.004 633 3573	113	.000 281 1484	173	.000 018 5502
54	.004 409 0120	114	.000 268 6479	174	.000 017 7299
55	.004 196 4252	115	.000 256 7062	175	.000 016 9459
56	.003 994 8970	116	.000 245 2982	176	.000 016 1965
57	.003 803 7766	117	.000 234 3997	177	.000 015 4803
58	.003 622 4589	118	.000 223 9878	178	.000 014 7957
59	.003 450 3799	119	.000 214 0405	179	.000 014 1415
60	.003 287 0141	120	.000 204 5369	180	.000 013 5162

NOMINAL INTEREST RATE COMPOUNDED

	YEARLY @ $4\frac{11}{16}\%$ 4.6875% PER ANNUM		HALF-YEARLY @ $9\frac{3}{8}\%$ 9.3750% PER ANNUM		QUARTERLY @ $18\frac{3}{4}\%$ 18.7500% PER ANNUM
Periods	Sinking Fund	Periods	Sinking Fund	Periods	Sinking Fund
1	1.000 000 0000	61	.003 053 2457	121	.000 184 2343
2	.488 549 6183	62	.002 908 0518	122	.000 175 9541
3	.318 185 3492	63	.002 770 1455	123	.000 168 0473
4	.233 092 5145	64	.002 639 1257	124	.000 160 4970
5	.182 108 1487	65	.002 514 6167	125	.000 153 2871
6	.148 177 9054	66	.002 396 2660	126	.000 146 4020
7	.123 992 7577	67	.002 283 7431	127	.000 139 8272
8	.105 898 1742	68	.002 176 7374	128	.000 133 5484
9	.091 863 8432	69	.002 074 9572	129	.000 127 5524
10	.080 671 5638	70	.001 978 1279	130	.000 121 8262
11	.071 546 1041	71	.001 885 9913	131	.000 116 3578
12	.063 970 6313	72	.001 798 3042	132	.000 111 1354
13	.057 587 3276	73	.001 714 8374	133	.000 106 1479
14	.052 140 5992	74	.001 635 3748	134	.000 101 3847
15	.047 443 0020	75	.001 559 7126	135	.000 096 8357
16	.043 353 9445	76	.001 487 6583	136	.000 092 4913
17	.039 765 9086	77	.001 419 0302	137	.000 088 3420
18	.036 595 2618	78	.001 353 6567	138	.000 084 3793
19	.033 775 9726	79	.001 291 3754	139	.000 080 5946
20	.031 255 2095	80	.001 232 0328	140	.000 076 9800
21	.028 990 1992	81	.001 175 4838	141	.000 073 5277
22	.026 945 9401	82	.001 121 5908	142	.000 070 2305
23	.025 093 5133	83	.001 070 2237	143	.000 067 0814
24	.023 408 8157	84	.001 021 2592	144	.000 064 0736
25	.021 871 5964	85	.000 974 5804	145	.000 061 2009
26	.020 464 7168	86	.000 930 0767	146	.000 058 4571
27	.019 173 5738	87	.000 887 6428	147	.000 055 8365
28	.017 985 6474	88	.000 847 1793	148	.000 053 3335
29	.016 890 1419	89	.000 808 5916	149	.000 050 9429
30	.015 877 6982	90	.000 771 7898	150	.000 048 6595
31	.014 940 1627	91	.000 736 6890	151	.000 046 4785
32	.014 070 3987	92	.000 703 2081	152	.000 044 3954
33	.013 262 1327	93	.000 671 2702	153	.000 042 4058
34	.012 509 8276	94	.000 640 8025	154	.000 040 5054
35	.011 808 5772	95	.000 611 7354	155	.000 038 6902
36	.011 154 0195	96	.000 584 0030	156	.000 036 9565
37	.010 542 2623	97	.000 557 5426	157	.000 035 3004
38	.009 969 8224	98	.000 532 2945	158	.000 033 7187
39	.009 433 5727	99	.000 508 2020	159	.000 032 2079
40	.008 930 6978	100	.000 485 2111	160	.000 030 7648
41	.008 458 6566	101	.000 463 2705	161	.000 029 3864
42	.008 015 1491	102	.000 442 3313	162	.000 028 0698
43	.007 598 0888	103	.000 422 3470	163	.000 026 8122
44	.007 205 5787	104	.000 403 2733	164	.000 025 6110
45	.006 835 8898	105	.000 385 0679	165	.000 024 4636
46	.006 487 4435	106	.000 367 6908	166	.000 023 3677
47	.006 158 7951	107	.000 351 1037	167	.000 022 3209
48	.005 848 6206	108	.000 335 2702	168	.000 021 3210
49	.005 555 7038	109	.000 320 1556	169	.000 020 3659
50	.005 278 9260	110	.000 305 7268	170	.000 019 4536
51	.005 017 2563	111	.000 291 9523	171	.000 018 5822
52	.004 769 7436	112	.000 278 8020	172	.000 017 7499
53	.004 535 5084	113	.000 266 2474	173	.000 016 9548
54	.004 313 7370	114	.000 254 2612	174	.000 016 1954
55	.004 103 6751	115	.000 242 8174	175	.000 015 4700
56	.003 904 6226	116	.000 231 8912	176	.000 014 7771
57	.003 715 9291	117	.000 221 4590	177	.000 014 1152
58	.003 536 9895	118	.000 211 4982	178	.000 013 4830
59	.003 367 2402	119	.000 201 9873	179	.000 012 8791
60	.003 206 1558	120	.000 192 9059	180	.000 012 3023

	NOMINAL INTEREST RATE COMPOUNDED				
	YEARLY @ 4¾% 4.7500% PER ANNUM		HALF-YEARLY @ 9½% 9.5000% PER ANNUM		QUARTERLY @ 19% 19.0000% PER ANNUM
Periods	Sinking Fund	Periods	Sinking Fund	Periods	Sinking Fund
1	1.000 000 0000	61	.002 976 4084	121	.000 173 6363
2	.488 400 4884	62	.002 833 3891	122	.000 165 7351
3	.317 989 6693	63	.002 697 6092	123	.000 158 1946
4	.232 875 9246	64	.002 568 6682	124	.000 150 9983
5	.181 880 8993	65	.002 446 1907	125	.000 144 1304
6	.147 945 1156	66	.002 329 8248	126	.000 137 5757
7	.123 757 3467	67	.002 219 2405	127	.000 131 3199
8	.105 661 9598	68	.002 114 1277	128	.000 125 3494
9	.091 628 0310	69	.002 014 1951	129	.000 119 6509
10	.080 436 9909	70	.001 919 1690	130	.000 114 2122
11	.071 313 3726	71	.001 828 7917	131	.000 109 0212
12	.063 740 1861	72	.001 742 8204	132	.000 104 0667
13	.057 359 5042	73	.001 661 0268	133	.000 099 3378
14	.051 915 6544	74	.001 583 1953	134	.000 094 8243
15	.047 221 1344	75	.001 509 1227	135	.000 090 5162
16	.043 135 3090	76	.001 438 6173	136	.000 086 4041
17	.039 550 6258	77	.001 371 4981	137	.000 082 4793
18	.036 383 4258	78	.001 307 5940	138	.000 078 7329
19	.033 567 6559	79	.001 246 7435	139	.000 075 1571
20	.031 050 4673	80	.001 188 7937	140	.000 071 7438
21	.028 789 0722	81	.001 133 6000	141	.000 068 4859
22	.026 748 4572	82	.001 081 0259	142	.000 065 3760
23	.024 899 6934	83	.001 030 9417	143	.000 062 4076
24	.023 218 6689	84	.000 983 2248	144	.000 059 5741
25	.021 685 1257	85	.000 937 7592	145	.000 056 8694
26	.020 281 9186	86	.000 894 4348	146	.000 054 2877
27	.018 994 4391	87	.000 853 1472	147	.000 051 8232
28	.017 810 1623	88	.000 813 7976	148	.000 049 4708
29	.016 718 2882	89	.000 776 2920	149	.000 047 2253
30	.015 709 4539	90	.000 740 5414	150	.000 045 0818
31	.014 775 5025	91	.000 706 4613	151	.000 043 0356
32	.013 909 2942	92	.000 673 9715	152	.000 041 0824
33	.013 104 5529	93	.000 642 9958	153	.000 039 2180
34	.012 355 7388	94	.000 613 4620	154	.000 037 4382
35	.011 657 9440	95	.000 585 3011	155	.000 035 7392
36	.011 006 8041	96	.000 558 4480	156	.000 034 1174
37	.010 398 4255	97	.000 532 8405	157	.000 032 5693
38	.009 829 3231	98	.000 508 4196	158	.000 031 0914
39	.009 296 3686	99	.000 485 1293	159	.000 029 6807
40	.008 796 7454	100	.000 462 9162	160	.000 028 3340
41	.008 327 9111	101	.000 441 7296	161	.000 027 0484
42	.007 887 5648	102	.000 421 5211	162	.000 025 8212
43	.007 473 6193	103	.000 402 2450	163	.000 024 6497
44	.007 084 1765	104	.000 383 8573	164	.000 023 5314
45	.006 717 5069	105	.000 366 3167	165	.000 022 4638
46	.006 372 0312	106	.000 349 5834	166	.000 021 4447
47	.006 046 3045	107	.000 333 6198	167	.000 020 4719
48	.005 739 0022	108	.000 318 3901	168	.000 019 5432
49	.005 448 9078	109	.000 303 8600	169	.000 018 6566
50	.005 174 9023	110	.000 289 9970	170	.000 017 8103
51	.004 915 9549	111	.000 276 7702	171	.000 017 0024
52	.004 671 1140	112	.000 264 1499	172	.000 016 2311
53	.004 439 5003	113	.000 252 1082	173	.000 015 4949
54	.004 220 3000	114	.000 240 6182	174	.000 014 7920
55	.004 012 7589	115	.000 229 6543	175	.000 014 1211
56	.003 816 1771	116	.000 219 1924	176	.000 013 4805
57	.003 629 9043	117	.000 209 2091	177	.000 012 8691
58	.003 453 3356	118	.000 199 6824	178	.000 012 2854
59	.003 285 9076	119	.000 190 5912	179	.000 011 7281
60	.003 127 0953	120	.000 181 9156	180	.000 011 1962

NOMINAL INTEREST RATE COMPOUNDED

YEARLY	HALF-YEARLY	QUARTERLY
@	@	@
$4\frac{13}{16}\%$	$9\frac{5}{8}\%$	$19\frac{1}{4}\%$
4.8125%	9.6250%	19.2500%
PER ANNUM	PER ANNUM	PER ANNUM

Periods	Sinking Fund	Periods	Sinking Fund	Periods	Sinking Fund
1	1.000 000 0000	61	.002 901 3252	121	.000 163 6297
2	.488 251 4495	62	.002 760 4687	122	.000 156 0922
3	.317 794 1511	63	.002 626 8026	123	.000 148 9030
4	.232 659 5617	64	.002 499 9268	124	.000 142 0459
5	.181 653 9399	65	.002 379 4665	125	.000 135 5055
6	.147 712 6774	66	.002 265 0703	126	.000 129 2670
7	.123 522 3477	67	.002 156 4087	127	.000 123 3164
8	.105 426 2172	68	.002 053 1723	128	.000 117 6405
9	.091 392 7493	69	.001 955 0705	129	.000 112 2264
10	.080 203 0064	70	.001 861 8299	130	.000 107 0620
11	.071 081 2866	71	.001 773 1936	131	.000 102 1358
12	.063 510 4425	72	.001 688 9195	132	.000 097 4367
13	.057 132 4376	73	.001 608 7799	133	.000 092 9542
14	.051 691 5206	74	.001 532 5599	134	.000 088 6783
15	.047 000 1310	75	.001 460 0570	135	.000 084 5995
16	.042 917 5897	76	.001 391 0802	136	.000 080 7086
17	.039 336 3102	77	.001 325 4492	137	.000 076 9969
18	.036 172 6066	78	.001 262 9936	138	.000 073 4561
19	.033 360 4043	79	.001 203 5525	139	.000 070 0785
20	.030 846 8373	80	.001 146 9740	140	.000 066 8563
21	.028 589 1033	81	.001 093 1141	141	.000 063 7825
22	.026 552 1769	82	.001 041 8368	142	.000 060 8502
23	.024 707 1190	83	.000 993 0135	143	.000 058 0529
24	.023 029 8092	84	.000 946 5222	144	.000 055 3843
25	.021 499 9821	85	.000 902 2476	145	.000 052 8385
26	.020 100 4861	86	.000 860 0802	146	.000 050 4099
27	.018 816 7071	87	.000 819 9165	147	.000 048 0930
28	.017 636 1154	88	.000 781 6583	148	.000 045 8827
29	.016 547 9066	89	.000 745 2125	149	.000 043 7740
30	.015 542 7141	90	.000 710 4906	150	.000 041 7624
31	.014 612 3775	91	.000 677 4090	151	.000 039 8433
32	.013 749 7539	92	.000 645 8881	152	.000 038 0124
33	.012 948 5647	93	.000 615 8525	153	.000 036 2657
34	.012 203 2676	94	.000 587 2304	154	.000 034 5994
35	.011 508 9525	95	.000 559 9538	155	.000 033 0097
36	.010 861 2530	96	.000 533 9580	156	.000 031 4930
37	.010 256 2739	97	.000 509 1818	157	.000 030 0461
38	.009 690 5285	98	.000 485 5666	158	.000 028 6657
39	.009 160 8869	99	.000 463 0572	159	.000 027 3488
40	.008 664 5316	100	.000 441 6007	160	.000 026 0924
41	.008 198 9188	101	.000 421 1470	161	.000 024 8937
42	.007 761 7468	102	.000 401 6485	162	.000 023 7501
43	.007 350 9274	103	.000 383 0599	163	.000 022 6591
44	.006 964 5619	104	.000 365 3380	164	.000 021 6183
45	.006 600 9201	105	.000 348 4420	165	.000 020 6252
46	.006 258 4222	106	.000 332 3327	166	.000 019 6778
47	.005 935 6227	107	.000 316 9730	167	.000 018 7740
48	.005 631 1967	108	.000 302 3277	168	.000 017 9116
49	.005 343 9275	109	.000 288 3630	169	.000 017 0889
50	.005 072 6959	110	.000 275 0470	170	.000 016 3040
51	.004 816 4707	111	.000 262 3493	171	.000 015 5552
52	.004 574 3005	112	.000 250 2408	172	.000 014 8407
53	.004 345 3059	113	.000 238 6940	173	.000 014 1591
54	.004 128 6732	114	.000 227 6824	174	.000 013 5088
55	.003 923 6482	115	.000 217 1811	175	.000 012 8884
56	.003 729 5311	116	.000 207 1662	176	.000 012 2964
57	.003 545 6720	117	.000 197 6151	177	.000 011 7317
58	.003 371 4660	118	.000 188 5060	178	.000 011 1929
59	.003 206 3503	119	.000 179 8183	179	.000 010 6789
60	.003 049 8000	120	.000 171 5325	180	.000 010 1885

NOMINAL INTEREST RATE COMPOUNDED

	YEARLY	HALF-YEARLY	QUARTERLY
	@	@	@
	$4\frac{7}{8}\%$	$9\frac{3}{4}\%$	$19\frac{1}{2}\%$
	4.8750%	9.7500%	19.5000%
	PER ANNUM	PER ANNUM	PER ANNUM

Periods	Sinking Fund	Periods	Sinking Fund	Periods	Sinking Fund
1	1.000 000 0000	61	.002 827 9634	121	.000 154 1832
2	.488 102 5015	62	.002 689 2570	122	.000 146 9946
3	.317 598 7943	63	.002 557 6913	123	.000 140 1421
4	.232 443 4256	64	.002 432 8665	124	.000 133 6099
5	.181 427 2700	65	.002 314 4084	125	.000 127 3829
6	.147 480 5904	66	.002 201 9663	126	.000 121 4469
7	.123 287 7604	67	.002 095 2112	127	.000 115 7882
8	.105 190 9457	68	.001 993 8343	128	.000 110 3937
9	.091 157 9973	69	.001 897 5455	129	.000 105 2511
10	.079 969 6094	70	.001 806 0724	130	.000 100 3485
11	.070 849 8451	71	.001 719 1585	131	.000 095 6748
12	.063 281 3995	72	.001 636 5626	132	.000 091 2191
13	.056 906 1265	73	.001 558 0574	133	.000 086 9713
14	.051 468 1962	74	.001 483 4290	134	.000 082 9217
15	.046 779 9900	75	.001 412 4755	135	.000 079 0609
16	.042 700 7845	76	.001 345 0066	136	.000 075 3802
17	.039 122 9592	77	.001 280 8428	137	.000 071 8711
18	.035 962 8014	78	.001 219 8145	138	.000 068 5255
19	.033 154 2150	79	.001 161 7615	139	.000 065 3359
20	.030 644 3163	80	.001 106 5325	140	.000 062 2950
21	.028 390 2887	81	.001 053 9845	141	.000 059 3957
22	.026 357 0948	82	.001 003 9821	142	.000 056 6316
23	.024 515 7854	83	.000 956 3976	143	.000 053 9962
24	.022 842 2314	84	.000 911 1096	144	.000 051 4836
25	.021 316 1599	85	.000 868 0036	145	.000 049 0880
26	.019 920 4131	86	.000 826 9709	146	.000 046 8040
27	.018 640 3711	87	.000 787 9088	147	.000 044 6264
28	.017 463 4994	88	.000 750 7197	148	.000 042 5502
29	.016 378 9892	89	.000 715 3113	149	.000 040 5706
30	.015 377 4701	90	.000 681 5959	150	.000 038 6833
31	.014 450 7783	91	.000 649 4906	151	.000 036 8837
32	.013 591 7680	92	.000 618 9164	152	.000 035 1680
33	.012 794 1576	93	.000 589 7987	153	.000 033 5321
34	.012 052 4026	94	.000 562 0664	154	.000 031 9724
35	.011 361 5906	95	.000 535 6523	155	.000 030 4853
36	.010 717 3534	96	.000 510 4924	156	.000 029 0674
37	.010 115 7939	97	.000 486 5259	157	.000 027 7154
38	.009 553 4240	98	.000 463 6951	158	.000 026 4264
39	.009 027 1125	99	.000 441 9454	159	.000 025 1974
40	.008 534 0403	100	.000 421 2245	160	.000 024 0255
41	.008 071 6628	101	.000 401 4831	161	.000 022 9082
42	.007 637 6773	102	.000 382 6741	162	.000 021 8429
43	.007 229 9947	103	.000 364 7528	163	.000 020 8271
44	.006 846 7156	104	.000 347 6768	164	.000 019 8586
45	.006 486 1092	105	.000 331 4055	165	.000 018 9351
46	.006 146 5952	106	.000 315 9007	166	.000 018 0546
47	.005 826 7277	107	.000 301 1257	167	.000 017 2151
48	.005 525 1814	108	.000 287 0458	168	.000 016 4146
49	.005 240 7393	109	.000 273 6279	169	.000 015 6513
50	.004 972 2821	110	.000 260 8405	170	.000 014 9235
51	.004 718 7786	111	.000 248 6538	171	.000 014 2296
52	.004 479 2771	112	.000 237 0392	172	.000 013 5680
53	.004 252 8984	113	.000 225 9696	173	.000 012 9371
54	.004 038 8287	114	.000 215 4192	174	.000 012 3356
55	.003 836 3142	115	.000 205 3635	175	.000 011 7621
56	.003 644 6552	116	.000 195 7791	176	.000 011 2152
57	.003 463 2020	117	.000 186 6437	177	.000 010 6938
58	.003 291 3500	118	.000 177 9361	178	.000 010 1966
59	.003 128 5368	119	.000 169 6361	179	.000 009 7225
60	.002 974 2377	120	.000 161 7246	180	.000 009 2705

NOMINAL INTEREST RATE COMPOUNDED

YEARLY	HALF-YEARLY	QUARTERLY
@	@	@
$4\frac{15}{16}\%$	$9\frac{7}{8}\%$	$19\frac{3}{4}\%$
4.9375%	9.8750%	19.7500%
PER ANNUM	PER ANNUM	PER ANNUM

Periods	Sinking Fund	Periods	Sinking Fund	Periods	Sinking Fund
1	1.000 000 0000	61	.002 756 2903	121	.000 145 2669
2	.487 953 6444	62	.002 619 7208	122	.000 138 4127
3	.317 403 5989	63	.002 490 2414	123	.000 131 8827
4	.232 227 5160	64	.002 367 4529	124	.000 125 6616
5	.181 200 8896	65	.002 250 9816	125	.000 119 7346
6	.147 248 8541	66	.002 140 4774	126	.000 114 0879
7	.123 053 5841	67	.002 035 6118	127	.000 108 7080
8	.104 956 1447	68	.001 936 0769	128	.000 103 5824
9	.090 923 7745	69	.001 841 5833	129	.000 098 6989
10	.079 736 7993	70	.001 751 8591	130	.000 094 0461
11	.070 619 0470	71	.001 666 6486	131	.000 089 6130
12	.063 053 0557	72	.001 585 7113	132	.000 085 3893
13	.056 680 5695	73	.001 508 8207	133	.000 081 3649
14	.051 245 6797	74	.001 435 7635	134	.000 077 5306
15	.046 560 7095	75	.001 366 3388	135	.000 073 8771
16	.042 484 8913	76	.001 300 3570	136	.000 070 3961
17	.038 910 5705	77	.001 237 6392	137	.000 067 0794
18	.035 754 0076	78	.001 178 0166	138	.000 063 9191
19	.032 949 0847	79	.001 121 3300	139	.000 060 9079
20	.030 442 9008	80	.001 067 4288	140	.000 058 0387
21	.028 192 6246	81	.001 016 1707	141	.000 055 3048
22	.026 163 2068	82	.000 967 4212	142	.000 052 6998
23	.024 325 6880	83	.000 921 0531	143	.000 050 2177
24	.022 655 9303	84	.000 876 9462	144	.000 047 8525
25	.021 133 6536	85	.000 834 9865	145	.000 045 5989
26	.019 741 6934	86	.000 795 0662	146	.000 043 4515
27	.018 465 4243	87	.000 757 0833	147	.000 041 4053
28	.017 292 3069	88	.000 720 9410	148	.000 039 4556
29	.016 211 5280	89	.000 686 5478	149	.000 037 5977
30	.015 213 7133	90	.000 653 8167	150	.000 035 8274
31	.014 290 6957	91	.000 622 6655	151	.000 034 1405
32	.013 435 3263	92	.000 593 0161	152	.000 032 5330
33	.012 641 3208	93	.000 564 7944	153	.000 031 0013
34	.011 903 1323	94	.000 537 9303	154	.000 029 5418
35	.011 215 8462	95	.000 512 3570	155	.000 028 1510
36	.010 575 0924	96	.000 488 0114	156	.000 026 8257
37	.009 976 9720	97	.000 464 8335	157	.000 025 5629
38	.009 417 9954	98	.000 442 7661	158	.000 024 3595
39	.008 895 0300	99	.000 421 7552	159	.000 023 2128
40	.008 405 2555	100	.000 401 7494	160	.000 022 1201
41	.007 946 1263	101	.000 382 6998	161	.000 021 0789
42	.007 515 3386	102	.000 364 5601	162	.000 020 0867
43	.007 110 8026	103	.000 347 2863	163	.000 019 1412
44	.006 730 6183	104	.000 330 8363	164	.000 018 2402
45	.006 373 0541	105	.000 315 1705	165	.000 017 3817
46	.006 036 5294	106	.000 300 2510	166	.000 016 5636
47	.005 719 5977	107	.000 286 0418	167	.000 015 7840
48	.005 420 9335	108	.000 272 5087	168	.000 015 0411
49	.005 139 3197	109	.000 259 6193	169	.000 014 3332
50	.004 873 6367	110	.000 247 3425	170	.000 013 6586
51	.004 622 8532	111	.000 235 6491	171	.000 013 0158
52	.004 386 0177	112	.000 224 5109	172	.000 012 4032
53	.004 162 2509	113	.000 213 9015	173	.000 011 8195
54	.003 950 7391	114	.000 203 7955	174	.000 011 2632
55	.003 750 7288	115	.000 194 1689	175	.000 010 7331
56	.003 561 5204	116	.000 184 9986	176	.000 010 2280
57	.003 382 4645	117	.000 176 2630	177	.000 009 7467
58	.003 212 9570	118	.000 167 9413	178	.000 009 2880
59	.003 052 4357	119	.000 160 0138	179	.000 008 8509
60	.002 900 3764	120	.000 152 4616	180	.000 008 4344

Sinking Fund

NOMINAL INTEREST RATE COMPOUNDED					
YEARLY @ 5% 5.0000% PER ANNUM		HALF-YEARLY @ 10% 10.0000% PER ANNUM		QUARTERLY @ 20% 20.0000% PER ANNUM	
Periods	Sinking Fund	Periods	Sinking Fund	Periods	Sinking Fund
1	1.000 000 0000	61	.002 686 2736	121	.000 136 8522
2	.487 804 8780	62	.002 551 8273	122	.000 130 3185
3	.317 208 5646	63	.002 424 4196	123	.000 124 0974
4	.232 011 8326	64	.002 303 6520	124	.000 118 1741
5	.180 974 7981	65	.002 189 1514	125	.000 112 5341
6	.147 017 4681	66	.002 080 5683	126	.000 107 1638
7	.122 819 8184	67	.001 977 5751	127	.000 102 0504
8	.104 721 8136	68	.001 879 8643	128	.000 097 1814
9	.090 690 0800	69	.001 787 1473	129	.000 092 5451
10	.079 504 5750	70	.001 699 1530	130	.000 088 1304
11	.070 388 8915	71	.001 615 6265	131	.000 083 9267
12	.062 825 4100	72	.001 536 3280	132	.000 079 9238
13	.056 455 7652	73	.001 461 0318	133	.000 076 1121
14	.051 023 9695	74	.001 389 5254	134	.000 072 4825
15	.046 342 2876	75	.001 321 6085	135	.000 069 0262
16	.042 269 9080	76	.001 257 0925	136	.000 065 7349
17	.038 699 1417	77	.001 195 7993	137	.000 062 6007
18	.035 546 2223	78	.001 137 5610	138	.000 059 6162
19	.032 745 0104	79	.001 082 2189	139	.000 056 7741
20	.030 242 5872	80	.001 029 6235	140	.000 054 0677
21	.027 996 1071	81	.000 979 6332	141	.000 051 4904
22	.025 970 5086	82	.000 932 1143	142	.000 049 0360
23	.024 136 8219	83	.000 886 9406	143	.000 046 6988
24	.022 470 9008	84	.000 843 9924	144	.000 044 4731
25	.020 952 4573	85	.000 803 1567	145	.000 042 3535
26	.019 564 3207	86	.000 764 3265	146	.000 040 3350
27	.018 291 8599	87	.000 727 4005	147	.000 038 4129
28	.017 122 5304	88	.000 692 2828	148	.000 036 5823
29	.016 045 5149	89	.000 658 8825	149	.000 034 8391
30	.015 051 4351	90	.000 627 1136	150	.000 033 1790
31	.014 132 1204	91	.000 596 8946	151	.000 031 5980
32	.013 280 4189	92	.000 568 1481	152	.000 030 0925
33	.012 490 0437	93	.000 540 8008	153	.000 028 6587
34	.011 755 4454	94	.000 514 7832	154	.000 027 2932
35	.011 071 7072	95	.000 490 0295	155	.000 025 9929
36	.010 434 4571	96	.000 466 4770	156	.000 024 7545
37	.009 839 7945	97	.000 444 0666	157	.000 023 5752
38	.009 284 2282	98	.000 422 7418	158	.000 022 4520
39	.008 764 6242	99	.000 402 4492	159	.000 021 3824
40	.008 278 1612	100	.000 383 1381	160	.000 020 3638
41	.007 822 2924	101	.000 364 7603	161	.000 019 3937
42	.007 394 7131	102	.000 347 2701	162	.000 018 4699
43	.006 993 3328	103	.000 330 6241	163	.000 017 5900
44	.006 616 2506	104	.000 314 7810	164	.000 016 7521
45	.006 261 7347	105	.000 299 7016	165	.000 015 9542
46	.005 928 2036	106	.000 285 3486	166	.000 015 1942
47	.005 614 2109	107	.000 271 6867	167	.000 014 4705
48	.005 318 4306	108	.000 258 6824	168	.000 013 7812
49	.005 039 6453	109	.000 246 3035	169	.000 013 1248
50	.004 776 7355	110	.000 234 5197	170	.000 012 4996
51	.004 528 6697	111	.000 223 3022	171	.000 011 9043
52	.004 294 4966	112	.000 212 6236	172	.000 011 3373
53	.004 073 3368	113	.000 202 4576	173	.000 010 7973
54	.003 864 3770	114	.000 192 7796	174	.000 010 2830
55	.003 666 8637	115	.000 183 5659	175	.000 009 7933
56	.003 480 0978	116	.000 174 7942	176	.000 009 3268
57	.003 303 4300	117	.000 166 4429	177	.000 008 8826
58	.003 136 2568	118	.000 158 4919	178	.000 008 4596
59	.002 978 0161	119	.000 150 9219	179	.000 008 0567
60	.002 828 1845	120	.000 143 7145	180	.000 007 6730

NOMINAL INTEREST RATE COMPOUNDED

YEARLY	HALF-YEARLY	QUARTERLY
@	@	@
$5\frac{1}{16}\%$	$10\frac{1}{8}\%$	$20\frac{1}{4}\%$
5.0625%	10.1250%	20.2500%
PER ANNUM	PER ANNUM	PER ANNUM

Periods	Sinking Fund	Periods	Sinking Fund	Periods	Sinking Fund
1	1.000 000 0000	61	.002 617 8814	121	.000 128 9122
2	.487 656 2024	62	.002 485 5439	122	.000 122 6855
3	.317 013 6914	63	.002 360 1928	123	.000 116 7601
4	.231 796 3753	64	.002 241 4302	124	.000 111 1216
5	.180 748 9954	65	.002 128 8837	125	.000 105 7560
6	.146 786 4322	66	.002 022 2046	126	.000 100 6499
7	.122 586 4629	67	.001 921 0658	127	.000 095 7909
8	.104 487 9519	68	.001 825 1608	128	.000 091 1668
9	.090 456 9131	69	.001 734 2016	129	.000 086 7664
10	.079 272 9357	70	.001 647 9180	130	.000 082 5787
11	.070 159 3774	71	.001 566 0557	131	.000 078 5934
12	.062 598 4612	72	.001 488 3758	132	.000 074 8007
13	.056 231 7121	73	.001 414 6534	133	.000 071 1913
14	.050 803 0638	74	.001 344 6769	134	.000 067 7563
15	.046 124 7225	75	.001 278 2468	135	.000 064 4873
16	.042 055 8324	76	.001 215 1753	136	.000 061 3762
17	.038 488 6704	77	.001 155 2851	137	.000 058 4153
18	.035 339 4429	78	.001 098 4091	138	.000 055 5975
19	.032 541 9890	79	.001 044 3897	139	.000 052 9157
20	.030 043 3722	80	.000 993 0780	140	.000 050 3633
21	.027 800 7323	81	.000 944 3333	141	.000 047 9343
22	.025 778 9957	82	.000 898 0229	142	.000 045 6224
23	.023 949 1825	83	.000 854 0211	143	.000 043 4222
24	.022 287 1374	84	.000 812 2094	144	.000 041 3282
25	.020 772 5653	85	.000 772 4754	145	.000 039 3352
26	.019 388 2887	86	.000 734 7130	146	.000 037 4384
27	.018 119 6709	87	.000 698 8217	147	.000 035 6331
28	.016 954 1626	88	.000 664 7065	148	.000 033 9150
29	.015 880 9419	89	.000 632 2772	149	.000 032 2797
30	.014 890 6267	90	.000 601 4485	150	.000 030 7234
31	.013 975 0430	91	.000 572 1399	151	.000 029 2421
32	.013 127 0359	92	.000 544 2746	152	.000 027 8323
33	.012 340 3157	93	.000 517 7801	153	.000 026 4905
34	.011 609 3305	94	.000 492 5878	154	.000 025 2134
35	.010 929 1615	95	.000 468 6324	155	.000 023 9979
36	.010 295 4346	96	.000 445 8522	156	.000 022 8410
37	.009 704 2476	97	.000 424 1886	157	.000 021 7399
38	.009 152 1079	98	.000 403 5858	158	.000 020 6919
39	.008 635 8799	99	.000 383 9913	159	.000 019 6945
40	.008 152 7413	100	.000 365 3549	160	.000 018 7451
41	.007 700 1442	101	.000 347 6292	161	.000 017 8416
42	.007 275 7831	102	.000 330 7690	162	.000 016 9816
43	.006 877 5666	103	.000 314 7316	163	.000 016 1631
44	.006 503 5933	104	.000 299 4764	164	.000 015 3840
45	.006 152 1307	105	.000 284 9647	165	.000 014 6425
46	.005 821 5972	106	.000 271 1600	166	.000 013 9367
47	.005 510 5456	107	.000 258 0274	167	.000 013 2650
48	.005 217 6500	108	.000 245 5338	168	.000 012 6257
49	.004 941 6928	109	.000 233 6480	169	.000 012 0172
50	.004 681 5543	110	.000 222 3401	170	.000 011 4380
51	.004 436 2032	111	.000 211 5818	171	.000 010 8867
52	.004 204 6880	112	.000 201 3460	172	.000 010 3620
53	.003 986 1297	113	.000 191 6073	173	.000 009 8626
54	.003 779 7152	114	.000 182 3413	174	.000 009 3873
55	.003 584 6911	115	.000 173 5250	175	.000 008 9349
56	.003 400 3587	116	.000 165 1363	176	.000 008 5043
57	.003 226 0692	117	.000 157 1544	177	.000 008 0944
58	.003 061 2192	118	.000 149 5595	178	.000 007 7043
59	.002 905 2475	119	.000 142 3326	179	.000 007 3330
60	.002 757 6308	120	.000 135 4559	180	.000 006 9796

NOMINAL INTEREST RATE COMPOUNDED

YEARLY	HALF-YEARLY	QUARTERLY
@	@	@
$5\frac{1}{8}\%$	**$10\frac{1}{4}\%$**	**$20\frac{1}{2}\%$**
5.1250%	10.2500%	20.5000%
PER ANNUM	PER ANNUM	PER ANNUM

Periods	Sinking Fund	Periods	Sinking Fund	Periods	Sinking Fund
1	1.000 000 0000	61	.002 551 0823	121	.000 121 4212
2	.487 507 6173	62	.002 420 8386	122	.000 115 4884
3	.316 818 9790	63	.002 297 5283	123	.000 109 8461
4	.231 581 1439	64	.002 180 7543	124	.000 104 4800
5	.180 523 4812	65	.002 070 1449	125	.000 099 3766
6	.146 555 7458	66	.001 965 3521	126	.000 094 5229
7	.122 353 5171	67	.001 866 0496	127	.000 089 9067
8	.104 254 5590	68	.001 771 9316	128	.000 085 5163
9	.090 224 2732	69	.001 682 7110	129	.000 081 3406
10	.079 041 8806	70	.001 598 1183	130	.000 077 3692
11	.069 930 5037	71	.001 517 9001	131	.000 073 5919
12	.062 372 2081	72	.001 441 8184	132	.000 069 9993
13	.056 008 4090	73	.001 369 6491	133	.000 066 5823
14	.050 582 9611	74	.001 301 1814	134	.000 063 3323
15	.045 908 0123	75	.001 236 2167	135	.000 060 2411
16	.041 842 6624	76	.001 174 5681	136	.000 057 3010
17	.038 279 1540	77	.001 116 0592	137	.000 054 5045
18	.035 133 6666	78	.001 060 5237	138	.000 051 8446
19	.032 340 0173	79	.001 007 8049	139	.000 049 3147
20	.029 845 2521	80	.000 957 7547	140	.000 046 9083
21	.027 606 4964	81	.000 910 2335	141	.000 044 6195
22	.025 588 6640	82	.000 865 1092	142	.000 042 4424
23	.023 762 7649	83	.000 822 2572	143	.000 040 3717
24	.022 104 6351	84	.000 781 5596	144	.000 038 4020
25	.020 593 9718	85	.000 742 9051	145	.000 036 5285
26	.019 213 5911	86	.000 706 1883	146	.000 034 7465
27	.017 948 8506	87	.000 671 3096	147	.000 033 0515
28	.016 787 1960	88	.000 638 1748	148	.000 031 4392
29	.015 717 8009	89	.000 606 6945	149	.000 029 9056
30	.014 731 2795	90	.000 576 7844	150	.000 028 4468
31	.013 819 4542	91	.000 548 3644	151	.000 027 0593
32	.012 975 1672	92	.000 521 3589	152	.000 025 7394
33	.012 192 1258	93	.000 495 6960	153	.000 024 4840
34	.011 464 7761	94	.000 471 3078	154	.000 023 2898
35	.010 788 1967	95	.000 448 1300	155	.000 022 1539
36	.010 158 0120	96	.000 426 1013	156	.000 021 0734
37	.009 570 3178	97	.000 405 1640	157	.000 020 0457
38	.009 021 6200	98	.000 385 2632	158	.000 019 0680
39	.008 508 7819	99	.000 366 3468	159	.000 018 1381
40	.008 028 9799	100	.000 348 3654	160	.000 017 2536
41	.007 579 6651	101	.000 331 2723	161	.000 016 4122
42	.007 158 5311	102	.000 315 0230	162	.000 015 6118
43	.006 763 4858	103	.000 299 5754	163	.000 014 8505
44	.006 392 6272	104	.000 284 8895	164	.000 014 1263
45	.006 044 2224	105	.000 270 9273	165	.000 013 4374
46	.005 716 6891	106	.000 257 6528	166	.000 012 7822
47	.005 408 5802	107	.000 245 0318	167	.000 012 1589
48	.005 118 5693	108	.000 233 0318	168	.000 011 5660
49	.004 845 4389	109	.000 221 6220	169	.000 011 0020
50	.004 588 0691	110	.000 210 7732	170	.000 010 4655
51	.004 345 4288	111	.000 200 4575	171	.000 009 9552
52	.004 116 5665	112	.000 190 6485	172	.000 009 4698
53	.003 900 6035	113	.000 181 3212	173	.000 009 0080
54	.003 696 7268	114	.000 172 4518	174	.000 008 5688
55	.003 504 1833	115	.000 164 0176	175	.000 008 1510
56	.003 322 2749	116	.000 155 9972	176	.000 007 7536
57	.003 150 3530	117	.000 148 3701	177	.000 007 3755
58	.002 987 8148	118	.000 141 1169	178	.000 007 0159
59	.002 834 0994	119	.000 134 2192	179	.000 006 6738
60	.002 688 6844	120	.000 127 6595	180	.000 006 3484

NOMINAL INTEREST RATE COMPOUNDED

	YEARLY @ $5\frac{3}{16}\%$ 5.1875% PER ANNUM		HALF-YEARLY @ $10\frac{3}{8}\%$ 10.3750% PER ANNUM		QUARTERLY @ $20\frac{3}{4}\%$ 20.7500% PER ANNUM
Periods	Sinking Fund	Periods	Sinking Fund	Periods	Sinking Fund
1	1.000 000 0000	61	.002 485 8451	121	.000 114 3548
2	.487 359 1228	62	.002 357 6797	122	.000 108 7034
3	.316 624 4274	63	.002 236 3940	123	.000 103 3318
4	.231 366 1380	64	.002 121 5917	124	.000 098 2262
5	.180 298 2551	65	.002 012 9019	125	.000 093 3732
6	.146 325 4086	66	.001 909 9772	126	.000 088 7605
7	.122 120 9804	67	.001 812 4924	127	.000 084 3760
8	.104 021 6342	68	.001 720 1422	128	.000 080 2084
9	.089 992 1594	69	.001 632 6406	129	.000 076 2470
10	.078 811 4087	70	.001 549 7188	130	.000 072 4815
11	.069 702 2695	71	.001 471 1244	131	.000 068 9022
12	.062 146 6495	72	.001 396 6202	132	.000 065 4999
13	.055 785 8544	73	.001 325 9829	133	.000 062 2658
14	.050 363 6597	74	.001 259 0027	134	.000 059 1915
15	.045 692 1550	75	.001 195 4820	135	.000 056 2692
16	.041 630 3958	76	.001 135 2345	136	.000 053 4914
17	.038 070 5902	77	.001 078 0850	137	.000 050 8507
18	.034 928 8905	78	.001 023 8680	138	.000 048 3406
19	.032 139 0923	79	.000 972 4277	139	.000 045 9545
20	.029 648 2237	80	.000 923 6169	140	.000 043 6863
21	.027 413 3953	81	.000 877 2969	141	.000 041 5301
22	.025 399 5090	82	.000 833 3364	142	.000 039 4804
23	.023 577 5643	83	.000 791 6119	143	.000 037 5320
24	.021 923 3884	84	.000 752 0063	144	.000 035 6797
25	.020 416 6710	85	.000 714 4091	145	.000 033 9190
26	.019 040 2216	86	.000 678 7158	146	.000 032 2452
27	.017 779 3920	87	.000 644 8277	147	.000 030 6540
28	.016 621 6230	88	.000 612 6514	148	.000 029 1414
29	.015 556 0838	89	.000 582 0984	149	.000 027 7035
30	.014 573 3847	90	.000 553 0851	150	.000 026 3365
31	.013 665 3446	91	.000 525 5325	151	.000 025 0371
32	.012 824 8026	92	.000 499 3655	152	.000 023 8018
33	.012 045 4635	93	.000 474 5131	153	.000 022 6274
34	.011 321 7707	94	.000 450 9083	154	.000 021 5111
35	.010 648 8008	95	.000 428 4873	155	.000 020 4498
36	.010 022 1763	96	.000 407 1899	156	.000 019 4409
37	.009 437 9913	97	.000 386 9588	157	.000 018 4818
38	.008 892 7502	98	.000 367 7400	158	.000 017 5700
39	.008 383 3150	99	.000 349 4821	159	.000 016 7032
40	.007 906 8609	100	.000 332 1365	160	.000 015 8792
41	.007 460 8381	101	.000 315 6569	161	.000 015 0959
42	.007 042 9394	102	.000 299 9997	162	.000 014 3512
43	.006 651 0719	103	.000 285 1234	163	.000 013 6433
44	.006 283 3331	104	.000 270 9886	164	.000 012 9703
45	.005 937 9895	105	.000 257 5580	165	.000 012 3305
46	.005 613 4587	106	.000 244 7961	166	.000 011 7222
47	.005 308 2931	107	.000 232 6695	167	.000 011 1440
48	.005 021 1663	108	.000 221 1461	168	.000 010 5943
49	.004 750 8605	109	.000 210 1957	169	.000 010 0717
50	.004 496 2562	110	.000 199 7896	170	.000 009 5749
51	.004 256 3220	111	.000 189 9006	171	.000 009 1026
52	.004 030 1067	112	.000 180 5027	172	.000 008 6537
53	.003 816 7319	113	.000 171 5715	173	.000 008 2268
54	.003 615 3849	114	.000 163 0835	174	.000 007 8210
55	.003 425 3129	115	.000 155 0168	175	.000 007 4353
56	.003 245 8182	116	.000 147 3501	176	.000 007 0685
57	.003 076 2526	117	.000 140 0637	177	.000 006 7199
58	.002 916 0140	118	.000 133 1385	178	.000 006 3885
59	.002 764 5419	119	.000 126 5565	179	.000 006 0734
60	.002 621 3145	120	.000 120 3007	180	.000 005 7738

NOMINAL INTEREST RATE COMPOUNDED

YEARLY	HALF-YEARLY	QUARTERLY
@	@	@
$5\frac{1}{4}$%	$10\frac{1}{2}$%	21%
5.2500%	10.5000%	21.0000%
PER ANNUM	PER ANNUM	PER ANNUM

Periods	Sinking Fund	Periods	Sinking Fund	Periods	Sinking Fund
1	1.000 000 0000	61	.002 422 1390	121	.000 107 6898
2	.487 210 7186	62	.002 296 0358	122	.000 102 3076
3	.316 430 0363	63	.002 176 7581	123	.000 097 1950
4	.231 151 3576	64	.002 063 9102	124	.000 092 3382
5	.180 073 3168	65	.001 957 1220	125	.000 087 7246
6	.146 095 4203	66	.001 856 0470	126	.000 083 3418
7	.121 888 8524	67	.001 760 3607	127	.000 079 1784
8	.103 789 1770	68	.001 669 7590	128	.000 075 2232
9	.089 760 5712	69	.001 583 9565	129	.000 071 4659
10	.078 581 5194	70	.001 502 6853	130	.000 067 8964
11	.069 474 6736	71	.001 425 6940	131	.000 064 5055
12	.061 921 7842	72	.001 352 7462	132	.000 061 2842
13	.055 564 0468	73	.001 283 6198	133	.000 058 2238
14	.050 145 1581	74	.001 218 1056	134	.000 055 3165
15	.045 477 1489	75	.001 156 0071	135	.000 052 5545
16	.041 419 0304	76	.001 097 1390	136	.000 049 9305
17	.037 862 9764	77	.001 041 3269	137	.000 047 4377
18	.034 725 1119	78	.000 988 4063	138	.000 045 0694
19	.031 939 2107	79	.000 938 2223	139	.000 042 8194
20	.029 452 2832	80	.000 890 6287	140	.000 040 6819
21	.027 221 4252	81	.000 845 4876	141	.000 038 6511
22	.025 211 5264	82	.000 802 6688	142	.000 036 7218
23	.023 393 5759	83	.000 762 0495	143	.000 034 8889
24	.021 743 3921	84	.000 723 5137	144	.000 033 1475
25	.020 240 6571	85	.000 686 9517	145	.000 031 4930
26	.018 868 1737	86	.000 652 2600	146	.000 029 9212
27	.017 611 2882	87	.000 619 3406	147	.000 028 4279
28	.016 457 4362	88	.000 588 1011	148	.000 027 0092
29	.015 395 7825	89	.000 558 4538	149	.000 025 6613
30	.014 416 9335	90	.000 530 3161	150	.000 024 3806
31	.013 512 7048	91	.000 503 6095	151	.000 023 1640
32	.012 675 9322	92	.000 478 2600	152	.000 022 0080
33	.011 900 3179	93	.000 454 1974	153	.000 020 9098
34	.011 180 3028	94	.000 431 3554	154	.000 019 8664
35	.010 510 9616	95	.000 409 6709	155	.000 018 8751
36	.009 887 9146	96	.000 389 0846	156	.000 017 9333
37	.009 307 2544	97	.000 369 5399	157	.000 017 0384
38	.008 765 4839	98	.000 350 9836	158	.000 016 1883
39	.008 259 4639	99	.000 333 3649	159	.000 015 3806
40	.007 786 3683	100	.000 316 6360	160	.000 014 6131
41	.007 343 6465	101	.000 300 7513	161	.000 013 8840
42	.006 928 9905	102	.000 285 6678	162	.000 013 1913
43	.006 540 3066	103	.000 271 3447	163	.000 012 5331
44	.006 175 6919	104	.000 257 7433	164	.000 011 9078
45	.005 833 4124	105	.000 244 8268	165	.000 011 3137
46	.005 511 8853	106	.000 232 5604	166	.000 010 7493
47	.005 209 6629	107	.000 220 9112	167	.000 010 2130
48	.004 925 4187	108	.000 209 8478	168	.000 009 7034
49	.004 657 9348	109	.000 199 3406	169	.000 009 2193
50	.004 406 0917	110	.000 189 3614	170	.000 008 7594
51	.004 168 8583	111	.000 179 8834	171	.000 008 3224
52	.003 945 2836	112	.000 170 8814	172	.000 007 9072
53	.003 734 4893	113	.000 162 3313	173	.000 007 5127
54	.003 535 6631	114	.000 154 2102	174	.000 007 1379
55	.003 348 0527	115	.000 146 4966	175	.000 006 7818
56	.003 170 9607	116	.000 139 1698	176	.000 006 4435
57	.003 003 7397	117	.000 132 2103	177	.000 006 1221
58	.002 845 7878	118	.000 125 5997	178	.000 005 8166
59	.002 696 5454	119	.000 119 3204	179	.000 005 5265
60	.002 555 4911	120	.000 113 3557	180	.000 005 2508

NOMINAL INTEREST RATE COMPOUNDED

	YEARLY @ $5\frac{5}{16}\%$ 5.3125% PER ANNUM		HALF-YEARLY @ $10\frac{5}{8}\%$ 10.6250% PER ANNUM		QUARTERLY @ $21\frac{1}{4}\%$ 21.2500% PER ANNUM
Periods	Sinking Fund	Periods	Sinking Fund	Periods	Sinking Fund
1	1.000 000 0000	61	.002 359 9337	121	.000 101 4043
2	.487 062 4049	62	.002 235 8762	122	.000 096 2797
3	.316 235 8057	63	.002 118 5893	123	.000 091 4145
4	.230 936 8023	64	.002 007 6779	124	.000 086 7956
5	.179 848 6661	65	.001 902 7730	125	.000 082 4104
6	.145 865 7805	66	.001 803 5288	126	.000 078 2470
7	.121 657 1327	67	.001 709 6218	127	.000 074 2943
8	.103 557 1867	68	.001 620 7486	128	.000 070 5416
9	.089 529 5077	69	.001 536 6250	129	.000 066 9786
10	.078 352 2115	70	.001 456 9839	130	.000 063 5958
11	.069 247 7150	71	.001 381 5748	131	.000 060 3841
12	.061 697 6109	72	.001 310 1623	132	.000 057 3347
13	.055 342 9849	73	.001 242 5252	133	.000 054 4395
14	.049 927 4545	74	.001 178 4555	134	.000 051 6906
15	.045 262 9921	75	.001 117 7574	135	.000 049 0807
16	.041 208 5642	76	.001 060 2467	136	.000 046 6026
17	.037 656 3102	77	.001 005 7499	137	.000 044 2498
18	.034 522 3280	78	.000 954 1036	138	.000 042 0158
19	.031 740 3695	79	.000 905 1537	139	.000 039 8947
20	.029 257 4271	80	.000 858 7550	140	.000 037 8808
21	.027 030 5821	81	.000 814 7706	141	.000 035 9686
22	.025 024 7118	82	.000 773 0713	142	.000 034 1530
23	.023 210 7949	83	.000 733 5352	143	.000 032 4291
24	.021 564 6409	84	.000 696 0471	144	.000 030 7923
25	.020 065 9242	85	.000 660 4984	145	.000 029 2381
26	.018 697 4412	86	.000 626 7864	146	.000 027 7624
27	.017 444 5323	87	.000 594 8141	147	.000 026 3612
28	.016 294 6280	88	.000 564 4898	148	.000 025 0308
29	.015 236 8889	89	.000 535 7269	149	.000 023 7676
30	.014 261 9173	90	.000 508 4434	150	.000 022 5681
31	.013 361 5253	91	.000 482 5620	151	.000 021 4292
32	.012 528 5458	92	.000 458 0092	152	.000 020 3478
33	.011 756 6782	93	.000 434 7158	153	.000 019 3210
34	.011 040 3610	94	.000 412 6162	154	.000 018 3460
35	.010 374 6668	95	.000 391 6483	155	.000 017 4202
36	.009 755 2140	96	.000 371 7533	156	.000 016 5412
37	.009 178 0935	97	.000 352 8756	157	.000 015 7065
38	.008 639 8068	98	.000 334 9625	158	.000 014 9140
39	.008 137 2134	99	.000 317 9642	159	.000 014 1614
40	.007 667 4862	100	.000 301 8333	160	.000 013 4469
41	.007 228 0736	101	.000 286 5252	161	.000 012 7684
42	.006 816 6668	102	.000 271 9974	162	.000 012 1241
43	.006 431 1717	103	.000 258 2098	163	.000 011 5124
44	.006 069 6845	104	.000 245 1242	164	.000 010 9315
45	.005 730 4711	105	.000 232 7048	165	.000 010 3800
46	.005 411 9483	106	.000 220 9171	166	.000 009 8563
47	.005 112 6683	107	.000 209 7289	167	.000 009 3590
48	.004 831 3044	108	.000 199 1095	168	.000 008 8868
49	.004 566 6389	109	.000 189 0297	169	.000 008 4384
50	.004 317 5522	110	.000 179 4618	170	.000 008 0127
51	.004 083 0135	111	.000 170 3798	171	.000 007 6084
52	.003 862 0720	112	.000 161 7588	172	.000 007 2246
53	.003 653 8498	113	.000 153 5753	173	.000 006 8601
54	.003 457 5350	114	.000 145 8069	174	.000 006 5140
55	.003 272 3757	115	.000 138 4325	175	.000 006 1853
56	.003 097 6749	116	.000 131 4320	176	.000 005 8733
57	.002 932 7859	117	.000 124 7863	177	.000 005 5770
58	.002 777 1074	118	.000 118 4774	178	.000 005 2956
59	.002 630 0803	119	.000 112 4881	179	.000 005 0284
60	.002 491 1842	120	.000 106 8023	180	.000 004 7748

Sinking Fund

NOMINAL INTEREST RATE COMPOUNDED

YEARLY	HALF-YEARLY	QUARTERLY
@	@	@
$5\frac{3}{8}\%$	$10\frac{3}{4}\%$	$21\frac{1}{2}\%$
5.3750%	10.7500%	21.5000%
PER ANNUM	PER ANNUM	PER ANNUM

Periods	Sinking Fund	Periods	Sinking Fund	Periods	Sinking Fund
1	1.000 000 0000	61	.002 299 1990	121	.000 095 4775
2	.486 914 1814	62	.002 177 1704	122	.000 090 5992
3	.316 041 7353	63	.002 061 8566	123	.000 085 9705
4	.230 722 4720	64	.001 952 8636	124	.000 081 5786
5	.179 624 3026	65	.001 849 8232	125	.000 077 4114
6	.145 636 4886	66	.001 752 3906	126	.000 073 4574
7	.121 425 8206	67	.001 660 2431	127	.000 069 7056
8	.103 325 6628	68	.001 573 0784	128	.000 066 1457
9	.089 298 9682	69	.001 490 6131	129	.000 062 7677
10	.078 123 4844	70	.001 412 5813	130	.000 059 5625
11	.069 021 3928	71	.001 338 7333	131	.000 056 5211
12	.061 474 1284	72	.001 268 8348	132	.000 053 6352
13	.055 122 6672	73	.001 202 6655	133	.000 050 8968
14	.049 710 5473	74	.001 140 0185	134	.000 048 2983
15	.045 049 6825	75	.001 080 6989	135	.000 045 8326
16	.040 998 9948	76	.001 024 5236	136	.000 043 4928
17	.037 450 5891	77	.000 971 3200	137	.000 041 2726
18	.034 320 5360	78	.000 920 9257	138	.000 039 1659
19	.031 542 5654	79	.000 873 1877	139	.000 037 1667
20	.029 063 6520	80	.000 827 9618	140	.000 035 2696
21	.026 840 8621	81	.000 785 1120	141	.000 033 4695
22	.024 839 0608	82	.000 744 5101	142	.000 031 7612
23	.023 029 2163	83	.000 706 0350	143	.000 030 1403
24	.021 387 1293	84	.000 669 5727	144	.000 028 6020
25	.019 892 4665	85	.000 635 0155	145	.000 027 1424
26	.018 528 0176	86	.000 602 2615	146	.000 025 7572
27	.017 279 1172	87	.000 571 2147	147	.000 024 4428
28	.016 133 1909	88	.000 541 7843	148	.000 023 1955
29	.015 079 3947	89	.000 513 8846	149	.000 022 0118
30	.014 108 3271	90	.000 487 4345	150	.000 020 8886
31	.013 211 7967	91	.000 462 3574	151	.000 019 8227
32	.012 382 6333	92	.000 438 5809	152	.000 018 8112
33	.011 614 5336	93	.000 416 0365	153	.000 017 8514
34	.010 901 9338	94	.000 394 6593	154	.000 016 9405
35	.010 239 9042	95	.000 374 3882	155	.000 016 0762
36	.009 624 0614	96	.000 355 1651	156	.000 015 2559
37	.009 050 4948	97	.000 336 9352	157	.000 014 4775
38	.008 515 7044	98	.000 319 6465	158	.000 013 7389
39	.008 016 5483	99	.000 303 2499	159	.000 013 0379
40	.007 550 1986	100	.000 287 6988	160	.000 012 3727
41	.007 114 1027	101	.000 272 9493	161	.000 011 7414
42	.006 705 9510	102	.000 258 9595	162	.000 011 1424
43	.006 323 6488	103	.000 245 6901	163	.000 010 5739
44	.005 965 2920	104	.000 233 1035	164	.000 010 0345
45	.005 629 1459	105	.000 221 1643	165	.000 009 5226
46	.005 313 6272	106	.000 209 8391	166	.000 009 0367
47	.005 017 2880	107	.000 199 0959	167	.000 008 5757
48	.004 738 8015	108	.000 188 9047	168	.000 008 1382
49	.004 476 9500	109	.000 179 2368	169	.000 007 7230
50	.004 230 6143	110	.000 170 0653	170	.000 007 3291
51	.003 998 7635	111	.000 161 3645	171	.000 006 9552
52	.003 780 4474	112	.000 153 1102	172	.000 006 6003
53	.003 574 7882	113	.000 145 2792	173	.000 006 2636
54	.003 380 9745	114	.000 137 8497	174	.000 005 9441
55	.003 198 2551	115	.000 130 8011	175	.000 005 6409
56	.003 025 9335	116	.000 124 1138	176	.000 005 3531
57	.002 863 3633	117	.000 117 7691	177	.000 005 0800
58	.002 709 9443	118	.000 111 7494	178	.000 004 8209
59	.002 565 1179	119	.000 106 0380	179	.000 004 5750
60	.002 428 3643	120	.000 100 6190	180	.000 004 3416

Sinking Fund

NOMINAL INTEREST RATE COMPOUNDED

YEARLY	HALF-YEARLY	QUARTERLY
@	@	@
$5\frac{7}{16}\%$	$10\frac{7}{8}\%$	$21\frac{3}{4}\%$
7.4375%	10.8750%	21.7500%
PER ANNUM	PER ANNUM	PER ANNUM

Periods	Sinking Fund	Periods	Sinking Fund	Periods	Sinking Fund
1	1.000 000 0000	61	.002 239 9055	121	.000 089 8896
2	.486 766 0481	62	.002 119 8882	122	.000 085 2467
3	.315 847 8250	63	.002 006 5295	123	.000 080 8439
4	.230 508 3664	64	.001 899 4364	124	.000 076 6688
5	.179 400 2261	65	.001 798 2414	125	.000 072 7097
6	.145 407 5445	66	.001 702 6008	126	.000 068 9552
7	.121 194 9158	67	.001 612 1929	127	.000 065 3949
8	.103 094 6047	68	.001 526 7163	128	.000 062 0185
9	.089 068 9521	69	.001 445 8887	129	.000 058 8167
10	.077 895 3371	70	.001 369 4450	130	.000 055 7804
11	.068 795 7059	71	.001 297 1368	131	.000 052 9010
12	.061 251 3356	72	.001 228 7308	132	.000 050 1703
13	.054 903 0923	73	.001 164 0076	133	.000 047 5807
14	.049 494 4348	74	.001 102 7613	134	.000 045 1249
15	.044 837 2183	75	.001 044 7983	135	.000 042 7959
16	.040 790 3202	76	.000 989 9362	136	.000 040 5873
17	.037 245 8107	77	.000 938 0037	137	.000 038 4927
18	.034 119 7331	78	.000 888 8393	138	.000 036 5062
19	.031 345 7953	79	.000 842 2911	139	.000 034 6224
20	.028 870 9541	80	.000 798 2158	140	.000 032 8358
21	.026 652 2612	81	.000 756 4784	141	.000 031 1415
22	.024 654 5690	82	.000 716 9518	142	.000 029 5346
23	.022 848 8354	83	.000 679 5159	143	.000 028 0107
24	.021 210 8520	84	.000 644 0577	144	.000 026 5654
25	.019 720 2780	85	.000 610 4702	145	.000 025 1948
26	.018 359 8964	86	.000 578 6527	146	.000 023 8949
27	.017 115 0360	87	.000 548 5101	147	.000 022 6621
28	.015 973 1173	88	.000 519 9524	148	.000 021 4930
29	.014 923 2918	89	.000 492 8950	149	.000 020 3841
30	.013 956 1542	90	.000 467 2576	150	.000 019 3325
31	.013 063 5095	91	.000 442 9644	151	.000 018 3352
32	.012 238 1846	92	.000 419 9439	152	.000 017 3893
33	.011 473 8733	93	.000 398 1285	153	.000 016 4923
34	.010 765 0096	94	.000 377 4541	154	.000 015 6415
35	.010 106 6615	95	.000 357 8604	155	.000 014 8346
36	.009 494 4440	96	.000 339 2901	156	.000 014 0694
37	.008 924 4447	97	.000 321 6891	157	.000 013 3437
38	.008 393 1622	98	.000 305 0063	158	.000 012 6554
39	.007 897 4535	99	.000 289 1932	159	.000 012 0026
40	.007 434 4896	100	.000 274 2040	160	.000 011 3835
41	.007 001 7171	101	.000 259 9955	161	.000 010 7963
42	.006 596 8256	102	.000 246 5265	162	.000 010 2394
43	.006 217 7198	103	.000 233 7583	163	.000 009 7113
44	.005 862 4953	104	.000 221 6540	164	.000 009 2104
45	.005 529 4171	105	.000 210 1790	165	.000 008 7353
46	.005 216 9016	106	.000 199 3001	166	.000 008 2847
47	.004 923 5008	107	.000 188 9863	167	.000 007 8574
48	.004 647 8881	108	.000 179 2080	168	.000 007 4522
49	.004 388 8457	109	.000 169 9372	169	.000 007 0678
50	.004 145 2546	110	.000 161 1475	170	.000 006 7033
51	.003 916 0844	111	.000 152 8136	171	.000 006 3575
52	.003 700 3849	112	.000 144 9119	172	.000 006 0296
53	.003 497 2791	113	.000 137 4198	173	.000 005 7186
54	.003 305 9559	114	.000 130 3159	174	.000 005 4237
55	.003 125 6646	115	.000 123 5801	175	.000 005 1440
56	.002 955 7093	116	.000 117 1933	176	.000 004 8787
57	.002 795 4445	117	.000 111 1372	177	.000 004 6270
58	.002 644 2704	118	.000 105 3946	178	.000 004 3884
59	.002 501 6293	119	.000 099 9493	179	.000 004 1621
60	.002 367 0022	120	.000 094 7859	180	.000 003 9474

NOMINAL INTEREST RATE COMPOUNDED

YEARLY	HALF-YEARLY	QUARTERLY
@	@	@
$5\frac{1}{2}\%$	11%	22%
5.5000%	11.0000%	22.0000%
PER ANNUM	PER ANNUM	PER ANNUM

Periods	Sinking Fund	Periods	Sinking Fund	Periods	Sinking Fund
1	1.000 000 0000	61	.002 182 0238	121	.000 084 6219
2	.486 618 0049	62	.002 064 0001	122	.000 080 2039
3	.315 654 0747	63	.001 952 5782	123	.000 076 0169
4	.230 294 4853	64	.001 847 3659	124	.000 072 0487
5	.179 176 4362	65	.001 747 9969	125	.000 068 2880
6	.145 178 9476	66	.001 654 1284	126	.000 064 7237
7	.120 964 4178	67	.001 565 4398	127	.000 061 3457
8	.102 864 0118	68	.001 481 6307	128	.000 058 1442
9	.088 839 4585	69	.001 402 4198	129	.000 055 1100
10	.077 667 7687	70	.001 327 5431	130	.000 052 2342
11	.068 570 6532	71	.001 256 7533	131	.000 049 5087
12	.061 029 2312	72	.001 189 8180	132	.000 046 9254
13	.054 684 2587	73	.001 126 5191	133	.000 044 4771
14	.049 279 1154	74	.001 066 6516	134	.000 042 1566
15	.044 625 5976	75	.001 010 0230	135	.000 039 9573
16	.040 582 5380	76	.000 956 4521	136	.000 037 8728
17	.037 041 9723	77	.000 905 7685	137	.000 035 8971
18	.033 919 9163	78	.000 857 8119	138	.000 034 0245
19	.031 150 0559	79	.000 812 4313	139	.000 032 2497
20	.028 679 3300	80	.000 769 4845	140	.000 030 5675
21	.026 464 7754	81	.000 728 8376	141	.000 028 9731
22	.024 471 2319	82	.000 690 3644	142	.000 027 4619
23	.022 669 6472	83	.000 653 9459	143	.000 026 0295
24	.021 035 8037	84	.000 619 4699	144	.000 024 6719
25	.019 549 3529	85	.000 586 8307	145	.000 023 3852
26	.018 193 0713	86	.000 555 9284	146	.000 022 1656
27	.016 952 2817	87	.000 526 6688	147	.000 021 0096
28	.015 814 3996	88	.000 498 9631	148	.000 019 9139
29	.014 768 5720	89	.000 472 7272	149	.000 018 8754
30	.013 805 3897	90	.000 447 8820	150	.000 017 8910
31	.012 916 6543	91	.000 424 3525	151	.000 016 9580
32	.012 095 1895	92	.000 402 0682	152	.000 016 0737
33	.011 334 6865	93	.000 380 9621	153	.000 015 2355
34	.010 629 5769	94	.000 360 9712	154	.000 014 4410
35	.009 974 9266	95	.000 342 0357	155	.000 013 6880
36	.009 366 3488	96	.000 324 0994	156	.000 012 9742
37	.008 799 9295	97	.000 307 1089	157	.000 012 2977
38	.008 272 1659	98	.000 291 0137	158	.000 011 6564
39	.007 779 9139	99	.000 275 7663	159	.000 011 0486
40	.007 320 3434	100	.000 261 3216	160	.000 010 4725
41	.006 890 9001	101	.000 247 6369	161	.000 009 9265
42	.006 489 2731	102	.000 234 6718	162	.000 009 4089
43	.006 113 3667	103	.000 222 3883	163	.000 008 9183
44	.005 761 2757	104	.000 210 7501	164	.000 008 4533
45	.005 431 2651	105	.000 199 7233	165	.000 008 0125
46	.005 121 7512	106	.000 189 2753	166	.000 007 5948
47	.004 831 2858	107	.000 179 3757	167	.000 007 1988
48	.004 558 5424	108	.000 169 9955	168	.000 006 8234
49	.004 302 3035	109	.000 161 1072	169	.000 006 4677
50	.004 061 4501	110	.000 152 6849	170	.000 006 1305
51	.003 834 9523	111	.000 144 7041	171	.000 005 8108
52	.003 621 8603	112	.000 137 1415	172	.000 005 5079
53	.003 421 2975	113	.000 129 9750	173	.000 005 2207
54	.003 232 4534	114	.000 123 1839	174	.000 004 9485
55	.003 054 5778	115	.000 116 7483	175	.000 004 6905
56	.002 886 9756	116	.000 110 6497	176	.000 004 4460
57	.002 729 0020	117	.000 104 8702	177	.000 004 2142
58	.002 580 0578	118	.000 099 3932	178	.000 003 9944
59	.002 439 5863	119	.000 094 2027	179	.000 003 7862
60	.002 307 0692	120	.000 089 2837	180	.000 003 5888

Sinking Fund

NOMINAL INTEREST RATE COMPOUNDED

YEARLY	HALF-YEARLY	QUARTERLY
@	@	@
$5\frac{9}{16}\%$	$11\frac{1}{8}\%$	$22\frac{1}{4}\%$
5.5625%	11.1250%	22.2500%
PER ANNUM	PER ANNUM	PER ANNUM

Periods	Sinking Fund	Periods	Sinking Fund	Periods	Sinking Fund
1	1.000 000 0000	61	.002 125 5252	121	.000 079 6566
2	.486 470 0517	62	.002 009 4768	122	.000 075 4535
3	.315 460 4842	63	.001 899 9729	123	.000 071 4724
4	.230 080 8285	64	.001 796 6223	124	.000 067 7017
5	.178 952 9326	65	.001 699 0595	125	.000 064 1301
6	.144 950 6977	66	.001 606 9430	126	.000 060 7472
7	.120 734 3260	67	.001 519 9531	127	.000 057 5428
8	.102 633 8835	68	.001 437 7907	128	.000 054 5077
9	.088 610 4868	69	.001 360 1753	129	.000 051 6328
10	.077 440 7784	70	.001 286 8442	130	.000 048 9097
11	.068 346 2336	71	.001 217 5511	131	.000 046 3303
12	.060 807 8139	72	.001 152 0648	132	.000 043 8871
13	.054 466 1651	73	.001 090 1683	133	.000 041 5728
14	.049 064 5875	74	.001 031 6576	134	.000 039 3806
15	.044 414 8184	75	.000 976 3414	135	.000 037 3041
16	.040 375 6461	76	.000 924 0395	136	.000 035 3371
17	.036 839 0715	77	.000 874 5827	137	.000 033 4739
18	.033 721 0829	78	.000 827 8117	138	.000 031 7091
19	.030 955 3441	79	.000 783 5766	139	.000 030 0373
20	.028 488 7761	80	.000 741 7363	140	.000 028 4537
21	.026 278 4006	81	.000 702 1580	141	.000 026 9536
22	.024 289 0452	82	.000 664 7164	142	.000 025 5327
23	.022 491 6467	83	.000 629 2936	143	.000 024 1867
24	.020 861 9789	84	.000 595 7785	144	.000 022 9117
25	.019 379 6853	85	.000 564 0663	145	.000 021 7039
26	.018 027 5357	86	.000 534 0580	146	.000 020 5598
27	.016 790 8472	87	.000 505 6606	147	.000 019 4761
28	.015 657 0301	88	.000 478 7860	148	.000 018 4494
29	.014 615 2270	89	.000 453 3513	149	.000 017 4770
30	.013 656 0248	90	.000 429 2781	150	.000 016 5558
31	.012 771 2214	91	.000 406 4925	151	.000 015 6831
32	.011 953 6378	92	.000 384 9246	152	.000 014 8565
33	.011 196 9623	93	.000 364 5085	153	.000 014 0735
34	.010 495 6241	94	.000 345 1819	154	.000 013 3317
35	.009 844 6873	95	.000 326 8860	155	.000 012 6290
36	.009 239 7629	96	.000 309 5653	156	.000 011 9634
37	.008 676 9355	97	.000 293 1671	157	.000 011 3329
38	.008 152 7011	98	.000 277 6419	158	.000 010 7356
39	.007 663 9142	99	.000 262 9427	159	.000 010 1698
40	.007 207 7439	100	.000 249 0252	160	.000 009 6338
41	.006 781 6352	101	.000 235 8474	161	.000 009 1261
42	.006 383 2764	102	.000 223 3698	162	.000 008 6451
43	.006 010 5712	103	.000 211 5548	163	.000 008 1895
44	.005 661 6144	104	.000 200 3670	164	.000 007 7579
45	.005 334 6705	105	.000 189 7729	165	.000 007 3491
46	.005 028 1558	106	.000 179 7407	166	.000 006 9618
47	.004 740 6221	107	.000 170 2405	167	.000 006 5949
48	.004 470 7429	108	.000 161 2438	168	.000 006 2473
49	.004 217 3011	109	.000 152 7239	169	.000 005 9181
50	.003 979 1779	110	.000 144 6554	170	.000 005 6062
51	.003 755 3437	111	.000 137 0142	171	.000 005 3108
52	.003 544 8494	112	.000 129 7775	172	.000 005 0309
53	.003 346 8186	113	.000 122 9239	173	.000 004 7658
54	.003 160 4416	114	.000 116 4330	174	.000 004 5146
55	.002 984 9689	115	.000 110 2855	175	.000 004 2767
56	.002 819 7060	116	.000 104 4632	176	.000 004 0514
57	.002 664 0088	117	.000 098 9489	177	.000 003 8379
58	.002 517 2791	118	.000 093 7261	178	.000 003 6356
59	.002 378 9609	119	.000 088 7794	179	.000 003 4440
60	.002 248 5369	120	.000 084 0942	180	.000 003 2625

Sinking Fund

NOMINAL INTEREST RATE COMPOUNDED

YEARLY	HALF-YEARLY	QUARTERLY
@	@	@
$5\frac{5}{8}\%$	$11\frac{1}{4}\%$	$22\frac{1}{2}\%$
5.6250%	11.2500%	22.5000%
PER ANNUM	PER ANNUM	PER ANNUM

Periods	Sinking Fund	Periods	Sinking Fund	Periods	Sinking Fund
1	1.000 000 0000	61	.002 070 3812	121	.000 074 9769
2	.486 322 1884	62	.001 956 2896	122	.000 070 9790
3	.315 267 0534	63	.001 848 6846	123	.000 067 1946
4	.229 867 3958	64	.001 747 1759	124	.000 063 6121
5	.178 729 7152	65	.001 651 3994	125	.000 060 2209
6	.144 722 7942	66	.001 561 0145	126	.000 057 0106
7	.120 504 6400	67	.001 475 7026	127	.000 053 9716
8	.102 404 2191	68	.001 395 1657	128	.000 051 0948
9	.088 382 0362	69	.001 319 1246	129	.000 048 3714
10	.077 214 3653	70	.001 247 3176	130	.000 045 7933
11	.068 122 4462	71	.001 179 4995	131	.000 043 3527
12	.060 587 0826	72	.001 115 4404	132	.000 041 0423
13	.054 248 8099	73	.001 054 9242	133	.000 038 8551
14	.048 850 8492	74	.000 997 7483	134	.000 036 7846
15	.044 204 8789	75	.000 943 7223	135	.000 034 8244
16	.040 169 6423	76	.000 892 6673	136	.000 032 9688
17	.036 637 1057	77	.000 844 4152	137	.000 031 2121
18	.033 523 2299	78	.000 798 8077	138	.000 029 5490
19	.030 761 6566	79	.000 755 6962	139	.000 027 9746
20	.028 299 2886	80	.000 714 9405	140	.000 026 4841
21	.026 093 1328	81	.000 676 4089	141	.000 025 0731
22	.024 108 0042	82	.000 639 9773	142	.000 023 7373
23	.022 314 8291	83	.000 605 5288	143	.000 022 4727
24	.020 689 3721	84	.000 572 9532	144	.000 021 2755
25	.019 211 2691	85	.000 542 1468	145	.000 020 1420
26	.017 863 2831	86	.000 513 0118	146	.000 019 0690
27	.016 630 7255	87	.000 485 4558	147	.000 018 0532
28	.015 501 0012	88	.000 459 3920	148	.000 017 0915
29	.014 463 2487	89	.000 434 7383	149	.000 016 1810
30	.013 508 0505	90	.000 411 4172	150	.000 015 3191
31	.012 627 2016	91	.000 389 3558	151	.000 014 5031
32	.011 813 5194	92	.000 368 4850	152	.000 013 7305
33	.011 060 6899	93	.000 348 7399	153	.000 012 9991
34	.010 363 1398	94	.000 330 0590	154	.000 012 3067
35	.009 715 9312	95	.000 312 3842	155	.000 011 6512
36	.009 114 6732	96	.000 295 6610	156	.000 011 0306
37	.008 555 4491	97	.000 279 8374	157	.000 010 4431
38	.008 034 7533	98	.000 264 8646	158	.000 009 8868
39	.007 549 4395	99	.000 250 6965	159	.000 009 3602
40	.007 096 6755	100	.000 237 2895	160	.000 008 8617
41	.006 673 9058	101	.000 224 6023	161	.000 008 3897
42	.006 278 8180	102	.000 212 5961	162	.000 007 9428
43	.005 909 3155	103	.000 201 2339	163	.000 007 5198
44	.005 563 4926	104	.000 190 4810	164	.000 007 1193
45	.005 239 6138	105	.000 180 3045	165	.000 006 7401
46	.004 936 0952	106	.000 170 6734	166	.000 006 3811
47	.004 651 4888	107	.000 161 5581	167	.000 006 0412
48	.004 384 4681	108	.000 152 9311	168	.000 005 7195
49	.004 133 8164	109	.000 144 7658	169	.000 005 4149
50	.003 898 4152	110	.000 137 0376	170	.000 005 1265
51	.003 677 2353	111	.000 129 7229	171	.000 004 8534
52	.003 469 3281	112	.000 122 7995	172	.000 004 5950
53	.003 273 8179	113	.000 116 2464	173	.000 004 3502
54	.003 089 8955	114	.000 110 0437	174	.000 004 1186
55	.002 916 8122	115	.000 104 1725	175	.000 003 8992
56	.002 753 8742	116	.000 098 6151	176	.000 003 6915
57	.002 600 4383	117	.000 093 3547	177	.000 003 4949
58	.002 455 9071	118	.000 088 3753	178	.000 003 3088
59	.002 319 7255	119	.000 083 6620	179	.000 003 1326
60	.002 191 3771	120	.000 079 2003	180	.000 002 9658

NOMINAL INTEREST RATE COMPOUNDED

YEARLY	HALF-YEARLY	QUARTERLY
@	@	@
$5\frac{11}{16}\%$	$11\frac{3}{8}\%$	$22\frac{3}{4}\%$
5.6875%	11.3750%	22.7500%
PER ANNUM	PER ANNUM	PER ANNUM

Periods	Sinking Fund	Periods	Sinking Fund	Periods	Sinking Fund
1	1.000 000 0000	61	.002 016 5638	121	.000 070 5669
2	.486 174 4151	62	.001 904 4101	122	.000 066 7650
3	.315 073 7820	63	.001 798 6845	123	.000 063 1681
4	.229 654 1869	64	.001 698 9980	124	.000 059 7652
5	.178 506 7834	65	.001 604 9875	125	.000 056 5457
6	.144 495 2369	66	.001 516 3135	126	.000 053 4999
7	.120 275 3593	67	.001 432 6587	127	.000 050 6183
8	.102 175 0181	68	.001 353 7261	128	.000 047 8920
9	.088 154 1060	69	.001 279 2377	129	.000 045 3127
10	.076 988 5285	70	.001 208 9331	130	.000 042 8724
11	.067 899 2900	71	.001 142 5682	131	.000 040 5636
12	.060 367 0359	72	.001 079 9142	132	.000 038 3792
13	.054 032 1918	73	.001 020 7564	133	.000 036 3125
14	.048 637 8990	74	.000 964 8932	134	.000 034 3572
15	.043 995 7770	75	.000 912 1354	135	.000 032 5072
16	.039 964 5244	76	.000 862 3052	136	.000 030 7569
17	.036 436 0724	77	.000 815 2357	137	.000 029 1009
18	.033 326 3546	78	.000 770 7698	138	.000 027 5341
19	.030 568 9902	79	.000 728 7599	139	.000 026 0517
20	.028 110 8641	80	.000 689 0670	140	.000 024 6492
21	.025 908 9681	81	.000 651 5606	141	.000 023 3221
22	.023 928 1046	82	.000 616 1174	142	.000 022 0666
23	.022 139 1894	83	.000 582 6219	143	.000 020 8787
24	.020 517 9780	84	.000 550 9647	144	.000 019 7547
25	.019 044 0985	85	.000 521 0433	145	.000 018 6913
26	.017 700 3071	86	.000 492 7608	146	.000 017 6851
27	.016 471 9094	87	.000 466 0259	147	.000 016 7331
28	.015 346 3054	88	.000 440 7527	148	.000 015 8324
29	.014 312 6286	89	.000 416 8601	149	.000 014 9801
30	.013 361 4581	90	.000 394 2715	150	.000 014 1738
31	.012 484 5851	91	.000 372 9150	151	.000 013 4109
32	.011 674 8241	92	.000 352 7223	152	.000 012 6890
33	.010 925 8584	93	.000 333 6295	153	.000 012 0060
34	.010 232 1124	94	.000 315 5758	154	.000 011 3598
35	.009 588 6461	95	.000 298 5042	155	.000 010 7483
36	.008 991 0670	96	.000 282 3606	156	.000 010 1698
37	.008 435 4566	97	.000 267 0942	157	.000 009 6225
38	.007 918 3083	98	.000 252 6569	158	.000 009 1045
39	.007 436 4745	99	.000 239 0032	159	.000 008 6145
40	.006 987 1224	100	.000 226 0903	160	.000 008 1509
41	.006 567 6954	101	.000 213 8776	161	.000 007 7122
42	.006 175 8809	102	.000 202 3270	162	.000 007 2971
43	.005 809 5816	103	.000 191 4023	163	.000 006 9044
44	.005 466 8918	104	.000 181 0693	164	.000 006 5328
45	.005 146 0757	105	.000 171 2958	165	.000 006 1812
46	.004 845 5495	106	.000 162 0514	166	.000 005 8485
47	.004 563 8653	107	.000 153 3072	167	.000 005 5337
48	.004 299 6968	108	.000 145 0361	168	.000 005 2359
49	.004 051 8274	109	.000 137 2122	169	.000 004 9541
50	.003 819 1394	110	.000 129 8114	170	.000 004 6875
51	.003 600 6038	111	.000 122 8106	171	.000 004 4352
52	.003 395 2727	112	.000 116 1881	172	.000 004 1965
53	.003 202 2709	113	.000 109 9235	173	.000 003 9707
54	.003 020 7901	114	.000 103 9972	174	.000 003 7570
55	.002 850 0822	115	.000 098 3910	175	.000 003 5548
56	.002 689 4543	116	.000 093 0875	176	.000 003 3635
57	.002 538 2640	117	.000 088 0703	177	.000 003 1825
58	.002 395 9149	118	.000 083 3239	178	.000 003 0112
59	.002 261 8528	119	.000 078 8336	179	.000 002 8491
60	.002 135 5624	120	.000 074 5857	180	.000 002 6958

Sinking Fund

NOMINAL INTEREST RATE COMPOUNDED

	YEARLY	HALF-YEARLY	QUARTERLY
	@	@	@
	$5\frac{3}{4}\%$	$11\frac{1}{2}\%$	23%
	5.7500%	11.5000%	23.0000%
	PER ANNUM	PER ANNUM	PER ANNUM

Periods	Sinking Fund	Periods	Sinking Fund	Periods	Sinking Fund
1	1.000 000 0000	61	.001 964 0454	121	.000 066 4116
2	.486 026 7315	62	.001 853 8103	122	.000 062 7966
3	.314 880 6701	63	.001 749 9444	123	.000 059 3786
4	.229 441 2017	64	.001 652 0600	124	.000 056 1468
5	.178 284 1371	65	.001 559 7949	125	.000 053 0911
6	.144 268 0253	66	.001 472 8110	126	.000 050 2018
7	.120 046 4834	67	.001 390 7921	127	.000 047 4699
8	.101 946 2799	68	.001 313 4424	128	.000 044 8868
9	.087 926 6954	69	.001 240 4852	129	.000 042 4443
10	.076 763 2671	70	.001 171 6612	130	.000 040 1349
11	.067 676 7637	71	.001 106 7277	131	.000 037 9512
12	.060 147 6727	72	.001 045 4569	132	.000 035 8863
13	.053 816 3092	73	.000 987 6353	133	.000 033 9339
14	.048 425 7351	74	.000 933 0627	134	.000 032 0878
15	.043 787 5108	75	.000 881 5510	135	.000 030 3421
16	.039 760 2900	76	.000 832 9236	136	.000 028 6915
17	.036 235 9691	77	.000 787 0147	137	.000 027 1307
18	.033 130 4539	78	.000 743 6685	138	.000 025 6549
19	.030 377 3417	79	.000 702 7384	139	.000 024 2593
20	.027 923 4988	80	.000 664 0868	140	.000 022 9397
21	.025 725 9022	81	.000 627 5839	141	.000 021 6920
22	.023 749 3418	82	.000 593 1080	142	.000 020 5121
23	.021 964 7226	83	.000 560 5442	143	.000 019 3964
24	.020 347 7910	84	.000 529 7847	144	.000 018 3414
25	.018 878 1674	85	.000 500 7275	145	.000 017 3438
26	.017 538 6012	86	.000 473 2771	146	.000 016 4005
27	.016 314 3920	87	.000 447 3432	147	.000 015 5085
28	.015 192 9348	88	.000 422 8407	148	.000 014 6650
29	.014 163 3587	89	.000 399 6895	149	.000 013 8674
30	.013 216 2386	90	.000 377 8142	150	.000 013 1133
31	.012 343 3625	91	.000 357 1435	151	.000 012 4001
32	.011 537 5417	92	.000 337 6103	152	.000 011 7257
33	.010 792 4570	93	.000 319 1514	153	.000 011 0880
34	.010 102 5304	94	.000 301 7070	154	.000 010 4850
35	.009 462 8198	95	.000 285 2207	155	.000 009 9148
36	.008 868 9312	96	.000 269 6395	156	.000 009 3756
37	.008 316 9445	97	.000 254 9133	157	.000 008 8658
38	.007 803 3517	98	.000 240 9947	158	.000 008 3836
39	.007 325 0044	99	.000 227 8390	159	.000 007 9277
40	.006 879 0687	100	.000 215 4042	160	.000 007 4966
41	.006 462 9876	101	.000 203 6504	161	.000 007 0889
42	.006 074 4478	102	.000 192 5401	162	.000 006 7034
43	.005 711 3517	103	.000 182 0379	163	.000 006 3389
44	.005 371 7934	104	.000 172 1102	164	.000 005 9942
45	.005 054 0370	105	.000 162 7255	165	.000 005 6682
46	.004 756 4988	106	.000 153 8539	166	.000 005 3600
47	.004 477 7310	107	.000 145 4671	167	.000 005 0685
48	.004 216 4076	108	.000 137 5387	168	.000 004 7929
49	.003 971 3125	109	.000 130 0433	169	.000 004 5323
50	.003 741 3281	110	.000 122 9573	170	.000 004 2858
51	.003 525 4263	111	.000 116 2581	171	.000 004 0528
52	.003 322 6596	112	.000 109 9247	172	.000 003 8324
53	.003 132 1537	113	.000 103 9369	173	.000 003 6240
54	.002 953 1008	114	.000 098 2758	174	.000 003 4270
55	.002 784 7538	115	.000 092 9236	175	.000 003 2406
56	.002 626 4207	116	.000 087 8633	176	.000 003 0644
57	.002 477 4599	117	.000 083 0789	177	.000 002 8978
58	.002 337 2760	118	.000 078 5555	178	.000 002 7402
59	.002 205 3159	119	.000 074 2786	179	.000 002 5912
60	.002 081 0653	120	.000 070 2349	180	.000 002 4503

NOMINAL INTEREST RATE COMPOUNDED

YEARLY	HALF-YEARLY	QUARTERLY
@	@	@
$5\frac{13}{16}\%$	$11\frac{5}{8}\%$	$23\frac{1}{4}\%$
5.8125%	11.6250%	23.2500%
PER ANNUM	PER ANNUM	PER ANNUM

Periods	Sinking Fund	Periods	Sinking Fund	Periods	Sinking Fund
1	1.000 000 0000	61	.001 912 7987	121	.000 062 4965
2	.485 879 1376	62	.001 804 4627	122	.000 059 0599
3	.314 687 7173	63	.001 702 4366	123	.000 055 8125
4	.229 228 4398	64	.001 606 3337	124	.000 052 7439
5	.178 061 7760	65	.001 515 7934	125	.000 049 8440
6	.144 041 1590	66	.001 430 4785	126	.000 047 1038
7	.119 818 0118	67	.001 350 0742	127	.000 044 5143
8	.101 718 0038	68	.001 274 2859	128	.000 042 0673
9	.087 699 8038	69	.001 202 8382	129	.000 039 7548
10	.076 538 5803	70	.001 135 4731	130	.000 037 5696
11	.067 454 8665	71	.001 071 9489	131	.000 035 5046
12	.059 928 9917	72	.001 012 0392	132	.000 033 5531
13	.053 601 1607	73	.000 955 5319	133	.000 031 7090
14	.048 214 3559	74	.000 902 2278	134	.000 029 9662
15	.043 580 0784	75	.000 851 9401	135	.000 028 3193
16	.039 556 9370	76	.000 804 4936	136	.000 026 7630
17	.036 036 7932	77	.000 759 7234	137	.000 025 2922
18	.032 935 5251	78	.000 717 4751	138	.000 023 9023
19	.030 186 7077	79	.000 677 6033	139	.000 022 5887
20	.027 737 1891	80	.000 639 9713	140	.000 021 3474
21	.025 543 9313	81	.000 604 4508	141	.000 020 1744
22	.023 571 7114	82	.000 570 9209	142	.000 019 0658
23	.021 791 4237	83	.000 539 2681	143	.000 018 0181
24	.020 178 8057	84	.000 509 3853	144	.000 017 0281
25	.018 713 4698	85	.000 481 1721	145	.000 016 0924
26	.017 378 1587	86	.000 454 5336	146	.000 015 2082
27	.016 158 1661	87	.000 429 3807	147	.000 014 3726
28	.015 040 8818	88	.000 405 6293	148	.000 013 5829
29	.014 015 4305	89	.000 383 2004	149	.000 012 8366
30	.013 072 3831	90	.000 362 0193	150	.000 012 1313
31	.012 203 5241	91	.000 342 0158	151	.000 011 4648
32	.011 401 6621	92	.000 323 1237	152	.000 010 8349
33	.010 660 4748	93	.000 305 2806	153	.000 010 2396
34	.009 974 3822	94	.000 288 4277	154	.000 009 6770
35	.009 338 4402	95	.000 272 5095	155	.000 009 1453
36	.008 748 2530	96	.000 257 4737	156	.000 008 6429
37	.008 199 8991	97	.000 243 2709	157	.000 008 1681
38	.007 689 8693	98	.000 229 8547	158	.000 007 7193
39	.007 215 0140	99	.000 217 1811	159	.000 007 2952
40	.006 772 4989	100	.000 205 2088	160	.000 006 8944
41	.006 359 7660	101	.000 193 8987	161	.000 006 5157
42	.005 974 5016	102	.000 183 2138	162	.000 006 1577
43	.005 614 6081	103	.000 173 1195	163	.000 005 8194
44	.005 278 1790	104	.000 163 5830	164	.000 005 4997
45	.004 963 4787	105	.000 154 5731	165	.000 005 1976
46	.004 668 9234	106	.000 146 0607	166	.000 004 9120
47	.004 393 0656	107	.000 138 0183	167	.000 004 6422
48	.004 134 5796	108	.000 130 4196	168	.000 004 3872
49	.003 892 2498	109	.000 123 2402	169	.000 004 1462
50	.003 664 9591	110	.000 116 4568	170	.000 003 9184
51	.003 451 6800	111	.000 110 0475	171	.000 003 7031
52	.003 251 4655	112	.000 103 9915	172	.000 003 4997
53	.003 063 4423	113	.000 098 2694	173	.000 003 3074
54	.002 886 8033	114	.000 092 8626	174	.000 003 1257
55	.002 720 8022	115	.000 087 7538	175	.000 002 9540
56	.002 564 7481	116	.000 082 9264	176	.000 002 7917
57	.002 418 0002	117	.000 078 3650	177	.000 002 6384
58	.002 279 9643	118	.000 074 0547	178	.000 002 4934
59	.002 150 0883	119	.000 069 9819	179	.000 002 3565
60	.002 027 8590	120	.000 066 1332	180	.000 002 2270

NOMINAL INTEREST RATE COMPOUNDED

YEARLY	HALF-YEARLY	QUARTERLY
@	@	@
$5\frac{7}{8}\%$	$11\frac{3}{4}\%$	$23\frac{1}{2}\%$
5.8750%	11.7500%	23.5000%
PER ANNUM	PER ANNUM	PER ANNUM

Periods	Sinking Fund	Periods	Sinking Fund	Periods	Sinking Fund
1	1.000 000 0000	61	.001 862 7969	121	.000 058 8082
2	.485 731 6333	62	.001 756 3402	122	.000 055 5419
3	.314 494 9236	63	.001 656 1336	123	.000 052 4571
4	.229 015 9011	64	.001 561 7918	124	.000 049 5438
5	.177 839 6997	65	.001 472 9552	125	.000 046 7924
6	.143 814 6377	66	.001 389 2882	126	.000 044 1940
7	.119 589 9440	67	.001 310 4770	127	.000 041 7399
8	.101 490 1893	68	.001 236 2286	128	.000 039 4222
9	.087 473 4303	69	.001 166 2685	129	.000 037 2333
10	.076 314 4671	70	.001 100 3402	130	.000 035 1660
11	.067 233 5972	71	.001 038 2034	131	.000 033 2135
12	.059 710 9916	72	.000 979 6329	132	.000 031 3695
13	.053 386 7449	73	.000 924 4178	133	.000 029 6279
14	.048 003 7596	74	.000 872 3602	134	.000 027 9831
15	.043 373 4778	75	.000 823 2746	135	.000 026 4296
16	.039 354 4631	76	.000 776 9870	136	.000 024 9624
17	.035 838 5422	77	.000 733 3338	137	.000 023 5767
18	.032 741 5652	78	.000 692 1617	138	.000 022 2679
19	.029 997 0850	79	.000 653 3266	139	.000 021 0318
20	.027 551 9314	80	.000 616 6930	140	.000 019 8644
21	.025 363 0511	81	.000 582 1336	141	.000 018 7618
22	.023 395 2087	82	.000 549 5289	142	.000 017 7204
23	.021 619 2878	83	.000 518 7663	143	.000 016 7368
24	.020 011 0166	84	.000 489 7400	144	.000 015 8078
25	.018 549 9998	85	.000 462 3505	145	.000 014 9304
26	.017 218 9732	86	.000 436 5041	146	.000 014 1017
27	.016 003 2246	87	.000 412 1126	147	.000 013 3190
28	.014 890 1387	88	.000 389 0930	148	.000 012 5798
29	.013 868 8358	89	.000 367 3672	149	.000 011 8816
30	.012 929 8827	90	.000 346 8617	150	.000 011 2222
31	.012 065 0606	91	.000 327 5070	151	.000 010 5994
32	.011 267 1749	92	.000 309 2380	152	.000 010 0111
33	.010 529 9010	93	.000 291 9931	153	.000 009 4555
34	.009 847 6563	94	.000 275 7144	154	.000 008 9307
35	.009 215 4950	95	.000 260 3472	155	.000 008 4351
36	.008 629 0194	96	.000 245 8401	156	.000 007 9670
37	.008 084 3068	97	.000 232 1446	157	.000 007 5248
38	.007 577 8466	98	.000 219 2148	158	.000 007 1072
39	.007 106 4885	99	.000 207 0077	159	.000 006 7128
40	.006 667 3972	100	.000 195 4826	160	.000 006 3403
41	.006 258 0142	101	.000 184 6012	161	.000 005 9884
42	.005 876 0254	102	.000 174 3273	162	.000 005 6561
43	.005 519 3329	103	.000 164 6268	163	.000 005 3422
44	.005 186 0302	104	.000 155 4675	164	.000 005 0457
45	.004 874 3816	105	.000 146 8190	165	.000 004 7657
46	.004 582 8035	106	.000 138 6528	166	.000 004 5012
47	.004 309 8487	107	.000 130 9418	167	.000 004 2515
48	.004 054 1920	108	.000 123 6606	168	.000 004 0155
49	.003 814 6180	109	.000 116 7850	169	.000 003 7927
50	.003 590 0104	110	.000 110 2925	170	.000 003 5822
51	.003 379 3421	111	.000 104 1615	171	.000 003 3834
52	.003 181 6673	112	.000 098 3719	172	.000 003 1957
53	.002 996 1130	113	.000 092 9046	173	.000 003 0183
54	.002 821 8733	114	.000 087 7416	174	.000 002 8508
55	.002 658 2028	115	.000 082 8660	175	.000 002 6926
56	.002 504 4114	116	.000 078 2616	176	.000 002 5432
57	.002 359 8595	117	.000 073 9134	177	.000 002 4021
58	.002 223 9540	118	.000 069 8071	178	.000 002 2688
59	.002 096 1438	119	.000 065 9292	179	.000 002 1429
60	.001 975 9169	120	.000 062 2669	180	.000 002 0240

NOMINAL INTEREST RATE COMPOUNDED

YEARLY	HALF-YEARLY	QUARTERLY
@	@	@
$5\frac{15}{16}\%$	$11\frac{7}{8}\%$	$23\frac{3}{4}\%$
5.9375%	11.8750%	23.7500%
PER ANNUM	PER ANNUM	PER ANNUM

Periods	Sinking Fund	Periods	Sinking Fund	Periods	Sinking Fund
1	1.000 000 0000	61	.001 814 0136	121	.000 055 3340
2	.485 584 2185	62	.001 709 4161	122	.000 052 2300
3	.314 302 2888	63	.001 611 0086	123	.000 049 3002
4	.228 803 5854	64	.001 518 4070	124	.000 046 5349
5	.177 617 9079	65	.001 431 2531	125	.000 043 9248
6	.143 588 4610	66	.001 349 2126	126	.000 041 4612
7	.119 362 2796	67	.001 271 9730	127	.000 039 1359
8	.101 262 8358	68	.001 199 2426	128	.000 036 9411
9	.087 247 5743	69	.001 130 7484	129	.000 034 8694
10	.076 090 9267	70	.001 066 2350	130	.000 032 9140
11	.067 012 9547	71	.001 005 4635	131	.000 031 0683
12	.059 493 6713	72	.000 948 2102	132	.000 029 3261
13	.053 173 0603	73	.000 894 2652	133	.000 027 6817
14	.047 793 9445	74	.000 843 4322	134	.000 026 1296
15	.043 167 7069	75	.000 795 5268	135	.000 024 6645
16	.039 152 8661	76	.000 750 3763	136	.000 023 2816
17	.035 641 2134	77	.000 707 8184	137	.000 021 9762
18	.032 548 5714	78	.000 667 7011	138	.000 020 7441
19	.029 808 4703	79	.000 629 8813	139	.000 019 5810
20	.027 367 7219	80	.000 594 2249	140	.000 018 4832
21	.025 183 2576	81	.000 560 6058	141	.000 017 4470
22	.023 219 8293	82	.000 528 9055	142	.000 016 4689
23	.021 448 3098	83	.000 499 0127	143	.000 015 5456
24	.019 844 4182	84	.000 470 8227	144	.000 014 6741
25	.018 387 7513	85	.000 444 2370	145	.000 013 8515
26	.017 061 0380	86	.000 419 1629	146	.000 013 0750
27	.015 849 5604	87	.000 395 5135	147	.000 012 3420
28	.014 740 6979	88	.000 373 2068	148	.000 011 6501
29	.013 723 5662	89	.000 352 1655	149	.000 010 9970
30	.012 788 7285	90	.000 332 3172	150	.000 010 3806
31	.011 927 9623	91	.000 313 5933	151	.000 009 7987
32	.011 134 0701	92	.000 295 9297	152	.000 009 2494
33	.010 400 7247	93	.000 279 2657	153	.000 008 7309
34	.009 722 3413	94	.000 263 5441	154	.000 008 2415
35	.009 093 9720	95	.000 248 7114	155	.000 007 7795
36	.008 511 2176	96	.000 234 7167	156	.000 007 3435
37	.007 970 1540	97	.000 221 5124	157	.000 006 9318
38	.007 467 2696	98	.000 209 0535	158	.000 006 5433
39	.006 999 4130	99	.000 197 2977	159	.000 006 1765
40	.006 563 7480	100	.000 186 2051	160	.000 005 8303
41	.006 157 7160	101	.000 175 7379	161	.000 005 5035
42	.005 779 0022	102	.000 165 8608	162	.000 005 1950
43	.005 425 5086	103	.000 156 5402	163	.000 004 9038
44	.005 095 3288	104	.000 147 7448	164	.000 004 6290
45	.004 786 7269	105	.000 139 4446	165	.000 004 3695
46	.004 498 1198	106	.000 131 6118	166	.000 004 1246
47	.004 228 0604	107	.000 124 2199	167	.000 003 8934
48	.003 975 2239	108	.000 117 2440	168	.000 003 6752
49	.003 738 3957	109	.000 110 6605	169	.000 003 4692
50	.003 516 4600	110	.000 104 4474	170	.000 003 2747
51	.003 308 3905	111	.000 098 5837	171	.000 003 0912
52	.003 113 2419	112	.000 093 0497	172	.000 002 9179
53	.002 930 1425	113	.000 087 8268	173	.000 002 7544
54	.002 758 2870	114	.000 082 8975	174	.000 002 6000
55	.002 596 9312	115	.000 078 2452	175	.000 002 4543
56	.002 445 3859	116	.000 073 8543	176	.000 002 3167
57	.002 303 0127	117	.000 069 7101	177	.000 002 1869
58	.002 169 2196	118	.000 065 7988	178	.000 002 0643
59	.002 043 4566	119	.000 062 1071	179	.000 001 9486
60	.001 925 2130	120	.000 058 6227	180	.000 001 8394

Sinking Fund

NOMINAL INTEREST RATE COMPOUNDED

YEARLY	HALF-YEARLY	QUARTERLY
@	@	@
6%	**12%**	**24%**
6.0000%	12.0000%	24.0000%
PER ANNUM	PER ANNUM	PER ANNUM

Periods	Sinking Fund	Periods	Sinking Fund	Periods	Sinking Fund
1	1,000 000 0000	61	,001 766 4228	121	,000 052 0617
2	,485 436 8932	62	,001 663 6642	122	,000 049 1124
3	,314 109 8128	63	,001 567 0351	123	,000 046 3303
4	,228 591 4924	64	,001 476 1528	124	,000 043 7059
5	,177 396 4004	65	,001 390 6603	125	,000 041 2303
6	,143 362 6285	66	,001 310 2248	126	,000 038 8950
7	,119 135 0181	67	,001 234 5351	127	,000 036 6920
8	,101 035 9426	68	,001 163 3009	128	,000 034 6139
9	,087 022 2350	69	,001 096 2506	129	,000 032 6536
10	,075 867 9582	70	,001 033 1302	130	,000 030 8043
11	,066 792 9381	71	,000 973 7022	131	,000 029 0598
12	,059 277 0294	72	,000 917 7439	132	,000 027 4142
13	,052 960 1053	73	,000 865 0472	133	,000 025 8618
14	,047 584 9090	74	,000 815 4168	134	,000 024 3973
15	,042 962 7640	75	,000 768 6698	135	,000 023 0158
16	,038 952 1436	76	,000 724 6347	136	,000 021 7125
17	,035 444 8042	77	,000 683 1507	137	,000 020 4831
18	,032 356 5406	78	,000 644 0667	138	,000 019 3233
19	,029 620 8604	79	,000 607 2411	139	,000 018 2292
20	,027 184 5570	80	,000 572 5410	140	,000 017 1971
21	,025 004 5467	81	,000 539 8414	141	,000 016 2234
22	,023 045 5685	82	,000 509 0251	142	,000 015 3049
23	,021 278 4847	83	,000 479 9819	143	,000 014 4383
24	,019 679 0050	84	,000 452 6081	144	,000 013 6209
25	,018 226 7182	85	,000 426 8066	145	,000 012 8497
26	,016 904 3467	86	,000 402 4856	146	,000 012 1222
27	,015 697 1663	87	,000 379 5593	147	,000 011 4359
28	,014 592 5515	88	,000 357 9467	148	,000 010 7885
29	,013 579 6135	89	,000 337 5715	149	,000 010 1777
30	,012 648 9115	90	,000 318 3623	150	,000 009 6015
31	,011 792 2196	91	,000 300 2516	151	,000 009 0580
32	,011 002 3374	92	,000 283 1761	152	,000 008 5452
33	,010 272 9350	93	,000 267 0759	153	,000 008 0614
34	,009 598 4254	94	,000 251 8949	154	,000 007 6051
35	,008 973 8590	95	,000 237 5802	155	,000 007 1745
36	,008 394 8348	96	,000 224 0821	156	,000 006 7684
37	,007 857 4274	97	,000 211 3535	157	,000 006 3852
38	,007 358 1240	98	,000 199 3504	158	,000 006 0238
39	,006 893 7724	99	,000 188 0310	159	,000 005 6828
40	,006 461 5359	100	,000 177 3563	160	,000 005 3611
41	,006 058 8551	101	,000 167 2893	161	,000 005 0576
42	,005 683 4152	102	,000 157 7952	162	,000 004 7713
43	,005 333 1178	103	,000 148 8412	163	,000 004 5012
44	,005 006 0565	104	,000 140 3965	164	,000 004 2464
45	,004 700 4958	105	,000 132 4320	165	,000 004 0060
46	,004 414 8527	106	,000 124 9202	166	,000 003 7792
47	,004 147 6805	107	,000 117 8354	167	,000 003 5653
48	,003 897 6549	108	,000 111 1531	168	,000 003 3635
49	,003 663 5619	109	,000 104 8504	169	,000 003 1731
50	,003 444 2864	110	,000 098 9057	170	,000 002 9935
51	,003 238 8028	111	,000 093 2986	171	,000 002 8240
52	,003 046 1669	112	,000 088 0098	172	,000 002 6642
53	,002 865 5076	113	,000 083 0212	173	,000 002 5134
54	,002 696 0209	114	,000 078 3157	174	,000 002 3711
55	,002 536 9634	115	,000 073 8773	175	,000 002 2369
56	,002 387 6472	116	,000 069 6907	176	,000 002 1103
57	,002 247 4350	117	,000 065 7417	177	,000 001 9908
58	,002 115 7359	118	,000 062 0166	178	,000 001 8781
59	,001 992 0012	119	,000 058 5028	179	,000 001 7718
60	,001 875 7215	120	,000 055 1883	180	,000 001 6715

Amount of 1

The amount of 1 accumulated at compound interest

$$s = (1+i)^n$$

Note: Since the values tabulated are used for nominal annual rates as well as for effective rates compounded *m* times a year these can be expressed as values of

$$\left[1 + \frac{j^{(m)}}{m}\right]^{mn}$$

Effective Rates	***Number of periods***
3% increasing by $\frac{1}{16}$% to 6%	180

NOTE

Nominal annual rates at these effective rates, compounded half yearly and quarterly, are shown in the heading to each table.

Amount of 1

NOMINAL INTEREST RATE COMPOUNDED

YEARLY	HALF-YEARLY	QUARTERLY
@	@	@
3%	**6%**	**12%**
3.0000%	6.0000%	12.0000%
PER ANNUM	PER ANNUM	PER ANNUM

Periods	Amount	Periods	Amount	Periods	Amount
1	1.030 000 0000	61	6.068 351 1972	121	35.752 316 7497
2	1.060 900 0000	62	6.250 401 7331	122	36.824 886 2522
3	1.092 727 0000	63	6.437 913 7851	123	37.929 632 8397
4	1.125 508 8100	64	6.631 051 1986	124	39.067 521 8249
5	1.159 274 0743	65	6.829 982 7346	125	40.239 547 4797
6	1.194 052 2965	66	7.034 882 2166	126	41.446 733 9041
7	1.229 873 8654	67	7.245 928 6831	127	42.690 135 9212
8	1.266 770 0814	68	7.463 306 5436	128	43.970 839 9988
9	1.304 773 1838	69	7.687 205 7399	129	45.289 965 1988
10	1.343 916 3793	70	7.917 821 9121	130	46.648 664 1547
11	1.384 233 8707	71	8.155 356 5695	131	48.048 124 0794
12	1.425 760 8868	72	8.400 017 2666	132	49.489 567 8018
13	1.468 533 7135	73	8.652 017 7846	133	50.974 254 8358
14	1.512 589 7249	74	8.911 578 3181	134	52.503 482 4809
15	1.557 967 4166	75	9.178 925 6676	135	54.078 586 9553
16	1.604 706 4391	76	9.454 293 4377	136	55.700 944 5640
17	1.652 847 6323	77	9.737 922 2408	137	57.371 972 9009
18	1.702 433 0612	78	10.030 059 9080	138	59.093 132 0879
19	1.753 506 0531	79	10.330 961 7053	139	60.865 926 0506
20	1.806 111 2347	80	10.640 890 5564	140	62.691 903 8321
21	1.860 294 5717	81	10.960 117 2731	141	64.572 660 9470
22	1.916 103 4089	82	11.288 920 7913	142	66.509 840 7754
23	1.973 586 5111	83	11.627 588 4151	143	68.505 135 9987
24	2.032 794 1065	84	11.976 416 0675	144	70.560 290 0787
25	2.093 777 9297	85	12.335 708 5495	145	72.677 098 7810
26	2.156 591 2675	86	12.705 779 8060	146	74.857 411 7445
27	2.221 289 0056	87	13.086 953 2002	147	77.103 134 0968
28	2.287 927 6757	88	13.479 561 7962	148	79.416 228 1197
29	2.356 565 5060	89	13.883 948 6501	149	81.798 714 9633
30	2.427 262 4712	90	14.300 467 1096	150	84.252 676 4122
31	2.500 080 3453	91	14.729 481 1229	151	86.780 256 7046
32	2.575 082 7557	92	15.171 365 5566	152	89.383 664 4057
33	2.652 335 2384	93	15.626 506 5233	153	92.065 174 3379
34	2.731 905 2955	94	16.095 301 7190	154	94.827 129 5680
35	2.813 862 4544	95	16.578 160 7705	155	97.671 943 4550
36	2.898 278 3280	96	17.075 505 5936	156	100.602 101 7587
37	2.985 226 6778	97	17.587 770 7615	157	103.620 164 8115
38	3.074 783 4782	98	18.115 403 8843	158	106.728 769 7558
39	3.167 026 9825	99	18.658 866 0008	159	109.930 632 8485
40	3.262 037 7920	100	19.218 631 9809	160	113.228 551 8339
41	3.359 898 9258	101	19.795 190 9403	161	116.625 408 3889
42	3.460 695 8935	102	20.389 046 6685	162	120.124 170 6406
43	3.564 516 7703	103	21.000 718 0685	163	123.727 895 7598
44	3.671 452 2734	104	21.630 739 6106	164	127.439 732 6326
45	3.781 595 8417	105	22.279 661 7989	165	131.262 924 6116
46	3.895 043 7169	106	22.948 051 6529	166	135.200 812 3500
47	4.011 895 0284	107	23.636 493 2025	167	139.256 836 7205
48	4.132 251 8793	108	24.345 587 9985	168	143.434 541 8221
49	4.256 219 4356	109	25.075 955 6385	169	147.737 578 0767
50	4.383 906 0187	110	25.828 234 3077	170	152.169 705 4190
51	4.515 423 1993	111	26.603 081 3369	171	156.734 796 5816
52	4.650 885 8952	112	27.401 173 7770	172	161.436 840 4790
53	4.790 412 4721	113	28.223 208 9903	173	166.279 945 6934
54	4.934 124 8463	114	29.069 905 2600	174	171.268 344 0642
55	5.082 148 5917	115	29.942 002 4178	175	176.406 394 3861
56	5.234 613 0494	116	30.840 262 4903	176	181.698 586 2177
57	5.391 651 4409	117	31.765 470 3651	177	187.149 543 8043
58	5.553 400 9841	118	32.718 434 4760	178	192.764 030 1184
59	5.720 003 0136	119	33.699 987 5103	179	198.546 951 0219
60	5.891 603 1040	120	34.710 987 1356	180	204.503 359 5526

NOMINAL INTEREST RATE COMPOUNDED

	YEARLY @ $3\frac{1}{16}\%$ 3.0625% PER ANNUM		HALF-YEARLY @ $6\frac{1}{8}\%$ 6.1250% PER ANNUM		QUARTERLY @ $12\frac{1}{4}\%$ 12.2500% PER ANNUM
Periods	**Amount**	**Periods**	**Amount**	**Periods**	**Amount**
1	1,030 625 0000	61	6,297 106 7019	121	38,475 248 3344
2	1,062 187 8906	62	6,489 955 5946	122	39,653 552 8146
3	1,094 717 3948	63	6,688 710 4847	123	40,867 942 8696
4	1,128 243 1150	64	6,893 552 2433	124	42,119 523 6199
5	1,162 795 5604	65	7,104 667 2807	125	43,409 434 0308
6	1,198 406 1744	66	7,322 247 7162	126	44,738 847 9480
7	1,235 107 3635	67	7,546 491 5525	127	46,108 975 1664
8	1,272 932 5265	68	7,777 602 8563	128	47,521 062 5309
9	1,311 916 0851	69	8,015 791 9438	129	48,976 395 0709
10	1,352 093 5153	70	8,261 275 5721	130	50,476 297 1699
11	1,393 501 3792	71	8,514 277 1365	131	52,022 133 7708
12	1,436 177 3589	72	8,775 026 8738	132	53,615 311 6175
13	1,480 160 2905	73	9,043 762 0718	133	55,257 280 5358
14	1,525 490 1994	74	9,320 727 2852	134	56,949 534 7522
15	1,572 208 3368	75	9,606 174 5583	135	58,693 614 2540
16	1,620 357 2171	76	9,900 363 6542	136	60,491 106 1905
17	1,669 980 6569	77	10,203 562 2911	137	62,343 646 3176
18	1,721 123 8145	78	10,516 046 3863	138	64,252 920 4861
19	1,773 833 2313	79	10,838 100 3068	139	66,220 666 1759
20	1,828 156 8740	80	11,170 017 1287	140	68,248 674 0776
21	1,884 144 1783	81	11,512 098 9033	141	70,338 789 7212
22	1,941 846 0937	82	11,864 656 9322	142	72,492 915 1564
23	2,001 315 1303	83	12,228 012 0508	143	74,713 010 6831
24	2,062 605 4062	84	12,602 494 9198	144	77,001 096 6353
25	2,125 772 6968	85	12,988 446 3267	145	79,359 255 2197
26	2,190 874 4856	86	13,386 217 4955	146	81,789 632 4108
27	2,257 970 0167	87	13,796 170 4063	147	84,294 439 9034
28	2,327 120 3485	88	14,218 678 1250	148	86,875 957 1254
29	2,398 388 4092	89	14,654 125 1426	149	89,536 533 3124
30	2,471 839 0542	90	15,102 907 7250	150	92,278 589 6451
31	2,547 539 1252	91	15,565 434 2741	151	95,104 621 4530
32	2,625 557 5109	92	16,042 125 6988	152	98,017 200 4850
33	2,705 965 2097	93	16,533 415 7983	153	101,018 977 2498
34	2,788 835 3943	94	17,039 751 6571	154	104,112 683 4281
35	2,874 243 4782	95	17,561 594 0516	155	107,301 134 3581
36	2,962 267 1847	96	18,099 417 8694	156	110,587 231 5978
37	3,052 986 6173	97	18,653 712 5417	157	113,973 965 5655
38	3,146 484 3324	98	19,224 982 4883	158	117,464 418 2609
39	3,242 845 4151	99	19,813 747 5770	159	121,061 766 0702
40	3,342 157 5559	100	20,420 543 5965	160	124,769 282 6561
41	3,444 511 1311	101	21,045 922 7442	161	128,590 341 9374
42	3,549 999 2845	102	21,690 454 1282	162	132,528 421 1592
43	3,658 718 0126	103	22,354 724 2859	163	136,587 104 0572
44	3,770 766 2517	104	23,039 337 7172	164	140,770 084 1190
45	3,886 245 9682	105	23,744 917 4347	165	145,081 167 9451
46	4,005 262 2509	106	24,472 105 5312	166	149,524 278 7135
47	4,127 923 4074	107	25,221 563 7631	167	154,103 459 7491
48	4,254 341 0617	108	25,993 974 1533	168	158,822 878 2039
49	4,384 630 2567	109	26,790 039 6118	169	163,686 828 8489
50	4,518 909 5583	110	27,610 484 5749	170	168,699 737 9824
51	4,657 301 1636	111	28,456 055 6650	171	173,866 167 4581
52	4,799 931 0117	112	29,327 522 3697	172	179,190 818 8365
53	4,946 928 8989	113	30,225 677 7423	173	184,678 537 6634
54	5,098 428 5965	114	31,151 339 1232	174	190,334 317 8793
55	5,254 567 9722	115	32,105 348 8838	175	196,163 306 3643
56	5,415 489 1164	116	33,088 575 1934	176	202,170 807 6218
57	5,581 338 4706	117	34,101 912 8087	177	208,362 288 6052
58	5,752 266 9612	118	35,146 283 8884	178	214,743 383 6937
59	5,928 430 1369	119	36,222 638 8325	179	221,319 899 8193
60	6,109 988 3099	120	37,331 957 1468	180	228,097 821 7513

Amount of 1

NOMINAL INTEREST RATE COMPOUNDED

	YEARLY @ $3\frac{1}{8}\%$ 3.1250% PER ANNUM		HALF-YEARLY @ $6\frac{1}{4}\%$ 6.2500% PER ANNUM		QUARTERLY @ $12\frac{1}{2}\%$ 12.5000% PER ANNUM
Periods	Amount	Periods	Amount	Periods	Amount
1	1,031 250 0000	61	6,534 338 8979	121	41,403 718 6258
2	1,063 476 5625	62	6,738 536 9885	122	42,697 584 8329
3	1,096 710 2051	63	6,949 116 2694	123	44,031 884 3589
4	1,130 982 3990	64	7,166 276 1528	124	45,407 880 7451
5	1,166 325 5990	65	7,390 222 2826	125	46,826 877 0184
6	1,202 773 2739	66	7,621 166 7289	126	48,290 216 9252
7	1,240 359 9387	67	7,859 328 1892	127	49,799 286 2041
8	1,279 121 1868	68	8,104 932 1951	128	51,355 513 8980
9	1,319 093 7239	69	8,358 211 3262	129	52,960 373 7073
10	1,360 315 4028	70	8,619 405 4301	130	54,615 385 3857
11	1,402 825 2591	71	8,888 761 8498	131	56,322 116 1790
12	1,446 663 5485	72	9,156 535 6576	132	58,082 182 3096
13	1,491 871 7844	73	9,452 989 8969	133	59,897 250 5068
14	1,538 492 7776	74	9,748 395 8312	134	61,769 039 5851
15	1,586 570 6769	75	10,053 033 2009	135	63,699 322 0721
16	1,636 151 0106	76	10,367 190 4885	136	65,689 925 8869
17	1,687 280 7296	77	10,691 165 1912	137	67,742 736 0708
18	1,740 008 2524	78	11,025 264 1034	138	69,859 696 5731
19	1,794 383 5103	79	11,369 803 6067	139	72,042 812 0910
20	1,850 457 9950	80	11,725 109 9694	140	74,294 149 9688
21	1,908 284 8074	81	12,091 519 6559	141	76,615 842 1553
22	1,967 918 7076	82	12,469 379 6452	142	79,010 087 2227
23	2,029 416 1672	83	12,859 047 7591	143	81,479 152 4484
24	2,092 835 4224	84	13,260 893 0016	144	84,025 375 9624
25	2,158 236 5294	85	13,675 295 9079	145	86,651 168 9612
26	2,225 681 4209	86	14,102 648 9050	146	89,359 017 9913
27	2,295 233 9653	87	14,543 356 6833	147	92,151 487 3035
28	2,366 960 0268	88	14,997 836 5796	148	95,031 221 2817
29	2,440 927 5276	89	15,466 518 9727	149	98,000 946 9468
30	2,517 206 5128	90	15,949 847 6906	150	101,063 476 5389
31	2,595 869 2164	91	16,448 280 4310	151	104,221 710 1807
32	2,676 990 1294	92	16,962 289 1944	152	107,478 638 6239
33	2,760 646 0709	93	17,492 360 7317	153	110,837 346 0809
34	2,846 916 2606	94	18,038 997 0046	154	114,301 013 1459
35	2,935 882 3938	95	18,602 715 6610	155	117,872 919 8067
36	3,027 628 7186	96	19,184 050 5254	156	121,556 448 5507
37	3,122 242 1160	97	19,783 552 1043	157	125,355 087 5679
38	3,219 812 1822	98	20,401 788 1076	158	129,272 434 0544
39	3,320 431 3129	99	21,039 343 9860	159	133,312 197 6186
40	3,424 194 7914	100	21,696 823 4855	160	137,478 203 7941
41	3,531 200 8786	101	22,374 849 2194	161	141,774 397 6627
42	3,641 550 9061	102	23,074 063 2575	162	146,204 847 5897
43	3,755 349 3719	103	23,795 127 7343	163	150,773 749 0769
44	3,872 704 0398	104	24,538 725 4760	164	155,485 428 7355
45	3,993 726 0410	105	25,305 560 6472	165	160,344 348 3835
46	4,118 529 9798	106	26,096 359 4174	166	165,355 109 2705
47	4,247 234 0417	107	26,911 870 6492	167	170,522 456 4352
48	4,379 960 1055	108	27,752 866 6070	168	175,851 283 1988
49	4,516 833 8588	109	28,620 143 6884	169	181,346 635 7987
50	4,657 984 9168	110	29,514 523 1787	170	187,013 718 1674
51	4,803 546 9455	111	30,436 852 0280	171	192,857 896 8602
52	4,953 657 7875	112	31,388 003 6539	172	198,884 706 1371
53	5,108 459 5934	113	32,368 878 7681	173	205,099 853 2038
54	5,268 098 9557	114	33,380 406 2296	174	211,509 223 6165
55	5,432 727 0481	115	34,423 543 9243	175	218,118 886 8545
56	5,602 499 7683	116	35,499 279 6719	176	224,935 102 0687
57	5,777 577 8861	117	36,608 632 1617	177	231,964 324 0083
58	5,958 127 1950	118	37,752 651 9167	178	239,213 209 1336
59	6,144 318 6699	119	38,932 422 2891	179	246,688 621 9190
60	6,336 328 6283	120	40,149 060 4856	180	254,397 641 3540

Amount of 1

NOMINAL INTEREST RATE COMPOUNDED

YEARLY @ $3\frac{3}{16}\%$ 3.1875% PER ANNUM		HALF-YEARLY @ $6\frac{3}{8}\%$ 6.3750% PER ANNUM		QUARTERLY @ $12\frac{3}{4}\%$ 12.7500% PER ANNUM	
Periods	Amount	Periods	Amount	Periods	Amount
1	1.031 875 0000	61	6.780 356 4697	121	44.553 103 6770
2	1.064 766 0156	62	6.996 480 3322	122	45.973 233 8567
3	1.098 705 4324	63	7.219 493 1428	123	47.438 630 6859
4	1.133 726 6680	64	7.449 614 4867	124	48.950 737 0390
5	1.169 864 2056	65	7.687 070 9485	125	50.511 041 7821
6	1.207 153 6271	66	7.932 096 3350	126	52.121 081 2389
7	1.245 631 6490	67	8.184 931 9057	127	53.782 440 7034
8	1.285 336 1578	68	8.445 826 6101	128	55.496 756 0008
9	1.326 306 2478	69	8.715 037 3333	129	57.265 715 0984
10	1.368 582 2595	70	8.992 829 1483	130	59.091 059 7671
11	1.412 205 8190	71	9.279 475 5774	131	60.974 587 2972
12	1.457 219 8795	72	9.575 258 8615	132	62.918 152 2673
13	1.503 668 7631	73	9.880 470 2377	133	64.923 668 3708
14	1.551 598 2050	74	10.195 410 2265	134	66.993 110 3001
15	1.601 055 3978	75	10.520 388 9275	135	69.128 515 6910
16	1.652 089 0386	76	10.855 726 3245	136	71.331 987 1286
17	1.704 749 3767	77	11.201 752 6011	137	73.605 694 2183
18	1.759 088 2630	78	11.558 808 4653	138	75.951 875 7215
19	1.815 159 2014	79	11.927 245 4851	139	78.372 841 7602
20	1.873 017 4010	80	12.307 426 4350	140	80.870 976 0913
21	1.932 719 8306	81	12.699 725 6526	141	83.448 738 4542
22	1.994 325 2752	82	13.104 529 4078	142	86.108 666 9924
23	2.057 894 3934	83	13.522 236 2826	143	88.853 380 7528
24	2.123 489 7772	84	13.953 257 5641	144	91.685 582 2643
25	2.191 176 0138	85	14.398 017 6490	145	94.608 060 1990
26	2.261 019 7492	86	14.856 954 4616	146	97.623 692 1178
27	2.333 089 7538	87	15.330 519 8850	147	100.735 447 3040
28	2.407 456 9897	88	15.819 180 2064	148	103.946 389 6869
29	2.484 194 6812	89	16.323 416 5754	149	107.259 680 8581
30	2.563 378 3867	90	16.843 725 4788	150	110.678 583 1855
31	2.645 086 0727	91	17.380 619 2284	151	114.206 463 0245
32	2.729 398 1913	92	17.934 626 4663	152	117.846 794 0334
33	2.816 397 7587	93	18.506 292 6849	153	121.603 160 5932
34	2.906 170 4372	94	19.096 180 7643	154	125.479 261 3372
35	2.998 804 6199	95	19.704 871 5261	155	129.478 912 7923
36	3.094 391 5172	96	20.332 964 3060	156	133.606 053 1375
37	3.193 025 2468	97	20.981 077 5433	157	137.864 746 0813
38	3.294 802 9265	98	21.649 849 3900	158	142.259 184 8626
39	3.399 824 7698	99	22.339 938 3393	159	146.793 696 3801
40	3.508 194 1843	100	23.052 023 8738	160	151.472 745 4522
41	3.620 017 8740	101	23.786 807 1348	161	156.300 939 2135
42	3.735 405 9437	102	24.545 011 6122	162	161.283 031 6510
43	3.854 472 0081	103	25.327 383 8574	163	166.423 928 2848
44	3.977 333 3034	104	26.134 694 2178	164	171.728 690 9989
45	4.104 110 8024	105	26.967 737 5960	165	177.202 543 0245
46	4.234 929 3343	106	27.827 334 2319	166	182.850 874 0834
47	4.369 917 7068	107	28.714 330 5105	167	188.679 245 6948
48	4.509 208 8337	108	29.629 599 7956	168	194.693 396 6514
49	4.652 939 8653	109	30.574 043 2891	169	200.899 248 6696
50	4.801 252 3235	110	31.548 590 9189	170	207.302 912 2210
51	4.954 292 2413	111	32.554 202 2544	171	213.910 692 5480
52	5.112 210 3065	112	33.591 867 4513	172	220.729 095 8730
53	5.275 162 0100	113	34.662 608 2263	173	227.764 835 8039
54	5.443 307 7991	114	35.767 478 8635	174	235.024 839 9452
55	5.616 813 2352	115	36.907 567 2523	175	242.516 256 7184
56	5.795 849 1571	116	38.083 995 9585	176	250.246 462 4013
57	5.980 591 8489	117	39.297 923 3296	177	258.223 068 3904
58	6.171 223 2141	118	40.550 544 6358	178	266.453 928 6953
59	6.367 930 9541	119	41.843 093 2460	179	274.947 147 6725
60	6.570 908 7532	120	43.176 841 8432	180	283.711 088 0045

Amount of 1

NOMINAL INTEREST RATE COMPOUNDED

YEARLY	HALF-YEARLY	QUARTERLY
@	@	@
$3\frac{1}{4}\%$	$6\frac{1}{2}\%$	13%
3.2500%	6.5000%	13.0000%
PER ANNUM	PER ANNUM	PER ANNUM

Periods	Amount	Periods	Amount	Periods	Amount
1	1,032 500 0000	61	7,035 479 1453	121	47,939 919 4231
2	1,066 056 2500	62	7,264 132 2176	122	49,497 966 8044
3	1,100 703 0781	63	7,500 216 5146	123	51,106 650 7255
4	1,136 475 9282	64	7,743 973 5513	124	52,767 616 8741
5	1,173 411 3958	65	7,995 652 6918	125	54,482 564 4225
6	1,211 547 2662	66	8,255 511 4043	126	56,253 247 7662
7	1,250 922 5523	67	8,523 815 5249	127	58,081 478 3187
8	1,291 577 5353	68	8,800 839 5294	128	59,969 126 3640
9	1,333 553 8052	69	9,086 866 8142	129	61,918 122 9708
10	1,376 894 3039	70	9,382 189 9856	130	63,930 461 9674
11	1,421 643 3687	71	9,687 111 1601	131	66,008 201 9813
12	1,467 846 7782	72	10,001 942 2729	132	68,153 468 5457
13	1,515 551 7985	73	10,327 005 3967	133	70,368 456 2735
14	1,564 807 2320	74	10,662 633 0721	134	72,655 431 1023
15	1,615 663 4670	75	11,009 168 6470	135	75,016 732 6132
16	1,668 172 5297	76	11,366 966 6280	136	77,454 776 4231
17	1,722 388 1369	77	11,736 393 0434	137	79,972 056 6569
18	1,778 365 7513	78	12,117 825 8173	138	82,571 148 4982
19	1,836 162 6383	79	12,511 655 1564	139	85,254 710 8244
20	1,895 837 9240	80	12,918 283 9489	140	88,025 488 9262
21	1,957 452 6565	81	13,338 128 1773	141	90,886 317 3163
22	2,021 069 8679	82	13,771 617 3431	142	93,840 122 6291
23	2,086 754 6386	83	14,219 194 9067	143	96,889 926 6145
24	2,154 574 1643	84	14,681 318 7412	144	100,038 849 2295
25	2,224 597 8247	85	15,158 461 6003	145	103,290 111 8294
26	2,296 897 2540	86	15,651 111 6023	146	106,647 040 4639
27	2,371 546 4147	87	16,159 772 7293	147	110,113 069 2790
28	2,448 621 6732	88	16,684 965 3430	148	113,691 744 0305
29	2,528 201 8776	89	17,227 226 7167	149	117,386 725 7115
30	2,610 368 4386	90	17,787 111 5850	150	121,201 794 2972
31	2,695 205 4129	91	18,365 192 7115	151	125,140 852 6118
32	2,782 799 5888	92	18,962 061 4746	152	129,207 930 3217
33	2,873 240 5754	93	19,578 328 4725	153	133,407 188 0572
34	2,966 620 8941	94	20,214 624 1479	154	137,742 921 6690
35	3,063 036 0732	95	20,871 599 4327	155	142,219 566 6233
36	3,162 584 7456	96	21,549 926 4143	156	146,841 702 5385
37	3,265 368 7498	97	22,250 299 0227	157	151,614 057 8710
38	3,371 493 2342	98	22,973 433 7410	158	156,541 514 7518
39	3,481 066 7643	99	23,720 070 3376	159	161,629 113 9813
40	3,594 201 4341	100	24,490 972 6235	160	166,882 060 1856
41	3,711 012 9807	101	25,286 929 2338	161	172,305 727 1417
42	3,831 620 9026	102	26,108 754 4339	162	177,905 663 2738
43	3,956 148 5819	103	26,957 288 9530	163	183,687 597 3302
44	4,084 723 4108	104	27,833 400 8440	164	189,657 444 2434
45	4,217 476 9217	105	28,737 986 3714	165	195,821 311 1813
46	4,354 544 9216	106	29,671 970 9285	166	202,185 503 7947
47	4,496 067 6316	107	30,636 309 9836	167	208,756 532 6680
48	4,642 189 8296	108	31,631 990 0581	168	215,541 119 9798
49	4,793 060 9991	109	32,660 029 7350	169	222,546 206 3791
50	4,948 835 4816	110	33,721 480 7014	170	229,778 958 0864
51	5,109 672 6347	111	34,817 428 8242	171	237,246 774 2242
52	5,275 736 9953	112	35,948 995 2610	172	244,957 294 3865
53	5,447 198 4477	113	37,117 337 6069	173	252,918 406 4541
54	5,624 232 3972	114	38,323 651 0792	174	261,138 254 6638
55	5,807 019 9501	115	39,569 169 7392	175	269,625 247 9404
56	5,995 748 0985	116	40,855 167 7558	176	278,388 068 4985
57	6,190 609 9117	117	42,182 960 7078	177	287,435 680 7247
58	6,391 804 7339	118	43,553 906 9308	178	296,777 340 3482
59	6,599 538 3877	119	44,969 408 9061	179	306,422 603 9095
60	6,814 023 3853	120	46,430 914 6955	180	316,381 338 5366

Amount of 1

NOMINAL INTEREST RATE COMPOUNDED

	YEARLY @ $3\frac{5}{16}\%$ 3.3125% PER ANNUM		HALF-YEARLY @ $6\frac{5}{8}\%$ 6.6250% PER ANNUM		QUARTERLY @ $13\frac{1}{4}\%$ 12.2500% PER ANNUM
Periods	Amount	Periods	Amount	Periods	Amount
1	1.033 125 0000	61	7.300 038 0844	121	51.581 905 4168
2	1.067 347 2656	62	7.541 851 8459	122	53.290 556 0337
3	1.102 703 1438	63	7.791 675 6883	123	55.055 805 7024
4	1.139 230 1854	64	8.049 774 9455	124	56.879 529 2662
5	1.176 967 1853	65	8.316 423 7406	125	58.763 663 6732
6	1.215 954 2233	66	8.591 905 2770	126	60.710 210 0324
7	1.256 232 7070	67	8.876 512 1393	127	62.721 235 7397
8	1.297 845 4154	68	9.170 546 6039	128	64.798 876 6736
9	1.340 836 5448	69	9.474 320 9602	129	66.945 339 4634
10	1.385 251 7553	70	9.788 157 8420	130	69.162 903 8331
11	1.431 138 2197	71	10.112 390 5705	131	71.453 925 0226
12	1.478 544 6733	72	10.447 363 5081	132	73.820 836 2889
13	1.527 521 4656	73	10.793 432 4243	133	76.266 151 4910
14	1.578 120 6141	74	11.150 964 8734	134	78.792 467 7592
15	1.630 395 8595	75	11.520 340 5848	135	81.402 468 2537
16	1.684 402 7223	76	11.901 951 8667	136	84.098 925 0146
17	1.740 198 5625	77	12.296 204 0223	137	86.884 701 9057
18	1.797 842 6399	78	12.703 515 7805	138	89.762 757 6563
19	1.857 396 1773	79	13.124 319 7408	139	92.736 149 0037
20	1.918 922 4257	80	13.559 062 8322	140	95.808 033 9394
21	1.982 486 7310	81	14.008 206 7885	141	98.981 675 0637
22	2.048 156 6040	82	14.472 228 6384	142	102.260 443 0501
23	2.116 001 7915	83	14.951 621 2120	143	105.647 820 2262
24	2.186 094 3508	84	15.446 893 6646	144	109.147 404 2712
25	2.258 508 7262	85	15.958 572 0173	145	112.762 912 0377
26	2.333 321 8278	86	16.487 199 7154	146	116.498 183 4989
27	2.410 613 1133	87	17.033 338 2059	147	120.357 185 8273
28	2.490 464 6727	88	17.597 567 5340	148	124.344 017 6078
29	2.572 961 3150	89	18.180 486 9586	149	128.462 913 1911
30	2.658 190 6585	90	18.782 715 5891	150	132.718 247 1906
31	2.746 243 2241	91	19.404 893 0430	151	137.114 539 1287
32	2.837 212 5309	92	20.047 680 1250	152	141.656 458 2374
33	2.931 195 1960	93	20.711 759 5291	153	146.348 828 4165
34	3.028 291 0369	94	21.397 836 5636	154	151.196 633 3578
35	3.128 603 1775	95	22.106 639 8997	155	156.205 021 8378
36	3.232 238 1577	96	22.838 922 3464	156	161.379 313 1861
37	3.339 306 0467	97	23.595 461 6491	157	166.725 002 9354
38	3.449 920 5595	98	24.377 061 3163	158	172.247 768 6577
39	3.564 199 1780	99	25.184 551 4724	159	177.953 475 9945
40	3.682 263 2758	100	26.018 789 7399	160	183.848 184 8868
41	3.804 238 2468	101	26.880 662 1500	161	189.938 156 0111
42	3.930 253 6387	102	27.771 084 0837	162	196.229 857 4290
43	4.060 443 2905	103	28.691 001 2440	163	202.729 971 4563
44	4.194 945 4745	104	29.641 390 6602	164	209.445 401 7608
45	4.333 903 0433	105	30.623 261 7258	165	216.383 280 6942
46	4.477 463 5817	106	31.637 657 2705	166	223.550 976 8672
47	4.625 779 5628	107	32.685 654 6676	167	230.956 102 9759
48	4.779 008 5108	108	33.768 366 9784	168	238.606 523 8870
49	4.937 313 1677	109	34.886 944 1346	169	246.510 364 9907
50	5.100 861 6664	110	36.042 574 1591	170	254.676 020 8310
51	5.269 827 7091	111	37.236 484 4281	171	263.112 164 0211
52	5.444 390 7520	112	38.469 942 9748	172	271.827 754 4543
53	5.624 736 1956	113	39.744 259 8358	173	280.832 048 8206
54	5.811 055 5821	114	41.060 788 4429	174	290.134 610 4377
55	6.003 546 7983	115	42.420 927 0600	175	299.745 319 4085
56	6.202 414 2860	116	43.826 120 2689	176	309.674 383 1139
57	6.407 869 2592	117	45.277 860 5028	177	319.932 347 0545
58	6.620 129 9284	118	46.777 689 6320	178	330.530 106 0507
59	6.839 421 7323	119	48.327 200 6010	179	341.478 915 8137
60	7.065 977 5772	120	49.928 039 1209	180	352.790 404 9000

Amount of 1

NOMINAL INTEREST RATE COMPOUNDED

YEARLY	HALF-YEARLY	QUARTERLY
@	@	@
$3\frac{3}{8}\%$	$6\frac{3}{4}\%$	$13\frac{1}{2}\%$
3.3750%	6.7500%	13.5000%
PER ANNUM	PER ANNUM	PER ANNUM

Periods	Amount	Periods	Amount	Periods	Amount
1	1,033 750 0000	61	7,574 376 2798	121	55,498 114 6579
2	1,068 639 0625	62	7,830 011 4792	122	57,371 176 0276
3	1,104 705 6309	63	8,094 274 3666	123	59,307 453 2185
4	1,141 989 4459	64	8,367 456 1265	124	61,309 079 7647
5	1,180 531 5897	65	8,649 857 7708	125	63,378 261 2067
6	1,220 374 5309	66	8,941 790 4705	126	65,517 277 5224
7	1,261 562 1713	67	9,243 575 8989	127	67,728 485 6388
8	1,304 139 8945	68	9,555 546 5855	128	70,014 322 0291
9	1,348 154 6160	69	9,878 046 2828	129	72,377 305 3976
10	1,393 654 8343	70	10,211 430 3448	130	74,820 039 4548
11	1,440 690 6849	71	10,556 066 1190	131	77,345 215 7864
12	1,489 313 9956	72	10,912 333 3505	132	79,955 616 8192
13	1,539 578 3429	73	11,280 624 6011	133	82,654 118 8868
14	1,591 539 1120	74	11,661 345 6813	134	85,443 695 3993
15	1,645 253 5570	75	12,054 916 0981	135	88,327 420 1190
16	1,700 780 8646	76	12,461 769 5164	136	91,308 470 5480
17	1,758 182 2187	77	12,882 354 2376	137	94,390 131 4290
18	1,817 520 8686	78	13,317 133 6931	138	97,575 798 3647
19	1,878 862 1979	79	13,766 586 9552	139	100,868 981 5595
20	1,942 273 7971	80	14,231 209 2650	140	104,273 309 6872
21	2,007 825 5378	81	14,711 512 5777	141	107,792 533 8891
22	2,075 589 6497	82	15,208 026 1272	142	111,430 531 9079
23	2,145 640 8003	83	15,721 297 0090	143	115,191 312 3598
24	2,218 056 1774	84	16,251 890 7830	144	119,079 019 1519
25	2,292 915 5733	85	16,800 392 0969	145	123,097 936 0483
26	2,370 301 4739	86	17,367 405 3302	146	127,252 491 3899
27	2,450 299 1487	87	17,953 555 2601	147	131,547 262 9743
28	2,532 996 7449	88	18,559 487 7501	148	135,986 983 0997
29	2,618 485 3851	89	19,185 870 4617	149	140,576 543 7793
30	2,706 859 2668	90	19,833 393 5898	150	145,321 002 1319
31	2,798 215 7671	91	20,502 770 6234	151	150,225 585 9538
32	2,892 655 5492	92	21,194 739 1320	152	155,295 699 4798
33	2,990 282 6740	93	21,910 061 5777	153	160,536 929 3372
34	3,091 204 7143	94	22,649 526 1559	154	165,955 050 7023
35	3,195 532 8734	95	23,413 947 6637	155	171,556 033 6635
36	3,303 382 1079	96	24,204 168 3973	156	177,346 049 7997
37	3,414 871 2540	97	25,021 059 0807	157	183,331 478 9804
38	3,530 123 1588	98	25,865 519 8247	158	189,518 916 3960
39	3,649 264 8154	99	26,738 481 1188	159	195,915 179 8244
40	3,772 427 5029	100	27,640 904 8566	160	202,527 317 1434
41	3,899 746 9312	101	28,573 785 3955	161	209,362 614 0970
42	4,031 363 3901	102	29,538 150 6526	162	216,428 602 3228
43	4,167 421 9045	103	30,535 063 2371	163	223,733 067 6512
44	4,308 072 3938	104	31,565 621 6213	164	231,284 058 6844
45	4,453 469 8371	105	32,630 961 3511	165	239,089 895 6650
46	4,603 774 4441	106	33,732 256 2967	166	247,159 179 6437
47	4,759 151 8316	107	34,870 719 9467	167	255,500 801 9567
48	4,919 773 2059	108	36,047 606 7449	168	264,123 954 0227
49	5,085 815 5516	109	37,264 213 4725	169	273,038 137 4710
50	5,257 461 8264	110	38,521 880 6772	170	282,253 174 6106
51	5,434 901 1631	111	39,821 994 1501	171	291,779 219 2538
52	5,618 329 0773	112	41,165 986 4526	172	301,626 767 9036
53	5,807 947 6837	113	42,555 338 4954	173	311,806 671 3203
54	6,003 965 9180	114	43,991 581 1696	174	322,330 146 4774
55	6,206 599 7678	115	45,476 297 0341	175	333,208 788 9210
56	6,416 072 5099	116	47,011 122 0590	176	344,454 585 5471
57	6,632 614 9571	117	48,597 747 4285	177	356,079 927 8093
58	6,856 465 7119	118	50,237 921 4042	178	368,097 625 3728
59	7,087 871 4297	119	51,933 451 2516	179	380,520 920 2292
60	7,327 087 0905	120	53,686 205 2313	180	393,363 501 2869

NOMINAL INTEREST RATE COMPOUNDED

YEARLY @ $3\frac{7}{16}\%$ 3.4375% PER ANNUM		HALF-YEARLY @ $6\frac{7}{8}\%$ 6.8750% PER ANNUM		QUARTERLY @ $13\frac{3}{4}\%$ 13.7500% PER ANNUM	
Periods	Amount	Periods	Amount	Periods	Amount
1	1.034 375 0000	61	7.858 848 9727	121	59.709 009 9578
2	1.069 931 6406	62	8.128 996 9061	122	61.761 507 1751
3	1.106 710 5408	63	8.408 431 1747	123	63.884 558 9843
4	1.144 753 7156	64	8.697 470 9964	124	66.080 590 6994
5	1.184 104 6246	65	8.996 446 5619	125	68.352 111 0047
6	1.224 808 2211	66	9.305 699 4124	126	70.701 714 8205
7	1.266 911 0037	67	9.625 582 8297	127	73.132 086 2674
8	1.310 461 0694	68	9.956 462 2395	128	75.646 001 7329
9	1.355 508 1687	69	10.298 715 6290	129	78.246 333 0424
10	1.402 103 7620	70	10.652 733 9787	130	80.936 050 7408
11	1.450 301 0788	71	11.018 921 7093	131	83.718 227 4850
12	1.500 155 1784	72	11.397 697 1430	132	86.596 041 5548
13	1.551 723 0126	73	11.789 492 9823	133	89.572 780 4832
14	1.605 063 4912	74	12.194 756 8036	134	92.651 844 8123
15	1.660 237 5487	75	12.613 951 5687	135	95.836 751 9777
16	1.717 308 2144	76	13.047 556 1539	136	99.131 140 3270
17	1.776 340 6843	77	13.496 065 8967	137	102.538 773 2757
18	1.837 402 3953	78	13.959 993 1619	138	106.063 543 6071
19	1.900 563 1027	79	14.439 867 9268	139	109.709 477 9186
20	1.965 894 9593	80	14.936 238 3868	140	113.480 741 2220
21	2.033 472 5985	81	15.449 671 5813	141	117.381 641 7015
22	2.103 373 2191	82	15.980 754 0419	142	121.416 635 6350
23	2.175 676 6735	83	16.530 092 4621	143	125.590 332 4850
24	2.250 465 5592	84	17.098 314 3905	144	129.907 500 1641
25	2.327 825 3128	85	17.686 068 9477	145	134.373 070 4823
26	2.407 844 3079	86	18.294 027 5678	146	138.992 144 7801
27	2.490 613 9560	87	18.922 884 7654	147	143.769 999 7569
28	2.576 228 8107	88	19.573 358 9292	148	148.712 093 4986
29	2.664 786 6761	89	20.246 193 1424	149	153.824 071 7126
30	2.756 388 7181	90	20.942 156 0317	150	159.111 774 1777
31	2.851 139 5803	91	21.662 042 6453	151	164.581 241 4151
32	2.949 147 5033	92	22.406 675 3612	152	170.238 721 5887
33	3.050 524 4488	93	23.176 904 8268	153	176.090 677 6433
34	3.155 386 2267	94	23.973 610 9302	154	182.143 794 6873
35	3.263 852 6282	95	24.797 703 8059	155	188.404 987 6297
36	3.376 047 5623	96	25.650 124 8742	156	194.881 409 0794
37	3.492 099 1973	97	26.531 847 9168	157	201.580 457 5165
38	3.612 140 1072	98	27.443 880 1889	158	208.509 785 7437
39	3.736 307 4234	99	28.387 263 5704	159	215.677 309 6286
40	3.864 742 9910	100	29.363 075 7556	160	223.091 217 1471
41	3.997 593 5314	101	30.372 431 4847	161	230.759 977 7365
42	4.135 010 8090	102	31.416 483 8170	162	238.692 351 9712
43	4.277 151 8056	103	32.496 425 4482	163	246.897 401 5702
44	4.424 178 8989	104	33.613 490 0730	164	255.384 499 7492
45	4.576 260 0485	105	34.768 953 7943	165	264.163 341 9281
46	4.733 568 9877	106	35.964 136 5810	166	273.243 956 8069
47	4.896 285 4216	107	37.200 403 7759	167	282.636 717 8221
48	5.064 595 2330	108	38.479 167 6557	168	292.352 354 9972
49	5.238 690 6941	109	39.801 889 0439	169	302.401 967 2003
50	5.418 770 6868	110	41.170 078 9798	170	312.797 034 8228
51	5.605 040 9291	111	42.585 300 4447	171	323.549 432 8948
52	5.797 714 2111	112	44.049 170 1475	172	334.671 444 6506
53	5.997 010 6371	113	45.563 360 3713	173	346.175 775 5604
54	6.203 157 8777	114	47.129 600 8841	174	358.075 567 8453
55	6.416 391 4298	115	48.749 680 9145	175	370.384 415 4900
56	6.636 954 8851	116	50.425 451 1959	176	383.116 379 7725
57	6.865 100 2093	117	52.158 826 0808	177	396.286 005 3272
58	7.101 088 0290	118	53.951 785 7273	178	409.908 336 7603
59	7.345 187 9300	119	55.806 378 3617	179	423.998 935 8364
60	7.597 678 7651	120	57.724 722 6179	180	438.573 899 2558

Amount of 1

NOMINAL INTEREST RATE COMPOUNDED

YEARLY	HALF-YEARLY	QUARTERLY
@	@	@
3½%	**7%**	**14%**
3.5000%	7.0000%	14.0000%
PER ANNUM	PER ANNUM	PER ANNUM

Periods	Amount	Periods	Amount	Periods	Amount
1	1,035 000 0000	61	8,153 824 0823	121	64,236 567 3090
2	1,071 225 0000	62	8,439 207 9252	122	66,484 847 1648
3	1,108 717 8750	63	8,734 580 2025	123	68,811 816 8156
4	1,147 523 0006	64	9,040 290 5096	124	71,220 230 4042
5	1,187 686 3056	65	9,356 700 6775	125	73,712 938 4683
6	1,229 255 3263	66	9,684 185 2012	126	76,292 891 3147
7	1,272 279 2628	67	10,023 131 6832	127	78,963 142 5107
8	1,316 809 0370	68	10,373 941 2921	128	81,726 852 4986
9	1,362 897 3533	69	10,737 029 2374	129	84,587 292 3360
10	1,410 598 7606	70	11,112 825 2607	130	87,547 847 5678
11	1,459 969 7172	71	11,501 774 1448	131	90,612 022 2327
12	1,511 068 6573	72	11,904 336 2399	132	93,783 443 0108
13	1,563 956 0604	73	12,320 988 0083	133	97,065 863 5162
14	1,618 694 5225	74	12,752 222 5885	134	100,463 168 7393
15	1,675 348 8308	75	13,198 550 3791	135	103,979 379 6451
16	1,733 986 0398	76	13,660 499 6424	136	107,618 657 9327
17	1,794 675 5512	77	14,138 617 1299	137	111,385 310 9604
18	1,857 489 1955	78	14,633 468 7294	138	115,283 796 8440
19	1,922 501 3174	79	15,145 640 1350	139	119,318 729 7335
20	1,989 788 8635	80	15,675 737 5397	140	123,494 885 2742
21	2,059 431 4737	81	16,224 388 3536	141	127,817 206 2588
22	2,131 511 5753	82	16,792 241 94[illegible]0	142	132,290 808 4778
23	2,206 114 4804	83	17,379 970 4141	143	136,920 986 7746
24	2,283 328 4872	84	17,988 269 3786	144	141,713 221 3117
25	2,363 244 9843	85	18,617 858 8068	145	146,673 184 0576
26	2,445 958 5587	86	19,269 483 8[illegible]51	146	151,806 745 4996
27	2,531 567 1083	87	19,943 915 8003	147	157,119 981 5921
28	2,620 171 9571	88	20,641 952 8533	148	162,619 180 9478
29	2,711 877 9756	89	21,364 421 2032	149	168,310 852 2810
30	2,806 793 7047	90	22,112 175 9453	150	174,201 732 1108
31	2,905 031 4844	91	22,886 102 1034	151	180,298 792 7347
32	3,006 707 5863	92	23,687 115 6770	152	186,609 250 4804
33	3,111 942 3518	93	24,516 164 7257	153	193,140 574 2472
34	3,220 860 3342	94	25,374 230 4911	154	199,900 494 3459
35	3,333 590 4459	95	26,262 328 5583	155	206,897 011 6480
36	3,450 266 1115	96	27,181 510 0579	156	214,138 407 0557
37	3,571 025 4254	97	28,132 862 9099	157	221,633 251 3026
38	3,696 011 3152	98	29,117 513 1117	158	229,390 415 0982
39	3,825 371 7113	99	30,136 626 0706	159	237,419 079 6266
40	3,959 259 7212	100	31,191 407 9831	160	245,728 747 4136
41	4,097 833 8114	101	32,283 107 2625	161	254,329 253 5731
42	4,241 257 9948	102	33,413 016 0167	162	263,230 777 4481
43	4,389 702 0246	103	34,582 471 5773	163	272,443 854 6588
44	4,543 341 5955	104	35,792 858 0825	164	281,979 389 5719
45	4,702 358 5513	105	37,045 608 1154	165	291,848 668 2069
46	4,866 941 1006	106	38,342 204 3994	166	302,063 371 5941
47	5,037 284 0392	107	39,684 181 5534	167	312,635 589 5999
48	5,213 588 9805	108	41,073 127 9078	168	323,577 835 2359
49	5,396 064 5948	109	42,510 687 3845	169	334,903 059 4692
50	5,584 926 8557	110	43,998 561 4430	170	346,624 666 5506
51	5,780 399 2956	111	45,538 511 0935	171	358,756 529 8798
52	5,982 713 2710	112	47,132 358 9818	172	371,313 008 4256
53	6,192 108 2354	113	48,781 991 5461	173	384,308 963 7205
54	6,408 832 0237	114	50,489 361 2503	174	397,759 777 4508
55	6,633 141 1445	115	52,256 488 8940	175	411,681 369 6615
56	6,865 301 0846	116	54,085 466 0053	176	426,090 217 5997
57	7,105 586 6225	117	55,978 457 3155	177	441,003 375 2157
58	7,354 282 1543	118	57,937 703 3215	178	456,438 493 3482
59	7,611 682 0297	119	59,965 522 9378	179	472,413 840 6154
60	7,878 090 9008	120	62,064 316 2406	180	488,948 325 0369

NOMINAL INTEREST RATE COMPOUNDED

	YEARLY	HALF-YEARLY	QUARTERLY
	@	@	@
	$3\frac{9}{16}\%$	$7\frac{1}{8}\%$	$14\frac{1}{4}\%$
	3.5625%	7.1250%	14.2500%
	PER ANNUM	PER ANNUM	PER ANNUM

Periods	Amount	Periods	Amount	Periods	Amount
1	1.035 625 0000	61	8.459 682 6502	121	69.104 386 7640
2	1.072 519 1406	62	8.761 058 8446	122	71.566 230 5424
3	1.110 727 6350	63	9.073 171 5660	123	74.115 777 5055
4	1.150 297 3070	64	9.396 403 3030	124	76.756 152 0791
5	1.191 276 6486	65	9.731 150 1707	125	79.490 589 9969
6	1.233 715 8792	66	10.077 822 3955	126	82.322 442 2656
7	1.277 667 0074	67	10.436 844 8184	127	85.255 179 2713
8	1.323 183 8945	68	10.808 657 4150	128	88.292 395 0328
9	1.370 322 3207	69	11.193 715 8354	129	91.437 811 6059
10	1.419 140 0534	70	11.592 491 9621	130	94.695 283 6443
11	1.469 696 9178	71	12.005 474 4882	131	98.068 803 1242
12	1.522 054 8705	72	12.433 169 5168	132	101.562 504 2355
13	1.576 278 0753	73	12.876 101 1809	133	105.180 668 4489
14	1.632 432 9817	74	13.334 812 2854	134	108.927 729 7623
15	1.690 588 4067	75	13.809 864 9731	135	112.808 280 1351
16	1.750 815 6187	76	14.301 841 4128	136	116.827 075 1149
17	1.813 188 4251	77	14.811 344 5131	137	120.989 039 6659
18	1.877 783 2627	78	15.338 998 6614	138	125.299 274 2040
19	1.944 679 2915	79	15.885 450 4887	139	129.763 060 8475
20	2.013 958 4912	80	16.451 369 6624	140	134.385 869 8902
21	2.085 705 7625	81	17.037 449 7066	141	139.173 366 5051
22	2.160 009 0303	82	17.644 408 8524	142	144.131 417 6868
23	2.236 959 3520	83	18.272 990 9178	143	149.266 099 4419
24	2.316 651 0289	84	18.923 966 2192	144	154.583 704 2345
25	2.399 181 7218	85	19.598 132 5158	145	160.090 748 6979
26	2.484 652 5706	86	20.296 315 9866	146	165.793 981 6202
27	2.573 168 3185	87	21.019 372 2437	147	171.700 392 2155
28	2.664 837 4398	88	21.768 187 3798	148	177.817 218 6881
29	2.759 772 2736	89	22.543 679 0552	149	184.151 957 1039
30	2.858 089 1609	90	23.346 797 6216	150	190.712 370 5757
31	2.959 908 5872	91	24.178 527 2869	151	197.506 498 7775
32	3.065 355 3306	92	25.039 887 3214	152	204.542 667 7964
33	3.174 558 6143	93	25.931 933 3073	153	211.829 500 3367
34	3.287 652 2649	94	26.855 758 4313	154	219.375 926 2862
35	3.404 774 8769	95	27.812 494 8255	155	227.191 193 6601
36	3.526 069 9818	96	28.803 314 9536	156	235.284 879 9343
37	3.651 686 2249	97	29.829 433 0488	157	243.666 903 7819
38	3.781 777 5467	98	30.892 106 6012	158	252.347 537 2291
39	3.916 503 3718	99	31.992 637 8989	159	261.337 418 2429
40	4.056 028 8044	100	33.132 375 6240	160	270.647 563 7678
41	4.200 524 8306	101	34.312 716 5056	161	280.289 383 2271
42	4.350 168 5277	102	35.535 107 0311	162	290.274 692 5045
43	4.505 143 2815	103	36.801 045 2191	163	300.615 728 4250
44	4.665 639 0109	104	38.112 082 4551	164	311.325 163 7501
45	4.831 852 4006	105	39.469 825 3925	165	322.416 122 7087
46	5.003 987 1424	106	40.875 937 9221	166	333.902 197 0802
47	5.182 254 1844	107	42.332 143 2106	167	345.797 462 8512
48	5.366 871 9897	108	43.840 225 8125	168	358.116 497 4653
49	5.558 066 8043	109	45.402 033 8570	169	370.874 397 6875
50	5.756 072 9342	110	47.019 481 3132	170	384.086 798 1051
51	5.961 133 0325	111	48.694 550 3350	171	397.769 890 2876
52	6.173 498 3968	112	50.429 293 6907	172	411.940 442 6291
53	6.393 429 2772	113	52.225 837 2784	173	426.615 820 8978
54	6.621 195 1952	114	54.086 382 7314	174	441.814 009 5173
55	6.857 075 2740	115	56.013 210 1163	175	457.553 633 6063
56	7.101 358 5806	116	58.008 680 7266	176	473.853 981 8035
57	7.354 344 4801	117	60.075 239 9775	177	490.735 029 9053
58	7.616 343 0022	118	62.215 420 4017	178	508.217 465 3457
59	7.887 675 2216	119	64.431 844 7535	179	526.322 712 5486
60	8.168 673 6514	120	66.727 229 2229	180	545.072 959 1831

NOMINAL INTEREST RATE COMPOUNDED

YEARLY @ $3\frac{5}{8}\%$ 3.6250% PER ANNUM		HALF-YEARLY @ $7\frac{1}{4}\%$ 7.2500% PER ANNUM		QUARTERLY @ $14\frac{1}{2}\%$ 14.5000% PER ANNUM	
Periods	**Amount**	**Periods**	**Amount**	**Periods**	**Amount**
1	1.036 250 0000	61	8.776 819 3001	121	74.337 811 3647
2	1.073 814 0625	62	9.094 978 9997	122	77.032 557 0266
3	1.112 739 8223	63	9.424 671 9885	123	79.824 987 2189
4	1.153 076 6408	64	9.766 316 3481	124	82.718 643 0055
5	1.194 875 6691	65	10.120 345 3157	125	85.717 193 8145
6	1.238 189 9121	66	10.487 207 8334	126	88.824 442 0903
7	1.283 074 2964	67	10.867 369 1173	127	92.044 328 1160
8	1.329 585 7396	68	11.261 311 2478	128	95.380 935 0102
9	1.377 783 2227	69	11.669 533 7806	129	98.838 493 9044
10	1.427 727 8645	70	12.092 554 3801	130	102.421 389 3084
11	1.479 482 9996	71	12.530 909 4764	131	106.134 164 6708
12	1.533 114 2583	72	12.985 154 9449	132	109.981 528 1401
13	1.588 689 6502	73	13.455 866 8117	133	113.968 358 5352
14	1.646 279 6500	74	13.943 641 9836	134	118.099 711 5321
15	1.705 957 2873	75	14.449 099 0055	135	122.380 826 0752
16	1.767 798 2390	76	14.972 878 8444	136	126.817 131 0204
17	1.831 880 9251	77	15.515 645 7025	137	131.414 252 0199
18	1.898 286 6087	78	16.078 087 8593	138	136.178 018 6556
19	1.967 099 4982	79	16.660 918 5442	139	141.114 471 8319
20	2.038 406 8551	80	17.264 876 8414	140	146.229 871 4358
21	2.112 299 1035	81	17.890 728 6269	141	151.530 704 2753
22	2.188 869 9461	82	18.539 267 5396	142	157.023 692 3053
23	2.268 216 4816	83	19.211 315 9879	143	162.715 801 1514
24	2.350 439 3291	84	19.907 726 1925	144	168.614 248 9431
25	2.435 642 7547	85	20.629 381 2670	145	174.726 515 4673
26	2.523 934 8046	86	21.377 196 3379	146	181.060 351 6530
27	2.615 427 4413	87	22.152 119 7051	147	187.623 789 4004
28	2.710 236 6860	88	22.955 134 0444	148	194.425 151 7662
29	2.808 482 7659	89	23.787 257 6536	149	201.473 063 5177
30	2.910 290 2661	90	24.649 545 7435	150	208.776 462 0702
31	3.015 788 2883	91	25.543 091 7767	151	216.344 608 8202
32	3.125 110 6137	92	26.469 028 8536	152	224.187 100 8900
33	3.238 395 8735	93	27.428 531 1495	153	232.313 883 2972
34	3.355 787 7239	94	28.422 815 4037	154	240.735 261 5668
35	3.477 435 0289	95	29.453 142 4621	155	249.461 914 7986
36	3.603 492 0487	96	30.520 818 8764	156	258.504 909 2100
37	3.734 118 6354	97	31.627 198 5606	157	267.875 712 1689
38	3.869 480 4360	98	32.775 684 5084	158	277.586 206 7350
39	4.009 749 1018	99	33.961 730 5719	159	287.648 706 7291
40	4.155 102 5067	100	35.192 843 3051	160	298.075 972 3481
41	4.305 724 9726	101	36.468 583 8749	161	308.881 226 3457
42	4.461 807 5028	102	37.790 570 0404	162	320.078 170 8007
43	4.623 548 0248	103	39.160 478 2043	163	331.681 004 4922
44	4.791 151 6407	104	40.580 045 5392	164	343.704 440 9051
45	4.964 830 8877	105	42.051 072 1900	165	356.163 726 8879
46	5.144 806 0074	106	43.575 423 5569	166	369.074 661 9876
47	5.331 305 2252	107	45.155 032 6609	167	382.453 618 4846
48	5.524 565 0396	108	46.791 902 5948	168	396.317 562 1547
49	5.724 830 5222	109	48.488 109 0639	169	410.684 073 7828
50	5.932 355 6287	110	50.245 803 0175	170	425.571 371 4574
51	6.147 403 5202	111	52.067 213 3768	171	440.998 333 6728
52	6.370 246 8978	112	53.954 649 8618	172	456.984 523 2684
53	6.601 168 3479	113	55.910 505 9192	173	473.550 212 2369
54	6.840 460 7005	114	57.937 261 7588	174	490.716 407 4305
55	7.088 427 4009	115	60.037 487 4976	175	508.504 877 1998
56	7.345 382 8942	116	62.213 846 4194	176	526.938 178 9983
57	7.611 653 0241	117	64.469 098 3521	177	546.039 687 9870
58	7.887 575 4462	118	66.806 103 1673	178	565.833 626 6765
59	8.173 500 0561	119	69.227 824 4071	179	586.345 095 6435
60	8.469 789 4331	120	71.737 333 0419	180	607.600 105 3606

NOMINAL INTEREST RATE COMPOUNDED

	YEARLY		HALF-YEARLY		QUARTERLY
	@ $3\frac{11}{16}\%$ 3.6875% PER ANNUM		@ $7\frac{3}{8}\%$ 7.3750% PER ANNUM		@ $14\frac{3}{4}\%$ 14.7500% PER ANNUM
Periods	Amount	Periods	Amount	Periods	Amount
1	1.036 875 0000	61	9.105 642 7131	121	79.964 054 7016
2	1.075 109 7656	62	9.441 413 2882	122	82.912 729 2187
3	1.114 754 4382	63	9.789 565 4032	123	85.970 136 1087
4	1.155 861 0081	64	10.150 555 6274	124	89.140 284 8777
5	1.198 483 3828	65	10.524 857 3662	125	92.427 332 8825
6	1.242 677 4576	66	10.912 961 4815	126	95.835 590 7826
7	1.288 501 1888	67	11.315 376 9362	127	99.369 528 1927
8	1.336 014 6701	68	11.732 631 4607	128	103.033 779 5448
9	1.385 280 2111	69	12.165 272 2458	129	106.833 150 1655
10	1.436 362 4189	70	12.613 866 6599	130	110.772 622 5779
11	1.489 328 2831	71	13.079 002 9929	131	114.857 363 0354
12	1.544 247 2635	72	13.561 291 2283	132	119.092 728 2974
13	1.601 191 3814	73	14.061 363 8423	133	123.484 272 6533
14	1.660 235 3136	74	14.579 876 6340	134	128.037 755 2074
15	1.721 456 4907	75	15.117 509 5849	135	132.759 147 4307
16	1.784 935 1988	76	15.674 967 7509	136	137.654 640 9922
17	1.850 754 6843	77	16.252 982 1867	137	142.730 655 8788
18	1.919 001 2633	78	16.852 310 9048	138	147.993 848 8143
19	1.989 764 4349	79	17.473 739 8694	139	153.451 121 9893
20	2.063 136 9984	80	18.118 084 0271	140	159.109 632 1127
21	2.139 215 1752	81	18.786 188 3756	141	164.976 799 7969
22	2.218 098 7348	82	19.478 929 0720	142	171.060 319 2894
23	2.299 891 1256	83	20.197 214 5815	143	177.368 168 5632
24	2.384 699 6109	84	20.941 986 8692	144	183.908 619 7789
25	2.472 635 4091	85	21.714 222 6350	145	190.690 250 1333
26	2.563 813 8398	86	22.514 934 5946	146	197.721 953 1069
27	2.658 354 4751	87	23.345 172 8078	147	205.012 950 1278
28	2.756 381 2964	88	24.206 026 0551	148	212.572 802 6637
29	2.858 022 8567	89	25.098 623 2659	149	220.411 424 7619
30	2.963 412 4495	90	26.024 134 9988	150	228.539 096 0500
31	3.072 688 2836	91	26.983 774 9769	151	236.966 475 2169
32	3.185 993 6641	92	27.978 801 6792	152	245.704 613 9905
33	3.303 477 1804	93	29.010 519 9911	153	254.764 971 6314
34	3.425 292 9014	94	30.080 282 9158	154	264.159 429 9603
35	3.551 600 5772	95	31.189 493 3483	155	273.900 308 9401
36	3.682 565 8485	96	32.339 605 9155	156	284.000 382 8323
37	3.818 360 4641	97	33.532 128 8836	157	294.472 896 9492
38	3.959 162 5062	98	34.768 626 1362	158	305.331 585 0242
39	4.105 156 6237	99	36.050 719 2250	159	316.590 687 2220
40	4.256 534 2742	100	37.380 089 4964	160	328.264 968 8133
41	4.413 493 9755	101	38.758 480 2966	161	340.369 739 5383
42	4.576 241 5659	102	40.187 699 2575	162	352.920 873 6837
43	4.744 990 4736	103	41.669 620 6677	163	365.934 830 9008
44	4.919 961 9973	104	43.206 187 9298	164	379.428 677 7903
45	5.101 385 5960	105	44.799 416 1097	165	393.420 110 2838
46	5.289 499 1898	106	46.451 394 5787	166	407.927 476 8505
47	5.484 549 4725	107	48.164 289 7538	167	422.969 802 5594
48	5.686 792 2342	108	49.940 347 9385	168	438.566 814 0288
49	5.896 492 6979	109	51.781 898 2687	169	454.738 965 2961
50	6.113 925 8661	110	53.691 355 7674	170	471.507 464 6414
51	6.339 376 8824	111	55.671 224 5113	171	488.894 302 4000
52	6.573 141 4050	112	57.724 100 9152	172	506.922 279 8010
53	6.815 525 9943	113	59.852 677 1364	173	525.615 038 8687
54	7.066 848 5153	114	62.059 744 6058	174	544.997 093 4270
55	7.327 438 5543	115	64.348 197 6882	175	565.093 861 2471
56	7.597 637 8510	116	66.721 037 4779	176	585.931 697 3806
57	7.877 800 7468	117	69.181 375 7349	177	607.537 928 7215
58	8.168 294 6493	118	71.732 438 9651	178	629.940 889 8431
59	8.469 500 5145	119	74.377 572 6520	179	653.169 960 1561
60	8.781 813 3460	120	77.120 245 6435	180	677.255 602 4368

Amount of 1

NOMINAL INTEREST RATE COMPOUNDED

YEARLY	HALF-YEARLY	QUARTERLY
@	@	@
$3\frac{3}{4}\%$	$7\frac{1}{2}\%$	15%
3.7500%	7.5000%	15.0000%
PER ANNUM	PER ANNUM	PER ANNUM

Periods	Amount	Periods	Amount	Periods	Amount
1	1,037 500 0000	61	9,446 576 1198	121	86,012 337 7221
2	1,076 406 2500	62	9,800 822 7243	122	89,237 800 3867
3	1,116 771 4844	63	10,168 353 5764	123	92,584 217 9012
4	1,158 650 4150	64	10,549 666 8355	124	96,056 126 0725
5	1,202 099 8056	65	10,945 279 3419	125	99,658 230 8002
6	1,247 178 5483	66	11,355 727 3172	126	103,395 414 4552
7	1,293 947 7439	67	11,781 567 0916	127	107,272 742 4973
8	1,342 470 7843	68	12,223 375 8575	128	111,295 470 3409
9	1,392 813 4387	69	12,681 752 4522	129	115,469 050 4787
10	1,445 043 9426	70	13,157 318 1691	130	119,799 139 8716
11	1,499 233 0905	71	13,650 717 6005	131	124,291 607 6168
12	1,555 454 3314	72	14,162 619 5105	132	128,952 542 9025
13	1,613 783 8688	73	14,693 717 7421	133	133,788 263 2613
14	1,674 300 7639	74	15,244 732 1575	134	138,805 323 1336
15	1,737 087 0425	75	15,816 409 6134	135	144,010 522 7511
16	1,802 227 8066	76	16,409 524 9739	136	149,410 917 3543
17	1,869 811 3494	77	17,024 882 1604	137	155,013 826 7551
18	1,939 929 2750	78	17,663 315 2414	138	160,826 845 2584
19	2,012 676 6228	79	18,325 689 5630	139	166,857 851 9556
20	2,088 151 9961	80	19,012 902 9216	140	173,115 021 4039
21	2,166 457 6960	81	19,725 886 7811	141	179,606 834 7066
22	2,247 699 8596	82	20,465 607 5354	142	186,342 091 0080
23	2,331 988 6043	83	21,233 067 8180	143	193,329 919 4209
24	2,419 438 1770	84	22,029 307 8612	144	200,579 791 3991
25	2,510 167 1086	85	22,855 406 9060	145	208,101 533 5766
26	2,604 298 3752	86	23,712 484 6650	146	215,905 341 0857
27	2,701 959 5643	87	24,601 702 8399	147	224,001 791 3764
28	2,803 283 0479	88	25,524 266 6964	148	232,401 858 5531
29	2,908 406 1622	89	26,481 426 6975	149	241,116 928 2488
30	3,017 471 3933	90	27,474 480 1987	150	250,158 813 0581
31	3,130 626 5706	91	28,504 773 2061	151	259,539 768 5478
32	3,248 025 0670	92	29,573 702 2013	152	269,272 509 8683
33	3,369 826 0070	93	30,682 716 0339	153	279,370 228 9884
34	3,496 194 4822	94	31,833 317 8852	154	289,846 612 5755
35	3,627 301 7753	95	33,027 067 3058	155	300,715 860 5471
36	3,763 325 5919	96	34,265 582 3298	156	311,992 705 3176
37	3,904 450 3016	97	35,550 541 6672	157	323,692 431 7670
38	4,050 867 1879	98	36,883 686 9797	158	335,830 897 9582
39	4,202 774 7074	99	38,266 825 2414	159	348,424 556 6317
40	4,360 378 7590	100	39,701 831 1880	160	361,490 477 5054
41	4,523 892 9624	101	41,190 649 8575	161	375,046 370 4118
42	4,693 538 9485	102	42,735 299 2272	162	389,110 609 3023
43	4,869 546 6591	103	44,337 872 9482	163	403,702 257 1511
44	5,052 154 6588	104	46,000 543 1838	164	418,841 091 7943
45	5,241 610 4585	105	47,725 563 5532	165	434,547 632 7365
46	5,438 170 8507	106	49,515 272 1864	166	450,843 168 9642
47	5,642 102 2576	107	51,372 094 8934	167	467,749 787 8003
48	5,853 681 0923	108	53,298 548 4519	168	485,290 404 8428
49	6,073 194 1332	109	55,297 244 0189	169	503,488 795 0244
50	6,300 938 9132	110	57,370 890 6696	170	522,369 624 8378
51	6,537 224 1225	111	59,522 299 0697	171	541,958 485 7693
52	6,782 370 0270	112	61,754 385 2848	172	562,281 928 9856
53	7,036 708 9031	113	64,070 174 7330	173	583,367 501 3226
54	7,300 585 4869	114	66,472 806 2855	174	605,243 782 6222
55	7,574 357 4427	115	68,965 536 5212	175	627,940 424 4705
56	7,858 395 8468	116	71,551 744 1407	176	651,488 190 3881
57	8,153 085 6910	117	74,234 934 5460	177	675,918 997 5277
58	8,458 826 4045	118	77,018 744 5915	178	701,265 959 9350
59	8,776 032 3946	119	79,906 947 5136	179	727,563 433 4326
60	9,105 133 6094	120	82,903 458 0454	180	754,847 062 1863

Amount of 1

NOMINAL INTEREST RATE COMPOUNDED

	YEARLY @ $3\frac{13}{16}\%$ 3.8125% PER ANNUM		HALF-YEARLY @ $7\frac{5}{8}\%$ 7.6250% PER ANNUM		QUARTERLY @ $15\frac{1}{4}\%$ 15.2500% PER ANNUM
Periods	Amount	Periods	Amount	Periods	Amount
1	1,038 125 0000	61	9,800 057 8087	121	92,514 035 4531
2	1,077 703 5156	62	10,173 685 0127	122	96,041 133 0548
3	1,118 790 9622	63	10,561 556 7538	123	99,702 701 2525
4	1,161 444 8676	64	10,964 216 1051	124	103,503 866 7377
5	1,205 724 9532	65	11,382 226 8441	125	107,449 951 6571
6	1,251 693 2170	66	11,816 174 2425	126	111,546 481 0640
7	1,299 414 0209	67	12,266 665 8855	127	115,799 190 6546
8	1,348 954 1805	68	12,734 332 5224	128	120,214 034 7983
9	1,400 383 0586	69	13,219 828 9498	129	124,797 194 8750
10	1,453 772 6627	70	13,723 834 9285	130	129,555 087 9296
11	1,509 197 7455	71	14,247 056 1351	131	134,494 375 6569
12	1,566 735 9095	72	14,790 225 1503	132	139,621 973 7288
13	1,626 467 7161	73	15,354 102 4841	133	144,945 061 4772
14	1,688 476 7977	74	15,939 477 6414	134	150,471 091 9461
15	1,752 849 9756	75	16,547 170 2264	135	156,207 802 3265
16	1,819 677 3810	76	17,178 031 0913	136	162,163 224 7902
17	1,889 052 5811	77	17,832 943 5267	137	168,345 697 7353
18	1,961 072 7108	78	18,512 824 4986	138	174,763 877 4615
19	2,035 838 6079	79	19,218 625 9326	139	181,426 750 2897
20	2,113 454 9548	80	19,951 336 0463	140	188,343 645 1445
21	2,194 030 4249	81	20,711 980 7331	141	195,524 246 6156
22	2,277 677 8349	82	21,501 624 9985	142	202,978 608 5179
23	2,364 514 3023	83	22,321 374 4516	143	210,717 167 9676
24	2,454 661 4101	84	23,172 376 8526	144	218,750 759 9964
25	2,548 245 3764	85	24,055 823 7201	145	227,090 632 7212
26	2,645 397 2314	86	24,972 951 9994	146	235,748 463 0937
27	2,746 253 0008	87	25,925 045 7944	147	244,736 373 2492
28	2,850 953 8965	88	26,913 438 1653	148	254,066 947 4793
29	2,959 646 5138	89	27,939 512 9953	149	263,753 249 8519
30	3,072 483 0371	90	29,004 706 9283	150	273,808 842 5026
31	3,189 621 4529	91	30,110 511 3799	151	284,247 804 6230
32	3,311 225 7708	92	31,258 474 6263	152	295,084 752 1742
33	3,437 466 2533	93	32,450 203 9714	153	306,334 858 3509
34	3,568 519 6542	94	33,687 367 9978	154	318,013 874 8255
35	3,704 569 4660	95	34,971 698 9027	155	330,138 153 8032
36	3,845 806 1769	96	36,304 994 9234	156	342,724 670 9170
37	3,992 427 5374	97	37,689 122 8549	157	355,791 048 9957
38	4,144 638 8373	98	39,126 020 6637	158	369,355 582 7386
39	4,302 653 1929	99	40,617 700 2015	159	383,437 264 3305
40	4,466 691 8459	100	42,166 250 0217	160	398,055 810 0331
41	4,636 984 4725	101	43,773 838 3038	161	413,231 687 7906
42	4,813 769 5056	102	45,442 715 8891	162	428,986 145 8877
43	4,997 294 4679	103	47,175 219 4324	163	445,341 242 6996
44	5,187 816 3195	104	48,973 774 6732	164	462,319 877 5776
45	5,385 601 8167	105	50,840 899 8327	165	479,945 822 9102
46	5,590 927 8860	106	52,779 209 1388	166	498,243 757 4087
47	5,804 082 0116	107	54,791 416 4872	167	517,239 300 6599
48	6,025 362 6383	108	56,880 339 2408	168	536,959 048 9975
49	6,255 079 5889	109	59,048 902 1743	169	557,430 612 7405
50	6,493 554 4982	110	61,300 141 5697	170	578,682 654 8513
51	6,741 121 2635	111	63,637 209 4671	171	600,744 931 0675
52	6,998 126 5117	112	66,063 378 0780	172	623,648 331 5644
53	7,264 930 0849	113	68,582 044 3672	173	647,424 924 2053
54	7,541 905 5444	114	71,196 734 8087	174	672,107 999 4407
55	7,829 440 6933	115	73,911 110 3233	175	697,732 116 9193
56	8,127 938 1197	116	76,728 971 4044	176	724,333 153 8769
57	8,437 815 7605	117	79,654 263 4392	177	751,948 355 3684
58	8,759 507 4864	118	82,691 082 2328	178	780,616 386 4169
59	9,093 463 7093	119	85,843 679 7429	179	810,377 386 1490
60	9,440 152 0132	120	89,116 470 0331	180	841,273 023 9959

Amount of 1

NOMINAL INTEREST RATE COMPOUNDED

YEARLY	HALF-YEARLY	QUARTERLY
@	@	@
$3\frac{7}{8}\%$	$7\frac{3}{4}\%$	$15\frac{1}{2}\%$
3.8750%	7.7500%	15.5000%
PER ANNUM	PER ANNUM	PER ANNUM

Periods	Amount	Periods	Amount	Periods	Amount
1	1.038 750 0000	61	10.166 541 6530	121	99.502 834 3502
2	1.079 001 5625	62	10.560 495 1420	122	103.358 569 1812
3	1.120 812 8730	63	10.969 714 3288	123	107.363 713 7370
4	1.164 244 3719	64	11.394 790 7590	124	111.524 057 6443
5	1.209 358 8413	65	11.836 338 9009	125	115.845 614 8780
6	1.256 221 4964	66	12.294 997 0333	126	120.334 632 4545
7	1.304 900 0794	67	12.771 428 1684	127	124.997 599 4622
8	1.355 464 9574	68	13.266 321 0099	128	129.841 256 4413
9	1.407 989 2245	69	13.780 390 9490	129	134.872 605 1284
10	1.462 548 8070	70	14.314 381 0983	130	140.098 918 5771
11	1.519 222 5733	71	14.869 063 3658	131	145.527 751 6720
12	1.578 092 4480	72	15.445 239 5713	132	151.166 952 0493
13	1.639 243 5303	73	16.043 742 6047	133	157.024 671 4412
14	1.702 764 2171	74	16.665 437 6306	134	163.109 377 4596
15	1.768 746 3306	75	17.311 223 3388	135	169.429 865 8361
16	1.837 285 2509	76	17.982 033 2432	136	175.995 273 1373
17	1.908 480 0543	77	18.678 837 0313	137	182.815 089 9713
18	1.982 433 6564	78	19.402 641 9663	138	189.899 174 7077
19	2.059 252 9606	79	20.154 494 3425	139	197.257 767 7276
20	2.139 049 0129	80	20.935 480 9983	140	204.901 506 2271
21	2.221 937 1621	81	21.746 730 8869	141	212.841 439 5934
22	2.308 037 2271	82	22.589 416 7088	142	221.089 045 3776
23	2.397 473 6697	83	23.464 756 6063	143	229.656 245 8860
24	2.490 375 7744	84	24.374 015 9248	144	238.555 425 4141
25	2.586 877 8356	85	25.318 509 0419	145	247.799 448 1489
26	2.687 119 3518	86	26.299 601 2672	146	257.401 676 7647
27	2.791 245 2267	87	27.318 710 8163	147	267.375 991 7393
28	2.899 405 9792	88	28.377 310 8605	148	277.736 811 4192
29	3.011 757 9609	89	29.475 931 6563	149	288.499 112 8617
30	3.128 463 5819	90	30.619 162 7580	150	299.678 453 4851
31	3.249 691 5457	91	31.805 655 3149	151	311.290 993 5576
32	3.375 617 0931	92	33.038 124 4583	152	323.353 519 5580
33	3.506 422 2554	93	34.318 351 7811	153	335.883 468 4409
34	3.642 296 1178	94	35.648 187 9126	154	348.898 952 8429
35	3.783 435 0924	95	37.029 555 1942	155	362.418 787 2656
36	3.930 043 2022	96	38.464 450 4580	156	376.462 515 2721
37	4.082 332 3763	97	39.954 947 9132	157	391.050 437 7389
38	4.240 522 7559	98	41.503 202 1449	158	406.203 642 2013
39	4.404 843 0127	99	43.111 451 2280	159	421.944 033 3366
40	4.575 530 6794	100	44.782 019 9631	160	438.294 364 6284
41	4.752 832 4932	101	46.517 323 2366	161	455.278 271 2578
42	4.937 004 7524	102	48.319 869 5120	162	472.920 304 2690
43	5.128 313 6865	103	50.192 264 4556	163	491.245 966 0594
44	5.327 035 8419	104	52.137 214 7033	164	510.281 747 2442
45	5.533 458 4807	105	54.157 531 7730	165	530.055 164 9500
46	5.747 879 9969	106	56.256 136 1292	166	550.594 802 5918
47	5.970 610 3467	107	58.436 061 4043	167	571.930 351 1922
48	6.201 971 4977	108	60.700 458 7837	168	594.092 652 3009
49	6.442 297 8932	109	63.052 601 5615	169	617.113 742 5775
50	6.691 936 9366	110	65.495 889 8720	170	641.026 900 1024
51	6.951 249 4929	111	68.033 855 6046	171	665.866 692 4814
52	7.220 610 4107	112	70.670 167 5093	172	691.669 026 8151
53	7.500 409 0641	113	73.408 636 5003	173	718.471 201 6041
54	7.791 049 9154	114	76.253 221 1646	174	746.311 960 6663
55	8.092 953 0996	115	79.208 033 4848	175	775.231 549 1421
56	8.406 555 0322	116	82.277 344 7823	176	805.271 771 6714
57	8.732 309 0397	117	85.465 591 8926	177	836.476 052 8236
58	9.070 686 0150	118	88.777 383 5785	178	868.889 499 8706
59	9.422 175 0981	119	92.217 507 1921	179	902.558 967 9905
60	9.787 284 3831	120	95.790 935 5958	180	937.533 128 0002

Amount of 1

NOMINAL INTEREST RATE COMPOUNDED

YEARLY	HALF-YEARLY	QUARTERLY
@	@	@
$3\frac{15}{16}\%$	$7\frac{7}{8}\%$	$15\frac{3}{4}\%$
3.9375%	7.8750%	15.7500%
PER ANNUM	PER ANNUM	PER ANNUM

Periods	Amount	Periods	Amount	Periods	Amount
1	1,039 375 0000	61	10,546 497 6539	121	107,014 901 0346
2	1,080 300 3906	62	10,961 765 9990	122	111,228 612 7629
3	1,122 837 2185	63	11,393 385 5352	123	115,608 239 3904
4	1,167 048 9340	64	11,842 000 0906	124	120,160 313 8164
5	1,213 001 4858	65	12,308 278 8442	125	124,891 626 1729
6	1,260 763 4193	66	12,792 917 3237	126	129,809 233 9535
7	1,310 405 9789	67	13,296 638 4433	127	134,920 472 5404
8	1,362 003 2143	68	13,820 193 5820	128	140,232 966 1467
9	1,415 632 0909	69	14,364 363 7043	129	145,754 639 1887
10	1,471 372 6045	70	14,929 960 5252	130	151,493 728 1067
11	1,529 307 9008	71	15,517 827 7209	131	157,458 793 6510
12	1,589 524 3993	72	16,128 842 1874	132	163,658 733 6510
13	1,652 111 9226	73	16,763 915 3485	133	170,102 796 2885
14	1,717 163 8295	74	17,423 994 5153	134	176,800 593 8923
15	1,784 777 1553	75	18,110 064 2994	135	183,762 117 2768
16	1,855 052 7558	76	18,823 148 0812	136	190,997 750 6446
17	1,928 095 4581	77	19,564 309 5369	137	198,518 287 0762
18	2,004 014 2167	78	20,334 654 2249	138	206,334 944 6299
19	2,082 922 2765	79	21,135 331 2350	139	214,459 383 0747
20	2,164 937 3411	80	21,967 534 9024	140	222,903 721 2832
21	2,250 181 7490	81	22,832 506 5891	141	231,680 555 3088
22	2,338 782 6553	82	23,731 536 5361	142	240,802 977 1740
23	2,430 872 2224	83	24,665 965 7872	143	250,284 594 4003
24	2,526 587 8161	84	25,637 188 1901	144	260,139 550 3048
25	2,626 072 2114	85	26,646 652 4750	145	270,382 545 0980
26	2,729 473 8047	86	27,695 864 4163	146	281,028 857 8113
27	2,836 946 8358	87	28,786 389 0776	147	292,094 369 0876
28	2,948 651 6174	88	29,919 853 1476	148	303,595 584 8704
29	3,064 754 7749	89	31,097 947 3653	149	315,549 661 0247
30	3,185 429 4941	90	32,322 429 0428	150	327,974 428 9275
31	3,310 855 7805	91	33,595 124 6863	151	340,888 422 0666
32	3,441 220 7268	92	34,917 932 7208	152	354,310 903 6854
33	3,576 718 7929	93	36,292 826 3217	153	368,261 895 5180
34	3,717 552 0954	94	37,721 856 3581	154	382,762 207 6541
35	3,863 930 7092	95	39,207 154 4523	155	397,833 469 5804
36	4,016 072 9808	96	40,750 936 1588	156	413,498 162 4452
37	4,174 205 8545	97	42,355 504 2701	157	429,779 652 5914
38	4,338 565 2100	98	44,023 252 2507	158	446,702 226 4122
39	4,509 396 2151	99	45,756 667 8081	159	464,291 126 5772
40	4,686 953 6911	100	47,558 336 6030	160	482,572 589 6862
41	4,871 502 4927	101	49,430 946 1068	161	501,573 885 4051
42	5,063 317 9033	102	51,377 289 6097	162	521,323 357 1429
43	5,262 686 0458	103	53,400 270 3881	163	541,850 464 3304
44	5,469 904 3088	104	55,502 906 0346	164	563,185 826 3634
45	5,685 281 7910	105	57,688 332 9597	165	585,361 268 2765
46	5,909 139 7615	106	59,959 811 0700	166	608,409 868 2149
47	6,141 812 1396	107	62,320 728 6309	167	632,366 006 7758
48	6,383 645 9926	108	64,774 607 3207	168	657,265 418 2926
49	6,635 002 0536	109	67,325 107 4840	169	683,145 244 1379
50	6,896 255 2594	110	69,976 033 5912	170	710,044 088 1258
51	7,167 795 3103	111	72,731 339 9138	171	738,002 074 0958
52	7,450 027 2506	112	75,595 136 4229	172	767,060 905 7633
53	7,743 372 0736	113	78,571 694 9196	173	797,263 928 9277
54	8,048 267 3490	114	81,665 455 4071	174	828,656 196 1293
55	8,365 167 8759	115	84,881 032 7137	175	861,284 533 8519
56	8,694 546 3610	116	88,223 223 3768	176	895,197 612 3723
57	9,036 894 1239	117	91,697 012 7973	177	930,446 018 3594
58	9,392 721 8301	118	95,307 582 6762	178	967,082 330 3323
59	9,762 560 2521	119	99,060 318 7440	179	1005,161 197 0892
60	10,146 961 0620	120	102,960 818 7946	180	1044,739 419 2246

NOMINAL INTEREST RATE COMPOUNDED

YEARLY @ **4%** 4.0000% PER ANNUM	HALF-YEARLY @ **8%** 8.0000% PER ANNUM	QUARTERLY @ **16%** 16.0000% PER ANNUM

Periods	Amount	Periods	Amount	Periods	Amount
1	1,040 000 0000	61	10,940 412 5044	121	115,089 063 2364
2	1,081 600 0000	62	11,378 029 0045	122	119,692 625 7659
3	1,124 864 0000	63	11,833 150 1647	123	124,480 330 7965
4	1,169 858 5600	64	12,306 476 1713	124	129,459 544 0284
5	1,216 652 9024	65	12,798 735 2182	125	134,637 925 7895
6	1,265 319 0185	66	13,310 684 6269	126	140,023 442 8211
7	1,315 931 7792	67	13,843 112 0120	127	145,624 380 5339
8	1,368 569 0504	68	14,396 836 4925	128	151,449 355 7553
9	1,423 311 8124	69	14,972 709 9522	129	157,507 329 9855
10	1,480 244 2849	70	15,571 618 3502	130	163,807 623 1849
11	1,539 454 0563	71	16,194 483 0843	131	170,359 928 1123
12	1,601 032 2186	72	16,842 262 4076	132	177,174 325 2368
13	1,665 073 5073	73	17,515 952 9039	133	184,261 298 2463
14	1,731 676 4476	74	18,216 591 0201	134	191,631 750 1761
15	1,800 943 5055	75	18,945 254 6609	135	199,297 020 1832
16	1,872 981 2457	76	19,703 064 8473	136	207,268 900 9905
17	1,947 900 4956	77	20,491 187 4412	137	215,559 657 0301
18	2,025 816 5154	78	21,310 834 9389	138	224,182 043 3113
19	2,106 849 1760	79	22,163 268 3364	139	233,149 325 0438
20	2,191 123 1430	80	23,049 799 0699	140	242,475 298 0455
21	2,278 768 0688	81	23,971 791 0327	141	252,174 309 9674
22	2,369 918 7915	82	24,930 662 6740	142	262,261 282 3661
23	2,464 715 5432	83	25,927 889 1809	143	272,751 733 6607
24	2,563 304 1649	84	26,965 004 7482	144	283,661 803 0071
25	2,665 836 3315	85	28,043 604 9381	145	295,008 275 1274
26	2,772 469 7847	86	29,165 349 1356	146	306,808 606 1325
27	2,883 368 5761	87	30,331 963 1010	147	319,080 950 3778
28	2,998 703 3192	88	31,545 241 6251	148	331,844 188 3929
29	3,118 651 4519	89	32,807 051 2901	149	345,117 955 9287
30	3,243 397 5100	90	34,119 333 3417	150	358,922 674 1658
31	3,373 133 4104	91	35,484 106 6754	151	373,279 581 1324
32	3,508 058 7468	92	36,903 470 9424	152	388,210 764 3777
33	3,648 381 0967	93	38,379 609 7801	153	403,739 194 9528
34	3,794 316 3406	94	39,914 794 1713	154	419,888 762 7509
35	3,946 088 9942	95	41,511 385 9381	155	436,684 313 2610
36	4,103 932 5540	96	43,171 841 3757	156	454,151 685 7914
37	4,268 089 8561	97	44,898 715 0307	157	472,317 753 2231
38	4,438 813 4504	98	46,694 663 6319	158	491,210 463 3520
39	4,616 365 9884	99	48,562 450 1772	159	510,858 881 8861
40	4,801 020 6279	100	50,504 948 1843	160	531,293 237 1615
41	4,993 061 4531	101	52,525 146 1116	161	552,544 966 6480
42	5,192 783 9112	102	54,626 151 9561	162	574,646 765 3139
43	5,400 495 2676	103	56,811 198 0344	163	597,632 635 9265
44	5,616 515 0783	104	59,083 645 9557	164	621,537 941 3635
45	5,841 175 6815	105	61,446 991 7940	165	646,399 459 0181
46	6,074 822 7087	106	63,904 871 4657	166	672,255 437 3788
47	6,317 815 6171	107	66,461 066 3243	167	699,145 654 8739
48	6,570 528 2418	108	69,119 508 9773	168	727,111 481 0689
49	6,833 349 3714	109	71,884 289 3364	169	756,195 940 3117
50	7,106 683 3463	110	74,759 660 9099	170	786,443 777 9241
51	7,390 950 6801	111	77,750 047 3463	171	817,901 529 0411
52	7,686 588 7073	112	80,860 049 2401	172	850,617 590 2027
53	7,994 052 2556	113	84,094 451 2097	173	884,642 293 8108
54	8,313 814 3459	114	87,458 229 2581	174	920,027 985 5633
55	8,646 366 9197	115	90,956 558 4284	175	956,829 104 9858
56	8,992 221 5965	116	94,594 820 7656	176	995,102 269 1852
57	9,351 910 4603	117	98,378 613 5962	177	1034,906 359 9526
58	9,725 986 8787	118	102,313 758 1400	178	1076,302 614 3507
59	10,115 026 3539	119	106,406 308 4656	179	1119,354 718 9248
60	10,519 627 4081	120	110,662 560 8043	180	1164,128 907 6818

Amount of 1

NOMINAL INTEREST RATE COMPOUNDED

YEARLY	HALF-YEARLY	QUARTERLY
@	@	@
$4\frac{1}{16}\%$	$8\frac{1}{8}\%$	$16\frac{1}{4}\%$
4.0625%	8.1250%	16.2500%
PER ANNUM	PER ANNUM	PER ANNUM

Periods	Amount	Periods	Amount	Periods	Amount
1	1,040 625 0000	61	11,348 790 1711	121	123,767 003 8165
2	1,082 900 3906	62	11,809 834 7717	122	128,795 038 3465
3	1,126 893 2190	63	12,289 609 3094	123	134,027 336 7794
4	1,172 673 2560	64	12,788 874 6875	124	139,472 197 3360
5	1,220 313 1070	65	13,308 422 7217	125	145,138 255 3528
6	1,269 888 3270	66	13,849 077 3948	126	151,034 496 9765
7	1,321 477 5403	67	14,411 696 1640	127	157,170 273 4162
8	1,375 162 5654	68	14,997 171 3206	128	163,555 315 7737
9	1,431 028 5446	69	15,606 431 4055	129	170,199 750 4770
10	1,489 164 0792	70	16,240 442 6814	130	177,114 115 3401
11	1,549 661 3699	71	16,900 210 6653	131	184,309 376 2758
12	1,612 616 3631	72	17,586 781 7236	132	191,796 944 6870
13	1,678 128 9028	73	18,301 244 7311	133	199,588 695 5649
14	1,746 302 8895	74	19,044 732 7983	134	207,696 986 3223
15	1,817 246 4444	75	19,818 425 0682	135	216,134 676 3916
16	1,891 072 0812	76	20,623 548 5866	136	224,915 147 6200
17	1,967 896 8845	77	21,461 380 2480	137	234,052 325 4921
18	2,047 842 6954	78	22,333 248 8205	138	243,560 701 2152
19	2,131 036 3049	79	23,240 537 0539	139	253,455 354 7021
20	2,217 609 6548	80	24,184 683 8717	140	263,751 978 4868
21	2,307 700 0471	81	25,167 186 6540	141	274,466 902 6129
22	2,401 450 3615	82	26,189 603 6118	142	285,617 120 5315
23	2,499 009 2824	83	27,253 556 2585	143	297,220 316 0531
24	2,600 531 5345	84	28,360 731 9815	144	309,294 891 3928
25	2,706 178 1281	85	29,512 886 7183	145	321,859 996 3556
26	2,816 116 6145	86	30,711 847 7412	146	334,935 558 7075
27	2,930 521 3520	87	31,959 516 5557	147	348,542 315 7800
28	3,049 573 7819	88	33,257 871 9158	148	362,701 847 3586
29	3,173 462 7168	89	34,608 972 9623	149	377,436 609 9075
30	3,302 384 6397	90	36,014 962 4889	150	392,769 972 1850
31	3,436 544 0157	91	37,478 070 3400	151	408,726 252 3050
32	3,576 153 6163	92	39,000 616 9476	152	425,330 756 3049
33	3,721 434 8570	93	40,585 017 0111	153	442,609 818 2798
34	3,872 618 1481	94	42,233 783 3272	154	460,590 842 1474
35	4,029 943 2603	95	43,949 530 7748	155	479,302 345 1097
36	4,193 659 7053	96	45,734 980 4626	156	498,774 002 8798
37	4,364 027 1308	97	47,592 964 0439	157	519,036 696 7468
38	4,541 315 7330	98	49,526 428 2081	158	540,122 562 5521
39	4,725 806 6846	99	51,538 439 3541	159	562,065 041 6558
40	4,917 792 5812	100	53,632 188 4529	160	584,898 933 9730
41	5,117 577 9048	101	55,810 996 1088	161	608,660 453 1657
42	5,325 479 5072	102	58,078 317 8257	162	633,387 284 0755
43	5,541 827 1122	103	60,437 749 4873	163	659,118 642 4911
44	5,766 963 8386	104	62,893 033 0603	164	685,895 337 3423
45	6,001 246 7445	105	65,448 062 5283	165	713,759 835 4219
46	6,245 047 3935	106	68,106 890 0686	166	742,756 328 7359
47	6,498 752 4439	107	70,873 732 4776	167	772,930 804 5908
48	6,762 764 2619	108	73,752 977 8595	168	804,331 118 5273
49	7,037 501 5601	109	76,749 192 5850	169	837,007 070 2174
50	7,323 400 0610	110	79,867 128 5338	170	871,010 482 4450
51	7,620 913 1884	111	83,111 730 6305	171	906,395 283 2943
52	7,930 512 7867	112	86,488 144 6873	172	943,217 591 6782
53	8,252 689 8687	113	90,001 725 5653	173	981,535 806 3401
54	8,587 955 3946	114	93,658 045 6664	174	1021,410 698 4727
55	8,936 841 0825	115	97,462 903 7716	175	1062,905 508 0981
56	9,299 900 2515	116	101,422 334 2373	176	1106,086 044 3646
57	9,677 708 6992	117	105,542 616 5657	177	1151,020 789 9169
58	10,070 865 6151	118	109,830 285 3636	178	1197,781 009 5073
59	10,479 994 5307	119	114,292 140 7065	179	1246,440 863 0185
60	10,905 744 3085	120	118,935 258 9227	180	1297,077 523 0786

Amount of 1

	NOMINAL INTEREST RATE COMPOUNDED				
	YEARLY @ $4\frac{1}{8}\%$ 4.1250% PER ANNUM		HALF-YEARLY @ $8\frac{1}{4}\%$ 8.2500% PER ANNUM		QUARTERLY @ $16\frac{1}{2}\%$ 16.5000% PER ANNUM
Periods	Amount	Periods	Amount	Periods	Amount
1	1.041 250 0000	61	11.772 152 4962	121	133.093 468 8058
2	1.084 201 5625	62	12.257 753 7867	122	138.583 574 3941
3	1.128 924 8770	63	12.763 386 1304	123	144.300 146 8378
4	1.175 493 0281	64	13.289 875 8083	124	150.252 527 8949
5	1.223 982 1155	65	13.838 083 1854	125	156.450 444 6706
6	1.274 471 3778	66	14.408 904 1167	126	162.904 025 5132
7	1.327 043 3221	67	15.003 271 4116	127	169.623 816 5657
8	1.381 783 8592	68	15.622 156 3573	128	176.620 798 9990
9	1.438 782 4434	69	16.266 570 3070	129	183.906 406 9577
10	1.498 132 2192	70	16.937 566 3322	130	191.492 546 2447
11	1.559 930 1732	71	17.636 240 9434	131	199.391 613 7773
12	1.624 277 2928	72	18.363 735 8823	132	207.616 517 8456
13	1.691 278 7312	73	19.121 239 9875	133	216.180 699 2067
14	1.761 043 9788	74	19.909 991 1369	134	225.098 153 0490
15	1.833 687 0430	75	20.731 278 2713	135	234.383 451 8623
16	1.909 326 6335	76	21.585 443 5000	136	244.051 769 2516
17	1.988 086 3571	77	22.475 884 2944	137	254.118 904 7332
18	2.070 094 9193	78	23.404 055 7716	138	264.601 309 5535
19	2.155 486 3348	79	24.369 473 0721	139	275.516 113 5726
20	2.244 400 1461	80	25.374 713 8364	140	286.881 153 2574
21	2.336 981 6521	81	26.421 420 7821	141	298.715 000 8293
22	2.433 382 1452	82	27.511 304 3894	142	311.036 994 6135
23	2.533 759 1587	83	28.646 145 6954	143	323.867 270 6413
24	2.638 276 7240	84	29.827 799 2054	144	337.226 795 5553
25	2.747 105 6389	85	31.058 195 9226	145	351.137 400 8719
26	2.860 423 7465	86	32.339 346 5044	146	365.621 818 6579
27	2.978 416 2261	87	33.673 344 5477	147	380.703 718 6775
28	3.101 275 8954	88	35.062 370 0103	148	396.407 747 0730
29	3.229 203 5261	89	36.508 692 7732	149	412.759 566 6397
30	3.362 408 1715	90	38.014 676 3501	150	429.785 898 7636
31	3.501 107 5086	91	39.582 781 7495	151	447.514 567 0876
32	3.645 528 1933	92	41.215 571 4967	152	465.974 542 9800
33	3.795 906 2313	93	42.915 713 8210	153	485.195 992 8779
34	3.952 487 3633	94	44.685 987 0161	154	505.210 327 5841
35	4.115 527 4671	95	46.529 283 9805	155	526.050 253 5970
36	4.285 292 9751	96	48.448 616 9447	156	547.749 826 5579
37	4.462 061 3103	97	50.447 122 3936	157	570.344 506 9034
38	4.646 121 3394	98	52.528 066 1924	158	593.871 217 8131
39	4.837 773 8446	99	54.694 848 9228	159	618.368 405 5479
40	5.037 332 0157	100	56.951 011 4409	160	643.876 102 2768
41	5.245 121 9613	101	59.300 240 6628	161	670.435 991 4957
42	5.461 483 2422	102	61.746 375 5902	162	698.091 476 1449
43	5.686 769 4260	103	64.293 413 5833	163	726.887 749 5359
44	5.921 348 6648	104	66.945 516 8936	164	756.871 869 2042
45	6.165 604 2972	105	69.707 019 4654	165	788.092 833 8089
46	6.419 935 4745	106	72.582 434 0184	166	820.601 663 2035
47	6.684 757 8128	107	75.576 459 4216	167	854.451 481 8107
48	6.960 504 0726	108	78.693 988 3728	168	889.697 605 4353
49	7.247 624 8656	109	81.940 115 3932	169	926.397 631 6595
50	7.546 589 3913	110	85.320 145 1531	170	964.611 533 9655
51	7.857 886 2037	111	88.839 601 1407	171	1004.401 759 7416
52	8.182 024 0096	112	92.504 234 6877	172	1045.833 332 3309
53	8.519 532 5000	113	96.320 034 3686	173	1088.973 957 2896
54	8.870 963 2156	114	100.293 235 7863	174	1133.894 133 0278
55	9.236 890 4483	115	104.430 331 7625	175	1180.667 266 0152
56	9.617 912 1792	116	108.738 082 9477	176	1229.369 790 7383
57	10.014 651 0566	117	113.223 528 8693	177	1280.081 294 6062
58	10.427 755 4127	118	117.893 999 4352	178	1332.884 648 0087
59	10.857 900 3235	119	122.757 126 9119	179	1387.866 139 7391
60	11.305 788 7118	120	127.820 858 3970	180	1445.115 618 0033

NOMINAL INTEREST RATE COMPOUNDED

YEARLY @ $4\frac{3}{16}\%$ 4.1875% PER ANNUM		HALF-YEARLY @ $8\frac{3}{8}\%$ 8.3750% PER ANNUM		QUARTERLY @ $16\frac{3}{4}\%$ 16.7500% PER ANNUM	
Periods	Amount	Periods	Amount	Periods	Amount
1	1.041 875 0000	61	12.211 039 8207	121	143.116 490 4648
2	1.085 503 5156	62	12.722 377 1132	122	149.109 493 5031
3	1.130 958 9753	63	13.255 126 6548	123	155.353 453 5435
4	1.178 317 8824	64	13.810 185 0835	124	161.858 879 4106
5	1.227 659 9438	65	14.388 486 5839	125	168.636 719 9860
6	1.279 068 2039	66	14.991 004 4596	126	175.698 382 6354
7	1.332 629 1849	67	15.618 752 7713	127	183.055 752 4082
8	1.388 433 0321	68	16.272 788 0436	128	190.721 212 0403
9	1.446 573 6653	69	16.954 211 0429	129	198.707 662 7945
10	1.507 148 9375	70	17.664 168 6304	130	207.028 546 1740
11	1.570 260 7993	71	18.403 855 6918	131	215.697 866 5451
12	1.636 015 4702	72	19.174 517 1488	132	224.730 214 7066
13	1.704 523 6181	73	19.977 450 0545	133	234.140 792 4475
14	1.775 900 5446	74	20.814 005 7755	134	243.945 438 1312
15	1.850 266 3799	75	21.685 592 2673	135	254.160 653 3530
16	1.927 746 2845	76	22.593 676 4435	136	264.803 630 7121
17	2.008 470 6602	77	23.539 786 6446	137	275.892 282 7482
18	2.092 575 3691	78	24.525 515 2103	138	287.445 272 0883
19	2.180 201 9627	79	25.552 521 1598	139	299.482 042 8570
20	2.271 497 9199	80	26.622 532 9833	140	312.022 853 4016
21	2.366 616 8952	81	27.737 351 5520	141	325.088 810 3878
22	2.465 718 9777	82	28.898 853 1483	142	338.701 904 3228
23	2.568 970 9599	83	30.108 992 6238	143	352.885 046 5663
24	2.676 546 6189	84	31.369 806 6900	144	367.662 107 8913
25	2.788 627 0085	85	32.683 417 3451	145	383.057 958 6592
26	2.905 400 7645	86	34.052 035 4464	146	399.098 510 6781
27	3.027 064 4215	87	35.477 964 4307	147	415.810 760 8127
28	3.153 822 7442	88	36.963 604 1913	148	433.222 836 4217
29	3.285 889 0716	89	38.511 455 1168	149	451.364 042 6969
30	3.423 485 6765	90	40.124 122 2998	150	470.264 911 9848
31	3.566 844 1392	91	41.804 319 9211	151	489.957 255 1742
32	3.716 205 7375	92	43.554 875 8178	152	510.474 215 2346
33	3.871 821 8528	93	45.378 736 2427	153	531.850 322 9975
34	4.033 954 3929	94	47.278 970 8228	154	554.121 555 2731
35	4.202 876 2331	95	49.258 777 7261	155	577.325 395 4001
36	4.378 871 6753	96	51.321 489 0433	156	601.500 896 3325
37	4.562 236 9267	97	53.470 576 3970	157	626.688 746 3664
38	4.753 280 5980	98	55.709 656 7836	158	652.931 337 6205
39	4.952 324 2231	99	58.042 498 6615	159	680.272 837 3834
40	5.159 702 7999	100	60.473 028 2929	160	708.759 262 4488
41	5.375 765 3546	101	63.005 336 3527	161	738.438 556 5639
42	5.600 875 5289	102	65.643 684 8124	162	769.360 671 1200
43	5.835 412 1916	103	68.392 514 1140	163	801.577 649 2231
44	6.079 770 0772	104	71.256 450 6425	164	835.143 713 2843
45	6.334 360 4492	105	74.240 314 5131	165	870.115 356 2781
46	6.599 611 7930	106	77.349 127 6834	166	906.551 436 8223
47	6.875 970 5368	107	80.588 122 4051	167	944.513 278 2392
48	7.163 901 8030	108	83.962 750 0308	168	984.064 771 7655
49	7.463 890 1910	109	87.478 690 1884	169	1025.272 484 0831
50	7.776 440 5928	110	91.141 860 3400	170	1068.205 769 3541
51	8.102 079 0426	111	94.958 425 7418	171	1112.936 885 9458
52	8.441 353 6025	112	98.934 809 8197	172	1159.541 118 0448
53	8.794 835 2846	113	103.077 704 9809	173	1208.096 902 3629
54	9.163 119 0122	114	107.394 083 8770	174	1258.685 960 1494
55	9.546 824 6208	115	111.891 211 1393	175	1311.393 434 7306
56	9.946 597 9018	116	116.576 655 6058	176	1366.308 034 8100
57	10.363 111 6889	117	121.458 303 0593	177	1423.522 183 7677
58	10.797 066 9909	118	126.544 369 4999	178	1483.132 175 2129
59	11.249 194 1711	119	131.843 414 9727	179	1545.238 335 0500
60	11.720 254 1770	120	137.364 357 9747	180	1609.945 190 3302

Amount of 1

NOMINAL INTEREST RATE COMPOUNDED

YEARLY @ $4\frac{1}{4}\%$ 4.2500% PER ANNUM		HALF-YEARLY @ $8\frac{1}{2}\%$ 8.5000% PER ANNUM		QUARTERLY @ 17% 17.0000% PER ANNUM	
Periods	Amount	Periods	Amount	Periods	Amount
1	1,042 500 0000	61	12,666 011 6280	121	153,887 626 4364
2	1,086 806 2500	62	13,204 317 1222	122	160,427 850 5599
3	1,132 995 5156	63	13,765 500 5999	123	167,246 034 2087
4	1,181 147 8250	64	14,350 534 3753	124	174,353 990 6626
5	1,231 346 6076	65	14,960 432 0863	125	181,764 035 2658
6	1,283 678 8384	66	15,596 250 4500	126	189,489 006 7646
7	1,338 235 1891	67	16,259 091 0941	127	197,542 289 5521
8	1,395 110 1846	68	16,950 102 4656	128	205,937 836 8580
9	1,454 402 3674	69	17,670 481 8204	129	214,690 194 9245
10	1,516 214 4681	70	18,421 477 2977	130	223,814 528 2088
11	1,580 653 5829	71	19,204 390 0829	131	233,326 645 6577
12	1,647 831 3602	72	20,020 576 6614	132	243,243 028 0981
13	1,717 864 1930	73	20,871 451 1695	133	253,580 856 7923
14	1,790 873 4212	74	21,758 487 8442	134	264,358 043 2059
15	1,866 985 5416	75	22,683 223 5776	135	275,593 260 0422
16	1,946 332 4272	76	23,647 260 5797	136	287,305 973 5940
17	2,029 051 5553	77	24,652 269 1543	137	299,516 477 4717
18	2,115 286 2464	78	25,699 990 5934	138	312,245 927 7643
19	2,205 185 9119	79	26,792 240 1936	139	325,516 379 6943
20	2,298 906 3131	80	27,930 910 4018	140	339,350 825 8313
21	2,396 609 8315	81	29,117 974 0939	141	353,773 235 9291
22	2,498 465 7493	82	30,355 487 9929	142	368,808 598 4561
23	2,604 650 5436	83	31,645 596 2326	143	384,482 963 8905
24	2,715 348 1917	84	32,990 534 0725	144	400,823 489 8558
25	2,830 750 4899	85	34,392 631 7705	145	417,858 488 1747
26	2,951 057 3857	86	35,854 318 6208	146	435,617 473 9221
27	3,076 477 3246	87	37,378 127 1622	147	454,131 216 5638
28	3,207 227 6109	88	38,966 697 5666	148	473,431 793 2678
29	3,343 534 7844	89	40,622 782 2131	149	493,552 644 4816
30	3,485 635 0127	90	42,349 250 4572	150	514,528 631 8721
31	3,633 774 5007	91	44,149 093 6016	151	536,396 098 7267
32	3,788 209 9170	92	46,025 430 0797	152	559,192 932 9226
33	3,949 208 8385	93	47,981 510 8581	153	582,958 632 5718
34	4,117 050 2141	94	50,020 725 0695	154	607,734 374 4561
35	4,292 024 8482	95	52,146 605 8850	155	633,563 085 3705
36	4,474 435 9043	96	54,362 836 6351	156	660,489 516 4987
37	4,664 599 4302	97	56,673 257 1921	157	688,560 320 9499
38	4,862 844 9060	98	59,081 870 6228	158	717,824 134 5903
39	5,069 515 8145	99	61,592 850 1242	159	748,331 660 3104
40	5,284 970 2366	100	64,210 546 2545	160	780,135 755 8735
41	5,509 581 4717	101	66,939 494 4703	161	813,291 525 4982
42	5,743 738 6842	102	69,784 422 9853	162	847,856 415 3318
43	5,987 847 5783	103	72,750 260 9622	163	883,890 312 9834
44	6,242 331 1004	104	75,842 147 0531	164	921,455 651 2852
45	6,507 630 1721	105	79,065 438 3028	165	960,617 516 4649
46	6,784 204 4544	106	82,425 719 4307	166	1001,443 760 9146
47	7,072 533 1438	107	85,928 812 5065	167	1044,005 120 7535
48	7,373 115 8024	108	89,580 787 0381	168	1088,375 338 3855
49	7,686 473 2240	109	93,387 970 4872	169	1134,631 290 2669
50	8,013 148 3360	110	97,356 959 2329	170	1182,853 120 1032
51	8,353 707 1403	111	101,494 630 0003	171	1233,124 377 7076
52	8,708 739 6937	112	105,808 151 7753	172	1285,532 163 7602
53	9,078 861 1307	113	110,304 998 2257	173	1340,167 280 7200
54	9,464 712 7288	114	114,992 960 6503	174	1397,124 390 1506
55	9,866 963 0197	115	119,880 161 4780	175	1456,502 176 7320
56	10,286 308 9481	116	124,975 068 3408	176	1518,403 519 2431
57	10,723 477 0784	117	130,286 508 7453	177	1582,935 668 8110
58	11,179 224 8542	118	135,823 685 3669	178	1650,210 434 7354
59	11,654 341 9105	119	141,596 191 9950	179	1720,344 378 2117
60	12,149 651 4417	120	147,614 030 1548	180	1793,459 014 2857

Amount of 1

NOMINAL INTEREST RATE COMPOUNDED

Periods	Amount	Periods	Amount	Periods	Amount
	YEARLY @ $4\frac{5}{16}\%$ 4.3125% PER ANNUM		HALF-YEARLY @ $8\frac{5}{8}\%$ 8.6250% PER ANNUM		QUARTERLY @ $17\frac{1}{4}\%$ 17.2500% PER ANNUM
1	1.043 125 0000	61	13.137 647 2100	121	165.462 216 1443
2	1.088 109 7656	62	13.704 208 2460	122	172.597 774 2155
3	1.135 034 4993	63	14.295 202 2266	123	180.041 053 2286
4	1.183 982 8620	64	14.911 682 8226	124	187.805 323 6490
5	1.235 042 1230	65	15.554 749 1443	125	195.904 428 2314
6	1.288 303 3145	66	16.225 547 7012	126	204.352 806 6989
7	1.343 861 3950	67	16.925 274 4458	127	213.165 521 4878
8	1.401 815 4176	68	17.655 176 9063	128	222.358 284 6019
9	1.462 268 7075	69	18.416 556 4103	129	231.947 485 6254
10	1.525 329 0455	70	19.210 770 4055	130	241.950 220 9430
11	1.591 108 8606	71	20.039 234 8793	131	252.384 324 2212
12	1.659 725 4302	72	20.903 426 8835	132	263.268 398 2032
13	1.731 301 0894	73	21.804 887 1678	133	274.621 847 8757
14	1.805 963 4489	74	22.745 222 9269	134	286.464 915 0653
15	1.883 845 6226	75	23.726 110 6656	135	298.818 714 5275
16	1.965 086 4651	76	24.749 299 1881	136	311.705 271 5915
17	2.049 830 8189	77	25.816 612 7156	137	325.147 561 4289
18	2.138 229 7730	78	26.929 954 1389	138	339.169 550 0155
19	2.230 440 9319	79	28.091 308 4112	139	353.796 236 8600
20	2.326 628 6971	80	29.302 746 0864	140	369.053 699 5745
21	2.426 964 5597	81	30.566 427 0114	141	384.969 140 3687
22	2.531 627 4063	82	31.884 604 1763	142	401.570 934 5471
23	2.640 803 8382	83	33.259 627 7314	143	418.888 681 0994
24	2.754 688 5037	84	34.693 949 1773	144	436.953 255 4719
25	2.873 484 4455	85	36.190 125 7355	145	455.796 864 6141
26	2.997 403 4622	86	37.750 824 9079	146	475.453 104 4006
27	3.126 666 4865	87	39.378 829 2320	147	495.957 019 5278
28	3.261 503 9787	88	41.077 041 2427	148	517.345 165 9950
29	3.402 156 3378	89	42.848 488 6463	149	539.655 676 2785
30	3.548 874 3298	90	44.696 329 7191	150	562.928 327 3180
31	3.701 919 5353	91	46.623 858 9383	151	587.204 611 4336
32	3.861 564 8153	92	48.634 512 8550	152	612.527 810 3017
33	4.028 094 7979	93	50.731 876 2218	153	638.943 072 1209
34	4.201 806 3861	94	52.919 688 3839	154	666.497 492 1062
35	4.383 009 2865	95	55.201 849 9455	155	695.240 196 4532
36	4.572 026 5620	96	57.582 429 7244	156	725.222 429 9253
37	4.769 195 2075	97	60.065 672 0062	157	756.497 647 2158
38	4.974 866 7508	98	62.656 004 1115	158	789.121 608 2520
39	5.189 407 8794	99	65.358 044 2888	159	823.152 477 6079
40	5.413 201 0942	100	68.176 609 9488	160	858.650 928 2047
41	5.646 645 3914	101	71.116 726 2528	161	895.680 249 4835
42	5.890 156 9739	102	74.183 635 0725	162	934.306 460 2425
43	6.144 169 9934	103	77.382 804 3350	163	974.598 426 3405
44	6.409 137 3244	104	80.719 937 7719	164	1016.627 983 4764
45	6.685 531 3715	105	84.200 985 0883	165	1060.470 065 2638
46	6.973 844 9119	106	87.832 152 5703	166	1106.202 836 8283
47	7.274 591 9737	107	91.619 914 1498	167	1153.907 834 1665
48	7.588 308 7526	108	95.571 022 9476	168	1203.670 109 5150
49	7.915 554 5675	109	99.692 523 3122	169	1255.578 382 9878
50	8.256 912 8583	110	103.991 763 3800	170	1309.725 200 7541
51	8.612 992 2253	111	108.476 408 1758	171	1366.207 100 0367
52	8.984 427 5150	112	113.154 453 2784	172	1425.124 781 2257
53	9.371 880 9516	113	118.034 239 0760	173	1486.583 287 4161
54	9.776 043 3176	114	123.124 465 6361	174	1550.692 191 6859
55	10.197 635 1857	115	128.434 208 2167	175	1617.565 792 4524
56	10.637 408 2031	116	133.972 933 4460	176	1687.323 317 2519
57	11.096 146 4318	117	139.750 516 2009	177	1760.089 135 3084
58	11.574 667 7467	118	145.777 257 2121	178	1835.992 979 2686
59	12.073 825 2933	119	152.063 901 4293	179	1915.170 176 4995
60	12.594 509 0090	120	158.621 657 1785	180	1997.761 890 3610

	NOMINAL INTEREST RATE COMPOUNDED				
	YEARLY @ $4\frac{3}{8}\%$ 4.3750% PER ANNUM		HALF-YEARLY @ $8\frac{3}{4}\%$ 8.7500% PER ANNUM		QUARTERLY @ $17\frac{1}{2}\%$ 17.5000% PER ANNUM
Periods	Amount	Periods	Amount	Periods	Amount
1	1.043 750 0000	61	13.626 546 3564	121	177.899 655 6682
2	1.089 414 0625	62	14.222 707 7595	122	185.682 765 6037
3	1.137 075 9277	63	14.844 951 2240	123	193.806 386 5989
4	1.186 822 9996	64	15.494 417 8400	124	202.285 416 0126
5	1.238 746 5058	65	16.172 298 6205	125	211.135 402 9631
6	1.292 941 6654	66	16.879 836 6852	126	220.372 576 8427
7	1.349 507 8633	67	17.618 329 5402	127	230.013 877 0796
8	1.408 548 8323	68	18.389 131 4576	128	240.076 984 2019
9	1.470 172 8437	69	19.193 655 9588	129	250.580 352 2607
10	1.534 492 9056	70	20.033 378 4070	130	261.543 242 6721
11	1.601 626 9703	71	20.909 838 7123	131	272.985 759 5390
12	1.671 698 1502	72	21.824 644 1560	132	284.928 886 5188
13	1.744 834 9443	73	22.779 472 3378	133	297.394 525 3040
14	1.821 171 4731	74	23.775 074 2526	134	310.405 535 7861
15	1.900 847 7250	75	24.816 277 5011	135	323.985 777 9767
16	1.984 009 8130	76	25.901 989 6418	136	338.160 155 7632
17	2.070 810 2423	77	27.035 201 6887	137	352.954 662 5778
18	2.161 408 1904	78	28.217 991 7625	138	368.396 429 0656
19	2.255 969 7988	79	29.452 528 9021	139	384.513 772 8372
20	2.354 668 4775	80	30.741 077 0416	140	401.336 250 3989
21	2.457 685 2234	81	32.085 999 1622	141	418.894 711 3538
22	2.565 208 9519	82	33.489 761 6255	142	437.221 354 9755
23	2.677 436 8435	83	34.954 938 6966	143	456.349 789 2557
24	2.794 574 7054	84	36.484 217 2646	144	476.315 092 5357
25	2.916 837 3488	85	38.080 401 7699	145	497.153 877 8341
26	3.044 448 9828	86	39.746 419 3474	146	518.904 359 9893
27	3.177 643 6258	87	41.485 325 1938	147	541.606 425 7389
28	3.316 665 5344	88	43.300 308 1711	148	565.301 706 8649
29	3.461 769 6516	89	45.194 696 6535	149	590.033 656 5403
30	3.613 222 0738	90	47.171 964 6321	150	615.847 629 0139
31	3.771 300 5395	91	49.235 738 0848	151	642.790 962 7833
32	3.936 294 9381	92	51.389 801 6260	152	670.913 067 4051
33	4.108 507 8417	93	53.638 105 4471	153	700.265 514 1040
34	4.288 255 0598	94	55.984 772 5605	154	730.902 130 3461
35	4.475 866 2186	95	58.434 106 3600	155	762.879 098 5487
36	4.671 685 3657	96	60.990 598 5132	156	796.255 059 1102
37	4.876 071 6004	97	63.658 937 1982	157	831.091 217 9463
38	5.089 399 7330	98	66.444 015 7006	158	867.451 458 7314
39	5.312 060 9713	99	69.350 941 3875	159	905.402 460 0509
40	5.544 463 6388	100	72.385 045 0732	160	945.013 817 6782
41	5.787 033 9230	101	75.551 890 7952	161	986.358 172 2016
42	6.040 216 6571	102	78.857 286 0174	162	1029.511 342 2354
43	6.304 476 1358	103	82.307 292 2807	163	1074.552 463 4582
44	6.580 296 9668	104	85.908 236 3180	164	1121.564 133 7345
45	6.868 184 9591	105	89.666 721 6569	165	1170.632 564 5854
46	7.168 668 0510	106	93.589 640 7294	166	1221.847 739 2860
47	7.482 297 2783	107	97.684 187 5113	167	1275.303 577 8798
48	7.809 647 7842	108	101.957 870 7149	168	1331.098 109 4120
49	8.151 319 8748	109	106.418 527 5587	169	1389.333 651 6988
50	8.507 940 1193	110	111.074 338 1394	170	1450.116 998 9606
51	8.880 162 4995	111	115.933 340 4330	171	1513.559 617 6651
52	9.268 669 6088	112	121.005 945 9519	172	1579.777 850 9380
53	9.674 173 9042	113	126.299 956 0873	173	1648.893 131 9165
54	10.097 419 0125	114	131.825 579 1661	174	1721.032 206 4379
55	10.539 181 0943	115	137.592 948 2547	175	1796.327 365 4695
56	11.000 270 2672	116	143.612 639 7408	176	1874.916 687 7088
57	11.481 532 0914	117	149.895 692 7295	177	1956.944 292 7961
58	11.983 849 1204	118	156.453 629 2864	178	2042.560 605 6059
59	12.508 142 5194	119	163.298 475 5677	179	2131.922 632 1012
60	13.055 373 7547	120	170.442 783 8737	180	2225.194 247 2556

NOMINAL INTEREST RATE COMPOUNDED

YEARLY @ $4\frac{7}{16}\%$ 4.4375% PER ANNUM		HALF-YEARLY @ $8\frac{7}{8}\%$ 8.8750% PER ANNUM		QUARTERLY @ $17\frac{3}{4}\%$ 17.7500% PER ANNUM	
Periods	Amount	Periods	Amount	Periods	Amount
1	1.044 375 0000	61	14.133 330 0664	121	191.263 692 4149
2	1.090 719 1406	62	14.760 496 5881	122	199.751 018 7658
3	1.139 119 8025	63	15.415 493 6242	123	208.614 970 2235
4	1.189 668 2437	64	16.099 556 1538	124	217.872 259 5272
5	1.242 459 7720	65	16.813 973 9581	125	227.540 341 0437
6	1.297 593 9244	66	17.560 094 0525	126	237.637 443 6775
7	1.355 174 6548	67	18.339 323 2261	127	248.182 605 2407
8	1.415 310 5301	68	19.153 130 6942	128	259.195 708 3483
9	1.478 114 9349	69	20.003 050 8688	129	270.697 517 9062
10	1.543 706 2851	70	20.890 686 2511	130	282.709 720 2633
11	1.612 208 2515	71	21.817 710 4535	131	295.254 964 1000
12	1.683 749 9927	72	22.785 871 3548	132	308.356 903 1319
13	1.758 466 3986	73	23.796 994 3962	133	322.040 240 7084
14	1.836 498 3451	74	24.852 986 0225	134	336.330 776 3898
15	1.917 992 9591	75	25.955 837 2773	135	351.255 454 5921
16	2.003 103 8967	76	27.107 627 5565	136	366.842 415 3897
17	2.091 991 6321	77	28.310 528 5293	137	383.121 047 5726
18	2.184 823 7608	78	29.566 808 2328	138	400.122 044 0586
19	2.281 775 3152	79	30.878 835 3481	139	417.877 459 7637
20	2.383 029 0948	80	32.249 083 6667	140	436.420 772 0407
21	2.488 776 0109	81	33.680 136 7544	141	455.786 943 8001
22	2.599 215 4463	82	35.174 692 8229	142	476.012 489 4312
23	2.714 555 6318	83	36.735 569 8169	143	497.135 543 6497
24	2.835 014 0379	84	38.365 710 7275	144	519.195 933 3991
25	2.960 817 7859	85	40.068 189 1410	145	542.235 252 9437
26	3.092 204 0751	86	41.846 215 0342	146	566.296 942 2931
27	3.229 420 6310	87	43.703 140 8263	147	591.426 369 1074
28	3.372 726 1714	88	45.642 467 7005	148	617.670 914 2365
29	3.522 390 8953	89	47.667 852 2047	149	645.080 061 0557
30	3.678 696 9913	90	49.783 113 1463	150	673.705 488 7651
31	3.841 939 1703	91	51.992 238 7921	151	703.601 169 8290
32	4.012 425 2210	92	54.299 394 3885	152	734.823 471 7402
33	4.190 476 5901	93	56.708 930 0145	153	767.431 263 2987
34	4.376 428 9888	94	59.225 388 7839	154	801.486 025 6076
35	4.570 633 0252	95	61.853 515 4112	155	837.051 967 9939
36	4.773 454 8657	96	64.598 265 1576	156	874.196 149 0736
37	4.985 276 9254	97	67.464 813 1739	157	912.988 603 1888
38	5.206 498 5889	98	70.458 564 2585	158	953.502 472 4553
39	5.437 536 9638	99	73.585 163 0475	159	995.814 144 6705
40	5.678 827 6666	100	76.850 504 6577	160	1040.003 397 3402
41	5.930 825 6443	101	80.260 745 8019	161	1086.153 548 0972
42	6.194 006 0322	102	83.822 316 3969	162	1134.351 611 7940
43	6.468 865 0499	103	87.541 931 6870	163	1184.688 464 5674
44	6.755 920 9365	104	91.426 604 9056	164	1237.259 015 1825
45	7.055 714 9281	105	95.483 660 4983	165	1292.162 383 9813
46	7.368 812 2780	106	99.720 747 9329	166	1349.502 089 7704
47	7.695 803 3228	107	104.145 856 1224	167	1409.386 245 0040
48	8.037 304 5953	108	108.767 328 4879	168	1471.927 759 6261
49	8.393 959 9867	109	113.593 878 6895	169	1537.244 553 9595
50	8.766 441 9611	110	118.634 607 0564	170	1605.459 781 0414
51	9.155 452 8231	111	123.899 017 7445	171	1676.702 058 8251
52	9.561 726 0422	112	129.397 036 6569	172	1751.105 712 6855
53	9.986 027 6353	113	135.139 030 1585	173	1828.811 028 6859
54	10.429 157 6116	114	141.135 824 6218	174	1909.964 518 0839
55	10.891 951 4806	115	147.398 726 8394	175	1994.719 193 5738
56	11.375 281 8276	116	153.939 545 3429	176	2083.234 857 7887
57	11.880 059 9587	117	160.770 612 6675	177	2175.678 404 6030
58	12.407 237 6193	118	167.904 808 6046	178	2272.224 133 8073
59	12.957 808 7887	119	175.355 584 4865	179	2373.054 079 7450
60	13.532 811 5537	120	183.136 988 5481	180	2478.358 354 5337

Amount of 1

NOMINAL INTEREST RATE COMPOUNDED

YEARLY	HALF-YEARLY	QUARTERLY
@	@	@
$4\frac{1}{2}\%$	9%	18%
4.5000%	9.0000%	18.0000%
PER ANNUM	PER ANNUM	PER ANNUM

Periods	Amount	Periods	Amount	Periods	Amount
1	1.045 000 0000	61	14.658 641 2857	121	205.622 740 9977
2	1.092 025 0000	62	15.318 280 1435	122	214.875 764 3426
3	1.141 166 1250	63	16.007 602 7500	123	224.545 173 7380
4	1.192 518 6006	64	16.727 944 8738	124	234.649 706 5562
5	1.246 181 9377	65	17.480 702 3931	125	245.208 943 3512
6	1.302 260 1248	66	18.267 334 0008	126	256.243 345 8020
7	1.360 861 8305	67	19.089 364 0308	127	267.774 296 3631
8	1.422 100 6128	68	19.948 385 4122	128	279.824 139 6994
9	1.486 095 1404	69	20.846 062 7557	129	292.416 225 9859
10	1.552 969 4217	70	21.784 135 5797	130	305.574 956 1553
11	1.622 853 0457	71	22.764 421 6808	131	319.325 829 1823
12	1.695 881 4328	72	23.788 820 6565	132	333.695 491 4955
13	1.772 196 0972	73	24.859 317 5860	133	348.711 788 6128
14	1.851 944 9216	74	25.977 986 8774	134	364.403 819 1003
15	1.935 282 4431	75	27.146 996 2869	135	380.801 990 9599
16	2.022 370 1530	76	28.368 611 1198	136	397.938 080 5531
17	2.113 376 8099	77	29.645 198 6202	137	415.845 294 1779
18	2.208 478 7664	78	30.979 232 5581	138	434.558 332 4160
19	2.307 860 3108	79	32.373 298 0232	139	454.113 457 3747
20	2.411 714 0248	80	33.830 096 4342	140	474.548 562 9565
21	2.520 241 1560	81	35.352 450 7738	141	495.903 248 2896
22	2.633 652 0080	82	36.943 311 0586	142	518.218 894 4626
23	2.752 166 3483	83	38.605 760 0562	143	541.538 744 7134
24	2.876 013 8340	84	40.343 019 2587	144	565.907 988 2255
25	3.005 434 4565	85	42.158 455 1254	145	591.373 847 6957
26	3.140 679 0071	86	44.055 585 6060	146	617.985 670 8420
27	3.282 009 5624	87	46.038 086 9583	147	645.795 026 0299
28	3.429 699 9927	88	48.109 800 8714	148	674.855 802 2012
29	3.584 036 4924	89	50.274 741 9106	149	705.224 313 3003
30	3.745 318 1345	90	52.537 105 2966	150	736.959 407 3988
31	3.913 857 4506	91	54.901 275 0350	151	770.122 580 7317
32	4.089 981 0359	92	57.371 832 4115	152	804.778 096 8647
33	4.274 030 1825	93	59.953 564 8701	153	840.993 111 2236
34	4.466 361 5407	94	62.651 475 2892	154	878.837 801 2286
35	4.667 347 8100	95	65.470 791 6772	155	918.385 502 2839
36	4.877 378 4615	96	68.416 977 3027	156	959.712 849 8867
37	5.096 860 4922	97	71.495 741 2813	157	1002.899 928 1316
38	5.326 219 2144	98	74.713 049 6390	158	1048.030 424 8975
39	5.565 899 0790	99	78.075 136 8727	159	1095.191 794 0179
40	5.816 364 5376	100	81.588 518 0320	160	1144.475 424 7487
41	6.078 100 9418	101	85.260 001 3435	161	1195.976 818 8624
42	6.351 615 4842	102	89.096 701 4039	162	1249.795 775 7112
43	6.637 438 1810	103	93.106 052 9671	163	1306.036 585 6182
44	6.936 122 8991	104	97.295 825 3506	164	1364.808 231 9710
45	7.248 248 4296	105	101.674 137 4914	165	1426.224 602 4097
46	7.574 419 6089	106	106.249 473 6785	166	1490.404 709 5182
47	7.915 268 4913	107	111.030 699 9940	167	1557.472 921 4465
48	8.271 455 5734	108	116.027 081 4938	168	1627.559 202 9116
49	8.643 671 0742	109	121.248 300 1610	169	1700.799 367 0426
50	9.032 636 2725	110	126.704 473 6682	170	1777.335 338 5595
51	9.439 104 9048	111	132.406 174 9833	171	1857.315 428 7947
52	9.863 864 6255	112	138.364 452 8575	172	1940.894 623 0905
53	10.307 738 5337	113	144.590 853 2361	173	2028.234 881 1295
54	10.771 586 7677	114	151.097 441 6318	174	2119.505 450 7804
55	11.256 308 1722	115	157.896 826 5052	175	2214.883 196 0655
56	11.762 842 0400	116	165.002 183 6979	176	2314.552 939 8884
57	12.292 169 9318	117	172.427 281 9643	177	2418.707 822 1834
58	12.845 317 5787	118	180.186 509 6527	178	2527.549 674 1816
59	13.423 356 8698	119	188.294 902 5871	179	2641.289 409 5198
60	14.027 407 9289	120	196.768 173 2035	180	2760.147 432 9482

Amount of 1

NOMINAL INTEREST RATE COMPOUNDED

YEARLY	HALF-YEARLY	QUARTERLY
@	@	@
$4\frac{9}{16}\%$	$9\frac{1}{8}\%$	$18\frac{1}{4}\%$
4.5625%	9.1250%	18.2500%
PER ANNUM	PER ANNUM	PER ANNUM

Periods	Amount	Periods	Amount	Periods	Amount
1	1.045 625 0000	61	15.203 145 6682	121	221.050 221 8372
2	1.093 331 6406	62	15.896 789 1893	122	231.135 638 2086
3	1.143 214 8967	63	16.622 080 1961	123	241.681 201 7018
4	1.195 374 0764	64	17.380 462 6050	124	252.707 906 5295
5	1.249 913 0186	65	18.173 446 2114	125	264.237 704 7649
6	1.306 940 3001	66	19.002 609 6948	126	276.293 550 0448
7	1.366 569 4513	67	19.869 603 7621	127	288.899 443 2656
8	1.428 919 1825	68	20.776 154 4337	128	302.080 480 3646
9	1.494 113 6202	69	21.724 066 4798	129	315.862 902 2812
10	1.562 282 5541	70	22.715 227 0129	130	330.274 147 1978
11	1.633 561 6957	71	23.751 609 2454	131	345.342 905 1637
12	1.708 092 9480	72	24.835 276 4172	132	361.099 175 2118
13	1.786 024 6888	73	25.968 385 9037	133	377.574 325 0808
14	1.867 512 0652	74	27.153 193 5106	134	394.801 153 6626
15	1.952 717 3032	75	28.392 057 9645	135	412.813 956 2985
16	2.041 810 0301	76	29.687 445 6091	136	431.648 593 0546
17	2.134 967 6128	77	31.041 935 3151	137	451.342 560 1127
18	2.232 375 5101	78	32.458 223 6138	138	471.935 064 4179
19	2.334 227 6427	79	33.939 130 0662	139	493.467 101 7319
20	2.440 726 7790	80	35.487 602 8755	140	515.981 538 2484
21	2.552 084 9382	81	37.106 724 7567	141	539.523 195 9310
22	2.668 523 8135	82	38.799 719 0737	142	564.138 941 7454
23	2.790 275 2125	83	40.569 956 2564	143	589.877 780 9625
24	2.917 581 5191	84	42.420 960 5106	144	616.790 954 7189
25	3.050 696 1759	85	44.356 416 8339	145	644.932 042 0280
26	3.189 884 1889	86	46.380 178 3520	146	674.357 066 4455
27	3.335 422 6551	87	48.496 273 9893	147	705.124 607 6021
28	3.487 601 3137	88	50.708 916 4900	148	737.295 917 8239
29	3.646 723 1236	89	53.022 510 8049	149	770.935 044 0746
30	3.813 104 8662	90	55.441 662 8604	150	806.108 955 4605
31	3.987 077 7757	91	57.971 188 7284	151	842.887 676 5534
32	4.168 988 1992	92	60.616 124 2141	152	881.344 426 7962
33	4.359 198 2858	93	63.381 734 8814	153	921.555 766 2688
34	4.558 086 7076	94	66.273 526 5353	154	963.601 748 1048
35	4.766 049 4136	95	69.297 256 1835	155	1007.566 077 8620
36	4.983 500 4181	96	72.458 943 4969	156	1053.536 280 1645
37	5.210 872 6247	97	75.764 882 7939	157	1101.603 872 9470
38	5.448 618 6882	98	79.221 655 5714	158	1151.864 549 6502
39	5.697 211 9158	99	82.836 143 6068	159	1204.418 369 7280
40	5.957 147 2095	100	86.615 542 6589	160	1259.369 957 8468
41	6.228 942 0509	101	90.567 376 7927	161	1316.828 712 1736
42	6.513 137 5320	102	94.699 513 3589	162	1376.909 022 1665
43	6.810 299 4319	103	99.020 178 6559	163	1439.730 496 3029
44	7.121 019 3435	104	103.537 974 3071	164	1505.418 200 1967
45	7.445 915 8510	105	108.261 894 3848	165	1574.102 905 5807
46	7.785 635 7617	106	113.201 343 3161	166	1645.921 350 6478
47	8.140 855 3933	107	118.366 154 6049	167	1721.016 512 2711
48	8.512 281 9207	108	123.766 610 4088	168	1799.537 890 6435
49	8.900 654 7833	109	129.413 462 0087	169	1881.641 806 9041
50	9.306 747 1578	110	135.317 951 2128	170	1967.491 714 3441
51	9.731 367 4969	111	141.491 832 7369	171	2057.258 523 8110
52	10.175 361 1389	112	147.947 397 6055	172	2151.120 943 9599
53	10.639 611 9909	113	154.697 497 6213	173	2249.265 837 0281
54	11.125 044 2879	114	161.755 570 9502	174	2351.888 590 8425
55	11.632 624 4336	115	169.135 668 8748	175	2459.193 507 7997
56	12.163 362 9234	116	176.852 483 7673	176	2571.394 211 5930
57	12.718 316 3567	117	184.921 378 3391	177	2688.714 072 4969
58	13.298 589 5405	118	193.358 416 2259	178	2811.386 652 0546
59	13.905 337 6883	119	202.180 393 9662	179	2939.656 168 0546
60	14.539 768 7203	120	211.404 874 4409	180	3073.777 980 7221

NOMINAL INTEREST RATE COMPOUNDED

	YEARLY @ $4\frac{5}{8}\%$ 4.6250% PER ANNUM		HALF-YEARLY @ $9\frac{1}{4}\%$ 9.2500% PER ANNUM		QUARTERLY @ $18\frac{1}{2}\%$ 18.5000% PER ANNUM
Periods	Amount	Periods	Amount	Periods	Amount
1	1,046 250 0000	61	15,767 532 3638	121	237,624 924 1023
2	1,094 639 0625	62	16,496 780 7356	122	248,615 076 8420
3	1,145 266 1191	63	17,259 756 8446	123	260,113 524 1460
4	1,198 234 6772	64	18,058 020 5987	124	272,143 774 6377
5	1,253 653 0310	65	18,893 204 0513	125	284,730 424 2147
6	1,311 634 4837	66	19,767 014 7387	126	297,899 206 3346
7	1,372 297 5785	67	20,681 239 1704	127	311,677 044 6276
8	1,435 766 3415	68	21,637 746 4820	128	326,092 107 9416
9	1,502 170 5348	69	22,638 492 2568	129	341,173 867 9339
10	1,571 645 9221	70	23,685 522 5237	130	356,953 159 3259
11	1,644 334 5460	71	24,780 977 9404	131	373,462 242 9447
12	1,720 385 0187	72	25,927 098 1702	132	390,734 871 6809
13	1,799 952 8258	73	27,126 226 4605	133	408,806 359 4961
14	1,883 200 6440	74	28,380 814 4343	134	427,713 653 6228
15	1,970 298 6738	75	29,693 427 1019	135	447,495 410 1029
16	2,061 424 9875	76	31,066 748 1054	136	468,192 072 8201
17	2,156 765 8931	77	32,503 585 2052	137	489,845 956 1881
18	2,256 516 3157	78	34,006 876 0210	138	512,501 331 6618
19	2,360 880 1953	79	35,579 694 0370	139	536,204 518 2511
20	2,470 070 9043	80	37,225 254 8862	140	561,003 977 2202
21	2,584 311 6836	81	38,946 922 9247	141	586,950 411 1667
22	2,703 836 0990	82	40,748 218 1099	142	614,096 867 6831
23	2,828 888 5186	83	42,632 823 1975	143	642,498 847 8135
24	2,959 724 6126	84	44,604 591 2704	144	672,214 419 5249
25	3,096 611 8759	85	46,667 553 6166	145	703,304 336 4279
26	3,239 830 1752	86	48,825 927 9714	146	735,832 161 9877
27	3,389 672 3208	87	51,084 127 1401	147	769,864 399 4796
28	3,546 444 6656	88	53,446 768 0203	148	805,470 627 9555
29	3,710 467 7314	89	55,918 681 0413	149	842,723 644 4985
30	3,882 076 8640	90	58,504 920 0394	150	881,699 613 0565
31	4,061 622 9189	91	61,210 772 5912	151	922,478 220 1604
32	4,249 472 9789	92	64,041 770 8236	152	965,142 837 8428
33	4,446 011 1042	93	67,003 702 7242	153	1009,780 694 0931
34	4,651 639 1178	94	70,102 623 9752	154	1056,483 051 1949
35	4,866 777 4270	95	73,344 870 3340	155	1105,345 392 3126
36	5,091 865 8830	96	76,737 070 5870	156	1156,467 616 7071
37	5,327 364 6801	97	80,286 160 1016	157	1209,954 243 9798
38	5,573 755 2965	98	83,999 395 0063	158	1265,914 627 7638
39	5,831 541 4790	99	87,884 367 0254	159	1324,463 179 2979
40	6,101 250 2724	100	91,949 019 0003	160	1385,719 601 3404
41	6,383 433 0975	101	96,201 661 1291	161	1449,809 132 9024
42	6,678 666 8782	102	100,650 987 9563	162	1516,862 805 2992
43	6,987 555 2214	103	105,306 096 1492	163	1587,017 710 0443
44	7,310 729 6503	104	110,176 503 0962	164	1660,417 279 1338
45	7,648 850 8967	105	115,272 166 3643	165	1737,211 578 2938
46	8,002 610 2506	106	120,603 504 0587	166	1817,557 613 7898
47	8,372 730 9747	107	126,181 416 1214	167	1901,619 653 4276
48	8,759 969 7823	108	132,017 306 6170	168	1989,569 562 3987
49	9,165 118 3847	109	138,123 107 0481	169	2081,587 154 6596
50	9,589 005 1100	110	144,511 300 7490	170	2177,860 560 5626
51	10,032 496 5964	111	151,194 948 4087	171	2278,586 611 4886
52	10,496 499 5640	112	158,187 714 7726	172	2383,971 242 2700
53	10,981 962 6688	113	165,503 896 5808	173	2494,229 912 2249
54	11,489 878 4422	114	173,158 451 7977	174	2609,588 045 6654
55	12,021 285 3202	115	181,167 030 1933	175	2730,281 492 7774
56	12,577 269 7662	116	189,546 005 3398	176	2856,557 011 8183
57	13,158 968 4929	117	198,312 508 0867	177	2988,672 773 6149
58	13,767 570 7857	118	207,484 461 5857	178	3126,898 889 3946
59	14,404 320 9346	119	217,080 617 9341	179	3271,517 963 0291
60	15,070 520 7778	120	227,120 596 5135	180	3422,825 668 8192

Amount of 1

NOMINAL INTEREST RATE COMPOUNDED

	YEARLY	HALF-YEARLY	QUARTERLY
	@	@	@
	$4\frac{11}{16}\%$	$9\frac{3}{8}\%$	$18\frac{3}{4}\%$
	4.6875%	9.3750%	18.7500%
	PER ANNUM	PER ANNUM	PER ANNUM

Periods	Amount	Periods	Amount	Periods	Amount
1	1,046 875 0000	61	16,352 514 8326	121	255,431 394 7239
2	1,095 947 2656	62	17,119 038 9654	122	267,404 741 3516
3	1,147 319 7937	63	17,921 493 9169	123	279,939 338 6024
4	1,201 100 4090	64	18,761 563 9443	124	293,061 495 0994
5	1,257 401 9907	65	19,641 012 2542	125	306,798 752 6822
6	1,316 342 7090	66	20,561 684 7036	126	321,179 944 2142
7	1,378 046 2735	67	21,525 513 6741	127	336,235 254 0992
8	1,442 642 1926	68	22,534 522 1275	128	351,996 281 6351
9	1,510 266 0454	69	23,590 827 8523	129	368,496 107 3367
10	1,581 059 7662	70	24,696 647 9078	130	385,769 362 3682
11	1,655 171 9428	71	25,854 303 2785	131	403,852 301 2292
12	1,732 758 1276	72	27,066 223 7447	132	422,782 877 8493
13	1,813 981 1648	73	28,334 952 9827	133	442,600 825 2485
14	1,899 011 5319	74	29,663 153 9038	134	463,347 738 9320
15	1,988 027 6975	75	31,053 614 2430	135	485,067 164 1944
16	2,081 216 4958	76	32,509 252 4107	136	507,804 687 5160
17	2,178 773 5190	77	34,033 123 6174	137	531,608 032 2434
18	2,280 903 5277	78	35,628 426 2870	138	556,527 158 7548
19	2,387 820 8806	79	37,298 508 7692	139	582,614 369 3214
20	2,499 749 9844	80	39,046 876 3677	140	609,924 417 8833
21	2,616 925 7649	81	40,877 198 6975	141	638,514 624 9716
22	2,739 594 1601	82	42,793 317 3864	142	668,444 998 0172
23	2,868 012 6364	83	44,799 254 1389	143	699,778 357 2992
24	3,002 450 7287	84	46,899 219 1767	144	732,580 467 7976
25	3,143 190 6066	85	49,097 620 0756	145	766,920 177 2256
26	3,290 527 6663	86	51,399 071 0166	146	802,869 560 5331
27	3,444 771 1507	87	53,808 402 4705	147	840,504 071 1831
28	3,606 244 7984	88	56,330 671 3363	148	879,902 699 5198
29	3,775 287 5233	89	58,971 171 5552	149	921,148 138 5598
30	3,952 254 1259	90	61,735 445 2219	150	964,326 957 5547
31	4,137 516 0381	91	64,629 294 2167	151	1009,529 783 6901
32	4,331 462 1024	92	67,658 792 3831	152	1056,851 492 3006
33	4,534 499 3884	93	70,830 298 2760	153	1106,391 406 0022
34	4,747 054 0473	94	74,150 468 5077	154	1158,253 503 1585
35	4,969 572 2057	95	77,626 271 7190	155	1212,546 636 1191
36	5,202 520 9029	96	81,265 003 2058	156	1269,384 759 6872
37	5,446 389 0702	97	85,074 300 2311	157	1328,887 170 2975
38	5,701 688 5578	98	89,062 158 0544	158	1391,178 756 4052
39	5,968 955 2090	99	93,236 946 7132	159	1456,390 260 6117
40	6,248 749 9844	100	97,607 428 5904	160	1524,658 554 0779
41	6,541 660 1399	101	102,182 776 8056	161	1596,126 923 8003
42	6,848 300 4590	102	106,972 594 4684	162	1670,945 373 3534
43	7,169 314 5430	103	111,986 934 8341	163	1749,270 937 7294
44	7,505 376 1622	104	117,236 322 4044	164	1831,268 012 9354
45	7,857 190 6698	105	122,731 775 0171	165	1917,108 701 0418
46	8,225 496 4825	106	128,484 826 9710	166	2006,973 171 4031
47	8,611 066 6301	107	134,507 553 2353	167	2101,050 038 8126
48	9,014 710 3784	108	140,812 594 7932	168	2199,536 759 3820
49	9,437 274 9274	109	147,413 185 1742	169	2302,640 044 9780
50	9,879 647 1896	110	154,323 178 2292	170	2410,576 297 0863
51	10,342 755 6516	111	161,557 077 2087	171	2523,572 061 0123
52	10,827 572 3228	112	169,130 065 2028	172	2641,864 501 3722
53	11,335 114 7754	113	177,058 037 0092	173	2765,701 899 8740
54	11,866 448 2805	114	185,357 632 4940	174	2895,344 176 4306
55	12,422 688 0436	115	194,046 271 5172	175	3031,063 434 7008
56	13,005 001 5457	116	203,142 190 4946	176	3173,144 533 2024
57	13,614 610 9931	117	212,664 480 6740	177	3321,885 683 1963
58	14,252 795 8834	118	222,633 128 2056	178	3477,599 074 5961
59	14,920 895 6905	119	233,069 056 0902	179	3640,611 531 2178
60	15,620 312 6760	120	243,994 168 0944	180	3811,265 196 7436

Amount of 1

NOMINAL INTEREST RATE COMPOUNDED

YEARLY	HALF-YEARLY	QUARTERLY
@	@	@
$4\frac{3}{4}\%$	$9\frac{1}{2}\%$	19%
4.7500%	9.5000%	19.0000%
PER ANNUM	PER ANNUM	PER ANNUM

Periods	Amount	Periods	Amount	Periods	Amount
1	1,047 500 0000	61	16,958 831 6879	121	274,560 355 3394
2	1,097 256 2500	62	17,764 376 1931	122	287,601 972 2180
3	1,149 375 9219	63	18,608 184 0622	123	301,263 065 8984
4	1,203 971 2782	64	19,492 072 8052	124	315,573 061 5286
5	1,261 159 9139	65	20,417 946 2634	125	330,562 781 9512
6	1,321 065 0098	66	21,387 798 7109	126	346,264 514 0939
7	1,383 815 5978	67	22,403 719 1497	127	362,712 078 5133
8	1,449 546 8386	68	23,467 895 8093	128	379,940 902 2427
9	1,518 400 3135	69	24,582 620 8603	129	397,988 095 0992
10	1,590 524 3284	70	25,750 295 3511	130	416,892 529 6164
11	1,666 074 2340	71	26,973 434 3803	131	436,694 924 7732
12	1,745 212 7601	72	28,254 672 5134	132	457,437 933 7000
13	1,828 110 3662	73	29,596 769 4578	133	479,166 235 5507
14	1,914 945 6086	74	31,002 616 0070	134	501,926 631 7394
15	2,005 905 5250	75	32,475 240 2673	135	525,768 146 7470
16	2,101 186 0374	76	34,017 814 1800	136	550,742 133 7175
17	2,200 992 3742	77	35,633 660 3536	137	576,902 385 0690
18	2,305 539 5120	78	37,326 259 2204	138	604,305 248 3598
19	2,415 052 6388	79	39,099 256 5334	139	633,009 747 6569
20	2,529 767 6391	80	40,956 471 2187	140	663,077 710 6706
21	2,649 931 6020	81	42,901 903 6016	141	694,573 901 9275
22	2,775 803 3531	82	44,939 744 0227	142	727,566 162 2690
23	2,907 654 0124	83	47,074 381 8637	143	762,125 554 9768
24	3,045 767 5779	84	49,310 415 0023	144	798,326 518 8382
25	3,190 441 5379	85	51,652 659 7149	145	836,247 028 4830
26	3,341 987 5110	86	54,106 161 0513	146	875,968 762 3360
27	3,500 731 9177	87	56,676 203 7013	147	917,577 278 5469
28	3,667 016 6838	88	59,368 323 3771	148	961,162 199 2779
29	3,841 199 9763	89	62,188 318 7375	149	1006,817 403 7436
30	4,023 656 9752	90	65,142 263 8775	150	1054,641 230 4214
31	4,214 780 6815	91	68,236 521 4117	151	1104,736 688 8664
32	4,414 982 7639	92	71,477 756 1787	152	1157,211 681 5876
33	4,624 694 4451	93	74,872 949 5972	153	1212,179 236 4630
34	4,844 367 4313	94	78,429 414 7031	154	1269,757 750 1950
35	5,074 474 8843	95	82,154 811 9015	155	1330,071 243 3293
36	5,315 512 4413	96	86,057 165 4668	156	1393,249 627 3874
37	5,567 999 2822	97	90,144 880 8265	157	1459,428 984 6883
38	5,832 479 2481	98	94,426 762 6657	158	1528,751 861 4610
39	6,109 522 0124	99	98,912 033 8924	159	1601,367 574 8804
40	6,399 724 3080	100	103,610 355 5023	160	1677,432 534 6872
41	6,703 711 2127	101	108,531 847 3886	161	1757,110 580 0848
42	7,022 137 4953	102	113,687 110 1396	162	1840,573 332 6389
43	7,355 689 0263	103	119,087 247 8712	163	1928,000 565 9392
44	7,705 084 2550	104	124,743 892 1451	164	2019,580 592 8213
45	8,071 075 7571	105	130,669 227 0220	165	2115,510 670 9803
46	8,454 451 8556	106	136,876 015 3055	166	2215,997 427 8519
47	8,856 038 3187	107	143,377 626 0325	167	2321,257 305 6749
48	9,276 700 1389	108	150,188 063 2691	168	2431,517 027 6944
49	9,717 343 3955	109	157,321 996 2744	169	2547,014 086 5099
50	10,178 917 2068	110	164,794 791 0974	170	2667,997 255 6191
51	10,662 415 7741	111	172,622 543 6745	171	2794,727 125 2610
52	11,168 880 5234	112	180,822 114 4991	172	2927,476 663 7109
53	11,699 402 3482	113	189,411 164 9378	173	3066,531 805 2372
54	12,255 123 9598	114	198,408 195 2723	174	3212,192 065 9860
55	12,837 242 3478	115	207,832 584 5477	175	3364,771 189 1203
56	13,447 011 3594	116	217,704 632 3138	176	3524,597 820 6035
57	14,085 744 3989	117	228,045 602 3487	177	3692,016 217 0822
58	14,754 817 2579	118	238,877 768 4602	178	3867,386 987 3936
59	15,455 671 0776	119	250,224 462 4621	179	4051,087 869 2948
60	16,189 815 4538	120	262,110 124 4290	180	4243,514 543 0863

NOMINAL INTEREST RATE COMPOUNDED

YEARLY	HALF-YEARLY	QUARTERLY
@	@	@
$4\frac{13}{16}\%$	$9\frac{5}{8}\%$	$19\frac{1}{4}\%$
4.8125%	9.6250%	19.2500%
PER ANNUM	PER ANNUM	PER ANNUM

Periods	Amount	Periods	Amount	Periods	Amount
1	1,048 125 0000	61	17,587 247 5662	121	295,109 149 1527
2	1,098 566 0156	62	18,433 633 8554	122	309,311 276 9557
3	1,151 434 5051	63	19,320 752 4846	123	324,196 882 1592
4	1,206 847 2907	64	20,250 563 6980	124	339,798 857 1131
5	1,264 926 8166	65	21,225 122 0759	125	356,151 677 1117
6	1,325 801 4196	66	22,246 581 0758	126	373,291 476 5727
7	1,389 605 6129	67	23,317 197 7901	127	391,256 128 8827
8	1,456 480 3830	68	24,439 337 9338	128	410,085 330 0852
9	1,526 573 5015	69	25,615 481 0718	129	429,820 686 5956
10	1,600 039 8512	70	26,848 226 0984	130	450,505 807 1380
11	1,677 041 7691	71	28,140 296 9794	131	472,186 399 1065
12	1,757 749 4042	72	29,494 548 7715	132	494,910 369 5635
13	1,842 341 0943	73	30,913 973 9311	133	518,727 931 0988
14	1,931 003 7594	74	32,401 708 9266	134	543,691 712 7829
15	2,023 933 3154	75	33,961 041 1687	135	569,856 876 4606
16	2,121 335 1062	76	35,595 416 2749	136	597,281 238 6402
17	2,223 424 3582	77	37,308 445 6831	137	626,025 398 2498
18	2,330 426 6554	78	39,103 914 6316	138	656,152 870 5406
19	2,442 578 4382	79	40,985 790 5233	139	687,730 227 4353
20	2,560 127 5255	80	42,958 231 6922	140	720,827 244 6306
21	2,683 333 6627	81	45,025 596 5924	141	755,517 055 7785
22	2,812 469 0952	82	47,192 453 4284	142	791,876 314 0878
23	2,947 819 1704	83	49,463 590 2497	143	829,985 361 7033
24	3,089 682 9680	84	51,844 025 5304	144	869,928 407 2353
25	3,238 373 9608	85	54,339 019 2591	145	911,793 711 8335
26	3,394 220 7077	86	56,954 084 5609	146	955,673 784 2155
27	3,557 567 5792	87	59,694 999 8804	147	1001,665 585 0808
28	3,728 775 5190	88	62,567 821 7497	148	1049,870 741 3629
29	3,908 222 8408	89	65,578 898 1714	149	1100,395 770 7909
30	4,096 306 0651	90	68,734 882 6459	150	1153,352 317 2603
31	4,293 440 7944	91	72,042 748 8732	151	1208,857 397 5284
32	4,500 062 6327	92	75,509 806 1627	152	1267,033 659 7845
33	4,716 628 1469	93	79,143 715 5843	153	1328,009 654 6616
34	4,943 615 8764	94	82,952 506 8968	154	1391,920 119 2922
35	5,181 527 3905	95	86,944 596 2912	155	1458,906 275 0331
36	5,430 888 3962	96	91,128 804 9877	156	1529,116 139 5191
37	5,692 249 9002	97	95,514 378 7278	157	1602,704 853 7334
38	5,966 189 4267	98	100,111 008 2040	158	1679,835 024 8194
39	6,253 312 2928	99	104,928 850 4739	159	1760,677 085 3888
40	6,554 252 9469	100	109,978 551 4029	160	1845,409 670 1231
41	6,869 676 3700	101	115,271 269 1892	161	1934,220 010 4978
42	7,200 279 5453	102	120,818 699 0189	162	2027,304 348 5030
43	7,546 792 9984	103	126,633 098 9092	163	2124,868 370 2747
44	7,909 982 4115	104	132,727 316 7942	164	2227,127 660 5942
45	8,290 650 3150	105	139,114 818 9149	165	2334,308 179 2603
46	8,689 637 8614	106	145,809 719 5752	166	2446,646 760 3872
47	9,107 826 6835	107	152,826 812 3297	167	2564,391 635 7308
48	9,546 140 8427	108	160,181 602 6731	168	2687,802 983 2004
49	10,005 548 8707	109	167,890 342 3018	169	2817,153 501 7669
50	10,487 065 9101	110	175,970 065 0250	170	2952,729 014 0394
51	10,991 755 9570	111	184,438 624 4044	171	3094,829 097 8400
52	11,520 734 2125	112	193,314 733 2038	172	3243,767 748 1736
53	12,075 169 5464	113	202,618 004 7393	173	3399,874 071 0545
54	12,656 287 0809	114	212,368 996 2173	174	3563,493 010 7239
55	13,265 370 8966	115	222,589 254 1603	175	3734,986 111 8650
56	13,903 766 8710	116	233,301 362 0168	176	3914,732 318 4985
57	14,572 885 6517	117	244,528 990 0638	177	4103,128 811 3263
58	15,274 205 7737	118	256,296 947 7106	178	4300,591 885 3714
59	16,009 276 9265	119	268,631 238 3192	179	4507,557 869 8549
60	16,779 723 3786	120	281,559 116 6633	180	4724,484 092 3416

NOMINAL INTEREST RATE COMPOUNDED

	YEARLY		HALF-YEARLY		QUARTERLY
	@		@		@
	$4\frac{7}{8}\%$		$9\frac{3}{4}\%$		$19\frac{1}{2}\%$
	4.8750%		9.7500%		19.5000%
	PER ANNUM		PER ANNUM		PER ANNUM
Periods	Amount	Periods	Amount	Periods	Amount
1	1,048 750 0000	61	18,238 554 0286	121	317,182 219 8371
2	1,099 876 5625	62	19,127 683 5375	122	332,644 853 0542
3	1,153 495 5449	63	20,060 158 1099	123	348,861 289 6406
4	1,209 728 4527	64	21,038 090 8178	124	365,868 277 5106
5	1,268 702 7148	65	22,063 697 7452	125	383,704 356 0392
6	1,330 551 9722	66	23,139 303 0103	126	402,409 943 3961
7	1,395 416 3808	67	24,267 344 0320	127	422,027 428 1367
8	1,463 442 9294	68	25,450 377 0536	128	442,601 265 2583
9	1,534 785 7722	69	26,691 082 9349	129	464,178 076 9397
10	1,609 606 5786	70	27,992 273 2280	130	486,806 758 1905
11	1,688 074 8993	71	29,356 896 5479	131	510,538 587 6523
12	1,770 368 5506	72	30,788 045 2546	132	535,427 343 8003
13	1,856 674 0174	73	32,288 962 4607	133	561,529 426 8106
14	1,947 186 8758	74	33,863 049 3807	134	588,903 986 3676
15	2,042 112 2360	75	35,513 873 0380	135	617,613 055 7030
16	2,141 665 2075	76	37,245 174 3486	136	647,721 692 1685
17	2,246 071 3864	77	39,060 876 5981	137	679,298 124 6618
18	2,355 567 3664	78	40,965 094 3323	138	712,413 908 2390
19	2,470 401 2756	79	42,962 142 6810	139	747,144 086 2657
20	2,590 833 3377	80	45,056 547 1367	140	783,567 360 4711
21	2,717 136 4630	81	47,253 053 8096	141	821,766 269 2941
22	2,849 596 8655	82	49,556 640 1828	142	861,827 374 9222
23	2,988 514 7127	83	51,972 526 3917	143	903,841 459 4496
24	3,134 204 8050	84	54,506 187 0533	144	947,903 730 5978
25	3,286 997 2892	85	57,163 363 6721	145	994,114 037 4645
26	3,447 238 4071	86	59,950 077 6512	146	1042,577 096 7908
27	3,615 291 2794	87	62,872 643 9366	147	1093,402 730 2594
28	3,791 536 7293	88	65,937 685 3286	148	1146,706 113 3595
29	3,976 374 1448	89	69,152 147 4883	149	1202,608 036 3858
30	4,170 222 3844	90	72,523 314 6784	150	1261,235 178 1596
31	4,373 520 7256	91	76,058 826 2690	151	1322,720 393 0949
32	4,586 729 8610	92	79,766 694 0496	152	1387,203 012 2583
33	4,810 332 9417	93	83,655 320 3845	153	1454,829 159 1059
34	5,044 836 6726	94	87,733 517 2532	154	1525,752 080 6123
35	5,290 772 4604	95	92,010 526 2193	155	1600,132 494 5421
36	5,548 697 6179	96	96,496 039 3725	156	1678,138 953 6511
37	5,819 196 6267	97	101,200 221 2919	157	1759,948 227 6416
38	6,102 882 4623	98	106,133 732 0799	158	1845,745 703 7391
39	6,400 397 9823	99	111,307 751 5188	159	1935,725 806 7964
40	6,712 417 3840	100	116,734 004 4053	160	2030,092 439 8777
41	7,039 647 7314	101	122,424 787 1201	161	2129,059 446 3217
42	7,382 830 5583	102	128,392 995 4922	162	2232,851 094 3299
43	7,742 743 5481	103	134,652 154 0225	163	2341,702 585 1785
44	8,120 202 2960	104	141,216 446 5310	164	2455,860 586 2059
45	8,516 062 1580	105	148,100 748 2994	165	2575,583 789 7835
46	8,931 220 1882	106	155,320 659 7790	166	2701,143 499 5354
47	9,366 617 1723	107	162,892 541 9433	167	2832,824 245 1378
48	9,823 239 7595	108	170,833 553 3630	168	2970,924 427 0882
49	10,302 122 6978	109	179,161 689 0894	169	3115,756 992 9088
50	10,804 351 1793	110	187,895 821 4325	170	3267,650 146 3131
51	11,331 063 2993	111	197,055 742 7274	171	3426,948 090 9459
52	11,883 452 6351	112	206,662 210 1853	172	3594,011 810 3795
53	12,462 770 9511	113	216,736 992 9319	173	3769,219 886 1355
54	13,070 331 0349	114	227,302 921 3373	174	3952,969 355 5846
55	13,707 509 6729	115	238,383 938 7525	175	4145,676 611 6693
56	14,375 750 7695	116	250,005 155 7667	176	4347,778 346 4882
57	15,076 568 6195	117	262,192 907 1103	177	4559,732 540 8795
58	15,811 551 3397	118	274,974 811 3319	178	4782,019 502 2474
59	16,582 364 4675	119	288,379 833 3844	179	5015,142 952 9819
60	17,390 754 7353	120	302,438 350 2619	180	5259,631 171 9398

NOMINAL INTEREST RATE COMPOUNDED

	YEARLY @ $4\frac{15}{16}\%$ 4.9375% PER ANNUM		HALF-YEARLY @ $9\frac{7}{8}\%$ 9.8750% PER ANNUM		QUARTERLY @ $19\frac{3}{4}\%$ 19.7500% PER ANNUM
Periods	Amount	Periods	Amount	Periods	Amount
1	1,049 375 0000	61	18,913 570 4913	121	340,891 624 7578
2	1,101 187 8906	62	19,847 428 0343	122	357,723 148 7302
3	1,155 559 0427	63	20,827 394 7935	123	375,385 729 1988
4	1,212 614 7705	64	21,855 747 4115	124	393,920 399 5780
5	1,272 487 6248	65	22,934 874 9399	125	413,370 219 3071
6	1,335 316 7012	66	24,067 284 3901	126	433,780 373 8854
7	1,401 247 9633	67	25,255 606 5568	127	455,198 279 8460
8	1,470 434 5815	68	26,502 602 1306	128	477,673 694 9134
9	1,543 037 2890	69	27,811 168 1108	129	501,258 833 5998
10	1,619 224 7551	70	29,184 344 5362	130	526,008 488 5088
11	1,699 173 9774	71	30,625 321 5477	131	551,980 157 6289
12	1,783 070 6926	72	32,137 446 7991	132	579,234 177 9118
13	1,871 109 8080	73	33,724 233 2348	133	607,833 865 4462
14	1,963 495 8548	74	35,389 367 2508	134	637,845 662 5526
15	2,060 443 4626	75	37,136 717 2588	135	669,339 292 1412
16	2,162 177 8586	76	38,970 342 6735	136	702,387 919 6906
17	2,268 935 3903	77	40,894 503 3430	137	737,068 323 2253
18	2,380 964 0752	78	42,913 669 4455	138	773,461 071 6846
19	2,498 524 1765	79	45,032 531 8744	139	811,650 712 0990
20	2,621 888 8077	80	47,256 013 1357	140	851,725 966 0089
21	2,751 344 5675	81	49,589 278 7843	141	893,779 935 5806
22	2,887 192 2056	82	52,037 749 4242	142	937,910 319 8999
23	3,029 747 3207	83	54,607 113 3021	143	984,219 641 9450
24	3,179 341 0947	84	57,303 339 5213	144	1032,815 486 7660
25	3,336 321 0612	85	60,132 691 9102	145	1083,810 751 4251
26	3,501 051 9136	86	63,101 743 5733	146	1137,323 907 2767
27	3,673 916 3519	87	66,217 392 1622	147	1193,479 275 1985
28	3,855 315 9717	88	69,486 875 9002	148	1252,407 314 4114
29	4,045 672 1978	89	72,917 790 3978	149	1314,244 925 5604
30	4,245 427 2626	90	76,518 106 2987	150	1379,135 768 7600
31	4,455 045 2337	91	80,296 187 7972	151	1447,230 597 3425
32	4,675 013 0921	92	84,260 812 0697	152	1518,687 608 0863
33	4,905 841 8635	93	88,421 189 6656	153	1593,672 808 7356
34	5,148 067 8056	94	92,786 985 9053	154	1672,360 403 6669
35	5,402 253 6535	95	97,368 343 3344	155	1754,933 198 5979
36	5,668 989 9276	96	102,175 905 2865	156	1841,583 025 2787
37	5,948 896 3053	97	107,220 840 6101	157	1932,511 187 1518
38	6,242 623 0603	98	112,514 869 6152	158	2027,928 927 0175
39	6,550 852 5739	99	118,070 291 3024	159	2128,057 917 7890
40	6,874 300 9198	100	123,900 011 9355	160	2233,130 777 4798
41	7,213 719 5277	101	130,017 575 0248	161	2343,391 609 6178
42	7,569 896 9294	102	136,437 192 7917	162	2459,096 570 3427
43	7,943 660 5903	103	143,173 779 1858	163	2580,514 463 5034
44	8,335 878 8319	104	150,242 984 5331	164	2707,927 365 1389
45	8,747 462 8492	105	157,661 231 8944	165	2841,631 278 7926
46	9,179 368 8274	106	165,445 755 2192	166	2981,936 823 1830
47	9,632 600 1633	107	173,614 639 3831	167	3129,169 953 8277
48	10,108 209 7963	108	182,186 862 2026	168	3283,672 720 2979
49	10,607 302 6550	109	191,182 338 5239	169	3445,804 060 8626
50	11,131 038 2236	110	200,621 966 4885	170	3615,940 636 3677
51	11,680 633 2359	111	210,527 676 0839	171	3794,477 705 2884
52	12,257 364 5019	112	220,922 480 0905	172	3981,830 041 9870
53	12,862 571 8742	113	231,830 527 5450	173	4178,432 900 3101
54	13,497 661 3605	114	243,277 159 8425	174	4384,743 024 7629
55	14,164 108 3902	115	255,288 969 6098	175	4601,239 711 6106
56	14,863 461 2419	116	267,893 862 4842	176	4828,425 922 3713
57	15,597 344 6408	117	281,121 121 9444	177	5066,829 452 2884
58	16,367 463 5324	118	295,001 477 3404	178	5317,004 156 4951
59	17,175 607 0443	119	309,567 175 2841	179	5579,531 236 7221
60	18,023 652 6421	120	324,852 054 5637	180	5855,020 591 5352

Amount of 1

NOMINAL INTEREST RATE COMPOUNDED

	YEARLY @ 5% 5.0000% PER ANNUM		HALF-YEARLY @ 10% 10.0000% PER ANNUM		QUARTERLY @ 20% 20.0000% PER ANNUM
Periods	Amount	Periods	Amount	Periods	Amount
1	1,050 000 0000	61	19,613 145 1888	121	366,357 584 9506
2	1,102 500 0000	62	20,593 802 4483	122	384,675 464 1981
3	1,157 625 0000	63	21,623 492 5707	123	403,909 237 4080
4	1,215 506 2500	64	22,704 667 1992	124	424,104 699 2784
5	1,276 281 5625	65	23,839 900 5592	125	445,309 934 2423
6	1,340 095 6406	66	25,031 895 5871	126	467,575 430 9544
7	1,407 100 4227	67	26,283 490 3665	127	490,954 202 5022
8	1,477 455 4438	68	27,597 664 8848	128	515,501 912 6273
9	1,551 328 2160	69	28,977 548 1291	129	541,277 008 2586
10	1,628 894 6268	70	30,426 425 5355	130	568,340 858 6716
11	1,710 339 3581	71	31,947 746 8123	131	596,757 901 6051
12	1,795 856 3260	72	33,545 134 1529	132	626,595 796 6854
13	1,885 649 1423	73	35,222 390 8605	133	657,925 586 5197
14	1,979 931 5994	74	36,983 510 4036	134	690,821 865 8456
15	2,078 928 1794	75	38,832 685 9238	135	725,362 959 1379
16	2,182 874 5884	76	40,774 320 2199	136	761,631 107 0948
17	2,292 018 3178	77	42,813 036 2309	137	799,712 662 4496
18	2,406 619 2337	78	44,953 688 0425	138	839,698 295 5720
19	2,526 950 1954	79	47,201 372 4446	139	881,683 210 3506
20	2,653 297 7051	80	49,561 441 0668	140	925,767 370 8682
21	2,785 962 5904	81	52,039 513 1202	141	972,055 739 4116
22	2,925 260 7199	82	54,641 488 7762	142	1020,658 526 3822
23	3,071 523 7559	83	57,373 563 2150	143	1071,691 452 7013
24	3,225 099 9437	84	60,242 241 3758	144	1125,276 025 3363
25	3,386 354 9409	85	63,254 353 4445	145	1181,539 826 6031
26	3,555 672 6879	86	66,417 071 1168	146	1240,616 817 9333
27	3,733 456 3223	87	69,737 924 6726	147	1302,647 658 8300
28	3,920 129 1385	88	73,224 820 9062	148	1367,780 041 7715
29	4,116 135 5954	89	76,886 061 9515	149	1436,169 043 8600
30	4,321 942 3752	90	80,730 365 0491	150	1507,977 496 0530
31	4,538 039 4939	91	84,766 883 3016	151	1583,376 370 8557
32	4,764 941 4686	92	89,005 227 4667	152	1662,545 189 3985
33	5,003 188 5420	93	93,455 488 8400	153	1745,672 448 8684
34	5,253 347 9691	94	98,128 263 2820	154	1832,956 071 3118
35	5,516 015 3676	95	103,034 676 4461	155	1924,603 874 8774
36	5,791 816 1360	96	108,186 410 2684	156	2020,834 068 6213
37	6,081 406 9428	97	113,595 730 7818	157	2121,875 772 0523
38	6,385 477 2899	98	119,275 517 3209	158	2227,969 560 6550
39	6,704 751 1544	99	125,239 293 1870	159	2339,368 038 6877
40	7,039 988 7121	100	131,501 257 8463	160	2456,336 440 6221
41	7,391 988 1477	101	138,076 320 7386	161	2579,153 262 6532
42	7,761 587 5551	102	144,980 136 7755	162	2708,110 925 7859
43	8,149 666 9329	103	152,229 143 6143	163	2843,516 472 0752
44	8,557 150 2795	104	159,840 600 7950	164	2985,692 295 6789
45	8,985 007 7935	105	167,832 630 8348	165	3134,976 910 4629
46	9,434 258 1832	106	176,224 262 3765	166	3291,725 755 9860
47	9,905 971 0923	107	185,035 475 4954	167	3456,312 043 7853
48	10,401 269 6469	108	194,287 249 2701	168	3629,127 645 9746
49	10,921 333 1293	109	204,001 611 7336	169	3810,584 028 2733
50	11,467 399 7858	110	214,201 692 3203	170	4001,113 229 6870
51	12,040 769 7750	111	224,911 776 9363	171	4201,168 891 1713
52	12,642 808 2638	112	236,157 365 7832	172	4411,227 335 7299
53	13,274 948 6770	113	247,965 234 0723	173	4631,788 702 5164
54	13,938 696 1108	114	260,363 495 7759	174	4863,378 137 6422
55	14,635 630 9164	115	273,381 670 5647	175	5106,547 044 5243
56	15,367 412 4622	116	287,050 754 0930	176	5361,874 396 7505
57	16,135 783 0853	117	301,403 291 7976	177	5629,968 116 5880
58	16,942 572 2396	118	316,473 456 3875	178	5911,466 522 4174
59	17,789 700 8515	119	332,297 129 2069	179	6207,039 848 5383
60	18,679 185 8941	120	348,911 985 6672	180	6517,391 840 9652

Amount of 1

NOMINAL INTEREST RATE COMPOUNDED

YEARLY	HALF-YEARLY	QUARTERLY
@	@	@
$5\frac{1}{16}\%$	$10\frac{1}{8}\%$	$20\frac{1}{4}\%$
5.0625%	10.1250%	20.2500%
PER ANNUM	PER ANNUM	PER ANNUM

Periods	Amount	Periods	Amount	Periods	Amount
1	1.050 625 0000	61	20.338 156 1691	121	393.709 074 4645
2	1.103 812 8906	62	21.367 775 3252	122	413.640 596 3592
3	1.159 693 4182	63	22.449 518 9510	123	434.581 151 5499
4	1.218 402 8975	64	23.586 025 8479	124	456.581 822 3471
5	1.280 084 5442	65	24.780 068 4065	125	479.696 277 1035
6	1.344 888 8242	66	26.034 559 3695	126	503.980 901 1318
7	1.412 973 8210	67	27.352 558 9376	127	529.494 934 2516
8	1.484 505 6207	68	28.737 282 2338	128	556.300 615 2981
9	1.559 658 7177	69	30.192 107 1469	129	584.463 333 9476
10	1.638 616 4403	70	31.720 582 5712	130	614.051 790 2287
11	1.721 571 3976	71	33.326 437 0639	131	645.138 162 1090
12	1.808 725 9496	72	35.013 587 9403	132	677.798 281 5658
13	1.900 292 7008	73	36.786 150 8297	133	712.111 819 5700
14	1.996 495 0188	74	38.648 449 7155	134	748.162 480 4358
15	2.097 567 5791	75	40.605 027 4823	135	786.038 206 0078
16	2.203 756 9378	76	42.660 656 9986	136	825.831 390 1870
17	2.315 322 1327	77	44.820 352 7592	137	867.639 104 3152
18	2.432 535 3157	78	47.089 383 1176	138	911.563 333 9711
19	2.555 682 4161	79	49.473 283 1380	139	957.711 227 7534
20	2.685 063 8384	80	51.977 868 0968	140	1006.195 358 6584
21	2.820 995 1952	81	54.609 247 6692	141	1057.133 998 6905
22	2.963 808 0770	82	57.373 840 8325	142	1110.651 407 3742
23	3.113 850 8609	83	60.278 391 5246	143	1166.878 134 8725
24	3.271 489 5607	84	63.329 985 0955	144	1225.951 340 4505
25	3.437 108 7197	85	66.536 065 5910	145	1288.015 127 0608
26	3.611 112 3486	86	69.904 453 9116	146	1353.220 892 8682
27	3.793 924 9113	87	73.443 366 8908	147	1421.727 700 5697
28	3.985 992 3599	88	77.161 437 3397	148	1493.702 665 4110
29	4.187 783 2231	89	81.067 735 1050	149	1569.321 362 8475
30	4.399 789 7488	90	85.171 789 1947	150	1648.768 256 8416
31	4.622 529 1048	91	89.483 611 0227	151	1732.237 149 8442
32	4.856 544 6408	92	94.013 718 8307	152	1819.931 655 5551
33	5.102 407 2132	93	98.773 163 3465	153	1912.065 695 6176
34	5.360 716 5784	94	103.773 554 7409	154	2008.864 021 4582
35	5.632 102 8552	95	109.027 090 9497	155	2110.562 762 5445
36	5.917 228 0622	96	114.546 587 4290	156	2217.410 002 3983
37	6.216 787 7329	97	120.345 508 4176	157	2329.666 383 7697
38	6.531 512 6118	98	126.437 999 7812	158	2447.605 744 4481
39	6.862 170 4378	99	132.838 923 5201	159	2571.515 785 2608
40	7.209 567 8162	100	139.563 894 0234	160	2701.698 771 8896
41	7.574 552 1869	101	146.629 316 1583	161	2838.472 272 2165
42	7.958 013 8914	102	154.052 425 2888	162	2982.169 930 9975
43	8.360 888 3446	103	161.851 329 3190	163	3133.142 283 7542
44	8.784 158 3171	104	170.045 052 8658	164	3291.757 611 8693
45	9.228 856 3319	105	178.653 583 6672	165	3458.402 840 9702
46	9.696 067 1837	106	187.697 921 3403	166	3633.484 484 7943
47	10.186 930 5849	107	197.200 128 6082	167	3817.429 636 8370
48	10.702 643 9457	108	207.183 385 1189	168	4010.687 012 2019
49	11.244 465 2955	109	217.672 043 9906	169	4213.728 042 1946
50	11.813 716 3511	110	228.691 691 2176	170	4427.048 024 3307
51	12.411 785 7413	111	240.269 208 0855	171	4651.167 330 5624
52	13.040 132 3945	112	252.432 836 7448	172	4886.632 676 6721
53	13.700 289 0970	113	265.212 249 1050	173	5134.018 455 9287
54	14.393 866 2325	114	278.638 619 2160	174	5393.928 140 2600
55	15.122 555 7105	115	292.744 699 3138	175	5666.995 752 3607
56	15.888 135 0934	116	307.564 899 7166	176	5953.887 412 3240
57	16.692 471 9325	117	323.135 372 7647	177	6255.302 962 5729
58	17.537 528 3240	118	339.494 101 0109	178	6571.977 675 0531
59	18.425 365 6954	119	356.680 989 8746	179	6904.684 044 8527
60	19.358 149 8338	120	374.737 964 9870	180	7254.233 674 6234

NOMINAL INTEREST RATE COMPOUNDED	YEARLY @ $5\frac{1}{8}\%$ 5.1250% PER ANNUM		HALF-YEARLY @ $10\frac{1}{4}\%$ 10.2500% PER ANNUM		QUARTERLY @ $20\frac{1}{2}\%$ 20.5000% PER ANNUM
Periods	**Amount**	**Periods**	**Amount**	**Periods**	**Amount**
1	1.051 250 0000	61	21.089 512 3229	121	423.084 451 8606
2	1.105 126 5625	62	22.170 349 8295	122	444.767 530 0184
3	1.161 764 2988	63	23.306 580 2582	123	467.561 865 9319
4	1.221 304 7191	64	24.501 042 4965	124	491.524 411 5609
5	1.283 896 5860	65	25.756 720 9244	125	516.715 037 6534
6	1.349 696 2860	66	27.076 752 8718	126	543.196 683 3331
7	1.418 868 2207	67	28.464 436 4565	127	571.035 513 3539
8	1.491 585 2170	68	29.923 238 8249	128	600.301 083 4133
9	1.568 028 9594	69	31.456 804 8146	129	631.066 513 9383
10	1.648 390 4435	70	33.068 966 0614	130	663.408 672 7776
11	1.732 870 4538	71	34.763 750 5720	131	697.408 367 2574
12	1.821 680 0645	72	36.545 392 7888	132	733.150 546 0794
13	1.915 041 1678	73	38.418 344 1693	133	770.724 511 5660
14	2.013 187 0277	74	40.387 284 3079	134	810.224 142 7837
15	2.116 362 8629	75	42.457 132 6287	135	851.748 130 1014
16	2.224 826 4596	76	44.633 060 6759	136	895.400 221 7691
17	2.338 848 8156	77	46.920 505 0356	137	941.289 483 1347
18	2.458 714 8174	78	49.325 180 9187	138	989.530 569 1454
19	2.584 723 9518	79	51.853 096 4407	139	1040.244 010 8141
20	2.717 191 0544	80	54.510 567 6333	140	1093.556 516 3683
21	2.856 447 0959	81	57.304 234 2245	141	1149.601 287 8322
22	3.002 840 0096	82	60.241 076 2285	142	1208.518 353 8336
23	3.156 735 5600	83	63.328 431 3853	143	1270.454 919 4676
24	3.318 518 2575	84	66.574 013 4937	144	1335.565 734 0903
25	3.488 592 3182	85	69.985 931 6853	145	1404.013 477 9624
26	3.667 382 6745	86	73.572 710 6842	146	1475.969 168 7080
27	3.855 336 0366	87	77.343 312 1067	147	1551.612 588 6043
28	4.052 922 0084	88	81.307 156 8522	148	1631.132 733 7702
29	4.260 634 2614	89	85.474 148 6409	149	1714.728 286 3760
30	4.478 991 7673	90	89.854 698 7587	150	1802.608 111 0527
31	4.708 540 0953	91	94.459 752 0701	151	1894.991 776 7442
32	4.949 852 7752	92	99.300 814 3637	152	1992.110 105 3023
33	5.203 532 7300	93	104.389 981 0999	153	2094.205 748 1991
34	5.470 213 7824	94	109.739 967 6312	154	2201.533 792 7943
35	5.750 562 2387	95	115.364 140 9723	155	2314.362 399 6750
36	6.045 278 5535	96	121.276 553 1971	156	2432.973 472 6583
37	6.355 099 0793	97	127.491 976 5485	157	2557.663 363 1321
38	6.680 797 9071	98	134.025 940 3466	158	2688.743 610 4926
39	7.023 188 7999	99	140.894 769 7894	159	2826.541 720 5303
40	7.383 127 2259	100	148.115 626 7411	160	2971.401 983 7075
41	7.761 512 4962	101	155.706 552 6116	161	3123.686 335 3725
42	8.159 290 0116	102	163.686 513 4329	162	3283.775 260 0604
43	8.577 453 6247	103	172.075 447 2463	163	3452.068 742 1385
44	9.017 048 1230	104	180.894 313 9177	164	3628.987 265 1730
45	9.479 171 8393	105	190.165 147 5060	165	3814.972 862 5132
46	9.964 979 3961	106	199.911 111 3157	166	4010.490 221 7170
47	10.475 684 5901	107	210.156 555 7706	167	4216.027 845 5800
48	11.012 563 4253	108	220.927 079 2539	168	4432.099 272 6659
49	11.576 957 3009	109	232.249 592 0656	169	4659.244 360 3901
50	12.170 276 3626	110	244.152 383 6590	170	4898.030 633 8601
51	12.794 003 0261	111	256.665 193 3215	171	5149.054 703 8454
52	13.449 695 6812	112	269.819 284 4792	172	5412.943 757 4175
53	14.138 992 5849	113	283.647 522 8088	173	5690.357 124 9851
54	14.863 615 9549	114	298.184 458 3527	174	5981.987 927 6406
55	15.625 376 2726	115	313.466 411 8433	175	6288.564 808 9322
56	16.426 176 8065	116	329.531 565 4503	176	6610.853 755 3899
57	17.268 018 3679	117	346.420 058 1796	177	6949.660 010 3537
58	18.153 004 3092	118	364.174 086 1613	178	7305.830 085 8843
59	19.083 345 7801	119	382.838 008 0771	179	7680.253 877 7859
60	20.061 367 2513	120	402.458 455 9910	180	8073.866 889 0224

NOMINAL INTEREST RATE COMPOUNDED

	YEARLY @ $5\frac{3}{16}\%$ 5.1875% PER ANNUM		HALF-YEARLY @ $10\frac{3}{8}\%$ 10.3750% PER ANNUM		QUARTERLY @ $20\frac{3}{4}\%$ 20.7500% PER ANNUM
Periods	Amount	Periods	Amount	Periods	Amount
1	1,051 875 0000	61	21,868 154 4478	121	454,632 136 8537
2	1,106 441 0156	62	23,002 564 9598	122	478,216 178 9530
3	1,163 837 6433	63	24,195 823 0171	123	503,023 643 2362
4	1,224 211 7211	64	25,450 981 3361	124	529,117 994 7291
5	1,287 717 7041	65	26,771 250 9929	125	556,565 990 7057
6	1,354 518 0600	66	28,160 009 6381	126	585,437 851 4735
7	1,424 783 6843	67	29,620 810 1381	127	615,807 440 0187
8	1,498 694 3380	68	31,157 389 6640	128	647,752 450 9697
9	1,576 439 1068	69	32,773 679 2529	129	681,354 609 3637
10	1,658 216 8854	70	34,473 813 8641	130	716,699 879 7245
11	1,744 236 8864	71	36,262 142 9583	131	753,878 685 9852
12	1,834 719 1748	72	38,143 241 6243	132	792,986 142 8207
13	1,929 895 2320	73	40,121 922 2835	133	834,122 298 9795
14	2,030 008 5472	74	42,203 247 0020	134	877,392 393 2390
15	2,135 315 2406	75	44,392 540 4402	135	922,907 123 6383
16	2,246 084 7187	76	46,695 403 4756	136	970,782 930 6771
17	2,362 600 3635	77	49,117 727 5308	137	1021,142 295 2059
18	2,485 160 2573	78	51,665 709 6465	138	1074,114 051 7697
19	2,614 077 9457	79	54,345 868 3344	139	1129,833 718 2053
20	2,749 683 2391	80	57,165 060 2543	140	1188,443 842 3372
21	2,892 323 0571	81	60,130 497 7550	141	1250,094 366 6584
22	3,042 362 3157	82	63,249 767 3260	142	1314,943 011 9288
23	3,200 184 8608	83	66,530 849 0060	143	1383,155 680 6726
24	3,366 194 4505	84	69,982 136 7982	144	1454,906 881 6075
25	3,540 815 7876	85	73,612 460 1446	145	1530,380 176 0909
26	3,724 495 6066	86	77,431 106 5146	146	1609,768 647 7256
27	3,917 703 8162	87	81,447 845 1651	147	1693,275 396 3264
28	4,120 934 7016	88	85,672 952 1330	148	1781,114 057 5108
29	4,334 708 1893	89	90,117 236 5249	149	1873,509 349 2442
30	4,559 571 1766	90	94,792 068 1697	150	1970,697 646 7363
31	4,796 098 9314	91	99,709 406 7060	151	2072,927 587 1607
32	5,044 896 5635	92	104,881 832 1788	152	2180,460 705 7447
33	5,306 600 5727	93	110,322 577 2231	153	2293,572 104 8552
34	5,581 880 4774	94	116,045 560 9165	154	2412,551 157 7945
35	5,871 440 5272	95	122,065 424 3891	155	2537,702 249 1051
36	6,176 021 5045	96	128,397 568 2793	156	2669,345 553 2774
37	6,496 402 6201	97	135,058 192 1338	157	2807,817 853 8537
38	6,833 403 5060	98	142,064 335 8507	158	2953,473 405 0224
39	7,187 886 3129	99	149,433 923 2730	159	3106,684 837 9079
40	7,560 757 9153	100	157,185 808 0427	160	3267,844 113 8744
41	7,952 972 2322	101	165,339 821 8350	161	3437,363 527 2816
42	8,365 532 6667	102	173,916 825 0926	162	3615,676 760 2594
43	8,799 494 6738	103	182,938 760 3943	163	3803,239 992 1978
44	9,255 968 4600	104	192,428 708 5898	164	4000,533 066 7931
45	9,736 121 8239	105	202,410 947 8479	165	4208,060 719 6330
46	10,241 183 1435	106	212,911 015 7675	166	4426,353 869 4639
47	10,772 444 5191	107	223,955 774 7104	167	4655,970 976 4424
48	11,331 265 0785	108	235,573 480 5235	168	4897,499 470 8453
49	11,919 074 4544	109	247,793 854 8257	169	5151,557 255 8954
50	12,537 376 4418	110	260,648 161 0448	170	5418,794 288 5450
51	13,187 752 8447	111	274,169 284 3990	171	5699,894 242 2633
52	13,871 867 5235	112	288,391 816 0272	172	5995,576 256 0807
53	14,591 470 6513	113	303,352 141 4836	173	6306,596 774 3648
54	15,348 403 1913	114	319,088 533 8230	174	6633,751 482 0350
55	16,144 601 6069	115	335,641 251 5151	175	6977,877 340 1656
56	16,982 102 8152	116	353,052 641 4375	176	7339,854 727 1867
57	17,863 049 3988	117	371,367 247 2120	177	7720,609 691 1595
58	18,789 695 0863	118	390,631 923 1611	178	8121,116 318 8884
59	19,764 410 5189	119	410,895 954 1751	179	8542,399 227 9307
60	20,789 689 3146	120	432,211 181 7980	180	8985,536 187 8796

Amount of 1

NOMINAL INTEREST RATE COMPOUNDED

YEARLY	HALF-YEARLY	QUARTERLY
@	@	@
$5\frac{1}{4}\%$	$10\frac{1}{2}\%$	21%
5.2500%	10.5000%	21.0000%
PER ANNUM	PER ANNUM	PER ANNUM

Periods	Amount	Periods	Amount	Periods	Amount
1	1.052 500 0000	61	22.675 056 3483	121	488.511 335 2950
2	1.107 756 2500	62	23.865 496 8066	122	514.158 180 3980
3	1.165 913 4531	63	25.118 435 3889	123	541.151 484 8689
4	1.227 123 9094	64	26.437 153 2468	124	569.561 937 8245
5	1.291 547 9147	65	27.825 103 7923	125	599.463 939 5603
6	1.359 354 1802	66	29.285 921 7414	126	630.935 796 3872
7	1.430 720 2746	67	30.823 432 6328	127	664.059 925 6976
8	1.505 833 0891	68	32.441 662 8460	128	698.923 071 7967
9	1.584 889 3262	69	34.144 850 1455	129	735.616 533 0660
10	1.668 096 0159	70	35.937 454 7781	130	774.236 401 0520
11	1.755 671 0567	71	37.824 171 1539	131	814.883 812 1072
12	1.847 843 7872	72	39.809 940 1395	132	857.665 212 2428
13	1.944 855 5860	73	41.899 961 9968	133	902.692 635 8856
14	2.046 960 5043	74	44.099 710 0017	134	950.083 999 2696
15	2.154 425 9307	75	46.414 944 7768	135	999.963 409 2312
16	2.267 533 2921	76	48.851 729 3775	136	1052.461 488 2159
17	2.386 578 7899	77	51.416 445 1699	137	1107.715 716 3472
18	2.511 874 1764	78	54.115 808 5413	138	1165.870 791 4554
19	2.643 747 5707	79	56.956 888 4897	139	1227.079 008 0069
20	2.782 544 3181	80	59.947 125 1354	140	1291.500 655 9272
21	2.928 627 8948	81	63.094 349 2050	141	1359.304 440 3634
22	3.082 380 8593	82	66.406 802 5383	142	1430.667 923 4825
23	3.244 205 8544	83	69.893 159 6715	143	1505.777 989 4653
24	3.414 526 6618	84	73.562 550 5543	144	1584.831 333 9122
25	3.593 789 3115	85	77.424 584 4584	145	1668.034 978 9426
26	3.782 463 2504	86	81.489 375 1425	146	1755.606 815 3371
27	3.981 042 5710	87	85.767 567 3375	147	1847.776 173 1423
28	4.190 047 3060	88	90.270 364 6227	148	1944.784 422 2323
29	4.410 024 7896	89	95.009 558 7654	149	2046.885 604 3995
30	4.641 551 0910	90	99.997 560 6005	150	2154.347 098 6305
31	4.885 232 5233	91	105.247 432 5321	151	2267.450 321 3086
32	5.141 707 2308	92	110.772 922 7400	152	2386.491 463 1773
33	5.411 646 8604	93	116.588 501 1839	153	2511.782 264 9941
34	5.695 758 3205	94	122.709 397 4960	154	2643.650 833 9062
35	5.994 785 6324	95	129.151 640 8645	155	2782.442 502 6863
36	6.309 511 8781	96	135.932 102 0099	156	2928.520 734 0774
37	6.640 761 2517	97	143.068 537 3655	157	3082.268 072 6164
38	6.989 401 2174	98	150.579 635 5771	158	3244.087 146 4288
39	7.356 344 7813	99	158.485 066 4449	159	3414.401 721 6163
40	7.742 552 8823	100	166.805 532 4333	160	3593.657 812 0011
41	8.149 036 9086	101	175.562 822 8860	161	3782.324 847 1312
42	8.576 861 3463	102	184.779 871 0876	162	3980.896 901 6056
43	9.027 146 5670	103	194.480 814 3197	163	4189.893 988 9399
44	9.501 071 7618	104	204.691 057 0714	164	4409.863 423 3592
45	9.999 878 0293	105	215.437 337 5677	165	4641.381 253 0856
46	10.524 871 6258	106	226.747 797 7900	166	4885.053 768 8726
47	11.077 427 3862	107	238.652 057 1740	167	5141.519 091 7384
48	11.658 992 3240	108	251.181 290 1756	168	5411.448 844 0547
49	12.271 089 4210	109	264.368 307 9098	169	5695.549 908 3675
50	12.915 321 6156	110	278.247 644 0751	170	5994.566 278 5568
51	13.593 376 0004	111	292.855 645 3890	171	6309.281 008 1811
52	14.307 028 2404	112	308.230 566 7720	172	6640.518 261 1106
53	15.058 147 2230	113	324.412 671 5275	173	6989.145 469 8189
54	15.848 699 9522	114	341.444 336 7827	174	7356.075 606 9844
55	16.680 756 6997	115	359.370 164 4638	175	7742.269 576 3510
56	17.556 496 4265	116	378.237 098 0981	176	8148.738 729 1095
57	18.478 212 4888	117	398.094 545 7483	177	8576.547 512 3877
58	19.448 318 6445	118	418.994 509 4001	178	9026.816 256 7881
59	20.469 355 3733	119	440.991 721 1436	179	9500.724 110 2694
60	21.543 996 5304	120	464.143 786 5036	180	9999.512 126 0586

NOMINAL INTEREST RATE COMPOUNDED

YEARLY @ $5\frac{5}{16}\%$ 5.3125% PER ANNUM		HALF-YEARLY @ $10\frac{5}{8}\%$ 10.6250% PER ANNUM		QUARTERLY @ $21\frac{1}{4}\%$ 21.2500% PER ANNUM	
Periods	Amount	Periods	Amount	Periods	Amount
1	1,053 125 0000	61	23,511 225 9732	121	524,892 815 9166
2	1,109 072 2656	62	24,760 259 8530	122	552,777 746 7622
3	1,167 991 7297	63	26,075 648 6577	123	582,144 064 5590
4	1,230 041 2904	64	27,460 917 4926	124	613,070 467 9887
5	1,295 387 2339	65	28,919 778 7344	125	645,639 836 6006
6	1,364 204 6807	66	30,456 141 9797	126	679,939 452 9200
7	1,436 678 0544	67	32,074 124 5224	127	716,061 236 3563
8	1,513 001 5760	68	33,778 062 3876	128	754,101 989 5378
9	1,593 379 7848	69	35,572 521 9520	129	794,163 657 7320
10	1,678 028 0858	70	37,462 312 1807	130	836,353 602 0490
11	1,767 173 3279	71	39,452 497 5153	131	880,784 887 1578
12	1,861 054 4109	72	41,548 411 4458	132	927,576 584 2881
13	1,959 922 9265	73	43,755 670 8038	133	976,854 090 3284
14	2,064 043 8320	74	46,080 190 8153	134	1028,749 463 8771
15	2,173 696 1606	75	48,528 200 9523	135	1083,401 779 1455
16	2,289 173 7691	76	51,106 261 6279	136	1140,957 498 6626
17	2,410 786 1256	77	53,821 281 7769	137	1201,570 865 7791
18	2,538 859 1385	78	56,680 537 3713	138	1265,404 318 0236
19	2,673 736 0302	79	59,691 690 9192	139	1332,628 922 4186
20	2,815 778 2568	80	62,862 811 9992	140	1403,424 833 9221
21	2,965 366 4767	81	66,202 398 8867	141	1477,981 778 2242
22	3,122 901 5708	82	69,719 401 3276	142	1556,499 560 1924
23	3,288 805 7167	83	73,423 244 5231	143	1639,188 599 3276
24	3,463 523 5205	84	77,323 854 3884	144	1726,270 493 6669
25	3,647 523 2075	85	81,431 684 1528	145	1817,978 613 6429
26	3,841 297 8779	86	85,757 742 3734	146	1914,558 727 4927
27	4,045 366 8276	87	90,313 622 4370	147	2016,269 659 8908
28	4,260 276 9404	88	95,111 533 6289	148	2123,383 985 5725
29	4,486 604 1528	89	100,164 333 8530	149	2236,188 759 8060
30	4,724 954 9984	90	105,485 564 0889	150	2354,986 287 6707
31	4,975 968 2327	91	111,089 484 6811	151	2480,094 934 2032
32	5,240 316 5451	92	116,991 113 5548	152	2611,849 977 5827
33	5,518 708 3615	93	123,206 266 4624	153	2750,604 507 6418
34	5,811 889 7432	94	129,751 599 3682	154	2896,730 372 1103
35	6,120 646 3859	95	136,644 653 0847	155	3050,619 173 1287
36	6,445 805 7251	96	143,903 900 2798	156	3212,683 316 7011
37	6,788 239 1542	97	151,548 794 9821	157	3383,357 117 9009
38	7,148 864 3593	98	159,599 824 7156	158	3563,097 964 7893
39	7,528 647 7784	99	168,078 565 4036	159	3752,387 544 1688
40	7,928 607 1916	100	177,007 739 1907	160	3951,733 132 4527
41	8,349 814 4487	101	186,411 275 3352	161	4161,668 955 1143
42	8,793 398 3413	102	196,314 374 3373	162	4382,757 618 3547
43	9,260 547 6282	103	206,743 575 4740	163	4615,591 616 8298
44	9,752 514 2209	104	217,726 827 9211	164	4860,794 921 4739
45	10,270 616 5389	105	229,293 565 6544	165	5119,024 651 6772
46	10,816 243 0425	106	241,474 786 3298	166	5390,972 836 2976
47	11,390 855 9542	107	254,303 134 3535	167	5677,368 268 2259
48	11,995 995 1767	108	267,812 988 3661	168	5978,978 457 4754
49	12,633 282 4205	109	282,040 553 3730	169	6296,611 688 0288
50	13,304 425 5491	110	297,023 957 7710	170	6631,119 183 9553
51	14,011 223 1564	111	312,803 355 5275	171	6983,397 390 6029
52	14,755 569 3865	112	329,421 033 7899	172	7354,390 376 9787
53	15,539 459 0102	113	346,921 526 2100	173	7745,092 365 7557
54	16,364 992 7701	114	365,351 732 2899	174	8156,550 397 6865
55	17,234 383 0110	115	384,761 043 0678	175	8589,867 137 5636
56	18,149 959 6085	116	405,201 473 4808	176	9046,203 829 2466
57	19,114 176 2127	117	426,727 801 7595	177	9526,783 407 6754
58	20,129 616 8240	118	449,397 716 2280	178	10032,893 776 2081
59	21,199 002 7178	119	473,271 969 9026	179	10565,891 258 0692
60	22,325 199 7371	120	498,414 543 3036	180	11127,204 231 1541

Amount of 1

NOMINAL INTEREST RATE COMPOUNDED

YEARLY	HALF-YEARLY	QUARTERLY
@	@	@
$5\frac{3}{8}\%$	$10\frac{3}{4}\%$	$21\frac{1}{2}\%$
5.3750%	10.7500%	21.5000%
PER ANNUM	PER ANNUM	PER ANNUM

Periods	Amount	Periods	Amount	Periods	Amount
1	1,053 750 0000	61	24,377 706 5915	121	563,959 742 5005
2	1,110 389 0625	62	25,688 008 3208	122	594,272 578 6599
3	1,170 072 4746	63	27,068 738 7680	123	626,214 729 7629
4	1,232 963 8701	64	28,523 683 4768	124	659,873 771 4876
5	1,299 235 6781	65	30,056 831 4637	125	695,341 986 7051
6	1,369 069 5958	66	31,672 386 1548	126	732,716 618 4905
7	1,442 657 0866	67	33,374 776 9107	127	772,100 136 7344
8	1,520 199 9050	68	35,168 671 1696	128	813,600 519 0838
9	1,601 910 6499	69	37,058 987 2450	129	857,331 546 9846
10	1,688 013 3473	70	39,050 907 8094	130	903,413 117 6350
11	1,778 744 0648	71	41,149 894 1041	131	951,971 572 7079
12	1,874 351 5582	72	43,361 700 9122	132	1003,140 044 7410
13	1,975 097 9545	73	45,692 392 3363	133	1057,058 822 1458
14	2,081 259 4696	74	48,148 358 4243	134	1113,875 733 8361
15	2,193 127 1660	75	50,736 332 6897	135	1173,746 554 5298
16	2,311 007 7512	76	53,463 410 5717	136	1236,835 431 8358
17	2,435 224 4179	77	56,337 068 8900	137	1303,315 336 2970
18	2,566 117 7303	78	59,365 186 3428	138	1373,368 535 6229
19	2,704 046 5583	79	62,556 065 1087	139	1447,187 094 4127
20	2,849 389 0608	80	65,918 453 6083	140	1524,973 400 7373
21	3,002 543 7228	81	69,461 570 4898	141	1606,940 721 0270
22	3,163 930 4479	82	73,195 129 9036	142	1693,313 784 7822
23	3,333 991 7095	83	77,129 368 1359	143	1784,329 400 7142
24	3,513 193 7639	84	81,275 071 6732	144	1880,237 106 0026
25	3,702 027 9287	85	85,643 606 7756	145	1981,299 850 4502
26	3,901 011 9299	86	90,246 950 6398	146	2087,794 717 4119
27	4,110 691 3211	87	95,097 724 2367	147	2200,013 683 4728
28	4,331 640 9796	88	100,209 226 9144	148	2318,264 418 9595
29	4,564 466 6823	89	105,595 472 8611	149	2442,871 131 4786
30	4,809 806 7665	90	111,271 229 5274	150	2574,175 454 7955
31	5,068 333 8802	91	117,252 058 1145	151	2712,537 385 4908
32	5,340 756 8262	92	123,554 356 2381	152	2858,336 269 9609
33	5,627 822 5056	93	130,195 402 8859	153	3011,971 844 4713
34	5,930 317 9653	94	137,193 405 7910	154	3173,865 331 1117
35	6,249 072 5559	95	144,567 551 3523	155	3344,460 592 6589
36	6,584 960 2058	96	152,338 057 2375	156	3524,225 349 5143
37	6,938 901 8169	97	160,526 227 8140	157	3713,652 462 0507
38	7,311 867 7895	98	169,154 512 5590	158	3913,261 281 8859
39	7,704 880 6832	99	178,246 567 6091	159	4123,599 075 7873
40	8,119 018 0200	100	187,827 320 6181	160	4345,242 526 1109
41	8,555 415 2385	101	197,923 039 1013	161	4578,799 311 8893
42	9,015 268 8076	102	208,561 402 4530	162	4824,909 774 9034
43	9,499 839 5060	103	219,771 577 8348	163	5084,248 675 3045
44	10,010 455 8795	104	231,584 300 1434	164	5357,527 041 6021
45	10,548 517 8830	105	244,031 956 2761	165	5645,494 120 0882
46	11,115 500 7192	106	257,148 673 9260	166	5948,939 429 0429
47	11,712 958 8828	107	270,970 415 1495	167	6268,694 923 3540
48	12,342 530 4228	108	285,535 074 9638	168	6605,637 275 4843
49	13,005 941 4330	109	300,882 585 2431	169	6960,690 279 0415
50	13,705 010 7850	110	317,055 024 1999	170	7334,827 381 5400
51	14,441 655 1147	111	334,096 731 7507	171	7729,074 353 2978
52	15,217 894 0772	112	352,054 431 0823	172	8144,512 099 7875
53	16,035 855 8838	113	370,977 356 7529	173	8582,279 625 1511
54	16,897 783 1376	114	390,917 389 6784	174	9043,577 155 0030
55	17,806 038 9812	115	411,929 199 3736	175	9529,669 427 0844
56	18,763 113 5764	116	434,070 393 8399	176	10041,889 158 7902
57	19,771 630 9312	117	457,401 677 5088	177	10581,640 701 0752
58	20,834 356 0937	118	481,987 017 6749	178	11150,403 888 7580
59	21,954 202 7338	119	507,893 819 8750	179	11749,738 097 7787
60	23,134 241 1307	120	535,193 112 6933	180	12381,286 520 5343

Amount of 1

NOMINAL INTEREST RATE COMPOUNDED

	YEARLY @ $5\frac{7}{16}\%$ 7.4375% PER ANNUM		HALF-YEARLY @ $10\frac{7}{8}\%$ 10.8750% PER ANNUM		QUARTERLY @ $21\frac{3}{4}\%$ 21.7500% PER ANNUM
Periods	Amount	Periods	Amount	Periods	Amount
1	1.054 375 0000	61	25.275 578 0079	121	605.908 565 3893
2	1.111 706 6406	62	26.649 937 5621	122	638.854 843 6323
3	1.172 155 6892	63	28.099 027 9170	123	673.592 575 7549
4	1.235 891 6548	64	29.626 912 5600	124	710.219 172 0615
5	1.303 093 2635	65	31.237 875 9304	125	748.837 339 5424
6	1.373 948 9597	66	32.936 435 4341	126	789.555 369 8800
7	1.448 657 4344	67	34.727 354 1109	127	832.487 443 1172
8	1.527 428 1824	68	36.615 653 9907	128	877.753 947 8367
9	1.610 482 0898	69	38.606 630 1764	129	925.481 818 7503
10	1.698 052 0535	70	40.705 865 6922	130	975.804 892 6449
11	1.790 383 6339	71	42.919 247 1393	131	1028.864 283 6824
12	1.887 735 7440	72	45.252 981 2025	132	1084.808 779 1077
13	1.990 381 3751	73	47.713 612 0553	133	1143.795 256 4717
14	2.098 608 3623	74	50.308 039 7108	134	1205.989 123 5423
15	2.212 720 1920	75	53.043 539 3701	135	1271.564 782 1349
16	2.333 036 8525	76	55.927 781 8234	136	1340.706 117 1635
17	2.459 895 7313	77	58.968 854 9600	137	1413.607 012 2843
18	2.593 652 5617	78	62.175 286 4485	138	1490.471 893 5772
19	2.734 682 4198	79	65.556 067 6491	139	1571.516 302 7905
20	2.883 380 7763	80	69.120 678 8275	140	1656.967 501 7547
21	3.040 164 6061	81	72.879 115 7388	141	1747.065 109 6626
22	3.205 473 5565	82	76.841 917 6571	142	1842.061 775 0005
23	3.379 771 1811	83	81.020 196 9297	143	1942.223 884 0162
24	3.563 546 2391	84	85.425 670 1377	144	2047.832 307 7096
25	3.757 314 0659	85	90.070 690 9515	145	2159.183 189 4413
26	3.961 618 0182	86	94.968 284 7719	146	2276.588 775 3671
27	4.177 030 9979	87	100.132 185 2564	147	2400.378 290 0277
28	4.404 157 0585	88	105.576 872 8297	148	2530.898 859 5480
29	4.643 633 0985	89	111.317 615 2899	149	2668.516 485 0359
30	4.896 130 6482	90	117.370 510 6212	150	2813.617 068 9097
31	5.162 357 7522	91	123.752 532 1363	151	2966.607 497 0317
32	5.443 060 9550	92	130.481 576 0712	152	3127.916 779 6828
33	5.739 027 3944	93	137.576 511 7701	153	3297.997 254 5781
34	6.051 087 0090	94	145.057 234 5975	154	3477.325 855 2957
35	6.380 114 8651	95	152.944 721 7288	155	3666.405 448 6775
36	6.727 033 6109	96	161.261 090 9728	156	3865.766 244 9493
37	7.092 816 0635	97	170.029 662 7944	157	4075.967 284 5184
38	7.478 487 9370	98	179.275 025 7089	158	4297.598 005 6141
39	7.885 130 7185	99	189.023 105 2318	159	4531.279 897 1694
40	8.313 884 7014	100	199.301 236 5788	160	4777.668 241 5779
41	8.765 952 1820	101	210.138 241 3178	161	5037.453 952 2137
42	9.242 600 8319	102	221.564 508 1894	162	5311.365 510 8654
43	9.745 167 2521	103	233.612 078 3222	163	5600.171 010 5187
44	10.275 060 7215	104	246.314 735 0810	164	5904.680 309 2156
45	10.833 767 1482	105	259.708 098 8010	165	6225.747 301 0292
46	11.422 853 2369	106	273.829 726 6733	166	6564.272 310 5227
47	12.043 970 8816	107	288.719 218 0612	167	6921.204 617 4074
48	12.698 861 7983	108	304.418 325 5433	168	7297.545 118 4789
49	13.389 362 4086	109	320.971 071 9947	169	7694.349 134 2962
50	14.117 408 9896	110	338.423 874 0344	170	8112.729 368 4735
51	14.885 043 1034	111	356.825 672 1850	171	8553.859 027 8843
52	15.694 417 3221	112	376.228 068 1101	172	9018.975 112 5255
53	16.547 801 2640	113	396.685 469 3135	173	9509.381 884 2691
54	17.447 587 9577	114	418.255 241 7075	174	10026.454 524 2262
55	18.396 300 5529	115	440.997 870 4753	175	10571.642 988 9810
56	19.396 599 3955	116	464.977 129 6824	176	11146.476 076 5068
57	20.451 289 4876	117	490.260 261 1089	177	11752.565 713 1669
58	21.563 328 3535	118	516.918 162 8067	178	12391.611 473 8203
59	22.735 834 3328	119	545.025 587 9093	179	13065.405 347 7093
60	23.972 095 3246	120	574.661 354 2519	180	13775.836 763 4910

Amount of 1

NOMINAL INTEREST RATE COMPOUNDED

YEARLY	HALF-YEARLY	QUARTERLY
@	@	@
$5\frac{1}{2}\%$	11%	22%
5.5000%	11.0000%	22.0000%
PER ANNUM	PER ANNUM	PER ANNUM

Periods	Amount	Periods	Amount	Periods	Amount
1	1.055 000 0000	61	26.205 957 8196	121	650.949 976 5321
2	1.113 025 0000	62	27.647 285 4997	122	686.752 225 2413
3	1.174 241 3750	63	29.167 886 2021	123	724.523 597 6296
4	1.238 824 6506	64	30.772 119 9432	124	764.372 395 4993
5	1.306 960 0064	65	32.464 586 5401	125	806.412 877 2517
6	1.378 842 8068	66	34.250 138 7998	126	850.765 585 5006
7	1.454 679 1611	67	36.133 896 4338	127	897.557 692 7031
8	1.534 686 5150	68	38.121 260 7377	128	946.923 365 8018
9	1.619 094 2733	69	40.217 930 0783	129	999.004 150 9208
10	1.708 144 4584	70	42.429 916 2326	130	1053.949 379 2215
11	1.802 092 4036	71	44.763 561 6254	131	1111.916 595 0787
12	1.901 207 4858	72	47.225 557 5147	132	1173.072 007 8080
13	2.005 773 8975	73	49.822 963 1781	133	1237.590 968 2374
14	2.116 091 4618	74	52.563 226 1529	134	1305.658 471 4905
15	2.232 476 4922	75	55.454 203 5913	135	1377.469 687 4225
16	2.355 262 6993	76	58.504 184 7888	136	1453.230 520 2307
17	2.484 802 1478	77	61.721 914 9522	137	1533.158 198 8434
18	2.621 466 2659	78	65.116 620 2745	138	1617.481 899 7798
19	2.765 646 9105	79	68.698 034 3896	139	1706.443 404 2677
20	2.917 757 4906	80	72.476 426 2811	140	1800.297 791 5024
21	3.078 234 1526	81	76.462 629 7265	141	1899.314 170 0350
22	3.247 537 0310	82	80.668 074 3615	142	2003.776 449 3870
23	3.426 151 5677	83	85.104 818 4514	143	2113.984 154 1033
24	3.614 589 9039	84	89.785 583 4662	144	2230.253 282 5789
25	3.813 392 3486	85	94.723 790 5568	145	2352.917 213 1208
26	4.023 128 9278	86	99.933 599 0375	146	2482.327 659 8424
27	4.244 401 0188	87	105.429 946 9845	147	2618.855 681 1337
28	4.477 843 0749	88	111.228 594 0687	148	2762.892 743 5961
29	4.724 124 4440	89	117.346 166 7424	149	2914.851 844 4939
30	4.983 951 2884	90	123.800 205 9133	150	3075.168 695 9411
31	5.258 068 6093	91	130.609 217 2385	151	3244.302 974 2178
32	5.547 262 3828	92	137.792 724 1866	152	3422.739 637 7998
33	5.852 361 8138	93	145.371 324 0169	153	3610.990 317 8788
34	6.174 241 7136	94	153.366 746 8378	154	3809.594 785 3621
35	6.513 825 0078	95	161.801 917 9139	155	4019.122 498 5570
36	6.872 085 3833	96	170.701 023 3992	156	4240.174 235 9777
37	7.250 050 0793	97	180.089 579 6861	157	4473.383 818 9564
38	7.648 802 8337	98	189.994 506 5688	158	4719.419 928 9990
39	8.069 486 9896	99	200.444 204 4301	159	4978.988 025 0940
40	8.513 308 7740	100	211.468 635 6738	160	5252.832 366 4742
41	8.981 540 7565	101	223.099 410 6358	161	5541.738 146 6302
42	9.475 525 4982	102	235.369 878 2208	162	5846.533 744 6949
43	9.996 679 4006	103	248.315 221 5230	163	6168.093 100 6531
44	10.546 496 7676	104	261.972 558 7067	164	6507.338 221 1890
45	11.126 554 0898	105	276.381 049 4356	165	6865.241 823 3544
46	11.738 514 5647	106	291.582 007 1545	166	7242.830 123 6389
47	12.384 132 8658	107	307.619 017 5480	167	7641.185 780 4391
48	13.065 260 1734	108	324.538 063 5132	168	8061.450 998 3632
49	13.783 849 4830	109	342.387 657 0064	169	8504.830 803 2732
50	14.541 961 2045	110	361.218 978 1418	170	8972.596 497 4532
51	15.341 769 0708	111	381.086 021 9396	171	9466.089 304 8131
52	16.185 566 3697	112	402.045 753 1462	172	9986.724 216 5779
53	17.075 772 5200	113	424.158 269 5693	173	10535.994 048 4897
54	18.014 940 0086	114	447.486 974 3956	174	11115.473 721 1566
55	19.005 761 7091	115	472.098 757 9874	175	11726.824 775 8202
56	20.051 078 6031	116	498.064 189 6767	176	12371.800 138 4903
57	21.153 887 9262	117	525.457 720 1089	177	13052.249 146 1073
58	22.317 351 7622	118	554.357 894 7149	178	13770.122 849 1432
59	23.544 806 1091	119	584.847 578 9242	179	14527.479 605 8461
60	24.839 770 4451	120	617.014 195 7650	180	15326.490 984 1676

NOMINAL INTEREST RATE COMPOUNDED

	YEARLY @ $5\frac{9}{16}\%$ 5.5625% PER ANNUM		HALF-YEARLY @ $11\frac{1}{8}\%$ 11.1250% PER ANNUM		QUARTERLY @ $22\frac{1}{4}\%$ 22.2500% PER ANNUM
Periods	Amount	Periods	Amount	Periods	Amount
1	1,055 625 0000	61	27,170 002 7153	121	699,309 932 5511
2	1,114 344 1406	62	28,681 334 1163	122	738,209 047 5493
3	1,176 329 5334	63	30,276 733 3266	123	779,271 925 8192
4	1,241 762 8637	64	31,960 876 6178	124	822,618 926 6929
5	1,310 835 9230	65	33,738 700 3797	125	868,377 104 4902
6	1,383 751 1713	66	35,615 415 5883	126	916,680 580 9274
7	1,460 722 3302	67	37,596 523 0804	127	967,670 938 2415
8	1,541 975 0098	68	39,687 829 6768	128	1021,497 634 1812
9	1,627 747 3697	69	41,895 465 2026	129	1078,318 440 0825
10	1,718 290 8171	70	44,225 900 4544	130	1138,299 903 3121
11	1,813 870 7438	71	46,685 966 1672	131	1201,617 835 4339
12	1,914 767 3040	72	49,282 873 0353	132	1268,457 827 5299
13	2,021 276 2352	73	52,024 232 8479	133	1339,015 794 1862
14	2,133 709 7258	74	54,918 080 8000	134	1413,498 547 7378
15	2,252 397 3293	75	57,972 899 0445	135	1492,124 404 4557
16	2,377 686 9308	76	61,197 641 5539	136	1575,123 824 4536
17	2,509 945 7663	77	64,601 760 3653	137	1662,740 087 1888
18	2,649 561 4996	78	68,195 233 2856	138	1755,230 004 5387
19	2,796 943 3580	79	71,988 593 1372	139	1852,864 673 5412
20	2,952 523 3323	80	75,992 958 6304	140	1955,930 271 0069
21	3,116 757 4426	81	80,220 066 9542	141	2064,728 892 3316
22	3,290 127 0754	82	84,682 308 1786	142	2179,579 436 9676
23	3,473 140 3939	83	89,392 761 5710	143	2300,818 543 1489
24	3,666 333 8283	84	94,365 233 9334	144	2428,801 574 6116
25	3,870 273 6475	85	99,614 300 0709	145	2563,903 662 1993
26	4,085 557 6192	86	105,155 345 5124	146	2706,520 803 4092
27	4,312 816 7617	87	111,004 611 6065	147	2857,071 023 0988
28	4,552 717 1941	88	117,179 243 1271	148	3015,995 598 7587
29	4,805 962 0880	89	123,697 338 5260	149	3183,760 353 9396
30	5,073 293 7292	90	130,578 002 9816	150	3360,857 023 6275
31	5,355 495 6929	91	137,841 404 3974	151	3547,804 695 5668
32	5,653 395 1408	92	145,508 832 5170	152	3745,151 331 7577
33	5,967 865 2455	93	153,602 761 3258	153	3953,475 374 5867
34	6,299 827 7498	94	162,146 914 9245	154	4173,387 442 2981
35	6,650 255 6684	95	171,166 337 0672	155	4405,532 118 7760
36	7,020 176 1399	96	180,687 464 5665	156	4650,589 842 8829
37	7,410 673 4377	97	190,738 204 7831	157	4909,278 902 8932
38	7,822 892 1477	98	201,348 017 4241	158	5182,357 541 8667
39	8,258 040 5234	99	212,548 000 8933	159	5470,626 180 1330
40	8,717 394 0275	100	224,370 983 4430	160	5774,929 761 4029
41	9,202 299 0703	101	236,851 619 3970	161	6096,160 229 3809
42	9,714 176 9560	102	250,026 490 7260	162	6435,259 142 1403
43	10,254 528 0492	103	263,934 214 2726	163	6793,220 431 9218
44	10,824 936 1720	104	278,615 554 9416	164	7171,093 318 4475
45	11,427 073 2465	105	294,113 545 1852	165	7569,985 384 2861
46	12,062 704 1959	106	310,473 611 1361	166	7991,065 821 2870
47	12,733 692 1168	107	327,743 705 7556	167	8435,568 857 5961
48	13,442 003 7408	108	345,974 449 3882	168	8904,797 375 2999
49	14,189 715 1988	109	365,219 278 1354	169	9400,126 729 3009
50	14,979 018 1068	110	385,534 600 4817	170	9923,008 778 6183
51	15,812 225 9890	111	406,979 962 6335	171	10474,976 141 9290
52	16,691 781 0596	112	429,618 223 0550	172	11057,646 689 8238
53	17,620 261 3810	113	453,515 736 7124	173	11672,728 286 9452
54	18,600 388 4204	114	478,742 549 5671	174	12322,023 797 9065
55	19,635 035 0262	115	505,372 603 8867	175	13007,436 371 6651
56	20,727 233 8496	116	533,483 954 9779	176	13730,975 019 8389
57	21,880 186 2325	117	563,158 999 9736	177	14494,760 505 3175
58	23,097 271 5916	118	594,484 719 3471	178	15301,031 558 4258
59	24,382 057 3239	119	627,552 931 8608	179	16152,151 438 8632
60	25,738 309 2626	120	662,460 563 6955	180	17050,614 862 6500

Amount of 1

NOMINAL INTEREST RATE COMPOUNDED

YEARLY	HALF-YEARLY	QUARTERLY
@	@	@
$5\frac{5}{8}\%$	$11\frac{1}{4}\%$	$22\frac{1}{2}\%$
5.6250%	11.2500%	22.5000%
PER ANNUM	PER ANNUM	PER ANNUM

Periods	Amount	Periods	Amount	Periods	Amount
1	1,056 250 0000	61	28,168 909 8183	121	751,230 750 6294
2	1,115 664 0625	62	29,753 410 9956	122	793,487 480 3523
3	1,178 420 1660	63	31,427 040 3641	123	838,121 151 1221
4	1,244 706 3004	64	33,194 811 3846	124	885,265 465 8727
5	1,314 721 0297	65	35,062 019 5250	125	935,061 648 3280
6	1,388 674 0877	66	37,034 258 1232	126	987,658 866 0465
7	1,466 787 0051	67	39,117 435 1427	127	1043,214 677 2616
8	1,549 293 7741	68	41,317 790 8694	128	1101,895 502 8576
9	1,636 441 5489	69	43,641 916 6059	129	1163,877 124 8933
10	1,728 491 3861	70	46,096 774 4149	130	1229,345 213 1686
11	1,825 719 0265	71	48,689 717 9758	131	1298,495 881 4093
12	1,928 415 7218	72	51,428 514 6119	132	1371,536 274 7386
13	2,036 889 1061	73	54,321 368 5588	133	1448,685 190 1926
14	2,151 464 1183	74	57,376 945 5403	134	1530,173 732 1409
15	2,272 483 9750	75	60,604 398 7269	135	1616,246 004 5739
16	2,400 311 1986	76	64,013 396 1553	136	1707,159 842 3312
17	2,535 328 7035	77	67,614 149 6890	137	1803,187 583 4623
18	2,677 940 9431	78	71,417 445 6090	138	1904,616 885 0320
19	2,828 575 1211	79	75,434 676 9245	139	2011,751 584 8151
20	2,987 682 4717	80	79,677 877 5015	140	2124,912 611 4609
21	3,155 739 6107	81	84,159 758 1110	141	2244,438 945 8556
22	3,333 249 9638	82	88,893 744 5047	142	2370,688 636 5600
23	3,520 745 2743	83	93,894 017 6331	143	2504,039 872 3665
24	3,718 787 1960	84	99,175 556 1250	144	2644,892 115 1871
25	3,927 968 9758	85	104,754 181 1570	145	2793,667 296 6664
26	4,148 917 2306	86	110,646 603 8471	146	2950,811 082 1039
27	4,382 293 8249	87	116,870 475 3135	147	3116,794 205 4722
28	4,628 797 8525	88	123,444 439 5499	148	3292,113 879 5300
29	4,889 167 7317	89	130,388 189 2746	149	3477,295 285 2536
30	5,164 183 4166	90	137,722 524 9213	150	3672,893 145 0491
31	5,454 668 7338	91	145,469 416 9481	151	3879,493 384 4581
32	5,761 493 8501	92	153,652 071 6514	152	4097,714 887 3339
33	6,085 577 8792	93	162,295 000 6818	153	4328,211 349 7464
34	6,427 891 6349	94	171,424 094 4702	154	4571,673 238 1696
35	6,789 460 5393	95	181,066 699 7841	155	4828,829 857 8167
36	7,171 367 6947	96	191,251 701 6470	156	5100,451 537 3189
37	7,574 757 1275	97	202,009 609 8646	157	5387,351 936 2931
38	8,000 837 2159	98	213,372 650 4195	158	5690,390 482 7095
39	8,450 884 3093	99	225,374 862 0056	159	6010,474 947 3619
40	8,926 246 5517	100	238,052 197 9934	160	6348,564 163 1511
41	9,428 347 9202	101	251,442 634 1306	161	6705,670 897 3283
42	9,958 692 4907	102	265,586 282 3004	162	7082,864 885 3030
43	10,518 868 9433	103	280,525 510 6798	163	7481,276 035 1013
44	11,110 555 3214	104	296,305 070 6555	164	7902,097 812 0758
45	11,735 524 0582	105	312,972 230 8799	165	8346,590 814 0050
46	12,395 647 2865	106	330,576 918 8669	166	8816,086 547 2928
47	13,092 902 4464	107	349,171 870 5532	167	9311,991 415 5780
48	13,829 378 2090	108	368,812 788 2718	168	9835,790 932 7043
49	14,607 280 7332	109	389,558 507 6121	169	10389,054 172 6689
50	15,428 940 2745	110	411,471 173 6653	170	10973,438 469 8815
51	16,296 818 1649	111	434,616 427 1839	171	11590,694 383 8124
52	17,213 514 1867	112	459,063 601 2130	172	12242,670 942 9018
53	18,181 774 3597	113	484,885 928 7813	173	12931,321 183 4401
54	19,204 499 1674	114	512,160 762 2752	174	13658,708 000 0086
55	20,284 752 2456	115	540,969 805 1532	175	14427,010 325 0090
56	21,425 769 5594	116	571,399 356 6931	176	15238,529 655 7908
57	22,630 969 0971	117	603,540 570 5070	177	16095,696 948 9290
58	23,903 961 1088	118	637,489 727 5981	178	17001,079 902 3063
59	25,248 558 9212	119	673,348 524 7755	179	17957,390 646 8110
60	26,668 790 3605	120	711,224 379 2941	180	18967,493 870 6941

NOMINAL INTEREST RATE COMPOUNDED

YEARLY @ $5\frac{11}{16}\%$ 5.6875% PER ANNUM		HALF-YEARLY @ $11\frac{3}{8}\%$ 11.3750% PER ANNUM		QUARTERLY @ $22\frac{3}{4}\%$ 22.7500% PER ANNUM	
Periods	Amount	Periods	Amount	Periods	Amount
1	1,056 875 0000	61	29,203 918 0747	121	806,972 282 3548
2	1,116 984 7656	62	30,864 890 9152	122	852,868 830 9137
3	1,180 513 2742	63	32,620 331 5860	123	901,375 745 6719
4	1,247 654 9666	64	34,475 612 9450	124	952,641 491 2070
5	1,318 615 3429	65	36,436 413 4312	125	1006,822 976 0194
6	1,393 611 5905	66	38,508 734 4451	126	1064,086 032 7805
7	1,472 873 2497	67	40,698 918 7167	127	1124,605 925 8949
8	1,556 642 9158	68	43,013 669 7187	128	1188,567 887 9302
9	1,645 176 9816	69	45,460 072 1839	129	1256,167 686 5562
10	1,738 746 4224	70	48,045 613 7894	130	1327,612 223 7291
11	1,837 637 6252	71	50,778 208 0737	131	1403,120 168 9537
12	1,942 153 2652	72	53,666 218 6578	132	1482,922 628 5629
13	2,052 613 2321	73	56,718 484 8440	133	1567,263 853 0624
14	2,169 355 6097	74	59,944 348 6695	134	1656,401 984 7053
15	2,292 737 7100	75	63,353 683 5001	135	1750,609 847 5854
16	2,423 137 1672	76	66,956 924 2492	136	1850,175 782 6669
17	2,560 953 0936	77	70,765 099 3158	137	1955,404 530 3060
18	2,706 607 3008	78	74,789 864 3394	138	2066,618 162 9672
19	2,860 545 5911	79	79,043 537 8737	139	2184,157 070 9860
20	3,023 239 1216	80	83,539 139 0903	140	2308,381 004 3983
21	3,195 185 8466	81	88,290 427 6260	141	2439,670 174 0234
22	3,376 912 0416	82	93,311 945 6973	142	2578,426 415 1710
23	3,568 973 9140	83	98,619 062 6088	143	2725,074 417 5339
24	3,771 959 3053	84	104,228 021 7947	144	2880,063 025 0311
25	3,986 489 4908	85	110,155 990 5343	145	3043,866 609 5798
26	4,213 221 0806	86	116,421 112 4959	146	3216,986 522 9996
27	4,452 848 0296	87	123,042 563 2691	147	3399,952 631 4952
28	4,706 103 7613	88	130,040 609 0550	148	3593,324 937 4115
29	4,973 763 4127	89	137,436 668 6950	149	3797,695 293 2268
30	5,256 646 2068	90	145,253 379 2271	150	4013,689 213 0291
31	5,555 617 9598	91	153,514 665 1706	151	4241,967 787 0201
32	5,871 593 7313	92	162,245 811 7522	152	4483,229 704 9069
33	6,205 540 6247	93	171,473 542 2956	153	4738,213 394 3734
34	6,558 480 7478	94	181,226 100 0136	154	5007,699 281 1784
35	6,931 494 3403	95	191,533 334 4519	155	5292,512 177 7954
36	7,325 723 0809	96	202,426 792 8489	156	5593,523 807 9076
37	7,742 373 5811	97	213,939 816 6921	157	5911,655 474 4823
38	8,182 721 0785	98	226,107 643 7665	158	6247,880 879 5935
39	8,648 113 3399	99	238,967 516 0057	159	6603,229 104 6204
40	9,139 974 7861	100	252,558 793 4786	160	6978,787 759 9456
41	9,659 810 8520	101	266,923 074 8577	161	7375,706 313 7926
42	10,209 212 5943	102	282,104 324 7402	162	7795,199 610 3895
43	10,789 861 5606	103	298,149 008 2098	163	8238,551 588 2304
44	11,403 534 9368	104	315,106 233 0517	164	8707,119 209 8110
45	12,052 110 9863	105	333,027 900 0565	165	9202,336 614 8690
46	12,737 574 7987	106	351,968 861 8722	166	9725,719 509 8397
47	13,462 024 3654	107	371,987 090 8912	167	10278,869 806 9618
48	14,227 677 0011	108	393,143 856 6857	168	10863,480 527 2328
49	15,036 876 1306	109	415,503 913 5347	169	11481,340 982 2191
50	15,892 098 4605	110	439,135 698 6169	170	12134,342 250 5829
51	16,795 961 5605	111	464,111 541 4758	171	12824,482 966 0848
52	17,751 231 8742	112	490,507 885 3972	172	13553,875 434 7808
53	18,760 833 1870	113	518,405 521 3792	173	14324,752 100 1340
54	19,827 855 5746	114	547,889 835 4076	174	15139,472 375 8291
55	20,955 564 8604	115	579,051 069 7964	175	16000,529 867 2044
56	22,147 412 6118	116	611,984 599 3911	176	16910,560 003 4016
57	23,407 046 7041	117	646,791 223 4815	177	17872,348 103 5951
58	24,738 322 4854	118	683,577 474 3170	178	18888,837 901 9871
59	26,145 314 5767	119	722,455 943 1688	179	19963,140 557 6626
60	27,632 329 3433	120	763,545 624 9365	180	21098,544 176 8796

Amount of 1

NOMINAL INTEREST RATE COMPOUNDED

YEARLY	HALF-YEARLY	QUARTERLY
@	@	@
5¾%	**11½%**	**23%**
5.7500%	11.5000%	23.0000%
PER ANNUM	PER ANNUM	PER ANNUM

Periods	Amount	Periods	Amount	Periods	Amount
1	1,057 500 0000	61	30,276 309 6884	121	866,813 171 0148
2	1,118 306 2500	62	32,017 197 4955	122	916,654 928 3481
3	1,182 608 8594	63	33,858 186 3515	123	969,362 586 7281
4	1,250 608 8688	64	35,805 032 0667	124	1025,100 935 4650
5	1,322 518 8787	65	37,863 821 4105	125	1084,044 239 2543
6	1,398 563 7143	66	40,040 991 1416	126	1146,376 783 0114
7	1,478 981 1278	67	42,343 348 1323	127	1212,293 448 0345
8	1,564 022 5427	68	44,778 090 6499	128	1282,000 321 2965
9	1,653 953 8389	69	47,352 830 8622	129	1355,715 339 7711
10	1,749 056 1846	70	50,075 618 6368	130	1433,668 971 8079
11	1,849 626 9153	71	52,954 966 7084	131	1516,104 937 6868
12	1,955 980 4629	72	55,999 877 2942	132	1603,280 971 6038
13	2,068 449 3395	73	59,219 870 2386	133	1695,469 627 4711
14	2,187 385 1765	74	62,625 012 7773	134	1792,959 131 0506
15	2,313 159 8242	75	66,225 951 0120	135	1896,054 281 0861
16	2,446 166 5141	76	70,033 943 1952	136	2005,077 402 2485
17	2,586 821 0886	77	74,060 894 9289	137	2120,369 352 8778
18	2,735 563 3012	78	78,319 396 3873	138	2242,290 590 6683
19	2,892 858 1910	79	82,822 761 6796	139	2371,222 299 6317
20	3,059 197 5370	80	87,585 070 4762	140	2507,567 581 8605
21	3,235 101 3954	81	92,621 212 0286	141	2651,752 717 8175
22	3,421 119 7256	82	97,946 931 7202	142	2804,228 499 0920
23	3,617 834 1098	83	103,578 880 2941	143	2965,471 637 7898
24	3,825 859 5712	84	109,534 665 9110	144	3135,986 256 9627
25	4,045 846 4965	85	115,832 909 2009	145	3316,305 466 7381
26	4,278 482 6701	86	122,493 301 4800	146	3506,993 031 0755
27	4,524 495 4236	87	129,536 666 3151	147	3708,645 130 3623
28	4,784 653 9104	88	136,985 024 6282	148	3921,892 225 3582
29	5,059 771 5103	89	144,861 663 5443	149	4147,401 028 3163
30	5,350 708 3721	90	153,191 209 1981	150	4385,876 587 4445
31	5,658 374 1035	91	161,999 703 7270	151	4638,064 491 2225
32	5,983 730 6145	92	171,314 586 6913	152	4904,753 199 4678
33	6,327 795 1248	93	181,165 281 1760	153	5186,776 508 4372
34	6,691 643 3445	94	191,582 284 8437	154	5485,016 157 6724
35	7,076 412 8368	95	202,598 266 2222	155	5800,404 586 7385
36	7,483 306 5749	96	214,247 666 5299	156	6133,927 850 4760
37	7,913 596 7030	97	226,566 907 3554	157	6486,628 701 8783
38	8,368 628 5134	98	239,594 504 5283	158	6859,609 852 2364
39	8,849 824 6529	99	253,371 188 5387	159	7254,037 418 7399
40	9,358 689 5705	100	267,940 031 8797	160	7671,144 570 3175
41	9,896 814 2208	101	283,346 583 7128	161	8112,235 383 1107
42	10,465 881 0385	102	299,639 012 2763	162	8578,688 917 6396
43	11,067 669 1982	103	316,868 255 4822	163	9071,963 530 4039
44	11,704 060 1771	104	335,088 180 1724	164	9593,601 433 4021
45	12,377 043 6372	105	354,355 750 5323	165	10145,233 515 8227
46	13,088 723 6464	106	374,731 206 1879	166	10728,584 442 9825
47	13,841 325 2560	107	396,278 250 5437	167	11345,478 048 4540
48	14,637 201 4583	108	419,064 249 9500	168	11997,843 036 2401
49	15,478 840 5421	109	443,160 444 3221	169	12687,719 010 8240
50	16,368 873 8733	110	468,642 159 8706	170	13417,262 853 9463
51	17,310 084 1210	111	495,589 094 6382	171	14188,755 468 0482
52	18,305 413 9580	112	524,085 467 5799	172	15004,608 907 4610
53	19,357 975 2605	113	554,220 381 9657	173	15867,373 919 6400
54	20,471 058 8380	114	586,088 053 9287	174	16779,747 920 0193
55	21,648 144 7212	115	619,788 117 0296	175	17744,583 425 4204
56	22,892 913 0427	116	655,425 933 7588	176	18764,896 972 3821
57	24,209 255 5426	117	693,112 924 9500	177	19843,878 548 2941
58	25,601 287 7363	118	732,966 918 1346	178	20984,901 564 8210
59	27,073 361 7812	119	775,112 515 9273	179	22191,533 404 7982
60	28,630 080 0836	120	819,681 485 5932	180	23467,546 575 5741

Amount of 1

NOMINAL INTEREST RATE COMPOUNDED

YEARLY @ $5\frac{13}{16}\%$ 5.8125% PER ANNUM	HALF-YEARLY @ $11\frac{5}{8}\%$ 11.6250% PER ANNUM	QUARTERLY @ $23\frac{1}{4}\%$ 23.2500% PER ANNUM

Periods	Amount	Periods	Amount	Periods	Amount
1	1.058 125 0000	61	31.387 411 6047	121	931.052 198 2200
2	1.119 628 5156	62	33.211 804 9042	122	985.169 607 2416
3	1.184 706 9231	63	35.142 241 0643	123	1042.432 590 6625
4	1.253 568 0130	64	37.184 883 8261	124	1103.023 984 9948
5	1.326 431 6538	65	39.346 255 1985	125	1167.137 254 1226
6	1.403 530 4936	66	41.633 256 2819	126	1234.977 107 0184
7	1.485 110 7036	67	44.053 189 3033	127	1306.760 151 3639
8	1.571 432 7632	68	46.613 780 9316	128	1382.715 585 1619
9	1.662 772 2926	69	49.323 206 9482	129	1463.085 928 5495
10	1.759 420 9321	70	52.190 118 3521	130	1548.127 798 1464
11	1.861 687 2738	71	55.223 668 9813	131	1638.112 726 4137
12	1.969 897 8466	72	58.433 544 7408	132	1733.328 028 6364
13	2.084 398 1589	73	61.829 994 5289	133	1834.077 720 3009
14	2.205 553 8019	74	65.423 862 9609	134	1940.683 487 7934
15	2.333 751 6166	75	69.226 624 9955	135	2053.485 715 5214
16	2.469 400 9293	76	73.250 422 5733	136	2172.844 572 7361
17	2.612 934 8583	77	77.508 103 3854	137	2299.141 163 5264
18	2.764 811 6970	78	82.013 261 8947	138	2432.778 743 6564
19	2.925 516 3769	79	86.780 282 7423	139	2574.184 008 1314
20	3.095 562 0163	80	91.824 386 6767	140	2723.808 453 6040
21	3.275 491 5585	81	97.161 679 1523	141	2882.129 819 9698
22	3.465 879 5053	82	102.809 201 7530	142	3049.653 615 7555
23	3.667 333 7515	83	108.784 986 6049	143	3226.914 732 1713
24	3.880 497 5258	84	115.108 113 9514	144	3414.479 150 9788
25	4.106 051 4445	85	121.798 773 0748	145	3612.945 751 6294
26	4.344 715 6848	86	128.878 326 7597	146	3822.948 223 4429
27	4.597 252 2839	87	136.369 379 5027	147	4045.157 088 9305
28	4.864 467 5729	88	144.295 849 6862	148	4280.281 844 7246
29	5.147 214 7506	89	152.683 045 9493	149	4529.073 226 9492
30	5.446 396 6080	90	161.557 747 9951	150	4792.325 608 2656
31	5.762 968 4108	91	170.948 292 0973	151	5070.879 534 2460
32	6.097 940 9497	92	180.884 661 5754	152	5365.624 407 1741
33	6.452 383 7674	93	191.398 582 5295	153	5677.501 325 8411
34	6.827 428 5739	94	202.523 625 1390	154	6007.506 090 4056
35	7.224 272 8597	95	214.295 310 8502	155	6356.692 381 9104
36	7.644 183 7197	96	226.751 225 7934	156	6726.175 126 6090
37	8.088 501 8984	97	239.931 140 7926	157	7117.134 055 8431
38	8.558 646 0713	98	253.877 138 3512	158	7530.817 472 8390
39	9.056 117 3742	99	268.633 747 0179	159	7968.546 238 4477
40	9.582 504 1965	100	284.248 083 5633	160	8431.717 988 5575
41	10.139 487 2530	101	300.770 003 4204	161	8921.811 596 6424
42	10.728 844 9495	102	318.252 259 8692	162	9440.391 895 6973
43	11.352 459 0622	103	336.750 672 4741	163	9989.114 674 6347
44	12.012 320 7452	104	356.324 305 3117	164	10569.731 965 0978
45	12.710 536 8885	105	377.035 655 5579	165	11184.097 635 5691
46	13.449 336 8452	106	398.950 853 0372	166	11834.173 310 6366
47	14.231 079 5493	107	422.139 871 3700	167	12522.034 634 3173
48	15.058 261 0481	108	446.676 751 3934	168	13249.877 897 4370
49	15.933 522 4715	109	472.639 837 5681	169	14020.027 050 2255
50	16.859 658 4652	110	500.112 028 1268	170	14834.941 122 5199
51	17.839 626 1135	111	529.181 039 7616	171	15697.222 075 2664
52	18.876 554 3813	112	559.939 687 6978	172	16609.623 108 3912
53	19.973 754 1048	113	592.486 182 0452	173	17575.057 451 5665
54	21.134 728 5621	114	626.924 441 3766	174	18596.607 665 9388
55	22.363 184 6598	115	663.364 424 5316	175	19677.535 486 5215
56	23.663 044 7681	116	701.922 481 7075	176	20821.292 236 6755
57	25.038 459 2453	117	742.721 725 9568	177	22031.529 847 9323
58	26.493 819 6889	118	785.892 426 2780	178	23312.112 520 3434
59	28.033 772 9583	119	831.572 423 5554	179	24667.129 060 5883
60	29.663 236 0115	120	879.907 570 6746	180	26100.905 937 2350

Amount of 1

NOMINAL INTEREST RATE COMPOUNDED

YEARLY	HALF-YEARLY	QUARTERLY
@	@	@
$5\frac{7}{8}\%$	$11\frac{3}{4}\%$	$23\frac{1}{2}\%$
5.8750%	11.7500%	23.5000%
PER ANNUM	PER ANNUM	PER ANNUM

Periods	Amount	Periods	Amount	Periods	Amount
1	1,058 750 0000	61	32.538 597 0434	121	1000,009 726 1445
2	1,120 951 5625	62	34.450 239 6197	122	1058,760 297 5555
3	1,186 807 4668	63	36.474 191 1974	123	1120,962 465 0369
4	1,256 532 4055	64	38.617 049 9303	124	1186,819 009 8578
5	1,330 353 6843	65	40.885 801 6137	125	1256,544 626 6870
6	1,408 511 9632	66	43.287 842 4585	126	1330,366 623 5048
7	1,491 262 0411	67	45.831 003 2029	127	1408,525 662 6358
8	1,578 873 6860	68	48.523 574 6411	128	1491,276 545 3156
9	1,671 632 5151	69	51.374 334 6512	129	1578,889 042 3529
10	1,769 840 9253	70	54.392 576 8120	130	1671,648 773 5911
11	1,873 819 0797	71	57.588 140 6997	131	1769,858 139 0396
12	1,983 905 9506	72	60.971 443 9658	132	1873,837 304 7082
13	2,100 460 4252	73	64.553 516 2988	133	1983,925 246 3598
14	2,223 862 4752	74	68.346 035 3813	134	2100,480 854 5834
15	2,354 514 3956	75	72.361 364 9600	135	2223,884 104 7902
16	2,492 842 1163	76	76.612 595 1514	136	2354,537 295 9466
17	2,639 296 5907	77	81.113 585 1165	137	2492,866 362 0835
18	2,794 355 2654	78	85.879 008 2421	138	2639,322 260 8559
19	2,958 523 6372	79	90.924 399 9764	139	2794,382 443 6812
20	3,132 336 9009	80	96.266 208 4750	140	2958,552 412 2475
21	3,316 361 6938	81	101.921 848 2229	141	3132,367 366 4670
22	3,511 197 9433	82	107.909 756 8060	142	3316,393 949 2469
23	3,717 480 8225	83	114.249 455 0183	143	3511,232 093 7652
24	3,935 882 8208	84	120.961 610 5006	144	3717,516 979 2739
25	4,167 115 9366	85	128.068 105 1176	145	3935,921 101 8062
26	4,411 933 9978	86	135.592 106 2932	146	4167,156 466 5374
27	4,671 135 1202	87	143.558 142 5379	147	4411,976 908 9464
28	4,945 564 3085	88	151.992 183 4120	148	4671,180 552 3470
29	5,236 116 2116	89	160.921 724 1875	149	4945,612 409 7974
30	5,543 738 0391	90	170.375 875 4835	150	5236,167 138 8730
31	5,869 432 6489	91	180.385 458 1682	151	5543,791 958 2818
32	6,214 261 8170	92	190.983 103 8355	152	5869,489 735 8309
33	6,579 349 6988	93	202.203 361 1859	153	6214,322 257 8109
34	6,965 886 4936	94	214.082 808 6556	154	6579,413 690 4573
35	7,375 132 3250	95	226.660 173 6641	155	6965,954 244 7717
36	7,808 421 3491	96	239.976 458 8668	156	7375,204 056 6520
37	8,267 166 1034	97	254.075 075 8253	157	7808,497 294 9803
38	8,752 862 1120	98	269.001 986 5300	158	8267,246 511 0604
39	9,267 092 7611	99	284.805 853 2386	159	8752,947 243 5852
40	9,811 534 4608	100	301.538 197 1164	160	9267,182 894 1458
41	10,387 962 1103	101	319.253 566 1970	161	9811,629 889 1769
42	10,998 254 8843	102	338.009 713 2111	162	10388,063 145 1661
43	11,644 402 3588	103	357.867 783 8622	163	10998,361 854 9446
44	12,328 510 9974	104	378.892 516 1641	164	11644,515 613 9226
45	13,052 811 0185	105	401.152 451 4888	165	12328,630 906 2405
46	13,819 663 6658	106	424.720 158 0137	166	13052,937 971 9821
47	14,631 568 9062	107	449.672 467 2970	167	13819,798 077 8361
48	15,491 173 5794	108	476.090 724 7507	168	14631,711 214 9090
49	16,401 280 0272	109	504.061 054 8298	169	15491,324 248 7849
50	17,364 855 2288	110	533.674 641 8011	170	16401,439 548 4010
51	18,385 040 4735	111	565.028 027 0069	171	17365,024 121 8695
52	19,465 161 6013	112	598.223 423 5936	172	18385,219 289 0294
53	20,608 739 8454	113	633.369 049 7297	173	19465,350 922 2598
54	21,819 503 3113	114	670.579 481 4013	174	20608,940 288 9426
55	23,101 399 1308	115	709.976 025 9336	175	21819,715 530 9180
56	24,458 606 3297	116	751.687 117 4572	176	23101,623 818 3594
57	25,895 549 4516	117	795.848 735 6079	177	24458,844 217 6880
58	27,416 912 9819	118	842.604 848 8248	178	25895,801 315 4772
59	29,027 656 6196	119	892.107 883 6933	179	27417,179 642 7615
60	30,733 031 4460	120	944.519 221 8603	180	29027,938 946 7737

NOMINAL INTEREST RATE COMPOUNDED

	YEARLY @ $5\frac{15}{16}\%$ 5.9375% PER ANNUM		HALF-YEARLY @ $11\frac{7}{8}\%$ 11.8750% PER ANNUM		QUARTERLY @ $23\frac{3}{4}\%$ 23.7500% PER ANNUM
Periods	Amount	Periods	Amount	Periods	Amount
1	1,059 375 0000	61	33,731 287 0842	121	1074,029 242 1093
2	1,122 275 3906	62	35,734 082 2549	122	1137,799 728 3596
3	1,188 910 4919	63	37,855 793 3888	123	1205,356 587 2309
4	1,259 502 0524	64	40,103 481 1212	124	1276,924 634 5978
5	1,334 284 9868	65	42,484 625 3128	125	1352,742 034 7770
6	1,413 508 1579	66	45,007 149 9407	126	1433,061 093 0919
7	1,497 435 2047	67	47,679 449 4685	127	1518,149 095 4942
8	1,586 345 4200	68	50,510 416 7806	128	1608,289 198 0392
9	1,680 534 6793	69	53,509 472 7770	129	1703,781 369 1728
10	1,780 316 4259	70	56,686 597 7231	130	1804,943 387 9674
11	1,886 022 7137	71	60,052 364 4629	131	1912,111 901 6280
12	1,998 005 3123	72	63,617 973 6029	132	2025,643 545 7871
13	2,116 636 8777	73	67,395 290 7856	133	2145,916 131 3182
14	2,242 312 1924	74	71,396 886 1760	134	2273,329 901 6153
15	2,375 449 4788	75	75,636 076 2927	135	2408,308 864 5237
16	2,516 491 7916	76	80,126 968 3226	136	2551,302 203 3548
17	2,665 908 4917	77	84,884 507 0667	137	2702,785 771 6790
18	2,824 196 8084	78	89,924 524 6738	138	2863,263 676 8724
19	2,991 883 4939	79	95,263 793 3263	139	3033,269 957 6867
20	3,169 526 5763	80	100,920 081 0551	140	3213,370 361 4243
21	3,357 717 2168	81	106,912 210 8677	141	3404,164 226 6339
22	3,557 081 6766	82	113,260 123 3880	142	3606,286 477 5903
23	3,768 283 4011	83	119,984 943 2142	143	3820,409 737 1972
24	3,992 025 2280	84	127,109 049 2175	144	4047,246 565 3433
25	4,229 051 7260	85	134,656 149 0148	145	4287,551 830 1606
26	4,480 151 6722	86	142,651 357 8625	146	4542,125 220 0763
27	4,746 160 6777	87	151,121 282 2356	147	4811,813 905 0184
28	5,027 963 9680	88	160,094 108 3684	148	5097,515 355 6288
29	5,326 499 3286	89	169,599 696 0527	149	5400,180 329 8693
30	5,642 760 2262	90	179,669 678 0059	150	5720,816 036 9553
31	5,977 799 1146	91	190,337 565 1375	151	6060,489 489 1495
32	6,332 730 9371	92	201,638 858 0675	152	6420,331 052 5678
33	6,708 736 8364	93	213,611 165 2653	153	6801,538 208 8140
34	7,107 068 0861	94	226,294 328 2029	154	7205,379 539 9623
35	7,529 050 2537	95	239,730 553 9399	155	7633,198 950 1476
36	7,976 087 6125	96	253,964 555 5801	156	8086,420 137 8126
37	8,449 667 8145	97	269,043 701 0677	157	8566,551 333 4952
38	8,951 366 8410	98	285,018 170 8186	158	9075,190 318 9215
39	9,482 854 2472	99	301,941 124 7109	159	9614,029 744 1074
40	10,045 898 7181	100	319,868 878 9907	160	10184,862 760 1638
41	10,642 373 9545	101	338,861 093 6807	161	10789,588 986 5486
42	11,274 264 9081	102	358,980 971 1180	162	11430,220 832 6249
43	11,943 674 3870	103	380,295 466 2781	163	12108,890 194 5620
44	12,652 830 0537	104	402,875 509 5884	164	12827,855 549 8641
45	13,404 091 8382	105	426,796 242 9702	165	13589,509 473 1373
46	14,199 959 7911	106	452,137 269 8966	166	14396,386 598 1048
47	15,043 082 4036	107	478,982 920 2967	167	15251,172 052 3673
48	15,936 265 4214	108	507,422 531 1893	168	16156,710 392 9766
49	16,882 481 1808	109	537,550 743 9787	169	17116,015 072 5596
50	17,884 878 5009	110	569,467 819 4024	170	18132,278 467 4928
51	18,946 793 1619	111	603,279 971 1794	171	19208,882 501 5002
52	20,071 759 0058	112	639,099 719 4682	172	20349,409 900 0267
53	21,263 519 6968	113	677,046 265 3116	173	21557,656 112 8408
54	22,526 041 1788	114	717,245 887 3145	174	22837,641 944 5408
55	23,863 524 8738	115	759,832 361 8738	175	24193,626 934 9979
56	25,280 421 6632	116	804,947 408 3601	176	25630,123 534 2634
57	26,781 446 6994	117	852,741 160 7314	177	27151,912 119 1103
58	28,371 595 0972	118	903,372 667 1499	178	28764,056 901 1824
59	30,056 158 5561	119	957,010 419 2619	179	30471,922 779 6901
60	31,840 742 9704	120	1013,832 912 9056	180	32281,193 194 7342

Amount of 1

NOMINAL INTEREST RATE COMPOUNDED

YEARLY	HALF-YEARLY	QUARTERLY
@	@	@
6%	**12%**	**24%**
6.0000%	12.0000%	24.0000%
PER ANNUM	PER ANNUM	PER ANNUM

Periods	Amount	Periods	Amount	Periods	Amount
1	1.060 000 0000	61	34.966 952 3045	121	1153.479 012 7051
2	1.123 600 0000	62	37.064 969 4428	122	1222.687 753 4674
3	1.191 016 0000	63	39.288 867 6094	123	1296.049 018 6755
4	1.262 476 9600	64	41.646 199 6659	124	1373.811 959 7960
5	1.338 225 5776	65	44.144 971 6459	125	1456.240 677 3838
6	1.418 519 1123	66	46.793 669 9446	126	1543.615 118 0268
7	1.503 630 2590	67	49.601 290 1413	127	1636.232 025 1084
8	1.593 848 0745	68	52.577 367 5498	128	1734.405 946 6149
9	1.689 478 9590	69	55.732 009 6028	129	1838.470 303 4118
10	1.790 847 6965	70	59.075 930 1790	130	1948.778 521 6165
11	1.898 298 5583	71	62.620 485 9897	131	2065.705 232 9135
12	2.012 196 4718	72	66.377 715 1491	132	2189.647 546 8883
13	2.132 928 2601	73	70.360 378 0580	133	2321.026 399 7016
14	2.260 903 9558	74	74.582 000 7415	134	2460.287 983 6837
15	2.396 558 1931	75	79.056 920 7860	135	2607.905 262 7047
16	2.540 351 6847	76	83.800 336 0332	136	2764.379 578 4670
17	2.692 772 7858	77	88.828 356 1951	137	2930.242 353 1751
18	2.854 339 1529	78	94.158 057 5669	138	3106.056 894 3656
19	3.025 599 5021	79	99.807 541 0209	139	3292.420 308 0275
20	3.207 135 4722	80	105.795 993 4821	140	3489.965 526 5091
21	3.399 563 6005	81	112.143 753 0910	141	3699.363 458 0997
22	3.603 537 4166	82	118.872 378 2765	142	3921.325 265 5857
23	3.819 749 6616	83	126.004 720 9731	143	4156.604 781 5208
24	4.048 934 6413	84	133.565 004 2315	144	4406.001 068 4121
25	4.291 870 7197	85	141.578 904 4854	145	4670.361 132 5168
26	4.549 382 9629	86	150.073 638 7545	146	4950.582 800 4678
27	4.822 345 9407	87	159.078 057 0798	147	5247.617 768 4958
28	5.111 686 6971	88	168.622 740 5045	148	5562.474 834 6056
29	5.418 387 8990	89	178.740 104 9348	149	5896.223 324 6819
30	5.743 491 1729	90	189.464 511 2309	150	6249.996 724 1629
31	6.088 100 6433	91	200.832 381 9048	151	6624.996 527 6126
32	6.453 386 6819	92	212.882 324 8190	152	7022.496 319 2694
33	6.840 589 8828	93	225.655 264 3082	153	7443.846 098 4255
34	7.251 025 2758	94	239.194 580 1667	154	7890.476 864 3311
35	7.686 086 7923	95	253.546 254 9767	155	8363.905 476 1909
36	8.147 251 9999	96	268.759 030 2753	156	8865.739 804 7624
37	8.636 087 1198	97	284.884 572 0918	157	9397.684 193 0481
38	9.154 252 3470	98	301.977 646 4173	158	9961.545 244 6310
39	9.703 507 4879	99	320.096 305 2023	159	10559.237 959 3089
40	10.285 717 9371	100	339.302 083 5145	160	11192.792 236 8674
41	10.902 861 0134	101	359.660 208 5254	161	11864.359 771 0795
42	11.557 032 6742	102	381.239 821 0369	162	12576.221 357 3442
43	12.250 454 6346	103	404.114 210 2991	163	13330.794 638 7849
44	12.985 481 9127	104	428.361 062 9170	164	14130.642 317 1120
45	13.764 610 8274	105	454.062 726 6921	165	14978.480 856 1387
46	14.590 487 4771	106	481.306 490 2936	166	15877.189 707 5070
47	15.465 916 7257	107	510.184 879 7112	167	16829.821 089 9575
48	16.393 871 7293	108	540.795 972 4939	168	17839.610 355 3549
49	17.377 504 0330	109	573.243 730 8435	169	18909.986 976 6762
50	18.420 154 2750	110	607.638 354 6941	170	20044.586 195 2768
51	19.525 363 5315	111	644.096 655 9758	171	21247.261 366 9934
52	20.696 885 3434	112	682.742 455 3343	172	22522.097 049 0130
53	21.938 698 4640	113	723.707 002 6544	173	23873.422 871 9538
54	23.255 020 3718	114	767.129 422 8136	174	25305.828 244 2710
55	24.650 321 5941	115	813.157 188 1824	175	26824.177 938 9272
56	26.129 340 8898	116	861.946 619 4734	176	28433.628 615 2629
57	27.697 101 3432	117	913.663 416 6418	177	30139.646 332 1786
58	29.358 927 4238	118	968.483 221 6403	178	31948.025 112 1094
59	31.120 463 0692	119	1026.592 214 9387	179	33864.906 618 8359
60	32.987 690 8533	120	1088.187 747 8350	180	35896.801 015 9661

Present Value of 1

The present value of 1 due at the end of a period

$$v^n = \frac{1}{(1+i)^n}$$

Effective Rates	*Number of periods*
3% increasing by $\frac{1}{16}$% to 6%	180

NOTE

Nominal annual rates at these effective rates, compounded half yearly and quarterly, are shown in the heading to each table.

Present Value of 1

NOMINAL INTEREST RATE COMPOUNDED

YEARLY	HALF-YEARLY	QUARTERLY
@	@	@
3%	**6%**	**12%**
3.0000%	6.0000%	12.0000%
PER ANNUM	PER ANNUM	PER ANNUM

Periods	Present Value	Periods	Present Value	Periods	Present Value
1	.970 873 7864	61	.164 789 4078	121	.027 970 2154
2	.942 595 9091	62	.159 989 7163	122	.027 155 5489
3	.915 141 6594	63	.155 329 8216	123	.026 364 6106
4	.888 487 0479	64	.150 805 6521	124	.025 596 7093
5	.862 608 7844	65	.146 413 2544	125	.024 851 1741
6	.837 484 2567	66	.142 148 7907	126	.024 127 3535
7	.813 091 5113	67	.138 008 5347	127	.023 424 6150
8	.789 409 2343	68	.133 988 8686	128	.022 742 3447
9	.766 416 7323	69	.130 086 2802	129	.022 079 9463
10	.744 093 9149	70	.126 297 3594	130	.021 436 8411
11	.722 421 2766	71	.122 618 7956	131	.020 812 4671
12	.701 379 8802	72	.119 047 3743	132	.020 206 2787
13	.680 951 3400	73	.115 579 9751	133	.019 617 7463
14	.661 117 8058	74	.112 213 5680	134	.019 046 3556
15	.641 861 9474	75	.108 945 2117	135	.018 491 6074
16	.623 166 9392	76	.105 772 0502	136	.017 953 0169
17	.605 016 4458	77	.102 691 3109	137	.017 430 1135
18	.587 394 6076	78	.099 700 3018	138	.016 922 4403
19	.570 286 0268	79	.096 796 4095	139	.016 429 5537
20	.553 675 7542	80	.093 977 0966	140	.015 951 0230
21	.537 549 2759	81	.091 239 8996	141	.015 486 4301
22	.521 892 5009	82	.088 582 4268	142	.015 035 3690
23	.506 691 7484	83	.086 002 3561	143	.014 597 4457
24	.491 933 7363	84	.083 497 4332	144	.014 172 2773
25	.477 605 5693	85	.081 065 4691	145	.013 759 4926
26	.463 694 7274	86	.078 704 3389	146	.013 358 7306
27	.450 189 0558	87	.076 411 9795	147	.012 969 6414
28	.437 076 7532	88	.074 186 3879	148	.012 591 8849
29	.424 346 3623	89	.072 025 6193	149	.012 225 1309
30	.411 986 7595	90	.069 927 7857	150	.011 869 0592
31	.399 987 1452	91	.067 891 0541	151	.011 523 3584
32	.388 337 0341	92	.065 913 6448	152	.011 187 7266
33	.377 026 2467	93	.063 993 8299	153	.010 861 8705
34	.366 044 8997	94	.062 129 9319	154	.010 545 5053
35	.355 383 3978	95	.060 320 3223	155	.010 238 3547
36	.345 032 4251	96	.058 563 4197	156	.009 940 1502
37	.334 982 9369	97	.056 857 6890	157	.009 650 6312
38	.325 226 1524	98	.055 201 6398	158	.009 369 5449
39	.315 753 5460	99	.053 593 8250	159	.009 096 6455
40	.306 556 8408	100	.052 032 8399	160	.008 831 6947
41	.297 628 0008	101	.050 517 3202	161	.008 574 4609
42	.288 959 2240	102	.049 045 9420	162	.008 324 7193
43	.280 542 9360	103	.047 617 4194	163	.008 082 2517
44	.272 371 7825	104	.046 230 5043	164	.007 846 8463
45	.264 438 6238	105	.044 883 9847	165	.007 618 2974
46	.256 736 5279	106	.043 576 6842	166	.007 396 4053
47	.249 258 7650	107	.042 307 4604	167	.007 180 9760
48	.241 998 8009	108	.041 075 2043	168	.006 971 8213
49	.234 950 2922	109	.039 878 8391	169	.006 768 7586
50	.228 107 0798	110	.038 717 3195	170	.006 571 6103
51	.221 463 1843	111	.037 589 6306	171	.006 380 2042
52	.215 012 8003	112	.036 494 7870	172	.006 194 3730
53	.208 750 2915	113	.035 431 8320	173	.006 013 9543
54	.202 670 1859	114	.034 399 8369	174	.005 838 7906
55	.196 767 1708	115	.033 397 8999	175	.005 668 7288
56	.191 036 0882	116	.032 425 1455	176	.005 503 6201
57	.185 471 9303	117	.031 480 7238	177	.005 343 3205
58	.180 069 8352	118	.030 563 8095	178	.005 187 6898
59	.174 825 0827	119	.029 673 6015	179	.005 036 5921
60	.169 733 0900	120	.028 809 3218	180	.004 889 8952

Present Value of 1

NOMINAL INTEREST RATE COMPOUNDED

YEARLY	HALF-YEARLY	QUARTERLY
@	@	@
$3\frac{1}{16}\%$	$6\frac{1}{8}\%$	$12\frac{1}{4}\%$
3.0625%	6.1250%	12.2500%
PER ANNUM	PER ANNUM	PER ANNUM

Periods	Present Value	Periods	Present Value	Periods	Present Value
1	.970 285 0212	61	.158 803 0896	121	.025 990 7354
2	.941 453 0224	62	.154 084 2592	122	.025 218 4213
3	.913 477 7658	63	.149 505 6487	123	.024 469 0564
4	.886 333 7934	64	.145 063 0915	124	.023 741 9589
5	.859 996 4036	65	.140 752 5448	125	.023 036 4671
6	.834 441 6287	66	.136 570 0860	126	.022 351 9390
7	.809 646 2134	67	.132 511 9088	127	.021 687 7516
8	.785 587 5933	68	.128 574 3202	128	.021 043 3005
9	.762 243 8747	69	.124 753 7370	129	.020 417 9993
10	.739 593 8141	70	.121 046 6824	130	.019 811 2789
11	.717 616 7996	71	.117 449 7828	131	.019 222 5871
12	.696 292 8317	72	.113 959 7650	132	.018 651 3884
13	.675 602 5050	73	.110 573 4530	133	.018 097 1628
14	.655 526 9909	74	.107 287 7651	134	.017 559 4060
15	.636 048 0202	75	.104 099 7115	135	.017 037 6286
16	.617 147 8668	76	.101 006 3908	136	.016 531 3558
17	.598 809 3311	77	.098 004 9880	137	.016 040 1269
18	.581 015 7245	78	.095 092 7719	138	.015 563 4949
19	.563 750 8546	79	.092 267 0922	139	.015 101 0260
20	.546 999 0099	80	.089 525 3775	140	.014 652 2993
21	.530 744 9459	81	.086 865 1328	141	.014 216 9065
22	.514 973 8711	82	.084 283 9372	142	.013 794 4515
23	.499 671 4335	83	.081 779 4418	143	.013 384 5496
24	.484 823 7074	84	.079 349 3674	144	.012 986 8280
25	.470 417 1813	85	.076 991 5027	145	.012 600 9247
26	.456 438 7447	86	.074 703 7018	146	.012 226 4885
27	.442 875 6771	87	.072 483 8829	147	.011 863 1787
28	.429 715 6357	88	.070 330 0258	148	.011 510 6646
29	.416 946 6447	89	.068 240 1706	149	.011 168 6254
30	.404 557 0840	90	.066 212 4154	150	.010 836 7499
31	.392 535 6789	91	.064 244 9149	151	.010 514 7361
32	.380 871 4895	92	.062 335 8786	152	.010 202 2910
33	.369 553 9013	93	.060 483 5693	153	.009 899 1301
34	.358 572 6150	94	.058 686 3013	154	.009 604 9777
35	.347 917 6373	95	.056 942 4391	155	.009 319 5660
36	.337 579 2721	96	.055 250 3957	156	.009 042 6353
37	.327 548 1112	97	.053 608 6314	157	.008 773 9335
38	.317 815 0260	98	.052 015 6521	158	.008 513 2163
39	.308 371 1593	99	.050 470 0081	159	.008 260 2463
40	.299 207 9168	100	.048 970 2928	160	.008 014 7932
41	.290 316 9599	101	.047 515 1416	161	.007 776 6338
42	.281 690 1976	102	.046 103 2302	162	.007 545 5513
43	.273 319 7794	103	.044 733 2737	163	.007 321 3354
44	.265 198 0879	104	.043 404 0254	164	.007 103 7821
45	.257 317 7324	105	.042 114 2757	165	.006 892 6933
46	.249 671 5414	106	.040 862 8509	166	.006 687 8771
47	.242 252 5569	107	.039 648 6122	167	.006 489 1470
48	.235 054 0273	108	.038 470 4545	168	.006 296 3221
49	.228 069 4019	109	.037 327 3058	169	.006 109 2270
50	.221 292 3244	110	.036 218 1257	170	.005 927 6915
51	.214 716 6277	111	.035 141 9048	171	.005 751 5503
52	.208 336 3277	112	.034 097 6639	172	.005 580 6431
53	.202 145 6181	113	.033 084 4525	173	.005 414 8144
54	.196 138 8654	114	.032 101 3487	174	.005 253 9133
55	.190 310 6031	115	.031 147 4578	175	.005 097 7934
56	.184 655 5276	116	.030 221 9118	176	.004 946 3125
57	.179 168 4925	117	.029 323 8683	177	.004 799 3330
58	.173 844 5046	118	.028 452 5102	178	.004 656 7209
59	.168 678 7188	119	.027 607 0444	179	.004 518 3465
60	.163 666 4343	120	.026 786 7017	180	.004 384 0840

Present Value of 1

NOMINAL INTEREST RATE COMPOUNDED

YEARLY	HALF-YEARLY	QUARTERLY
@	@	@
$3\frac{1}{8}\%$	$6\frac{1}{4}\%$	$12\frac{1}{2}\%$
3.1250%	6.2500%	12.5000%
PER ANNUM	PER ANNUM	PER ANNUM

Periods	Present Value	Periods	Present Value	Periods	Present Value
1	.969 696 9697	61	.153 037 6700	121	.024 152 4200
2	.940 312 2130	62	.148 400 1649	122	.023 420 5284
3	.911 817 9036	63	.143 903 1902	123	.022 710 8155
4	.884 187 0580	64	.139 542 4874	124	.022 022 6089
5	.857 393 5108	65	.135 313 9272	125	.021 355 2571
6	.831 411 8892	66	.131 213 5052	126	.020 708 1281
7	.806 217 5896	67	.127 237 3383	127	.020 080 6091
8	.781 786 7535	68	.123 381 6614	128	.019 472 1058
9	.758 096 2458	69	.119 642 8232	129	.018 882 0420
10	.735 123 6323	70	.116 017 2831	130	.018 309 8589
11	.712 847 1586	71	.112 501 6079	131	.017 755 0147
12	.691 245 7296	72	.109 092 4682	132	.017 216 9839
13	.670 298 8893	73	.105 786 6359	133	.016 695 2572
14	.649 986 8017	74	.102 580 9802	134	.016 189 3403
15	.630 290 2320	75	.099 472 4657	135	.015 698 7542
16	.611 190 5280	76	.096 458 1485	136	.015 223 0344
17	.592 669 6029	77	.093 535 1743	137	.014 761 7303
18	.574 709 9180	78	.090 700 7751	138	.014 314 4051
19	.557 294 4659	79	.087 952 2668	139	.013 880 6353
20	.540 406 7548	80	.085 287 0466	140	.013 460 0100
21	.524 030 7925	81	.082 702 5906	141	.013 052 1309
22	.508 151 0716	82	.080 196 4515	142	.012 656 6118
23	.492 752 5542	83	.077 766 2560	143	.012 273 0781
24	.477 820 6586	84	.075 409 7028	144	.011 901 1666
25	.463 341 2448	85	.073 124 5603	145	.011 540 5252
26	.449 300 6010	86	.070 908 6645	146	.011 190 8123
27	.435 685 4312	87	.068 759 9171	147	.010 851 6968
28	.422 482 8424	88	.066 676 2833	148	.010 522 8575
29	.409 680 3320	89	.064 655 7898	149	.010 203 9830
30	.397 265 7765	90	.062 696 5235	150	.009 894 7714
31	.385 227 4197	91	.060 796 6288	151	.009 594 9299
32	.373 553 8615	92	.058 954 3067	152	.009 304 1744
33	.362 234 0475	93	.057 167 8126	153	.009 022 2297
34	.351 257 2582	94	.055 435 4546	154	.008 748 8288
35	.340 613 0988	95	.053 755 5924	155	.008 483 7128
36	.330 291 4898	96	.052 126 6350	156	.008 226 6306
37	.320 282 6568	97	.050 547 0400	157	.007 977 3388
38	.310 577 1217	98	.049 015 3115	158	.007 735 6012
39	.301 165 6938	99	.047 529 9991	159	.007 501 1891
40	.292 039 4606	100	.046 089 6961	160	.007 273 8803
41	.283 189 7800	101	.044 693 0386	161	.007 053 4597
42	.274 608 2715	102	.043 338 7041	162	.006 839 7185
43	.266 286 8088	103	.042 025 4100	163	.006 632 4543
44	.258 217 5115	104	.040 751 9128	164	.006 431 4708
45	.250 392 7384	105	.039 517 0063	165	.006 236 5778
46	.242 805 0797	106	.038 319 5213	166	.006 047 5906
47	.235 447 3500	107	.037 158 3237	167	.005 864 3303
48	.228 312 5818	108	.036 032 3139	168	.005 686 6233
49	.221 394 0187	109	.034 940 4256	169	.005 514 3014
50	.214 685 1091	110	.033 881 6248	170	.005 347 2013
51	.208 179 4997	111	.032 854 9089	171	.005 185 1649
52	.201 871 0300	112	.031 859 3056	172	.005 028 0387
53	.195 753 7261	113	.030 893 8721	173	.004 875 6739
54	.189 821 7950	114	.029 957 6941	174	.004 727 9262
55	.184 069 6194	115	.029 049 8852	175	.004 584 6557
56	.178 491 7521	116	.028 169 5857	176	.004 445 7267
57	.173 082 9112	117	.027 315 9619	177	.004 311 0078
58	.167 837 9745	118	.026 488 2054	178	.004 180 3712
59	.162 751 9752	119	.025 685 5326	179	.004 053 6932
60	.157 820 0972	120	.024 907 1831	180	.003 930 8541

Present Value of 1

NOMINAL INTEREST RATE COMPOUNDED

	YEARLY @ $3\frac{3}{16}\%$ 3.1875% PER ANNUM		HALF-YEARLY @ $6\frac{3}{8}\%$ 6.3750% PER ANNUM		QUARTERLY @ $12\frac{3}{4}\%$ 12.7500% PER ANNUM
Periods	Present Value	Periods	Present Value	Periods	Present Value
1	.969 109 6305	61	.147 484 8711	121	.022 445 1254
2	.939 173 4760	62	.142 929 0089	122	.021 751 7872
3	.910 162 0603	63	.138 513 8791	123	.021 079 8665
4	.882 046 8180	64	.134 235 1342	124	.020 428 7016
5	.854 800 0659	65	.130 088 5613	125	.019 797 6515
6	.828 394 9760	66	.126 070 0775	126	.019 186 0947
7	.802 805 5491	67	.122 175 7263	127	.018 593 4291
8	.778 006 5891	68	.118 401 6729	128	.018 019 0712
9	.753 973 6781	69	.114 744 2015	129	.017 462 4555
10	.730 683 1526	70	.111 199 7107	130	.016 923 0338
11	.708 112 0801	71	.107 764 7106	131	.016 400 2750
12	.686 238 2363	72	.104 435 8189	132	.015 893 6645
13	.665 040 0836	73	.101 209 7578	133	.015 402 7033
14	.644 496 7497	74	.098 083 3510	134	.014 926 9081
15	.624 588 0070	75	.095 053 5201	135	.014 465 8104
16	.605 294 2527	76	.092 117 2817	136	.014 018 9562
17	.586 596 4896	77	.089 271 7448	137	.013 585 9054
18	.568 476 3073	78	.086 514 1077	138	.013 166 2318
19	.550 915 8641	79	.083 841 6549	139	.012 759 5220
20	.533 897 8695	80	.081 251 7552	140	.012 365 3757
21	.517 405 5671	81	.078 741 8585	141	.011 983 4046
22	.501 422 7180	82	.076 309 4934	142	.011 613 2328
23	.485 933 5849	83	.073 952 2649	143	.011 254 4958
24	.470 922 9170	84	.071 667 8521	144	.010 906 8403
25	.456 375 9341	85	.069 454 0057	145	.010 569 9239
26	.442 278 3128	86	.067 308 5458	146	.010 243 4151
27	.428 616 1723	87	.065 229 3600	147	.009 926 9922
28	.415 376 0604	88	.063 214 4009	148	.009 620 3437
29	.402 544 9404	89	.061 261 6847	149	.009 323 1678
30	.390 110 1785	90	.059 369 2887	150	.009 035 1717
31	.378 059 5310	91	.057 535 3494	151	.008 756 0719
32	.366 381 1324	92	.055 758 0612	152	.008 485 5936
33	.355 063 4838	93	.054 035 6741	153	.008 223 4705
34	.344 095 4416	94	.052 366 4921	154	.007 969 4444
35	.333 466 2063	95	.050 748 8719	155	.007 723 2653
36	.323 165 3120	96	.049 181 2205	156	.007 484 6908
37	.313 182 6161	97	.047 661 9944	157	.007 253 4860
38	.303 508 2894	98	.046 189 6978	158	.007 029 4231
39	.294 132 8062	99	.044 762 8809	159	.006 812 2816
40	.285 046 9351	100	.043 380 1390	160	.006 601 8477
41	.276 241 7300	101	.042 040 1105	161	.006 397 9142
42	.267 708 5209	102	.040 741 4759	162	.006 200 2803
43	.259 438 9057	103	.039 482 9567	163	.006 008 7513
44	.251 424 7421	104	.038 263 3136	164	.005 823 1388
45	.243 658 1389	105	.037 081 3457	165	.005 643 2599
46	.236 131 4490	106	.035 935 8892	166	.005 468 9375
47	.228 837 2613	107	.034 825 8163	167	.005 300 0000
48	.221 768 3937	108	.033 750 0340	168	.005 136 2810
49	.214 917 8861	109	.032 707 4830	169	.004 977 6194
50	.208 278 9932	110	.031 697 1367	170	.004 823 8589
51	.201 845 1781	111	.030 718 0005	171	.004 674 8481
52	.195 610 1060	112	.029 769 1101	172	.004 530 4403
53	.189 567 6376	113	.028 849 5313	173	.004 390 4934
54	.183 711 8232	114	.027 958 3586	174	.004 254 8694
55	.178 036 8971	115	.027 094 7146	175	.004 123 4349
56	.172 537 2716	116	.026 257 7488	176	.003 996 0605
57	.167 207 5315	117	.025 446 6373	177	.003 872 6207
58	.162 042 4291	118	.024 660 5812	178	.003 752 9940
59	.157 036 8786	119	.023 898 8068	179	.003 637 0626
60	.152 185 9514	120	.023 160 5638	180	.003 524 7124

Present Value of 1

NOMINAL INTEREST RATE COMPOUNDED

YEARLY	HALF-YEARLY	QUARTERLY
@	@	@
$3\frac{1}{4}\%$	$6\frac{1}{2}\%$	13%
3.2500%	6.5000%	13.0000%
PER ANNUM	PER ANNUM	PER ANNUM

Periods	Present Value	Periods	Present Value	Periods	Present Value
1	.968 523 0024	61	.142 136 7300	121	.020 859 4427
2	.938 036 8062	62	.137 662 6925	122	.020 202 8500
3	.908 510 2239	63	.133 329 4843	123	.019 566 9250
4	.879 913 0498	64	.129 132 6724	124	.018 951 0169
5	.852 216 0289	65	.125 067 9636	125	.018 354 4958
6	.825 390 8270	66	.121 131 1996	126	.017 776 7514
7	.799 410 0019	67	.117 318 3532	127	.017 217 1926
8	.774 246 9752	68	.113 625 5236	128	.016 675 2471
9	.749 876 0051	69	.110 048 9333	129	.016 150 3604
10	.726 272 1599	70	.106 584 9233	130	.015 641 9955
11	.703 411 2929	71	.103 229 9499	131	.015 149 6325
12	.681 270 0173	72	.099 980 5810	132	.014 672 7675
13	.659 825 6826	73	.096 833 4925	133	.014 210 9129
14	.639 056 3512	74	.093 785 4649	134	.013 763 5960
15	.618 940 7760	75	.090 833 3801	135	.013 330 3593
16	.599 458 3787	76	.087 974 2180	136	.012 910 7596
17	.580 589 2287	77	.085 205 0537	137	.012 504 3677
18	.562 314 0230	78	.082 523 0545	138	.012 110 7677
19	.544 614 0659	79	.079 925 4765	139	.011 729 5571
20	.527 471 2502	80	.077 409 6625	140	.011 360 3459
21	.510 868 0390	81	.074 973 0387	141	.011 002 7563
22	.494 787 4469	82	.072 613 1125	142	.010 656 4226
23	.479 213 0237	83	.070 327 4698	143	.010 320 9904
24	.464 128 8365	84	.068 113 7722	144	.009 996 1166
25	.449 519 4542	85	.065 969 7551	145	.009 681 4688
26	.435 369 9314	86	.063 893 2253	146	.009 376 7253
27	.421 665 7932	87	.061 882 0584	147	.009 081 5741
28	.408 393 0200	88	.059 934 1970	148	.008 795 7134
29	.395 538 0339	89	.058 047 6484	149	.008 518 8508
30	.383 087 6842	90	.056 220 4827	150	.008 250 7029
31	.371 029 2341	91	.054 450 8307	151	.007 990 9956
32	.359 350 3478	92	.052 736 8821	152	.007 739 4630
33	.348 039 0777	93	.051 076 8834	153	.007 495 8480
34	.337 083 8525	94	.049 469 1364	154	.007 259 9012
35	.326 473 4649	95	.047 911 9965	155	.007 031 3813
36	.316 197 0605	96	.046 403 8708	156	.006 810 0545
37	.306 244 1264	97	.044 943 2162	157	.006 595 6944
38	.296 604 4807	98	.043 528 5387	158	.006 388 0818
39	.287 268 2622	99	.042 158 3910	159	.006 187 0042
40	.278 225 9198	100	.040 831 3714	160	.005 992 2558
41	.269 468 2032	101	.039 546 1225	161	.005 803 6376
42	.260 986 1532	102	.038 301 3293	162	.005 620 9565
43	.252 771 0927	103	.037 095 7184	163	.005 444 0257
44	.244 814 6176	104	.035 928 0566	164	.005 272 6641
45	.237 108 5885	105	.034 797 1492	165	.005 106 6965
46	.229 645 1220	106	.033 701 8394	166	.004 945 9530
47	.222 416 5831	107	.032 641 0067	167	.004 790 2693
48	.215 415 5769	108	.031 613 5658	168	.004 639 4860
49	.208 634 9413	109	.030 618 4657	169	.004 493 4489
50	.202 067 7397	110	.029 654 6883	170	.004 352 0086
51	.195 707 2540	111	.028 721 2478	171	.004 215 0204
52	.189 546 9772	112	.027 817 1891	172	.004 082 3442
53	.183 580 6075	113	.026 941 5875	173	.003 953 8443
54	.177 802 0411	114	.026 093 5472	174	.003 829 3892
55	.172 205 3667	115	.025 272 2007	175	.003 708 8515
56	.166 784 8588	116	.024 476 7077	176	.003 592 1080
57	.161 534 9722	117	.023 706 2545	177	.003 479 0392
58	.156 450 3363	118	.022 960 0527	178	.003 369 5295
59	.151 525 7494	119	.022 237 3392	179	.003 263 4668
60	.146 756 1738	120	.021 537 3745	180	.003 160 7427

Present Value of 1

	NOMINAL INTEREST RATE COMPOUNDED				
	YEARLY @ $3\frac{5}{16}\%$ 3.3125% PER ANNUM		HALF-YEARLY @ $6\frac{5}{8}\%$ 6.6250% PER ANNUM		QUARTERLY @ $13\frac{1}{4}\%$ 12.2500% PER ANNUM
Periods	Present Value	Periods	Present Value	Periods	Present Value
1	.967 937 0841	61	.136 985 5867	121	.019 386 6433
2	.936 902 1988	62	.132 593 4294	122	.018 765 0510
3	.906 862 3823	63	.128 342 0974	123	.018 163 3887
4	.877 785 7300	64	.124 227 0755	124	.017 581 0175
5	.849 641 3600	65	.120 243 9932	125	.017 017 3188
6	.822 399 3805	66	.116 388 6202	126	.016 471 6940
7	.796 030 8583	67	.112 656 8616	127	.015 943 5634
8	.770 507 7879	68	.109 044 7542	128	.015 432 3663
9	.745 803 0614	69	.105 548 4614	129	.014 937 5596
10	.721 890 4406	70	.102 164 2699	130	.014 458 6179
11	.698 744 5281	71	.098 888 5855	131	.013 995 0325
12	.676 340 7411	72	.095 717 9291	132	.013 546 3109
13	.654 655 2847	73	.092 648 9332	133	.013 111 9767
14	.633 665 1274	74	.089 678 3383	134	.012 691 5685
15	.613 347 9757	75	.086 802 9893	135	.012 284 6398
16	.593 682 2511	76	.084 019 8323	136	.011 890 7584
17	.574 647 0670	77	.081 325 9115	137	.011 509 5060
18	.556 222 2065	78	.078 718 3656	138	.011 140 4777
19	.538 388 1006	79	.076 194 4253	139	.010 783 2815
20	.521 125 8082	80	.073 751 4098	140	.010 437 5381
21	.504 416 9953	81	.071 386 7246	141	.010 102 8801
22	.488 243 9156	82	.069 097 8580	142	.009 778 9524
23	.472 589 3919	83	.066 882 3792	143	.009 465 4106
24	.457 436 7980	84	.064 737 9351	144	.009 161 9220
25	.442 770 0404	85	.062 662 2482	145	.008 868 1640
26	.428 573 5418	86	.060 653 1138	146	.008 583 8248
27	.414 832 2244	87	.058 708 3981	147	.008 308 6024
28	.401 531 4937	88	.056 826 0356	148	.008 042 2044
29	.388 657 2232	89	.055 004 0272	149	.007 784 3478
30	.376 195 7393	90	.053 240 4377	150	.007 534 7589
31	.364 133 8069	91	.051 533 3941	151	.007 293 1726
32	.352 458 6153	92	.049 881 0832	152	.007 059 3322
33	.341 157 7644	93	.048 281 7502	153	.006 832 9894
34	.330 219 2517	94	.046 733 6965	154	.006 613 9039
35	.319 631 4596	95	.045 235 2779	155	.006 401 8428
36	.309 383 1430	96	.043 784 9030	156	.006 196 5811
37	.299 463 4173	97	.042 381 0314	157	.005 997 9006
38	.289 861 7469	98	.041 022 1719	158	.005 805 5904
39	.280 567 9341	99	.039 706 8815	159	.005 619 4463
40	.271 572 1080	100	.038 433 7631	160	.005 439 2705
41	.262 864 7143	101	.037 201 4645	161	.005 264 8716
42	.254 436 5051	102	.036 008 6771	162	.005 096 0644
43	.246 278 5288	103	.034 854 1339	163	.004 932 6698
44	.238 382 1211	104	.033 736 6088	164	.004 774 5140
45	.230 738 8952	105	.032 654 9147	165	.004 621 4291
46	.223 340 7334	106	.031 607 9029	166	.004 473 2527
47	.216 179 7782	107	.030 594 4614	167	.004 329 8271
48	.209 248 4242	108	.029 613 5138	168	.004 191 0002
49	.202 539 3095	109	.028 664 0182	169	.004 056 6246
50	.196 045 3087	110	.027 744 9661	170	.003 926 5573
51	.189 759 5244	111	.026 855 3816	171	.003 800 6605
52	.183 675 2808	112	.025 994 3198	172	.003 678 8002
53	.177 786 1157	113	.025 160 8661	173	.003 560 8471
54	.172 085 7744	114	.024 354 1354	174	.003 446 6760
55	.166 568 2027	115	.023 573 2708	175	.003 336 1655
56	.161 227 5404	116	.022 817 4430	176	.003 229 1983
57	.156 058 1154	117	.022 085 8492	177	.003 125 6608
58	.151 054 4371	118	.021 377 7125	178	.003 025 4430
59	.146 211 1914	119	.020 692 2807	179	.002 928 4385
60	.141 523 2343	120	.020 028 8258	180	.002 834 5442

Present Value of 1

NOMINAL INTEREST RATE COMPOUNDED

YEARLY	HALF-YEARLY	QUARTERLY
@	@	@
$3\frac{3}{8}\%$	$6\frac{3}{4}\%$	$13\frac{1}{2}\%$
3.3750%	6.7500%	13.5000%
PER ANNUM	PER ANNUM	PER ANNUM

Periods	Present Value	Periods	Present Value	Periods	Present Value
1	.967 351 8742	61	.132 024 0721	121	.018 018 6301
2	.935 769 6486	62	.127 713 7336	122	.017 430 3556
3	.905 218 5234	63	.123 544 1195	123	.016 861 2872
4	.875 664 8352	64	.119 510 6356	124	.016 310 7977
5	.847 076 0196	65	.115 608 8373	125	.015 778 2808
6	.819 420 5752	66	.111 834 4255	126	.015 263 1495
7	.792 668 0292	67	.108 183 2411	127	.014 764 8363
8	.766 788 9037	68	.104 651 2610	128	.014 282 7920
9	.741 754 6831	69	.101 234 5935	129	.013 816 4856
10	.717 537 7830	70	.097 929 4738	130	.013 365 4033
11	.694 111 5192	71	.094 732 2600	131	.012 929 0479
12	.671 450 0790	72	.091 639 4292	132	.012 506 9387
13	.649 528 4924	73	.088 647 5736	133	.012 098 6106
14	.628 322 6045	74	.085 753 3965	134	.011 703 6137
15	.607 809 0491	75	.082 953 7088	135	.011 321 5126
16	.587 965 2228	76	.080 245 4257	136	.010 951 8864
17	.568 769 2603	77	.077 625 5630	137	.010 594 3279
18	.550 200 0100	78	.075 091 2338	138	.010 248 4429
19	.532 237 0108	79	.072 639 6458	139	.009 913 8505
20	.514 860 4700	80	.070 268 0975	140	.009 590 1818
21	.498 051 2406	81	.067 973 9758	141	.009 277 0804
22	.481 790 8011	82	.065 754 7529	142	.008 974 2011
23	.466 061 2344	83	.063 607 9835	143	.008 681 2102
24	.450 845 2086	84	.061 531 3020	144	.008 397 7850
25	.436 125 9575	85	.059 522 4203	145	.008 123 6131
26	.421 887 2624	86	.057 579 1249	146	.007 858 3923
27	.408 113 4340	87	.055 699 2744	147	.007 601 8305
28	.394 789 2953	88	.053 880 7974	148	.007 353 6450
29	.381 900 1648	89	.052 121 6904	149	.007 113 5623
30	.369 431 8402	90	.050 420 0149	150	.006 881 3178
31	.357 370 5830	91	.048 773 8959	151	.006 656 6557
32	.345 703 1032	92	.047 181 5196	152	.006 439 3283
33	.334 416 5449	93	.045 641 1314	153	.006 229 0963
34	.323 498 4714	94	.044 151 0340	154	.006 025 7280
35	.312 936 8527	95	.042 709 5855	155	.005 828 9993
36	.302 720 0510	96	.041 315 1976	156	.005 638 6934
37	.292 836 8087	97	.039 966 3338	157	.005 454 6006
38	.283 276 2357	98	.038 661 5079	158	.005 276 5181
39	.274 027 7975	99	.037 399 2822	159	.005 104 2497
40	.265 081 3035	100	.036 178 2657	160	.004 937 6055
41	.256 426 8958	101	.034 997 1131	161	.004 776 4020
42	.248 055 0383	102	.033 854 5230	162	.004 620 4614
43	.239 956 5062	103	.032 749 2363	163	.004 469 6120
44	.232 122 3760	104	.031 680 0351	164	.004 323 6875
45	.224 544 0155	105	.030 645 7413	165	.004 182 5272
46	.217 213 0742	106	.029 645 2153	166	.004 045 9756
47	.210 121 4745	107	.028 677 3546	167	.003 913 8820
48	.203 261 4021	108	.027 741 0927	168	.003 786 1011
49	.196 625 2983	109	.026 835 3980	169	.003 662 4920
50	.190 205 8508	110	.025 959 2726	170	.003 542 9185
51	.183 995 9863	111	.025 111 7510	171	.003 427 2489
52	.177 988 8622	112	.024 291 8994	172	.003 315 3556
53	.172 177 8595	113	.023 498 8144	173	.003 207 1155
54	.166 556 5750	114	.022 731 6221	174	.003 102 4092
55	.161 118 8150	115	.021 989 4773	175	.003 001 1213
56	.155 858 5877	116	.021 271 5621	176	.002 903 1403
57	.150 770 0969	117	.020 577 0854	177	.002 808 3582
58	.145 847 7358	118	.019 905 2821	178	.002 716 6706
59	.141 086 0806	119	.019 255 4120	179	.002 627 9764
60	.136 479 8845	120	.018 626 7589	180	.002 542 1779

Present Value of 1

NOMINAL INTEREST RATE COMPOUNDED

YEARLY	HALF-YEARLY	QUARTERLY
@	@	@
$3\frac{7}{16}\%$	$6\frac{7}{8}\%$	$13\frac{3}{4}\%$
3.4375%	6.8750%	13.7500%
PER ANNUM	PER ANNUM	PER ANNUM

Periods	Present Value	Periods	Present Value	Periods	Present Value
1	.966 767 3716	61	.127 245 0970	121	.016 747 8912
2	.934 639 1508	62	.123 016 4080	122	.016 191 3147
3	.903 578 6352	63	.118 928 2494	123	.015 653 2348
4	.873 550 3422	64	.114 975 9511	124	.015 133 0366
5	.844 519 9683	65	.111 154 9980	125	.014 630 1261
6	.816 454 3500	66	.107 461 0253	126	.014 143 9285
7	.789 321 4260	67	.103 889 8130	127	.013 673 8886
8	.763 090 2003	68	.100 437 2814	128	.013 219 4693
9	.737 730 7073	69	.097 099 4866	129	.012 780 1516
10	.713 213 9768	70	.093 872 6154	130	.012 355 4336
11	.689 512 0018	71	.090 752 9817	131	.011 944 8301
12	.666 597 7056	72	.087 737 0216	132	.011 547 8720
13	.644 444 9118	73	.084 821 2897	133	.011 164 1058
14	.623 028 3135	74	.082 002 4553	134	.010 793 0932
15	.602 323 4451	75	.079 277 2982	135	.010 434 4104
16	.582 306 6539	76	.076 642 7052	136	.010 087 6475
17	.562 955 0732	77	.074 095 6667	137	.009 752 4085
18	.544 246 5965	78	.071 633 2729	138	.009 428 3103
19	.526 159 8516	79	.069 252 7110	139	.009 114 9828
20	.508 674 1767	80	.066 951 2614	140	.008 812 0679
21	.491 769 5969	81	.064 726 2950	141	.008 519 2197
22	.475 426 8006	82	.062 575 2701	142	.008 236 1037
23	.459 627 1184	83	.060 495 7294	143	.007 962 3963
24	.444 352 5012	84	.058 485 2973	144	.007 697 7850
25	.429 585 4996	85	.056 541 6771	145	.007 441 9673
26	.415 309 2443	86	.054 662 6486	146	.007 194 6512
27	.401 507 4266	87	.052 846 0651	147	.006 955 5540
28	.388 164 2794	88	.051 089 8514	148	.006 724 4027
29	.375 264 5602	89	.049 392 0014	149	.006 500 9331
30	.362 793 5325	90	.047 750 5754	150	.006 284 8900
31	.350 736 9499	91	.046 163 6982	151	.006 076 0266
32	.339 081 0391	92	.044 629 5572	152	.005 874 1043
33	.327 812 4850	93	.043 146 3997	153	.005 678 8923
34	.316 918 4145	94	.041 712 5315	154	.005 490 1678
35	.306 386 3826	95	.040 326 3144	155	.005 307 7151
36	.296 204 3578	96	.038 986 1650	156	.005 131 3258
37	.286 360 7084	97	.037 690 5522	157	.004 960 7983
38	.276 844 1894	98	.036 437 9961	158	.004 795 9380
39	.267 643 9293	99	.035 227 0657	159	.004 636 5564
40	.258 749 4181	100	.034 056 3778	160	.004 482 4714
41	.250 150 4948	101	.032 924 5948	161	.004 333 5071
42	.241 837 3364	102	.031 830 4240	162	.004 189 4933
43	.233 800 4461	103	.030 772 6153	163	.004 050 2654
44	.226 030 6427	104	.029 749 9604	164	.003 915 6644
45	.218 519 0504	105	.028 761 2911	165	.003 785 5366
46	.211 257 0880	106	.027 805 4778	166	.003 659 7333
47	.204 236 4597	107	.026 881 4287	167	.003 538 1107
48	.197 449 1453	108	.025 988 0881	168	.003 420 5300
49	.190 887 3912	109	.025 124 4356	169	.003 306 8568
50	.184 543 7015	110	.024 289 4846	170	.003 196 9613
51	.178 410 8292	111	.023 482 2812	171	.003 090 7178
52	.172 481 7684	112	.022 701 9033	172	.002 988 0051
53	.166 749 7459	113	.021 947 4594	173	.002 888 7059
54	.161 208 2136	114	.021 218 0876	174	.002 792 7066
55	.155 850 8409	115	.020 512 9548	175	.002 699 8976
56	.150 671 5078	116	.019 831 2554	176	.002 610 1729
57	.145 664 2976	117	.019 172 2106	177	.002 523 4300
58	.140 823 4901	118	.018 535 0677	178	.002 439 5698
59	.136 143 5554	119	.017 919 0987	179	.002 358 4965
60	.131 619 1472	120	.017 323 5999	180	.002 280 1174

Present Value of 1

NOMINAL INTEREST RATE COMPOUNDED

YEARLY	HALF-YEARLY	QUARTERLY
@	@	@
$3\frac{1}{2}\%$	7%	14%
3.5000%	7.0000%	14.0000%
PER ANNUM	PER ANNUM	PER ANNUM

Periods	Present Value	Periods	Present Value	Periods	Present Value
1	.966 183 5749	61	.122 641 8414	121	.015 567 4570
2	.933 510 7004	62	.118 494 5328	122	.015 041 0213
3	.901 942 7057	63	.114 487 4713	123	.014 532 3877
4	.871 442 2277	64	.110 615 9143	124	.014 040 9543
5	.841 973 1669	65	.106 875 2795	125	.013 566 1394
6	.813 500 6443	66	.103 261 1396	126	.013 107 3811
7	.785 990 9607	67	.099 769 2170	127	.012 664 1363
8	.759 411 5562	68	.096 395 3788	128	.012 235 8805
9	.733 730 9722	69	.093 135 6316	129	.011 822 1068
10	.708 918 8137	70	.089 986 1175	130	.011 422 3254
11	.684 945 7137	71	.086 943 1087	131	.011 036 0632
12	.661 783 2983	72	.084 003 0036	132	.010 662 8630
13	.639 404 1529	73	.081 162 3223	133	.010 302 2830
14	.617 781 7903	74	.078 417 7027	134	.009 953 8967
15	.596 890 6186	75	.075 765 8964	135	.009 617 2915
16	.576 705 9117	76	.073 203 7646	136	.009 292 0690
17	.557 203 7794	77	.070 728 2750	137	.008 977 8445
18	.538 361 1396	78	.068 336 4976	138	.008 674 2459
19	.520 155 6904	79	.066 025 6015	139	.008 380 9139
20	.502 565 8844	80	.063 792 8517	140	.008 097 5013
21	.485 570 9028	81	.061 635 6055	141	.007 823 6728
22	.469 150 6308	82	.059 551 3097	142	.007 559 1042
23	.453 285 6336	83	.057 537 4973	143	.007 303 4823
24	.437 957 1339	84	.055 591 7848	144	.007 056 5046
25	.423 146 9893	85	.053 711 8694	145	.006 817 8789
26	.408 837 6708	86	.051 895 5260	146	.006 587 3226
27	.395 012 2423	87	.050 140 6048	147	.006 364 5629
28	.381 654 3404	88	.048 445 0288	148	.006 149 3361
29	.368 748 1550	89	.046 806 7911	149	.005 941 3875
30	.356 278 4106	90	.045 223 9527	150	.005 740 4710
31	.344 230 3484	91	.043 694 6403	151	.005 546 3488
32	.332 589 7086	92	.042 217 0438	152	.005 358 7912
33	.321 342 7136	93	.040 789 4143	153	.005 177 5760
34	.310 476 0518	94	.039 410 0621	154	.005 002 4889
35	.299 976 8617	95	.038 077 3547	155	.004 833 3226
36	.289 832 7166	96	.036 789 7147	156	.004 669 8769
37	.280 031 6102	97	.035 545 6181	157	.004 511 9584
38	.270 561 9422	98	.034 343 5923	158	.004 359 3801
39	.261 412 5046	99	.033 182 2148	159	.004 211 9614
40	.252 572 4682	100	.032 060 1109	160	.004 069 5279
41	.244 031 3702	101	.030 975 9526	161	.003 931 9110
42	.235 779 1017	102	.029 928 4566	162	.003 798 9479
43	.227 805 8953	103	.028 916 3832	163	.003 670 4810
44	.220 102 3143	104	.027 938 5345	164	.003 546 3585
45	.212 659 2409	105	.026 993 7531	165	.003 426 4333
46	.205 467 8656	106	.026 080 9209	166	.003 310 5636
47	.198 519 6769	107	.025 198 9574	167	.003 198 6122
48	.191 806 4511	108	.024 346 8187	168	.003 090 4465
49	.185 320 2426	109	.023 523 4964	169	.002 985 9387
50	.179 053 3745	110	.022 728 0158	170	.002 884 9649
51	.172 998 4295	111	.021 959 4356	171	.002 787 4057
52	.167 148 2411	112	.021 216 8460	172	.002 693 1456
53	.161 495 8851	113	.020 499 3681	173	.002 602 0731
54	.156 034 6716	114	.019 806 1527	174	.002 514 0802
55	.150 758 1368	115	.019 136 3794	175	.002 429 0630
56	.145 660 0355	116	.018 489 2555	176	.002 346 9208
57	.140 734 3339	117	.017 864 0150	177	.002 267 5563
58	.135 975 2018	118	.017 259 9179	178	.002 190 8757
59	.131 377 0066	119	.016 676 2491	179	.002 116 7881
60	.126 934 3059	120	.016 112 3180	180	.002 045 2059

Present Value of 1

	NOMINAL INTEREST RATE COMPOUNDED				
	YEARLY @ $3\frac{9}{16}\%$ 3.5625% PER ANNUM		HALF-YEARLY @ $7\frac{1}{8}\%$ 7.1250% PER ANNUM		QUARTERLY @ $14\frac{1}{4}\%$ 14.2500% PER ANNUM
Periods	Present Value	Periods	Present Value	Periods	Present Value
1	.965 600 4828	61	.118 207 7439	121	.014 470 8614
2	.932 384 2924	62	.114 141 4546	122	.013 973 0707
3	.900 310 7229	63	.110 215 0436	123	.013 492 4038
4	.869 340 4687	64	.106 423 6993	124	.013 028 2716
5	.839 435 5763	65	.102 762 7755	125	.012 580 1054
6	.810 559 3977	66	.099 227 7856	126	.012 147 3558
7	.782 676 5458	67	.095 814 3977	127	.011 729 4927
8	.755 752 8505	68	.092 518 4287	128	.011 326 0038
9	.729 755 3173	69	.089 335 8394	129	.010 936 3947
10	.704 652 0867	70	.086 262 7296	130	.010 560 1880
11	.680 412 3951	71	.083 295 3334	131	.010 196 9227
12	.657 006 5373	72	.080 430 0141	132	.009 846 1534
13	.634 405 8296	73	.077 663 2605	133	.009 507 4505
14	.612 582 5753	74	.074 991 6818	134	.009 180 3988
15	.591 510 0305	75	.072 412 0042	135	.008 864 5975
16	.571 162 3710	76	.069 921 0662	136	.008 559 6596
17	.551 514 6612	77	.067 515 8153	137	.008 265 2115
18	.532 542 8231	78	.065 193 3038	138	.007 980 8922
19	.514 223 6071	79	.062 950 6856	139	.007 706 3534
20	.496 534 5633	80	.060 785 2124	140	.007 441 2585
21	.479 454 0141	81	.058 694 2305	141	.007 185 2828
22	.462 961 0275	82	.056 675 1773	142	.006 938 1126
23	.447 035 3916	83	.054 725 5786	143	.006 699 4448
24	.431 657 5900	84	.052 843 0451	144	.006 468 9872
25	.416 808 7773	85	.051 025 2698	145	.006 246 4571
26	.402 470 7566	86	.049 270 0252	146	.006 031 5820
27	.388 625 9569	87	.047 575 1601	147	.005 824 0985
28	.375 257 4116	88	.045 938 5976	148	.005 623 7523
29	.362 348 7378	89	.044 358 3320	149	.005 430 2980
30	.349 884 1162	90	.042 832 4268	150	.005 243 4983
31	.337 848 2715	91	.041 359 0120	151	.005 063 1245
32	.326 226 4541	92	.039 936 2819	152	.004 888 9555
33	.315 004 4216	93	.038 562 4931	153	.004 720 7778
34	.304 168 4215	94	.037 235 9620	154	.004 558 3853
35	.293 705 1747	95	.035 955 0629	155	.004 401 5791
36	.283 601 8585	96	.034 718 2261	156	.004 250 1669
37	.273 846 0915	97	.033 523 9359	157	.004 103 9632
38	.264 425 9181	98	.032 370 7286	158	.003 962 7888
39	.255 329 7942	99	.031 257 1912	159	.003 826 4708
40	.246 546 5726	100	.030 181 9589	160	.003 694 8421
41	.238 065 4895	101	.029 143 7141	161	.003 567 7413
42	.229 876 1516	102	.028 141 1844	162	.003 445 0127
43	.221 968 5230	103	.027 173 1413	163	.003 326 5059
44	.214 332 9130	104	.026 238 3983	164	.003 212 0757
45	.206 959 9642	105	.025 335 8101	165	.003 101 5819
46	.199 840 6414	106	.024 464 2704	166	.002 994 8889
47	.192 966 2198	107	.023 622 7114	167	.002 891 8662
48	.186 328 2750	108	.022 810 1015	168	.002 792 3874
49	.179 918 6723	109	.022 025 4450	169	.002 696 3306
50	.173 729 5568	110	.021 267 7803	170	.002 603 5782
51	.167 753 3440	111	.020 536 1790	171	.002 514 0163
52	.161 982 7099	112	.019 829 7443	172	.002 427 5354
53	.156 410 5829	113	.019 147 6107	173	.002 344 0293
54	.151 030 1344	114	.018 488 9421	174	.002 263 3959
55	.145 834 7707	115	.017 852 9314	175	.002 185 5361
56	.140 818 1250	116	.017 238 7992	176	.002 110 3547
57	.135 974 0494	117	.016 645 7928	177	.002 037 7596
58	.131 296 6078	118	.016 073 1856	178	.001 967 6616
59	.126 780 0679	119	.015 520 2758	179	.001 899 9750
60	.122 418 8948	120	.014 986 3858	180	.001 834 6168

NOMINAL INTEREST RATE COMPOUNDED

YEARLY	HALF-YEARLY	QUARTERLY
@	@	@
$3\frac{5}{8}\%$	$7\frac{1}{4}\%$	$14\frac{1}{2}\%$
3.6250%	7.2500%	14.5000%
PER ANNUM	PER ANNUM	PER ANNUM

Periods	Present Value	Periods	Present Value	Periods	Present Value
1	.965 018 0941	61	.113 936 4918	121	.013 452 1044
2	.931 259 9219	62	.109 950 7761	122	.012 981 5242
3	.898 682 6750	63	.106 104 4884	123	.012 527 4057
4	.867 245 0422	64	.102 392 7512	124	.012 089 1732
5	.836 907 1577	65	.098 810 8576	125	.011 666 2709
6	.807 630 5503	66	.095 354 2655	126	.011 258 1625
7	.779 378 0943	67	.092 018 5915	127	.010 864 3305
8	.752 113 9632	68	.088 799 6058	128	.010 484 2755
9	.725 803 5833	69	.085 693 2264	129	.010 117 5156
10	.700 413 5906	70	.082 695 5140	130	.009 763 5856
11	.675 911 7883	71	.079 802 6673	131	.009 422 0368
12	.652 267 1057	72	.077 011 0179	132	.009 092 4359
13	.629 449 5592	73	.074 317 0257	133	.008 774 3652
14	.607 430 2139	74	.071 717 2745	134	.008 467 4212
15	.586 181 1473	75	.069 208 4676	135	.008 171 2147
16	.565 675 4136	76	.066 787 4235	136	.007 885 3700
17	.545 887 0095	77	.064 451 0721	137	.007 609 5247
18	.526 790 8415	78	.062 196 4508	138	.007 343 3290
19	.508 362 6939	79	.060 020 7004	139	.007 086 4454
20	.490 579 1979	80	.057 921 0619	140	.006 838 5480
21	.473 417 8026	81	.055 894 8727	141	.006 599 3226
22	.456 856 7456	82	.053 939 5636	142	.006 368 4657
23	.440 875 0259	83	.052 052 6548	143	.006 145 6846
24	.425 452 3772	84	.050 231 7538	144	.005 930 6969
25	.410 569 2422	85	.048 474 5513	145	.005 723 2298
26	.396 206 7476	86	.046 778 8191	146	.005 523 0203
27	.382 346 6804	87	.045 142 4068	147	.005 329 8145
28	.368 971 4648	88	.043 563 2394	148	.005 143 3675
29	.356 064 1397	89	.042 039 3143	149	.004 963 4427
30	.343 608 3375	90	.040 568 6989	150	.004 789 8120
31	.331 588 2630	91	.039 149 5285	151	.004 622 2552
32	.319 988 6736	92	.037 780 0034	152	.004 460 5599
33	.308 794 8599	93	.036 458 3869	153	.004 304 5210
34	.297 992 6271	94	.035 183 0030	154	.004 153 9407
35	.287 568 2771	95	.033 952 2345	155	.004 008 6279
36	.277 508 5907	96	.032 764 5206	156	.003 868 3985
37	.267 800 8113	97	.031 618 3553	157	.003 733 0745
38	.258 432 6285	98	.030 512 2849	158	.003 602 4845
39	.249 392 1626	99	.029 444 9071	159	.003 476 4627
40	.240 667 9494	100	.028 414 8681	160	.003 354 8494
41	.232 248 9259	101	.027 420 8618	161	.003 237 4904
42	.224 124 4158	102	.026 461 6278	162	.003 124 2368
43	.216 284 1166	103	.025 535 9497	163	.003 014 9450
44	.208 718 0860	104	.024 642 6535	164	.002 909 4765
45	.201 416 7295	105	.023 780 6065	165	.002 807 6975
46	.194 370 7884	106	.022 948 7155	166	.002 709 4789
47	.187 571 3278	107	.022 145 9257	167	.002 614 6961
48	.181 009 7253	108	.021 371 2190	168	.002 523 2291
49	.174 677 6601	109	.020 623 6131	169	.002 434 9617
50	.168 567 1026	110	.019 902 1598	170	.002 349 7821
51	.162 670 3041	111	.019 205 9443	171	.002 267 5823
52	.156 979 7868	112	.018 534 0838	172	.002 188 2579
53	.151 488 3347	113	.017 885 7262	173	.002 111 7085
54	.146 188 9840	114	.017 260 0494	174	.002 037 8369
55	.141 075 0147	115	.016 656 2600	175	.001 966 5495
56	.136 139 9418	116	.016 073 5923	176	.001 897 7558
57	.131 377 5072	117	.015 511 3074	177	.001 831 3687
58	.126 781 6716	118	.014 968 6923	178	.001 767 3039
59	.122 346 6071	119	.014 445 0589	179	.001 705 4803
60	.118 066 6896	120	.013 939 7432	180	.001 645 8193

NOMINAL INTEREST RATE COMPOUNDED

	YEARLY @ $3\frac{11}{16}\%$ 3.6875% PER ANNUM		HALF-YEARLY @ $7\frac{3}{8}\%$ 7.3750% PER ANNUM		QUARTERLY @ $14\frac{3}{4}\%$ 14.7500% PER ANNUM
Periods	Present Value	Periods	Present Value	Periods	Present Value
1	.964 436 4075	61	.109 822 0116	121	.012 505 6190
2	.930 137 5841	62	.105 916 3464	122	.012 060 8742
3	.897 058 5500	63	.102 149 5806	123	.011 631 9462
4	.865 155 9253	64	.098 516 7745	124	.011 218 2724
5	.834 387 8725	65	.095 013 1641	125	.010 819 3104
6	.804 714 0422	66	.091 634 1546	126	.010 434 5368
7	.776 095 5199	67	.088 375 3149	127	.010 063 4472
8	.748 494 7751	68	.085 232 3712	128	.009 705 5549
9	.721 875 6119	69	.082 201 2019	129	.009 360 3905
10	.696 203 1218	70	.079 277 8318	130	.009 027 5014
11	.671 443 6376	71	.076 458 4273	131	.008 706 4510
12	.647 564 6897	72	.073 739 2910	132	.008 396 8183
13	.624 534 9629	73	.071 116 8569	133	.008 098 1973
14	.602 324 2560	74	.068 587 6860	134	.007 810 1963
15	.580 903 4416	75	.066 148 4615	135	.007 532 4376
16	.560 244 4283	76	.063 795 9845	136	.007 264 5571
17	.540 320 1237	77	.061 527 1701	137	.007 006 2034
18	.521 104 3990	78	.059 339 0429	138	.006 757 0376
19	.502 572 0545	79	.057 228 7334	139	.006 516 7331
20	.484 698 7867	80	.055 193 4740	140	.006 284 9746
21	.467 461 1566	81	.053 230 5958	141	.006 061 4583
22	.450 836 5585	82	.051 337 5246	142	.005 845 8911
23	.434 803 1908	83	.049 511 7778	143	.005 637 9902
24	.419 340 0273	84	.047 750 9611	144	.005 437 4830
25	.404 426 7895	85	.046 052 7654	145	.005 244 1066
26	.390 043 9199	86	.044 414 9636	146	.005 057 6073
27	.376 172 5569	87	.042 835 4079	147	.004 877 7406
28	.362 794 5093	88	.041 312 0269	148	.004 704 2707
29	.349 892 2332	89	.039 842 8228	149	.004 536 9699
30	.337 448 8084	90	.038 425 8689	150	.004 375 6190
31	.325 447 9165	91	.037 059 3070	151	.004 220 0062
32	.313 873 8194	92	.035 741 3449	152	.004 069 9276
33	.302 711 3388	93	.034 470 2542	153	.003 925 1864
34	.291 945 8361	94	.033 244 3682	154	.003 785 5927
35	.281 563 1933	95	.032 062 0790	155	.003 650 9634
36	.271 549 7947	96	.030 921 8363	156	.003 521 1220
37	.261 892 5084	97	.029 822 1447	157	.003 395 8983
38	.252 578 6700	98	.028 761 5621	158	.003 275 1279
39	.243 596 0651	99	.027 738 6976	159	.003 158 6526
40	.234 932 9139	100	.026 752 2099	160	.003 046 3196
41	.226 577 8554	101	.025 800 8052	161	.002 937 9815
42	.218 519 9329	102	.024 883 2359	162	.002 833 4963
43	.210 748 5791	103	.023 998 2986	163	.002 732 7270
44	.203 253 6025	104	.023 144 8329	164	.002 635 5414
45	.196 025 1742	105	.022 321 7195	165	.002 541 8121
46	.189 053 8148	106	.021 527 8790	166	.002 451 4161
47	.182 330 3819	107	.020 762 2702	167	.002 364 2350
48	.175 846 0585	108	.020 023 8893	168	.002 280 1543
49	.169 592 3409	109	.019 311 7679	169	.002 199 0638
50	.163 561 0280	110	.018 624 9720	170	.002 120 8572
51	.157 744 2103	111	.017 962 6011	171	.002 045 4319
52	.152 134 2595	112	.017 323 7865	172	.001 972 6890
53	.146 723 8187	113	.016 707 6904	173	.001 902 5331
54	.141 505 7926	114	.016 113 5049	174	.001 834 8722
55	.136 473 3382	115	.015 540 4508	175	.001 769 6175
56	.131 619 8560	116	.014 987 7765	176	.001 706 6836
57	.126 938 9811	117	.014 454 7574	177	.001 645 9878
58	.122 424 5749	118	.013 940 6943	178	.001 587 4505
59	.118 070 7172	119	.013 444 9131	179	.001 530 9951
60	.113 871 6983	120	.012 966 7637	180	.001 476 5474

Present Value of 1

NOMINAL INTEREST RATE COMPOUNDED

YEARLY	HALF-YEARLY	QUARTERLY
@	@	@
$3\frac{3}{4}\%$	$7\frac{1}{2}\%$	15%
3.7500%	7.5000%	15.0000%
PER ANNUM	PER ANNUM	PER ANNUM

Periods	Present Value	Periods	Present Value	Periods	Present Value
1	.963 855 4217	61	.105 858 4600	121	.011 626 2391
2	.929 017 2739	62	.102 032 2506	122	.011 206 0135
3	.895 438 3363	63	.098 344 3379	123	.010 800 9769
4	.863 073 0952	64	.094 789 7233	124	.010 410 5802
5	.831 877 6822	65	.091 363 5887	125	.010 034 2941
6	.801 809 8141	66	.088 061 2903	126	.009 671 6088
7	.772 828 7365	67	.084 878 3521	127	.009 322 0326
8	.744 895 1677	68	.081 810 4599	128	.008 985 0916
9	.717 971 2460	69	.078 853 4553	129	.008 660 3293
10	.692 020 4781	70	.076 003 3304	130	.008 347 3053
11	.667 007 6897	71	.073 256 2221	131	.008 045 5955
12	.642 898 9780	72	.070 608 4068	132	.007 754 7909
13	.619 661 6656	73	.068 056 2957	133	.007 474 4972
14	.597 264 2560	74	.065 596 4296	134	.007 204 3347
15	.575 676 3913	75	.063 225 4743	135	.006 943 9370
16	.554 868 8109	76	.060 940 2162	136	.006 692 9513
17	.534 813 3117	77	.058 737 5578	137	.006 451 0374
18	.515 482 7101	78	.056 614 5135	138	.006 217 8674
19	.496 850 8049	79	.054 568 2058	139	.005 993 1252
20	.478 892 3421	80	.052 595 8610	140	.005 776 5062
21	.461 582 9803	81	.050 694 8058	141	.005 567 7169
22	.444 899 2581	82	.048 862 4634	142	.005 366 4741
23	.428 818 5620	83	.047 096 3503	143	.005 172 5051
24	.413 319 0959	84	.045 394 0726	144	.004 985 5471
25	.398 379 8515	85	.043 753 3230	145	.004 805 3466
26	.383 980 5798	86	.042 171 8776	146	.004 631 6594
27	.370 101 7636	87	.040 647 5928	147	.004 464 2500
28	.356 724 5915	88	.039 178 4027	148	.004 302 8916
29	.343 830 9315	89	.037 762 3159	149	.004 147 3654
30	.331 403 3075	90	.036 397 4129	150	.003 997 4606
31	.319 424 8747	91	.035 081 8438	151	.003 852 9741
32	.307 879 3973	92	.033 813 8253	152	.003 713 7100
33	.296 751 2263	93	.032 591 6389	153	.003 579 4795
34	.286 025 2784	94	.031 413 6278	154	.003 450 1007
35	.275 687 0153	95	.030 278 1955	155	.003 325 3983
36	.265 722 4244	96	.029 183 8029	156	.003 205 2031
37	.256 117 9994	97	.028 128 9666	157	.003 089 3524
38	.246 860 7223	98	.027 112 2570	158	.002 977 6891
39	.237 938 0456	99	.026 132 2959	159	.002 870 0618
40	.229 337 8753	100	.025 187 7551	160	.002 766 3246
41	.221 048 5545	101	.024 277 3543	161	.002 666 3370
42	.213 058 8477	102	.023 399 8596	162	.002 569 9633
43	.205 357 9255	103	.022 554 0815	163	.002 477 0731
44	.197 935 3499	104	.021 738 8737	164	.002 387 5403
45	.190 781 0601	105	.020 953 1313	165	.002 301 2437
46	.183 885 3592	106	.020 195 7892	166	.002 218 0662
47	.177 238 9004	107	.019 465 8209	167	.002 137 8951
48	.170 832 6751	108	.018 762 2370	168	.002 060 6218
49	.164 658 0001	109	.018 084 0839	169	.001 986 1415
50	.158 706 5061	110	.017 430 4423	170	.001 914 3533
51	.152 970 1264	111	.016 800 4263	171	.001 845 1598
52	.147 441 0856	112	.016 193 1820	172	.001 778 4673
53	.142 111 8898	113	.015 607 8863	173	.001 714 1853
54	.136 975 3154	114	.015 043 7458	174	.001 652 2268
55	.132 024 4004	115	.014 499 9959	175	.001 592 5078
56	.127 252 4341	116	.013 975 8997	176	.001 534 9472
57	.122 652 9486	117	.013 470 7467	177	.001 479 4672
58	.118 219 7095	118	.012 983 8522	178	.001 425 9925
59	.113 946 7079	119	.012 514 5564	179	.001 374 4506
60	.109 828 1522	120	.012 062 2230	180	.001 324 7717

NOMINAL INTEREST RATE COMPOUNDED

YEARLY	HALF-YEARLY	QUARTERLY
@	@	@
$3\frac{13}{16}\%$	$7\frac{5}{8}\%$	$15\frac{1}{4}\%$
3.8125%	7.6250%	15.2500%
PER ANNUM	PER ANNUM	PER ANNUM

Periods	Present Value	Periods	Present Value	Periods	Present Value
1	.963 275 1355	61	.102 040 2144	121	.010 809 1707
2	.927 898 9866	62	.098 292 8014	122	.010 412 2054
3	.893 822 0220	63	.094 683 0115	123	.010 029 8185
4	.860 996 5293	64	.091 205 7908	124	.009 661 4748
5	.829 376 5484	65	.087 856 2705	125	.009 306 6584
6	.798 917 8070	66	.084 629 7608	126	.008 964 8727
7	.769 577 6588	67	.081 521 7443	127	.008 635 6389
8	.741 315 0235	68	.078 527 8693	128	.008 318 4963
9	.714 090 3297	69	.075 643 9439	129	.008 013 0006
10	.687 865 4591	70	.072 865 9303	130	.007 718 7243
11	.662 603 6933	71	.070 189 9389	131	.007 435 2552
12	.638 269 6624	72	.067 612 2229	132	.007 162 1964
13	.614 829 2955	73	.065 129 1732	133	.006 899 1657
14	.592 249 7729	74	.062 737 3131	134	.006 645 7948
15	.570 499 4802	75	.060 433 2938	135	.006 401 7289
16	.549 547 9641	76	.058 213 8893	136	.006 166 6263
17	.529 365 8895	77	.056 075 9921	137	.005 940 1577
18	.509 924 9990	78	.054 016 6089	138	.005 722 0063
19	.491 198 0724	79	.052 032 8562	139	.005 511 8664
20	.473 158 8898	80	.050 121 9566	140	.005 309 4438
21	.455 782 1936	81	.048 281 2346	141	.005 114 4552
22	.439 043 6543	82	.046 508 1128	142	.004 926 6275
23	.422 919 8356	83	.044 800 1086	143	.004 745 6978
24	.407 388 1619	84	.043 154 8307	144	.004 571 4127
25	.392 426 8869	85	.041 569 9754	145	.004 403 5282
26	.378 015 0626	86	.040 043 3237	146	.004 241 8092
27	.364 132 5106	87	.038 572 7380	147	.004 086 0293
28	.350 759 7935	88	.037 156 1595	148	.003 935 9705
29	.337 878 1876	89	.035 791 6045	149	.003 791 4225
30	.325 469 6569	90	.034 477 1627	150	.003 652 1830
31	.313 516 8279	91	.033 210 9936	151	.003 518 0571
32	.302 002 9648	92	.031 991 3243	152	.003 388 8569
33	.290 911 9469	93	.030 816 4473	153	.003 264 4016
34	.280 228 2450	94	.029 684 7174	154	.003 144 5169
35	.269 936 9007	95	.028 594 5502	155	.003 029 0349
36	.260 023 5046	96	.027 544 4192	156	.002 917 7940
37	.250 474 1766	97	.026 532 8542	157	.002 810 6384
38	.241 275 5464	98	.025 558 4387	158	.002 707 4181
39	.232 414 7346	99	.024 619 8085	159	.002 607 9886
40	.223 879 3350	100	.023 715 6494	160	.002 512 2105
41	.215 657 3967	101	.022 844 6953	161	.002 419 9499
42	.207 737 4080	102	.022 005 7270	162	.002 331 0776
43	.200 108 2799	103	.021 197 5697	163	.002 245 4691
44	.192 759 3304	104	.020 419 0918	164	.002 163 0046
45	.185 680 2701	105	.019 669 2034	165	.002 083 5685
46	.178 861 1873	106	.018 946 8546	166	.002 007 0497
47	.172 292 5345	107	.018 251 0339	167	.001 933 3411
48	.165 965 1145	108	.017 580 7672	168	.001 862 3394
49	.159 870 0681	109	.016 935 1159	169	.001 793 9453
50	.153 998 8615	110	.016 313 1760	170	.001 728 0629
51	.148 343 2742	111	.015 714 0768	171	.001 664 6000
52	.142 895 3875	112	.015 136 9795	172	.001 603 4678
53	.137 647 5738	113	.014 581 0760	173	.001 544 5806
54	.132 592 4853	114	.014 045 5879	174	.001 487 8561
55	.127 723 0442	115	.013 529 7656	175	.001 433 2148
56	.123 032 4327	116	.013 032 8868	176	.001 380 5802
57	.118 514 0833	117	.012 554 2558	177	.001 329 8786
58	.114 161 6697	118	.012 093 2025	178	.001 281 0390
59	.109 969 0978	119	.011 649 0812	179	.001 233 9930
60	.105 930 4976	120	.011 221 2703	180	.001 188 6747

Present Value of 1

NOMINAL INTEREST RATE COMPOUNDED

YEARLY	HALF-YEARLY	QUARTERLY
@	@	@
$3\frac{7}{8}\%$	$7\frac{3}{4}\%$	$15\frac{1}{2}\%$
3.8750%	7.7500%	15.5000%
PER ANNUM	PER ANNUM	PER ANNUM

Periods	Present Value	Periods	Present Value	Periods	Present Value
1	.962 695 5475	61	.098 361 8652	121	.010 049 9650
2	.926 782 7172	62	.094 692 5297	122	.009 675 0565
3	.892 209 5954	63	.091 160 0767	123	.009 314 1338
4	.858 926 2050	64	.087 759 4000	124	.008 966 6752
5	.826 884 4332	65	.084 485 5836	125	.008 632 1783
6	.796 037 9622	66	.081 333 8952	126	.008 310 1596
7	.766 342 2018	67	.078 299 7788	127	.008 000 1536
8	.737 754 2256	68	.075 378 8484	128	.007 701 7123
9	.710 232 7082	69	.072 566 8817	129	.007 414 4041
10	.683 737 8658	70	.069 859 8139	130	.007 137 8138
11	.658 231 3991	71	.067 253 7318	131	.006 871 5416
12	.633 676 4372	72	.064 744 8682	132	.006 615 2025
13	.610 037 4847	73	.062 329 5963	133	.006 368 4260
14	.587 280 3703	74	.060 004 4249	134	.006 130 8554
15	.565 372 1977	75	.057 765 9926	135	.005 902 1472
16	.544 281 2974	76	.055 611 0639	136	.005 681 9708
17	.523 977 1816	77	.053 536 5236	137	.005 470 0080
18	.504 430 4997	78	.051 539 3729	138	.005 265 9523
19	.485 612 9961	79	.049 616 7248	139	.005 069 5089
20	.467 497 4692	80	.047 765 8001	140	.004 880 3936
21	.450 057 7321	81	.045 983 9231	141	.004 698 3332
22	.433 268 5748	82	.044 268 5180	142	.004 523 0644
23	.417 105 7279	83	.042 617 1052	143	.004 354 3340
24	.401 545 8271	84	.041 027 2974	144	.004 191 8980
25	.386 566 3798	85	.039 496 7965	145	.004 035 5215
26	.372 145 7327	86	.038 023 3902	146	.003 884 9786
27	.358 263 0399	87	.036 604 9484	147	.003 740 0516
28	.344 898 2334	88	.035 239 4208	148	.003 600 5310
29	.332 031 9936	89	.033 924 8335	149	.003 466 2152
30	.319 645 7219	90	.032 659 2862	150	.003 336 9099
31	.307 721 5132	91	.031 440 9494	151	.003 212 4283
32	.296 242 1307	92	.030 268 0620	152	.003 092 5904
33	.285 190 9802	93	.029 138 9285	153	.002 977 2230
34	.274 552 0868	94	.028 051 9168	154	.002 866 1594
35	.264 310 0716	95	.027 005 4554	155	.002 759 2389
36	.254 450 1291	96	.025 998 0316	156	.002 656 3070
37	.244 958 0063	97	.025 028 1893	157	.002 557 2149
38	.235 819 9820	98	.024 094 5264	158	.002 461 8194
39	.227 022 8467	99	.023 195 6933	159	.002 369 9826
40	.218 553 8837	100	.022 330 3907	160	.002 281 5717
41	.210 400 8507	101	.021 497 3677	161	.002 196 4589
42	.202 551 9622	102	.020 695 4201	162	.002 114 5212
43	.194 995 8722	103	.019 923 3888	163	.002 035 6401
44	.187 721 6579	104	.019 180 1577	164	.001 959 7017
45	.180 718 8042	105	.018 464 6524	165	.001 886 5961
46	.173 977 1882	106	.017 775 8387	166	.001 816 2177
47	.167 487 0645	107	.017 112 7207	167	.001 748 4646
48	.161 239 0512	108	.016 474 3401	168	.001 683 2391
49	.155 224 1167	109	.015 859 7738	169	.001 620 4468
50	.149 433 5660	110	.015 268 1336	170	.001 559 9969
51	.143 859 0287	111	.014 698 5643	171	.001 501 8021
52	.138 492 4464	112	.014 150 2424	172	.001 445 7782
53	.133 326 0615	113	.013 622 3753	173	.001 391 8442
54	.128 352 4058	114	.013 114 2001	174	.001 339 9222
55	.123 564 2895	115	.012 624 9820	175	.001 289 9372
56	.118 954 7914	116	.012 154 0140	176	.001 241 8168
57	.114 517 2480	117	.011 700 6152	177	.001 195 4915
58	.110 245 2448	118	.011 264 1301	178	.001 150 8943
59	.106 132 6063	119	.010 843 9279	179	.001 107 9608
60	.102 173 3875	120	.010 439 4011	180	.001 066 6290

Present Value of 1

NOMINAL INTEREST RATE COMPOUNDED

YEARLY	HALF-YEARLY	QUARTERLY
@	@	@
$3\frac{15}{16}\%$	$7\frac{7}{8}\%$	$15\frac{3}{4}\%$
3.9375%	7.8750%	15.7500%
PER ANNUM	PER ANNUM	PER ANNUM

Periods	Present Value	Periods	Present Value	Periods	Present Value
1	.962 116 6566	61	.094 818 2072	121	.009 344 4931
2	.925 668 4610	62	.091 226 1765	122	.008 990 4924
3	.890 601 0449	63	.087 770 2240	123	.008 649 9025
4	.856 862 0997	64	.084 445 1944	124	.008 322 2153
5	.824 401 2985	65	.081 246 1281	125	.008 006 9419
6	.793 170 2211	66	.078 168 2532	126	.007 703 6122
7	.763 122 2813	67	.075 206 9784	127	.007 411 7736
8	.734 212 6579	68	.072 357 8866	128	.007 130 9909
9	.706 398 2276	69	.069 616 7279	129	.006 860 8451
10	.679 637 5010	70	.066 979 4135	130	.006 600 9333
11	.653 890 5602	71	.064 442 0094	131	.006 350 8679
12	.629 118 9996	72	.062 000 7306	132	.006 110 2758
13	.605 285 8686	73	.059 651 9357	133	.005 878 7981
14	.582 355 6162	74	.057 392 1209	134	.005 656 0896
15	.560 294 0384	75	.055 217 9155	135	.005 441 8180
16	.539 068 2270	76	.053 126 0762	136	.005 235 6638
17	.518 646 5202	77	.051 113 4829	137	.005 037 3193
18	.498 998 4560	78	.049 177 1332	138	.004 846 4888
19	.480 094 7262	79	.047 314 1390	139	.004 662 8876
20	.461 907 1328	80	.045 521 7212	140	.004 486 2418
21	.444 408 5463	81	.043 797 2062	141	.004 316 2880
22	.427 572 8648	82	.042 138 0216	142	.004 152 7726
23	.411 374 9751	83	.040 541 6925	143	.003 995 4517
24	.395 790 7157	84	.039 005 8376	144	.003 844 0906
25	.380 796 8401	85	.037 528 1661	145	.003 698 4636
26	.366 370 9827	86	.036 106 4737	146	.003 558 3534
27	.352 491 6249	87	.034 738 6398	147	.003 423 5511
28	.339 138 0637	88	.033 422 6239	148	.003 293 8555
29	.326 290 3800	89	.032 156 4632	149	.003 169 0733
30	.313 929 4095	90	.030 938 2689	150	.003 049 0182
31	.302 036 7139	91	.029 766 2238	151	.002 933 5112
32	.290 594 5533	92	.028 638 5797	152	.002 822 3800
33	.279 585 8601	93	.027 553 6546	153	.002 715 4588
34	.268 994 2129	94	.026 509 8300	154	.002 612 5881
35	.258 803 8128	95	.025 505 5490	155	.002 513 6146
36	.248 999 4591	96	.024 539 3136	156	.002 418 3904
37	.239 566 5271	97	.023 609 6823	157	.002 326 7737
38	.230 490 9461	98	.022 715 2686	158	.002 238 6277
39	.221 759 1785	99	.021 854 7383	159	.002 153 8210
40	.213 358 1994	100	.021 026 8077	160	.002 072 2271
41	.205 275 4774	101	.020 230 2420	161	.001 993 7242
42	.197 498 9560	102	.019 463 8528	162	.001 918 1953
43	.190 017 0353	103	.018 726 4969	163	.001 845 5276
44	.182 818 5547	104	.018 017 0746	164	.001 775 6129
45	.175 892 7766	105	.017 334 5276	165	.001 708 3467
46	.169 229 3702	106	.016 677 8377	166	.001 643 6288
47	.162 818 3958	107	.016 046 0255	167	.001 581 3627
48	.156 650 2906	108	.015 438 1484	168	.001 521 4554
49	.150 715 8539	109	.014 853 2997	169	.001 463 8176
50	.145 006 2334	110	.014 290 6071	170	.001 408 3633
51	.139 512 9125	111	.013 749 2311	171	.001 355 0097
52	.134 227 6969	112	.013 228 3642	172	.001 303 6774
53	.129 142 7030	113	.012 727 2296	173	.001 254 2898
54	.124 250 3457	114	.012 245 0796	174	.001 206 7731
55	.119 543 3271	115	.011 781 1950	175	.001 161 0565
56	.115 014 6262	116	.011 334 8840	176	.001 117 0718
57	.110 657 4877	117	.010 905 4807	177	.001 074 7534
58	.106 465 4121	118	.010 492 3446	178	.001 034 0381
59	.102 432 1463	119	.010 094 8595	179	.000 994 8653
60	.098 551 6741	120	.009 712 4325	180	.000 957 1765

Present Value of 1

NOMINAL INTEREST RATE COMPOUNDED

YEARLY	HALF-YEARLY	QUARTERLY
@	@	@
4%	8%	16%
4.0000%	8.0000%	16.0000%
PER ANNUM	PER ANNUM	PER ANNUM

Periods	Present Value	Periods	Present Value	Periods	Present Value
1	.961 538 4615	61	.091 404 2318	121	.008 688 9229
2	.924 556 2130	62	.087 888 6844	122	.008 354 7336
3	.888 996 3587	63	.084 508 3504	123	.008 033 3977
4	.854 804 1910	64	.081 258 0292	124	.007 724 4208
5	.821 927 1068	65	.078 132 7204	125	.007 427 3277
6	.790 314 5257	66	.075 127 6157	126	.007 141 6613
7	.759 917 8132	67	.072 238 0921	127	.006 866 9820
8	.730 690 2050	68	.069 459 7039	128	.006 602 8673
9	.702 586 7356	69	.066 788 1768	129	.006 348 9109
10	.675 564 1688	70	.064 219 4008	130	.006 104 7220
11	.649 580 9316	71	.061 749 4238	131	.005 869 9250
12	.624 597 0496	72	.059 374 4460	132	.005 644 1586
13	.600 574 0861	73	.057 090 8135	133	.005 427 0756
14	.577 475 0828	74	.054 895 0130	134	.005 218 3419
15	.555 264 5027	75	.052 783 6663	135	.005 017 6365
16	.533 908 1757	76	.050 753 5253	136	.004 824 6505
17	.513 373 2459	77	.048 801 4666	137	.004 639 0870
18	.493 628 1210	78	.046 924 4871	138	.004 460 6606
19	.474 642 4240	79	.045 119 6992	139	.004 289 0967
20	.456 386 9462	80	.043 384 3261	140	.004 124 1314
21	.438 833 6021	81	.041 715 6982	141	.003 965 5110
22	.421 955 3867	82	.040 111 2483	142	.003 812 9913
23	.405 726 3333	83	.038 568 5079	143	.003 666 3378
24	.390 121 4743	84	.037 085 1038	144	.003 525 3248
25	.375 116 8023	85	.035 658 7537	145	.003 389 7354
26	.360 689 2329	86	.034 287 2631	146	.003 259 3610
27	.346 816 5701	87	.032 968 5222	147	.003 134 0009
28	.333 477 4713	88	.031 700 5022	148	.003 013 4624
29	.320 651 4147	89	.030 481 2521	149	.002 897 5600
30	.308 318 6680	90	.029 308 8962	150	.002 786 1154
31	.296 460 2577	91	.028 181 6310	151	.002 678 9571
32	.285 057 9401	92	.027 097 7221	152	.002 575 9203
33	.274 094 1731	93	.026 055 5020	153	.002 476 8465
34	.263 552 0896	94	.025 053 3673	154	.002 381 5831
35	.253 415 4707	95	.024 089 7763	155	.002 289 9838
36	.243 668 7219	96	.023 163 2464	156	.002 201 9075
37	.234 296 8479	97	.022 272 3523	157	.002 117 2187
38	.225 285 4307	98	.021 415 7234	158	.002 035 7873
39	.216 620 6064	99	.020 592 0417	159	.001 957 4877
40	.208 289 0447	100	.019 800 0401	160	.001 882 1998
41	.200 277 9276	101	.019 038 5001	161	.001 809 8075
42	.192 574 9303	102	.018 306 2501	162	.001 740 1995
43	.185 168 2023	103	.017 602 1636	163	.001 673 2687
44	.178 046 3483	104	.016 925 1573	164	.001 608 9122
45	.171 198 4118	105	.016 274 1897	165	.001 547 0310
46	.164 613 8575	106	.015 648 2593	166	.001 487 5298
47	.158 282 5553	107	.015 046 4032	167	.001 430 3171
48	.152 194 7647	108	.014 467 6954	168	.001 375 3049
49	.146 341 1199	109	.013 911 2455	169	.001 322 4086
50	.140 712 6153	110	.013 376 1976	170	.001 271 5467
51	.135 300 5917	111	.012 861 7285	171	.001 222 6411
52	.130 096 7228	112	.012 367 0466	172	.001 175 6164
53	.125 093 0027	113	.011 891 3910	173	.001 130 4004
54	.120 281 7333	114	.011 434 0298	174	.001 086 9235
55	.115 655 5128	115	.010 994 2594	175	.001 045 1187
56	.111 207 2239	116	.010 571 4033	176	.001 004 9218
57	.106 930 0229	117	.010 164 8109	177	.000 966 2710
58	.102 817 3297	118	.009 773 8566	178	.000 929 1067
59	.098 862 8171	119	.009 397 9390	179	.000 893 3719
60	.095 060 4010	120	.009 036 4798	180	.000 859 0114

Present Value of 1

NOMINAL INTEREST RATE COMPOUNDED

YEARLY	HALF-YEARLY	QUARTERLY
@	@	@
$4\frac{1}{16}\%$	$8\frac{1}{8}\%$	$16\frac{1}{4}\%$
4.0625%	8.1250%	16.2500%
PER ANNUM	PER ANNUM	PER ANNUM

Periods	Present Value	Periods	Present Value	Periods	Present Value
1	.960 960 9610	61	.088 115 1193	121	.008 079 6979
2	.923 445 9685	62	.084 675 1897	122	.007 764 2743
3	.887 395 5253	63	.081 369 5517	123	.007 461 1644
4	.852 752 4567	64	.078 192 9626	124	.007 169 8878
5	.819 461 8203	65	.075 140 3845	125	.006 889 9822
6	.787 470 8183	66	.072 206 9761	126	.006 621 0039
7	.756 728 7143	67	.069 388 0851	127	.006 362 5263
8	.727 186 7524	68	.066 679 2409	128	.006 114 1394
9	.698 798 0804	69	.064 076 1475	129	.005 875 4493
10	.671 517 6749	70	.061 574 6762	130	.005 646 0774
11	.645 302 2702	71	.059 170 8600	131	.005 425 6599
12	.620 110 2896	72	.056 860 8865	132	.005 213 8474
13	.595 901 7798	73	.054 641 0922	133	.005 010 3038
14	.572 638 3470	74	.052 507 9564	134	.004 814 7064
15	.550 283 0962	75	.050 458 0963	135	.004 626 7448
16	.528 800 5729	76	.048 488 2607	136	.004 446 1212
17	.508 156 7067	77	.046 595 3256	137	.004 272 5489
18	.488 318 7572	78	.044 776 2888	138	.004 105 7527
19	.469 255 2622	79	.043 028 2656	139	.003 945 4680
20	.450 935 9877	80	.041 348 4834	140	.003 791 4408
21	.433 331 8801	81	.039 734 2784	141	.003 643 4265
22	.416 415 0199	82	.038 183 0903	142	.003 501 1907
23	.400 158 5777	83	.036 692 4592	143	.003 364 5076
24	.384 536 7713	84	.035 260 0208	144	.003 233 1604
25	.369 524 8253	85	.033 883 5035	145	.003 106 9409
26	.355 098 9312	86	.032 560 7241	146	.002 985 6490
27	.341 236 2102	87	.031 289 5847	147	.002 869 0921
28	.327 914 6764	88	.030 068 0694	148	.002 757 0855
29	.315 113 2026	89	.028 894 2408	149	.002 649 4515
30	.302 811 4860	90	.027 766 2374	150	.002 546 0195
31	.290 990 0166	91	.026 682 2702	151	.002 446 6253
32	.279 630 0459	92	.025 640 6200	152	.002 351 1114
33	.268 713 5577	93	.024 639 6349	153	.002 259 3263
34	.258 223 2386	94	.023 677 7272	154	.002 171 1244
35	.248 142 4515	95	.022 753 3715	155	.002 086 3658
36	.238 455 2086	96	.021 865 1017	156	.002 004 9160
37	.229 146 1464	97	.021 011 5092	157	.001 926 6460
38	.220 200 5011	98	.020 191 2400	158	.001 851 4316
39	.211 604 0851	99	.019 402 9934	159	.001 779 1535
40	.203 343 2650	100	.018 645 5192	160	.001 709 6971
41	.195 404 9393	101	.017 917 6161	161	.001 642 9521
42	.187 776 5183	102	.017 218 1295	162	.001 578 8129
43	.180 445 9034	103	.016 545 9503	163	.001 517 1775
44	.173 401 4688	104	.015 900 0123	164	.001 457 9484
45	.166 632 0421	105	.015 279 2911	165	.001 401 0315
46	.160 126 8873	106	.014 682 8023	166	.001 346 3366
47	.153 875 6875	107	.014 109 5998	167	.001 293 7769
48	.147 868 5285	108	.013 558 7746	168	.001 243 2691
49	.142 095 8832	109	.013 029 4530	169	.001 194 7330
50	.136 548 5965	110	.012 520 7957	170	.001 148 0918
51	.131 217 8705	111	.012 031 9959	171	.001 103 2714
52	.126 095 2509	112	.011 562 2783	172	.001 060 2008
53	.121 172 6135	113	.011 110 8981	173	.001 018 8115
54	.116 442 1511	114	.010 677 1393	174	.000 979 0381
55	.111 896 3615	115	.010 260 3140	175	.000 940 8174
56	.107 528 0350	116	.009 859 7612	176	.000 904 0888
57	.103 330 2439	117	.009 474 8456	177	.000 868 7940
58	.099 296 3304	118	.009 104 9568	178	.000 834 8772
59	.095 419 8971	119	.008 749 5080	179	.000 802 2844
60	.091 694 7960	120	.008 407 9356	180	.000 770 9639

Present Value of 1

	NOMINAL INTEREST RATE COMPOUNDED	
YEARLY	HALF-YEARLY	QUARTERLY
@	@	@
$4\frac{1}{8}\%$	$8\frac{1}{4}\%$	$16\frac{1}{2}\%$
4.1250%	8.2500%	16.5000%
PER ANNUM	PER ANNUM	PER ANNUM

Periods	Present Value	Periods	Present Value	Periods	Present Value
1	.960 384 1537	61	.084 946 2322	121	.007 513 5167
2	.922 337 7226	62	.081 581 0154	122	.007 215 8624
3	.885 798 5331	63	.078 349 1144	123	.006 929 9999
4	.850 706 8745	64	.075 245 2479	124	.006 655 4621
5	.817 005 4017	65	.072 264 3437	125	.006 391 8003
6	.784 639 0413	66	.069 401 5306	126	.006 138 5837
7	.753 554 9016	67	.066 652 1302	127	.005 895 3985
8	.723 702 1864	68	.064 011 6497	128	.005 661 8473
9	.695 032 1118	69	.061 475 7740	129	.005 437 5485
10	.667 497 8264	70	.059 040 3592	130	.005 222 1354
11	.641 054 3351	71	.056 701 4254	131	.005 015 2561
12	.615 658 4251	72	.054 455 1504	132	.004 816 5724
13	.591 268 5955	73	.052 297 8636	133	.004 625 7599
14	.567 844 9897	74	.050 226 0394	134	.004 442 5065
15	.545 349 3298	75	.048 236 2924	135	.004 266 5128
16	.523 744 8546	76	.046 325 3708	136	.004 097 4913
17	.502 996 2589	77	.044 490 1521	137	.003 935 1657
18	.483 069 6364	78	.042 727 6370	138	.003 779 2708
19	.463 932 4239	79	.041 034 9455	139	.003 629 5518
20	.445 553 3483	80	.039 409 3114	140	.003 485 7640
21	.427 902 3753	81	.037 848 0782	141	.003 347 6725
22	.410 950 6606	82	.036 348 6946	142	.003 215 0516
23	.394 670 5023	83	.034 908 7103	143	.003 087 6846
24	.379 035 2964	84	.033 525 7722	144	.002 965 3634
25	.364 019 4923	85	.032 197 6203	145	.002 847 8880
26	.349 598 5520	86	.030 922 0843	146	.002 735 0665
27	.335 748 9095	87	.029 697 0798	147	.002 626 7146
28	.322 447 9323	88	.028 520 6048	148	.002 522 6550
29	.309 673 8846	89	.027 390 7369	149	.002 422 7179
30	.297 405 8915	90	.026 305 6297	150	.002 326 7399
31	.285 623 9054	91	.025 263 5099	151	.002 234 5641
32	.274 308 6727	92	.024 262 6746	152	.002 146 0400
33	.263 441 7025	93	.023 301 4882	153	.002 061 0228
34	.253 005 2365	94	.022 378 3800	154	.001 979 3736
35	.242 982 2199	95	.021 491 8416	155	.001 900 9591
36	.233 356 2736	96	.020 640 4241	156	.001 825 6510
37	.224 111 6673	97	.019 822 7362	157	.001 753 3263
38	.215 233 2940	98	.019 037 4417	158	.001 683 8668
39	.206 706 6449	99	.018 283 2574	159	.001 617 1589
40	.198 517 7862	100	.017 558 9507	160	.001 553 0938
41	.190 653 3361	101	.016 863 3380	161	.001 491 5667
42	.183 100 4428	102	.016 195 2826	162	.001 432 4770
43	.175 846 7638	103	.015 553 6927	163	.001 375 7282
44	.168 880 4454	104	.014 937 5200	164	.001 321 2276
45	.162 190 1036	105	.014 345 7575	165	.001 268 8860
46	.155 764 8054	106	.013 777 4382	166	.001 218 6181
47	.149 594 0508	107	.013 231 6333	167	.001 170 3415
48	.143 667 7559	108	.012 707 4510	168	.001 123 9774
49	.137 976 2362	109	.012 204 0346	169	.001 079 4501
50	.132 510 1908	110	.011 720 5614	170	.001 036 6868
51	.127 260 6874	111	.011 256 2414	171	.000 995 6175
52	.122 219 1476	112	.010 810 3159	172	.000 956 1753
53	.117 377 3326	113	.010 382 0561	173	.000 918 2956
54	.112 727 3302	114	.009 970 7622	174	.000 881 9165
55	.108 261 5417	115	.009 575 7620	175	.000 846 9787
56	.103 972 6691	116	.009 196 4101	176	.000 813 4249
57	.099 853 7038	117	.008 832 0865	177	.000 781 2004
58	.095 897 9148	118	.008 482 1959	178	.000 750 2525
59	.092 098 8377	119	.008 146 1665	179	.000 720 5306
60	.088 450 2643	120	.007 823 4493	180	.000 691 9862

Present Value of 1

NOMINAL INTEREST RATE COMPOUNDED

	YEARLY	HALF-YEARLY	QUARTERLY
	@	@	@
	$4\frac{3}{16}\%$	$8\frac{3}{8}\%$	$16\frac{3}{4}\%$
	4.1875%	8.3750%	16.7500%
	PER ANNUM	PER ANNUM	PER ANNUM

Periods	Present Value	Periods	Present Value	Periods	Present Value
1	.959 808 0384	61	.081 893 1078	121	.006 987 3150
2	.921 231 4706	62	.078 601 6631	122	.006 706 4811
3	.884 205 3707	63	.075 442 5081	123	.006 436 9345
4	.848 667 4224	64	.072 410 3257	124	.006 178 2214
5	.814 557 8139	65	.069 500 0127	125	.005 929 9066
6	.781 819 1375	66	.066 706 6708	126	.005 691 5720
7	.750 396 2928	67	.064 025 5989	127	.005 462 8166
8	.720 236 3938	68	.061 452 2845	128	.005 243 2553
9	.691 288 6803	69	.058 982 3966	129	.005 032 5186
10	.663 504 4322	70	.056 611 7784	130	.004 830 2518
11	.636 836 8875	71	.054 336 4400	131	.004 636 1145
12	.611 241 1638	72	.052 152 5519	132	.004 449 7799
13	.586 674 1824	73	.050 056 4385	133	.004 270 9345
14	.563 094 5962	74	.048 044 5720	134	.004 099 2773
15	.540 462 7198	75	.046 113 5664	135	.003 934 5193
16	.518 740 4629	76	.044 260 1718	136	.003 776 3833
17	.497 891 2661	77	.042 481 2686	137	.003 624 6030
18	.477 880 0395	78	.040 773 8631	138	.003 478 9231
19	.458 673 1033	79	.039 135 0816	139	.003 339 0984
20	.440 238 1315	80	.037 562 1659	140	.003 204 8935
21	.422 544 0974	81	.036 052 4687	141	.003 076 0825
22	.405 561 2213	82	.034 603 4493	142	.002 952 4487
23	.389 260 9203	83	.033 212 6688	143	.002 833 7840
24	.373 615 7603	84	.031 877 7865	144	.002 719 8887
25	.358 599 4100	85	.030 596 5557	145	.002 610 5710
26	.344 186 5963	86	.029 366 8201	146	.002 505 6470
27	.330 353 0618	87	.028 186 5100	147	.002 404 9402
28	.317 075 5242	88	.027 053 6389	148	.002 308 2809
29	.304 331 6370	89	.025 966 3001	149	.002 215 5066
30	.292 099 9515	90	.024 922 6635	150	.002 126 4610
31	.280 359 8814	91	.023 920 9728	151	.002 040 9944
32	.269 091 6679	92	.022 959 5420	152	.001 958 9628
33	.258 276 3459	93	.022 036 7530	153	.001 880 2282
34	.247 895 7129	94	.021 151 0526	154	.001 804 6582
35	.237 932 2979	95	.020 300 9503	155	.001 732 1254
36	.228 369 3321	96	.019 485 0153	156	.001 662 5079
37	.219 190 7207	97	.018 701 8743	157	.001 595 6885
38	.210 381 0157	98	.017 950 2093	158	.001 531 5546
39	.201 925 3900	99	.017 228 7552	159	.001 469 9984
40	.193 809 6124	100	.016 536 2977	160	.001 410 9163
41	.186 020 0239	101	.015 871 6715	161	.001 354 2088
42	.178 543 5143	102	.015 233 7579	162	.001 299 7805
43	.171 367 5002	103	.014 621 4833	163	.001 247 5398
44	.164 479 9042	104	.014 033 8172	164	.001 197 3987
45	.157 869 1342	105	.013 469 7705	165	.001 149 2729
46	.151 524 0640	106	.012 928 3940	166	.001 103 0814
47	.145 434 0147	107	.012 408 7765	167	.001 058 7464
48	.139 588 7363	108	.011 910 0434	168	.001 016 1933
49	.133 978 3912	109	.011 431 3554	169	.000 975 3505
50	.128 593 5369	110	.010 971 9068	170	.000 936 1492
51	.123 425 1104	111	.010 530 9244	171	.000 898 5235
52	.118 464 4131	112	.010 107 6659	172	.000 862 4101
53	.113 703 0959	113	.009 701 4189	173	.000 827 7482
54	.109 133 1455	114	.009 311 4999	174	.000 794 4793
55	.104 746 8703	115	.008 937 2524	175	.000 762 5477
56	.100 536 8881	116	.008 578 0467	176	.000 731 8994
57	.096 496 1133	117	.008 233 2782	177	.000 702 4829
58	.092 617 7452	118	.007 902 3666	178	.000 674 2487
59	.088 895 2564	119	.007 584 7550	179	.000 647 1494
60	.085 322 3817	120	.007 279 9088	180	.000 621 1392

Present Value of 1

NOMINAL INTEREST RATE COMPOUNDED

YEARLY	HALF-YEARLY	QUARTERLY
@	@	@
$4\frac{1}{4}\%$	$8\frac{1}{2}\%$	17%
4.2500%	8.5000%	17.0000%
PER ANNUM	PER ANNUM	PER ANNUM

Periods	Present Value	Periods	Present Value	Periods	Present Value
1	.959 232 6139	61	.078 951 4513	121	.006 498 2483
2	.920 127 2076	62	.075 732 8070	122	.006 233 3317
3	.882 616 0265	63	.072 645 3784	123	.005 979 2150
4	.846 634 0781	64	.069 683 8162	124	.005 735 4581
5	.812 119 0198	65	.066 842 9892	125	.005 501 6384
6	.779 011 0502	66	.064 117 9752	126	.005 277 3510
7	.747 252 8059	67	.061 504 0530	127	.005 062 2072
8	.716 789 2623	68	.058 996 6935	128	.004 855 8342
9	.687 567 6377	69	.056 591 5525	129	.004 657 8746
10	.659 537 3023	70	.054 284 4628	130	.004 467 9852
11	.632 649 6905	71	.052 071 4272	131	.004 285 8371
12	.606 858 2163	72	.049 948 6112	132	.004 111 1147
13	.582 118 1931	73	.047 912 3369	133	.003 943 5153
14	.558 386 7559	74	.045 959 0762	134	.003 782 7485
15	.535 622 7875	75	.044 085 4448	135	.003 628 5358
16	.513 786 8465	76	.042 288 1964	136	.003 480 6098
17	.492 841 0998	77	.040 564 2172	137	.003 338 7145
18	.472 749 2564	78	.038 910 5201	138	.003 202 6038
19	.453 476 5049	79	.037 324 2399	139	.003 072 0420
20	.434 989 4532	80	.035 802 6282	140	.002 946 8029
21	.417 256 0702	81	.034 343 0486	141	.002 826 6695
22	.400 245 6309	82	.032 942 9723	142	.002 711 4335
23	.383 928 6627	83	.031 599 9734	143	.002 600 8955
24	.368 276 8947	84	.030 311 7251	144	.002 494 8638
25	.353 263 2083	85	.029 075 9953	145	.002 393 1547
26	.338 861 5907	86	.027 890 6430	146	.002 295 5920
27	.325 047 0894	87	.026 753 6144	147	.002 202 0067
28	.311 795 7692	88	.025 662 9394	148	.002 112 2367
29	.299 084 6707	89	.024 616 7285	149	.002 026 1263
30	.286 891 7705	90	.023 613 1688	150	.001 943 5264
31	.275 195 9429	91	.022 650 5216	151	.001 864 2939
32	.263 976 9236	92	.021 727 1191	152	.001 788 2916
33	.253 215 2745	93	.020 841 3612	153	.001 715 3876
34	.242 892 3496	94	.019 991 7134	154	.001 645 4557
35	.232 990 2634	95	.019 176 7035	155	.001 578 3748
36	.223 491 8594	96	.018 394 9194	156	.001 514 0286
37	.214 380 6805	97	.017 645 0066	157	.001 452 3056
38	.205 640 9405	98	.016 925 6659	158	.001 393 0989
39	.197 257 4969	99	.016 235 6507	159	.001 336 3059
40	.189 215 8244	100	.015 573 7657	160	.001 281 8282
41	.181 501 9898	101	.014 938 8639	161	.001 229 5714
42	.174 102 6281	102	.014 329 8455	162	.001 179 4450
43	.167 004 9190	103	.013 745 6552	163	.001 131 3621
44	.160 196 5650	104	.013 185 2807	164	.001 085 2394
45	.153 665 7698	105	.012 647 7513	165	.001 040 9970
46	.147 401 2180	106	.012 132 1355	166	.000 998 5583
47	.141 392 0557	107	.011 637 5401	167	.000 957 8497
48	.135 627 8711	108	.011 163 1080	168	.000 918 8007
49	.130 098 6774	109	.010 708 0173	169	.000 881 3436
50	.124 794 8943	110	.010 271 4794	170	.000 845 4135
51	.119 707 3327	111	.009 852 7380	171	.000 810 9482
52	.114 827 1777	112	.009 451 0676	172	.000 777 8880
53	.110 145 9738	113	.009 065 7723	173	.000 746 1755
54	.105 655 6103	114	.008 696 1845	174	.000 715 7559
55	.101 348 3073	115	.008 341 6638	175	.000 686 5764
56	.097 216 6017	116	.008 001 5959	176	.000 658 5865
57	.093 253 3350	117	.007 675 3918	177	.000 631 7376
58	.089 451 6403	118	.007 362 4861	178	.000 605 9833
59	.085 804 9307	119	.007 062 3368	179	.000 581 2790
60	.082 306 8880	120	.006 774 4238	180	.000 557 5817

Present Value of 1

NOMINAL INTEREST RATE COMPOUNDED

YEARLY	HALF-YEARLY	QUARTERLY
@	@	@
$4\frac{5}{16}\%$	$8\frac{5}{8}\%$	$17\frac{1}{4}\%$
4.3125%	8.6250%	17.2500%
PER ANNUM	PER ANNUM	PER ANNUM

Periods	Present Value	Periods	Present Value	Periods	Present Value
1	.958 657 8790	61	.076 117 1300	121	.006 043 6759
2	.919 024 9289	62	.072 970 2864	122	.005 793 8175
3	.881 030 4891	63	.069 953 5399	123	.005 554 2888
4	.844 606 8200	64	.067 061 5122	124	.005 324 6627
5	.809 688 9826	65	.064 289 0471	125	.005 104 5298
6	.776 214 7227	66	.061 631 2015	126	.004 893 4978
7	.744 124 3597	67	.059 083 2369	127	.004 691 1902
8	.713 360 6803	68	.056 640 6106	128	.004 497 2464
9	.683 868 8367	69	.054 298 9676	129	.004 311 3207
10	.655 596 2485	70	.052 054 1331	130	.004 133 0816
11	.628 492 5091	71	.049 902 1048	131	.003 962 2112
12	.602 509 2957	72	.047 839 0460	132	.003 798 4050
13	.577 600 2835	73	.045 861 2784	133	.003 641 3709
14	.553 721 0626	74	.043 965 2758	134	.003 490 8289
15	.530 829 0594	75	.042 147 6581	135	.003 346 5106
16	.508 883 4602	76	.040 405 1845	136	.003 208 1588
17	.487 845 1386	77	.038 734 7485	137	.003 075 5267
18	.467 676 5859	78	.037 133 3718	138	.002 948 3779
19	.448 341 8438	79	.035 598 1995	139	.002 826 4857
20	.429 806 4411	80	.034 126 4944	140	.002 709 6328
21	.412 037 3312	81	.032 715 6327	141	.002 597 6108
22	.395 002 8340	82	.031 363 0991	142	.002 490 2201
23	.378 672 5790	83	.030 066 4820	143	.002 387 2691
24	.363 017 4514	84	.028 823 4699	144	.002 288 5743
25	.348 009 5400	85	.027 631 8465	145	.002 193 9598
26	.333 622 0875	86	.026 489 4874	146	.002 103 2569
27	.319 829 4427	87	.025 394 3558	147	.002 016 3038
28	.306 607 0152	88	.024 344 4993	148	.001 932 9455
29	.293 931 2309	89	.023 338 0460	149	.001 853 0334
30	.281 779 4904	90	.022 373 2017	150	.001 776 4251
31	.270 130 1286	91	.021 448 2461	151	.001 702 9839
32	.258 962 3761	92	.020 561 5301	152	.001 632 5789
33	.248 256 3222	93	.019 711 4728	153	.001 565 0847
34	.237 992 8793	94	.018 896 5587	154	.001 500 3807
35	.228 153 7489	95	.018 115 3349	155	.001 438 3518
36	.218 721 3890	96	.017 366 4086	156	.001 378 8873
37	.209 678 9828	97	.016 648 4444	157	.001 321 8812
38	.201 010 4089	98	.015 960 1624	158	.001 267 2318
39	.192 700 2123	99	.015 300 3354	159	.001 214 8418
40	.184 733 5768	100	.014 667 7871	160	.001 164 6176
41	.177 096 2989	101	.014 061 3897	161	.001 116 4699
42	.169 774 7623	102	.013 480 0620	162	.001 070 3126
43	.162 755 9135	103	.012 922 7676	163	.001 026 0636
44	.156 027 2388	104	.012 388 5130	164	.000 983 6440
45	.149 576 7418	105	.011 876 3456	165	.000 942 9781
46	.143 392 9221	106	.011 385 3523	166	.000 903 9933
47	.137 464 7545	107	.010 914 6577	167	.000 866 6203
48	.131 781 6700	108	.010 463 4226	168	.000 830 7924
49	.126 333 5363	109	.010 030 8425	169	.000 796 4457
50	.121 110 6399	110	.009 616 1462	170	.000 763 5189
51	.116 103 6692	111	.009 218 5943	171	.000 731 9534
52	.111 303 6972	112	.008 837 4781	172	.000 701 6929
53	.106 702 1663	113	.008 472 1180	173	.000 672 6835
54	.102 290 8724	114	.008 121 8627	174	.000 644 8733
55	.098 061 9508	115	.007 786 0876	175	.000 618 2129
56	.094 007 8618	116	.007 464 1943	176	.000 592 6546
57	.090 121 3774	117	.007 155 6086	177	.000 568 1530
58	.086 395 5685	118	.006 859 7806	178	.000 544 6644
59	.082 823 7924	119	.006 576 1827	179	.000 522 1468
60	.079 399 6812	120	.006 304 3094	180	.000 500 5602

Present Value of 1

NOMINAL INTEREST RATE COMPOUNDED

YEARLY	HALF-YEARLY	QUARTERLY
@	@	@
$4\frac{3}{8}\%$	$8\frac{3}{4}\%$	$17\frac{1}{2}\%$
4.3750%	8.7500%	17.5000%
PER ANNUM	PER ANNUM	PER ANNUM

Periods	Present Value	Periods	Present Value	Periods	Present Value
1	.958 083 8323	61	.073 386 1665	121	.005 621 1463
2	.917 924 6298	62	.070 310 0997	122	.005 385 5294
3	.879 448 7471	63	.067 362 9697	123	.005 159 7887
4	.842 585 6260	64	.064 539 3722	124	.004 943 5101
5	.807 267 6656	65	.061 834 1291	125	.004 736 2971
6	.773 430 0988	66	.059 242 2793	126	.004 537 7697
7	.741 010 8731	67	.056 759 0700	127	.004 347 5638
8	.709 950 5371	68	.054 379 9473	128	.004 165 3306
9	.680 192 1313	69	.052 100 5483	129	.003 990 7359
10	.651 681 0839	70	.049 916 6930	130	.003 823 4595
11	.624 365 1103	71	.047 824 3765	131	.003 663 1947
12	.598 194 1177	72	.045 819 7620	132	.003 509 6477
13	.573 120 1128	73	.043 899 1731	133	.003 362 5367
14	.549 097 1140	74	.042 059 0880	134	.003 221 5920
15	.526 081 0673	75	.040 296 1322	135	.003 086 5552
16	.504 029 7651	76	.038 607 0728	136	.002 957 1787
17	.482 902 7690	77	.036 988 8123	137	.002 833 2251
18	.462 661 3355	78	.035 438 3830	138	.002 714 4671
19	.443 268 3454	79	.033 952 9418	139	.002 600 6871
20	.424 688 2351	80	.032 529 7646	140	.002 491 6762
21	.406 886 9319	81	.031 166 2415	141	.002 387 2347
22	.389 831 7910	82	.029 859 8721	142	.002 287 1710
23	.373 491 5363	83	.028 608 2607	143	.002 191 3015
24	.357 836 2024	84	.027 409 1121	144	.002 099 4506
25	.342 837 0802	85	.026 260 2271	145	.002 011 4497
26	.328 466 6636	86	.025 159 4991	146	.001 927 1374
27	.314 698 5999	87	.024 104 9093	147	.001 846 3592
28	.301 507 6406	88	.023 094 5239	148	.001 768 9669
29	.288 869 5958	89	.022 126 4899	149	.001 694 8186
30	.276 761 2894	90	.021 199 0323	150	.001 623 7783
31	.265 160 5168	91	.020 310 4501	151	.001 555 7157
32	.254 046 0041	92	.019 459 1138	152	.001 490 5061
33	.243 397 3692	93	.018 643 4624	153	.001 428 0298
34	.233 195 0843	94	.017 861 9999	154	.001 368 1722
35	.223 420 4400	95	.017 113 2933	155	.001 310 8237
36	.214 055 5114	96	.016 395 9696	156	.001 255 8790
37	.205 083 1247	97	.015 708 7134	157	.001 203 2374
38	.196 486 8260	98	.015 050 2643	158	.001 152 8023
39	.188 250 8513	99	.014 419 4149	159	.001 104 4812
40	.180 360 0971	100	.013 815 0083	160	.001 058 1856
41	.172 800 0930	101	.013 235 9361	161	.001 013 8305
42	.165 556 9753	102	.012 681 1364	162	.000 971 3346
43	.158 617 4614	103	.012 149 5918	163	.000 930 6200
44	.151 968 8253	104	.011 640 3274	164	.000 891 6120
45	.145 598 8745	105	.011 152 4095	165	.000 854 2390
46	.139 495 9277	106	.010 684 9433	166	.000 818 4326
47	.133 648 7930	107	.010 237 0714	167	.000 784 1270
48	.128 046 7478	108	.009 807 9726	168	.000 751 2594
49	.122 679 5188	109	.009 396 8600	169	.000 719 7695
50	.117 537 2635	110	.009 002 9796	170	.000 689 5995
51	.112 610 5519	111	.008 625 6092	171	.000 660 6942
52	.107 890 3491	112	.008 264 0567	172	.000 633 0004
53	.103 367 9992	113	.007 917 6591	173	.000 606 4674
54	.099 035 2088	114	.007 585 7812	174	.000 581 0467
55	.094 884 0324	115	.007 267 8143	175	.000 556 6914
56	.090 906 8574	116	.006 963 1754	176	.000 533 3570
57	.087 096 3903	117	.006 671 3058	177	.000 511 0007
58	.083 445 6434	118	.006 391 6702	178	.000 489 5816
59	.079 947 9218	119	.006 123 7559	179	.000 469 0602
60	.076 596 8113	120	.005 867 0715	180	.000 449 3990

Present Value of 1

NOMINAL INTEREST RATE COMPOUNDED

	YEARLY @ $4\frac{7}{16}\%$ 4.4375% PER ANNUM		HALF-YEARLY @ $8\frac{7}{8}\%$ 8.8750% PER ANNUM		QUARTERLY @ $17\frac{3}{4}\%$ 17.7500% PER ANNUM
Periods	Present Value	Periods	Present Value	Periods	Present Value
1	.957 510 4728	61	.070 754 7333	121	.005 228 3838
2	.916 826 3055	62	.067 748 3982	122	.005 006 2323
3	.877 870 7892	63	.064 869 8008	123	.004 793 5198
4	.840 570 4744	64	.062 113 5136	124	.004 589 8455
5	.804 855 0323	65	.059 474 3398	125	.004 394 8251
6	.770 657 1225	66	.056 947 3032	126	.004 208 0911
7	.737 912 2657	67	.054 527 6392	127	.004 029 2913
8	.706 558 7224	68	.052 210 7856	128	.003 858 0886
9	.676 537 3763	69	.049 992 3740	129	.003 694 1602
10	.647 791 6231	70	.047 868 2217	130	.003 537 1971
11	.620 267 2633	71	.045 834 3235	131	.003 386 9033
12	.593 912 4005	72	.043 886 8448	132	.003 242 9953
13	.568 677 3434	73	.042 022 1135	133	.003 105 2020
14	.544 514 5119	74	.040 236 6138	134	.002 973 2634
15	.521 378 3477	75	.038 526 9791	135	.002 846 9309
16	.499 225 2282	76	.036 889 9860	136	.002 725 9661
17	.478 013 3843	77	.035 322 5479	137	.002 610 1411
18	.457 702 8216	78	.033 821 7095	138	.002 499 2375
19	.438 255 2451	79	.032 384 6411	139	.002 393 0460
20	.419 633 9869	80	.031 008 6330	140	.002 291 3666
21	.401 803 9372	81	.029 691 0908	141	.002 194 0076
22	.384 731 4779	82	.028 429 5304	142	.002 100 7852
23	.368 384 4193	83	.027 221 5731	143	.002 011 5238
24	.352 731 9395	84	.026 064 9414	144	.001 926 0551
25	.337 744 5261	85	.024 957 4543	145	.001 844 2180
26	.323 393 9209	86	.023 897 0239	146	.001 765 8580
27	.309 653 0661	87	.022 881 6506	147	.001 690 8276
28	.296 496 0537	88	.021 909 4201	148	.001 618 9851
29	.283 898 0765	89	.020 978 4992	149	.001 550 1952
30	.271 835 3815	90	.020 087 1327	150	.001 484 3281
31	.260 285 2246	91	.019 233 6399	151	.001 421 2597
32	.249 225 8285	92	.018 416 4117	152	.001 360 8711
33	.238 636 3409	93	.017 633 9070	153	.001 303 0483
34	.228 496 7956	94	.016 884 6507	154	.001 247 6824
35	.218 788 0748	95	.016 167 2298	155	.001 194 6690
36	.209 491 8729	96	.015 480 2919	156	.001 143 9080
37	.200 590 6623	97	.014 822 5416	157	.001 095 3039
38	.192 067 6599	98	.014 192 7388	158	.001 048 7650
39	.183 906 7958	99	.013 589 6961	159	.001 004 2035
40	.176 092 6830	100	.013 012 2763	160	.000 961 5353
41	.168 610 5881	101	.012 459 3908	161	.000 920 6801
42	.161 446 4040	102	.011 929 9972	162	.000 881 5609
43	.154 586 6226	103	.011 423 0973	163	.000 844 1038
44	.148 018 3101	104	.010 937 7353	164	.000 808 2382
45	.141 729 0821	105	.010 472 9961	165	.000 773 8965
46	.135 707 0804	106	.010 028 0034	166	.000 741 0140
47	.129 940 9507	107	.009 601 9183	167	.000 709 5287
48	.124 419 8211	108	.009 193 9373	168	.000 679 3812
49	.119 133 2817	109	.008 803 2913	169	.000 650 5146
50	.114 071 3649	110	.008 429 2436	170	.000 622 8745
51	.109 224 5266	111	.008 071 0890	171	.000 596 4089
52	.104 583 6281	112	.007 728 1523	172	.000 571 0678
53	.100 139 9191	113	.007 399 7867	173	.000 546 8034
54	.095 885 0213	114	.007 085 3733	174	.000 523 5699
55	.091 810 9121	115	.006 784 3191	175	.000 501 3237
56	.087 909 9099	116	.006 496 0566	176	.000 480 0227
57	.084 174 6593	117	.006 220 0422	177	.000 459 6268
58	.080 598 1179	118	.005 955 7556	178	.000 440 0974
59	.077 173 5419	119	.005 702 6983	179	.000 421 3979
60	.073 894 4746	120	.005 460 3934	180	.000 403 4929

Present Value of 1

NOMINAL INTEREST RATE COMPOUNDED

YEARLY	HALF-YEARLY	QUARTERLY
@	@	@
$4\frac{1}{2}\%$	9%	18%
4.5000%	9.0000%	18.0000%
PER ANNUM	PER ANNUM	PER ANNUM

Periods	Present Value	Periods	Present Value	Periods	Present Value
1	.956 937 7990	61	.068 219 1467	121	.004 863 2753
2	.915 729 9512	62	.065 281 4801	122	.004 653 8520
3	.876 296 6041	63	.062 470 3159	123	.004 453 4469
4	.838 561 3436	64	.059 780 2066	124	.004 261 6716
5	.802 451 0465	65	.057 205 9393	125	.004 078 1547
6	.767 895 7383	66	.054 742 5256	126	.003 902 5404
7	.734 828 4577	67	.052 385 1920	127	.003 734 4884
8	.703 185 1270	68	.050 129 3703	128	.003 573 6731
9	.672 904 4277	69	.047 970 6893	129	.003 419 7829
10	.643 927 6820	70	.045 904 9659	130	.003 272 5195
11	.616 198 7388	71	.043 928 1970	131	.003 131 5976
12	.589 663 8649	72	.042 036 5521	132	.002 996 7441
13	.564 271 6410	73	.040 226 3657	133	.002 867 6977
14	.539 972 8622	74	.038 494 1298	134	.002 744 2083
15	.516 720 4423	75	.036 836 4879	135	.002 626 0367
16	.494 469 3228	76	.035 250 2276	136	.002 512 9538
17	.473 176 3854	77	.033 732 2753	137	.002 404 7405
18	.452 800 3688	78	.032 279 6892	138	.002 301 1870
19	.433 301 7884	79	.030 889 6548	139	.002 202 0929
20	.414 642 8597	80	.029 559 4783	140	.002 107 2659
21	.396 787 4255	81	.028 286 5821	141	.002 016 5224
22	.379 700 8857	82	.027 068 4996	142	.001 929 6865
23	.363 350 1298	83	.025 902 8704	143	.001 846 5899
24	.347 703 4735	84	.024 787 4358	144	.001 767 0717
25	.332 730 5967	85	.023 720 0343	145	.001 690 9777
26	.318 402 4849	86	.022 698 5974	146	.001 618 1605
27	.304 691 3731	87	.021 721 1458	147	.001 548 4789
28	.291 570 6919	88	.020 785 7855	148	.001 481 7980
29	.279 015 0162	89	.019 890 7038	149	.001 417 9885
30	.267 000 0155	90	.019 034 1663	150	.001 356 9268
31	.255 502 4072	91	.018 214 5132	151	.001 298 4946
32	.244 499 9112	92	.017 430 1562	152	.001 242 5785
33	.233 971 2069	93	.016 679 5753	153	.001 189 0704
34	.223 895 8917	94	.015 961 3161	154	.001 137 8664
35	.214 254 4419	95	.015 273 9867	155	.001 088 8674
36	.205 028 1740	96	.014 616 2552	156	.001 041 9783
37	.196 199 2096	97	.013 986 8471	157	.000 997 1085
38	.187 750 4398	98	.013 384 5427	158	.000 954 1708
39	.179 665 4926	99	.012 808 1748	159	.000 913 0821
40	.171 928 7011	100	.012 256 6266	160	.000 873 7628
41	.164 525 0728	101	.011 728 8293	161	.000 836 1366
42	.157 440 2611	102	.011 223 7601	162	.000 800 1307
43	.150 660 5369	103	.010 740 4403	163	.000 765 6753
44	.144 172 7626	104	.010 277 9333	164	.000 732 7037
45	.137 964 3661	105	.009 835 3428	165	.000 701 1518
46	.132 023 3169	106	.009 411 8113	166	.000 670 9587
47	.126 338 1023	107	.009 006 5180	167	.000 642 0657
48	.120 897 7055	108	.008 618 6775	168	.000 614 4170
49	.115 691 5842	109	.008 247 5383	169	.000 587 9588
50	.110 709 6500	110	.007 892 3812	170	.000 562 6400
51	.105 942 2488	111	.007 552 5178	171	.000 538 4115
52	.101 380 1424	112	.007 227 2898	172	.000 515 2263
53	.097 014 4903	113	.006 916 0668	173	.000 493 0395
54	.092 836 8328	114	.006 618 2457	174	.000 471 8082
55	.088 839 0745	115	.006 333 2495	175	.000 451 4911
56	.085 013 4684	116	.006 060 5259	176	.000 432 0489
57	.081 352 6013	117	.005 799 5463	177	.000 413 4439
58	.077 849 3793	118	.005 549 8050	178	.000 395 6401
59	.074 497 0137	119	.005 310 8182	179	.000 378 6030
60	.071 289 0083	120	.005 082 1227	180	.000 362 2995

Present Value of 1

NOMINAL INTEREST RATE COMPOUNDED

YEARLY	HALF-YEARLY	QUARTERLY
@	@	@
$4\frac{9}{16}\%$	$9\frac{1}{8}\%$	$18\frac{1}{4}\%$
4.5625%	9.1250%	18.2500%
PER ANNUM	PER ANNUM	PER ANNUM

Periods	Present Value	Periods	Present Value	Periods	Present Value
1	.956 365 8099	61	.065 775 8612	121	.004 523 8588
2	.914 635 5624	62	.062 905 7848	122	.004 326 4639
3	.874 726 1804	63	.060 160 9418	123	.004 137 6822
4	.836 558 2120	64	.057 535 8679	124	.003 957 1378
5	.800 055 6720	65	.055 025 3369	125	.003 784 4713
6	.765 145 8907	66	.052 624 3509	126	.003 619 3389
7	.731 759 3695	67	.050 328 1299	127	.003 461 4120
8	.699 829 6420	68	.048 132 1028	128	.003 310 3761
9	.669 293 1424	69	.046 031 8974	129	.003 165 9305
10	.640 089 0782	70	.044 023 3329	130	.003 027 7877
11	.612 159 3097	71	.042 102 4104	131	.002 895 6726
12	.585 448 2340	72	.040 265 3058	132	.002 769 3223
13	.559 902 6745	73	.038 508 3618	133	.002 648 4852
14	.535 471 7748	74	.036 828 0806	134	.002 532 9207
15	.512 106 8976	75	.035 221 1172	135	.002 422 3987
16	.489 761 5279	76	.033 684 2722	136	.002 316 6993
17	.468 391 1803	77	.032 214 4863	137	.002 215 6120
18	.447 953 3105	78	.030 808 8333	138	.002 118 9356
19	.428 407 2306	79	.029 464 5148	139	.002 026 4775
20	.409 714 0281	80	.028 178 8546	140	.001 938 0538
21	.391 836 4883	81	.026 949 2931	141	.001 853 4884
22	.374 739 0205	82	.025 773 3825	142	.001 772 6130
23	.358 387 5868	83	.024 648 7818	143	.001 695 2664
24	.342 749 6347	84	.023 573 2522	144	.001 621 2949
25	.327 794 0320	85	.022 544 6524	145	.001 550 5510
26	.313 491 0049	86	.021 560 9348	146	.001 482 8939
27	.299 812 0788	87	.020 620 1408	147	.001 418 1891
28	.286 730 0216	88	.019 720 3977	148	.001 356 3075
29	.274 218 7893	89	.018 859 9141	149	.001 297 1261
30	.262 253 4746	90	.018 036 9770	150	.001 240 5271
31	.250 810 2566	91	.017 249 9482	151	.001 186 3977
32	.239 866 3542	92	.016 497 2606	152	.001 134 6302
33	.229 399 9801	93	.015 777 4160	153	.001 085 1215
34	.219 390 2978	94	.015 088 9813	154	.001 037 7731
35	.209 817 3798	95	.014 430 5858	155	.000 992 4907
36	.200 662 1684	96	.013 800 9189	156	.000 949 1842
37	.191 906 4372	97	.013 198 7269	157	.000 907 7673
38	.183 532 7552	98	.012 622 8112	158	.000 868 1576
39	.175 524 4521	99	.012 072 0250	159	.000 830 2763
40	.167 865 5848	100	.011 545 2720	160	.000 794 0478
41	.160 540 9060	101	.011 041 5034	161	.000 759 4002
42	.153 535 8336	102	.010 559 7164	162	.000 726 2644
43	.146 836 4218	103	.010 098 9517	163	.000 694 5744
44	.140 429 3335	104	.009 658 2921	164	.000 664 2672
45	.134 301 8132	105	.009 236 8604	165	.000 635 2825
46	.128 441 6624	106	.008 833 8174	166	.000 607 5624
47	.122 837 2145	107	.008 448 3610	167	.000 581 0519
48	.117 477 3121	108	.008 079 7236	168	.000 555 6982
49	.112 351 2847	109	.007 727 1714	169	.000 531 4508
50	.107 448 9274	110	.007 390 0025	170	.000 508 2614
51	.102 760 4805	111	.007 067 5457	171	.000 486 0838
52	.098 276 6102	112	.006 759 1591	172	.000 464 8739
53	.093 988 3899	113	.006 464 2287	173	.000 444 5895
54	.089 887 2826	114	.006 182 1673	174	.000 425 1902
55	.085 965 1238	115	.005 912 4134	175	.000 406 6374
56	.082 214 1053	116	.005 654 4301	176	.000 388 8941
57	.078 626 7594	117	.005 407 7036	177	.000 371 9250
58	.075 195 9444	118	.005 171 7428	178	.000 355 6964
59	.071 914 8303	119	.004 946 0780	179	.000 340 1758
60	.068 776 8849	120	.004 730 2599	180	.000 325 3325

Present Value of 1

NOMINAL INTEREST RATE COMPOUNDED

YEARLY	HALF-YEARLY	QUARTERLY
@	@	@
$4\frac{5}{8}\%$	$9\frac{1}{4}\%$	$18\frac{1}{2}\%$
4.6250%	9.2500%	18.5000%
PER ANNUM	PER ANNUM	PER ANNUM

Periods	Present Value	Periods	Present Value	Periods	Present Value
1	.955 794 5042	61	.063 421 4649	121	.004 208 3128
2	.913 543 1342	62	.060 617 8876	122	.004 022 2822
3	.873 159 5070	63	.057 938 2438	123	.003 844 4752
4	.834 561 0581	64	.055 377 0550	124	.003 674 5283
5	.797 668 8727	65	.052 929 0848	125	.003 512 0939
6	.762 407 5247	66	.050 589 3284	126	.003 356 8401
7	.728 704 9221	67	.048 353 0020	127	.003 208 4493
8	.696 492 1597	68	.046 215 5336	128	.003 066 6182
9	.665 703 3784	69	.044 172 5530	129	.002 931 0568
10	.636 275 6305	70	.042 219 8834	130	.002 801 4880
11	.608 148 7508	71	.040 353 5326	131	.002 677 6469
12	.581 265 2337	72	.038 569 6846	132	.002 559 2801
13	.555 570 1159	73	.036 864 6926	133	.002 446 1459
14	.531 010 8634	74	.035 235 0706	134	.002 338 0128
15	.507 537 2649	75	.033 677 4868	135	.002 234 6598
16	.485 101 3285	76	.032 188 7568	136	.002 135 8755
17	.463 657 1837	77	.030 765 8369	137	.002 041 4581
18	.443 160 9880	78	.029 405 8178	138	.001 951 2144
19	.423 570 8368	79	.028 105 9190	139	.001 864 9600
20	.404 846 6780	80	.026 863 4830	140	.001 782 5186
21	.386 950 2299	81	.025 675 9694	141	.001 703 7214
22	.369 844 9031	82	.024 540 9504	142	.001 628 4076
23	.353 495 7258	83	.023 456 1055	143	.001 556 4230
24	.337 869 2719	84	.022 419 2168	144	.001 487 6206
25	.322 933 5933	85	.021 428 1642	145	.001 421 8596
26	.308 658 1536	86	.020 480 9215	146	.001 359 0056
27	.295 013 7669	87	.019 575 5523	147	.001 298 9300
28	.281 972 5371	88	.018 710 2053	148	.001 241 5102
29	.269 507 8013	89	.017 883 1114	149	.001 186 6286
30	.257 594 0753	90	.017 092 5796	150	.001 134 1731
31	.246 207 0015	91	.016 336 9936	151	.001 084 0364
32	.235 323 2989	92	.015 614 8087	152	.001 036 1161
33	.224 920 7158	93	.014 924 5483	153	.000 990 3140
34	.214 977 9840	94	.014 264 8013	154	.000 946 5367
35	.205 474 7757	95	.013 634 2187	155	.000 904 6946
36	.196 391 6613	96	.013 031 5113	156	.000 864 7021
37	.187 710 0706	97	.012 455 4469	157	.000 826 4775
38	.179 412 2538	98	.011 904 8476	158	.000 789 9427
39	.171 481 2462	99	.011 378 5880	159	.000 755 0229
40	.163 900 8327	100	.010 875 5918	160	.000 721 6467
41	.156 655 5151	101	.010 394 8309	161	.000 689 7460
42	.149 730 4804	102	.009 935 3222	162	.000 659 2554
43	.143 111 5703	103	.009 496 1264	163	.000 630 1127
44	.136 785 2523	104	.009 076 3454	164	.000 602 2582
45	.130 738 5924	105	.008 675 1211	165	.000 575 6351
46	.124 959 2281	106	.008 291 6330	166	.000 550 1889
47	.119 435 3435	107	.007 925 0973	167	.000 525 8675
48	.114 155 6449	108	.007 574 7644	168	.000 502 6213
49	.109 109 3380	109	.007 239 9182	169	.000 480 4027
50	.104 286 1057	110	.006 919 8741	170	.000 459 1662
51	.099 676 0866	111	.006 613 9776	171	.000 438 8685
52	.095 269 8558	112	.006 321 6034	172	.000 419 4681
53	.091 058 4046	113	.006 042 1538	173	.000 400 9253
54	.087 033 1227	114	.005 775 0574	174	.000 383 2022
55	.083 185 7803	115	.005 519 7681	175	.000 366 2626
56	.079 508 5117	116	.005 275 7640	176	.000 350 0718
57	.075 993 7985	117	.005 042 5463	177	.000 334 5967
58	.072 634 4549	118	.004 819 6380	178	.000 319 8057
59	.069 423 6129	119	.004 606 5835	179	.000 305 6685
60	.066 354 7076	120	.004 402 9472	180	.000 292 1563

Present Value of 1

NOMINAL INTEREST RATE COMPOUNDED

YEARLY	HALF-YEARLY	QUARTERLY
@	@	@
$4\frac{11}{16}\%$	$9\frac{3}{8}\%$	$18\frac{3}{4}\%$
4.6875%	9.3750%	18.7500%
PER ANNUM	PER ANNUM	PER ANNUM

Periods	Present Value	Periods	Present Value	Periods	Present Value
1	.955 223 8806	61	.061 152 6735	121	.003 914 9455
2	.912 452 6621	62	.058 414 4941	122	.003 739 6495
3	.871 596 5727	63	.055 798 9197	123	.003 572 2025
4	.832 569 8605	64	.053 300 4606	124	.003 412 2531
5	.795 290 6130	65	.050 913 8728	125	.003 259 4657
6	.759 680 5856	66	.048 634 1472	126	.003 113 5194
7	.725 665 0370	67	.046 456 4988	127	.002 974 1081
8	.693 172 5726	68	.044 376 3571	128	.002 840 9391
9	.662 134 9947	69	.042 389 3560	129	.002 713 7329
10	.632 487 1592	70	.040 491 3251	130	.002 592 2224
11	.604 166 8386	71	.038 678 2807	131	.002 476 1528
12	.577 114 5921	72	.036 946 4174	132	.002 365 2803
13	.551 273 6402	73	.035 292 1002	133	.002 259 3722
14	.526 589 7459	74	.033 711 8569	134	.002 158 2063
15	.503 011 1005	75	.032 202 3708	135	.002 061 5702
16	.480 488 2154	76	.030 760 4736	136	.001 969 2611
17	.458 973 8177	77	.029 383 1389	137	.001 881 0852
18	.438 422 7513	78	.028 067 4760	138	.001 796 8575
19	.418 791 8818	79	.026 810 7234	139	.001 716 4012
20	.400 040 0065	80	.025 610 2432	140	.001 639 5474
21	.382 127 7674	81	.024 463 5159	141	.001 566 1348
22	.365 017 5689	82	.023 368 1346	142	.001 496 0094
23	.348 673 4986	83	.022 321 8002	143	.001 429 0239
24	.333 061 2524	84	.021 322 3166	144	.001 365 0378
25	.318 148 0620	85	.020 367 5860	145	.001 303 9167
26	.303 902 6264	86	.019 455 6046	146	.001 245 5323
27	.290 295 0461	87	.018 584 4581	147	.001 189 7622
28	.277 296 7605	88	.017 752 3182	148	.001 136 4893
29	.264 880 4876	89	.016 957 4382	149	.001 085 6017
30	.253 020 1673	90	.016 198 1500	150	.001 036 9927
31	.241 690 9060	91	.015 472 8597	151	.000 990 5602
32	.230 868 9252	92	.014 780 0451	152	.000 946 2067
33	.220 531 5106	93	.014 118 2520	153	.000 903 8393
34	.210 656 9654	94	.013 486 0915	154	.000 863 3689
35	.201 224 5639	95	.012 882 2366	155	.000 824 7105
36	.192 214 5088	96	.012 305 4201	156	.000 787 7832
37	.183 607 8890	97	.011 754 4311	157	.000 752 5093
38	.175 386 6403	98	.011 228 1133	158	.000 718 8149
39	.167 533 5071	99	.010 725 3619	159	.000 686 6291
40	.160 032 0068	100	.010 245 1219	160	.000 655 8846
41	.152 866 3946	101	.009 786 3851	161	.000 626 5166
42	.146 021 6306	102	.009 348 1887	162	.000 598 4636
43	.139 483 3487	103	.008 929 6131	163	.000 571 6667
44	.133 237 8256	104	.008 529 7797	164	.000 546 0697
45	.127 271 9528	105	.008 147 8492	165	.000 521 6188
46	.121 573 2086	106	.007 783 0202	166	.000 498 2628
47	.116 129 6321	107	.007 434 5267	167	.000 475 9525
48	.110 929 7979	108	.007 101 6375	168	.000 454 6412
49	.105 962 7920	109	.006 783 6537	169	.000 434 2841
50	.101 218 1894	110	.006 479 9080	170	.000 414 8386
51	.096 686 0316	111	.006 189 7629	171	.000 396 2637
52	.092 356 8063	112	.005 912 6093	172	.000 378 5205
53	.088 221 4269	113	.005 647 8656	173	.000 361 5719
54	.084 271 2138	114	.005 394 9761	174	.000 345 3821
55	.080 497 8759	115	.005 153 4100	175	.000 329 9172
56	.076 893 4934	116	.004 922 6603	176	.000 315 1448
57	.073 450 5011	117	.004 702 2427	177	.000 301 0338
58	.070 161 6727	118	.004 491 6945	178	.000 287 5547
59	.067 020 1053	119	.004 290 5739	179	.000 274 6791
60	.064 019 2050	120	.004 098 4586	180	.000 262 3801

Present Value of 1

NOMINAL INTEREST RATE COMPOUNDED

YEARLY	HALF-YEARLY	QUARTERLY
@	@	@
$4\frac{3}{4}\%$	$9\frac{1}{2}\%$	19%
4.7500%	9.5000%	19.0000%
PER ANNUM	PER ANNUM	PER ANNUM

Periods	Present Value	Periods	Present Value	Periods	Present Value
1	.954 653 9379	61	.058 966 3261	121	.003 642 1864
2	.911 364 1412	62	.056 292 4354	122	.003 477 0276
3	.870 037 3663	63	.053 739 7952	123	.003 319 3581
4	.830 584 5979	64	.051 302 9071	124	.003 168 8383
5	.792 920 8572	65	.048 976 5223	125	.003 025 1440
6	.756 965 0188	66	.046 755 6299	126	.002 887 9656
7	.722 639 6361	67	.044 635 4462	127	.002 757 0077
8	.689 870 7743	68	.042 611 4045	128	.002 631 9883
9	.658 587 8514	69	.040 679 1451	129	.002 512 6380
10	.628 723 4858	70	.038 834 5060	130	.002 398 6997
11	.600 213 3516	71	.037 073 5141	131	.002 289 9281
12	.572 996 0397	72	.035 392 3762	132	.002 186 0889
13	.547 012 9257	73	.033 787 4713	133	.002 086 9584
14	.522 208 0437	74	.032 255 3426	134	.001 992 3231
15	.498 527 9653	75	.030 792 6898	135	.001 901 9790
16	.475 921 6853	76	.029 396 3626	136	.001 815 7318
17	.454 340 5110	77	.028 063 3533	137	.001 733 3955
18	.433 737 9580	78	.026 790 7907	138	.001 654 7928
19	.414 069 6496	79	.025 575 9339	139	.001 579 7545
20	.395 293 2216	80	.024 416 1660	140	.001 508 1189
21	.377 368 2307	81	.023 308 9890	141	.001 439 7316
22	.360 256 0675	82	.022 252 0182	142	.001 374 4454
23	.343 919 8735	83	.021 242 9768	143	.001 312 1198
24	.328 324 4615	84	.020 279 6914	144	.001 252 6203
25	.313 436 2401	85	.019 360 0873	145	.001 195 8189
26	.299 223 1409	86	.018 482 1836	146	.001 141 5932
27	.285 654 5498	87	.017 644 0893	147	.001 089 8265
28	.272 701 2409	88	.016 843 9993	148	.001 040 4071
29	.260 335 3135	89	.016 080 1903	149	.000 993 2288
30	.248 530 1322	90	.015 351 0170	150	.000 948 1897
31	.237 260 2694	91	.014 654 9088	151	.000 905 1931
32	.226 501 4505	92	.013 990 3664	152	.000 864 1461
33	.216 230 5017	93	.013 355 9584	153	.000 824 9605
34	.206 425 2999	94	.012 750 3183	154	.000 787 5518
35	.197 064 7255	95	.012 172 1416	155	.000 751 8394
36	.188 128 6162	96	.011 620 1829	156	.000 717 7465
37	.179 597 7243	97	.011 093 2533	157	.000 685 1995
38	.171 453 6748	98	.010 590 2180	158	.000 654 1284
39	.163 678 9258	99	.010 109 9933	159	.000 624 4662
40	.156 256 7311	100	.009 651 5449	160	.000 596 1492
41	.149 171 1036	101	.009 213 8854	161	.000 569 1161
42	.142 406 7815	102	.008 796 0719	162	.000 543 3090
43	.135 949 1948	103	.008 397 2047	163	.000 518 6720
44	.129 784 4341	104	.008 016 4246	164	.000 495 1523
45	.123 899 2211	105	.007 652 9113	165	.000 472 6991
46	.118 280 8794	106	.007 305 8819	166	.000 451 2641
47	.112 917 3073	107	.006 974 5889	167	.000 430 8010
48	.107 796 9520	108	.006 658 3188	168	.000 411 2659
49	.102 908 7848	109	.006 356 3902	169	.000 392 6166
50	.098 242 2766	110	.006 068 1530	170	.000 374 8130
51	.093 787 3763	111	.005 792 9861	171	.000 357 8167
52	.089 534 4881	112	.005 530 2970	172	.000 341 5911
53	.085 474 4516	113	.005 279 5198	173	.000 326 1013
54	.081 598 5218	114	.005 040 1144	174	.000 311 3139
55	.077 898 3502	115	.004 811 5650	175	.000 297 1970
56	.074 365 9668	116	.004 593 3795	176	.000 283 7203
57	.070 993 7630	117	.004 385 0878	177	.000 270 8547
58	.067 774 4754	118	.004 186 2414	178	.000 258 5725
59	.064 701 1699	119	.003 996 4118	179	.000 246 8473
60	.061 767 2266	120	.003 815 1903	180	.000 235 6537

Present Value of 1

NOMINAL INTEREST RATE COMPOUNDED

	YEARLY		HALF-YEARLY		QUARTERLY
	@		@		@
	$4\frac{13}{16}\%$		$9\frac{5}{8}\%$		$19\frac{1}{4}\%$
	4.8125%		9.6250%		19.2500%
	PER ANNUM		PER ANNUM		PER ANNUM

Periods	Present Value	Periods	Present Value	Periods	Present Value
1	.954 084 6750	61	.056 859 3804	121	.003 388 5767
2	.910 277 5671	62	.054 248 6635	122	.003 232 9891
3	.868 481 8768	63	.051 757 8185	123	.003 084 5454
4	.828 605 2492	64	.049 381 3414	124	.002 942 9175
5	.790 559 5699	65	.047 113 9811	125	.002 807 7925
6	.754 260 7703	66	.044 950 7273	126	.002 678 8718
7	.719 628 6419	67	.042 886 8001	127	.002 555 8705
8	.686 586 6589	68	.040 917 6387	128	.002 438 5169
9	.655 061 8094	69	.039 038 8920	129	.002 326 5516
10	.624 984 4335	70	.037 246 4086	130	.002 219 7272
11	.596 288 0701	71	.035 536 2277	131	.002 117 8077
12	.568 909 3096	72	.033 904 5702	132	.002 020 5679
13	.542 787 6538	73	.032 347 8309	133	.001 927 7929
14	.517 865 3822	74	.030 862 5697	134	.001 839 2776
15	.494 087 4249	75	.029 445 5048	135	.001 754 8266
16	.471 401 2402	76	.028 093 5049	136	.001 674 2532
17	.449 756 6991	77	.026 803 5825	137	.001 597 3793
18	.429 105 9741	78	.025 572 8873	138	.001 524 0351
19	.409 403 4338	79	.024 398 6998	139	.001 454 0585
20	.390 605 5421	80	.023 278 4256	140	.001 387 2950
21	.372 670 7617	81	.022 209 5891	141	.001 323 5969
22	.355 559 4626	82	.021 189 8286	142	.001 262 8235
23	.339 233 8343	83	.020 216 8907	143	.001 204 8405
24	.323 657 8026	84	.019 288 6256	144	.001 149 5199
25	.308 796 9494	85	.018 402 9821	145	.001 096 7393
26	.294 618 4371	86	.017 558 0032	146	.001 046 3822
27	.281 090 9358	87	.016 751 8218	147	.000 998 3372
28	.268 184 5541	88	.015 982 6565	148	.000 952 4982
29	.255 870 7732	89	.015 248 8076	149	.000 908 7639
30	.244 122 3835	90	.014 548 6536	150	.000 867 0378
31	.232 913 4249	91	.013 880 6475	151	.000 827 2274
32	.222 219 1293	92	.013 243 3130	152	.000 789 2450
33	.212 015 8658	93	.012 635 2420	153	.000 753 0066
34	.202 281 0884	94	.012 055 0908	154	.000 718 4320
35	.192 993 2865	95	.011 501 5774	155	.000 685 4450
36	.184 131 9370	96	.010 973 4787	156	.000 653 9726
37	.175 677 4593	97	.010 469 6279	157	.000 623 9452
38	.167 611 1716	98	.009 988 9115	158	.000 595 2966
39	.159 915 2502	99	.009 530 2674	159	.000 567 9633
40	.152 572 6895	100	.009 092 6820	160	.000 541 8851
41	.145 567 2649	101	.008 675 1886	161	.000 517 0043
42	.138 883 4966	102	.008 276 8645	162	.000 493 2658
43	.132 506 6158	103	.007 896 8296	163	.000 470 6174
44	.126 422 5314	104	.007 534 2441	164	.000 449 0088
45	.120 617 7998	105	.007 188 3068	165	.000 428 3925
46	.115 079 5943	106	.006 858 2534	166	.000 408 7227
47	.109 795 6774	107	.006 543 3544	167	.000 389 9560
48	.104 754 3732	108	.006 242 9142	168	.000 372 0511
49	.099 944 5421	109	.005 956 2688	169	.000 354 9682
50	.095 355 5559	110	.005 682 7847	170	.000 338 6698
51	.090 977 2746	111	.005 421 8578	171	.000 323 1196
52	.086 800 0235	112	.005 172 9115	172	.000 308 2835
53	.082 814 5722	113	.004 935 3956	173	.000 294 1285
54	.079 012 1142	114	.004 708 7853	174	.000 280 6235
55	.075 384 2473	115	.004 492 5799	175	.000 267 7386
56	.071 922 9551	116	.004 286 3016	176	.000 255 4453
57	.068 620 5892	117	.004 089 4947	177	.000 243 7165
58	.065 469 8526	118	.003 901 7242	178	.000 232 5261
59	.062 463 7830	119	.003 722 5753	179	.000 221 8496
60	.059 595 7381	120	.003 551 6520	180	.000 211 6633

Present Value of 1

NOMINAL INTEREST RATE COMPOUNDED

YEARLY	HALF-YEARLY	QUARTERLY
@	@	@
$4\frac{7}{8}\%$	$9\frac{3}{4}\%$	$19\frac{1}{2}\%$
4.8750%	9.7500%	19.5000%
PER ANNUM	PER ANNUM	PER ANNUM

Periods	Present Value	Periods	Present Value	Periods	Present Value
1	.953 516 0906	61	.054 828 9080	121	.003 152 7618
2	.909 192 9350	62	.052 280 2460	122	.003 006 2091
3	.866 930 0930	63	.049 850 0557	123	.002 866 4688
4	.826 631 7931	64	.047 532 8303	124	.002 733 2241
5	.788 206 7157	65	.045 323 3185	125	.002 606 1732
6	.751 567 7861	66	.043 216 5135	126	.002 485 0281
7	.716 631 9772	67	.041 207 6410	127	.002 369 5142
8	.683 320 1213	68	.039 292 1487	128	.002 259 3700
9	.651 556 7307	69	.037 465 6960	129	.002 154 3456
10	.621 269 8266	70	.035 724 1440	130	.002 054 2032
11	.592 390 7763	71	.034 063 5461	131	.001 958 7158
12	.564 854 1371	72	.032 480 1393	132	.001 867 6670
13	.538 597 5086	73	.030 970 3355	133	.001 780 8506
14	.513 561 3908	74	.029 530 7132	134	.001 698 0697
15	.489 689 0496	75	.028 158 0102	135	.001 619 1368
16	.466 926 3882	76	.026 849 1158	136	.001 543 8730
17	.445 221 8242	77	.025 601 0640	137	.001 472 1077
18	.424 526 1733	78	.024 411 0264	138	.001 403 6784
19	.404 792 5371	79	.023 276 3065	139	.001 338 4299
20	.385 976 1975	80	.022 194 3328	140	.001 276 2145
21	.368 034 5149	81	.021 162 6534	141	.001 216 8910
22	.350 926 8318	82	.020 178 9305	142	.001 160 3252
23	.334 614 3808	83	.019 240 9350	143	.001 106 3887
24	.319 060 1962	84	.018 346 5411	144	.001 054 9595
25	.304 229 0309	85	.017 493 7221	145	.001 005 9208
26	.290 087 2762	86	.016 680 5455	146	.000 959 1617
27	.276 602 8856	87	.015 905 1686	147	.000 914 5761
28	.263 745 3021	88	.015 165 8342	148	.000 872 0630
29	.251 485 3893	89	.014 460 8669	149	.000 831 5261
30	.239 795 3653	90	.013 788 6693	150	.000 792 8735
31	.228 648 7393	91	.013 147 7180	151	.000 756 0177
32	.218 020 2520	92	.012 536 5607	152	.000 720 8750
33	.207 885 8183	93	.011 953 8123	153	.000 687 3659
34	.198 222 4728	94	.011 398 1524	154	.000 655 4145
35	.189 008 3173	95	.010 868 3217	155	.000 624 9482
36	.180 222 4718	96	.010 363 1196	156	.000 595 8982
37	.171 845 0268	97	.009 881 4013	157	.000 568 1985
38	.163 856 9981	98	.009 422 0752	158	.000 541 7864
39	.156 240 2842	99	.008 984 1003	159	.000 516 6021
40	.148 977 6250	100	.008 566 4842	160	.000 492 5884
41	.142 052 5626	101	.008 168 2805	161	.000 469 6910
42	.135 449 4041	102	.007 788 5869	162	.000 447 8579
43	.129 153 1863	103	.007 426 5429	163	.000 427 0397
44	.123 149 6413	104	.007 081 3282	164	.000 407 1892
45	.117 425 1645	105	.006 752 1603	165	.000 388 2615
46	.111 966 7838	106	.006 438 2935	166	.000 370 2136
47	.106 762 1300	107	.006 139 0165	167	.000 353 0046
48	.101 799 4088	108	.005 853 6510	168	.000 336 5956
49	.097 067 3743	109	.005 581 5504	169	.000 320 9493
50	.092 555 3033	110	.005 322 0981	170	.000 306 0303
51	.088 252 9709	111	.005 074 7062	171	.000 291 8048
52	.084 150 6278	112	.004 838 8140	172	.000 278 2406
53	.080 238 9777	113	.004 613 8870	173	.000 265 3069
54	.076 509 1563	114	.004 399 4155	174	.000 252 9744
55	.072 952 7116	115	.004 194 9135	175	.000 241 2151
56	.069 561 5844	116	.003 999 9175	176	.000 230 0025
57	.066 328 0900	117	.003 813 9857	177	.000 219 3111
58	.063 244 9011	118	.003 636 6967	178	.000 209 1167
59	.060 305 0308	119	.003 467 6489	179	.000 199 3961
60	.057 501 8172	120	.003 306 4590	180	.000 190 1274

Present Value of 1

NOMINAL INTEREST RATE COMPOUNDED		
YEARLY @ $4\frac{15}{16}\%$ 4.9375% PER ANNUM	HALF-YEARLY @ $9\frac{7}{8}\%$ 9.8750% PER ANNUM	QUARTERLY @ $19\frac{3}{4}\%$ 19.7500% PER ANNUM

Periods	Present Value	Periods	Present Value	Periods	Present Value
1	.952 948 1834	61	.052 872 0899	121	.002 933 4836
2	.908 110 2403	62	.050 384 3621	122	.002 795 4579
3	.865 382 0039	63	.048 013 6863	123	.002 663 9265
4	.824 664 2086	64	.045 754 5551	124	.002 538 5839
5	.785 862 2595	65	.043 601 7202	125	.002 419 1390
6	.748 886 0126	66	.041 550 1801	126	.002 305 3141
7	.713 649 5654	67	.039 595 1686	127	.002 196 8449
8	.680 071 0569	68	.037 732 1440	128	.002 093 4793
9	.648 072 4783	69	.035 956 7781	129	.001 994 9773
10	.617 579 4909	70	.034 264 9464	130	.001 901 1100
11	.588 521 2540	71	.032 652 7184	131	.001 811 6593
12	.560 830 2599	72	.031 116 3487	132	.001 726 4175
13	.534 442 1774	73	.029 652 2679	133	.001 645 1864
14	.509 295 7021	74	.028 257 0749	134	.001 567 7774
15	.485 332 4142	75	.026 927 5282	135	.001 494 0106
16	.462 496 6425	76	.025 660 5391	136	.001 423 7147
17	.440 735 3353	77	.024 453 1641	137	.001 356 7263
18	.419 997 9371	78	.023 302 5983	138	.001 292 8899
19	.400 236 2712	79	.022 206 1687	139	.001 232 0571
20	.381 404 4276	80	.021 161 3281	140	.001 174 0865
21	.363 458 6565	81	.020 165 6492	141	.001 118 8436
22	.346 357 2664	82	.019 216 8188	142	.001 066 2000
23	.330 060 5279	83	.018 312 6325	143	.001 016 0334
24	.314 530 5805	84	.017 450 9899	144	.000 968 2272
25	.299 731 3453	85	.016 629 8891	145	.000 922 6703
26	.285 628 4410	86	.015 847 4226	146	.000 879 2570
27	.272 189 1040	87	.015 101 7726	147	.000 837 8864
28	.259 382 1122	88	.014 391 2068	148	.000 798 4623
29	.247 177 7127	89	.013 714 0744	149	.000 760 8932
30	.235 547 5523	90	.013 068 8023	150	.000 725 0918
31	.224 464 6120	91	.012 453 8914	151	.000 690 9749
32	.213 903 1443	92	.011 867 9132	152	.000 658 4633
33	.203 838 6128	93	.011 309 5063	153	.000 627 4814
34	.194 247 6358	94	.010 777 3735	154	.000 597 9572
35	.185 107 9316	95	.010 270 2785	155	.000 569 8223
36	.176 398 2672	96	.009 787 0432	156	.000 543 0111
37	.168 098 4083	97	.009 326 5450	157	.000 517 4614
38	.160 189 0728	98	.008 887 7142	158	.000 493 1139
39	.152 651 8860	99	.008 469 5311	159	.000 469 9120
40	.145 469 3374	100	.008 071 0242	160	.000 447 8018
41	.138 624 7408	101	.007 691 2679	161	.000 426 7319
42	.132 102 1950	102	.007 329 3798	162	.000 406 6534
43	.125 886 5467	103	.006 984 5191	163	.000 387 5196
44	.119 963 3560	104	.006 655 8848	164	.000 369 2861
45	.114 318 8622	105	.006 342 7133	165	.000 351 9105
46	.108 939 9521	106	.006 044 2772	166	.000 335 3525
47	.103 814 1294	107	.005 759 8829	167	.000 319 5736
48	.098 929 4860	108	.005 488 8700	168	.000 304 5370
49	.094 274 6740	109	.005 230 6087	169	.000 290 2080
50	.089 838 8793	110	.004 984 4990	170	.000 276 5532
51	.085 611 7969	111	.004 749 9693	171	.000 263 5409
52	.081 583 6063	112	.004 526 4746	172	.000 251 1408
53	.077 744 9494	113	.004 313 4958	173	.000 239 3242
54	.074 086 9083	114	.004 110 5380	174	.000 228 0635
55	.070 600 9847	115	.003 917 1297	175	.000 217 3327
56	.067 279 0801	116	.003 732 8216	176	.000 207 1068
57	.064 113 4772	117	.003 557 1856	177	.000 197 3621
58	.061 096 8216	118	.003 389 8135	178	.000 188 0758
59	.058 222 1052	119	.003 230 3166	179	.000 179 2265
60	.055 482 6494	120	.003 078 3244	180	.000 170 7936

Present Value of 1

NOMINAL INTEREST RATE COMPOUNDED

YEARLY @ 5% 5.0000% PER ANNUM	HALF-YEARLY @ 10% 10.0000% PER ANNUM	QUARTERLY @ 20% 20.0000% PER ANNUM

Periods	Present Value	Periods	Present Value	Periods	Present Value
1	.952 380 9524	61	.050 986 2131	121	.002 729 5736
2	.907 029 4785	62	.048 558 2982	122	.002 599 5939
3	.863 837 5985	63	.046 245 9983	123	.002 475 8037
4	.822 702 4748	64	.044 043 8079	124	.002 357 9083
5	.783 526 1665	65	.041 946 4837	125	.002 245 6270
6	.746 215 3966	66	.039 949 0321	126	.002 138 6924
7	.710 681 3301	67	.038 046 6972	127	.002 036 8499
8	.676 839 3620	68	.036 234 9497	128	.001 939 8570
9	.644 608 9162	69	.034 509 4759	129	.001 847 4829
10	.613 913 2535	70	.032 866 1676	130	.001 759 5075
11	.584 679 2891	71	.031 301 1120	131	.001 675 7214
12	.556 837 4182	72	.029 810 5828	132	.001 595 9252
13	.530 321 3506	73	.028 391 0313	133	.001 519 9287
14	.505 067 9530	74	.027 039 0774	134	.001 447 5512
15	.481 017 0981	75	.025 751 5023	135	.001 378 6202
16	.458 111 5220	76	.024 525 2403	136	.001 312 9716
17	.436 296 6876	77	.023 357 3717	137	.001 250 4491
18	.415 520 6549	78	.022 245 1159	138	.001 190 9039
19	.395 733 9570	79	.021 185 8247	139	.001 134 1942
20	.376 889 4829	80	.020 176 9759	140	.001 080 1850
21	.358 942 3646	81	.019 216 1675	141	.001 028 7476
22	.341 849 8711	82	.018 301 1119	142	.000 979 7596
23	.325 571 3058	83	.017 429 6304	143	.000 933 1044
24	.310 067 9103	84	.016 599 6480	144	.000 888 6708
25	.295 302 7717	85	.015 809 1885	145	.000 846 3532
26	.281 240 7350	86	.015 056 3700	146	.000 806 0507
27	.267 848 3190	87	.014 339 4000	147	.000 767 6673
28	.255 093 6371	88	.013 656 5715	148	.000 731 1117
29	.242 946 3211	89	.013 006 2585	149	.000 696 2969
30	.231 377 4487	90	.012 386 9129	150	.000 663 1399
31	.220 359 4749	91	.011 797 0599	151	.000 631 5618
32	.209 866 1666	92	.011 235 2951	152	.000 601 4874
33	.199 872 5396	93	.010 700 2811	153	.000 572 8452
34	.190 354 7996	94	.010 190 7439	154	.000 545 5668
35	.181 290 2854	95	.009 705 4704	155	.000 519 5874
36	.172 657 4146	96	.009 243 3051	156	.000 494 8452
37	.164 435 6330	97	.008 803 1477	157	.000 471 2811
38	.156 605 3647	98	.008 383 9502	158	.000 448 8392
39	.149 147 9664	99	.007 984 7145	159	.000 427 4659
40	.142 045 6823	100	.007 604 4900	160	.000 407 1104
41	.135 281 6022	101	.007 242 3714	161	.000 387 7241
42	.128 839 6211	102	.006 897 4966	162	.000 369 2611
43	.122 704 4011	103	.006 569 0444	163	.000 351 6772
44	.116 861 3344	104	.006 256 2327	164	.000 334 9307
45	.111 296 5089	105	.005 958 3169	165	.000 318 9816
46	.105 996 6752	106	.005 674 5875	166	.000 303 7920
47	.100 949 2144	107	.005 404 3691	167	.000 289 3257
48	.096 142 1090	108	.005 147 0182	168	.000 275 5483
49	.091 563 9133	109	.004 901 9221	169	.000 262 4270
50	.087 203 7270	110	.004 668 4972	170	.000 249 9304
51	.083 051 1685	111	.004 446 1878	171	.000 238 0290
52	.079 096 3510	112	.004 234 4646	172	.000 226 6943
53	.075 329 8581	113	.004 032 8234	173	.000 215 8993
54	.071 742 7220	114	.003 840 7842	174	.000 205 6184
55	.068 326 4019	115	.003 657 8897	175	.000 195 8270
56	.065 072 7637	116	.003 483 7045	176	.000 186 5019
57	.061 974 0607	117	.003 317 8138	177	.000 177 6209
58	.059 022 9149	118	.003 159 8227	178	.000 169 1628
59	.056 212 2999	119	.003 009 3549	179	.000 161 1074
60	.053 535 5237	120	.002 866 0523	180	.000 153 4356

Present Value of 1

NOMINAL INTEREST RATE COMPOUNDED		
YEARLY @ $5\frac{1}{16}\%$ 5.0625% PER ANNUM	HALF-YEARLY @ $10\frac{1}{8}\%$ 10.1250% PER ANNUM	QUARTERLY @ $20\frac{1}{4}\%$ 20.2500% PER ANNUM

Periods	Present Value	Periods	Present Value	Periods	Present Value
1	.951 814 3962	61	.049 168 6656	121	.002 539 9465
2	.905 950 6448	62	.046 799 4438	122	.002 417 5577
3	.862 296 8660	63	.044 544 3843	123	.002 301 0662
4	.820 746 5708	64	.042 397 9863	124	.002 190 1879
5	.781 198 4017	65	.040 355 0137	125	.002 084 6524
6	.743 555 8850	66	.038 410 4830	126	.001 984 2022
7	.707 727 1958	67	.036 559 6507	127	.001 888 5922
8	.673 624 9335	68	.034 798 0018	128	.001 797 5892
9	.641 165 9093	69	.033 121 2391	129	.001 710 9713
10	.610 270 9429	70	.031 525 2722	130	.001 628 5271
11	.580 864 6690	71	.030 006 2079	131	.001 550 0556
12	.552 875 3542	72	.028 560 3407	132	.001 475 3652
13	.526 234 7214	73	.027 184 1434	133	.001 404 2738
14	.500 877 7836	74	.025 874 2591	134	.001 336 6081
15	.476 742 6852	75	.024 627 4923	135	.001 272 2028
16	.453 770 5510	76	.023 440 8017	136	.001 210 9009
17	.431 905 3430	77	.022 311 2925	137	.001 152 5529
18	.411 093 7233	78	.021 236 2094	138	.001 097 0165
19	.391 284 9240	79	.020 212 9298	139	.001 044 1561
20	.372 430 6237	80	.019 238 9576	140	.000 993 8428
21	.354 484 8292	81	.018 311 9168	141	.000 945 9539
22	.337 403 7637	82	.017 429 5460	142	.000 900 3725
23	.321 145 7596	83	.016 589 6928	143	.000 856 9875
24	.305 671 1573	84	.015 790 3085	144	.000 815 6931
25	.290 942 2080	85	.015 029 4429	145	.000 776 3884
26	.276 922 9820	86	.014 305 2401	146	.000 738 9777
27	.263 579 2809	87	.013 615 9335	147	.000 703 3696
28	.250 878 5541	88	.012 959 8415	148	.000 669 4773
29	.238 789 8195	89	.012 335 3637	149	.000 637 2181
30	.227 283 5879	90	.011 740 9768	150	.000 606 5134
31	.216 331 7910	91	.011 175 2307	151	.000 577 2882
32	.205 907 7130	92	.010 636 7455	152	.000 549 4712
33	.195 985 9255	93	.010 124 2075	153	.000 522 9946
34	.186 542 2253	94	.009 636 3664	154	.000 497 7938
35	.177 553 5756	95	.009 172 0323	155	.000 473 8073
36	.168 998 0493	96	.008 730 0724	156	.000 450 9766
37	.160 854 7763	97	.008 309 4086	157	.000 429 2460
38	.153 103 8918	98	.007 909 0147	158	.000 408 5625
39	.145 726 4883	99	.007 527 9141	159	.000 388 8757
40	.138 704 5695	100	.007 165 1770	160	.000 370 1375
41	.132 021 0060	101	.006 819 9186	161	.000 352 3022
42	.125 659 4941	102	.006 491 2967	162	.000 335 3263
43	.119 604 5155	103	.006 178 5096	163	.000 319 1684
44	.113 841 2997	104	.005 880 7944	164	.000 303 7891
45	.108 355 7880	105	.005 597 4248	165	.000 289 1508
46	.103 134 5989	106	.005 327 7095	166	.000 275 2179
47	.098 164 9960	107	.005 070 9906	167	.000 261 9564
48	.093 434 8564	108	.004 826 6419	168	.000 249 3338
49	.088 932 6414	109	.004 594 0672	169	.000 237 3195
50	.084 647 3684	110	.004 372 6993	170	.000 225 8842
51	.080 568 5838	111	.004 161 9982	171	.000 214 9998
52	.076 686 3380	112	.003 961 4498	172	.000 204 6399
53	.072 991 1605	113	.003 770 5649	173	.000 194 7792
54	.069 474 0373	114	.003 588 8780	174	.000 185 3936
55	.066 126 3889	115	.003 415 9457	175	.000 176 4603
56	.062 940 0489	116	.003 251 3463	176	.000 167 9575
57	.059 907 2447	117	.003 094 6782	177	.000 159 8644
58	.057 020 5779	118	.002 945 5593	178	.000 152 1612
59	.054 273 0069	119	.002 803 6257	179	.000 144 8292
60	.051 657 8293	120	.002 668 5313	180	.000 137 8505

Present Value of 1

NOMINAL INTEREST RATE COMPOUNDED

	YEARLY	HALF-YEARLY	QUARTERLY
	@	@	@
	$5\frac{1}{8}\%$	**$10\frac{1}{4}\%$**	**$20\frac{1}{2}\%$**
	5.1250%	10.2500%	20.5000%
	PER ANNUM	PER ANNUM	PER ANNUM

Periods	Present Value	Periods	Present Value	Periods	Present Value
1	.951 248 5137	61	.047 416 9333	121	.002 363 5943
2	.904 873 7348	62	.045 105 2874	122	.002 248 3656
3	.860 759 7953	63	.042 906 3376	123	.002 138 7544
4	.818 796 4759	64	.040 814 5898	124	.002 034 4869
5	.778 878 9307	65	.038 824 8179	125	.001 935 3027
6	.740 907 4251	66	.036 932 0503	126	.001 840 9538
7	.704 787 0869	67	.035 131 5580	127	.001 751 2046
8	.670 427 6689	68	.033 418 8423	128	.001 665 8307
9	.637 743 3236	69	.031 789 6241	129	.001 584 6190
10	.606 652 3886	70	.030 239 8327	130	.001 507 3665
11	.577 077 1830	71	.028 765 5959	131	.001 433 8801
12	.548 943 8126	72	.027 363 2303	132	.001 363 9763
13	.522 181 9858	73	.026 029 2322	133	.001 297 4805
14	.496 724 8379	74	.024 760 2684	134	.001 234 2264
15	.472 508 7638	75	.023 553 1685	135	.001 174 0560
16	.449 473 2592	76	.022 404 9166	136	.001 116 8190
17	.427 560 7698	77	.021 312 6436	137	.001 062 3724
18	.406 716 5468	78	.020 273 6205	138	.001 010 5802
19	.386 888 5106	79	.019 285 2514	139	.000 961 3129
20	.368 027 1207	80	.018 345 0667	140	.000 914 4475
21	.350 085 2515	81	.017 450 7174	141	.000 869 8668
22	.333 018 0752	82	.016 599 9690	142	.000 827 4595
23	.316 782 9490	83	.015 790 6959	143	.000 787 1196
24	.301 339 3094	84	.015 020 8760	144	.000 748 7464
25	.286 648 5702	85	.014 288 5859	145	.000 712 2439
26	.272 674 0263	86	.013 591 9961	146	.000 677 5209
27	.259 380 7623	87	.012 929 3661	147	.000 644 4908
28	.246 735 5646	88	.012 299 0403	148	.000 613 0709
29	.234 706 8391	89	.011 699 4438	149	.000 583 1828
30	.223 264 5318	90	.011 129 0785	150	.000 554 7517
31	.212 380 0541	91	.010 586 5194	151	.000 527 7068
32	.202 026 2108	92	.010 070 4109	152	.000 501 9803
33	.192 177 1327	93	.009 579 4634	153	.000 477 5080
34	.182 808 2119	94	.009 112 4503	154	.000 454 2288
35	.173 896 0398	95	.008 668 2048	155	.000 432 0844
36	.165 418 3494	96	.008 245 6169	156	.000 411 0197
37	.157 353 9590	97	.007 843 6308	157	.000 390 9819
38	.149 682 7196	98	.007 461 2422	158	.000 371 9209
39	.142 385 4646	99	.007 097 4955	159	.000 353 7892
40	.135 443 9615	100	.006 751 4821	160	.000 336 5415
41	.128 840 8671	101	.006 422 3373	161	.000 320 1346
42	.122 559 6833	102	.006 109 2388	162	.000 304 5275
43	.116 584 7166	103	.005 811 4043	163	.000 289 6814
44	.110 901 0384	104	.005 528 0897	164	.000 275 5590
45	.105 494 4479	105	.005 258 5871	165	.000 262 1251
46	.100 351 4368	106	.005 002 2232	166	.000 249 3461
47	.095 459 1551	107	.004 758 3574	167	.000 237 1901
48	.090 805 3794	108	.004 526 3804	168	.000 225 6267
49	.086 378 4822	109	.004 305 7126	169	.000 214 6271
50	.082 167 4028	110	.004 095 8027	170	.000 204 1637
51	.078 161 6198	111	.003 896 1263	171	.000 194 2104
52	.074 351 1246	112	.003 706 1843	172	.000 184 7424
53	.070 726 3968	113	.003 525 5023	173	.000 175 7359
54	.067 278 3798	114	.003 353 6288	174	.000 167 1685
55	.063 998 4588	115	.003 190 1345	175	.000 159 0188
56	.060 878 4388	116	.003 034 6107	176	.000 151 2664
57	.057 910 5245	117	.002 886 6689	177	.000 143 8919
58	.055 087 3003	118	.002 745 9395	178	.000 136 8770
59	.052 401 7125	119	.002 612 0708	179	.000 130 2040
60	.049 847 0512	120	.002 484 7285	180	.000 123 8564

NOMINAL INTEREST RATE COMPOUNDED

YEARLY	HALF-YEARLY	QUARTERLY
@	@	@
$5\frac{3}{16}\%$	$10\frac{3}{8}\%$	$20\frac{3}{4}\%$
5.1875%	10.3750%	20.7500%
PER ANNUM	PER ANNUM	PER ANNUM

Periods	Present Value	Periods	Present Value	Periods	Present Value
1	.950 683 3036	61	.045 728 5960	121	.002 199 5805
2	.903 798 7438	62	.043 473 4127	122	.002 091 1045
3	.859 226 3756	63	.041 329 4476	123	.001 987 9781
4	.816 852 1693	64	.039 291 2158	124	.001 889 9376
5	.776 567 7189	65	.037 353 5028	125	.001 796 7321
6	.738 269 9645	66	.035 511 3515	126	.001 708 1232
7	.701 860 9288	67	.033 760 0489	127	.001 623 8842
8	.667 247 4665	68	.032 095 1149	128	.001 543 7996
9	.634 341 0257	69	.030 512 2898	129	.001 467 6645
10	.603 057 4220	70	.029 007 5245	130	.001 395 2842
11	.573 316 6222	71	.027 576 9692	131	.001 326 4734
12	.545 042 5404	72	.026 216 9642	132	.001 261 0561
13	.518 162 8429	73	.024 924 0301	133	.001 198 8650
14	.492 608 7633	74	.023 694 8593	134	.001 139 7409
15	.468 314 9265	75	.022 526 3071	135	.001 083 5326
16	.445 219 1815	76	.021 415 3841	136	.001 030 0964
17	.423 262 4423	77	.020 359 2481	137	.000 979 2954
18	.402 388 5369	78	.019 355 1972	138	.000 930 9998
19	.382 544 0636	79	.018 400 6628	139	.000 885 0860
20	.363 678 2542	80	.017 493 2029	140	.000 841 4365
21	.345 742 8442	81	.016 630 4960	141	.000 799 9396
22	.328 691 9493	82	.015 810 3348	142	.000 760 4892
23	.312 481 9482	83	.015 030 6214	143	.000 722 9844
24	.297 071 3709	84	.014 289 3608	144	.000 687 3292
25	.282 420 7923	85	.013 584 6567	145	.000 653 4324
26	.268 492 7318	86	.012 914 7063	146	.000 621 2073
27	.255 251 5573	87	.012 277 7957	147	.000 590 5714
28	.242 663 3937	88	.011 672 2953	148	.000 561 4464
29	.230 696 0368	89	.011 096 6563	149	.000 533 7577
30	.219 318 8704	90	.010 549 4059	150	.000 507 4345
31	.208 502 7883	91	.010 029 1440	151	.000 482 4095
32	.198 220 1196	92	.009 534 5398	152	.000 458 6187
33	.188 444 5581	93	.009 064 3278	153	.000 436 0011
34	.179 151 0951	94	.008 617 3051	154	.000 414 4990
35	.170 315 9549	95	.008 192 3280	155	.000 394 0573
36	.161 916 5347	96	.007 788 3095	156	.000 374 6237
37	.153 931 3461	97	.007 404 2158	157	.000 356 1485
38	.146 339 9606	98	.007 039 0643	158	.000 338 5844
39	.139 122 9572	99	.006 691 9209	159	.000 321 8865
40	.132 261 8726	100	.006 361 8975	160	.000 306 0121
41	.125 739 1540	101	.006 048 1497	161	.000 290 9206
42	.119 538 1143	102	.005 749 8750	162	.000 276 5734
43	.113 642 8894	103	.005 466 3101	163	.000 262 9337
44	.108 038 3975	104	.005 196 7298	164	.000 249 9667
45	.102 710 3007	105	.004 940 4442	165	.000 237 6392
46	.097 644 9680	106	.004 696 7978	166	.000 225 9196
47	.092 829 4407	107	.004 465 1673	167	.000 214 7780
48	.088 251 3994	108	.004 244 9600	168	.000 204 1858
49	.083 899 1319	109	.004 035 6126	169	.000 194 1161
50	.079 761 5039	110	.003 836 5895	170	.000 184 5429
51	.075 827 9300	111	.003 647 3816	171	.000 175 4419
52	.072 088 3470	112	.003 467 5048	172	.000 166 7896
53	.068 533 1879	113	.003 296 4989	173	.000 158 5641
54	.065 153 3575	114	.003 133 9265	174	.000 150 7443
55	.061 940 2091	115	.002 979 3716	175	.000 143 3101
56	.058 885 5227	116	.002 832 4388	176	.000 136 2425
57	.055 981 4832	117	.002 692 7523	177	.000 129 5234
58	.053 220 6614	118	.002 559 9546	178	.000 123 1358
59	.050 595 9942	119	.002 433 7061	179	.000 117 0631
60	.048 100 7669	120	.002 313 6838	180	.000 111 2900

Present Value of 1

NOMINAL INTEREST RATE COMPOUNDED

YEARLY	HALF-YEARLY	QUARTERLY
@	@	@
$5\frac{1}{4}\%$	$10\frac{1}{2}\%$	21 %
5.2500%	10.5000%	21.0000%
PER ANNUM	PER ANNUM	PER ANNUM

Periods	Present Value	Periods	Present Value	Periods	Present Value
1	.950 118 7648	61	.044 101 3237	121	.002 047 0354
2	.902 725 6673	62	.041 901 4952	122	.001 944 9268
3	.857 696 5960	63	.039 811 3969	123	.001 847 9114
4	.814 913 6304	64	.037 825 5552	124	.001 755 7353
5	.774 264 7320	65	.035 938 7698	125	.001 668 1571
6	.735 643 4508	66	.034 146 0996	126	.001 584 9473
7	.698 948 6469	67	.032 442 8500	127	.001 505 8882
8	.664 084 2250	68	.030 824 5605	128	.001 430 7726
9	.630 958 8837	69	.029 286 9934	129	.001 359 4039
10	.599 485 8752	70	.027 826 1220	130	.001 291 5952
11	.569 582 7793	71	.026 438 1206	131	.001 227 1688
12	.541 171 2867	72	.025 119 3545	132	.001 165 9561
13	.514 176 9945	73	.023 866 3701	133	.001 107 7968
14	.488 529 2110	74	.022 675 8861	134	.001 052 5385
15	.464 160 7705	75	.021 544 7849	135	.001 000 0366
16	.441 007 8580	76	.020 470 1044	136	.000 950 1535
17	.419 009 8413	77	.019 449 0303	137	.000 902 7587
18	.398 109 1129	78	.018 478 8886	138	.000 857 7280
19	.378 250 9386	79	.017 557 1389	139	.000 814 9434
20	.359 383 3146	80	.016 681 3671	140	.000 774 2931
21	.341 456 8310	81	.015 849 2799	141	.000 735 6704
22	.324 424 5425	82	.015 058 6982	142	.000 698 9742
23	.308 241 8456	83	.014 307 5518	143	.000 664 1085
24	.292 866 3616	84	.013 593 8734	144	.000 630 9820
25	.278 257 8257	85	.012 915 7942	145	.000 599 5078
26	.264 377 9817	86	.012 271 5384	146	.000 569 6036
27	.251 190 4814	87	.011 659 4190	147	.000 541 1911
28	.238 660 7900	88	.011 077 8327	148	.000 514 1958
29	.226 756 0950	89	.010 525 2568	149	.000 488 5471
30	.215 445 2209	90	.010 000 2439	150	.000 464 1778
31	.204 698 5471	91	.009 501 4194	151	.000 441 0240
32	.194 487 9308	92	.009 027 4769	152	.000 419 0252
33	.184 786 6326	93	.008 577 1752	153	.000 398 1237
34	.175 569 2471	94	.008 149 3351	154	.000 378 2648
35	.166 811 6362	95	.007 742 8362	155	.000 359 3965
36	.158 490 8657	96	.007 356 6140	156	.000 341 4693
37	.150 585 1456	97	.006 989 6570	157	.000 324 4364
38	.143 073 7725	98	.006 641 0043	158	.000 308 2531
39	.135 937 0761	99	.006 309 7428	159	.000 292 8771
40	.129 156 3668	100	.005 995 0050	160	.000 278 2680
41	.122 713 8877	101	.005 695 9667	161	.000 264 3877
42	.116 592 7674	102	.005 411 8449	162	.000 251 1997
43	.110 776 9762	103	.005 141 8954	163	.000 238 6695
44	.105 251 2838	104	.004 885 4113	164	.000 226 7644
45	.100 001 2197	105	.004 641 7209	165	.000 215 4531
46	.095 013 0354	106	.004 410 1862	166	.000 204 7060
47	.090 273 6678	107	.004 190 2006	167	.000 194 4950
48	.085 770 7058	108	.003 981 1862	168	.000 184 7934
49	.081 492 3570	109	.003 782 6017	169	.000 175 5757
50	.077 427 4176	110	.003 593 9208	170	.000 166 8177
51	.073 565 2424	111	.003 414 6516	171	.000 158 4967
52	.069 895 7172	112	.003 244 3246	172	.000 150 5907
53	.066 409 2325	113	.003 082 4937	173	.000 143 0790
54	.063 096 6580	114	.002 928 7351	174	.000 135 9421
55	.059 949 3187	115	.002 782 6461	175	.000 129 1611
56	.056 958 9727	116	.002 643 8443	176	.000 122 7184
57	.054 117 7888	117	.002 511 9661	177	.000 116 5970
58	.051 418 3266	118	.002 386 6661	178	.000 110 7810
59	.048 853 5170	119	.002 267 6163	179	.000 105 2551
60	.046 416 6432	120	.002 154 5048	180	.000 100 0049

Present Value of 1

NOMINAL INTEREST RATE COMPOUNDED

YEARLY	HALF-YEARLY	QUARTERLY
@	@	@
$5\frac{5}{16}\%$	$10\frac{5}{8}\%$	$21\frac{1}{4}\%$
5.3125%	10.6250%	21.2500%
PER ANNUM	PER ANNUM	PER ANNUM

Periods	Present Value	Periods	Present Value	Periods	Present Value
1	.949 554 8961	61	.042 532 8735	121	.001 905 1509
2	.901 654 5008	62	.040 387 2983	122	.001 809 0453
3	.856 170 4459	63	.038 349 9568	123	.001 717 7878
4	.812 980 8388	64	.036 415 3893	124	.001 631 1339
5	.771 969 9359	65	.034 578 4112	125	.001 548 8511
6	.733 027 8324	66	.032 834 0996	126	.001 470 7192
7	.696 050 1672	67	.031 177 7801	127	.001 396 5286
8	.660 937 8442	68	.029 605 0137	128	.001 326 0806
9	.627 596 7660	69	.028 111 5857	129	.001 259 1863
10	.595 937 5820	70	.026 693 4939	130	.001 195 6665
11	.565 875 4488	71	.025 346 9378	131	.001 135 3510
12	.537 329 8030	72	.024 068 3089	132	.001 078 0781
13	.510 224 1453	73	.022 854 1805	133	.001 023 6943
14	.484 485 8353	74	.021 701 2990	134	.000 972 0540
15	.460 045 8970	75	.020 606 5747	135	.000 923 0186
16	.436 838 8340	76	.019 567 0739	136	.000 876 4568
17	.414 802 4536	77	.018 580 0109	137	.000 832 2439
18	.393 877 7008	78	.017 642 7403	138	.000 790 2613
19	.374 008 4992	79	.016 752 7504	139	.000 750 3964
20	.355 141 6016	80	.015 907 6562	140	.000 712 5426
21	.337 226 4467	81	.015 105 1928	141	.000 676 5983
22	.320 215 0235	82	.014 343 2098	142	.000 642 4673
23	.304 061 7434	83	.013 619 6651	143	.000 610 0579
24	.288 723 3172	84	.012 932 6197	144	.000 579 2835
25	.274 158 6395	85	.012 280 2323	145	.000 550 0615
26	.260 328 6784	86	.011 660 7547	146	.000 522 3136
27	.247 196 3712	87	.011 072 5267	147	.000 495 9654
28	.234 726 5246	88	.010 513 9720	148	.000 470 9464
29	.222 885 7207	89	.009 983 5936	149	.000 447 1894
30	.211 642 2274	90	.009 479 9702	150	.000 424 6309
31	.200 965 9132	91	.009 001 7521	151	.000 403 2104
32	.190 828 1668	92	.008 547 6578	152	.000 382 8704
33	.181 201 8202	93	.008 116 4703	153	.000 363 5564
34	.172 061 0755	94	.007 707 0341	154	.000 345 2168
35	.163 381 4367	95	.007 318 2520	155	.000 327 8023
36	.155 139 6431	96	.006 949 0820	156	.000 311 2663
37	.147 313 6077	97	.006 598 5348	157	.000 295 5644
38	.139 882 3575	98	.006 265 6710	158	.000 280 6546
39	.132 825 9774	99	.005 949 5986	159	.000 266 4970
40	.126 125 5572	100	.005 649 4705	160	.000 253 0535
41	.119 763 1404	101	.005 364 4824	161	.000 240 2882
42	.113 721 6763	102	.005 093 8705	162	.000 228 1668
43	.107 984 9746	103	.004 836 9097	163	.000 216 6569
44	.102 537 6613	104	.004 592 9113	164	.000 205 7277
45	.097 365 1383	105	.004 361 2214	165	.000 195 3497
46	.092 453 5438	106	.004 141 2191	166	.000 185 4953
47	.087 789 7152	107	.003 932 3149	167	.000 176 1379
48	.083 361 1539	108	.003 733 9489	168	.000 167 2527
49	.079 155 9918	109	.003 545 5894	169	.000 158 8156
50	.075 162 9596	110	.003 366 7318	170	.000 150 8041
51	.071 371 3563	111	.003 196 8967	171	.000 143 1968
52	.067 771 0208	112	.003 035 6289	172	.000 135 9732
53	.064 352 3046	113	.002 882 4963	173	.000 129 1140
54	.061 106 0459	114	.002 737 0884	174	.000 122 6008
55	.058 023 5451	115	.002 599 0157	175	.000 116 4162
56	.055 096 5413	116	.002 467 9081	176	.000 110 5436
57	.052 317 1906	117	.002 343 4142	177	.000 104 9672
58	.049 678 0445	118	.002 225 2004	178	.000 099 6721
59	.047 172 0304	119	.002 112 9500	179	.000 094 6442
60	.044 792 4324	120	.002 006 3620	180	.000 089 8698

Present Value of 1

NOMINAL INTEREST RATE COMPOUNDED					
YEARLY @ 5⅜% 5.3750% PER ANNUM		HALF-YEARLY @ 10¾% 10.7500% PER ANNUM		QUARTERLY @ 21½% 21.5000% PER ANNUM	
Periods	**Present Value**	**Periods**	**Present Value**	**Periods**	**Present Value**
1	.948 991 6963	61	.041 021 0861	121	.001 773 1762
2	.900 585 2397	62	.038 928 6700	122	.001 682 7295
3	.854 647 9143	63	.036 942 9846	123	.001 596 8963
4	.811 053 7739	64	.035 058 5856	124	.001 515 4414
5	.769 683 2967	65	.033 270 3067	125	.001 438 1413
6	.730 423 0574	66	.031 573 2448	126	.001 364 7841
7	.693 165 4163	67	.029 962 7471	127	.001 295 1688
8	.657 808 2242	68	.028 434 3982	128	.001 229 1044
9	.624 254 5426	69	.026 984 0078	129	.001 166 4099
10	.592 412 3773	70	.025 607 5993	130	.001 106 9133
11	.562 194 4268	71	.024 301 3991	131	.001 050 4515
12	.533 517 8428	72	.023 061 8260	132	.000 996 8698
13	.506 304 0027	73	.021 885 4813	133	.000 946 0211
14	.480 478 2943	74	.020 769 1401	134	.000 897 7662
15	.455 969 9116	75	.019 709 7415	135	.000 851 9727
16	.432 711 6599	76	.018 704 3810	136	.000 808 5150
17	.410 639 7721	77	.017 750 3022	137	.000 767 2740
18	.389 693 7339	78	.016 844 8894	138	.000 728 1367
19	.369 816 1176	79	.015 985 6602	139	.000 690 9957
20	.350 952 4248	80	.015 170 2588	140	.000 655 7491
21	.333 050 9369	81	.014 396 4496	141	.000 622 3005
22	.316 062 5736	82	.013 662 1111	142	.000 590 5580
23	.299 940 7578	83	.012 965 2300	143	.000 560 4346
24	.284 641 2886	84	.012 303 8956	144	.000 531 8478
25	.270 122 2193	85	.011 676 2948	145	.000 504 7192
26	.256 343 7431	86	.011 080 7068	146	.000 478 9743
27	.243 268 0836	87	.010 515 4987	147	.000 454 5426
28	.230 859 3913	88	.009 979 1210	148	.000 431 3572
29	.219 083 6454	89	.009 470 1030	149	.000 409 3544
30	.207 908 5603	90	.008 987 0491	150	.000 388 4739
31	.197 303 4973	91	.008 528 6349	151	.000 368 6585
32	.187 239 3806	92	.008 093 6037	152	.000 349 8539
33	.177 688 6174	93	.007 680 7627	153	.000 332 0084
34	.168 625 0224	94	.007 288 9801	154	.000 315 0732
35	.160 023 7461	95	.006 917 1816	155	.000 299 0019
36	.151 861 2063	96	.006 564 3479	156	.000 283 7503
37	.144 115 0237	97	.006 229 5116	157	.000 269 2767
38	.136 763 9608	98	.005 911 7548	158	.000 255 5413
39	.129 787 8632	99	.005 610 2062	159	.000 242 5066
40	.123 167 6044	100	.005 324 0391	160	.000 230 1368
41	.116 885 0339	101	.005 052 4689	161	.000 218 3979
42	.110 922 9266	102	.004 794 7510	162	.000 207 2578
43	.105 264 9363	103	.004 550 1789	163	.000 196 6859
44	.099 895 5504	104	.004 318 0820	164	.000 186 6533
45	.094 800 0478	105	.004 097 8240	165	.000 177 1324
46	.089 964 4582	106	.003 888 8009	166	.000 168 0972
47	.085 375 5238	107	.003 690 4398	167	.000 159 5228
48	.081 020 6632	108	.003 502 1967	168	.000 151 3858
49	.076 887 9366	109	.003 323 5556	169	.000 143 6639
50	.072 966 0134	110	.003 154 0267	170	.000 136 3359
51	.069 244 1408	111	.002 993 1451	171	.000 129 3816
52	.065 712 1146	112	.002 840 4699	172	.000 122 7821
53	.062 360 2511	113	.002 695 5823	173	.000 116 5192
54	.059 179 3605	114	.002 558 0852	174	.000 110 5757
55	.056 160 7217	115	.002 427 6016	175	.000 104 9354
56	.053 296 0586	116	.002 303 7738	176	.000 099 5829
57	.050 577 5170	117	.002 186 2622	177	.000 094 5033
58	.047 997 6437	118	.002 074 7447	178	.000 089 6829
59	.045 549 3653	119	.001 968 9155	179	.000 085 1083
60	.043 225 9694	120	.001 868 4844	180	.000 080 7671

Present Value of 1

NOMINAL INTEREST RATE COMPOUNDED

	YEARLY @ $5\frac{7}{16}\%$ 7.4375% PER ANNUM		HALF-YEARLY @ $10\frac{7}{8}\%$ 10.8750% PER ANNUM		QUARTERLY @ $21\frac{3}{4}\%$ 21.7500% PER ANNUM
Periods	Present Value	Periods	Present Value	Periods	Present Value
1	.948 429 1642	61	.039 563 8826	121	.001 650 4140
2	.899 517 8795	62	.037 523 5401	122	.001 565 3008
3	.853 128 9906	63	.035 588 4197	123	.001 484 5769
4	.809 132 4155	64	.033 753 0952	124	.001 408 0161
5	.767 404 7806	65	.032 012 4199	125	.001 335 4035
6	.727 829 0747	66	.030 361 5126	126	.001 266 5356
7	.690 294 3210	67	.028 795 7440	127	.001 201 2193
8	.654 695 2659	68	.027 310 7234	128	.001 139 2714
9	.620 932 0838	69	.025 902 2866	129	.001 080 5183
10	.588 910 0973	70	.024 566 4840	130	.001 024 7950
11	.558 539 5113	71	.023 299 5699	131	.000 971 9455
12	.529 735 1619	72	.022 097 9916	132	.000 921 8214
13	.502 416 2769	73	.020 958 3797	133	.000 874 2823
14	.476 506 2495	74	.019 877 5386	134	.000 829 1949
15	.451 932 4240	75	.018 852 4373	135	.000 786 4326
16	.428 625 8912	76	.017 880 2013	136	.000 745 8756
17	.406 521 2957	77	.016 958 1044	137	.000 707 4102
18	.385 556 6527	78	.016 083 5608	138	.000 670 9285
19	.365 673 1739	79	.015 254 1181	139	.000 636 3281
20	.346 815 1027	80	.014 467 4505	140	.000 603 5121
21	.328 929 5580	81	.013 721 3520	141	.000 572 3885
22	.311 966 3857	82	.013 013 7304	142	.000 542 8700
23	.295 878 0185	83	.012 342 6014	143	.000 514 8737
24	.280 619 3418	84	.011 706 0832	144	.000 488 3212
25	.266 147 5678	85	.011 102 3907	145	.000 463 1381
26	.252 422 1153	86	.010 529 8311	146	.000 439 2537
27	.239 404 4958	87	.009 986 7989	147	.000 416 6010
28	.227 058 2059	88	.009 471 7714	148	.000 395 1165
29	.215 348 6244	89	.008 983 3042	149	.000 374 7400
30	.204 242 9159	90	.008 520 0277	150	.000 355 4144
31	.193 709 9380	91	.008 080 6427	151	.000 337 0854
32	.183 720 1546	92	.007 663 9172	152	.000 319 7016
33	.174 245 5526	93	.007 268 6826	153	.000 303 2143
34	.165 259 5639	94	.006 893 8306	154	.000 287 5773
35	.156 736 9900	95	.006 538 3100	155	.000 272 7467
36	.148 653 9325	96	.006 201 1239	156	.000 258 6809
37	.140 987 7249	97	.005 881 3267	157	.000 245 3405
38	.133 716 8701	98	.005 578 0218	158	.000 232 6881
39	.126 820 9793	99	.005 290 3585	159	.000 220 6882
40	.120 280 7154	100	.005 017 5303	160	.000 209 3071
41	.114 077 7384	101	.004 758 7721	161	.000 198 5130
42	.108 194 6541	102	.004 513 3582	162	.000 188 2755
43	.102 614 9654	103	.004 280 6006	163	.000 178 5660
44	.097 323 0258	104	.004 059 8464	164	.000 169 3572
45	.092 303 9960	105	.003 850 4768	165	.000 160 6233
46	.087 543 8018	106	.003 651 9045	166	.000 152 3398
47	.083 029 0948	107	.003 463 5727	167	.000 144 4835
48	.078 747 2150	108	.003 284 9534	168	.000 137 0324
49	.074 686 1553	109	.003 115 5456	169	.000 129 9655
50	.070 834 5278	110	.002 954 8743	170	.000 123 2631
51	.067 181 5320	111	.002 802 4889	171	.000 116 9063
52	.063 716 9243	112	.002 657 9622	172	.000 110 8773
53	.060 430 9892	113	.002 520 8889	173	.000 105 1593
54	.057 314 5126	114	.002 390 8846	174	.000 099 7362
55	.054 358 7553	115	.002 267 5846	175	.000 094 5927
56	.051 555 4288	116	.002 150 6434	176	.000 089 7145
57	.048 896 6723	117	.002 039 7329	177	.000 085 0878
58	.046 375 0300	118	.001 934 5422	178	.000 080 6998
59	.043 983 4310	119	.001 834 7762	179	.000 076 5380
60	.041 715 1687	120	.001 740 1553	180	.000 072 5909

Present Value of 1

NOMINAL INTEREST RATE COMPOUNDED

YEARLY	HALF-YEARLY	QUARTERLY
@	@	@
5½%	11%	22%
5.5000%	11.0000%	22.0000%
PER ANNUM	PER ANNUM	PER ANNUM

Periods	Present Value	Periods	Present Value	Periods	Present Value
1	.947 867 2986	61	.038 159 2616	121	.001 536 2164
2	.898 452 4157	62	.036 169 9162	122	.001 456 1292
3	.851 613 6642	63	.034 284 2808	123	.001 380 2173
4	.807 216 7433	64	.032 496 9486	124	.001 308 2628
5	.765 134 3538	65	.030 802 7949	125	.001 240 0596
6	.725 245 8330	66	.029 196 9620	126	.001 175 4119
7	.687 436 8086	67	.027 674 8455	127	.001 114 1345
8	.651 598 8707	68	.026 232 0810	128	.001 056 0517
9	.617 629 2613	69	.024 864 5318	129	.001 000 9968
10	.585 430 5794	70	.023 568 2766	130	.000 948 8122
11	.554 910 5018	71	.022 339 5986	131	.000 899 3480
12	.525 981 5183	72	.021 174 9750	132	.000 852 4626
13	.498 560 6809	73	.020 071 0664	133	.000 808 0214
14	.472 569 3658	74	.019 024 7074	134	.000 765 8971
15	.447 933 0481	75	.018 032 8981	135	.000 725 9688
16	.424 581 0883	76	.017 092 7944	136	.000 688 1221
17	.402 446 5292	77	.016 201 7008	137	.000 652 2484
18	.381 465 9044	78	.015 357 0624	138	.000 618 2449
19	.361 579 0563	79	.014 556 4572	139	.000 586 0142
20	.342 728 9633	80	.013 797 5898	140	.000 555 4637
21	.324 861 5766	81	.013 078 2842	141	.000 526 5058
22	.307 925 6650	82	.012 396 4779	142	.000 499 0577
23	.291 872 6683	83	.011 750 2160	143	.000 473 0404
24	.276 656 5576	84	.011 137 6455	144	.000 448 3796
25	.262 233 7039	85	.010 557 0100	145	.000 425 0043
26	.248 562 7525	86	.010 006 6445	146	.000 402 8477
27	.235 604 5047	87	.009 484 9711	147	.000 381 8462
28	.223 321 8055	88	.008 990 4939	148	.000 361 9395
29	.211 679 4364	89	.008 521 7952	149	.000 343 0706
30	.200 644 0156	90	.008 077 5310	150	.000 325 1854
31	.190 183 9010	91	.007 656 4275	151	.000 308 2326
32	.180 269 1005	92	.007 257 2772	152	.000 292 1636
33	.170 871 1853	93	.006 878 9358	153	.000 276 9323
34	.161 963 2088	94	.006 520 3183	154	.000 262 4951
35	.153 519 6292	95	.006 180 3965	155	.000 248 8105
36	.145 516 2362	96	.005 858 1957	156	.000 235 8394
37	.137 930 0817	97	.005 552 7921	157	.000 223 5444
38	.130 739 4140	98	.005 263 3101	158	.000 211 8904
39	.123 923 6151	99	.004 988 9195	159	.000 200 8440
40	.117 463 1423	100	.004 728 8336	160	.000 190 3735
41	.111 339 4714	101	.004 482 3068	161	.000 180 4488
42	.105 535 0440	102	.004 248 6320	162	.000 171 0415
43	.100 033 2170	103	.004 027 1394	163	.000 162 1247
44	.094 818 2152	104	.003 817 1937	164	.000 153 6727
45	.089 875 0855	105	.003 618 1931	165	.000 145 6613
46	.085 189 6545	106	.003 429 5669	166	.000 138 0676
47	.080 748 4877	107	.003 250 7743	167	.000 130 8697
48	.076 538 8509	108	.003 081 3027	168	.000 124 0471
49	.072 548 6738	109	.002 920 6660	169	.000 117 5802
50	.068 766 5155	110	.002 768 4038	170	.000 111 4505
51	.065 181 5312	111	.002 624 0795	171	.000 105 6402
52	.061 783 4419	112	.002 487 2791	172	.000 100 1329
53	.058 562 5042	113	.002 357 6105	173	.000 094 9127
54	.055 509 4827	114	.002 234 7019	174	.000 089 9647
55	.052 615 6234	115	.002 118 2009	175	.000 085 2746
56	.049 872 6288	116	.002 007 7733	176	.000 080 8290
57	.047 272 6339	117	.001 903 1027	177	.000 076 6151
58	.044 808 1838	118	.001 803 8888	178	.000 072 6210
59	.042 472 2121	119	.001 709 8472	179	.000 068 8351
60	.040 258 0210	120	.001 620 7083	180	.000 065 2465

Present Value of 1

NOMINAL INTEREST RATE COMPOUNDED

YEARLY	HALF-YEARLY	QUARTERLY
@	@	@
$5\frac{9}{16}\%$	$11\frac{1}{8}\%$	$22\frac{1}{4}\%$
5.5625%	11.1250%	22.2500%
PER ANNUM	PER ANNUM	PER ANNUM

Periods	Present Value	Periods	Present Value	Periods	Present Value
1	.947 306 0983	61	.036 805 2963	121	.001 429 9811
2	.897 388 8438	62	.034 865 8816	122	.001 354 6298
3	.850 101 9243	63	.033 028 6623	123	.001 283 2491
4	.805 306 7371	64	.031 288 2532	124	.001 215 6297
5	.762 871 9830	65	.029 639 5531	125	.001 151 5734
6	.722 673 2817	66	.028 077 7294	126	.001 090 8925
7	.684 592 8068	67	.026 598 2043	127	.001 033 4091
8	.648 518 9407	68	.025 196 6411	128	.000 978 9548
9	.614 345 9474	69	.023 868 9318	129	.000 927 3698
10	.581 973 6624	70	.022 611 1846	130	.000 878 5031
11	.551 307 1995	71	.021 419 7131	131	.000 832 2113
12	.522 256 6721	72	.020 291 0248	132	.000 788 3589
13	.494 736 9303	73	.019 221 8116	133	.000 746 8172
14	.468 667 3112	74	.018 208 9393	134	.000 707 4645
15	.443 971 4019	75	.017 249 4392	135	.000 670 1854
16	.420 576 8165	76	.016 340 4990	136	.000 634 8707
17	.398 414 9831	77	.015 479 4543	137	.000 601 4169
18	.377 420 9431	78	.014 663 7815	138	.000 569 7259
19	.357 533 1610	79	.013 891 0896	139	.000 539 7048
20	.338 693 3438	80	.013 159 1139	140	.000 511 2657
21	.320 846 2700	81	.012 465 7089	141	.000 484 3251
22	.303 939 6282	82	.011 808 8420	142	.000 458 8041
23	.287 923 8633	83	.011 186 5881	143	.000 434 6279
24	.272 752 0315	84	.010 597 1231	144	.000 411 7257
25	.258 379 6628	85	.010 038 7193	145	.000 390 0303
26	.244 764 6302	86	.009 509 7400	146	.000 369 4780
27	.231 867 0269	87	.009 008 6347	147	.000 350 0088
28	.219 649 0485	88	.008 533 9346	148	.000 331 5655
29	.208 074 8832	89	.008 084 2483	149	.000 314 0940
30	.197 110 6057	90	.007 658 2577	150	.000 297 5432
31	.186 724 0788	91	.007 254 7142	151	.000 281 8644
32	.176 884 8586	92	.006 872 4350	152	.000 267 0119
33	.167 564 1052	93	.006 510 2996	153	.000 252 9420
34	.158 734 4987	94	.006 167 2465	154	.000 239 6135
35	.150 370 1587	95	.005 842 2703	155	.000 226 9873
36	.142 446 5683	96	.005 534 4182	156	.000 215 0265
37	.134 940 5028	97	.005 242 7882	157	.000 203 6959
38	.127 829 9612	98	.004 966 5252	158	.000 192 9624
39	.121 094 1018	99	.004 704 8196	159	.000 182 7944
40	.114 713 1811	100	.004 456 9043	160	.000 173 1623
41	.108 668 4960	101	.004 222 0526	161	.000 164 0377
42	.102 942 3290	102	.003 999 5762	162	.000 155 3939
43	.097 517 8960	103	.003 788 8229	163	.000 147 2056
44	.092 379 2976	104	.003 589 1751	164	.000 139 4488
45	.087 511 4720	105	.003 400 0474	165	.000 132 1007
46	.082 900 1511	106	.003 220 8857	166	.000 125 1398
47	.078 531 8186	107	.003 051 1646	167	.000 118 5457
48	.074 393 6707	108	.002 890 3869	168	.000 112 2990
49	.070 473 5779	109	.002 738 0811	169	.000 106 3815
50	.066 760 0501	110	.002 593 8009	170	.000 100 7759
51	.063 242 2026	111	.002 457 1234	171	.000 095 4656
52	.059 909 7242	112	.002 327 6480	172	.000 090 4352
53	.056 752 8471	113	.002 204 9952	173	.000 085 6698
54	.053 762 3182	114	.002 088 8054	174	.000 081 1555
55	.050 929 3718	115	.001 978 7380	175	.000 076 8791
56	.048 245 7045	116	.001 874 4706	176	.000 072 8280
57	.045 703 4501	117	.001 775 6974	177	.000 068 9904
58	.043 295 1570	118	.001 682 1290	178	.000 065 3551
59	.041 013 7663	119	.001 593 4911	179	.000 061 9113
60	.038 852 5909	120	.001 509 5238	180	.000 058 6489

Present Value of 1

NOMINAL INTEREST RATE COMPOUNDED

YEARLY	HALF-YEARLY	QUARTERLY
@	@	@
$5\frac{5}{8}\%$	$11\frac{1}{4}\%$	$22\frac{1}{2}\%$
5.6250%	11.2500%	22.5000%
PER ANNUM	PER ANNUM	PER ANNUM

Periods	Present Value	Periods	Present Value	Periods	Present Value
1	.946 745 5621	61	.035 500 1314	121	.001 331 1489
2	.896 327 1594	62	.033 609 5919	122	.001 260 2593
3	.848 593 7604	63	.031 819 7319	123	.001 193 1449
4	.803 402 3767	64	.030 125 1900	124	.001 129 6047
5	.760 617 6347	65	.028 520 8899	125	.001 069 4482
6	.720 111 3702	66	.027 002 0260	126	.001 012 4953
7	.681 762 2440	67	.025 564 0483	127	.000 958 5755
8	.645 455 3789	68	.024 202 6492	128	.000 907 5271
9	.611 082 0155	69	.022 913 7508	129	.000 859 1972
10	.578 539 1863	70	.021 693 4918	130	.000 813 4412
11	.547 729 4071	71	.020 538 2171	131	.000 770 1218
12	.518 560 3855	72	.019 444 4659	132	.000 729 1094
13	.490 944 7436	73	.018 408 9618	133	.000 690 2811
14	.464 799 7573	74	.017 428 6029	134	.000 653 5206
15	.440 047 1075	75	.016 500 4525	135	.000 618 7177
16	.416 612 6461	76	.015 621 7301	136	.000 585 7682
17	.394 426 1739	77	.014 789 8037	137	.000 554 5735
18	.373 421 2297	78	.014 002 1810	138	.000 525 0400
19	.353 534 8920	79	.013 256 5027	139	.000 497 0793
20	.334 707 5901	80	.012 550 5351	140	.000 470 6076
21	.316 882 9255	81	.011 882 1634	141	.000 445 5456
22	.300 007 5034	82	.011 249 3855	142	.000 421 8184
23	.284 030 7725	83	.010 650 3058	143	.000 399 3547
24	.268 904 8734	84	.010 083 1297	144	.000 378 0873
25	.254 584 4955	85	.009 546 1583	145	.000 357 9524
26	.241 026 7413	86	.009 037 7830	146	.000 338 8899
27	.228 190 9977	87	.008 556 4810	147	.000 320 8425
28	.216 038 8144	88	.008 100 8104	148	.000 303 7562
29	.204 533 7887	89	.007 669 4063	149	.000 287 5798
30	.193 641 4568	90	.007 260 9764	150	.000 272 2649
31	.183 329 1899	91	.006 874 2972	151	.000 257 7656
32	.173 566 0969	92	.006 508 2103	152	.000 244 0385
33	.164 322 9320	93	.006 161 6192	153	.000 231 0423
34	.155 572 0066	94	.005 833 4857	154	.000 218 7383
35	.147 287 1069	95	.005 522 8267	155	.000 207 0895
36	.139 443 4148	96	.005 228 7116	156	.000 196 0611
37	.132 017 4341	97	.004 950 2595	157	.000 185 6200
38	.124 986 9199	98	.004 686 6363	158	.000 175 7349
39	.118 330 8117	99	.004 437 0521	159	.000 166 3762
40	.112 029 1709	100	.004 200 7594	160	.000 157 5159
41	.106 063 1203	101	.003 977 0503	161	.000 149 1275
42	.100 414 7885	102	.003 765 2547	162	.000 141 1858
43	.095 067 2554	103	.003 564 7382	163	.000 133 6670
44	.090 004 5021	104	.003 374 9001	164	.000 126 5487
45	.085 211 3630	105	.003 195 1717	165	.000 119 8094
46	.080 673 4797	106	.003 025 0146	166	.000 113 4290
47	.076 377 2589	107	.002 863 9191	167	.000 107 3884
48	.072 309 8309	108	.002 711 4027	168	.000 101 6695
49	.068 459 0115	109	.002 567 0085	169	.000 096 2552
50	.064 813 2653	110	.002 430 3039	170	.000 091 1291
51	.061 361 6713	111	.002 300 8794	171	.000 086 2761
52	.058 093 8900	112	.002 178 3474	172	.000 081 6815
53	.055 000 1326	113	.002 062 3407	173	.000 077 3316
54	.052 071 1314	114	.001 952 5119	174	.000 073 2134
55	.049 298 1126	115	.001 848 5320	175	.000 069 3144
56	.046 672 7693	116	.001 750 0895	176	.000 065 6231
57	.044 187 2372	117	.001 656 8894	177	.000 062 1284
58	.041 834 0707	118	.001 568 6527	178	.000 058 8198
59	.039 606 2208	119	.001 485 1150	179	.000 055 6874
60	.037 497 0138	120	.001 406 0260	180	.000 052 7218

Present Value of 1

NOMINAL INTEREST RATE COMPOUNDED		
YEARLY	HALF-YEARLY	QUARTERLY
@	@	@
$5\frac{11}{16}\%$	$11\frac{3}{8}\%$	$22\frac{3}{4}\%$
5.6875%	11.3750%	22.7500%
PER ANNUM	PER ANNUM	PER ANNUM

Periods	Present Value	Periods	Present Value	Periods	Present Value
1	.946 185 6889	61	.034 241 9807	121	.001 239 1999
2	.895 267 3580	62	.032 399 2721	122	.001 172 5132
3	.847 089 1619	63	.030 655 7276	123	.001 109 4153
4	.801 503 6422	64	.029 006 0108	124	.001 049 7128
5	.758 371 2759	65	.027 445 0723	125	.000 993 2233
6	.717 560 0482	66	.025 968 1346	126	.000 939 7736
7	.678 945 0485	67	.024 570 6773	127	.000 889 2004
8	.642 408 0885	68	.023 248 4233	128	.000 841 3487
9	.607 837 3398	69	.021 997 3254	129	.000 796 0721
10	.575 126 9921	70	.020 813 5545	130	.000 753 2320
11	.544 176 9293	71	.019 693 4874	131	.000 712 6973
12	.514 892 4227	72	.018 633 6959	132	.000 674 3440
13	.487 183 8417	73	.017 630 9364	133	.000 638 0547
14	.460 966 3789	74	.016 682 1397	134	.000 603 7182
15	.436 159 7908	75	.015 784 4019	135	.000 571 2295
16	.412 688 1522	76	.014 934 9752	136	.000 540 4892
17	.390 479 6236	77	.014 131 2598	137	.000 511 4031
18	.369 466 2317	78	.013 370 7957	138	.000 483 8823
19	.349 583 6609	79	.012 651 2556	139	.000 457 8425
20	.330 771 0571	80	.011 970 4370	140	.000 433 2040
21	.312 970 8405	81	.011 326 2562	141	.000 409 8915
22	.296 128 5303	82	.010 716 7415	142	.000 387 8334
23	.280 192 5775	83	.010 140 0274	143	.000 366 9625
24	.265 114 2070	84	.009 594 3488	144	.000 347 2146
25	.250 847 2686	85	.009 078 0356	145	.000 328 5295
26	.237 348 0956	86	.008 589 5073	146	.000 310 8499
27	.224 575 3714	87	.008 127 2689	147	.000 294 1217
28	.212 490 0025	88	.007 689 9055	148	.000 278 2938
29	.201 054 9994	89	.007 276 0786	149	.000 263 3176
30	.190 235 3631	90	.006 884 5214	150	.000 249 1473
31	.179 997 9781	91	.006 514 0356	151	.000 235 7396
32	.170 311 5109	92	.006 163 4873	152	.000 223 0535
33	.161 146 3143	93	.005 831 8035	153	.000 211 0500
34	.152 474 3364	94	.005 517 9690	154	.000 199 6925
35	.144 269 0351	95	.005 221 0233	155	.000 188 9462
36	.136 505 2963	96	.004 940 0575	156	.000 178 7782
37	.129 159 3579	97	.004 674 2117	157	.000 169 1574
38	.122 208 7360	98	.004 422 6722	158	.000 160 0543
39	.115 632 1571	99	.004 184 6692	159	.000 151 4411
40	.109 409 4922	100	.003 959 4741	160	.000 143 2914
41	.103 521 6957	101	.003 746 3977	161	.000 135 5802
42	.097 950 7470	102	.003 544 7879	162	.000 128 2841
43	.092 679 5950	103	.003 354 0276	163	.000 121 3806
44	.087 692 1065	104	.003 173 5329	164	.000 114 8485
45	.082 973 0162	105	.003 002 7514	165	.000 108 6681
46	.078 507 8805	106	.002 841 1604	166	.000 102 8202
47	.074 283 0330	107	.002 688 2653	167	.000 097 2870
48	.070 285 5427	108	.002 543 5982	168	.000 092 0515
49	.066 503 1747	109	.002 406 7162	169	.000 087 0978
50	.062 924 3522	110	.002 277 2004	170	.000 082 4107
51	.059 538 1215	111	.002 154 6545	171	.000 077 9759
52	.056 334 1185	112	.002 038 7032	172	.000 073 7796
53	.053 302 5367	113	.001 928 9918	173	.000 069 8092
54	.050 434 0974	114	.001 825 1844	174	.000 066 0525
55	.047 720 0212	115	.001 726 9634	175	.000 062 4979
56	.045 152 0012	116	.001 634 0280	176	.000 059 1346
57	.042 722 1773	117	.001 546 0940	177	.000 055 9524
58	.040 423 1128	118	.001 462 8920	178	.000 052 9413
59	.038 247 7708	119	.001 384 1674	179	.000 050 0923
60	.036 189 4934	120	.001 309 6794	180	.000 047 3966

Present Value of 1

	NOMINAL INTEREST RATE COMPOUNDED	
YEARLY	HALF-YEARLY	QUARTERLY
@	@	@
$5\frac{3}{4}\%$	$11\frac{1}{2}\%$	23%
5.7500%	11.5000%	23.0000%
PER ANNUM	PER ANNUM	PER ANNUM

Periods	Present Value	Periods	Present Value	Periods	Present Value
1	.945 626 4775	61	.033 029 1244	121	.001 153 6511
2	.894 209 4350	62	.031 233 2146	122	.001 090 9231
3	.845 588 1182	63	.029 534 9547	123	.001 031 6057
4	.799 610 5137	64	.027 929 0352	124	.000 975 5137
5	.756 132 8735	65	.026 410 4352	125	.000 922 4716
6	.715 019 2657	66	.024 974 4068	126	.000 872 3135
7	.676 141 1496	67	.023 616 4603	127	.000 824 8828
8	.639 376 9736	68	.022 332 3502	128	.000 780 0310
9	.604 611 7954	69	.021 118 0616	129	.000 737 6180
10	.571 736 9223	70	.019 969 7982	130	.000 697 5111
11	.540 649 5720	71	.018 883 9699	131	.000 659 5850
12	.511 252 5503	72	.017 857 1820	132	.000 623 7210
13	.483 453 9483	73	.016 886 2241	133	.000 589 8071
14	.457 166 8542	74	.015 968 0606	134	.000 557 7372
15	.432 309 0820	75	.015 099 8209	135	.000 527 4111
16	.408 802 9144	76	.014 278 7905	136	.000 498 7339
17	.386 574 8599	77	.013 502 4023	137	.000 471 6159
18	.365 555 4231	78	.012 768 2292	138	.000 445 9725
19	.345 678 8871	79	.012 073 9756	139	.000 421 7234
20	.326 883 1084	80	.011 417 4710	140	.000 398 7928
21	.309 109 3223	81	.010 796 6629	141	.000 377 1091
22	.292 301 9597	82	.010 209 6103	142	.000 356 6043
23	.276 408 4725	83	.009 654 4778	143	.000 337 2145
24	.261 379 1702	84	.009 129 5298	144	.000 318 8789
25	.247 167 0640	85	.008 633 1251	145	.000 301 5404
26	.233 727 7201	86	.008 163 7117	146	.000 285 1446
27	.221 019 1207	87	.007 719 8220	147	.000 269 6402
28	.209 001 5325	88	.007 300 0680	148	.000 254 9790
29	.197 637 3830	89	.006 903 1376	149	.000 241 1149
30	.186 891 1423	90	.006 527 7897	150	.000 228 0046
31	.176 729 2126	91	.006 172 8508	151	.000 215 6072
32	.167 119 8228	92	.005 837 2112	152	.000 203 8839
33	.158 032 9294	93	.005 519 8214	153	.000 192 7980
34	.149 440 1223	94	.005 219 6893	154	.000 182 3149
35	.141 314 5365	95	.004 935 8764	155	.000 172 4018
36	.133 630 7674	96	.004 667 4954	156	.000 163 0277
37	.126 364 7918	97	.004 413 7072	157	.000 154 1633
38	.119 493 8930	98	.004 173 7184	158	.000 145 7809
39	.112 996 5891	99	.003 946 7787	159	.000 137 8543
40	.106 852 5665	100	.003 732 1784	160	.000 130 3586
41	.101 042 6161	101	.003 529 2467	161	.000 123 2706
42	.095 548 5732	102	.003 337 3491	162	.000 116 5679
43	.090 353 2607	103	.003 155 8857	163	.000 110 2297
44	.085 440 4356	104	.002 984 2891	164	.000 104 2361
45	.080 794 7382	105	.002 822 0228	165	.000 098 5685
46	.076 401 6437	106	.002 668 5795	166	.000 093 2089
47	.072 247 4172	107	.002 523 4794	167	.000 088 1408
48	.068 319 0706	108	.002 386 2689	168	.000 083 3483
49	.064 604 3221	109	.002 256 5191	169	.000 078 8164
50	.061 091 5575	110	.002 133 8242	170	.000 074 5308
51	.057 769 7944	111	.002 017 8007	171	.000 070 4783
52	.054 628 6471	112	.001 908 0857	172	.000 066 6462
53	.051 658 2952	113	.001 804 3364	173	.000 063 0224
54	.048 849 4517	114	.001 706 2283	174	.000 059 5957
55	.046 193 3349	115	.001 613 4545	175	.000 056 3552
56	.043 681 6406	116	.001 525 7254	176	.000 053 2910
57	.041 306 5159	117	.001 442 7663	177	.000 050 3934
58	.039 060 5352	118	.001 364 3181	178	.000 047 6533
59	.036 936 6763	119	.001 290 1353	179	.000 045 0622
60	.034 928 2991	120	.001 219 9861	180	.000 042 6120

NOMINAL INTEREST RATE COMPOUNDED

	YEARLY @ $5\frac{13}{16}\%$ 5.8125% PER ANNUM		HALF-YEARLY @ $11\frac{5}{8}\%$ 11.6250% PER ANNUM		QUARTERLY @ $23\frac{1}{4}\%$ 23.2500% PER ANNUM
Periods	Present Value	Periods	Present Value	Periods	Present Value
1	.945 067 9268	61	.031 859 9065	121	.001 074 0536
2	.893 153 3862	62	.030 109 7758	122	.001 015 0536
3	.844 090 6190	63	.028 455 7834	123	.000 959 2946
4	.797 722 9713	64	.026 892 6482	124	.000 906 5986
5	.753 902 3946	65	.025 415 3793	125	.000 856 7973
6	.712 488 9730	66	.024 019 2598	126	.000 809 7316
7	.673 350 4766	67	.022 699 8321	127	.000 765 2514
8	.636 361 9389	68	.021 452 8832	128	.000 723 2145
9	.601 405 2582	69	.020 274 4319	129	.000 683 4869
10	.568 368 8205	70	.019 160 7153	130	.000 645 9415
11	.537 147 1429	71	.018 108 1775	131	.000 610 4586
12	.507 640 5367	72	.017 113 4578	132	.000 576 9248
13	.479 754 7895	73	.016 173 3800	133	.000 545 2332
14	.453 400 8643	74	.015 284 9428	134	.000 515 2824
15	.428 494 6148	75	.014 445 3092	135	.000 486 9768
16	.404 956 5172	76	.013 651 7984	136	.000 460 2262
17	.382 711 4162	77	.012 901 8768	137	.000 434 9450
18	.361 688 2846	78	.012 193 1499	138	.000 411 0526
19	.341 819 9973	79	.011 523 3549	139	.000 388 4726
20	.323 043 1162	80	.010 890 3532	140	.000 367 1330
21	.305 297 6880	81	.010 292 1235	141	.000 346 9656
22	.288 527 0531	82	.009 726 7558	142	.000 327 9061
23	.272 677 6639	83	.009 192 4449	143	.000 309 8935
24	.257 698 9145	84	.008 687 4849	144	.000 292 8704
25	.243 542 9788	85	.008 210 2633	145	.000 276 7825
26	.230 164 6581	86	.007 759 2565	146	.000 261 5782
27	.217 521 2362	87	.007 333 0245	147	.000 247 2092
28	.205 572 3437	88	.006 930 2063	148	.000 233 6295
29	.194 279 8287	89	.006 549 5157	149	.000 220 7957
30	.183 607 6349	90	.006 189 7372	150	.000 208 6670
31	.173 521 6869	91	.005 849 7221	151	.000 197 2044
32	.163 989 7809	92	.005 528 3847	152	.000 186 3716
33	.154 981 4822	93	.005 224 6991	153	.000 176 1338
34	.146 468 0281	94	.004 937 6955	154	.000 166 4584
35	.138 422 2356	95	.004 666 4577	155	.000 157 3145
36	.130 818 4152	96	.004 410 1195	156	.000 148 6729
37	.123 632 2885	97	.004 167 8625	157	.000 140 5060
38	.116 840 9105	98	.003 938 9132	158	.000 132 7877
39	.110 422 5971	99	.003 722 5405	159	.000 125 4934
40	.104 356 8549	100	.003 518 0536	160	.000 118 5998
41	.098 624 3165	101	.003 324 7996	161	.000 112 0849
42	.093 206 6783	102	.003 142 1615	162	.000 105 9278
43	.088 086 6422	103	.002 969 5561	163	.000 100 1090
44	.083 247 8604	104	.002 806 4322	164	.000 094 6098
45	.078 674 8828	105	.002 652 2691	165	.000 089 4127
46	.074 353 1084	106	.002 506 5744	166	.000 084 5010
47	.070 268 7380	107	.002 368 8831	167	.000 079 8592
48	.066 408 7305	108	.002 238 7554	168	.000 075 4724
49	.062 760 7613	109	.002 115 7759	169	.000 071 3265
50	.059 313 1825	110	.001 999 5520	170	.000 067 4084
51	.056 054 9864	111	.001 889 7125	171	.000 063 7055
52	.052 975 7698	112	.001 785 9066	172	.000 060 2061
53	.050 065 7010	113	.001 687 8031	173	.000 056 8988
54	.047 315 4882	114	.001 595 0886	174	.000 053 7732
55	.044 716 3503	115	.001 507 4670	175	.000 050 8194
56	.042 259 9885	116	.001 424 6587	176	.000 048 0278
57	.039 938 5597	117	.001 346 3993	177	.000 045 3895
58	.037 744 6518	118	.001 272 4388	178	.000 042 8962
59	.035 671 2599	119	.001 202 5411	179	.000 040 5398
60	.033 711 7636	120	.001 136 4830	180	.000 038 3128

Present Value of 1

NOMINAL INTEREST RATE COMPOUNDED

YEARLY	HALF-YEARLY	QUARTERLY
@	@	@
$5\frac{7}{8}\%$	$11\frac{3}{4}\%$	$23\frac{1}{2}\%$
5.8750%	11.7500%	23.5000%
PER ANNUM	PER ANNUM	PER ANNUM

Periods	Present Value	Periods	Present Value	Periods	Present Value
1	.944 510 0354	61	.030 732 7325	121	.000 999 9903
2	.892 099 2070	62	.029 027 3743	122	.000 944 5008
3	.842 596 6536	63	.027 416 6463	123	.000 892 0905
4	.795 840 9951	64	.025 895 2976	124	.000 842 5885
5	.751 679 8065	65	.024 458 3684	125	.000 795 8333
6	.709 969 1207	66	.023 101 1744	126	.000 751 6725
7	.670 572 9593	67	.021 819 2911	127	.000 709 9622
8	.633 362 8896	68	.020 608 5394	128	.000 670 5664
9	.598 217 6052	69	.019 464 9723	129	.000 633 3567
10	.565 022 5315	70	.018 384 8617	130	.000 598 2118
11	.533 669 4513	71	.017 364 6863	131	.000 565 0170
12	.504 056 1523	72	.016 401 1205	132	.000 533 6643
13	.476 086 0943	73	.015 491 0229	133	.000 504 0512
14	.449 668 0938	74	.014 631 4266	134	.000 476 0815
15	.424 716 0272	75	.013 819 5293	135	.000 449 6637
16	.401 148 5499	76	.013 052 6841	136	.000 424 7119
17	.378 888 8310	77	.012 328 3911	137	.000 401 1446
18	.357 864 3032	78	.011 644 2891	138	.000 378 8851
19	.338 006 4257	79	.010 998 1479	139	.000 357 8608
20	.319 250 4611	80	.010 387 8611	140	.000 338 0031
21	.301 535 2643	81	.009 811 4390	141	.000 319 2474
22	.284 803 0832	82	.009 267 0026	142	.000 301 5323
23	.268 999 3702	83	.008 752 7770	143	.000 284 8003
24	.254 072 6047	84	.008 267 0857	144	.000 268 9968
25	.239 974 1248	85	.007 808 3454	145	.000 254 0701
26	.226 657 9692	86	.007 375 0606	146	.000 239 9718
27	.214 080 7265	87	.006 965 8187	147	.000 226 6558
28	.202 201 3945	88	.006 579 2857	148	.000 214 0786
29	.190 981 2463	89	.006 214 2014	149	.000 202 1994
30	.180 383 7037	90	.005 869 3756	150	.000 190 9794
31	.170 374 2184	91	.005 543 6841	151	.000 180 3819
32	.160 920 1591	92	.005 236 0653	152	.000 170 3726
33	.151 990 7051	93	.004 945 5162	153	.000 160 9186
34	.143 556 7463	94	.004 671 0897	154	.000 151 9892
35	.135 590 7875	95	.004 411 8911	155	.000 143 5554
36	.128 066 8595	96	.004 167 0754	156	.000 135 5895
37	.120 960 4340	97	.003 935 8445	157	.000 128 0656
38	.114 248 3438	98	.003 717 4447	158	.000 120 9593
39	.107 908 7073	99	.003 511 1638	159	.000 114 2472
40	.101 920 8569	100	.003 316 3294	160	.000 107 9077
41	.096 265 2722	101	.003 132 3064	161	.000 101 9199
42	.090 923 5156	102	.002 958 4949	162	.000 096 2643
43	.085 878 1730	103	.002 794 3281	163	.000 090 9226
44	.081 112 7962	104	.002 639 2709	164	.000 085 8773
45	.076 611 8500	105	.002 492 8179	165	.000 081 1120
46	.072 360 6612	106	.002 354 4915	166	.000 076 6111
47	.068 345 3706	107	.002 223 8408	167	.000 072 3600
48	.064 552 8884	108	.002 100 4400	168	.000 068 3447
49	.060 970 8510	109	.001 983 8867	169	.000 064 5523
50	.057 587 5806	110	.001 873 8009	170	.000 060 9703
51	.054 392 0478	111	.001 769 8237	171	.000 057 5870
52	.051 373 8350	112	.001 671 6163	172	.000 054 3915
53	.048 523 1027	113	.001 578 8583	173	.000 051 3733
54	.045 830 5574	114	.001 491 2475	174	.000 048 5226
55	.043 287 4214	115	.001 408 4983	175	.000 045 8301
56	.040 885 4040	116	.001 330 3407	176	.000 043 2870
57	.038 616 6743	117	.001 256 5202	177	.000 040 8850
58	.036 473 8364	118	.001 186 7959	178	.000 038 6163
59	.034 449 9046	119	.001 120 9407	179	.000 036 4735
60	.032 538 2806	120	.001 058 7397	180	.000 034 4496

Present Value of 1

NOMINAL INTEREST RATE COMPOUNDED

YEARLY	HALF-YEARLY	QUARTERLY
@	@	@
$5\frac{15}{16}\%$	$11\frac{7}{8}\%$	$23\frac{3}{4}\%$
5.9375%	11.8750%	23.7500%
PER ANNUM	PER ANNUM	PER ANNUM

Periods	Present Value	Periods	Present Value	Periods	Present Value
1	.943 952 8024	61	.029 646 0671	121	.000 931 0733
2	.891 046 8931	62	.027 984 4881	122	.000 878 8893
3	.841 106 2118	63	.026 416 0360	123	.000 829 6300
4	.793 964 5657	64	.024 935 4912	124	.000 783 1316
5	.749 465 0767	65	.023 537 9268	125	.000 739 2392
6	.707 459 6595	66	.022 218 6919	126	.000 697 8070
7	.667 808 5281	67	.020 973 3965	127	.000 658 6968
8	.630 379 7315	68	.019 797 8964	128	.000 621 7787
9	.595 048 7141	69	.018 688 2798	129	.000 586 9298
10	.561 697 9013	70	.017 640 8541	130	.000 554 0340
11	.530 216 3080	71	.016 652 1337	131	.000 522 9819
12	.500 499 1698	72	.015 718 8282	132	.000 493 6703
13	.472 447 5939	73	.014 837 8320	133	.000 466 0014
14	.445 968 2302	74	.014 006 2131	134	.000 439 8834
15	.420 972 9607	75	.013 221 2041	135	.000 415 2291
16	.397 378 6059	76	.012 480 1926	136	.000 391 9567
17	.375 106 6487	77	.011 780 7128	137	.000 369 9886
18	.354 082 9722	78	.011 120 4369	138	.000 349 2518
19	.334 237 6139	79	.010 497 1676	139	.000 329 6772
20	.315 504 5323	80	.009 908 8307	140	.000 311 1997
21	.297 821 3874	81	.009 353 4685	141	.000 293 7579
22	.281 129 3332	82	.008 829 2328	142	.000 277 2936
23	.265 372 8219	83	.008 334 3791	143	.000 261 7520
24	.250 499 4189	84	.007 867 2605	144	.000 247 0816
25	.236 459 6285	85	.007 426 3226	145	.000 233 2333
26	.223 206 7290	86	.007 010 0980	146	.000 220 1613
27	.210 696 6173	87	.006 617 2017	147	.000 207 8218
28	.198 887 6624	88	.006 246 3261	148	.000 196 1740
29	.187 740 5662	89	.005 896 2370	149	.000 185 1790
30	.177 218 2336	90	.005 565 7694	150	.000 174 8002
31	.167 285 6483	91	.005 253 8236	151	.000 165 0032
32	.157 909 7565	92	.004 959 3616	152	.000 155 7552
33	.149 059 3571	93	.004 681 4032	153	.000 147 0256
34	.140 704 9979	94	.004 419 0237	154	.000 138 7852
35	.132 818 8771	95	.004 171 3498	155	.000 131 0067
36	.125 374 7512	96	.003 937 5573	156	.000 123 6641
37	.118 347 8477	97	.003 716 8683	157	.000 116 7331
38	.111 714 7825	98	.003 508 5482	158	.000 110 1905
39	.105 453 4820	99	.003 311 9039	159	.000 104 0147
40	.099 543 1099	100	.003 126 2810	160	.000 098 1849
41	.093 963 9975	101	.002 951 0617	161	.000 092 6819
42	.088 697 5788	102	.002 785 6630	162	.000 087 4874
43	.083 726 3281	103	.002 629 5344	163	.000 082 5840
44	.079 033 7020	104	.002 482 1563	164	.000 077 9554
45	.074 604 0845	105	.002 343 0384	165	.000 073 5862
46	.070 422 7346	106	.002 211 7177	166	.000 069 4619
47	.066 475 7377	107	.002 087 7571	167	.000 065 5687
48	.062 749 9589	108	.001 970 7442	168	.000 061 8938
49	.059 232 9995	109	.001 860 2895	169	.000 058 4248
50	.055 913 1559	110	.001 756 0255	170	.000 055 1503
51	.052 779 3802	111	.001 657 6052	171	.000 052 0592
52	.049 821 2439	112	.001 564 7010	172	.000 049 1415
53	.047 028 9028	113	.001 477 0039	173	.000 046 3872
54	.044 393 0645	114	.001 394 2220	174	.000 043 7874
55	.041 904 9577	115	.001 316 0798	175	.000 041 3332
56	.039 556 3022	116	.001 242 3172	176	.000 039 0166
57	.037 339 2823	117	.001 172 6888	177	.000 036 8298
58	.035 246 5202	118	.001 106 9629	178	.000 034 7656
59	.033 271 0515	119	.001 044 9207	179	.000 032 8171
60	.031 406 3023	120	.000 986 3558	180	.000 030 9778

Present Value of 1

NOMINAL INTEREST RATE COMPOUNDED

YEARLY	HALF-YEARLY	QUARTERLY
@	@	@
6%	**12%**	**24%**
6.0000%	12.0000%	24.0000%
PER ANNUM	PER ANNUM	PER ANNUM

Periods	Present Value	Periods	Present Value	Periods	Present Value
1	.943 396 2264	61	.028 598 4318	121	.000 866 9425
2	.889 996 4400	62	.026 979 6526	122	.000 817 8703
3	.839 619 2830	63	.025 452 5025	123	.000 771 5758
4	.792 093 6632	64	.024 011 7948	124	.000 727 9017
5	.747 258 1729	65	.022 652 6366	125	.000 686 6997
6	.704 960 5404	66	.021 370 4119	126	.000 647 8299
7	.665 057 1136	67	.020 160 7659	127	.000 611 1603
8	.627 412 3713	68	.019 019 5905	128	.000 576 5663
9	.591 898 4635	69	.017 943 0099	129	.000 543 9305
10	.558 394 7769	70	.016 927 3678	130	.000 513 1419
11	.526 787 5254	71	.015 969 2149	131	.000 484 0962
12	.496 969 3636	72	.015 065 2971	132	.000 456 6945
13	.468 839 0222	73	.014 212 5444	133	.000 430 8439
14	.442 300 9644	74	.013 408 0608	134	.000 406 4565
15	.417 265 0607	75	.012 649 1140	135	.000 383 4495
16	.393 646 2837	76	.011 933 1264	136	.000 361 7448
17	.371 364 4186	77	.011 257 6664	137	.000 341 2687
18	.350 343 7911	78	.010 620 4400	138	.000 321 9516
19	.330 513 0105	79	.010 019 2830	139	.000 303 7279
20	.311 804 7269	80	.009 452 1538	140	.000 286 5358
21	.294 155 4027	81	.008 917 1262	141	.000 270 3168
22	.277 505 0969	82	.008 412 3832	142	.000 255 0158
23	.261 797 2612	83	.007 936 2106	143	.000 240 5810
24	.246 978 5483	84	.007 486 9911	144	.000 226 9632
25	.232 998 6305	85	.007 063 1992	145	.000 214 1162
26	.219 810 0288	86	.006 663 3954	146	.000 201 9964
27	.207 367 9517	87	.006 286 2221	147	.000 190 5627
28	.195 630 1431	88	.005 930 3982	148	.000 179 7761
29	.184 556 7388	89	.005 594 7153	149	.000 169 6001
30	.174 110 1309	90	.005 278 0333	150	.000 160 0001
31	.164 254 8405	91	.004 979 2767	151	.000 150 9435
32	.154 957 3967	92	.004 697 4308	152	.000 142 3995
33	.146 186 2233	93	.004 431 5385	153	.000 134 3392
34	.137 911 5314	94	.004 180 6967	154	.000 126 7351
35	.130 105 2183	95	.003 944 0535	155	.000 119 5614
36	.122 740 7720	96	.003 720 8052	156	.000 112 7937
37	.115 793 1811	97	.003 510 1936	157	.000 106 4092
38	.109 238 8501	98	.003 311 5034	158	.000 100 3860
39	.103 055 5190	99	.003 124 0598	159	.000 094 7038
40	.097 222 1877	100	.002 947 2262	160	.000 089 3432
41	.091 719 0450	101	.002 780 4021	161	.000 084 2860
42	.086 527 4010	102	.002 623 0209	162	.000 079 5151
43	.081 629 6235	103	.002 474 5480	163	.000 075 0143
44	.077 009 0788	104	.002 334 4792	164	.000 070 7682
45	.072 650 0743	105	.002 202 3389	165	.000 066 7624
46	.068 537 8060	106	.002 077 6782	166	.000 062 9834
47	.064 658 3075	107	.001 960 0738	167	.000 059 4183
48	.060 998 4033	108	.001 849 1262	168	.000 056 0550
49	.057 545 6635	109	.001 744 4587	169	.000 052 8821
50	.054 288 3618	110	.001 645 7157	170	.000 049 8888
51	.051 215 4357	111	.001 552 5620	171	.000 047 0649
52	.048 316 4488	112	.001 464 6811	172	.000 044 4008
53	.045 581 5554	113	.001 381 7747	173	.000 041 8876
54	.043 001 4674	114	.001 303 5610	174	.000 039 5166
55	.040 567 4221	115	.001 229 7745	175	.000 037 2798
56	.038 271 1529	116	.001 160 1647	176	.000 035 1696
57	.036 104 8612	117	.001 094 4950	177	.000 033 1789
58	.034 061 1898	118	.001 032 5424	178	.000 031 3008
59	.032 133 1979	119	.000 974 0966	179	.000 029 5291
60	.030 314 3377	120	.000 918 9591	180	.000 027 8576

Amount of 1 Per Period

The amount of a periodical payment of 1 accumulated at compound interest

$$s_{\overline{n}|} = \frac{(1+i)^n - 1}{i}$$

Effective Rates	***Number of periods***
3% increasing by $\frac{1}{16}$% to 6%	180

NOTE

Nominal annual rates at these effective rates, compounded half yearly and quarterly, are shown in the heading to each table.

Amount of 1 Per Period

NOMINAL INTEREST RATE COMPOUNDED

	YEARLY	HALF-YEARLY	QUARTERLY
	@	@	@
	3%	**6%**	**12%**
	3.0000%	6.0000%	12.0000%
	PER ANNUM	PER ANNUM	PER ANNUM

Periods	Amount	Periods	Amount	Periods	Amount
1	1,000 000 0000	61	168.945 039 9056	121	1158,410 558 3223
2	2,030 000 0000	62	175.013 391 1027	122	1194,162 875 0720
3	3,090 900 0000	63	181.263 792 8358	123	1230,987 761 3241
4	4,183 627 0000	64	187.701 706 6209	124	1268,917 394 1639
5	5,309 135 8100	65	194.332 757 8195	125	1307,984 915 9888
6	6,468 409 8843	66	201.162 740 5541	126	1348,224 463 4684
7	7,662 462 1808	67	208.197 622 7707	127	1389,671 197 3725
8	8,892 336 0463	68	215.443 551 4539	128	1432,361 333 2937
9	10,159 106 1276	69	222.906 857 9975	129	1476,332 173 2925
10	11,463 879 3115	70	230.594 063 7374	130	1521,622 138 4913
11	12,807 795 6908	71	238.511 885 6495	131	1568,270 802 6460
12	14,192 029 5615	72	246.667 242 2190	132	1616,318 926 7254
13	15,617 790 4484	73	255.067 259 4856	133	1665,808 494 5271
14	17,086 324 1618	74	263.719 277 2701	134	1716,782 749 3630
15	18,598 913 8867	75	272.630 855 5882	135	1769,286 231 8438
16	20,156 881 3033	76	281.809 781 2559	136	1823,364 818 7992
17	21,761 587 7424	77	291.264 074 6936	137	1879,065 763 3631
18	23,414 435 3747	78	301.001 996 9344	138	1936,437 736 2640
19	25,116 868 4359	79	311.032 056 8424	139	1995,530 868 3519
20	26,870 374 4890	80	321.363 018 5477	140	2056,396 794 4025
21	28,676 485 7236	81	332.003 909 1041	141	2119,088 698 2346
22	30,536 780 2954	82	342.964 026 3772	142	2183,661 359 1816
23	32,452 883 7042	83	354.252 947 1685	143	2250,171 199 9571
24	34,426 470 2153	84	365.880 535 5836	144	2318,676 335 9558
25	36,459 264 3218	85	377.856 951 6511	145	2389,236 626 0344
26	38,553 042 2515	86	390.192 660 2006	146	2461,913 724 8155
27	40,709 633 5190	87	402.898 440 0067	147	2536,771 136 5599
28	42,930 922 5246	88	415.985 393 2069	148	2613,874 270 6567
29	45,218 850 2003	89	429.464 955 0031	149	2693,290 498 7764
30	47,575 415 7063	90	443.348 903 6532	150	2775,089 213 7397
31	50,002 678 1775	91	457.649 370 7628	151	2859,341 890 1519
32	52,502 758 5228	92	472.378 851 8856	152	2946,122 146 8565
33	55,077 841 2785	93	487.550 217 4422	153	3035,505 811 2622
34	57,730 176 5169	94	503.176 723 9655	154	3127,570 985 6001
35	60,462 081 8124	95	519.272 025 6844	155	3222,398 115 1681
36	63,275 944 2668	96	535.850 186 4550	156	3320,070 058 6231
37	66,174 222 5948	97	552.925 692 0486	157	3420,672 160 3818
38	69,159 449 2726	98	570.513 462 8101	158	3524,292 325 1932
39	72,234 232 7508	99	588.628 866 6944	159	3631,021 094 9490
40	75,401 259 7333	100	607.287 732 6952	160	3740,951 727 7975
41	78,663 297 5253	101	626.506 364 6761	161	3854,180 279 6314
42	82,023 196 4511	102	646.301 555 6163	162	3970,805 688 0204
43	85,483 892 3446	103	666.690 602 2848	163	4090,929 858 6610
44	89,048 409 1149	104	687.691 320 3534	164	4214,657 754 4208
45	92,719 861 3884	105	709.322 059 9640	165	4342,097 487 0534
46	96,501 457 2300	106	731.601 721 7629	166	4473,360 411 6650
47	100,396 500 9469	107	754.549 773 4158	167	4608,561 224 0150
48	104,408 395 9753	108	778.186 266 6183	168	4747,818 060 7355
49	108,540 647 8546	109	802.531 854 6168	169	4891,252 602 5575
50	112,796 867 2902	110	827.607 810 2553	170	5038,990 180 6342
51	117,180 773 3089	111	853.436 044 5630	171	5191,159 886 0533
52	121,696 196 5082	112	880.039 125 8999	172	5347,894 682 6349
53	126,347 082 4035	113	907.440 299 6769	173	5509,331 523 1139
54	131,137 494 8756	114	935.663 508 6672	174	5675,611 468 8073
55	136,071 619 7218	115	964.733 413 9272	175	5846,879 812 8715
56	141,153 768 3135	116	994.675 416 3450	176	6023,286 207 2577
57	146,388 381 3629	117	1025.515 678 8353	177	6204,984 793 4754
58	151,780 032 8038	118	1057.281 149 2004	178	6392,134 337 2797
59	157,333 433 7879	119	1089.999 583 6764	179	6584,898 367 3981
60	163,053 436 8015	120	1123.699 571 1867	180	6783,445 318 4200

Amount of 1 Per Period

NOMINAL INTEREST RATE COMPOUNDED

YEARLY @ $3\frac{1}{16}\%$ 3.0625% PER ANNUM		HALF-YEARLY @ $6\frac{1}{8}\%$ 6.1250% PER ANNUM		QUARTERLY @ $12\frac{1}{4}\%$ 12.2500% PER ANNUM	
Periods	**Amount**	**Periods**	**Amount**	**Periods**	**Amount**
1	1,000 000 0000	61	172,966 749 4485	121	1223,681 578 2654
2	2,030 625 0000	62	179,263 856 1504	122	1262,156 826 5998
3	3,092 812 8906	63	185,753 811 7450	123	1301,810 379 4144
4	4,187 530 2854	64	192,442 522 2297	124	1342,678 322 2840
5	5,315 773 4004	65	199,336 074 4729	125	1384,797 845 9039
6	6,478 568 9608	66	206,440 741 7537	126	1428,207 279 9347
7	7,676 975 1352	67	213,762 989 4699	127	1472,946 127 8827
8	8,912 082 4987	68	221,309 481 0224	128	1519,055 103 0491
9	10,185 015 0252	69	229,087 083 8787	129	1566,576 165 5800
10	11,496 931 1104	70	237,102 875 8225	130	1615,552 560 6509
11	12,849 024 6256	71	245,364 151 3946	131	1666,028 857 8208
12	14,242 526 0048	72	253,878 428 5310	132	1718,050 991 5916
13	15,678 703 3637	73	262,653 455 4048	133	1771,666 303 2091
14	17,158 863 6542	74	271,697 217 4766	134	1826,923 583 7449
15	18,684 353 8536	75	281,017 944 7618	135	1883,873 118 4970
16	20,256 562 1904	76	290,624 119 3201	136	1942,566 732 7510
17	21,876 919 4075	77	300,524 482 9743	137	2003,057 838 9415
18	23,546 900 0643	78	310,728 045 2654	138	2065,401 485 2591
19	25,268 023 8788	79	321,244 091 6516	139	2129,654 405 7452
20	27,041 857 1101	80	332,082 191 9585	140	2195,875 071 9211
21	28,870 013 9841	81	343,252 209 0872	141	2264,123 745 9987
22	30,754 158 1623	82	354,764 307 9905	142	2334,462 535 7199
23	32,696 004 2561	83	366,628 964 9227	143	2406,955 450 8763
24	34,697 319 3864	84	378,856 976 9734	144	2481,668 461 5594
25	36,759 924 7926	85	391,459 471 8933	145	2558,669 558 1947
26	38,885 697 4894	86	404,447 918 2200	146	2638,028 813 4144
27	41,076 571 9750	87	417,834 135 7155	147	2719,818 445 8252
28	43,334 541 9917	88	431,630 306 1218	148	2804,112 885 7286
29	45,661 662 3402	89	445,848 984 2467	149	2890,988 842 8540
30	48,060 050 7494	90	460,503 109 3893	150	2980,525 376 1664
31	50,531 889 8036	91	475,606 017 1143	151	3072,803 965 8115
32	53,079 428 9288	92	491,171 451 3885	152	3167,908 587 2645
33	55,704 986 4398	93	507,213 577 0872	153	3265,925 787 7495
34	58,410 951 6495	94	523,746 992 8855	154	3366,944 764 9993
35	61,199 787 0438	95	540,786 744 5427	155	3471,057 448 4274
36	64,074 030 5220	96	558,348 338 5943	156	3578,358 582 7855
37	67,036 297 7067	97	576,447 756 4637	157	3688,945 814 3833
38	70,089 284 3240	98	595,101 469 0054	158	3802,919 779 9488
39	73,235 768 6564	99	614,326 451 4937	159	3920,384 198 2097
40	76,478 614 0715	100	634,140 199 0707	160	4041,445 964 2799
41	79,820 771 6275	101	654,560 742 6673	161	4166,215 246 9360
42	83,265 282 7585	102	675,606 665 4114	162	4294,805 588 8734
43	86,815 282 0430	103	697,297 119 5397	163	4427,334 010 0326
44	90,474 000 0556	104	719,651 843 8256	164	4563,921 114 0899
45	94,244 766 3073	105	742,691 181 5427	165	4704,691 198 2089
46	98,131 012 2755	106	766,436 098 9775	166	4849,772 366 1540
47	102,136 274 5264	107	790,908 204 5087	167	4999,296 644 8675
48	106,264 197 9338	108	816,129 768 2717	168	5153,400 104 6166
49	110,518 538 9955	109	842,123 742 4251	169	5312,222 982 8204
50	114,903 169 2522	110	868,913 782 0368	170	5475,909 811 6693
51	119,422 078 8106	111	896,524 266 6117	171	5644,609 549 6517
52	124,079 379 9741	112	924,980 322 2767	172	5818,475 717 1098
53	128,879 310 9859	113	954,307 844 6464	173	5997,666 535 9463
54	133,826 239 8848	114	984,533 522 3887	174	6182,345 073 6096
55	138,924 668 4813	115	1015,684 861 5119	175	6372,679 391 4889
56	144,179 236 4535	116	1047,790 210 3957	176	6568,842 697 8532
57	149,594 725 5699	117	1080,878 785 5890	177	6771,013 505 4750
58	155,176 064 0405	118	1114,980 698 3977	178	6979,375 794 0802
59	160,928 331 0017	119	1150,126 982 2861	179	7194,119 177 7739
60	166,856 761 1386	120	1186,349 621 1186	180	7415,439 077 5932

NOMINAL INTEREST RATE COMPOUNDED

	YEARLY @ $3\frac{1}{8}\%$ 3.1250% PER ANNUM		HALF-YEARLY @ $6\frac{1}{4}\%$ 6.2500% PER ANNUM		QUARTERLY @ $12\frac{1}{2}\%$ 12.5000% PER ANNUM
Periods	**Amount**	**Periods**	**Amount**	**Periods**	**Amount**
1	1.000 000 0000	61	177.098 844 7335	121	1292.918 996 0262
2	2.031 250 0000	62	183.633 183 6314	122	1334.322 714 6520
3	3.094 726 5625	63	190.371 720 6199	123	1377.020 299 4849
4	4.191 436 7676	64	197.320 836 8892	124	1421.052 183 8438
5	5.322 419 1666	65	204.487 113 0420	125	1466.460 064 5889
6	6.488 744 7655	66	211.877 335 3246	126	1513.286 941 6073
7	7.691 518 0394	67	219.498 502 0535	127	1561.577 158 5325
8	8.931 877 9782	68	227.357 830 2426	128	1611.376 444 7367
9	10.210 999 1650	69	235.462 762 4377	129	1662.731 958 6347
10	11.530 092 8889	70	243.820 973 7639	130	1715.692 332 3420
11	12.890 408 2917	71	252.440 379 1940	131	1770.307 717 7277
12	14.293 233 5508	72	261.329 141 0438	132	1826.629 833 9067
13	15.739 897 0993	73	270.495 676 7015	133	1884.712 016 2163
14	17.231 768 8836	74	279.948 666 5984	134	1944.609 266 7231
15	18.770 261 6612	75	289.697 062 4296	135	2006.378 306 3082
16	20.356 832 3381	76	299.750 095 6305	136	2070.077 628 3803
17	21.992 983 3487	77	310.117 286 1190	137	2135.767 554 2672
18	23.680 264 0783	78	320.808 451 3102	138	2203.510 290 3380
19	25.420 272 3308	79	331.833 715 4136	139	2273.369 986 9111
20	27.214 655 8411	80	343.203 519 0203	140	2345.412 799 0020
21	29.065 113 8362	81	354.928 628 9897	141	2419.706 948 9709
22	30.973 398 6435	82	367.020 148 6456	142	2496.322 791 1262
23	32.941 317 3512	83	379.489 528 2908	143	2575.332 878 3489
24	34.970 733 5184	84	392.348 576 0499	144	2656.812 030 7973
25	37.063 568 9408	85	405.609 469 0514	145	2740.837 406 7597
26	39.221 805 4702	86	419.284 764 9593	146	2827.488 575 7210
27	41.447 486 8912	87	433.387 413 8643	147	2916.847 593 7122
28	43.742 720 8565	88	447.930 770 5475	148	3008.999 081 0157
29	46.109 680 8833	89	462.928 607 1271	149	3104.030 302 2975
30	48.550 608 4109	90	478.395 126 0998	150	3202.031 249 2443
31	51.067 814 9237	91	494.344 973 7905	151	3303.094 725 7832
32	53.663 684 1401	92	510.793 254 2214	152	3407.316 435 9639
33	56.340 674 2695	93	527.755 543 4158	153	3514.795 074 5878
34	59.101 320 3404	94	545.247 904 1476	154	3625.632 420 6686
35	61.948 236 6010	95	563.286 901 1522	155	3739.933 433 8145
36	64.884 118 9948	96	581.889 616 8132	156	3857.806 353 6212
37	67.911 747 7134	97	601.073 667 3386	157	3979.362 802 1719
38	71.033 989 8295	98	620.857 219 4429	158	4104.717 889 7398
39	74.253 802 0116	99	641.259 007 5505	159	4233.990 323 7941
40	77.574 233 3245	100	662.298 351 5365	160	4367.302 521 4127
41	80.998 428 1159	101	683.995 175 0220	161	4504.780 725 2068
42	84.529 628 9945	102	706.370 024 2414	162	4646.555 122 8696
43	88.171 179 9006	103	729.444 087 4990	163	4792.759 970 4592
44	91.926 529 2725	104	753.239 215 2333	164	4943.533 719 5361
45	95.799 233 3122	105	777.777 940 7094	165	5099.019 148 2716
46	99.792 959 3532	106	803.083 501 3565	166	5259.363 496 6551
47	103.911 489 3330	107	829.179 860 7739	167	5424.718 605 9255
48	108.158 723 3747	108	856.091 731 4231	168	5595.241 062 3607
49	112.538 683 4801	109	883.844 598 0301	169	5771.092 345 5595
50	117.055 517 3389	110	912.464 741 7185	170	5952.438 981 3582
51	121.713 502 2557	111	941.979 264 8972	171	6139.452 699 5257
52	126.517 049 2012	112	972.416 116 9253	172	6332.310 596 3858
53	131.470 706 9888	113	1003.804 120 5792	173	6531.195 302 5229
54	136.579 166 5822	114	1036.172 999 3473	174	6736.295 155 7267
55	141.847 265 5379	115	1069.553 405 5769	175	6947.804 379 3432
56	147.279 992 5859	116	1103.976 949 5012	176	7165.923 266 1977
57	152.882 492 3542	117	1139.476 229 1731	177	7390.858 368 2663
58	158.660 070 2403	118	1176.084 861 3347	178	7622.822 692 2747
59	164.618 197 4353	119	1213.837 513 2514	179	7862.035 901 4083
60	170.762 516 1052	120	1252.769 935 5405	180	8108.724 523 3273

Amount of 1 Per Period

NOMINAL INTEREST RATE COMPOUNDED

	YEARLY @ $3\frac{3}{16}\%$ 3.1875% PER ANNUM		HALF-YEARLY @ $6\frac{3}{8}\%$ 6.3750% PER ANNUM		QUARTERLY @ $12\frac{3}{4}\%$ 12.7500% PER ANNUM
Periods	Amount	Periods	Amount	Periods	Amount
1	1,000 000 0000	61	181,344 516 6976	121	1366,371 880 0628
2	2,031 875 0000	62	188,124 873 1674	122	1410,924 983 7398
3	3,096 641 0156	63	195,121 353 4996	123	1456,898 217 5965
4	4,195 346 4480	64	202,340 846 6424	124	1504,336 848 2824
5	5,329 073 1160	65	209,790 461 1291	125	1553,287 585 3214
6	6,498 937 3216	66	217,477 532 0776	126	1603,798 627 1035
7	7,706 090 9487	67	225,409 628 4126	127	1655,919 708 3424
8	8,951 722 5977	68	233,594 560 3182	128	1709,702 149 0458
9	10,237 058 7555	69	242,040 386 9284	129	1765,198 905 0466
10	11,563 365 0034	70	250,755 424 2617	130	1822,464 620 1450
11	12,931 947 2628	71	259,748 253 4100	131	1881,555 679 9121
12	14,344 153 0818	72	269,027 728 9875	132	1942,530 267 2093
13	15,801 372 9613	73	278,602 987 8490	133	2005,448 419 4766
14	17,305 041 7245	74	288,483 458 0867	134	2070,372 087 8474
15	18,856 639 9294	75	298,678 868 3132	135	2137,365 198 1476
16	20,457 695 3272	76	309,199 257 2406	136	2206,493 713 8385
17	22,109 784 3657	77	320,054 983 5652	137	2277,825 700 9671
18	23,814 533 7424	78	331,256 736 1663	138	2351,431 395 1855
19	25,573 622 0054	79	342,815 544 6316	139	2427,383 270 9070
20	27,388 781 2069	80	354,742 790 1168	140	2505,756 112 6672
21	29,261 798 6078	81	367,050 216 5517	141	2586,627 088 7584
22	31,194 518 4384	82	379,749 942 2043	142	2670,075 827 2126
23	33,188 843 7137	83	392,854 471 6121	143	2756,184 494 2050
24	35,246 738 1070	84	406,376 707 8947	144	2845,037 874 9578
25	37,370 227 8842	85	420,329 965 4589	145	2936,723 457 2221
26	39,561 403 8980	86	434,727 983 1079	146	3031,331 517 4210
27	41,822 423 6473	87	449,584 937 5694	147	3128,955 209 5388
28	44,155 513 4010	88	464,915 457 4545	148	3229,690 656 8429
29	46,562 970 3907	89	480,734 637 6608	149	3333,637 046 5297
30	49,047 165 0719	90	497,058 054 2363	150	3440,896 727 3879
31	51,610 543 4586	91	513,901 779 7150	151	3551,575 310 5734
32	54,255 629 5313	92	531,282 398 9435	152	3665,781 773 5979
33	56,985 027 7226	93	549,217 025 4098	153	3783,628 567 6313
34	59,801 425 4813	94	567,723 318 0947	154	3905,231 728 2246
35	62,707 595 9185	95	586,819 498 8590	155	4030,710 989 5617
36	65,706 400 5384	96	606,524 370 3851	156	4160,189 902 3540
37	68,800 792 0555	97	626,857 334 6911	157	4293,795 955 4915
38	71,993 817 3023	98	647,838 412 2344	158	4431,660 701 5728
39	75,288 620 2288	99	669,488 261 6244	159	4573,919 886 4355
40	78,688 444 9986	100	691,828 199 9637	160	4720,713 582 8156
41	82,196 639 1829	101	714,880 223 8375	161	4872,186 328 2678
42	85,816 657 0569	102	738,667 030 9723	162	5028,487 267 4814
43	89,552 063 0006	103	763,212 042 5846	163	5189,770 299 1323
44	93,406 535 0087	104	788,539 426 4420	164	5356,194 227 4172
45	97,383 868 3121	105	814,674 120 6598	165	5527,922 918 4161
46	101,487 979 1146	106	841,641 858 2558	166	5705,125 461 4406
47	105,722 908 4489	107	869,469 192 4877	167	5887,976 335 5240
48	110,092 826 1557	108	898,183 522 9983	168	6076,655 581 2189
49	114,602 034 9894	109	927,813 122 7938	169	6271,348 977 8702
50	119,254 974 8547	110	958,387 166 0829	170	6472,248 226 5398
51	124,056 227 1782	111	989,935 757 0018	171	6679,551 138 7608
52	129,010 519 4195	112	1022,489 959 2562	172	6893,461 831 3088
53	134,122 729 7260	113	1056,081 826 7075	173	7114,190 927 1818
54	139,397 891 7360	114	1090,744 434 9338	174	7341,955 762 9857
55	144,841 199 5351	115	1126,511 913 7973	175	7576,980 602 9308
56	150,458 012 7702	116	1163,419 481 0496	176	7819,496 859 6493
57	156,253 861 9273	117	1201,503 477 0081	177	8069,743 322 0506
58	162,234 453 7762	118	1240,801 400 3377	178	8327,966 390 4409
59	168,405 676 9903	119	1281,351 944 9735	179	8594,420 319 1362
60	174,773 607 9444	120	1323,195 038 2195	180	8869,367 466 8087

Amount of 1 Per Period

NOMINAL INTEREST RATE COMPOUNDED

YEARLY	HALF-YEARLY	QUARTERLY
@	@	@
$3\frac{1}{4}\%$	$6\frac{1}{2}\%$	13%
3.2500%	6.5000%	13.0000%
PER ANNUM	PER ANNUM	PER ANNUM

Periods	Amount	Periods	Amount	Periods	Amount
1	1,000 000 0000	61	185,707 050 6256	121	1444,305 213 0195
2	2,032 500 0000	62	192,742 529 7709	122	1492,245 132 4427
3	3,098 556 2500	63	200,006 661 9885	123	1541,743 099 2470
4	4,199 259 3281	64	207,506 878 5031	124	1592,849 749 9726
5	5,335 735 2563	65	215,250 852 0544	125	1645,617 366 8467
6	6,509 146 6521	66	223,246 504 7462	126	1700,099 931 2692
7	7,720 693 9183	67	231,502 016 1504	127	1756,353 179 0354
8	8,971 616 4707	68	240,025 831 6753	128	1814,434 657 3541
9	10,263 194 0060	69	248,825 671 2048	129	1874,403 783 7181
10	11,596 747 8111	70	257,913 538 0189	130	1936,321 906 6889
11	12,973 642 1150	71	267,295 728 0046	131	2000,252 368 6563
12	14,395 285 4837	72	276,982 839 1647	132	2066,260 570 6377
13	15,863 132 2620	73	286,984 781 4376	133	2134,414 039 1834
14	17,378 684 0605	74	297,311 786 8343	134	2204,782 495 4568
15	18,943 491 2924	75	307,974 419 9064	135	2277,437 926 5592
16	20,559 154 7595	76	318,983 588 5533	136	2352,454 659 1724
17	22,227 327 2891	77	330,350 555 1813	137	2429,909 435 5955
18	23,949 715 4260	78	342,086 948 2247	138	2509,881 492 2523
19	25,728 081 1774	79	354,204 774 0420	139	2592,452 640 7505
20	27,564 243 8156	80	366,716 429 1984	140	2677,707 351 5749
21	29,460 081 7397	81	379,634 713 1473	141	2765,732 840 5011
22	31,417 534 3962	82	392,972 841 3246	142	2856,619 157 8174
23	33,438 604 2641	83	406,744 458 6677	143	2950,459 280 4465
24	35,525 358 9026	84	420,963 653 5744	144	3047,349 207 0610
25	37,679 933 0670	85	435,644 972 3155	145	3147,388 056 2904
26	39,904 530 8917	86	450,803 433 9158	146	3250,678 168 1199
27	42,201 428 1456	87	466,454 545 5181	147	3357,325 208 5838
28	44,572 974 5604	88	482,614 318 2474	148	3467,438 277 8627
29	47,021 596 2336	89	499,299 283 5904	149	3581,130 021 8933
30	49,549 798 1112	90	516,526 510 3071	150	3698,516 747 6048
31	52,160 166 5498	91	534,313 621 8921	151	3819,718 541 9020
32	54,855 371 9627	92	552,678 814 6036	152	3944,859 394 5138
33	57,638 171 5514	93	571,640 876 0782	153	4074,067 324 8355
34	60,511 412 1269	94	591,219 204 5508	154	4207,474 512 8926
35	63,478 033 0210	95	611,433 828 6987	155	4345,217 434 5617
36	66,541 069 0942	96	632,305 428 1314	156	4487,437 001 1849
37	69,703 653 8397	97	653,855 354 5456	157	4634,278 703 7234
38	72,969 022 5895	98	676,105 653 5684	158	4785,892 761 5944
39	76,340 515 8237	99	699,079 087 3094	159	4942,434 276 3462
40	79,821 582 5880	100	722,799 157 6469	160	5104,063 390 3275
41	83,415 784 0221	101	747,290 130 2704	161	5270,945 450 5131
42	87,126 797 0028	102	772,577 059 5042	162	5443,251 177 6548
43	90,958 417 9054	103	798,685 813 9381	163	5621,156 840 9286
44	94,914 566 4873	104	825,643 102 8911	164	5804,844 438 2588
45	98,999 289 8981	105	853,476 503 7351	165	5994,501 882 5022
46	103,216 766 8198	106	882,214 490 1064	166	6190,323 193 6835
47	107,571 311 7415	107	911,886 461 0349	167	6392,508 697 4782
48	112,067 379 3731	108	942,522 771 0185	168	6601,265 230 1463
49	116,709 569 2027	109	974,154 761 0766	169	6816,806 350 1260
50	121,502 630 2018	110	1006,814 790 8116	170	7039,352 556 5051
51	126,451 465 6833	111	1040,536 271 5130	171	7269,131 514 5915
52	131,561 138 3180	112	1075,353 700 3372	172	7506,378 288 8158
53	136,836 875 3134	113	1111,302 695 5981	173	7751,335 583 2023
54	142,284 073 7611	114	1148,420 033 2051	174	8004,253 989 6563
55	147,908 306 1583	115	1186,743 684 2843	175	8265,392 244 3202
56	153,715 326 1084	116	1226,312 854 0235	176	8535,017 492 2606
57	159,711 074 2070	117	1267,168 021 7793	177	8813,405 560 7591
58	165,901 684 1187	118	1309,350 982 4871	178	9100,841 241 4837
59	172,293 488 8526	119	1352,904 889 4179	179	9397,618 581 8319
60	178,893 027 2403	120	1397,874 298 3240	180	9704,041 185 7415

Amount of 1 Per Period

NOMINAL INTEREST RATE COMPOUNDED

	YEARLY @ $3\frac{5}{16}\%$ 3.3125% PER ANNUM		HALF-YEARLY @ $6\frac{5}{8}\%$ 6.6250% PER ANNUM		QUARTERLY @ $13\frac{1}{4}\%$ 12.2500% PER ANNUM
Periods	Amount	Periods	Amount	Periods	Amount
1	1.000 000 0000	61	190.189 828 9631	121	1527.000 918 2431
2	2.033 125 0000	62	197.489 867 0475	122	1578.582 823 6599
3	3.100 472 2656	63	205.031 718 8935	123	1631.873 379 6936
4	4.203 175 4094	64	212.823 394 5818	124	1686.929 185 3960
5	5.342 405 5949	65	220.873 169 5273	125	1743.808 714 6622
6	6.519 372 7802	66	229.189 593 2679	126	1802.572 378 3354
7	7.735 327 0035	67	237.781 498 5449	127	1863.282 588 3678
8	8.991 559 7105	68	246.658 010 6842	128	1926.003 824 1075
9	10.289 405 1259	69	255.828 557 2881	129	1990.802 700 7810
10	11.630 241 6707	70	265.302 878 2483	130	2057.748 040 2444
11	13.015 493 4261	71	275.091 036 0903	131	2126.910 944 0775
12	14.446 631 6458	72	285.203 426 6608	132	2198.364 869 1001
13	15.925 176 3191	73	295.650 790 1689	133	2272.185 705 3890
14	17.452 697 7847	74	306.444 222 5933	134	2348.451 856 8800
15	19.030 818 3988	75	317.595 187 4667	135	2427.244 324 6392
16	20.661 214 2582	76	329.115 528 0515	136	2508.646 792 8928
17	22.345 616 9805	77	341.017 479 9182	137	2592.745 717 9074
18	24.085 815 5430	78	353.313 683 9405	138	2679.630 419 8131
19	25.883 658 1829	79	366.017 199 7210	139	2769.393 177 4694
20	27.741 054 3602	80	379.141 519 4618	140	2862.129 326 4731
21	29.659 976 7859	81	392.700 582 2939	141	2957.937 360 4125
22	31.642 463 5169	82	406.708 789 0824	142	3056.919 035 4762
23	33.690 620 1209	83	421.181 017 7208	143	3159.179 478 5263
24	35.806 621 9124	84	436.132 638 9328	144	3264.827 298 7525
25	37.992 716 2632	85	451.579 532 5974	145	3373.974 703 0237
26	40.251 224 9895	86	467.538 104 6147	146	3486.737 615 0613
27	42.584 546 8172	87	484.025 304 3301	147	3603.235 798 5602
28	44.995 159 9306	88	501.058 642 5360	148	3723.592 984 3875
29	47.485 624 6033	89	518.656 210 0700	149	3847.937 001 9954
30	50.058 585 9182	90	536.836 697 0286	150	3976.399 915 1865
31	52.716 776 5768	91	555.619 412 6177	151	4109.118 162 3770
32	55.463 019 8009	92	575.024 305 6606	152	4246.232 701 5058
33	58.300 232 3318	93	595.071 985 7856	153	4387.889 159 7431
34	61.231 427 5278	94	615.783 745 3148	154	4534.237 988 1596
35	64.259 718 5646	95	637.181 581 8783	155	4685.434 621 5174
36	67.388 321 7421	96	659.288 221 7781	156	4841.639 643 3552
37	70.620 559 8998	97	682.127 144 1245	157	5003.018 956 5413
38	73.959 865 9465	98	705.722 605 7736	158	5169.743 959 4768
39	77.409 786 5060	99	730.099 667 0898	159	5341.991 728 1344
40	80.973 985 6840	100	755.284 218 5622	160	5519.945 204 1289
41	84.656 248 9598	101	781.303 008 3021	161	5703.793 389 0157
42	88.460 487 2066	102	808.183 670 4521	162	5893.731 545 0268
43	92.390 740 8453	103	835.954 754 5358	163	6089.961 402 4558
44	96.451 184 1358	104	864.645 755 7798	164	6292.691 373 9122
45	100.646 129 6103	105	894.287 146 4400	165	6502.136 775 6730
46	104.980 032 6536	106	924.910 408 1658	166	6718.520 056 3672
47	109.457 496 2353	107	956.548 065 4363	167	6942.071 033 2343
48	114.083 275 7981	108	989.233 720 1039	168	7173.027 136 2102
49	118.862 284 3089	109	1023.002 087 0823	169	7411.633 660 0972
50	123.799 597 4766	110	1057.889 031 2169	170	7658.144 025 0879
51	128.900 459 1430	111	1093.931 605 3760	171	7912.820 045 9189
52	134.170 286 8521	112	1131.168 089 8041	172	8175.932 209 9400
53	139.614 677 6041	113	1169.638 032 7788	173	8447.759 964 3943
54	145.239 413 7997	114	1209.382 292 6146	174	8728.592 013 2148
55	151.050 469 3818	115	1250.443 081 0575	175	9018.726 623 6526
56	157.054 016 1801	116	1292.864 008 1175	176	9318.471 943 0611
57	163.256 430 4661	117	1336.690 128 3864	177	9628.146 326 1749
58	169.664 299 7253	118	1381.967 988 8892	178	9948.078 673 2295
59	176.284 429 6537	119	1428.745 678 5212	179	10278.608 779 2802
60	183.123 851 3860	120	1477.072 879 1222	180	10620.087 695 0939

Amount of 1 Per Period

NOMINAL INTEREST RATE COMPOUNDED

	YEARLY	HALF-YEARLY	QUARTERLY
	@	@	@
	$3\frac{3}{8}\%$	$6\frac{3}{4}\%$	$13\frac{1}{2}\%$
	3.3750%	6.7500%	13.5000%
	PER ANNUM	PER ANNUM	PER ANNUM

Periods	Amount	Periods	Amount	Periods	Amount
1	1,000 000 0000	61	194,796 334 2155	121	1614,758 952 8266
2	2,033 750 0000	62	202,370 710 4953	122	1670,257 067 4845
3	3,102 389 0625	63	210,200 721 9745	123	1727,628 243 5121
4	4,207 094 6934	64	218,294 996 3412	124	1786,935 696 7307
5	5,349 084 1393	65	226,662 452 4677	125	1848,244 776 4953
6	6,529 615 7290	66	235,312 310 2385	126	1911,623 037 7021
7	7,749 990 2598	67	244,254 100 7090	127	1977,140 315 2245
8	9,011 552 4311	68	253,497 676 6079	128	2044,868 800 8633
9	10,315 692 3256	69	263,053 223 1934	129	2114,883 122 8925
10	11,663 846 9416	70	272,931 269 4762	130	2187,260 428 2901
11	13,057 501 7759	71	283,142 699 8211	131	2262,080 467 7449
12	14,498 192 4608	72	293,698 765 9400	132	2339,425 683 5313
13	15,987 506 4564	73	304,611 099 2905	133	2419,381 300 3504
14	17,527 084 7993	74	315,891 723 8915	134	2502,035 419 2373
15	19,118 623 9113	75	327,553 069 5729	135	2587,479 114 6365
16	20,763 877 4683	76	339,607 985 6710	136	2675,806 534 7555
17	22,464 658 3328	77	352,069 755 1874	137	2767,115 005 3035
18	24,222 840 5516	78	364,952 109 4249	138	2861,505 136 7325
19	26,040 361 4202	79	378,269 243 1180	139	2959,080 935 0972
20	27,919 223 6181	80	392,035 830 0733	140	3059,949 916 6568
21	29,861 497 4152	81	406,267 039 3382	141	3164,223 226 3439
22	31,869 322 9530	82	420,978 551 9159	142	3272,015 760 2330
23	33,944 912 6026	83	436,186 578 0431	143	3383,446 292 1409
24	36,090 553 4030	84	451,907 875 0520	144	3498,637 604 5006
25	38,308 609 5803	85	468,159 765 8350	145	3617,716 623 6525
26	40,601 525 1537	86	484,960 157 9319	146	3740,814 559 7008
27	42,971 826 6276	87	502,327 563 2622	147	3868,067 051 0907
28	45,422 125 7763	88	520,281 118 5222	148	3999,614 314 0650
29	47,955 122 5212	89	538,840 606 2724	149	4135,601 297 1647
30	50,573 607 9063	90	558,026 476 7341	150	4276,177 840 9440
31	53,280 467 1732	91	577,859 870 3238	151	4421,498 843 0759
32	56,078 682 9403	92	598,362 640 9473	152	4571,724 429 0297
33	58,971 338 4895	93	619,557 380 0792	153	4727,020 128 5095
34	61,961 621 1635	94	641,467 441 6569	154	4887,557 057 8467
35	65,052 825 8778	95	664,116 967 8128	155	5053,512 108 5490
36	68,248 358 7512	96	687,530 915 4765	156	5225,068 142 2125
37	71,551 740 8590	97	711,735 083 8739	157	5402,414 192 0122
38	74,966 612 1130	98	736,756 142 9546	158	5585,745 670 9926
39	78,496 735 2718	99	762,621 662 7793	159	5775,264 587 3886
40	82,146 000 0872	100	789,360 143 8981	160	5971,179 767 2130
41	85,918 427 5902	101	817,001 048 7547	161	6173,707 084 3564
42	89,818 174 5214	102	845,574 834 1501	162	6383,069 698 4534
43	93,849 537 9115	103	875,112 984 8027	163	6599,498 300 7762
44	98,016 959 8160	104	905,648 048 0398	164	6823,231 368 4274
45	102,325 032 2098	105	937,213 669 6611	165	7054,515 427 1119
46	106,778 502 0468	106	969,844 631 0122	166	7293,605 322 7769
47	111,382 276 4909	107	1003,576 887 3089	167	7540,764 502 4206
48	116,141 428 3225	108	1038,447 607 2555	168	7796,265 304 3773
49	121,061 201 5284	109	1074,495 214 0004	169	8060,389 258 4000
50	126,147 017 0800	110	1111,759 427 4729	170	8333,427 395 8710
51	131,404 478 9064	111	1150,281 308 1501	171	8615,680 570 4817
52	136,839 380 0695	112	1190,103 302 3002	172	8907,459 789 7354
53	142,457 709 1468	113	1231,269 288 7528	173	9209,086 557 6390
54	148,265 656 8305	114	1273,824 627 2483	174	9520,893 228 9593
55	154,269 622 7486	115	1317,816 208 4179	175	9843,223 375 4367
56	160,476 222 5163	116	1363,292 505 4520	176	10176,432 164 3577
57	166,892 295 0263	117	1410,303 627 5110	177	10520,886 749 9048
58	173,524 909 9834	118	1458,901 374 9395	178	10876,966 677 7140
59	180,381 375 6953	119	1509,139 296 3437	179	11245,064 303 0869
60	187,469 247 1251	120	1561,072 747 5953	180	11625,585 223 3161

Amount of 1 Per Period

NOMINAL INTEREST RATE COMPOUNDED

Periods	YEARLY @ $3\frac{7}{16}\%$ 3.4375% PER ANNUM Amount	Periods	HALF-YEARLY @ $6\frac{7}{8}\%$ 6.8750% PER ANNUM Amount	Periods	QUARTERLY @ $13\frac{3}{4}\%$ 13.7500% PER ANNUM Amount
1	1,000 000 0000	61	199,530 151 9321	121	1707,898 471 5010
2	2,034 375 0000	62	207,389 000 9047	122	1767,607 481 4589
3	3,104 306 6406	63	215,517 997 8108	123	1829,368 988 6340
4	4,211 017 1814	64	223,926 428 9856	124	1893,253 547 6183
5	5,355 770 8970	65	232,623 899 9819	125	1959,334 138 3177
6	6,539 875 5216	66	241,620 346 5438	126	2027,686 249 3224
7	7,764 683 7426	67	250,926 045 9563	127	2098,387 964 1429
8	9,031 594 7463	68	260,551 628 7860	128	2171,520 050 4103
9	10,342 055 8157	69	270,508 091 0255	129	2247,166 052 1431
10	11,697 563 9844	70	280,806 806 6545	130	2325,412 385 1855
11	13,099 667 7463	71	291,459 540 6333	131	2406,348 435 9263
12	14,549 968 8251	72	302,478 462 3426	132	2490,066 663 4113
13	16,050 124 0035	73	313,876 159 4856	133	2576,662 704 9660
14	17,601 847 0161	74	325,665 652 4679	134	2666,235 485 4492
15	19,206 910 5073	75	337,860 409 2715	135	2758,887 330 2615
16	20,867 148 0560	76	350,474 360 8402	136	2854,724 082 2393
17	22,584 456 2704	77	363,521 916 9941	137	2953,855 222 5663
18	24,360 796 9547	78	377,017 982 8907	138	3056,393 995 8420
19	26,198 199 3500	79	390,977 976 0526	139	3162,457 539 4490
20	28,098 762 4527	80	405,417 843 9794	140	3272,167 017 3676
21	30,064 657 4120	81	420,354 082 3662	141	3385,647 758 5896
22	32,098 130 0105	82	435,803 753 9476	142	3503,029 400 2911
23	34,201 503 2296	83	451,784 507 9895	143	3624,446 035 9261
24	36,377 179 9031	84	468,314 600 4516	144	3750,036 368 4111
25	38,627 645 4623	85	485,412 914 8422	145	3879,943 868 5752
26	40,955 470 7751	86	503,098 983 7899	146	4014,316 939 0575
27	43,363 315 0830	87	521,393 011 3576	147	4153,309 083 8376
28	45,853 929 0389	88	540,315 896 1231	148	4297,079 083 5945
29	48,430 157 8496	89	559,889 255 0523	149	4445,791 177 0931
30	51,094 944 5257	90	580,135 448 1947	150	4599,615 248 8057
31	53,851 333 2438	91	601,077 604 2264	151	4758,727 022 9834
32	56,702 472 8241	92	622,739 646 8717	152	4923,308 264 3984
33	59,651 620 3274	93	645,146 322 2329	153	5093,546 985 9871
34	62,702 144 7761	94	668,323 227 0597	154	5269,637 663 6304
35	65,857 531 0028	95	692,296 837 9898	155	5451,781 458 3177
36	69,121 383 6310	96	717,094 541 7957	156	5640,186 445 9474
37	72,497 431 1934	97	742,744 666 6700	157	5835,067 855 0268
38	75,989 530 3906	98	769,276 514 5867	158	6036,648 312 5434
39	79,601 670 4978	99	796,720 394 7757	159	6245,158 098 2870
40	83,337 977 9212	100	825,107 658 3461	160	6460,835 407 9157
41	87,202 720 9122	101	854,470 734 1017	161	6683,926 625 0628
42	91,200 314 4436	102	884,843 165 5865	162	6914,686 602 7993
43	95,335 325 2526	103	916,259 649 4035	163	7153,378 954 7705
44	99,612 477 0581	104	948,756 074 8518	164	7400,276 356 3407
45	104,036 655 9570	105	982,369 564 9248	165	7655,660 856 0900
46	108,612 916 0055	106	1017,138 518 7191	166	7919,824 198 0181
47	113,346 484 9932	107	1053,102 655 3000	167	8193,068 154 8249
48	118,242 770 4148	108	1090,303 059 0760	168	8475,704 872 6470
49	123,307 365 6478	109	1128,782 226 7317	169	8768,057 227 6443
50	128,546 056 3420	110	1168,584 115 7756	170	9070,459 194 8445
51	133,964 827 0287	111	1209,754 194 7554	171	9383,256 229 6673
52	139,569 867 9579	112	1252,339 495 2001	172	9706,805 662 5621
53	145,367 582 1689	113	1296,388 665 3476	173	10041,477 107 2127
54	151,364 592 8060	114	1341,952 025 7190	174	10387,652 882 7732
55	157,567 750 6837	115	1389,081 626 6030	175	10745,728 450 6185
56	163,984 142 1134	116	1437,831 307 5175	176	11116,112 866 1085
57	170,621 096 9986	117	1488,256 758 7134	177	11499,229 245 8810
58	177,486 197 2079	118	1540,415 584 7942	178	11895,515 251 2081
59	184,587 285 2369	119	1594,367 370 5215	179	12305,423 587 9684
60	191,932 473 1669	120	1650,173 748 8832	180	12729,422 523 8048

Amount of 1 Per Period

NOMINAL INTEREST RATE COMPOUNDED

YEARLY @ $3\frac{1}{2}\%$ 3.5000% PER ANNUM	HALF-YEARLY @ 7% 7.0000% PER ANNUM	QUARTERLY @ 14% 14.0000% PER ANNUM

Periods	Amount	Periods	Amount	Periods	Amount
1	1.000 000 0000	61	204.394 973 7796	121	1806.759 065 9724
2	2.035 000 0000	62	212.548 797 8619	122	1870.995 633 2814
3	3.106 225 0000	63	220.988 005 7870	123	1937.480 480 4462
4	4.214 942 8750	64	229.722 585 9896	124	2006.292 297 2619
5	5.362 465 8756	65	238.762 876 4992	125	2077.512 527 6660
6	6.550 152 1813	66	248.119 577 1767	126	2151.225 466 1343
7	7.779 407 5076	67	257.803 762 3779	127	2227.518 357 4490
8	9.051 686 7704	68	267.826 894 0611	128	2306.481 499 9598
9	10.368 495 8073	69	278.200 835 3532	129	2388.208 352 4583
10	11.731 393 1606	70	288.937 864 5906	130	2472.795 644 7944
11	13.141 991 9212	71	300.050 689 8512	131	2560.343 492 3622
12	14.601 961 6385	72	311.552 463 9960	132	2650.955 514 5949
13	16.113 030 2958	73	323.456 800 2359	133	2744.738 957 6057
14	17.676 986 3562	74	335.777 788 2442	134	2841.804 821 1219
15	19.295 680 8786	75	348.530 010 8327	135	2942.267 989 8612
16	20.971 029 7094	76	361.728 561 2119	136	3046.247 369 5063
17	22.705 015 7492	77	375.389 060 8543	137	3153.866 027 4390
18	24.499 691 3004	78	389.527 677 9842	138	3265.251 338 3994
19	26.357 180 4960	79	404.161 146 7136	139	3380.535 135 2434
20	28.279 681 8133	80	419.306 786 8486	140	3499.853 864 9769
21	30.269 470 6768	81	434.982 524 3883	141	3623.348 750 2511
22	32.328 902 1505	82	451.206 912 7419	142	3751.165 956 5099
23	34.460 413 7257	83	467.999 154 6878	143	3883.456 764 9877
24	36.666 528 2061	84	485.379 125 1019	144	4020.377 751 7623
25	38.949 856 6933	85	503.367 394 4805	145	4162.090 973 0740
26	41.313 101 6776	86	521.985 253 2873	146	4308.764 157 1315
27	43.759 060 2363	87	541.254 737 1524	147	4460.570 902 6311
28	46.290 627 3446	88	561.198 652 9527	148	4617.690 884 2232
29	48.910 799 3017	89	581.840 605 8060	149	4780.310 065 1710
30	51.622 677 2772	90	603.205 027 0092	150	4948.620 917 4520
31	54.429 470 9819	91	625.317 202 9546	151	5122.822 649 5629
32	57.334 502 4663	92	648.203 305 0580	152	5303.121 442 2976
33	60.341 210 0526	93	671.890 420 7350	153	5489.730 692 7780
34	63.453 152 4044	94	696.406 585 4607	154	5682.871 267 0252
35	66.674 012 7386	95	721.780 815 9519	155	5882.771 761 3711
36	70.007 603 1845	96	748.043 144 5102	156	6089.668 773 0191
37	73.457 869 2959	97	775.224 654 5680	157	6303.807 180 0747
38	77.028 894 7213	98	803.357 517 4779	158	6525.440 431 3773
39	80.724 906 0365	99	832.475 030 5896	159	6754.830 846 4756
40	84.550 277 7478	100	862.611 656 6603	160	6992.249 926 1022
41	88.509 537 4690	101	893.803 064 6434	161	7237.978 673 5158
42	92.607 371 2804	102	926.086 171 9059	162	7492.307 927 0888
43	96.848 629 2752	103	959.499 187 9226	163	7755.538 704 5369
44	101.238 331 2998	104	994.081 659 4999	164	8027.982 559 1957
45	105.781 672 8953	105	1029.874 517 5824	165	8309.961 948 7676
46	110.484 031 4467	106	1066.920 125 6978	166	8601.810 616 9744
47	115.350 972 5473	107	1105.262 330 0972	167	8903.873 988 5686
48	120.388 256 5864	108	1144.946 511 6506	168	9216.509 578 1685
49	125.601 845 5670	109	1186.019 639 5584	169	9540.087 413 4043
50	130.997 910 1618	110	1228.530 326 9429	170	9874.990 472 8735
51	136.582 837 0175	111	1272.528 888 3859	171	10221.615 139 4241
52	142.363 236 3131	112	1318.067 399 4794	172	10580.371 669 3039
53	148.345 949 5840	113	1365.199 758 4612	173	10951.684 677 7296
54	154.538 057 8195	114	1413.981 750 0074	174	11335.993 641 4501
55	160.946 889 8432	115	1464.471 111 2576	175	11733.753 418 9008
56	167.580 030 9877	116	1516.727 600 1516	176	12145.434 788 5624
57	174.445 332 0722	117	1570.813 066 1569	177	12571.525 006 1621
58	181.550 918 6948	118	1626.791 523 4724	178	13012.528 381 3777
59	188.905 200 8491	119	1684.729 226 7940	179	13468.966 874 7259
60	196.516 882 8788	120	1744.694 749 7318	180	13941.380 715 3414

Amount of 1 Per Period

NOMINAL INTEREST RATE COMPOUNDED

	YEARLY	HALF-YEARLY	QUARTERLY
	@	@	@
	$3\frac{9}{16}\%$	$7\frac{1}{8}\%$	$14\frac{1}{4}\%$
	3.5625%	7.1250%	14.2500%
	PER ANNUM	PER ANNUM	PER ANNUM

Periods	Amount	Periods	Amount	Periods	Amount
1	1,000 000 0000	61	209,394 600 7079	121	1911,702 084 6021
2	2,035 625 0000	62	217,854 283 3581	122	1980,806 471 3661
3	3,108 144 1406	63	226,615 342 2028	123	2052,372 701 9085
4	4,218 871 7756	64	235,688 513 7687	124	2126,488 479 4140
5	5,369 169 0826	65	245,084 917 0717	125	2203,244 631 4931
6	6,560 445 7312	66	254,816 067 2424	126	2282,735 221 4901
7	7,794 161 6104	67	264,893 889 6379	127	2365,057 663 7557
8	9,071 828 6178	68	275,330 734 4563	128	2450,312 843 0270
9	10,395 012 5123	69	286,139 391 8713	129	2538,605 238 0598
10	11,765 334 8330	70	297,333 107 7067	130	2630,043 049 6657
11	13,184 474 8864	71	308,925 599 6688	131	2724,738 333 3100
12	14,654 171 8043	72	320,931 074 1570	132	2822,807 136 4342
13	16,176 226 6748	73	333,364 243 6738	133	2924,369 640 6696
14	17,752 504 7501	74	346,240 344 8547	134	3029,550 309 1185
15	19,384 937 7318	75	359,575 157 1401	135	3138,478 038 8808
16	21,075 526 1385	76	373,385 022 1132	136	3251,286 319 0160
17	22,826 341 7572	77	387,686 863 5260	137	3368,113 394 1309
18	24,639 530 1823	78	402,498 208 0391	138	3489,102 433 7968
19	26,517 313 4450	79	417,837 206 7005	139	3614,401 708 0008
20	28,461 992 7365	80	433,722 657 1892	140	3744,164 768 8484
21	30,475 951 2277	81	450,174 026 8516	141	3878,550 638 7386
22	32,561 656 9902	82	467,211 476 5582	142	4017,724 005 2437
23	34,721 666 0205	83	484,855 885 4106	143	4161,855 422 9305
24	36,958 625 3725	84	503,128 876 3283	144	4311,121 522 3724
25	39,275 276 4014	85	522,052 842 5475	145	4465,705 226 6069
26	41,674 458 1232	86	541,650 975 0633	146	4625,795 975 3048
27	44,159 110 6938	87	561,947 291 0499	147	4791,589 956 9250
28	46,732 279 0123	88	582,966 663 2936	148	4963,290 349 1404
29	49,397 116 4521	89	604,734 850 6734	149	5141,107 567 8286
30	52,156 888 7257	90	627,278 529 7286	150	5325,259 524 9325
31	55,014 977 8866	91	650,625 327 3502	151	5515,971 895 5082
32	57,974 886 4738	92	674,803 854 6371	152	5713,478 394 2857
33	61,040 241 8044	93	699,843 741 9585	153	5918,021 062 0821
34	64,214 800 4187	94	725,775 675 2658	154	6129,850 562 4188
35	67,502 452 6836	95	752,631 433 6971	155	6349,226 488 7049
36	70,907 227 5605	96	780,443 928 5226	156	6576,417 682 3650
37	74,433 297 5423	97	809,247 243 4762	157	6811,702 562 2993
38	78,084 983 7672	98	839,076 676 5251	158	7055,369 466 0812
39	81,866 761 3139	99	869,968 783 1263	159	7307,717 003 3103
40	85,783 264 6858	100	901,961 421 0251	160	7569,054 421 5533
41	89,839 293 4902	101	935,093 796 6491	161	7839,701 985 3211
42	94,039 818 3208	102	969,406 513 1548	162	8119,991 368 5482
43	98,389 986 8485	103	1004,941 620 1859	163	8410,266 061 0527
44	102,895 130 1299	104	1041,742 665 4050	164	8710,881 789 4777
45	107,560 769 1408	105	1079,854 747 8601	165	9022,206 953 2279
46	112,392 621 5414	106	1119,324 573 2526	166	9344,623 075 9366
47	117,396 608 6839	107	1160,200 511 1747	167	9678,525 273 0168
48	122,578 862 8682	108	1202,532 654 3853	168	10024,322 735 8681
49	127,945 734 8579	109	1246,372 880 1978	169	10382,439 233 3334
50	133,503 801 6622	110	1291,774 914 0549	170	10753,313 631 0209
51	139,259 874 5964	111	1338,794 395 3681	171	11137,400 429 1260
52	145,221 007 6289	112	1387,488 945 7030	172	11535,170 319 4136
53	151,394 506 0257	113	1437,918 239 3937	173	11947,110 762 0427
54	157,787 935 3029	114	1490,144 076 6721	174	12373,726 582 9405
55	164,409 130 4980	115	1544,230 459 4036	175	12815,540 592 4577
56	171,266 205 7720	116	1600,243 669 5198	176	13273,094 226 0640
57	178,367 564 3527	117	1658,252 350 2465	177	13746,948 207 8676
58	185,721 908 8327	118	1718,327 590 2240	178	14237,683 237 7728
59	193,338 251 8349	119	1780,543 010 6257	179	14745,900 703 1185
60	201,225 927 0565	120	1844,974 855 3793	180	15272,223 415 6671

Amount of 1 Per Period

NOMINAL INTEREST RATE COMPOUNDED

YEARLY	HALF-YEARLY	QUARTERLY
@	@	@
$3\frac{5}{8}\%$	$7\frac{1}{4}\%$	$14\frac{1}{2}\%$
3.6250%	7.2500%	14.5000%
PER ANNUM	PER ANNUM	PER ANNUM

Periods	Amount	Periods	Amount	Periods	Amount
1	1.000 000 0000	61	214.532 946 2097	121	2023.112 037 6460
2	2.036 250 0000	62	223.309 765 5098	122	2097.449 849 0106
3	3.110 064 0625	63	232.404 744 5095	123	2174.482 406 0373
4	4.222 803 8848	64	241.829 416 4980	124	2254.307 393 2561
5	5.375 880 5256	65	251.595 732 8461	125	2337.026 036 2617
6	6.570 756 1946	66	261.716 078 1617	126	2422.743 230 0762
7	7.808 946 1067	67	272.203 285 9951	127	2511.567 672 1664
8	9.092 020 4031	68	283.070 655 1124	128	2603.612 000 2824
9	10.421 606 1427	69	294.331 966 3602	129	2698.992 935 2927
10	11.799 389 3653	70	306.001 500 1408	130	2797.831 429 1970
11	13.227 117 2298	71	318.094 054 5209	131	2900.252 818 5054
12	14.706 600 2294	72	330.624 963 9973	132	3006.386 983 1763
13	16.239 714 4877	73	343.610 118 9422	133	3116.368 511 3164
14	17.828 404 1379	74	357.065 985 7538	134	3230.336 869 8516
15	19.474 683 7879	75	371.009 627 7374	135	3348.436 581 3837
16	21.180 641 0752	76	385.458 726 7429	136	3470.817 407 4589
17	22.948 439 3142	77	400.431 605 5873	137	3597.634 538 4793
18	24.780 320 2393	78	415.947 251 2899	138	3729.048 790 4992
19	26.678 606 8480	79	432.025 339 1491	139	3865.226 809 1548
20	28.645 706 3463	80	448.686 257 6933	140	4006.341 280 9866
21	30.684 113 2013	81	465.951 134 5347	141	4152.571 152 4224
22	32.796 412 3049	82	483.841 863 1615	142	4304.101 856 6977
23	34.985 282 2509	83	502.381 130 7011	143	4461.125 549 0030
24	37.253 498 7325	84	521.592 446 6891	144	4623.841 350 1543
25	39.603 938 0616	85	541.500 172 8815	145	4792.455 599 0974
26	42.039 580 8163	86	562.129 554 1485	146	4967.182 114 5647
27	44.563 515 6209	87	583.506 750 4864	147	5148.242 466 2177
28	47.178 943 0621	88	605.658 870 1915	148	5335.866 255 6181
29	49.889 179 7482	89	628.614 004 2359	149	5530.291 407 3842
30	52.697 662 5140	90	652.401 261 8895	150	5731.764 470 9019
31	55.607 952 7802	91	677.050 807 6330	151	5940.540 932 9721
32	58.623 741 0684	92	702.593 899 4097	152	6156.885 541 7923
33	61.748 851 6822	93	729.062 928 2633	153	6381.072 642 6823
34	64.987 247 5556	94	756.491 459 4128	154	6613.386 525 9795
35	68.343 035 2795	95	784.914 274 8166	155	6854.121 787 5463
36	71.820 470 3084	96	814.367 417 2787	156	7103.583 702 3449
37	75.423 962 3571	97	844.888 236 1550	157	7362.088 611 5549
38	79.158 080 9925	98	876.515 434 7156	158	7629.964 323 7237
39	83.027 561 4285	99	909.289 119 2241	159	7907.550 530 4587
40	87.037 310 5303	100	943.250 849 7959	160	8195.199 237 1878
41	91.192 413 0370	101	978.443 693 1010	161	8493.275 209 5359
42	95.498 138 0096	102	1014.912 276 9760	162	8802.156 435 8816
43	99.959 945 5125	103	1052.702 847 0163	163	9122.234 606 6823
44	104.583 493 5373	104	1091.863 325 2207	164	9453.915 611 1745
45	109.374 645 1780	105	1132.443 370 7599	165	9797.620 052 0796
46	114.339 476 0657	106	1174.494 442 9500	166	10153.783 778 9675
47	119.484 282 0731	107	1218.069 866 5069	167	10522.858 440 9550
48	124.815 587 2983	108	1263.224 899 1678	168	10905.312 059 4397
49	130.340 152 3378	109	1310.016 801 7626	169	11301.629 621 5943
50	136.064 982 8601	110	1358.504 910 8265	170	11712.313 695 3771
51	141.997 338 4887	111	1408.750 713 8440	171	12137.885 066 8346
52	148.144 742 0090	112	1460.817 927 2208	172	12578.883 400 5073
53	154.514 988 9068	113	1514.772 577 0826	173	13035.867 923 7757
54	161.116 157 2547	114	1570.683 083 0018	174	13509.418 136 0126
55	167.956 617 9551	115	1628.620 344 7606	175	14000.134 543 4430
56	175.045 045 3560	116	1688.657 832 2582	176	14508.639 420 6428
57	182.390 428 2502	117	1750.871 678 6776	177	15035.577 599 6411
58	190.002 081 2742	118	1815.340 777 0296	178	15581.617 287 6281
59	197.889 656 7204	119	1882.146 880 1969	179	16147.450 914 3047
60	206.063 156 7765	120	1951.374 704 6041	180	16733.796 009 9482

Amount of 1 Per Period

NOMINAL INTEREST RATE COMPOUNDED

	YEARLY @ $3\frac{11}{16}\%$ 3.6875% PER ANNUM		HALF-YEARLY @ $7\frac{3}{8}\%$ 7.3750% PER ANNUM		QUARTERLY @ $14\frac{3}{4}\%$ 14.7500% PER ANNUM
Periods	Amount	Periods	Amount	Periods	Amount
1	1,000 000 0000	61	219,814 039 6774	121	2141,398 093 6029
2	2,036 875 0000	62	228,919 682 3905	122	2221,362 148 3045
3	3,111 984 7656	63	238,361 095 6787	123	2304,274 877 5233
4	4,226 739 2039	64	248,150 661 0818	124	2390,245 013 6319
5	5,382 600 2120	65	258,301 216 7092	125	2479,385 298 5096
6	6,581 083 5948	66	268,826 074 0754	126	2571,812 631 3922
7	7,823 761 0524	67	279,739 035 5569	127	2667,648 222 1747
8	9,112 262 2412	68	291,054 412 4931	128	2767,017 750 3674
9	10,448 276 9113	69	302,787 043 9538	129	2870,051 529 9122
10	11,833 557 1224	70	314,952 316 1996	130	2976,884 680 0778
11	13,269 919 5413	71	327,566 182 8594	131	3087,657 302 6556
12	14,759 247 8244	72	340,645 185 8524	132	3202,514 665 6910
13	16,303 495 0879	73	354,206 477 0807	133	3321,607 393 9884
14	17,904 686 4693	74	368,267 840 9230	134	3445,091 666 6417
15	19,564 921 7829	75	382,847 717 5570	135	3573,129 421 8491
16	21,286 378 2736	76	397,965 227 1420	136	3705,888 569 2798
17	23,071 313 4724	77	413,640 194 8928	137	3843,543 210 2720
18	24,922 068 1567	78	429,893 177 0795	138	3986,273 866 1508
19	26,841 069 4200	79	446,745 487 9843	139	4134,267 714 9651
20	28,830 833 8549	80	464,219 227 8537	140	4287,718 836 9544
21	30,893 970 8533	81	482,337 311 8808	141	4446,828 469 0671
22	33,033 186 0285	82	501,123 500 2564	142	4611,805 268 8640
23	35,251 284 7633	83	520,602 429 3284	143	4782,865 588 1534
24	37,551 175 8889	84	540,799 643 9099	144	4960,233 756 7165
25	39,935 875 4998	85	561,741 630 7791	145	5144,142 376 4954
26	42,408 510 9089	86	583,455 853 4140	146	5334,832 626 6287
27	44,972 324 7487	87	605,970 788 0087	147	5532,554 579 7356
28	47,630 679 2238	88	629,315 960 8165	148	5737,567 529 8634
29	50,387 060 5201	89	653,521 986 8716	149	5950,140 332 5271
30	53,245 083 3768	90	678,620 610 1375	150	6170,551 757 2890
31	56,208 495 8263	91	704,644 745 1363	151	6399,090 853 3391
32	59,281 184 1099	92	731,628 520 1132	152	6636,057 328 5559
33	62,467 177 7740	93	759,607 321 7924	153	6881,761 942 5464
34	65,770 654 9544	94	788,617 841 7835	154	7136,526 914 1778
35	69,195 947 8559	95	818,698 124 6993	155	7400,686 344 1382
36	72,747 548 4330	96	849,887 618 0475	156	7674,586 653 0782
37	76,430 114 2815	97	882,227 223 9630	157	7958,587 035 9105
38	80,248 474 7456	98	915,759 352 8467	158	8253,059 932 8597
39	84,207 637 2519	99	950,527 978 9829	159	8558,391 517 8839
40	88,312 793 8755	100	986,578 698 2079	160	8874,982 205 1059
41	92,569 328 1497	101	1023,958 787 7043	161	9203,247 173 9192
42	96,982 822 1252	102	1062,717 268 0009	162	9543,616 913 4574
43	101,559 063 6911	103	1102,904 967 2584	163	9896,537 787 1412
44	106,304 054 1647	104	1144,574 587 9261	164	10262,472 618 0420
45	111,224 016 1620	105	1187,780 775 8559	165	10641,901 295 8323
46	116,325 401 7580	106	1232,580 191 9656	166	11035,321 406 1161
47	121,614 900 9478	107	1279,031 586 5443	167	11443,248 882 9666
48	127,099 450 4203	108	1327,195 876 2981	168	11866,218 685 5260
49	132,786 242 6545	109	1377,136 224 2366	169	12304,785 499 5548
50	138,682 735 3524	110	1428,918 122 5053	170	12759,524 464 8509
51	144,796 661 2185	111	1482,609 478 2727	171	13231,031 929 4923
52	151,136 038 1010	112	1538,280 702 7840	172	13719,926 231 8923
53	157,709 179 5059	113	1596,004 803 6992	173	14226,848 511 6933
54	164,524 705 5002	114	1655,857 480 8356	174	14752,463 550 5620
55	171,591 554 0155	115	1717,917 225 4414	175	15297,460 643 9890
56	178,918 992 5699	116	1782,265 423 1295	176	15862,554 505 2361
57	186,516 630 4209	117	1848,986 460 6074	177	16448,486 202 6167
58	194,394 431 1677	118	1918,167 836 3423	178	17056,024 131 3382
59	202,562 725 8170	119	1989,900 275 3075	179	17685,965 021 1813
60	211,032 226 3315	120	2064,277 847 9594	180	18339,134 981 3373

Amount of 1 Per Period

NOMINAL INTEREST RATE COMPOUNDED

	YEARLY @ $3\frac{3}{4}\%$ 3.7500% PER ANNUM		HALF-YEARLY @ $7\frac{1}{2}\%$ 7.5000% PER ANNUM		QUARTERLY @ 15% 15.0000% PER ANNUM
Periods	Amount	Periods	Amount	Periods	Amount
1	1,000 000 0000	61	225,242 029 8606	121	2266,995 672 5892
2	2,037 500 0000	62	234,688 605 9804	122	2353,008 010 3113
3	3,113 906 2500	63	244,489 428 7047	123	2442,245 810 6980
4	4,230 677 7344	64	254,657 782 2811	124	2534,830 028 5992
5	5,389 328 1494	65	265,207 449 1166	125	2630,886 154 6716
6	6,591 427 9550	66	276,152 728 4585	126	2730,544 385 4718
7	7,838 606 5033	67	287,508 455 7757	127	2833,939 799 9270
8	9,132 554 2472	68	299,290 022 8673	128	2941,212 542 4243
9	10,475 025 0315	69	311,513 398 7248	129	3052,508 012 7652
10	11,867 838 4702	70	324,195 151 1770	130	3167,977 063 2439
11	13,312 882 4128	71	337,352 469 3461	131	3287,776 203 1155
12	14,812 115 5033	72	351,003 186 9466	132	3412,067 810 7324
13	16,367 569 8346	73	365,165 806 4571	133	3541,020 353 6348
14	17,981 353 7034	74	379,859 524 1992	134	3674,808 616 8961
15	19,655 654 4673	75	395,104 256 3567	135	3813,613 940 0297
16	21,392 741 5098	76	410,920 665 9701	136	3957,624 462 7809
17	23,194 969 3165	77	427,330 190 9440	137	4107,035 380 1351
18	25,064 780 6658	78	444,355 073 1044	138	4262,049 206 8902
19	27,004 709 9408	79	462,018 388 3458	139	4422,876 052 1486
20	29,017 386 5636	80	480,344 077 9088	140	4589,733 904 1042
21	31,105 538 5597	81	499,356 980 8303	141	4762,848 925 5081
22	33,271 996 2557	82	519,082 867 6115	142	4942,455 760 2146
23	35,519 696 1153	83	539,548 475 1469	143	5128,797 851 2227
24	37,851 684 7196	84	560,781 542 9649	144	5322,127 770 6435
25	40,271 122 8966	85	582,810 850 8261	145	5522,707 562 0427
26	42,781 290 0052	86	605,666 257 7321	146	5730,809 095 6193
27	45,385 588 3804	87	629,378 742 3970	147	5946,714 436 7050
28	48,087 547 9447	88	653,980 445 2369	148	6170,716 228 0814
29	50,890 830 9926	89	679,504 711 9333	149	6403,118 086 6345
30	53,799 237 1548	90	705,986 138 6308	150	6644,235 014 8833
31	56,816 708 5481	91	733,460 618 8294	151	6894,393 827 9414
32	59,947 335 1187	92	761,965 392 0356	152	7153,933 596 4892
33	63,195 360 1856	93	791,539 094 2369	153	7423,206 106 3575
34	66,565 186 1926	94	822,221 810 2708	154	7702,576 335 3459
35	70,061 380 6748	95	854,055 128 1559	155	7992,422 947 9214
36	73,688 682 4501	96	887,082 195 4618	156	8293,138 808 4685
37	77,452 008 0420	97	921,347 777 7916	157	8605,131 513 7860
38	81,356 458 3436	98	956,898 319 4588	158	8928,823 945 5530
39	85,407 325 5315	99	993,782 006 4385	159	9264,654 843 5112
40	89,610 100 2389	100	1032,048 831 6799	160	9613,079 400 1429
41	93,970 478 9979	101	1071,750 662 8679	161	9974,569 877 6483
42	98,494 371 9603	102	1112,941 312 7255	162	10349,616 248 0601
43	103,187 910 9088	103	1155,676 611 9527	163	10738,726 857 3623
44	108,057 457 5679	104	1200,014 484 9009	164	11142,429 114 5134
45	113,109 612 2267	105	1246,015 028 0847	165	11561,270 206 3077
46	118,351 222 6852	106	1293,740 591 6379	166	11995,817 839 0442
47	123,789 393 5359	107	1343,255 863 8243	167	12446,661 008 0084
48	129,431 495 7935	108	1394,627 958 7177	168	12914,410 795 8087
49	135,285 176 8857	109	1447,926 507 1696	169	13399,701 200 6515
50	141,358 371 0189	110	1503,223 751 1885	170	13903,189 995 6759
51	147,659 309 9321	111	1560,594 641 8580	171	14425,559 620 5138
52	154,196 534 0546	112	1620,116 940 9277	172	14967,518 106 2831
53	160,978 904 0816	113	1681,871 326 2125	173	15529,800 035 2687
54	168,015 612 9847	114	1745,941 500 9455	174	16113,167 536 5913
55	175,316 198 4716	115	1812,414 307 2309	175	16718,411 319 2134
56	182,890 555 9143	116	1881,379 843 7521	176	17346,351 743 6839
57	190,748 951 7611	117	1952,931 587 8928	177	17997,839 934 0721
58	198,902 037 4521	118	2027,166 522 4387	178	18673,758 931 5998
59	207,360 863 8566	119	2104,185 267 0302	179	19375,024 891 5348
60	216,136 896 2512	120	2184,092 214 5438	180	20102,588 324 9673

NOMINAL INTEREST RATE COMPOUNDED

	YEARLY @ $3\frac{13}{16}\%$ 3.8125% PER ANNUM		HALF-YEARLY @ $7\frac{5}{8}\%$ 7.6250% PER ANNUM		QUARTERLY @ $15\frac{1}{4}\%$ 15.2500% PER ANNUM
Periods	Amount	Periods	Amount	Periods	Amount
1	1,000 000 0000	61	230,821 188 4261	121	2400,368 143 0325
2	2,038 125 0000	62	240,621 246 2349	122	2492,882 178 4856
3	3,115 828 5156	63	250,794 931 2476	123	2588,923 311 5403
4	4,234 619 4778	64	261,356 488 0014	124	2688,626 012 7928
5	5,396 064 3454	65	272,320 704 1064	125	2792,129 879 5306
6	6,601 789 2985	66	283,702 930 9505	126	2899,579 831 1877
7	7,853 482 5155	67	295,519 105 1930	127	3011,126 312 2517
8	9,152 896 5365	68	307,785 771 0785	128	3126,925 502 9063
9	10,501 850 7169	69	320,520 103 6008	129	3247,139 537 7046
10	11,902 233 7755	70	333,739 932 5506	130	3371,936 732 5796
11	13,356 006 4382	71	347,463 767 4791	131	3501,491 820 5092
12	14,865 204 1836	72	361,710 823 6143	132	3635,986 196 1661
13	16,431 940 0931	73	376,501 048 7645	133	3775,608 169 8949
14	18,058 407 8092	74	391,855 151 2487	134	3920,553 231 3722
15	19,746 884 6069	75	407,794 628 8900	135	4071,024 323 3182
16	21,499 734 5825	76	424,341 799 1165	136	4227,232 125 6447
17	23,319 411 9635	77	441,519 830 2078	137	4389,395 350 4349
18	25,208 464 5446	78	459,352 773 7345	138	4557,741 048 1703
19	27,169 537 2554	79	477,865 598 2331	139	4732,504 925 6317
20	29,205 375 8632	80	497,084 224 1657	140	4913,931 675 9215
21	31,318 830 8180	81	517,035 560 2121	141	5102,275 321 0660
22	33,512 861 2430	82	537,747 540 9451	142	5297,799 567 6816
23	35,790 539 0779	83	559,249 165 9437	143	5500,778 176 1995
24	38,155 053 3802	84	581,570 540 3953	144	5711,495 344 1671
25	40,609 714 7903	85	604,742 917 2478	145	5930,246 104 1634
26	43,157 960 1667	86	628,798 740 9679	146	6157,336 736 8847
27	45,803 357 3981	87	653,771 692 9673	147	6393,085 199 9784
28	48,549 610 3989	88	679,696 738 7617	148	6637,821 573 2276
29	51,400 564 2953	89	706,610 176 9270	149	6891,888 520 7069
30	54,360 210 8091	90	734,549 689 9223	150	7155,641 770 5588
31	57,432 693 8462	91	763,554 396 8506	151	7429,450 613 0614
32	60,622 315 2990	92	793,664 908 2305	152	7713,698 417 6843
33	63,933 541 0698	93	824,923 382 8568	153	8008,783 169 8586
34	67,371 007 3231	94	857,373 586 8283	154	8315,118 028 2094
35	70,939 526 9773	95	891,060 954 8261	155	8633,131 903 0349
36	74,644 096 4433	96	926,032 653 7288	156	8963,270 056 8381
37	78,489 902 6202	97	962,337 648 6522	157	9305,994 727 7551
38	82,482 330 1576	98	1000,026 771 5071	158	9661,785 776 7507
39	86,626 968 9949	99	1039,152 792 1708	159	10031,141 359 4893
40	90,929 622 1878	100	1079,770 492 3723	160	10414,578 623 8199
41	95,396 314 0337	101	1121,936 742 3940	161	10812,634 433 8530
42	100,033 298 5062	102	1165,710 580 6978	162	11225,866 121 6437
43	104,847 068 0118	103	1211,153 296 5869	163	11654,852 267 5313
44	109,844 362 4797	104	1258,328 516 0193	164	12100,193 510 2310
45	115,032 178 7993	105	1307,302 290 6925	165	12562,513 387 8085
46	120,417 780 6160	106	1358,143 190 5252	166	13042,459 210 7187
47	126,008 708 5020	107	1410,922 399 6639	167	13540,702 968 1274
48	131,812 790 5136	108	1465,713 816 1511	168	14057,942 268 7872
49	137,838 153 1520	109	1522,594 155 3919	169	14594,901 317 7847
50	144,093 232 7409	110	1581,643 057 5662	170	15152,331 930 5253
51	150,586 787 2391	111	1642,943 199 1359	171	15731,014 585 3765
52	157,327 908 5026	112	1706,580 408 6030	172	16331,759 516 4440
53	164,326 035 0143	113	1772,643 786 6809	173	16955,407 848 0085
54	171,590 965 0992	114	1841,225 831 0482	174	17602,832 772 2138
55	179,132 870 6436	115	1912,422 565 8569	175	18274,940 771 6544
56	186,962 311 3369	116	1986,333 676 1802	176	18972,672 888 5738
57	195,090 249 4566	117	2063,062 647 5845	177	19697,006 042 4506
58	203,528 065 2172	118	2142,716 911 0237	178	20448,954 397 8191
59	212,287 572 7036	119	2225,407 993 2565	179	21229,570 784 2359
60	221,381 036 4129	120	2311,251 672 9994	180	22039,948 170 3849

Amount of 1 Per Period

NOMINAL INTEREST RATE COMPOUNDED

	YEARLY	HALF-YEARLY	QUARTERLY
	@	@	@
	$3\frac{7}{8}\%$	$7\frac{3}{4}\%$	$15\frac{1}{2}\%$
	3.8750%	7.7500%	15.5000%
	PER ANNUM	PER ANNUM	PER ANNUM

Periods	Amount	Periods	Amount	Periods	Amount
1	1,000 000 0000	61	236,555 913 6246	121	2542,008 628 3911
2	2,038 750 0000	62	246,722 455 2775	122	2641,511 462 7412
3	3,117 751 5625	63	257,282 950 4195	123	2744,870 031 9225
4	4,238 564 4355	64	268,252 664 7483	124	2852,233 745 6594
5	5,402 808 8074	65	279,647 455 5073	125	2963,757 803 3038
6	6,612 167 6487	66	291,483 794 4082	126	3079,603 418 1818
7	7,868 389 1451	67	303,778 791 4415	127	3199,938 050 6363
8	9,173 289 2245	68	316,550 219 6099	128	3324,935 650 0985
9	10,528 754 1819	69	329,816 540 6198	129	3454,776 906 5398
10	11,936 743 4065	70	343,596 931 5688	130	3589,649 511 6682
11	13,399 292 2135	71	357,911 312 6671	131	3729,748 430 2453
12	14,918 514 7867	72	372,780 376 0329	132	3875,276 181 9174
13	16,496 607 2347	73	388,225 615 6042	133	4026,443 133 9667
14	18,135 850 7651	74	404,269 358 2089	134	4183,467 805 4079
15	19,838 614 9822	75	420,934 795 8395	135	4346,577 182 8674
16	21,607 361 3128	76	438,246 019 1782	136	4516,007 048 7035
17	23,444 646 5637	77	456,228 052 4214	137	4692,002 321 8408
18	25,353 126 6180	78	474,906 889 4527	138	4874,817 411 8121
19	27,335 560 2744	79	494,309 531 4190	139	5064,716 586 5198
20	29,394 813 2351	80	514,464 025 7615	140	5261,974 354 2475
21	31,533 862 2479	81	535,399 506 7598	141	5466,875 860 4746
22	33,755 799 4100	82	557,146 237 6467	142	5679,717 300 0680
23	36,063 836 6372	83	579,735 654 3555	143	5900,806 345 4456
24	38,461 310 3069	84	603,200 410 9618	144	6130,462 591 3316
25	40,951 686 0813	85	627,574 426 8865	145	6369,018 016 7457
26	43,538 563 9169	86	652,892 935 9284	146	6616,817 464 8946
27	46,225 683 2687	87	679,192 537 1956	147	6874,219 141 6593
28	49,016 928 4954	88	706,511 248 0120	148	7141,595 133 3986
29	51,916 334 4746	89	734,888 558 8724	149	7419,331 944 8178
30	54,928 092 4354	90	764,365 490 5287	150	7707,831 057 6795
31	58,056 556 0173	91	794,984 653 2867	151	8007,509 511 1645
32	61,306 247 5630	92	826,790 308 6016	152	8318,800 504 7222
33	64,681 864 6560	93	859,828 433 0599	153	8642,154 024 2801
34	68,188 286 9115	94	894,146 784 8410	154	8978,037 492 7210
35	71,830 583 0293	95	929,794 972 7535	155	9326,936 445 5639
36	75,614 018 1217	96	966,824 527 9477	156	9689,355 232 8295
37	79,544 061 3239	97	1005,288 978 4057	157	10065,817 748 1017
38	83,626 393 7002	98	1045,243 926 3189	158	10456,868 185 8406
39	87,866 916 4561	99	1086,747 128 4638	159	10863,071 828 0419
40	92,271 759 4687	100	1129,858 579 6918	160	11285,015 861 3786
41	96,847 290 1482	101	1174,640 599 6548	161	11723,310 226 0070
42	101,600 122 6414	102	1221,157 922 8915	162	12178,588 497 2648
43	106,537 127 3938	103	1269,477 792 4035	163	12651,508 801 5338
44	111,665 441 0803	104	1319,670 056 8591	164	13142,754 767 5932
45	116,992 476 9221	105	1371,807 271 5624	165	13653,036 514 8374
46	122,525 935 4029	106	1425,964 803 3355	166	14183,091 679 7874
47	128,273 815 3997	107	1482,220 939 4647	167	14733,686 482 3792
48	134,244 425 7465	108	1540,657 000 8690	168	15305,616 833 5713
49	140,446 397 2441	109	1601,357 459 6526	169	15899,709 485 8722
50	146,888 695 1373	110	1664,410 061 2142	170	16516,823 228 4498
51	153,580 632 0739	111	1729,905 951 0862	171	17157,850 128 5522
52	160,531 881 5668	112	1797,939 806 6908	172	17823,716 821 0336
53	167,752 491 9775	113	1868,609 974 2001	173	18515,385 847 8487
54	175,252 901 0416	114	1942,018 610 7004	174	19233,857 049 4528
55	183,043 950 9570	115	2018,271 831 8650	175	19980,169 010 1191
56	191,136 904 0566	116	2097,479 865 3498	176	20755,400 559 2612
57	199,543 459 0888	117	2179,757 210 1321	177	21560,672 330 9326
58	208,275 768 1284	118	2265,222 802 0247	178	22397,148 383 7562
59	217,346 454 1434	119	2354,000 185 6031	179	23266,037 883 6268
60	226,768 629 2415	120	2446,217 692 7953	180	24168,596 851 6173

NOMINAL INTEREST RATE COMPOUNDED

YEARLY @ $3\frac{15}{16}\%$ 3.9375% PER ANNUM		HALF-YEARLY @ $7\frac{7}{8}\%$ 7.8750% PER ANNUM		QUARTERLY @ $15\frac{3}{4}\%$ 15.7500% PER ANNUM	
Periods	Amount	Periods	Amount	Periods	Amount
1	1,000 000 0000	61	242,450 734 0663	121	2692,441 931 0380
2	2,039 375 0000	62	252,997 231 7201	122	2799,456 832 0726
3	3,119 675 3906	63	263,958 997 7191	123	2910,685 444 8355
4	4,242 512 6091	64	275,352 383 2543	124	3026,293 684 2259
5	5,409 561 5431	65	287,194 383 3449	125	3146,453 998 0423
6	6,622 563 0289	66	299,502 662 1891	126	3271,345 624 2152
7	7,883 326 4481	67	312,295 579 5128	127	3401,154 858 1687
8	9,193 732 4270	68	325,592 217 9562	128	3536,075 330 7091
9	10,555 735 6413	69	339,412 411 5382	129	3676,308 296 8557
10	11,971 367 7322	70	353,776 775 2425	130	3822,062 936 0444
11	13,442 740 3367	71	368,706 735 7677	131	3973,556 664 1512
12	14,972 048 2374	72	384,224 563 4885	132	4131,015 457 8021
13	16,561 572 6368	73	400,353 405 6759	133	4294,674 191 4531
14	18,213 684 5594	74	417,117 321 0244	134	4464,776 987 7416
15	19,930 848 3889	75	434,541 315 5397	135	4641,577 581 6339
16	21,715 625 5442	76	452,651 379 8391	136	4825,339 698 9107
17	23,570 678 3000	77	471,474 527 9202	137	5016,337 449 5553
18	25,498 773 7581	78	491,038 837 4571	138	5214,855 736 6316
19	27,502 787 9748	79	511,373 491 6820	139	5421,190 681 2614
20	29,585 710 2513	80	532,508 822 9170	140	5635,650 064 3361
21	31,750 647 5924	81	554,476 357 8193	141	5858,553 785 6193
22	34,000 829 3414	82	577,308 864 4084	142	6090,234 340 9281
23	36,339 611 9967	83	601,040 400 9445	143	6331,037 318 1021
24	38,770 484 2191	84	625,706 366 7317	144	6581,321 912 5024
25	41,297 072 0352	85	651,343 554 9218	145	6841,461 462 8072
26	43,923 144 2466	86	677,990 207 3968	146	7111,844 007 9052
27	46,652 618 0513	87	705,686 071 8131	147	7392,872 865 7165
28	49,489 564 8871	88	734,472 460 8907	148	7684,967 234 8041
29	52,438 216 5045	89	764,392 314 0383	149	7988,562 819 6745
30	55,502 971 2794	90	795,490 261 4035	150	8304,112 480 6992
31	58,688 400 7735	91	827,812 690 4463	151	8632,086 909 6267
32	61,999 256 5539	92	861,407 815 1326	152	8972,975 331 6933
33	65,440 477 2808	93	896,325 747 8535	153	9327,286 235 3787
34	69,017 196 0737	94	932,618 574 1752	154	9695,548 130 8967
35	72,734 748 1691	95	970,340 430 5334	155	10078,310 338 5508
36	76,598 678 8782	96	1009,547 584 9856	156	10476,143 808 1312
37	80,614 751 8591	97	1050,298 521 1444	157	10889,641 970 5764
38	84,788 957 7135	98	1092,654 025 4145	158	11319,421 623 1678
39	89,127 522 9235	99	1136,677 277 6652	159	11766,123 849 5801
40	93,636 919 1386	100	1182,433 945 4732	160	12230,414 976 1573
41	98,323 872 8297	101	1229,992 282 0763	161	12712,987 565 8435
42	103,195 375 3224	102	1279,423 228 1830	162	13214,561 451 2485
43	108,258 693 2257	103	1330,800 517 7927	163	13735,884 808 3915
44	113,521 379 2714	104	1384,200 788 1808	164	14277,735 272 7219
45	118,991 283 5803	105	1439,703 694 2154	165	14840,921 099 0853
46	124,676 565 3712	106	1497,392 027 1752	166	15426,282 367 3618
47	130,585 705 1327	107	1557,351 838 2452	167	16034,692 235 5766
48	136,727 517 2723	108	1619,672 566 8761	168	16667,058 242 3525
49	143,111 163 2649	109	1684,447 174 1968	169	17324,323 660 6451
50	149,746 165 3185	110	1751,772 281 6808	170	18007,468 904 7830
51	156,642 420 5779	111	1821,748 315 2720	171	18717,512 992 9088
52	163,810 215 8881	112	1894,479 655 1858	172	19455,515 067 0046
53	171,260 243 1387	113	1970,074 791 6088	173	20222,575 972 7679
54	179,003 615 2123	114	2048,646 486 5284	174	21019,839 901 6957
55	187,051 882 5613	115	2130,311 941 9354	175	21848,496 097 8249
56	195,417 050 4372	116	2215,192 974 6491	176	22709,780 631 6768
57	204,111 596 7981	117	2303,416 198 0260	177	23604,978 244 0491
58	213,148 490 9221	118	2395,113 210 8232	178	24535,424 262 4085
59	222,541 212 7521	119	2490,420 793 4994	179	25502,506 592 7408
60	232,303 773 0042	120	2589,481 112 2434	180	26507,667 789 8300

Amount of 1 Per Period

NOMINAL INTEREST RATE COMPOUNDED

YEARLY	HALF-YEARLY	QUARTERLY
@	@	@
4%	**8%**	**16%**
4.0000%	8.0000%	16.0000%
PER ANNUM	PER ANNUM	PER ANNUM

Periods	Amount	Periods	Amount	Periods	Amount
1	1,000 000 0000	61	248,510 312 6094	121	2852,226 580 9107
2	2,040 000 0000	62	259,450 725 1137	122	2967,315 644 1471
3	3,121 600 0000	63	270,828 754 1183	123	3087,008 269 9130
4	4,246 464 0000	64	282,661 904 2830	124	3211,488 600 7095
5	5,416 322 5600	65	294,968 380 4544	125	3340,948 144 7379
6	6,632 975 4624	66	307,767 115 6725	126	3475,586 070 5274
7	7,898 294 4809	67	321,077 800 2994	127	3615,609 513 3485
8	9,214 226 2601	68	334,920 912 3114	128	3761,233 893 8824
9	10,582 795 3105	69	349,317 748 8039	129	3912,683 249 6377
10	12,006 107 1230	70	364,290 458 7560	130	4070,190 579 6232
11	13,486 351 4079	71	379,862 077 1063	131	4233,998 202 8082
12	15,025 805 4642	72	396,056 560 1905	132	4404,358 130 9205
13	16,626 837 6828	73	412,898 822 5981	133	4581,532 456 1573
14	18,291 911 1901	74	430,414 775 5021	134	4765,793 754 4036
15	20,023 587 6377	75	448,631 366 5221	135	4957,425 504 5797
16	21,824 531 1432	76	467,576 621 1830	136	5156,722 524 7629
17	23,697 512 3889	77	487,279 686 0303	137	5363,991 425 7534
18	25,645 412 8845	78	507,770 873 4716	138	5579,551 082 7836
19	27,671 229 3998	79	529,081 708 4104	139	5803,733 126 0949
20	29,778 078 5758	80	551,244 976 7468	140	6036,882 451 1387
21	31,969 201 7189	81	574,294 775 8167	141	6279,357 749 1843
22	34,247 969 7876	82	598,266 566 8494	142	6531,532 059 1516
23	36,617 888 5791	83	623,197 229 5233	143	6793,793 341 5177
24	39,082 604 1223	84	649,125 118 7043	144	7066,545 075 1784
25	41,645 908 2872	85	676,090 123 4525	145	7350,206 878 1856
26	44,311 744 6187	86	704,133 728 3906	146	7645,215 153 3130
27	47,084 214 4034	87	733,299 077 5262	147	7952,023 759 4455
28	49,967 582 9796	88	763,631 040 6272	148	8271,104 709 8233
29	52,966 286 2987	89	795,176 282 2523	149	8602,948 898 2163
30	56,084 937 7507	90	827,983 333 5424	150	8948,066 854 1449
31	59,328 335 2607	91	862,102 666 8841	151	9306,989 528 3107
32	62,701 468 6711	92	897,586 773 5595	152	9680,269 109 4431
33	66,209 527 4180	93	934,490 244 5018	153	10068,479 873 8209
34	69,857 908 5147	94	972,869 854 2819	154	10472,219 068 7737
35	73,652 224 8553	95	1012,784 648 4532	155	10892,107 831 5246
36	77,598 313 8495	96	1054,296 034 3913	156	11328,792 144 7856
37	81,702 246 4035	97	1097,467 875 7670	157	11782,943 830 5770
38	85,970 336 2596	98	1142,366 590 7976	158	12255,261 583 8001
39	90,409 149 7100	99	1189,061 254 4296	159	12746,472 047 1521
40	95,025 515 6984	100	1237,623 704 6067	160	13257,330 929 0382
41	99,826 536 3264	101	1288,128 652 7910	161	13788,624 166 1997
42	104,819 597 7794	102	1340,653 798 9026	162	14341,169 132 8477
43	110,012 381 6906	103	1395,279 950 8588	163	14915,815 898 1616
44	115,412 876 9582	104	1452,091 148 8931	164	15513,448 534 0881
45	121,029 392 0365	105	1511,174 794 8488	165	16134,986 475 4516
46	126,870 567 7180	106	1572,621 786 6428	166	16781,385 934 4697
47	132,945 390 4267	107	1636,526 658 1085	167	17453,641 371 8485
48	139,263 206 0438	108	1702,987 724 4328	168	18152,787 026 7224
49	145,833 734 2855	109	1772,107 233 4101	169	18879,898 507 7913
50	152,667 083 6570	110	1843,991 522 7465	170	19636,094 448 1030
51	159,773 767 0032	111	1918,751 183 6564	171	20422,538 226 0271
52	167,164 717 6834	112	1996,501 231 0027	172	21240,439 755 0682
53	174,851 306 3907	113	2077,361 280 2428	173	22091,057 345 2709
54	182,845 358 6463	114	2161,455 731 4525	174	22975,699 639 0817
55	191,159 172 9922	115	2248,913 960 7106	175	23895,727 624 6450
56	199,805 539 9119	116	2339,870 519 1390	176	24852,556 729 6308
57	208,797 761 5083	117	2434,465 339 9046	177	25847,658 998 8160
58	218,149 671 9687	118	2532,843 953 5007	178	26882,565 358 7687
59	227,875 658 8474	119	2635,157 711 6408	179	27958,867 973 1194
60	237,990 685 2013	120	2741,564 020 1064	180	29078,222 692 0442

Amount of 1 Per Period

NOMINAL INTEREST RATE COMPOUNDED

YEARLY	HALF-YEARLY	QUARTERLY
@	@	@
$4\frac{1}{16}\%$	$8\frac{1}{8}\%$	$16\frac{1}{4}\%$
4.0625%	8.1250%	16.2500%
PER ANNUM	PER ANNUM	PER ANNUM

Periods	Amount	Periods	Amount	Periods	Amount
1	1,000 000 0000	61	254,739 450 3643	121	3021,957 017 0210
2	2,040 625 0000	62	266,088 240 5354	122	3145,724 020 8375
3	3,123 525 3906	63	277,898 075 3071	123	3274,519 059 1840
4	4,250 418 6096	64	290,187 684 6165	124	3408,546 395 9634
5	5,423 091 8656	65	302,976 559 3040	125	3548,018 593 2994
6	6,643 404 9727	66	316,284 982 0257	126	3693,156 848 6522
7	7,913 293 2997	67	330,134 059 4205	127	3844,191 345 6287
8	9,234 770 8400	68	344,545 755 5845	128	4001,361 619 0448
9	10,609 933 4054	69	359,542 926 9051	129	4164,916 934 8185
10	12,040 961 9500	70	375,149 358 3106	130	4335,116 685 2955
11	13,530 126 0292	71	391,389 800 9920	131	4512,230 800 6357
12	15,079 787 3991	72	408,290 011 6573	132	4696,540 176 9115
13	16,692 403 7622	73	425,876 793 3809	133	4888,337 121 5985
14	18,370 532 6650	74	444,178 038 1120	134	5087,925 817 1635
15	20,116 835 5546	75	463,222 770 9103	135	5295,622 803 4857
16	21,934 081 9990	76	483,041 195 9785	136	5511,757 479 8773
17	23,825 154 0802	77	503,664 744 5651	137	5736,672 627 4973
18	25,793 050 9647	78	525,126 124 8131	138	5970,724 952 9894
19	27,840 893 6601	79	547,459 373 6336	139	6214,285 654 2046
20	29,971 929 9651	80	570,699 910 6875	140	6467,741 008 9067
21	32,189 539 6199	81	594,884 594 5592	141	6731,492 987 3935
22	34,497 239 6669	82	620,051 781 2131	142	7005,959 890 0064
23	36,898 690 0284	83	646,241 384 8249	143	7291,577 010 5379
24	39,397 699 3108	84	673,494 941 0834	144	7588,797 326 5910
25	41,998 230 8453	85	701,855 673 0649	145	7898,092 217 9837
26	44,704 408 9734	86	731,368 559 7832	146	8219,952 214 3393
27	47,520 525 5880	87	762,080 407 5244	147	8554,887 773 0469
28	50,451 046 9400	88	794,039 924 0801	148	8903,430 088 8269
29	53,500 620 7219	89	827,297 795 9958	149	9266,131 936 1855
30	56,674 083 4387	90	861,906 768 9581	150	9643,568 546 0930
31	59,976 468 0784	91	897,921 731 4471	151	10036,338 518 2781
32	63,413 012 0941	92	935,399 801 7871	152	10445,064 770 5831
33	66,989 165 7104	93	974,400 418 7347	153	10870,395 526 8880
34	70,710 600 5674	94	1014,985 435 7458	154	11313,005 345 1679
35	74,583 218 7155	95	1057,219 219 0730	155	11773,596 187 3153
36	78,613 161 9758	96	1101,168 749 8478	156	12252,898 532 4250
37	82,806 821 6811	97	1146,903 730 3104	157	12751,672 535 3048
38	87,170 848 8119	98	1194,496 694 3542	158	13270,709 232 0515
39	91,712 164 5448	99	1244,023 122 5624	159	13810,831 794 6036
40	96,437 971 2295	100	1295,561 561 9165	160	14372,896 836 2594
41	101,355 763 8107	101	1349,193 750 3693	161	14957,795 770 2324
42	106,473 341 7155	102	1405,004 746 4781	162	15566,456 223 3981
43	111,798 821 2227	103	1463,083 064 3038	163	16199,843 507 4737
44	117,340 648 3348	104	1523,520 813 7911	164	16858,962 149 9648
45	123,107 612 1734	105	1586,413 846 8514	165	17544,857 487 3071
46	129,108 858 9180	106	1651,861 909 3797	166	18258,617 322 7290
47	135,353 906 3115	107	1719,968 799 4483	167	19001,373 651 4648
48	141,852 658 7554	108	1790,842 531 9258	168	19774,304 456 0556
49	148,615 423 0174	109	1864,595 509 7853	169	20578,635 574 5828
50	155,652 924 5775	110	1941,344 702 3704	170	21415,642 644 8003
51	162,976 324 6384	111	2021,211 830 9042	171	22286,653 127 2453
52	170,597 237 8269	112	2104,323 561 5346	172	23193,048 410 5396
53	178,527 750 6136	113	2190,811 706 2220	173	24136,266 002 2178
54	186,780 440 4822	114	2280,813 431 7873	174	25117,801 808 5579
55	195,368 395 8768	115	2374,471 477 4536	175	26139,212 507 0305
56	204,305 236 9593	116	2471,934 381 2252	176	27202,118 015 1287
57	213,605 137 2108	117	2573,356 715 4624	177	28308,204 059 4933
58	223,282 845 9100	118	2678,899 332 0281	178	29459,224 849 4102
59	233,353 711 5251	119	2788,729 617 3917	179	30657,005 858 9175
60	243,833 706 0558	120	2903,021 758 0983	180	31903,446 721 9360

NOMINAL INTEREST RATE COMPOUNDED

YEARLY	HALF-YEARLY	QUARTERLY
@	@	@
$4\frac{1}{8}\%$	$8\frac{1}{4}\%$	$16\frac{1}{2}\%$
4.1250%	8.2500%	16.5000%
PER ANNUM	PER ANNUM	PER ANNUM

Periods	Amount	Periods	Amount	Periods	Amount
1	1.000 000 0000	61	261.143 090 8173	121	3202.265 910 4448
2	2.041 250 0000	62	272.915 243 3135	122	3335.359 379 2506
3	3.125 451 5625	63	285.172 997 1002	123	3473.942 953 6447
4	4.254 376 4395	64	297.936 383 2306	124	3618.243 100 4826
5	5.429 869 4676	65	311.226 259 0388	125	3768.495 628 3775
6	6.653 851 5831	66	325.064 342 2242	126	3924.946 073 0481
7	7.928 322 9609	67	339.473 246 3409	127	4087.850 098 5613
8	9.255 366 2831	68	354.476 517 7525	128	4257.473 915 1269
9	10.637 150 1422	69	370.098 674 1098	129	4434.094 714 1259
10	12.075 932 5856	70	386.365 244 4168	130	4618.001 121 0836
11	13.574 064 8048	71	403.302 810 7490	131	4809.493 667 3283
12	15.133 994 9780	72	420.939 051 6924	132	5008.885 281 1056
13	16.758 272 2708	73	439.302 787 5747	133	5216.501 798 9512
14	18.449 551 0020	74	458.424 027 5622	134	5432.682 498 1580
15	20.210 594 9808	75	478.334 018 6991	135	5657.780 651 2070
16	22.044 282 0238	76	499.065 296 9704	136	5892.164 103 0693
17	23.953 608 6572	77	520.651 740 4705	137	6136.215 872 3209
18	25.941 695 0143	78	543.128 624 7649	138	6390.334 777 0541
19	28.011 789 9337	79	566.532 680 5364	139	6654.936 086 6076
20	30.167 276 2685	80	590.902 153 6085	140	6930.452 200 1802
21	32.411 676 4145	81	616.276 867 4449	141	7217.333 353 4376
22	34.748 658 0666	82	642.698 288 2270	142	7516.048 354 2669
23	37.182 040 2119	83	670.209 592 6164	143	7827.085 348 8804
24	39.715 799 3706	84	698.855 738 3118	144	8150.952 619 5217
25	42.354 076 0947	85	728.683 537 5171	145	8488.179 415 0770
26	45.101 181 7336	86	759.741 733 4397	146	8839.316 815 9489
27	47.961 605 4801	87	792.081 079 9441	147	9204.938 634 6068
28	50.940 021 7061	88	825.754 424 4918	148	9585.642 353 2843
29	54.041 297 6015	89	860.816 794 5021	149	9982.050 100 3573
30	57.270 501 1276	90	897.325 487 2753	150	10394.809 666 9971
31	60.632 909 2991	91	935.340 163 6254	151	10824.595 565 7607
32	64.134 016 8077	92	974.922 945 3750	152	11272.110 132 8483
33	67.779 545 0010	93	1016.138 516 8717	153	11738.084 675 8283
34	71.575 451 2323	94	1059.054 230 6926	154	12223.280 668 7062
35	75.527 938 5956	95	1103.740 217 7087	155	12728.490 996 2904
36	79.643 466 0627	96	1150.269 501 6892	156	13254.541 249 8873
37	83.928 759 0377	97	1198.718 118 6339	157	13802.291 076 4452
38	88.390 820 3481	98	1249.165 241 0275	158	14372.635 583 3485
39	93.036 941 6874	99	1301.693 307 2199	159	14966.506 801 1617
40	97.874 715 5320	100	1356.388 156 1427	160	15584.875 206 7096
41	102.912 047 5477	101	1413.339 167 5836	161	16228.751 308 9864
42	108.157 169 5091	102	1472.639 408 2464	162	16899.187 300 4820
43	113.618 652 7513	103	1534.385 783 8366	163	17597.278 776 6269
44	119.305 422 1773	104	1598.679 197 4199	164	18324.166 526 1628
45	125.226 770 8421	105	1665.624 714 3134	165	19081.038 395 3670
46	131.392 375 1393	106	1735.331 733 7789	166	19869.131 229 1759
47	137.812 310 6138	107	1807.914 167 7972	167	20689.732 892 3794
48	144.497 068 4267	108	1883.490 627 2189	168	21544.184 374 1901
49	151.457 572 4993	109	1962.184 615 5917	169	22433.881 979 6254
50	158.705 197 3649	110	2044.124 730 9848	170	23360.279 611 2849
51	166.251 786 7562	111	2129.444 876 1379	171	24324.891 145 2504
52	174.109 672 9598	112	2218.284 477 2786	172	25329.292 904 9920
53	182.291 696 9694	113	2310.788 711 9664	173	26375.126 237 3229
54	190.811 229 4694	114	2407.108 746 3350	174	27464.100 194 6125
55	199.682 192 6850	115	2507.401 982 1213	175	28597.994 327 6403
56	208.919 083 1333	116	2611.832 313 8838	176	29778.661 593 6554
57	218.536 995 3126	117	2720.570 396 8315	177	31008.031 384 3937
58	228.551 646 3692	118	2833.793 925 7008	178	32288.112 679 0000
59	238.979 401 7819	119	2951.687 925 1360	179	33620.997 327 0087
60	249.837 302 1054	120	3074.445 052 0478	180	35008.863 466 7478

Amount of 1 Per Period

NOMINAL INTEREST RATE COMPOUNDED

	YEARLY		HALF-YEARLY		QUARTERLY
	@		@		@
	$4\frac{3}{16}\%$		$8\frac{3}{8}\%$		$16\frac{3}{4}\%$
	4.1875%		8.3750%		16.7500%
	PER ANNUM		PER ANNUM		PER ANNUM
Periods	**Amount**	**Periods**	**Amount**	**Periods**	**Amount**
1	1,000 000 0000	61	267,726 324 0767	121	3393,826 637 9664
2	2,041 875 0000	62	279,937 363 8975	122	3536,943 128 4312
3	3,127 378 5156	63	292,659 741 0107	123	3686,052 621 9343
4	4,258 337 4910	64	305,914 867 6655	124	3841,406 075 4778
5	5,436 655 3734	65	319,725 052 7490	125	4003,264 954 8884
6	6,664 315 3172	66	334,113 539 3328	126	4171,901 674 8744
7	7,943 383 5211	67	349,104 543 7924	127	4347,600 057 5097
8	9,276 012 7060	68	364,723 296 5637	128	4530,655 809 9179
9	10,664 445 7381	69	380,996 084 6073	129	4721,377 021 9582
10	12,111 019 4034	70	397,950 295 6503	130	4920,084 684 7527
11	13,618 168 3409	71	415,614 464 2806	131	5127,113 230 9268
12	15,188 429 1401	72	434,018 319 9724	132	5342,811 097 4718
13	16,824 444 6104	73	453,192 837 1212	133	5567,541 312 1785
14	18,528 968 2285	74	473,170 287 1756	134	5801,682 104 6259
15	20,304 868 7730	75	493,984 292 9511	135	6045,627 542 7571
16	22,155 135 1529	76	515,669 885 2185	136	6299,788 196 1101
17	24,082 881 4374	77	538,263 561 6620	137	6564,591 826 8222
18	26,091 352 0976	78	561,803 348 3066	138	6840,484 109 5704
19	28,183 927 4667	79	586,328 863 5169	139	7127,929 381 6587
20	30,364 129 4294	80	611,881 384 6767	140	7427,411 424 5156
21	32,635 627 3492	81	638,503 917 6600	141	7739,434 277 9172
22	35,002 244 2445	82	666,241 269 2120	142	8064,523 088 3050
23	37,467 963 2222	83	695,140 122 3603	143	8403,224 992 6278
24	40,036 934 1821	84	725,249 114 9841	144	8756,110 039 1940
25	42,713 480 8010	85	756,618 921 6741	145	9123,772 147 0853
26	45,502 107 8096	86	789,302 339 0192	146	9506,830 105 7445
27	48,407 508 5741	87	823,354 374 4656	147	9905,928 616 4225
28	51,434 572 9956	88	858,832 338 8964	148	10321,739 377 2352
29	54,588 395 7398	89	895,795 943 0876	149	10754,962 213 6570
30	57,874 284 8114	90	934,307 398 2044	150	11206,326 256 3538
31	61,297 770 4879	91	974,431 520 5043	151	11676,591 168 3387
32	64,864 614 6271	92	1016,235 840 4254	152	12166,548 423 5128
33	68,580 820 3646	93	1059,790 716 2432	153	12677,022 638 7474
34	72,452 642 2173	94	1105,169 452 4859	154	13208,872 961 7450
35	76,486 596 6102	95	1152,448 423 3087	155	13762,994 517 0181
36	80,689 472 8433	96	1201,707 201 0348	156	14340,319 912 4182
37	85,068 344 5186	97	1253,028 690 0781	157	14941,820 808 7507
38	89,630 581 4453	98	1306,499 266 4751	158	15568,509 555 1171
39	94,383 862 0433	99	1362,208 923 2588	159	16221,440 892 7377
40	99,336 186 2664	100	1420,251 421 9202	160	16901,713 730 1211
41	104,495 889 0663	101	1480,724 450 2131	161	17610,472 992 5699
42	109,871 654 4209	102	1543,729 786 5658	162	18348,911 549 1337
43	115,472 529 9498	103	1609,373 471 3782	163	19118,272 220 2537
44	121,307 942 1414	104	1677,765 985 4922	164	19919,849 869 4768
45	127,387 712 2186	105	1749,022 436 1347	165	20754,993 582 7612
46	133,722 072 6678	106	1823,262 750 6478	166	21625,108 939 0393
47	140,321 684 4607	107	1900,611 878 3312	167	22531,660 375 8616
48	147,197 654 9975	108	1981,200 000 7363	168	23476,173 654 1008
49	154,361 556 8005	109	2065,162 750 7672	169	24460,238 425 8663
50	161,825 446 9916	110	2152,641 440 9555	170	25485,510 909 9494
51	169,601 887 5843	111	2243,783 301 2956	171	26553,716 679 3035
52	177,703 966 6269	112	2338,741 727 0373	172	27666,653 565 2494
53	186,145 320 2294	113	2437,676 536 8570	173	28826,194 683 2942
54	194,940 155 5140	114	2540,754 241 8379	174	30034,291 585 6571
55	204,103 274 5262	115	2648,148 325 7148	175	31292,977 545 8065
56	213,650 099 1470	116	2760,039 536 8542	176	32604,370 980 5372
57	223,596 697 0488	117	2876,616 192 4599	177	33970,679 015 3472
58	233,959 808 7377	118	2998,074 495 5192	178	35394,201 199 1148
59	244,756 875 7286	119	3124,618 865 0190	179	36877,333 374 3278
60	256,006 069 8997	120	3256,462 279 9917	180	38422,571 709 3777

Amount of 1 Per Period

NOMINAL INTEREST RATE COMPOUNDED

YEARLY	HALF-YEARLY	QUARTERLY
@	@	@
$4\frac{1}{4}\%$	$8\frac{1}{2}\%$	17%
4.2500%	8.5000%	17.0000%
PER ANNUM	PER ANNUM	PER ANNUM

Periods	Amount	Periods	Amount	Periods	Amount
1	1.000 000 0000	61	274.494 391 2464	121	3597.355 916 1505
2	2.042 500 0000	62	287.160 402 8744	122	3751.243 542 5869
3	3.129 306 2500	63	300.364 719 9966	123	3911.671 393 1468
4	4.262 301 7656	64	314.130 220 5964	124	4078.917 427 3555
5	5.443 449 5907	65	328.480 754 9718	125	4253.271 418 0182
6	6.674 796 1983	66	343.441 187 0581	126	4435.035 453 2839
7	7.958 475 0367	67	359.037 437 5080	127	4624.524 460 0485
8	9.296 710 2258	68	375.296 528 6021	128	4822.066 749 6006
9	10.691 820 4103	69	392.246 631 0677	129	5028.004 586 4586
10	12.146 222 7778	70	409.917 112 8881	130	5242.694 781 3831
11	13.662 437 2458	71	428.338 590 1858	131	5466.509 309 5919
12	15.243 090 8288	72	447.542 980 2687	132	5699.835 955 2495
13	16.890 922 1890	73	467.563 556 9301	133	5943.078 983 3476
14	18.608 786 3820	74	488.435 008 0997	134	6196.659 840 1399
15	20.399 659 8033	75	510.193 495 9439	135	6461.017 883 3458
16	22.266 645 3449	76	532.876 719 5215	136	6736.611 143 3880
17	24.212 977 7721	77	556.523 980 1012	137	7023.917 116 9820
18	26.242 029 3274	78	581.176 249 2555	138	7323.433 594 4538
19	28.357 315 5738	79	606.876 239 8488	139	7635.679 522 2180
20	30.562 501 4857	80	633.668 480 0424	140	7961.195 901 9123
21	32.861 407 7988	81	661.599 390 4442	141	8300.546 727 7436
22	35.258 017 6303	82	690.717 364 5381	142	8654.319 963 6727
23	37.756 483 3796	83	721.072 852 5310	143	9023.128 562 1288
24	40.361 133 9232	84	752.718 448 7635	144	9407.611 526 0192
25	43.076 482 1149	85	785.708 982 8360	145	9808.435 015 8751
26	45.907 232 6048	86	820.101 614 6065	146	10226.293 504 0498
27	48.858 289 9905	87	855.955 933 2273	147	10661.910 977 9719
28	51.934 767 3151	88	893.334 060 3895	148	11116.042 194 5357
29	55.141 994 9260	89	932.300 757 9560	149	11589.473 987 8034
30	58.485 529 7104	90	972.923 540 1691	150	12083.026 632 2851
31	61.971 164 7231	91	1015.272 790 6263	151	12597.555 264 1572
32	65.604 939 2238	92	1059.421 884 2279	152	13133.951 362 8839
33	69.393 149 1408	93	1105.447 314 3076	153	13693.144 295 8064
34	73.342 357 9793	94	1153.428 825 1657	154	14276.102 928 3782
35	77.459 408 1934	95	1203.449 550 2353	155	14883.837 302 8343
36	81.751 433 0416	96	1255.596 156 1203	156	15517.400 388 2048
37	86.225 868 9459	97	1309.958 992 7554	157	16177.889 904 7035
38	90.890 468 3761	98	1366.632 249 9475	158	16866.450 225 6534
39	95.753 313 2821	99	1425.714 120 5702	159	17584.274 360 2436
40	100.822 829 0966	100	1487.306 970 6945	160	18332.606 020 5540
41	106.107 799 3332	101	1551.517 516 9490	161	19112.741 776 4275
42	111.617 380 8049	102	1618.457 011 4193	162	19926.033 301 9257
43	117.361 119 4891	103	1688.241 434 4046	163	20773.889 717 2575
44	123.348 967 0674	104	1760.991 695 3668	164	21657.780 030 2410
45	129.591 298 1677	105	1836.833 842 4199	165	22579.235 681 5262
46	136.098 928 3398	106	1915.899 280 7228	166	23539.853 197 9911
47	142.883 132 7943	107	1998.325 000 1535	167	24541.296 958 9057
48	149.955 665 9380	108	2084.253 812 6600	168	25585.302 079 6592
49	157.328 781 7404	109	2173.834 599 6981	169	26673.677 418 0447
50	165.015 254 9644	110	2267.222 570 1852	170	27808.308 708 3116
51	173.028 403 3004	111	2364.579 529 4181	171	28991.161 828 4149
52	181.382 110 4406	112	2466.074 159 4184	172	30224.286 206 1225
53	190.090 850 1344	113	2571.882 311 1936	173	31509.818 369 8827
54	199.169 711 2651	114	2682.187 309 4194	174	32849.985 650 6027
55	208.634 423 9938	115	2797.180 270 0697	175	34247.110 040 7533
56	218.501 387 0136	116	2917.060 431 5477	176	35703.612 217 4853
57	228.787 695 9616	117	3042.035 499 8884	177	37222.015 736 7285
58	239.511 173 0400	118	3172.322 008 6337	178	38804.951 405 5394
59	250.690 397 8942	119	3308.145 694 0006	179	40455.161 840 2748
60	262.344 739 8047	120	3449.741 885 9957	180	42175.506 218 4865

Amount of 1 Per Period

NOMINAL INTEREST RATE COMPOUNDED

	YEARLY @ $4\frac{5}{16}\%$ 4.3125% PER ANNUM		HALF-YEARLY @ $8\frac{5}{8}\%$ 8.6250% PER ANNUM		QUARTERLY @ $17\frac{1}{4}\%$ 17.2500% PER ANNUM
Periods	Amount	Periods	Amount	Periods	Amount
1	1.000 000 0000	61	281.452 688 9285	121	3813.616 606 2444
2	2.043 125 0000	62	294.590 336 1385	122	3979.078 822 3887
3	3.131 234 7656	63	308.294 544 3845	123	4151.676 596 6042
4	4.266 269 2649	64	322.589 746 6111	124	4331.717 649 8328
5	5.450 252 1269	65	337.501 429 4337	125	4519.522 973 4818
6	6.685 294 2499	66	353.056 178 5780	126	4715.427 401 7132
7	7.973 597 5644	67	369.281 726 2792	127	4919.780 208 4121
8	9.317 458 9594	68	386.207 000 7250	128	5132.945 729 8998
9	10.719 274 3770	69	403.862 177 6313	129	5355.304 014 5018
10	12.181 543 0845	70	422.278 734 0416	130	5587.251 500 1272
11	13.706 872 1301	71	441.489 504 4472	131	5829.201 721 0702
12	15.297 980 9907	72	461.528 739 3264	132	6081.586 045 2913
13	16.957 706 4209	73	482.432 166 2099	133	6344.854 443 4945
14	18.689 007 5103	74	504.237 053 3777	134	6619.476 291 3702
15	20.494 970 9592	75	526.982 276 3046	135	6905.941 206 4355
16	22.378 816 5818	76	550.708 386 9702	136	7204.759 920 9631
17	24.343 903 0469	77	575.457 686 1583	137	7516.465 192 5546
18	26.393 733 8658	78	601.274 298 8739	138	7841.612 753 9835
19	28.531 963 6387	79	628.204 253 0129	139	8180.782 303 9990
20	30.762 404 5707	80	656.295 561 4240	140	8534.578 540 8590
21	33.089 033 2678	81	685.598 307 5104	141	8903.632 240 4336
22	35.515 997 8274	82	716.164 734 5218	142	9288.601 380 8023
23	38.047 625 2338	83	748.049 338 6981	143	9690.172 315 3493
24	40.688 429 0720	84	781.308 966 4294	144	10109.060 996 4488
25	43.443 117 5757	85	816.002 915 6067	145	10546.014 251 9206
26	46.316 602 0211	86	852.193 041 3422	146	11001.811 116 5347
27	49.314 005 4833	87	889.943 866 2501	147	11477.264 220 9353
28	52.440 671 9698	88	929.322 695 4822	148	11973.221 240 4631
29	55.702 175 9485	89	970.399 736 7248	149	12490.566 406 4581
30	59.104 332 2862	90	1013.248 225 3711	150	13030.222 082 7366
31	62.653 206 6161	91	1057.944 555 0902	151	13593.150 410 0546
32	66.355 126 1514	92	1104.568 414 0285	152	14180.355 021 4882
33	70.216 690 9667	93	1153.202 926 8835	153	14792.882 831 7899
34	74.244 785 7646	94	1203.934 803 1053	154	15431.825 903 9108
35	78.446 592 1507	95	1256.854 491 4892	155	16098.323 396 0170
36	82.829 601 4372	96	1312.056 341 4347	156	16793.563 592 4702
37	87.401 627 9992	97	1369.638 771 1591	157	17518.786 022 3955
38	92.170 823 2067	98	1429.704 443 1653	158	18275.283 669 6113
39	97.145 689 9575	99	1492.360 447 2768	159	19064.405 277 8633
40	102.335 097 8369	100	1557.718 491 5656	160	19887.557 755 4711
41	107.748 298 9311	101	1625.895 101 5144	161	20746.208 683 6758
42	113.394 944 3225	102	1697.011 827 7672	162	21641.888 933 1594
43	119.285 101 2964	103	1771.195 462 8397	163	22576.195 393 4019
44	125.429 271 2898	104	1848.578 267 1746	164	23550.793 819 7423
45	131.838 408 6142	105	1929.298 204 9465	165	24567.421 803 2187
46	138.523 939 9857	106	2013.499 190 0349	166	25627.891 868 4825
47	145.497 784 8975	107	2101.331 342 6051	167	26734.094 705 3108
48	152.772 376 8713	108	2192.951 256 7550	168	27888.002 539 4773
49	160.360 685 6238	109	2288.522 279 7025	169	29091.672 648 9923
50	168.276 240 1914	110	2388.214 803 0147	170	30347.251 031 9801
51	176.533 153 0496	111	2492.206 566 3947	171	31656.976 232 7342
52	185.146 145 2749	112	2600.682 974 5705	172	33023.183 332 7709
53	194.130 572 7898	113	2713.837 427 8488	173	34448.308 113 9966
54	203.502 453 7414	114	2831.871 666 9248	174	35934.891 401 4127
55	213.278 497 0590	115	2954.996 132 5609	175	37485.583 593 0987
56	223.476 132 2447	116	3083.430 340 7776	176	39103.149 385 5510
57	234.113 540 4477	117	3217.403 274 2236	177	40790.472 702 8029
58	245.209 686 8795	118	3357.153 790 4245	178	42550.561 838 1113
59	256.784 354 6262	119	3502.931 047 6366	179	44386.554 817 3799
60	268.858 179 9195	120	3654.994 949 0659	180	46301.724 993 8794

Amount of 1 Per Period

NOMINAL INTEREST RATE COMPOUNDED

YEARLY	HALF-YEARLY	QUARTERLY
@	@	@
$4\frac{3}{8}\%$	$8\frac{3}{4}\%$	$17\frac{1}{2}\%$
4.3750%	8.7500%	17.5000%
PER ANNUM	PER ANNUM	PER ANNUM

Periods	Amount	Periods	Amount	Periods	Amount
1	1.000 000 0000	61	288.606 773 8611	121	4043.420 700 9878
2	2.043 750 0000	62	302.233 320 2175	122	4221.320 356 6560
3	3.133 164 0625	63	316.456 027 9770	123	4407.003 122 2597
4	4.270 239 9902	64	331.300 979 2010	124	4600.809 508 8586
5	5.457 062 9898	65	346.795 397 0410	125	4803.094 924 8711
6	6.695 809 4956	66	362.967 695 6616	126	5014.230 327 8342
7	7.988 751 1610	67	379.847 532 3468	127	5234.602 904 6770
8	9.338 259 0243	68	397.465 861 8869	128	5464.616 781 7566
9	10.746 807 8567	69	415.854 993 3445	129	5704.693 765 9585
10	12.216 980 7004	70	435.048 649 3033	130	5955.274 118 2191
11	13.751 473 6060	71	455.082 027 7103	131	6216.817 360 8912
12	15.353 100 5763	72	475.991 866 4227	132	6489.803 120 4302
13	17.024 798 7265	73	497.816 510 5787	133	6774.732 006 9490
14	18.769 633 6708	74	520.595 982 9165	134	7072.126 532 2531
15	20.590 805 1439	75	544.372 057 1691	135	7382.532 068 0391
16	22.491 652 8689	76	569.188 334 6702	136	7706.517 846 0158
17	24.475 662 6819	77	595.090 324 3120	137	8044.678 001 7790
18	26.546 472 9243	78	622.125 526 0007	138	8397.632 664 3569
19	28.707 881 1147	79	650.343 517 7632	139	8766.029 093 4225
20	30.963 850 9135	80	679.796 046 6654	140	9150.542 866 2597
21	33.318 519 3909	81	710.537 123 7070	141	9551.879 116 6586
22	35.776 204 6143	82	742.623 122 8692	142	9970.773 828 0124
23	38.341 413 5662	83	776.112 884 4947	143	10407.995 182 9879
24	41.018 850 4097	84	811.067 823 1913	144	10864.344 972 2437
25	43.813 425 1151	85	847.552 040 4559	145	11340.660 064 7793
26	46.730 262 4639	86	885.632 442 2259	146	11837.813 942 6134
27	49.774 711 4467	87	925.378 861 5733	147	12356.718 302 6027
28	52.952 355 0725	88	966.864 186 7671	148	12898.324 728 3416
29	56.269 020 6069	89	1010.164 494 9382	149	13463.626 435 2066
30	59.730 790 2585	90	1055.359 191 5917	150	14053.660 091 7469
31	63.344 012 3323	91	1102.531 156 2238	151	14669.507 720 7608
32	67.115 312 8718	92	1151.766 894 3086	152	15312.298 683 5441
33	71.051 607 8100	93	1203.156 695 9346	153	15983.211 750 9491
34	75.160 115 6516	94	1256.794 801 3818	154	16683.477 265 0531
35	79.448 370 7114	95	1312.779 573 9422	155	17414.379 395 3992
36	83.924 236 9300	96	1371.213 680 3022	156	18177.258 493 9479
37	88.595 922 2957	97	1432.204 278 8154	157	18973.513 553 0582
38	93.471 993 8962	98	1495.863 216 0136	158	19804.604 771 0044
39	98.561 393 6291	99	1562.307 231 7142	159	20672.056 229 7359
40	103.873 454 6004	100	1631.658 173 1017	160	21577.458 689 7868
41	109.417 918 2392	101	1704.043 218 1749	161	22522.472 507 4650
42	115.204 952 1621	102	1779.595 108 9700	162	23508.830 679 6666
43	121.245 168 8192	103	1858.452 394 9875	163	24538.342 021 9020
44	127.549 644 9551	104	1940.759 687 2682	164	25612.894 485 3602
45	134.129 941 9218	105	2026.667 923 5862	165	26734.458 619 0947
46	140.998 126 8809	106	2116.334 645 2431	166	27905.091 183 6801
47	148.166 794 9320	107	2209.924 285 9724	167	29126.938 922 9661
48	155.649 092 2102	108	2307.608 473 4837	168	30402.242 500 8459
49	163.458 739 9944	109	2409.566 344 1986	169	31733.340 610 2579
50	171.610 059 8692	110	2515.984 871 7573	170	33122.674 261 9567
51	180.117 999 9885	111	2627.059 209 8967	171	34572.791 260 9173
52	188.998 162 4880	112	2742.993 050 3297	172	36086.350 878 5824
53	198.266 832 0968	113	2863.998 996 2816	173	37666.128 729 5204
54	207.941 006 0010	114	2990.298 952 3690	174	39315.021 861 4369
55	218.038 425 0136	115	3122.124 531 5351	175	41036.054 067 8748
56	228.577 606 1079	116	3259.717 479 7898	176	42832.381 433 3443
57	239.577 876 3751	117	3403.330 119 5306	177	44707.298 121 0531
58	251.059 408 4666	118	3553.225 812 2600	178	46664.242 413 8492
59	263.043 257 5870	119	3709.679 441 5464	179	48706.803 019 4551
60	275.551 400 1064	120	3872.977 917 1140	180	50838.725 651 5563

Amount of 1 Per Period

NOMINAL INTEREST RATE COMPOUNDED

YEARLY @ $4\frac{7}{16}\%$ 4.4375% PER ANNUM		HALF-YEARLY @ $8\frac{7}{8}\%$ 8.8750% PER ANNUM		QUARTERLY @ $17\frac{3}{4}\%$ 17.7500% PER ANNUM	
Periods	Amount	Periods	Amount	Periods	Amount
1	1.000 000 0000	61	295.962 367 6935	121	4287.632 505 1240
2	2.044 375 0000	62	310.095 697 7599	122	4478.896 197 5389
3	3.135 094 1406	63	324.856 194 3480	123	4678.647 216 3047
4	4.274 213 9431	64	340.271 687 9722	124	4887.262 186 5282
5	5.463 882 1868	65	356.371 244 1260	125	5105.134 446 0554
6	6.706 341 9589	66	373.185 218 0841	126	5332.674 787 0991
7	8.003 935 8833	67	390.745 312 1365	127	5570.312 230 7766
8	9.359 110 5381	68	409.084 635 3626	128	5818.494 836 0173
9	10.774 421 0683	69	428.237 766 0568	129	6077.690 544 3656
10	12.252 536 0032	70	448.240 816 9256	130	6348.388 062 2718
11	13.796 242 2883	71	469.131 503 1766	131	6631.097 782 5351
12	15.408 450 5398	72	490.949 213 6301	132	6926.352 746 6351
13	17.092 200 5326	73	513.735 084 9849	133	7234.709 649 7671
14	18.850 666 9312	74	537.532 079 3812	134	7556.749 890 4755
15	20.687 165 2763	75	562.385 065 4037	135	7893.080 666 8653
16	22.605 158 2354	76	588.340 902 6810	136	8244.336 121 4575
17	24.608 262 1321	77	615.448 530 2374	137	8611.178 536 8472
18	26.700 253 7642	78	643.759 058 7667	138	8994.299 584 4197
19	28.885 077 5250	79	673.325 866 9995	139	9394.421 628 4784
20	31.166 852 8402	80	704.204 702 3476	140	9812.299 088 2421
21	33.549 881 9349	81	736.453 786 0143	141	10248.719 860 2828
22	36.038 657 9458	82	770.133 922 7687	142	10704.506 804 0829
23	38.637 873 3921	83	805.308 615 5915	143	11180.519 293 5141
24	41.352 429 0239	84	842.044 185 4084	144	11677.654 837 1638
25	44.187 443 0619	85	880.409 896 1359	145	12196.850 770 5629
26	47.148 260 8477	86	920.478 085 2769	146	12739.086 023 5066
27	50.240 464 9228	87	962.324 300 3111	147	13305.382 965 7997
28	53.469 885 5538	88	1006.027 441 1374	148	13896.809 334 9071
29	56.842 611 7252	89	1051.669 908 8379	149	14514.480 249 1436
30	60.365 002 6206	90	1099.337 761 0426	150	15159.560 310 1994
31	64.043 699 6118	91	1149.120 874 1888	151	15833.265 798 9645
32	67.885 638 7821	92	1201.113 112 9810	152	16536.866 968 7935
33	71.898 064 0031	93	1255.412 507 3695	153	17271.690 440 5337
34	76.088 540 5932	94	1312.121 437 3840	154	18039.121 703 8324
35	80.464 969 5820	95	1371.346 826 1679	155	18840.607 729 4400
36	85.035 602 6072	96	1433.200 341 5791	156	19677.659 697 4339
37	89.809 057 4729	97	1497.798 606 7367	157	20551.855 846 5075
38	94.794 334 3983	98	1565.263 419 9106	158	21464.844 449 6963
39	100.000 832 9872	99	1635.721 984 1692	159	22418.346 922 1515
40	105.438 369 9510	100	1709.307 147 2167	160	23414.161 066 8220
41	111.117 197 6176	101	1786.157 651 8744	161	24454.164 464 1622
42	117.048 023 2619	102	1866.418 397 6763	162	25540.318 012 2594
43	123.242 029 2941	103	1950.240 714 0732	163	26674.669 624 0534
44	129.710 894 3441	104	2037.782 645 7602	164	27859.358 088 6208
45	136.466 815 2806	105	2129.209 250 6658	165	29096.617 103 8034
46	143.522 530 2086	106	2224.692 911 1641	166	30388.779 487 7846
47	150.891 342 4867	107	2324.413 659 0970	167	31738.281 577 5551
48	158.587 145 8095	108	2428.559 515 2195	168	33147.667 822 5591
49	166.624 450 4048	109	2537.326 843 7073	169	34619.595 582 1851
50	175.018 410 3915	110	2650.920 722 3968	170	36156.840 136 1446
51	183.784 852 3526	111	2769.555 329 4532	171	37762.299 917 1860
52	192.940 305 1758	112	2893.454 347 1977	172	39439.001 976 0111
53	202.502 031 2180	113	3022.851 383 8546	173	41190.107 688 6966
54	212.488 058 8532	114	3157.990 414 0131	174	43018.918 717 3826
55	222.917 216 4649	115	3299.126 238 6350	175	44928.883 235 4664
56	233.809 167 9455	116	3446.524 965 4744	176	46923.602 429 0402
57	245.184 449 7731	117	3600.464 510 8173	177	49006.837 286 8289
58	257.064 509 7318	118	3761.235 123 4848	178	51182.515 691 4319
59	269.471 747 3511	119	3929.139 932 0895	179	53454.739 825 2392
60	282.429 556 1398	120	4104.495 516 5760	180	55827.793 904 9842

Amount of 1 Per Period

NOMINAL INTEREST RATE COMPOUNDED

YEARLY	HALF-YEARLY	QUARTERLY
@	@	@
4½%	9%	18%
4.5000%	9.0000%	18.0000%
PER ANNUM	PER ANNUM	PER ANNUM

Periods	Amount	Periods	Amount	Periods	Amount
1	1,000 000 0000	61	303.525 361 9042	121	4547.172 022 1703
2	2,045 000 0000	62	318.184 003 1899	122	4752.794 763 1680
3	3,137 025 0000	63	333.502 283 3335	123	4967.670 527 5105
4	4,278 191 1250	64	349.509 886 0835	124	5192.215 701 2485
5	5,470 709 7256	65	366.237 830 9572	125	5426.865 407 8047
6	6,716 891 6633	66	383.718 533 3503	126	5672.074 351 1559
7	8,019 151 7881	67	401.985 867 3511	127	5928.317 696 9579
8	9,380 013 6186	68	421.075 231 3819	128	6196.091 993 3210
9	10,802 114 2314	69	441.023 616 7941	129	6475.916 133 0205
10	12,288 209 3718	70	461.869 679 5498	130	6768.332 359 0064
11	13,841 178 7936	71	483.653 815 1295	131	7073.907 315 1617
12	15,464 031 8393	72	506.418 236 8104	132	7393.233 144 3440
13	17,159 913 2721	73	530.207 057 4668	133	7726.928 635 8394
14	18,932 109 3693	74	555.066 375 0528	134	8075.640 424 4522
15	20,784 054 2909	75	581.044 361 9302	135	8440.044 243 5526
16	22,719 336 7340	76	608.191 358 2171	136	8820.846 234 5124
17	24,741 706 8870	77	636.559 969 3368	137	9218.784 315 0655
18	26,855 083 6970	78	666.205 167 9570	138	9634.629 609 2434
19	29,063 562 4633	79	697.184 400 5151	139	10069.187 941 6594
20	31,371 422 7742	80	729.557 698 5382	140	10523.301 399 0341
21	33,783 136 7990	81	763.387 794 9725	141	10997.849 961 9906
22	36,303 377 9550	82	798.740 245 7462	142	11493.753 210 2802
23	38,937 029 9629	83	835.683 556 8048	143	12011.972 104 7428
24	41,689 196 3113	84	874.289 316 8610	144	12553.510 849 4562
25	44,565 210 1453	85	914.632 336 1198	145	13119.418 837 6817
26	47,570 644 6018	86	956.790 791 2452	146	13710.792 685 3774
27	50,711 323 6089	87	1000.846 376 8512	147	14328.778 356 2194
28	53,993 333 1713	88	1046.884 463 8095	148	14974.573 382 2493
29	57,423 033 1640	89	1094.994 264 6809	149	15649.429 184 4505
30	61,007 069 6564	90	1145.269 006 5916	150	16354.653 497 7508
31	64,752 387 7909	91	1197.806 111 8882	151	17091.612 905 1496
32	68,666 245 2415	92	1252.707 386 9232	152	17861.735 485 8813
33	72,756 226 2774	93	1310.079 219 3347	153	18666.513 582 7459
34	77,030 256 4599	94	1370.032 784 2048	154	19507.506 693 9695
35	81,496 618 0005	95	1432.684 259 4940	155	20386.344 495 1981
36	86,163 965 8106	96	1498.155 051 1712	156	21304.729 997 4821
37	91,041 344 2720	97	1566.572 028 4739	157	22264.442 847 3687
38	96,138 204 7643	98	1638.067 769 7552	158	23267.342 775 5003
39	101,464 423 9787	99	1712.780 819 3942	159	24315.373 200 3979
40	107,030 323 0577	100	1790.855 956 2670	160	25410.564 994 4158
41	112,846 687 5953	101	1872.444 474 2990	161	26555.040 419 1645
42	118,924 788 5371	102	1957.704 475 6424	162	27751.017 238 0269
43	125,276 404 0213	103	2046.801 177 0463	163	29000.813 013 7381
44	131,913 842 2022	104	2139.907 230 0134	164	30306.849 599 3563
45	138,849 965 1013	105	2237.203 055 3640	165	31671.657 831 3273
46	146,098 213 5309	106	2338.877 192 8554	166	33097.882 433 7371
47	153,672 633 1398	107	2445.126 666 5339	167	34588.287 143 2552
48	161,587 901 6311	108	2556.157 366 5279	168	36145.760 064 7017
49	169,859 357 2045	109	2672.184 448 0217	169	37773.319 267 6133
50	178,503 028 2787	110	2793.432 748 1827	170	39474.118 634 6559
51	187,535 664 5512	111	2920.137 221 8509	171	41251.453 973 2154
52	196,974 769 4560	112	3052.543 396 8342	172	43108.769 402 0101
53	206,838 634 0815	113	3190.907 849 6917	173	45049.664 025 1005
54	217,146 372 6152	114	3335.498 702 9278	174	47077.898 906 2301
55	227,917 959 3829	115	3486.596 144 5596	175	49197.404 357 0104
56	239,174 267 5551	116	3644.492 971 0648	176	51412.287 553 0759
57	250,937 109 5951	117	3809.495 154 7627	177	53726.840 492 9643
58	263,229 279 5269	118	3981.922 436 7270	178	56145.548 315 1477
59	276,074 597 1056	119	4162.108 946 3797	179	58673.097 989 3293
60	289,497 953 9753	120	4350.403 848 9668	180	61314.387 398 8492

NOMINAL INTEREST RATE COMPOUNDED

	YEARLY @ $4\frac{9}{16}\%$ 4.5625% PER ANNUM		HALF-YEARLY @ $9\frac{1}{8}\%$ 9.1250% PER ANNUM		QUARTERLY @ $18\frac{1}{4}\%$ 18.2500% PER ANNUM
Periods	**Amount**	**Periods**	**Amount**	**Periods**	**Amount**
1	1.000 000 0000	61	311.301 822 8647	121	4823.018 560 8162
2	2.045 625 0000	62	326.504 968 5329	122	5044.068 782 6535
3	3.138 956 6406	63	342.401 757 7222	123	5275.204 420 8620
4	4.282 171 5374	64	359.023 837 9183	124	5516.885 622 5639
5	5.477 545 6137	65	376.404 300 5233	125	5769.593 529 0933
6	6.727 458 6324	66	394.577 746 7347	126	6033.831 233 8582
7	8.034 398 9325	67	413.580 356 4295	127	6310.124 783 9030
8	9.400 968 3838	68	433.449 960 1916	128	6599.024 227 1686
9	10.829 887 5663	69	454.226 114 6253	129	6901.104 707 5331
10	12.324 001 1865	70	475.950 181 1051	130	7216.967 609 8143
11	13.886 283 7406	71	498.665 408 1180	131	7547.241 757 0121
12	15.519 845 4363	72	522.417 017 3634	132	7892.584 662 1758
13	17.227 938 3843	73	547.252 293 7806	133	8253.683 837 3876
14	19.013 963 0731	74	573.220 679 6843	134	8631.258 162 4684
15	20.881 475 1383	75	600.373 873 1949	135	9026.059 316 1310
16	22.834 192 4415	76	628.765 931 1594	136	9438.873 272 4295
17	24.876 002 4716	77	658.453 376 7686	137	9870.521 865 4841
18	27.010 970 0844	78	689.495 312 0836	138	10321.864 425 5968
19	29.243 345 5945	79	721.953 535 6975	139	10793.799 490 0146
20	31.577 573 2373	80	755.892 665 7637	140	11287.266 591 7465
21	34.018 300 0162	81	791.380 268 6391	141	11803.248 129 9950
22	36.570 384 9545	82	828.486 993 3958	142	12342.771 325 9260
23	39.238 908 7680	83	867.286 712 4695	143	12906.910 267 6714
24	42.029 183 9805	84	907.856 668 7259	144	13496.788 048 6339
25	44.946 765 4997	85	950.277 629 2365	145	14113.579 003 3528
26	47.997 461 6756	86	994.634 046 0704	146	14758.511 045 3808
27	51.187 345 8645	87	1041.014 224 4224	147	15432.868 111 8263
28	54.522 768 5196	88	1089.510 498 4117	148	16137.992 719 4283
29	58.010 369 8333	89	1140.219 414 9017	149	16875.288 637 2523
30	61.657 092 9569	90	1193.241 925 7066	150	17646.223 681 3269
31	65.470 197 8231	91	1248.683 588 5669	151	18452.332 636 7874
32	69.457 275 5988	92	1306.654 777 2953	152	19295.220 313 3409
33	73.626 263 7980	93	1367.270 901 5094	153	20176.564 740 1370
34	77.985 462 0838	94	1430.652 636 3908	154	21098.120 506 4058
35	82.543 548 7913	95	1496.926 162 9261	155	22061.722 254 5106
36	87.309 598 2049	96	1566.223 419 1096	156	23069.288 332 3726
37	92.293 098 6230	97	1638.682 362 6065	157	24122.824 612 5371
38	97.503 971 2477	98	1714.447 245 4004	158	25224.428 485 4841
39	102.952 589 9359	99	1793.668 900 9718	159	26376.293 035 1343
40	108.649 801 8517	100	1876.505 044 5786	160	27580.711 404 8623
41	114.606 949 0612	101	1963.120 587 2375	161	28840.081 362 7092
42	120.835 891 1121	102	2053.687 964 0302	162	30156.910 074 8828
43	127.349 028 6441	103	2148.387 477 3891	163	31533.819 097 0493
44	134.159 328 0760	104	2247.407 656 0450	164	32973.549 593 3522
45	141.280 347 4195	105	2350.945 630 3521	165	34478.967 793 5489
46	148.726 263 2705	106	2459.207 524 7369	166	36053.070 699 1295
47	156.511 899 0322	107	2572.408 868 0530	167	37698.992 049 7773
48	164.652 754 4255	108	2690.775 022 6579	168	39420.008 562 0484
49	173.165 036 3462	109	2814.541 633 0667	169	41219.546 452 6919
50	182.065 691 1295	110	2943.955 095 0753	170	43101.188 259 5959
51	191.372 438 2873	111	3079.273 046 2881	171	45068.679 973 9400
52	201.103 805 7841	112	3220.764 879 0250	172	47125.938 497 7510
53	211.279 166 9230	113	3368.712 276 6306	173	49277.059 441 7109
54	221.918 778 9139	114	3523.409 774 2518	174	51526.325 278 7389
55	233.043 823 2018	115	3685.165 345 2021	175	53878.213 869 5814
56	244.676 447 6354	116	3854.301 014 0769	176	56337.407 377 3811
57	256.839 810 5588	117	4031.153 497 8442	177	58908.801 588 9741
58	269.558 126 9155	118	4216.074 876 1833	178	61597.515 661 4710
59	282.856 716 4561	119	4409.433 292 4092	179	64408.902 313 5256
60	296.762 054 1444	120	4611.613 686 3753	180	67348.558 481 5802

Amount of 1 Per Period

NOMINAL INTEREST RATE COMPOUNDED

	YEARLY	HALF-YEARLY	QUARTERLY
	@	@	@
	$4\frac{5}{8}\%$	$9\frac{1}{4}\%$	$18\frac{1}{2}\%$
	4.6250%	9.2500%	18.5000%
	PER ANNUM	PER ANNUM	PER ANNUM

Periods	Amount	Periods	Amount	Periods	Amount
1	1,000 000 0000	61	319,297 997 0541	121	5116,214 575 1845
2	2,046 250 0000	62	335,065 529 4179	122	5353,839 499 2868
3	3,140 889 0625	63	351,562 310 1535	123	5602,454 576 1288
4	4,286 155 1816	64	368,822 066 9981	124	5862,568 100 2747
5	5,484 389 8588	65	386,880 087 5967	125	6134,711 874 9124
6	6,738 042 8898	66	405,773 291 6481	126	6419,442 299 1271
7	8,049 677 3734	67	425,540 306 3868	127	6717,341 505 4618
8	9,421 974 9519	68	446,221 545 5572	128	7029,018 550 0894
9	10,857 741 2935	69	467,859 292 0392	129	7355,110 658 0310
10	12,359 911 8283	70	490,497 784 2960	130	7696,284 525 9649
11	13,931 557 7503	71	514,183 306 8197	131	8053,237 685 2908
12	15,575 892 2963	72	538,964 284 7601	132	8426,699 928 2355
13	17,296 277 3150	73	564,891 382 9303	133	8817,434 799 9164
14	19,096 230 1408	74	592,017 609 3908	134	9226,241 159 4126
15	20,979 430 7848	75	620,398 423 8251	135	9653,954 813 0354
16	22,949 729 4586	76	650,091 850 9270	136	10101,450 223 1383
17	25,011 154 4461	77	681,158 599 0324	137	10569,642 295 9584
18	27,167 920 3392	78	713,662 184 2377	138	11059,488 252 1465
19	29,424 436 6549	79	747,669 060 2586	139	11571,989 583 8083
20	31,785 316 8502	80	783,248 754 2956	140	12108,194 102 0594
21	34,255 387 7545	81	820,474 009 1818	141	12669,198 079 2797
22	36,839 699 4382	82	859,420 932 1064	142	13256,148 490 4463
23	39,543 535 5372	83	900,169 150 2164	143	13870,245 358 1295
24	42,372 424 0558	84	942,801 973 4139	144	14512,744 205 9430
25	45,332 148 6684	85	987,406 564 6843	145	15184,958 625 4678
26	48,428 760 5443	86	1034,074 118 3009	146	15888,262 961 8957
27	51,668 590 7194	87	1082,900 046 2723	147	16624,095 123 8834
28	55,058 263 0402	88	1133,984 173 4124	148	17393,959 523 3630
29	58,604 707 7058	89	1187,430 941 4327	149	18199,430 151 3185
30	62,315 175 4372	90	1243,349 622 4740	150	19042,153 795 8170
31	66,197 252 3012	91	1301,854 542 5134	151	19923,853 408 8736
32	70,258 875 2201	92	1363,065 315 1047	152	20846,331 629 0340
33	74,508 348 1990	93	1427,107 085 9283	153	21811,474 466 8768
34	78,954 359 3033	94	1494,110 788 6524	154	22821,255 160 9698
35	83,605 998 4210	95	1564,213 412 6276	155	23877,738 212 1647
36	88,472 775 8480	96	1637,558 282 9616	156	24983,083 604 4773
37	93,564 641 7310	97	1714,295 353 5486	157	26139,551 221 1844
38	98,892 006 4110	98	1794,581 513 6502	158	27349,505 465 1642
39	104,465 761 7075	99	1878,580 908 6566	159	28615,420 092 9280
40	110,297 303 1865	100	1966,465 275 6819	160	29939,883 272 2259
41	116,398 553 4589	101	2058,414 294 6822	161	31325,602 873 5664
42	122,781 986 5564	102	2154,615 955 8113	162	32775,412 006 4688
43	129,460 653 4346	103	2255,266 943 7675	163	34292,274 811 7680
44	136,448 208 6559	104	2360,573 039 9168	164	35879,292 521 8123
45	143,758 938 3063	105	2470,749 543 0129	165	37539,709 800 9461
46	151,407 789 2029	106	2586,021 709 3773	166	39276,921 379 2398
47	159,410 399 4536	107	2706,625 213 4360	167	41094,478 993 0297
48	167,783 130 4283	108	2832,806 629 5574	168	42996,098 646 4573
49	176,543 100 2106	109	2964,823 936 1744	169	44985,668 208 8559
50	185,708 218 5954	110	3102,947 043 2225	170	47067,255 363 5155
51	195,297 223 7054	111	3247,458 343 9715	171	49245,115 924 0781
52	205,329 720 3018	112	3398,653 292 3802	172	51523,702 535 5667
53	215,826 219 8657	113	3556,841 007 1528	173	53907,673 777 8367
54	226,808 182 5345	114	3722,344 903 7336	174	56401,903 690 0617
55	238,298 060 9767	115	3895,503 355 5313	175	59011,491 735 7270
56	250,319 346 2969	116	4076,670 385 7246	176	61741,773 228 5044
57	262,896 616 0632	117	4266,216 391 0644	177	64598,330 240 3227
58	276,055 584 5561	118	4464,528 899 1511	178	67587,003 013 9376
59	289,823 155 3418	119	4672,013 360 7369	179	70713,901 903 3322
60	304,227 476 2763	120	4889,093 978 6710	180	73985,419 866 3614

Amount of 1 Per Period

NOMINAL INTEREST RATE COMPOUNDED

YEARLY	HALF-YEARLY	QUARTERLY
@	@	@
$4\frac{11}{16}\%$	$9\frac{3}{8}\%$	$18\frac{3}{4}\%$
4.6875%	9.3750%	18.7500%
PER ANNUM	PER ANNUM	PER ANNUM

Periods	Amount	Periods	Amount	Periods	Amount
1	1.000 000 0000	61	327.520 316 4296	121	5427.869 754 1094
2	2.046 875 0000	62	343.872 831 2622	122	5683.301 148 8332
3	3.142 822 2656	63	360.991 870 2276	123	5950.705 890 1848
4	4.290 142 0593	64	378.913 364 1445	124	6230.645 228 7872
5	5.491 242 4684	65	397.674 928 0888	125	6523.706 723 8866
6	6.748 644 4591	66	417.315 940 3430	126	6830.505 476 5688
7	8.064 987 1681	67	437.877 625 0465	127	7151.685 420 7830
8	9.443 033 4416	68	459.403 138 7206	128	7487.920 674 8822
9	10.885 675 6342	69	481.937 660 8481	129	7839.916 956 5173
10	12.395 941 6795	70	505.528 488 7004	130	8208.413 063 8540
11	13.977 001 4457	71	530.225 136 6082	131	8594.182 426 2222
12	15.632 173 3885	72	556.079 439 8867	132	8998.034 727 4513
13	17.364 931 5161	73	583.145 663 6314	133	9420.817 605 3006
14	19.178 912 6809	74	611.480 616 6141	134	9863.418 430 5491
15	21.077 924 2128	75	641.143 770 5179	135	10326.766 169 4811
16	23.065 951 9103	76	672.197 384 7609	136	10811.833 333 6755
17	25.147 168 4061	77	704.706 637 1716	137	11319.638 021 1915
18	27.325 941 9251	78	738.739 760 7890	138	11851.246 053 4349
19	29.606 845 4529	79	774.368 187 0760	139	12407.773 212 1896
20	31.994 666 3335	80	811.666 695 8452	140	12990.387 581 5110
21	34.494 416 3179	81	850.713 572 2129	141	13600.311 999 3944
22	37.111 342 0828	82	891.590 770 9104	142	14238.826 624 3660
23	39.850 936 2429	83	934.384 088 2969	143	14907.271 622 3831
24	42.718 948 8793	84	979.183 342 4358	144	15607.049 979 6823
25	45.721 399 6080	85	1026.082 561 6124	145	16339.630 447 4799
26	48.864 590 2146	86	1075.180 181 6880	146	17106.550 624 7056
27	52.155 117 8809	87	1126.579 252 7047	147	17909.420 185 2386
28	55.599 889 0316	88	1180.387 655 1752	148	18749.924 256 4217
29	59.206 133 8299	89	1236.718 326 5115	149	19629.826 955 9415
30	62.981 421 3532	90	1295.689 498 0668	150	20550.975 094 5012
31	66.933 675 4792	91	1357.424 943 2886	151	21515.302 052 0560
32	71.071 191 5172	92	1422.054 237 5053	152	22524.831 855 7461
33	75.402 653 6196	93	1489.713 029 8883	153	23581.683 328 0467
34	79.937 153 0080	94	1560.543 328 1644	154	24688.074 734 0489
35	84.684 207 0553	95	1634.693 796 6721	155	25846.328 237 2074
36	89.653 779 2610	96	1712.320 068 3911	156	27058.874 873 3265
37	94.856 300 1639	97	1793.585 071 5969	157	28328.259 633 0137
38	100.302 689 2340	98	1878.659 371 8280	158	29657.146 803 3112
39	106.004 377 7919	99	1967.721 529 8824	159	31048.325 559 7164
40	111.973 333 0009	100	2060.958 476 5957	160	32504.715 820 3281
41	118.222 082 9853	101	2158.565 905 1861	161	34029.374 374 4060
42	124.763 743 1252	102	2260.748 681 9917	162	35625.501 298 2063
43	131.612 043 5842	103	2367.721 276 4601	163	37296.446 671 5597
44	138.781 358 1272	104	2479.708 211 2941	164	39045.717 609 2891
45	146.286 734 2895	105	2596.944 533 6985	165	40876.985 622 2245
46	154.143 924 9593	106	2719.676 308 7157	166	42794.094 323 2663
47	162.369 421 4417	107	2848.161 135 6867	167	44801.067 494 6694
48	170.980 488 0718	108	2982.668 688 9220	168	46902.117 533 4820
49	179.995 198 4502	109	3123.481 283 7152	169	49101.654 292 8640
50	189.432 473 3775	110	3270.894 468 8894	170	51404.294 337 8420
51	199.312 120 5671	111	3425.217 647 1186	171	53814.870 634 9283
52	209.654 876 2187	112	3586.774 724 3273	172	56338.442 695 9406
53	220.482 448 5414	113	3755.904 789 5301	173	58980.307 197 3128
54	231.817 563 3168	114	3932.962 826 5393	174	61746.009 097 1868
55	243.684 011 5973	115	4118.320 459 0334	175	64641.353 273 6175
56	256.106 699 6409	116	4312.366 730 5506	176	67672.416 708 3183
57	269.111 701 1866	117	4515.508 921 0451	177	70845.561 241 5207
58	282.726 312 1797	118	4728.173 401 7191	178	74167.446 924 7170
59	296.979 108 0631	119	4950.806 529 9247	179	77645.045 999 3131
60	311.900 003 7536	120	5183.875 586 0149	180	81285.657 530 5309

Amount of 1 Per Period

NOMINAL INTEREST RATE COMPOUNDED

	YEARLY	HALF-YEARLY	QUARTERLY
	@	@	@
	$4\frac{3}{4}\%$	$9\frac{1}{2}\%$	19%
	4.7500%	9.5000%	19.0000%
	PER ANNUM	PER ANNUM	PER ANNUM

Periods	Amount	Periods	Amount	Periods	Amount
1	1,000 000 0000	61	335.975 403 9555	121	5759.165 375 5667
2	2,047 500 0000	62	352.934 235 6434	122	6033.725 730 9061
3	3,144 756 2500	63	370.698 611 8364	123	6321.327 703 1242
4	4,294 132 1719	64	389.306 795 8987	124	6622.590 769 0226
5	5,498 103 4500	65	408.798 868 7039	125	6938.163 830 5512
6	6,759 263 3639	66	429.216 814 9673	126	7268.726 612 5023
7	8,080 328 3737	67	450.604 613 6782	127	7614.991 126 5962
8	9,464 143 9715	68	473.008 332 8280	128	7977.703 205 1095
9	10,913 690 8101	69	496.476 228 6373	129	8357.644 107 3522
10	12,432 091 1236	70	521.058 849 4975	130	8755.632 202 4514
11	14,022 615 4519	71	546.809 144 8487	131	9172.524 732 0679
12	15,688 689 6859	72	573.782 579 2290	132	9609.219 656 8411
13	17,433 902 4460	73	602.037 251 7424	133	10066.657 590 5411
14	19,262 012 8122	74	631.634 021 2001	134	10545.823 826 0918
15	21,176 958 4208	75	662.636 637 2071	135	11047.750 457 8311
16	23,182 863 9457	76	695.111 877 4745	136	11573.518 604 5781
17	25,284 049 9832	77	729.129 691 6545	137	12124.260 738 2956
18	27,485 042 3574	78	764.763 352 0081	138	12701.163 123 3646
19	29,790 581 8693	79	802.089 611 2285	139	13305.468 371 7244
20	32,205 634 5081	80	841.188 867 7618	140	13938.478 119 3813
21	34,735 402 1473	81	882.145 338 9805	141	14601.555 830 0519
22	37,385 333 7493	82	925.047 242 5821	142	15296.129 731 9794
23	40,161 137 1024	83	969.986 986 6048	143	16023.695 894 2484
24	43,068 791 1147	84	1017.061 368 4685	144	16785.821 449 2252
25	46,114 558 6927	85	1066.371 783 4707	145	17584.147 968 0634
26	49,305 000 2306	86	1118.024 443 1856	146	18420.394 996 5464
27	52,646 987 7415	87	1172.130 604 2369	147	19296.363 758 8824
28	56,147 719 6592	88	1228.806 807 9382	148	20213.941 037 4293
29	59,814 736 3431	89	1288.175 131 3152	149	21175.103 236 7072
30	63,655 936 3194	90	1350.363 450 0527	150	22181.920 640 4508
31	67,679 593 2945	91	1415.505 713 9302	151	23236.561 870 8722
32	71,894 373 9760	92	1483.742 235 3419	152	24341.298 559 7386
33	76,309 356 7399	93	1555.219 991 5206	153	25498.510 241 3262
34	80,934 051 1850	94	1630.092 941 1179	154	26710.689 477 7892
35	85,778 418 6163	95	1708.522 355 8210	155	27980.447 227 9842
36	90,852 893 5006	96	1790.677 167 7225	156	29310.518 471 3135
37	96,168 405 9419	97	1876.734 333 1893	157	30703.768 098 7009
38	101,736 405 2241	98	1966.879 214 0158	158	32163.197 083 3891
39	107,568 884 4722	99	2061.305 976 6815	159	33691.948 944 8501
40	113,678 406 4847	100	2160.218 010 5739	160	35293.316 519 7305
41	120,078 130 7927	101	2263.828 366 0761	161	36970.749 054 4177
42	126,781 842 0053	102	2372.360 213 4648	162	38727.859 634 5025
43	133,803 979 5006	103	2486.047 323 5043	163	40568.432 967 1414
44	141,159 668 5269	104	2605.134 571 4755	164	42496.433 533 0806
45	148,864 752 7819	105	2729.878 463 6206	165	44516.014 125 9020
46	156,935 828 5390	106	2860.547 690 6426	166	46631.524 796 8823
47	165,390 280 3947	107	2997.423 705 9481	167	48847.522 224 7342
48	174,246 318 7134	108	3140.801 331 9807	168	51168.779 530 4091
49	183,523 018 8523	109	3290.989 395 2498	169	53600.296 558 1035
50	193,240 362 2478	110	3448.311 391 5241	170	56147.310 644 6134
51	203,419 279 4545	111	3613.106 182 6215	171	58815.307 900 2326
52	214,081 695 2286	112	3785.728 726 2960	172	61610.035 025 4936
53	225,250 575 7520	113	3966.550 840 7951	173	64537.511 689 2046
54	236,949 978 1002	114	4155.962 005 7329	174	67604.043 494 4418
55	249,205 102 0600	115	4354.370 201 0052	175	70816.235 560 4278
56	262,042 344 4078	116	4562.202 785 5529	176	74181.006 749 5481
57	275,489 355 7672	117	4779.907 417 8667	177	77705.604 570 1516
58	289,575 100 1661	118	5007.953 020 2154	178	81397.620 787 2338
59	304,329 917 4240	119	5246.830 788 6756	179	85265.007 774 6274
60	319,785 588 5017	120	5497.055 251 1377	180	89316.095 643 9222

NOMINAL INTEREST RATE COMPOUNDED

YEARLY	HALF-YEARLY	QUARTERLY
@	@	@
$4\frac{13}{16}\%$	$9\frac{5}{8}\%$	$19\frac{1}{4}\%$
4.8125%	9.6250%	19.2500%
PER ANNUM	PER ANNUM	PER ANNUM

Periods	Amount	Periods	Amount	Periods	Amount
1	1,000 000 0000	61	344.670 079 2982	121	6111.358 943 4335
2	2,048 125 0000	62	362.257 326 8644	122	6406.468 092 5862
3	3,146 691 0156	63	380.690 960 7198	123	6715.779 369 5420
4	4,298 125 5208	64	400.011 713 2044	124	7039.976 251 7012
5	5,504 972 8114	65	420.262 276 9024	125	7379.775 108 8143
6	6,769 899 6280	66	441.487 398 9783	126	7735.926 785 9260
7	8,095 701 0476	67	463.733 980 0541	127	8109.218 262 4987
8	9,485 306 6605	68	487.051 177 8442	128	8500.474 391 3814
9	10,941 787 0435	69	511.490 515 7780	129	8910.559 721 4666
10	12,468 360 5450	70	537.105 996 8498	130	9340.380 408 0622
11	14,068 400 3962	71	563.954 222 9482	131	9790.886 215 2002
12	15,745 442 1653	72	592.094 519 9276	132	10263.072 614 3067
13	17,503 191 5695	73	621.589 068 6991	133	10757.982 983 8702
14	19,345 532 6638	74	652.503 042 6302	134	11276.710 914 9690
15	21,276 536 4232	75	684.904 751 5568	135	11820.402 627 7519
16	23,300 469 7386	76	718.865 792 7255	136	12390.259 504 2124
17	25,421 804 8448	77	754.461 209 0004	137	12987.540 742 8527
18	27,645 229 2029	78	791.769 654 6836	138	13613.566 141 1024
19	29,975 655 8583	79	830.873 569 3152	139	14269.719 011 6430
20	32,418 234 2965	80	871.859 359 8385	140	14957.449 239 0783
21	34,978 361 8220	81	914.817 591 5307	141	15678.276 483 7090
22	37,661 695 4847	82	959.843 188 1231	142	16433.793 539 4874
23	40,474 164 5799	83	1007.035 641 5516	143	17225.669 853 5753
24	43,421 983 7503	84	1056.499 231 8012	144	18055.655 215 2786
25	46,511 666 7183	85	1108.343 257 3317	145	18925.583 622 5139
26	49,750 040 6791	86	1162.682 276 5908	146	19837.377 334 3474
27	53,144 261 3868	87	1219.636 361 1517	147	20793.051 118 5628
28	56,701 828 9660	88	1279.331 361 0321	148	21794.716 703 6437
29	60,430 604 4850	89	1341.899 182 7818	149	22844.587 445 0065
30	64,338 827 3259	90	1407.478 080 9532	150	23944.983 215 7974
31	68,435 133 3909	91	1476.212 963 5990	151	25098.335 533 0577
32	72,728 574 1854	92	1548.255 712 4722	152	26307.192 930 5861
33	77,228 636 8180	93	1623.765 518 6350	153	27574.226 590 3706
34	81,945 264 9649	94	1702.909 234 2193	154	28902.236 245 0321
35	86,888 880 8413	95	1785.861 741 1161	155	30294.156 364 3243
36	92,070 408 2318	96	1872.806 337 4073	156	31753.062 639 3574
37	97,501 296 6280	97	1963.935 142 3950	157	33282.178 778 8765
38	103,193 546 5282	98	2059.449 521 1228	158	34884.883 632 6099
39	109,159 735 9549	99	2159.560 529 3268	159	36564.718 657 4293
40	115,413 048 2477	100	2264.489 379 8006	160	38325.395 742 8181
41	121,967 301 1946	101	2374.467 931 2036	161	40170.805 412 9412
42	128,836 977 5646	102	2489.739 200 3927	162	42105.025 423 4390
43	136,037 257 1099	103	2610.557 899 4116	163	44132.329 771 9420
44	143,584 050 1083	104	2737.190 998 3208	164	46257.198 142 2167
45	151,494 032 5198	105	2869.918 315 1150	165	48484.325 802 8109
46	159,784 682 8348	106	3009.033 134 0299	166	50818.633 982 0711
47	168,474 320 6962	107	3154.842 853 6051	167	53265.280 742 4583
48	177,582 147 3798	108	3307.669 665 9348	168	55829.672 378 1891
49	187,128 288 2224	109	3467.851 268 6080	169	58517.475 361 3895
50	197,133 837 0931	110	3635.741 610 9097	170	61334.628 863 1563
51	207,620 903 0032	111	3811.711 675 9347	171	64287.357 877 1957
52	218,612 658 9602	112	3996.150 300 3391	172	67382.186 975 0358
53	230,133 393 1727	113	4189.465 033 5429	173	70625.954 723 2094
54	242,208 562 7191	114	4392.083 038 2822	174	74025.828 794 2638
55	254,864 849 8000	115	4604.452 034 4995	175	77589.321 804 9878
56	268,130 220 6966	116	4827.041 288 6598	176	81324.307 916 8528
57	282,033 987 5677	117	5060.342 650 6765	177	85239.040 235 3513
58	296,606 873 2193	118	5304.871 640 7404	178	89342.169 046 6776
59	311,881 078 9930	119	5561.168 588 4510	179	93642.760 932 0490
60	327,890 355 9196	120	5829.799 826 7702	180	98150.318 801 9039

Amount of 1 Per Period

NOMINAL INTEREST RATE COMPOUNDED

YEARLY	HALF-YEARLY	QUARTERLY
@	@	@
$4\frac{7}{8}\%$	$9\frac{3}{4}\%$	$19\frac{1}{2}\%$
4.8750%	9.7500%	19.5000%
PER ANNUM	PER ANNUM	PER ANNUM

Periods	Amount	Periods	Amount	Periods	Amount
1	1,000 000 0000	61	353,611 364 6892	121	6485,789 124 8642
2	2,048 750 0000	62	371,849 918 7178	122	6802,971 344 7013
3	3,148 626 5625	63	390,977 602 2553	123	7135,616 197 7555
4	4,302 122 1074	64	411,037 760 3653	124	7484,477 487 3961
5	5,511 850 5602	65	432,075 851 1831	125	7850,345 764 9067
6	6,780 553 2750	66	454,139 548 9283	126	8234,050 120 9459
7	8,111 105 2471	67	477,278 851 9385	127	8636,460 064 3420
8	9,506 521 6279	68	501,546 195 9705	128	9058,487 492 4786
9	10,969 964 5573	69	526,996 573 0241	129	9501,088 757 7370
10	12,504 750 3294	70	553,687 655 9590	130	9965,266 834 6766
11	14,114 356 9080	71	581,679 929 1870	131	10452,073 592 8671
12	15,802 431 8073	72	611,036 825 7349	132	10962,612 180 5194
13	17,572 800 3579	73	641,824 870 9895	133	11498,039 524 3197
14	19,429 474 3753	74	674,113 833 4502	134	12059,568 951 1303
15	21,376 661 2511	75	707,976 882 8309	135	12648,472 937 4979
16	23,418 773 4871	76	743,490 755 8689	136	13266,085 993 2009
17	25,560 438 6946	77	780,735 930 2175	137	13913,807 685 3695
18	27,806 510 0810	78	819,796 806 8156	138	14593,105 810 0312
19	30,162 077 4474	79	860,761 901 1479	139	15305,519 718 2703
20	32,632 478 7230	80	903,724 043 8288	140	16052,663 804 5359
21	35,223 312 0607	81	948,780 590 9655	141	16836,231 165 0071
22	37,940 448 5237	82	996,033 644 7751	142	17657,997 434 3012
23	40,790 045 3892	83	1045,590 284 9578	143	18519,824 809 2233
24	43,778 560 1019	84	1097,562 811 3495	144	19423,666 268 6730
25	46,912 764 9069	85	1152,068 998 4028	145	20371,569 999 2708
26	50,199 762 1961	86	1209,232 362 0750	146	21365,684 036 7352
27	53,647 000 6032	87	1269,182 439 7261	147	22408,261 133 5261
28	57,262 291 8826	88	1332,055 083 6628	148	23501,663 863 7855
29	61,053 828 6119	89	1397,992 768 9913	149	24648,369 977 1450
30	65,030 202 7567	90	1467,144 916 4797	150	25850,978 013 5308
31	69,200 425 1411	91	1539,668 231 1580	151	27112,213 191 6905
32	73,573 945 8667	92	1615,727 057 4270	152	28434,933 584 7854
33	78,160 675 7277	93	1695,493 751 4766	153	29822,136 597 0437
34	82,971 008 6694	94	1779,149 071 8610	154	31276,965 756 1495
35	88,015 845 3421	95	1866,882 589 1143	155	32802,717 836 7618
36	93,306 617 8025	96	1958,893 115 3336	156	34402,850 331 3040
37	98,855 315 4204	97	2055,389 154 7061	157	36080,989 284 9550
38	104,674 512 0471	98	2156,589 375 9980	158	37840,937 512 5966
39	110,777 394 5094	99	2262,723 108 0779	159	39686,683 216 3357
40	117,177 792 4917	100	2374,030 859 5967	160	41622,409 023 1321
41	123,890 209 8757	101	2490,764 864 0021	161	43652,501 463 0097
42	130,929 857 6072	102	2613,189 651 1222	162	45781,560 909 3315
43	138,312 688 1655	103	2741,582 646 6144	163	48014,412 003 6614
44	146,055 431 7136	104	2876,234 800 6368	164	50356,114 588 8399
45	154,175 634 0096	105	3017,451 247 1679	165	52811,975 175 0458
46	162,691 696 1676	106	3165,551 995 4673	166	55387,558 964 8293
47	171,622 916 3557	107	3320,872 655 2463	167	58088,702 464 3647
48	180,989 533 5281	108	3483,765 197 1896	168	60921,526 709 5025
49	190,812 773 2876	109	3654,598 750 5526	169	63892,451 136 5908
50	201,114 895 9854	110	3833,760 439 6420	170	67008,208 129 4996
51	211,919 247 1646	111	4021,656 261 0746	171	70275,858 275 8127
52	223,250 310 4639	112	4218,712 003 8020	172	73702,806 366 7585
53	235,133 763 0990	113	4425,374 213 9873	173	77296,818 177 1380
54	247,596 534 0501	114	4642,111 206 9192	174	81066,038 063 2735
55	260,666 865 0851	115	4869,414 128 2565	175	85019,007 418 8581
56	274,374 374 7580	116	5107,798 067 0090	176	89164,684 030 5274
57	288,750 125 5274	117	5357,803 222 7757	177	93512,462 377 0156
58	303,826 694 1469	118	5619,996 129 8860	178	98072,194 917 8951
59	319,638 245 4865	119	5894,970 941 2180	179	102854,214 420 1425
60	336,220 609 9540	120	6183,350 774 6023	180	107869,357 373 1244

NOMINAL INTEREST RATE COMPOUNDED

YEARLY	HALF-YEARLY	QUARTERLY
@	@	@
$4\frac{15}{16}\%$	$9\frac{7}{8}\%$	$19\frac{3}{4}\%$
4.9375%	9.8750%	19.7500%
PER ANNUM	PER ANNUM	PER ANNUM

Periods	Amount	Periods	Amount	Periods	Amount
1	1,000 000 0000	61	362,806 490 9635	121	6883,881 007 7533
2	2,049 375 0000	62	381,720 061 4548	122	7224,772 632 5112
3	3,150 562 8906	63	401,567 489 4892	123	7582,495 781 2414
4	4,306 121 9333	64	422,394 884 2827	124	7957,881 510 4402
5	5,518 736 7038	65	444,250 631 6941	125	8351,801 910 0182
6	6,791 224 3286	66	467,185 506 6340	126	8765,172 129 3253
7	8,126 541 0298	67	491,252 791 0241	127	9198,952 503 2108
8	9,527 788 9931	68	516,508 397 5809	128	9654,150 783 0568
9	10,998 223 5747	69	543,010 999 7115	129	10131,824 477 9702
10	12,541 260 8637	70	570,822 167 8222	130	10633,083 311 5700
11	14,160 485 6188	71	600,006 512 3584	131	11159,091 800 0788
12	15,859 659 5962	72	630,631 833 9061	132	11711,071 957 7077
13	17,642 730 2888	73	662,769 280 7053	133	12290,306 135 6195
14	19,513 840 0968	74	696,493 513 9401	134	12898,140 001 0657
15	21,477 335 9516	75	731,882 881 1909	135	13535,985 663 6183
16	23,537 779 4142	76	769,019 598 4497	136	14205,324 955 7595
17	25,699 957 2728	77	807,989 941 1231	137	14907,712 875 4501
18	27,968 892 6631	78	848,884 444 4661	138	15644,781 198 6755
19	30,349 856 7384	79	891,798 113 9116	139	16418,242 270 3601
20	32,848 380 9148	80	936,830 645 7860	140	17229,892 982 4591
21	35,470 269 7225	81	984,086 658 9217	141	18081,618 948 4680
22	38,221 614 2900	82	1033,675 937 7059	142	18975,398 884 0486
23	41,108 806 4956	83	1085,713 687 1301	143	19913,309 203 9485
24	44,138 553 8163	84	1140,320 800 4322	144	20897,528 845 8935
25	47,317 894 9110	85	1197,624 139 9535	145	21930,344 332 6594
26	50,654 215 9722	86	1257,756 831 8637	146	23014,155 084 0845
27	54,155 267 8859	87	1320,858 575 4370	147	24151,478 991 3612
28	57,829 184 2377	88	1387,075 967 5992	148	25344,958 266 5596
29	61,684 500 2095	89	1456,562 843 4994	149	26597,365 580 9710
30	65,730 172 4073	90	1529,480 633 8972	150	27911,610 506 5315
31	69,975 599 6699	91	1605,998 740 1959	151	29290,746 275 2915
32	74,430 644 9036	92	1686,294 927 9931	152	30737,976 872 6340
33	79,105 657 9957	93	1770,555 740 0627	153	32256,664 480 7203
34	84,011 499 8593	94	1858,976 929 7283	154	33850,337 289 4558
35	89,159 567 6648	95	1951,763 915 6336	155	35522,697 693 1227
36	94,561 821 3183	96	2049,132 258 9680	156	37277,630 891 7207
37	100,230 811 2459	97	2151,308 164 2546	157	39119,213 916 9994
38	106,179 707 5511	98	2258,529 004 8647	158	41051,725 104 1512
39	112,422 330 6115	99	2371,043 874 4799	159	43079,654 031 1687
40	118,973 183 1854	100	2489,114 165 7823	160	45207,711 948 9576
41	125,847 484 1052	101	2613,014 177 7178	161	47440,842 726 4374
42	133,061 203 6329	102	2743,031 752 7426	162	49784,234 336 0553
43	140,631 100 5623	103	2879,468 945 5343	163	52243,330 906 3980
44	148,574 761 1525	104	3022,642 724 7200	164	54823,845 369 9014
45	156,910 639 9844	105	3172,885 709 2531	165	57531,772 735 0403
46	165,658 102 8337	106	3330,546 941 1475	166	60373,404 013 8329
47	174,837 471 6611	107	3495,992 696 3666	167	63355,340 837 0159
48	184,470 071 8243	108	3669,607 335 7497	168	66484,510 790 8435
49	194,578 281 6207	109	3851,794 197 9524	169	69768,183 511 1414
50	205,185 584 2757	110	4042,976 536 4763	170	73213,987 572 0040
51	216,316 622 4993	111	4243,598 502 9648	171	76829,928 208 3717
52	227,997 255 7352	112	4454,126 179 0487	172	80624,405 913 6601
53	240,254 620 2371	113	4675,048 659 1392	173	84606,235 955 6471
54	253,117 192 1113	114	4906,879 186 6842	174	88784,668 855 9571
55	266,614 853 4718	115	5150,156 346 5267	175	93169,411 880 7200
56	280,778 961 8620	116	5405,445 316 1365	176	97770,651 592 3306
57	295,642 423 1039	117	5673,339 178 6207	177	102599,077 514 7019
58	311,239 767 7447	118	5954,460 300 5651	178	107665,906 966 9903
59	327,607 231 2771	119	6249,461 777 9055	179	112982,911 123 4854
60	344,782 838 3214	120	6559,028 953 1896	180	118562,442 360 2075

NOMINAL INTEREST RATE COMPOUNDED

YEARLY	HALF-YEARLY	QUARTERLY
@	@	@
5%	10%	20%
5.0000%	10.0000%	20.0000%
PER ANNUM	PER ANNUM	PER ANNUM

Periods	Amount	Periods	Amount	Periods	Amount
1	1,000 000 0000	61	372.262 903 7766	121	7307.151 699 0112
2	2,050 000 0000	62	391.876 048 9654	122	7673.509 283 9618
3	3,152 500 0000	63	412.469 851 4137	123	8058.184 748 1599
4	4,310 125 0000	64	434.093 343 9844	124	8462.093 985 5679
5	5,525 631 2500	65	456.798 011 1836	125	8886.198 684 8463
6	6,801 912 8125	66	480.637 911 7428	126	9331.508 619 0886
7	8,142 008 4531	67	505.669 807 3299	127	9799.084 050 0430
8	9,549 108 8758	68	531.953 297 6964	128	10290.038 252 5452
9	11,026 564 3196	69	559.550 962 5812	129	10805.540 165 1724
10	12,577 892 5355	70	588.528 510 7103	130	11346.817 173 4310
11	14,206 787 1623	71	618.954 936 2458	131	11915.158 032 1026
12	15,917 126 5204	72	650.902 683 0581	132	12511.915 933 7077
13	17,712 982 8465	73	684.447 817 2110	133	13138.511 730 3931
14	19,598 631 9888	74	719.670 208 0715	134	13796.437 316 9128
15	21,578 563 5882	75	756.653 718 4751	135	14487.259 182 7584
16	23,657 491 7676	76	795.486 404 3989	136	15212.622 141 8963
17	25,840 366 3560	77	836.260 724 6188	137	15974.253 248 9911
18	28,132 384 6738	78	879.073 760 8497	138	16773.965 911 4407
19	30,539 003 9075	79	924.027 448 8922	139	17613.664 207 0127
20	33,065 954 1029	80	971.228 821 3368	140	18495.347 417 3634
21	35,719 251 8080	81	1020.790 262 4037	141	19421.114 788 2315
22	38,505 214 3984	82	1072.829 775 5239	142	20393.170 527 6431
23	41,430 475 1184	83	1127.471 264 3001	143	21413.829 054 0253
24	44,501 998 8743	84	1184.844 827 5151	144	22485.520 506 7265
25	47,727 098 8180	85	1245.087 068 8908	145	23610.796 532 0629
26	51,113 453 7589	86	1308.341 422 3354	146	24792.336 358 6660
27	54,669 126 4468	87	1374.758 493 4521	147	26032.953 176 5993
28	58,402 582 7692	88	1444.496 418 1247	148	27335.600 835 4293
29	62,322 711 9076	89	1517.721 239 0310	149	28703.380 877 2007
30	66,438 847 5030	90	1594.607 300 9825	150	30139.549 921 0608
31	70,760 789 8782	91	1675.337 666 0317	151	31647.527 417 1138
32	75,298 829 3721	92	1760.104 549 3332	152	33230.903 787 9695
33	80,063 770 8407	93	1849.109 776 7999	153	34893.448 977 3680
34	85,066 959 3827	94	1942.565 265 6399	154	36639.121 426 2364
35	90,320 307 3518	95	2040.693 528 9219	155	38472.077 497 5482
36	95,836 322 7194	96	2143.728 205 3680	156	40396.681 372 4256
37	101,628 138 8554	97	2251.914 615 6364	157	42417.515 441 0469
38	107,709 545 7982	98	2365.510 346 4182	158	44539.391 213 0992
39	114,095 023 0881	99	2484.785 863 7391	159	46767.360 773 7542
40	120,799 774 2425	100	2610.025 156 9261	160	49106.728 812 4419
41	127,839 762 9546	101	2741.526 414 7724	161	51563.065 253 0640
42	135,231 751 1023	102	2879.602 735 5110	162	54142.218 515 7172
43	142,993 338 6575	103	3024.582 872 2865	163	56850.329 441 5031
44	151,143 005 5903	104	3176.812 015 9009	164	59693.845 913 5782
45	159,700 155 8699	105	3336.652 616 6959	165	62679.538 209 2571
46	168,685 163 6633	106	3504.485 247 5307	166	65814.515 119 7200
47	178,119 421 8465	107	3680.709 509 9072	167	69106.240 875 7060
48	188,025 392 9388	108	3865.744 985 4026	168	72562.552 919 4913
49	198,426 662 5858	109	4060.032 234 6727	169	76191.680 565 4659
50	209,347 995 7151	110	4264.033 846 4064	170	80002.264 593 7392
51	220,815 395 5008	111	4478.235 538 7267	171	84003.377 823 4261
52	232,856 165 2759	112	4703.147 315 6630	172	88204.546 714 5974
53	245,498 973 5397	113	4939.304 681 4462	173	92615.774 050 3273
54	258,773 922 2166	114	5187.269 915 5185	174	97247.562 752 8437
55	272,712 618 3275	115	5447.633 411 2944	175	102110.940 890 4858
56	287,348 249 2439	116	5721.015 081 8591	176	107217.487 935 0101
57	302,715 661 7060	117	6008.065 835 9521	177	112579.362 331 7606
58	318,851 444 7913	118	6309.469 127 7497	178	118209.330 448 3487
59	335,794 017 0309	119	6625.942 584 1372	179	124120.796 970 7661
60	353,583 717 8825	120	6958.239 713 3440	180	130327.836 819 3044

Amount of 1 Per Period

NOMINAL INTEREST RATE COMPOUNDED

YEARLY	HALF-YEARLY	QUARTERLY
@	@	@
$5\frac{1}{16}\%$	$10\frac{1}{8}\%$	$20\frac{1}{4}\%$
5.0625%	10.1250%	20.2500%
PER ANNUM	PER ANNUM	PER ANNUM

Periods	Amount	Periods	Amount	Periods	Amount
1	1,000 000 0000	61	381,988 270 0072	121	7757,216 285 7178
2	2,050 625 0000	62	402,326 426 1763	122	8150,925 360 1823
3	3,154 437 8906	63	423,694 201 5015	123	8564,565 956 5415
4	4,314 131 3088	64	446,143 720 4525	124	8999,147 108 0914
5	5,532 534 2063	65	469,729 746 3004	125	9455,728 930 4386
6	6,812 618 7505	66	494,509 814 7068	126	9935,425 207 5420
7	8,157 507 5748	67	520,544 374 0764	127	10439,406 108 6738
8	9,570 481 3958	68	547,896 933 0140	128	10968,901 042 9254
9	11,054 987 0164	69	576,634 215 2478	129	11525,201 658 2235
10	12,614 645 7341	70	606,826 322 3947	130	12109,664 992 1711
11	14,253 262 1744	71	638,546 904 9660	131	12723,716 782 3998
12	15,974 833 5720	72	671,873 342 0299	132	13368,854 944 5088
13	17,783 559 5216	73	706,886 929 9701	133	14046,653 226 0745
14	19,683 852 2224	74	743,673 080 7999	134	14758,765 045 6445
15	21,680 347 2411	75	782,321 530 5154	135	15506,927 526 0803
16	23,777 914 8202	76	822,926 557 9977	136	16292,965 732 0881
17	25,981 671 7580	77	865,587 214 9963	137	17118,797 122 2751
18	28,296 993 8907	78	910,407 567 7555	138	17986,436 226 5903
19	30,729 529 2064	79	957,496 950 8732	139	18897,999 560 5614
20	33,285 211 6225	80	1006,970 234 0111	140	19855,710 788 3148
21	35,970 275 4609	81	1058,948 102 1079	141	20861,906 146 9732
22	38,791 270 6561	82	1113,557 349 7771	142	21919,040 145 6638
23	41,755 078 7331	83	1170,931 190 6096	143	23029,691 553 0380
24	44,868 929 5939	84	1231,209 582 1342	144	24196,569 687 9105
25	48,140 419 1546	85	1294,539 567 2298	145	25422,521 028 3610
26	51,577 527 8743	86	1361,075 632 8208	146	26710,536 155 4218
27	55,188 640 2230	87	1430,980 086 7323	147	28063,757 048 2900
28	58,982 565 1343	88	1504,423 453 6231	148	29485,484 748 8597
29	62,968 557 4942	89	1581,584 890 9628	149	30979,187 414 2707
30	67,156 340 7173	90	1662,652 626 0678	150	32548,508 777 1182
31	71,556 130 4661	91	1747,824 415 2625	151	34197,277 033 9598
32	76,178 659 5710	92	1837,308 026 2851	152	35929,514 183 8040
33	81,035 204 2118	93	1931,321 745 1158	153	37749,445 839 3591
34	86,137 611 4250	94	2030,094 908 4623	154	39661,511 534 9766
35	91,498 328 0034	95	2133,868 463 2032	155	41670,375 556 4348
36	97,130 430 8586	96	2242,895 554 1529	156	43780,938 318 9793
37	103,047 658 9208	97	2357,442 141 5819	157	45998,348 321 3777
38	109,264 446 6536	98	2477,787 649 9995	158	48328,014 705 1474
39	115,795 959 2655	99	2604,225 649 7807	159	50775,620 449 5955
40	122,658 129 7033	100	2737,064 573 3008	160	53347,136 234 8563
41	129,867 697 5195	101	2876,628 467 3242	161	56048,835 006 7459
42	137,442 249 7065	102	3023,257 783 4825	162	58887,307 278 9624
43	145,400 263 5978	103	3177,310 208 7713	163	61869,477 209 9598
44	153,761 151 9425	104	3339,161 538 0903	164	65002,619 493 7141
45	162,545 310 2596	105	3509,206 590 9561	165	68294,377 105 5833
46	171,774 166 5915	106	3687,860 174 6233	166	71752,779 946 5535
47	181,470 233 7752	107	3875,558 095 9636	167	75386,264 431 3478
48	191,657 164 3600	108	4072,758 224 5717	168	79203,694 068 1847
49	202,359 808 3057	109	4279,941 609 6907	169	83214,381 080 3866
50	213,604 273 6012	110	4497,613 653 6813	170	87428,109 122 5812
51	225,417 989 9523	111	4726,305 344 8989	171	91855,157 146 9118
52	237,829 775 6936	112	4966,574 552 9844	172	96506,324 477 4742
53	250,869 908 0881	113	5219,007 389 7292	173	101392,957 154 1464
54	264,570 197 1851	114	5484,219 638 8343	174	106526,975 610 0750
55	278,964 063 4176	115	5762,858 258 0503	175	111920,903 750 3351
56	294,086 619 1281	116	6055,602 957 3641	176	117587,899 502 6958
57	309,974 754 2214	117	6363,167 857 0806	177	123541,786 915 0198
58	326,667 226 1539	118	6686,303 229 8453	178	129797,089 877 5926
59	344,204 754 4779	119	7025,797 330 8562	179	136369,067 552 6458
60	362,630 120 1734	120	7382,478 320 7308	180	143273,751 597 4985

NOMINAL INTEREST RATE COMPOUNDED

YEARLY	HALF-YEARLY	QUARTERLY
@	@	@
$5\frac{1}{8}\%$	$10\frac{1}{4}\%$	$20\frac{1}{2}\%$
5.1250%	10.2500%	20.5000%
PER ANNUM	PER ANNUM	PER ANNUM

Periods	Amount	Periods	Amount	Periods	Amount
1	1,000 000 0000	61	391.990 484 3496	121	8235.794 182 6454
2	2,051 250 0000	62	413.079 996 6725	122	8658.878 634 5060
3	3,156 376 5625	63	435.250 346 5020	123	9103.646 164 5244
4	4,318 140 8613	64	458.556 926 7602	124	9571.208 030 4563
5	5,539 445 5805	65	483.057 969 2567	125	10062.732 442 0172
6	6,823 342 1665	66	508.814 690 1811	126	10579.447 479 6706
7	8,173 038 4525	67	535.891 443 0528	127	11122.644 163 0037
8	9,591 906 6732	68	564.355 879 5093	128	11693.679 676 3576
9	11,083 491 8902	69	594.279 118 3341	129	12293.980 759 7710
10	12,651 520 8496	70	625.735 923 1488	130	12925.047 273 7092
11	14,299 911 2931	71	658.804 889 2101	131	13588.455 946 4868
12	16,032 781 7469	72	693.568 639 7822	132	14285.864 313 7443
13	17,854 461 8114	73	730.114 032 5710	133	15019.014 859 8237
14	19,769 502 9792	74	768.532 376 7403	134	15789.739 371 3896
15	21,782 690 0069	75	808.919 661 0482	135	16599.963 514 1734
16	23,899 052 8698	76	851.376 793 6769	136	17451.711 644 2747
17	26,123 879 3294	77	896.009 854 3529	137	18347.111 866 0438
18	28,462 728 1450	78	942.930 359 3884	138	19288.401 349 1786
19	30,921 442 9624	79	992.255 540 3071	139	20277.931 918 3240
20	33,506 166 9142	80	1044.108 636 7478	140	21318.175 929 1381
21	36,223 357 9686	81	1098.619 204 3812	141	22411.732 445 5064
22	39,079 805 0645	82	1155.923 438 6057	142	23561.333 733 3386
23	42,082 645 0740	83	1216.164 514 8342	143	24769.852 087 1722
24	45,239 380 6341	84	1279.492 946 2195	144	26040.307 006 6398
25	48,557 898 8916	85	1346.066 959 7133	145	27375.872 740 7301
26	52,046 491 2098	86	1416.052 891 3986	146	28779.886 218 6925
27	55,713 873 8843	87	1489.625 602 0827	147	30255.855 387 4005
28	59,569 209 9208	88	1566.968 914 1895	148	31807.467 976 0047
29	63,622 131 9293	89	1648.276 071 0417	149	33438.600 709 7750
30	67,882 766 1907	90	1733.750 219 6826	150	35153.328 996 1510
31	72,361 757 9579	91	1823.604 918 4413	151	36955.937 107 2037
32	77,070 298 0533	92	1918.064 670 5114	152	38850.928 883 9479
33	82,020 150 8285	93	2017.365 484 8751	153	40843.038 989 2502
34	87,223 683 5585	94	2121.755 465 9750	154	42937.244 737 4493
35	92,693 897 3408	95	2231.495 433 6062	155	45138.778 530 2436
36	98,444 459 5796	96	2346.859 574 5785	156	47453.140 929 9185
37	104,489 738 1330	97	2468.136 127 7757	157	49886.114 402 5769
38	110,844 837 2123	98	2595.628 104 3242	158	52443.777 765 7089
39	117,525 635 1195	99	2729.654 044 6708	159	55132.521 376 2015
40	124,548 823 9193	100	2870.548 814 4602	160	57959.063 096 7318
41	131,931 951 1452	101	3018.664 441 2012	161	60930.465 080 4393
42	139,693 463 6414	102	3174.370 993 8128	162	64054.151 415 8119
43	147,852 753 6530	103	3338.057 507 2457	163	67337.926 675 8722
44	156,430 207 2777	104	3510.132 954 4920	164	70789.995 418 0107
45	165,447 255 4007	105	3691.027 268 4098	165	74418.982 683 1837
46	174,926 427 2400	106	3881.192 415 9158	166	78233.955 545 6969
47	184,891 406 6361	107	4081.103 527 2314	167	82244.445 767 4138
48	195,367 091 2262	108	4291.260 083 0021	168	86460.473 612 9938
49	206,379 654 6515	109	4512.187 162 2559	169	90892.572 885 6597
50	217,956 611 9524	110	4744.436 754 3215	170	95551.817 246 0498
51	230,126 888 3149	111	4988.589 137 9805	171	100449.847 879 9098
52	242,920 891 3411	112	5245.254 331 3020	172	105598.902 583 7552
53	256,370 587 0223	113	5515.073 615 7812	173	111011.846 341 1727
54	270,509 579 6072	114	5798.721 138 5900	174	116702.203 466 1578
55	285,373 195 5621	115	6096.905 596 9428	175	122684.191 393 7984
56	300,998 571 8346	116	6410.372 008 7861	176	128972.756 202 7305
57	317,424 748 6412	117	6739.903 574 2364	177	135583.609 958 1205
58	334,692 767 0090	118	7086.323 632 4160	178	142533.269 968 4741
59	352,845 771 3182	119	7450.497 718 5773	179	149839.100 054 3584
60	371,929 117 0983	120	7833.335 726 6544	180	157519.353 932 1443

Amount of 1 Per Period

NOMINAL INTEREST RATE COMPOUNDED

YEARLY	HALF-YEARLY	QUARTERLY
@	@	@
$5\frac{3}{16}\%$	$10\frac{3}{8}\%$	$20\frac{3}{4}\%$
5.1875%	10.3750%	20.7500%
PER ANNUM	PER ANNUM	PER ANNUM

Periods	Amount	Periods	Amount	Periods	Amount
1	1,000 000 0000	61	402,277 676 1023	121	8744,715 891 1563
2	2,051 875 0000	62	424,145 830 5501	122	9199,348 028 0100
3	3,158 316 0156	63	447,148 395 5098	123	9677,564 206 9631
4	4,322 153 6589	64	471,344 218 5269	124	10180,587 850 1993
5	5,546 365 3800	65	496,795 199 8630	125	10709,705 844 9284
6	6,834 083 0841	66	523,566 450 8559	126	11266,271 835 6340
7	8,188 601 1441	67	551,726 460 4940	127	11851,709 687 1075
8	9,613 384 8284	68	581,347 270 6322	128	12467,517 127 1262
9	11,112 079 1664	69	612,504 660 2962	129	13115,269 578 0959
10	12,688 518 2731	70	645,278 339 5491	130	13796,624 187 4596
11	14,346 735 1586	71	679,752 153 4132	131	14513,324 067 1841
12	16,090 972 0449	72	716,014 296 3715	132	15267,202 753 1693
13	17,925 691 2197	73	754,157 537 9958	133	16060,188 895 9899
14	19,855 586 4518	74	794,279 460 2793	134	16894,311 194 9694
15	21,885 594 9990	75	836,482 707 2813	135	17771,703 588 2085
16	24,020 910 2395	76	880,875 247 7215	136	18694,610 711 8468
17	26,266 994 9582	77	927,570 651 1971	137	19665,393 642 5238
18	28,629 595 3217	78	976,688 378 7279	138	20686,535 937 7297
19	31,114 755 5790	79	1028,354 088 3744	139	21760,649 989 4995
20	33,728 833 5246	80	1082,699 956 7088	140	22890,483 707 7048
21	36,478 516 7637	81	1139,865 016 9631	141	24078,927 550 0419
22	39,370 839 8208	82	1199,995 514 7181	142	25329,021 916 7004
23	42,413 202 1365	83	1263,245 282 0441	143	26643,964 928 6292
24	45,613 386 9974	84	1329,776 131 0501	144	28027,120 609 3018
25	48,979 581 4479	85	1399,758 267 8483	145	29482,027 490 9094
26	52,520 397 2355	86	1473,370 727 9930	146	31012,407 667 0003
27	56,244 892 8421	87	1550,801 834 5076	147	32622,176 314 7259
28	60,162 596 6582	88	1632,249 679 6727	148	34315,451 711 0523
29	64,283 531 3599	89	1717,922 631 8057	149	36096,565 768 5632
30	68,618 239 5492	90	1808,039 868 3306	150	37970,075 117 8074
31	73,177 810 7258	91	1902,831 936 5003	151	39940,772 764 5437
32	77,973 909 6572	92	2002,541 343 2062	152	42013,700 351 7044
33	83,018 806 2207	93	2107,423 175 3850	153	44194,161 057 4490
34	88,325 406 7934	94	2217,745 752 6081	154	46487,733 162 3042
35	93,907 287 2708	95	2333,791 313 5247	155	48900,284 320 0987
36	99,778 727 7979	96	2455,856 737 9138	156	51437,986 569 2038
37	105,954 749 3025	97	2584,254 306 1930	157	54107,332 122 4813
38	112,451 151 9225	98	2719,312 498 3268	158	56915,149 976 3350
39	119,284 555 4285	99	2861,376 834 1775	159	59868,623 381 3574
40	126,472 441 7414	100	3010,810 757 4505	160	62975,308 219 2653
41	134,033 199 6567	101	3167,996 565 4932	161	66243,152 333 1397
42	141,986 171 8889	102	3333,336 387 3282	162	69680,515 860 4213
43	150,351 704 5556	103	3507,253 212 4208	163	73296,192 620 6807
44	159,151 199 2294	104	3690,191 972 8152	164	77099,432 612 8785
45	168,407 167 6895	105	3882,620 681 4049	165	81099,965 679 6715
46	178,143 289 5134	106	4085,031 629 2528	166	85308,026 399 3045
47	188,384 472 6569	107	4297,942 645 0203	167	89734,380 268 7684
48	199,156 917 1759	108	4521,898 419 7307	168	94390,351 245 2108
49	210,488 182 2544	109	4757,471 900 2543	169	99287,850 716 0561
50	222,407 256 7089	110	5005,265 755 0800	170	104439,407 971 9515
51	234,944 633 1507	111	5265,913 916 1247	171	109858,202 260 4965
52	248,132 385 9954	112	5540,083 200 5237	172	115558,096 502 7598
53	262,004 253 5189	113	5828,475 016 5509	173	121553,672 758 8404
54	276,595 724 1702	114	6131,827 158 0345	174	127860,269 533 2053
55	291,944 127 3615	115	6450,915 691 8575	175	134494,021 015 2403
56	308,088 728 9684	116	6786,556 943 3726	176	141471,898 355 4059
57	325,070 831 7836	117	7139,609 584 8101	177	148811,753 082 5926
58	342,933 881 1824	118	7510,976 832 0221	178	156532,362 773 7520
59	361,723 576 2687	119	7901,608 755 1832	179	164653,479 092 6404
60	381,487 986 7876	120	8312,504 709 3583	180	173195,878 320 5712

Amount of 1 Per Period

NOMINAL INTEREST RATE COMPOUNDED

YEARLY	HALF-YEARLY	QUARTERLY
@	@	@
$5\frac{1}{4}\%$	$10\frac{1}{2}\%$	21 %
5.2500%	10.5000%	21.0000%
PER ANNUM	PER ANNUM	PER ANNUM

Periods	Amount	Periods	Amount	Periods	Amount
1	1,000 000 0000	61	412,853 216 1579	121	9285,930 196 0959
2	2,052 500 0000	62	435,533 272 5061	122	9774,441 531 3909
3	3,160 256 2500	63	459,393 769 3127	123	10288,599 711 7890
4	4,326 169 7031	64	484,517 204 7016	124	10829,751 196 6579
5	5,553 293 6125	65	510,954 357 9485	125	11399,313 134 4824
6	6,844 841 5272	66	538,779 461 7408	126	11998,777 074 0427
7	8,204 195 7074	67	568,065 383 4822	127	12629,712 870 4300
8	9,634 915 9820	68	598,888 816 1150	128	13293,772 796 1276
9	11,140 749 0711	69	631,330 478 9610	129	13992,695 867 9242
10	12,725 638 3973	70	665,475 329 1065	130	14728,312 400 9903
11	14,393 734 4132	71	701,412 783 8846	131	15502,548 802 0423
12	16,149 405 4698	72	739,236 955 0385	132	16317,432 614 1495
13	17,997 249 2570	73	779,046 895 1780	133	17175,097 826 3923
14	19,942 104 8430	74	820,946 857 1749	134	18077,790 462 2779
15	21,989 065 3473	75	865,046 567 1765	135	19027,874 461 5475
16	24,143 491 2780	76	911,461 511 9533	136	20027,837 870 7788
17	26,411 024 5701	77	960,313 241 3309	137	21080,299 358 9946
18	28,797 603 3600	78	1011,729 686 5007	138	22188,015 075 3419
19	31,309 477 5364	79	1065,845 495 0420	139	23353,885 866 7973
20	33,953 225 1071	80	1122,802 383 5317	140	24580,964 874 8042
21	36,735 769 4252	81	1182,749 508 6671	141	25872,465 530 7314
22	39,664 397 3200	82	1245,843 857 8722	142	27231,769 971 0948
23	42,746 778 1793	83	1312,250 660 4104	143	28662,437 894 5773
24	45,990 984 0337	84	1382,143 820 0820	144	30168,215 884 0426
25	49,405 510 6955	85	1455,706 370 6363	145	31753,047 217 9548
26	52,999 300 0070	86	1533,130 955 0947	146	33421,082 196 8974
27	56,781 763 2574	87	1614,620 330 2372	147	35176,689 012 2345
28	60,762 805 8284	88	1700,387 897 5746	148	37024,465 185 3769
29	64,952 853 1344	89	1790,658 262 1973	149	38969,249 607 6091
30	69,362 877 9240	90	1885,667 820 9627	150	41016,135 212 0086
31	74,004 429 0150	91	1985,665 381 5632	151	43170,482 310 6391
32	78,889 661 5383	92	2090,912 814 0953	152	45437,932 631 9476
33	84,031 368 7690	93	2201,685 736 8353	153	47824,424 095 1249
34	89,443 015 6294	94	2318,274 238 0191	154	50336,206 360 1189
35	95,138 773 9499	95	2440,983 635 5151	155	52979,857 194 0252
36	101,133 559 5823	96	2570,135 276 3797	156	55762,299 696 7115
37	107,443 071 4604	97	2706,067 378 3896	157	58690,820 430 7889
38	114,083 832 7120	98	2849,135 915 7551	158	61773,088 503 4053
39	121,073 233 9294	99	2999,715 551 3322	159	65017,175 649 8341
40	128,429 578 7107	100	3158,200 617 7771	160	68431,577 371 4503
41	136,172 131 5930	101	3325,006 150 2104	161	72025,235 183 4515
42	144,321 168 5017	102	3500,568 973 0965	162	75807,560 030 5827
43	152,898 029 8480	103	3685,348 844 1840	163	79788,456 932 1883
44	161,925 176 4150	104	3879,829 658 5037	164	83978,350 921 1282
45	171,426 248 1768	105	4084,520 715 5752	165	88388,214 344 4874
46	181,426 126 2061	106	4299,958 053 1428	166	93029,595 597 5730
47	191,950 997 8319	107	4526,705 850 9328	167	97914,649 366 4456
48	203,028 425 2181	108	4765,357 908 1068	168	103056,168 458 1840
49	214,687 417 5421	109	5016,539 198 2824	169	108467,617 302 2386
50	226,958 506 9630	110	5280,907 506 1923	170	114163,167 210 6061
51	239,873 828 5786	111	5559,155 150 2674	171	120157,733 489 1630
52	253,467 204 5789	112	5852,010 795 6564	172	126467,014 497 3440
53	267,774 232 8193	113	6160,241 362 4283	173	133107,532 758 4546
54	282,832 380 0424	114	6484,654 033 9558	174	140096,678 228 2734
55	298,681 079 9946	115	6826,098 370 7385	175	147452,753 835 2578
56	315,361 836 6943	116	7185,468 535 2023	176	155195,023 411 6088
57	332,918 333 1207	117	7563,705 633 3004	177	163343,762 140 7183
58	351,396 545 6096	118	7961,800 179 0487	178	171920,309 653 1060
59	370,844 864 2541	119	8380,794 688 4487	179	180947,125 909 8941
60	391,314 219 6274	120	8821,786 409 5923	180	190447,850 020 1635

Amount of 1 Per Period

NOMINAL INTEREST RATE COMPOUNDED

YEARLY	HALF-YEARLY	QUARTERLY
@	@	@
$5\frac{5}{16}\%$	$10\frac{5}{8}\%$	$21\frac{1}{4}\%$
5.3125%	10.6250%	21.2500%
PER ANNUM	PER ANNUM	PER ANNUM

Periods	Amount	Periods	Amount	Periods	Amount
1	1.000 000 0000	61	423.740 724 2011	121	9861.511 829 0192
2	2.053 125 0000	62	447.251 950 1743	122	10386.404 644 9358
3	3.162 197 2656	63	472.012 210 0273	123	10939.182 391 6980
4	4.330 188 9954	64	498.087 858 6850	124	11521.326 456 2570
5	5.560 230 2857	65	525.548 776 1777	125	12134.396 924 2457
6	6.855 617 5197	66	554.468 554 9121	126	12780.036 760 8462
7	8.219 822 2004	67	584.924 696 8918	127	13459.976 213 7662
8	9.656 500 2548	68	616.998 821 4142	128	14176.037 450 1225
9	11.169 501 8308	69	650.776 883 8018	129	14930.139 439 6602
10	12.762 881 6156	70	686.349 405 7538	130	15724.303 097 3922
11	14.440 909 7014	71	723.811 717 9345	131	16560.656 699 4412
12	16.208 083 0293	72	763.264 215 4498	132	17441.441 586 5990
13	18.069 137 4402	73	804.812 626 8955	133	18369.018 170 8870
14	20.029 060 3668	74	848.568 297 6994	134	19345.872 261 2154
15	22.093 104 1987	75	894.648 488 5146	135	20374.621 725 0925
16	24.266 800 3593	76	943.176 689 4670	136	21458.023 504 2380
17	26.555 974 1284	77	994.282 951 0949	137	22598.981 002 9007
18	28.966 760 2540	78	1048.104 232 8718	138	23800.551 868 6798
19	31.505 619 3925	79	1104.784 770 2431	139	25065.956 186 7034
20	34.179 355 4227	80	1164.476 461 1623	140	26398.585 109 1220
21	36.995 133 6795	81	1227.339 273 1616	141	27802.009 943 0441
22	39.960 500 1562	82	1293.541 672 0483	142	29279.991 721 2683
23	43.083 401 7270	83	1363.261 073 3758	143	30836.491 281 4607
24	46.372 207 4438	84	1436.684 317 8989	144	32475.679 880 7883
25	49.835 730 9642	85	1514.008 172 2873	145	34201.950 374 4552
26	53.483 254 1717	86	1595.439 856 4401	146	36019.928 988 0981
27	57.324 552 0496	87	1681.197 598 8134	147	37934.487 715 5908
28	61.369 918 8772	88	1771.511 221 2504	148	39950.757 375 4816
29	65.630 195 8176	89	1866.622 754 8793	149	42074.141 361 0540
30	70.116 799 9704	90	1966.787 088 7323	150	44310.330 120 8600
31	74.841 754 9688	91	2072.272 652 8212	151	46665.316 408 5307
32	79.817 723 2015	92	2183.362 137 5023	152	49145.411 342 7339
33	85.058 039 7466	93	2300.353 251 0571	153	51757.261 320 3167
34	90.576 748 1081	94	2423.559 517 5195	154	54507.865 827 9585
35	96.388 637 8514	95	2553.311 116 8878	155	57404.596 200 0688
36	102.509 284 2372	96	2689.955 769 9724	156	60455.215 373 1974
37	108.955 089 9623	97	2833.859 670 2522	157	63667.898 689 8985
38	115.743 329 1166	98	2985.408 465 2344	158	67051.255 807 7994
39	122.892 193 4759	99	3145.008 289 9499	159	70614.353 772 5888
40	130.420 841 2543	100	3313.086 855 3535	160	74366.741 316 7575
41	138.349 448 4459	101	3490.094 594 5442	161	78318.474 449 2103
42	146.699 262 8946	102	3676.505 869 8793	162	82480.143 404 3246
43	155.492 661 2359	103	3872.820 244 2167	163	86862.901 022 6793
44	164.753 208 8641	104	4079.563 819 6907	164	91478.492 639 5091
45	174.505 723 0850	105	4297.290 647 6118	165	96339.287 560 9831
46	184.776 339 6239	106	4526.584 213 2661	166	101458.312 212 6603
47	195.592 582 6664	107	4768.058 999 5959	167	106849.285 048 9579
48	206.983 438 6205	108	5022.362 133 9494	168	112526.653 317 1838
49	218.979 433 7972	109	5290.175 122 3155	169	118505.631 774 6592
50	231.612 716 2177	110	5572.215 675 6885	170	124802.243 462 6879
51	244.917 141 7668	111	5869.239 633 4595	171	131433.362 646 6432
52	258.928 364 9232	112	6182.042 988 9870	172	138416.760 037 2461
53	273.683 934 3097	113	6511.464 022 7769	173	145771.150 414 2248
54	289.223 393 3199	114	6858.385 548 9870	174	153516.242 779 9805
55	305.588 386 0900	115	7223.737 281 2769	175	161672.793 177 6670
56	322.822 769 1010	116	7608.498 324 3447	176	170262.660 315 2306
57	340.972 728 7095	117	8013.699 797 8255	177	179308.864 144 4772
58	360.086 904 9222	118	8440.427 599 5850	178	188835.647 552 1525
59	380.216 521 7462	119	8889.825 315 8130	179	198868.541 328 3606
60	401.415 524 4640	120	9363.097 285 7155	180	209434.432 586 4298

NOMINAL INTEREST RATE COMPOUNDED

YEARLY	HALF-YEARLY	QUARTERLY
@	@	@
$5\frac{3}{8}\%$	$10\frac{3}{4}\%$	$21\frac{1}{2}\%$
5.3750%	10.7500%	21.5000%
PER ANNUM	PER ANNUM	PER ANNUM

Periods	Amount	Periods	Amount	Periods	Amount
1	1,000 000 0000	61	434,934 076 1204	121	10473,669 627 9166
2	2,053 750 0000	62	459,311 782 7119	122	11037,629 370 4171
3	3,164 139 0625	63	484,999 791 0327	123	11631,901 949 0770
4	4,334 211 5371	64	512,068 529 8007	124	12258,116 678 8399
5	5,567 175 4072	65	540,592 213 2774	125	12917,990 450 3276
6	6,866 411 0854	66	570,649 044 7411	126	13613,332 437 0327
7	8,235 480 6812	67	602,321 430 8959	127	14346,049 055 5232
8	9,678 137 7678	68	635,696 207 8066	128	15118,149 192 2576
9	11,198 337 6728	69	670,864 878 9762	129	15931,749 711 3414
10	12,800 248 3228	70	707,923 866 2212	130	16789,081 258 3260
11	14,488 261 6701	71	746,974 774 0306	131	17692,494 375 9610
12	16,267 005 7349	72	788,124 668 1347	132	18644,465 948 6689
13	18,141 357 2931	73	831,486 369 0469	133	19647,605 993 4099
14	20,116 455 2476	74	877,178 761 3832	134	20704,664 815 5557
15	22,197 714 7172	75	925,327 119 8076	135	21818,540 549 3918
16	24,390 841 8832	76	976,063 452 4972	136	22992,287 103 9216
17	26,701 849 6345	77	1029,526 863 0690	137	24229,122 535 7574
18	29,137 074 0523	78	1085,863 931 9589	138	25532,437 872 0543
19	31,703 191 7826	79	1145,229 118 3017	139	26905,806 407 6773
20	34,407 238 3409	80	1207,785 183 4104	140	28352,993 502 0899
21	37,256 627 4018	81	1273,703 637 0187	141	29877,966 902 8273
22	40,259 171 1246	82	1343,165 207 5085	142	31484,907 623 8542
23	43,423 101 5726	83	1416,360 337 4121	143	33178,221 408 6364
24	46,757 093 2821	84	1493,489 705 5480	144	34962,550 809 3506
25	50,270 287 0460	85	1574,764 777 2212	145	36842,787 915 3532
26	53,972 314 9747	86	1660,408 383 9968	146	38824,087 765 8034
27	57,873 326 9046	87	1750,655 334 6366	147	40911,882 483 2153
28	61,984 018 2257	88	1845,753 058 8733	148	43111,896 166 6882
29	66,315 659 2054	89	1945,962 285 7878	149	45430,160 585 6477
30	70,880 125 8877	90	2051,557 758 6489	150	47873,031 717 1262
31	75,689 932 6541	91	2162,828 988 1763	151	50447,207 171 9218
32	80,758 266 5343	92	2280,081 046 2907	152	53159,744 557 4126
33	86,099 023 3605	93	2403,635 402 5289	153	56018,080 827 3735
34	91,726 845 8661	94	2533,830 805 4148	154	59030,052 671 8448
35	97,657 163 8314	95	2671,024 211 2058	155	62203,918 002 9565
36	103,906 236 3874	96	2815,591 762 5581	156	65548,378 595 6154
37	110,491 196 5932	97	2967,929 819 7956	157	69072,603 945 1297
38	117,430 098 4101	98	3128,456 047 6097	158	72786,256 407 1804
39	124,741 966 1996	99	3297,610 560 1687	159	76699,517 689 0664
40	132,446 846 8828	100	3475,857 127 7777	160	80823,116 764 8537
41	140,565 864 9028	101	3663,684 448 3958	161	85168,359 290 9646
42	149,121 280 1413	102	3861,607 487 4971	162	89747,158 602 8539
43	158,136 548 9489	103	4070,168 889 9500	163	94572,068 377 7573
44	167,636 388 4549	104	4289,940 467 7849	164	99656,317 053 0618
45	177,646 844 3344	105	4521,524 767 9283	165	105013,844 094 6638
46	188,195 362 2173	106	4765,556 724 2044	166	110659,338 214 7520
47	199,310 862 9365	107	5022,705 398 1304	167	116608,277 643 7949
48	211,023 821 8194	108	5293,675 813 2799	168	122876,972 567 1489
49	223,366 352 2421	109	5579,210 888 2437	169	129482,609 842 6332
50	236,372 293 6752	110	5880,093 473 4868	170	136443,300 121 6747
51	250,077 304 4602	111	6197,148 497 6868	171	143778,127 503 2147
52	264,518 959 5749	112	6531,245 229 4374	172	151507,201 856 5125
53	279,736 853 6521	113	6883,299 660 5197	173	159651,713 956 3001
54	295,772 709 5359	114	7254,277 017 2726	174	168233,993 581 4512
55	312,670 492 6734	115	7645,194 406 9510	175	177277,570 736 4542
56	330,476 531 6546	116	8057,123 606 3246	176	186807,240 163 5386
57	349,239 645 2311	117	8491,194 000 1646	177	196849,129 322 3288
58	369,011 276 1622	118	8948,595 677 6734	178	207430,770 023 4040
59	389,845 632 2560	119	9430,582 695 3484	179	218581,173 912 1619
60	411,799 834 9897	120	9938,476 515 2233	180	230330,912 009 9406

Amount of 1 Per Period

NOMINAL INTEREST RATE COMPOUNDED

YEARLY	HALF-YEARLY	QUARTERLY
@	@	@
$5\frac{7}{16}\%$	$10\frac{7}{8}\%$	$21\frac{3}{4}\%$
7.4375%	10.8750%	21.7500%
PER ANNUM	PER ANNUM	PER ANNUM

Periods	Amount	Periods	Amount	Periods	Amount
1	1,000 000 0000	61	446,447 411 6391	121	11124,755 225 5504
2	2,054 375 0000	62	471,722 989 6470	122	11730,663 790 9397
3	3,166 081 6406	63	498,372 927 2091	123	12369,518 634 5720
4	4,338 237 3298	64	526,471 955 1261	124	13043,111 210 3269
5	5,574 128 9846	65	556,098 867 6861	125	13753,330 382 3884
6	6,877 222 2482	66	587,336 743 6165	126	14502,167 721 9308
7	8,251 171 2079	67	620,273 179 0506	127	15291,723 091 8108
8	9,699 828 6424	68	655,000 533 1615	128	16124,210 534 9280
9	11,227 256 8248	69	691,616 187 1522	129	17001,964 482 7647
10	12,837 738 9146	70	730,222 817 3286	130	17927,446 301 5150
11	14,535 790 9681	71	770,928 683 0208	131	18903,251 194 1599
12	16,326 174 6020	72	813,847 930 1601	132	19932,115 477 8423
13	18,213 910 3460	73	859,100 911 3625	133	21016,924 256 9500
14	20,204 291 7211	74	906,814 523 4178	134	22160,719 513 4217
15	22,302 900 0834	75	957,122 563 1287	135	23366,708 636 9640
16	24,515 620 2754	76	1010,166 102 4988	136	24638,273 419 0989
17	26,848 657 1279	77	1066,093 884 3222	137	25978,979 536 2624
18	29,308 552 8592	78	1125,062 739 2822	138	27392,586 548 5466
19	31,902 205 4210	79	1187,238 025 7307	139	28883,058 442 1239
20	34,636 887 8407	80	1252,794 093 3798	140	30454,574 744 9144
21	37,520 268 6171	81	1321,914 772 2073	141	32111,542 246 6691
22	40,560 433 2231	82	1394,793 887 9461	142	33858,607 356 3317
23	43,765 906 7796	83	1471,635 805 6031	143	35700,669 131 3322
24	47,145 677 9608	84	1552,656 002 5328	144	37642,893 015 3484
25	50,709 224 1999	85	1638,081 672 6705	145	39690,725 323 0580
26	54,466 538 2657	86	1728,152 363 6220	146	41849,908 512 4993
27	58,428 156 2839	87	1823,120 648 3939	147	44126,497 287 8664
28	62,605 187 2819	88	1923,252 833 6504	148	46526,875 577 8942
29	67,009 344 3403	89	2028,829 706 4801	149	49057,774 437 4422
30	71,652 977 4388	90	2140,147 321 7700	150	51726,290 922 4781
31	76,549 108 0871	91	2257,517 832 3912	151	54539,907 991 3878
32	81,711 465 8393	92	2381,270 364 5275	152	57506,515 488 4195
33	87,154 526 7943	93	2511,751 940 5987	153	60634,432 268 1023
34	92,893 554 1888	94	2649,328 452 3687	154	63932,429 522 6804
35	98,944 641 1978	95	2794,385 686 9663	155	67409,755 377 9762
36	105,324 756 0629	96	2947,330 408 6950	156	71076,160 826 6536
37	112,051 789 6738	97	3108,591 499 6678	157	74941,927 071 6029
38	119,144 605 7373	98	3278,621 162 4623	158	79017,894 356 1213
39	126,623 093 6743	99	3457,896 188 1712	159	83315,492 361 7354
40	134,508 224 3928	100	3646,919 293 4030	160	87846,772 258 9048
41	142,822 109 0942	101	3846,220 529 9818	161	92624,440 500 4827
42	151,588 061 2762	102	4056,358 771 2995	162	97661,894 452 6965
43	160,830 662 1081	103	4277,923 279 4889	163	102973,259 963 5618
44	170,575 829 3602	104	4511,535 357 8111	164	108573,430 974 0805
45	180,850 890 0817	105	4757,850 092 8921	165	114478,111 283 2961
46	191,684 657 2299	106	5017,558 191 6931	166	120703,858 584 3254
47	203,107 510 4668	107	5291,387 918 3664	167	127268,130 894 8481
48	215,151 481 3484	108	5580,107 136 4276	168	134189,335 512 2554
49	227,850 343 1467	109	5884,525 461 9709	169	141486,880 630 7343
50	241,239 705 5553	110	6205,496 533 9655	170	149181,229 765 0305
51	255,357 114 5449	111	6543,920 407 9999	171	157293,959 133 5040
52	270,242 157 6483	112	6900,746 080 1849	172	165847,818 161 3883
53	285,936 574 9704	113	7276,974 148 2950	173	174866,793 273 9138
54	302,484 376 2344	114	7673,659 617 6085	174	184376,175 158 1828
55	319,931 964 1921	115	8091,914 859 3160	175	194402,629 682 4090
56	338,328 264 7451	116	8532,912 729 7913	176	204974,272 671 3900
57	357,724 864 1406	117	8997,889 859 4737	177	216120,748 747 8969
58	378,176 153 6282	118	9488,150 120 5826	178	227873,314 461 0638
59	399,739 481 9818	119	10005,068 283 3892	179	240264,925 934 8841
60	422,475 316 3145	120	10550,093 871 2985	180	253330,331 282 5934

Amount of 1 Per Period

NOMINAL INTEREST RATE COMPOUNDED

YEARLY	HALF-YEARLY	QUARTERLY
@	@	@
$5\frac{1}{2}\%$	11%	22%
5.5000%	11.0000%	22.0000%
PER ANNUM	PER ANNUM	PER ANNUM

Periods	Amount	Periods	Amount	Periods	Amount
1	1.000 000 0000	61	458.290 142 1741	121	11817.272 300 5833
2	2.055 000 0000	62	484.496 099 9937	122	12468.222 277 1154
3	3.168 025 0000	63	512.143 385 4933	123	13154.974 502 3567
4	4.342 266 3750	64	541.311 271 6955	124	13879.498 099 9864
5	5.581 091 0256	65	572.083 391 6387	125	14643.870 495 4856
6	6.888 051 0320	66	604.547 978 1788	126	15450.283 372 7373
7	8.266 893 8388	67	638.798 116 9787	127	16301.048 958 2379
8	9.721 572 9999	68	674.932 013 4125	128	17198.606 650 9410
9	11.256 259 5149	69	713.053 274 1502	129	18145.530 016 7427
10	12.875 353 7882	70	753.271 204 2284	130	19144.534 167 6636
11	14.583 498 2466	71	795.701 120 4610	131	20198.483 546 8851
12	16.385 590 6502	72	840.464 682 0864	132	21310.400 141 9637
13	18.286 798 1359	73	887.690 239 6011	133	22483.472 149 7717
14	20.292 572 0334	74	937.513 202 7792	134	23721.063 118 0092
15	22.408 663 4952	75	990.076 428 9320	135	25026.721 589 4997
16	24.641 139 9875	76	1045.530 632 5233	136	26404.191 276 9222
17	26.996 402 6868	77	1104.034 817 3121	137	27857.421 797 1529
18	29.481 204 8346	78	1165.756 732 2642	138	29390.579 995 9963
19	32.102 671 1005	79	1230.873 352 5388	139	31008.061 895 7761
20	34.868 318 0110	80	1299.571 386 9284	140	32714.505 300 0438
21	37.786 075 5016	81	1372.047 813 2095	141	34514.803 091 5462
22	40.864 309 6542	82	1448.510 442 9360	142	36414.117 261 5812
23	44.111 846 6852	83	1529.178 517 2975	143	38417.893 710 9682
24	47.537 998 2528	84	1614.283 335 7488	144	40531.877 865 0715
25	51.152 588 1567	85	1704.068 919 2150	145	42762.131 147 6504
26	54.965 980 5054	86	1798.792 709 7718	146	45115.048 360 7712
27	58.989 109 4332	87	1898.726 308 8093	147	47597.376 020 6136
28	63.233 510 4520	88	2004.156 255 7938	148	50216.231 701 7473
29	67.711 353 5268	89	2115.384 849 8624	149	52979.124 445 3434
30	72.435 477 9708	90	2232.731 016 6049	150	55893.976 289 8373
31	77.419 429 2592	91	2356.531 222 5181	151	58969.144 985 7784
32	82.677 497 8685	92	2487.140 439 7566	152	62213.447 959 9962
33	88.224 760 2512	93	2624.933 163 9433	153	65636.187 597 7960
34	94.077 122 0651	94	2770.304 487 9601	154	69247.177 915 6748
35	100.251 363 7786	95	2923.671 234 7979	155	73056.772 701 0369
36	106.765 188 7865	96	3085.473 152 7118	156	77075.895 199 5939
37	113.637 274 1697	97	3256.174 176 1110	157	81316.069 435 5716
38	120.887 324 2490	98	3436.263 755 7971	158	85789.453 254 5280
39	128.536 127 0827	99	3626.258 262 3659	159	90508.873 183 5270
40	136.605 614 0723	100	3826.702 466 7960	160	95487.861 208 6210
41	145.118 922 8463	101	4038.171 102 4698	161	100740.693 575 0952
42	154.100 463 6028	102	4261.270 513 1057	162	106282.431 721 7254
43	163.575 989 1010	103	4496.640 391 3265	163	112128.965 466 4203
44	173.572 668 5015	104	4744.955 612 8494	164	118297.058 567 0734
45	184.119 165 2691	105	5006.928 171 5562	165	124804.396 788 2625
46	195.245 719 3589	106	5283.309 220 9917	166	131669.638 611 6169
47	206.984 233 9237	107	5574.891 228 1463	167	138912.468 735 2558
48	219.368 366 7895	108	5882.510 245 6943	168	146553.654 515 6949
49	232.433 626 9629	109	6207.048 309 2075	169	154615.105 514 0581
50	246.217 476 4458	110	6549.435 966 2139	170	163119.936 317 3313
51	260.759 437 6504	111	6910.654 944 3557	171	172092.532 814 7845
52	276.101 206 7211	112	7291.740 966 2953	172	181558.622 119 5977
53	292.286 773 0908	113	7693.786 719 4415	173	191545.346 336 1755
54	309.362 545 6108	114	8117.944 989 0108	174	202081.340 384 6652
55	327.377 485 6194	115	8565.431 963 4064	175	213196.814 105 8218
56	346.383 247 3284	116	9037.530 721 3937	176	224923.638 881 6420
57	366.434 325 9315	117	9535.594 911 0704	177	237295.439 020 1323
58	387.588 213 8577	118	10061.052 631 1793	178	250347.688 166 2396
59	409.905 565 6199	119	10615.410 525 8941	179	264117.811 015 3828
60	433.450 371 7290	120	11200.258 104 8183	180	278645.290 621 2288

Amount of 1 Per Period

NOMINAL INTEREST RATE COMPOUNDED

YEARLY	HALF-YEARLY	QUARTERLY
@	@	@
$5\frac{9}{16}\%$	$11\frac{1}{8}\%$	$22\frac{1}{4}\%$
5.5625%	11.1250%	22.2500%
PER ANNUM	PER ANNUM	PER ANNUM

Periods	Amount	Periods	Amount	Periods	Amount
1	1.000 000 0000	61	470.471 958 9267	121	12553.886 427 8849
2	2.055 625 0000	62	497.641 961 6420	122	13253.196 360 4360
3	3.169 969 1406	63	526.323 295 7583	123	13991.405 407 9852
4	4.346 298 6741	64	556.600 029 0849	124	14770.677 333 8044
5	5.588 061 5378	65	588.560 905 7027	125	15593.296 260 4973
6	6.898 897 4609	66	622.299 606 0824	126	16461.673 364 9874
7	8.282 648 6321	67	657.915 021 6708	127	17378.353 945 9149
8	9.743 370 9623	68	695.511 544 7512	128	18346.024 884 1564
9	11.285 345 9721	69	735.199 374 4280	129	19367.522 518 3376
10	12.913 093 3418	70	777.094 839 6306	130	20445.840 958 4201
11	14.631 384 1589	71	821.320 740 0850	131	21584.140 861 7322
12	16.445 254 9027	72	868.006 706 2522	132	22785.758 697 1661
13	18.360 022 2067	73	917.289 579 2875	133	24054.216 524 6960
14	20.381 298 4419	74	969.313 812 1354	134	25393.232 318 8822
15	22.515 008 1678	75	1024.231 892 9354	135	26806.730 866 6200
16	24.767 405 4971	76	1082.204 791 9799	136	28298.855 271 0757
17	27.145 092 4279	77	1143.402 433 5338	137	29873.979 095 5293
18	29.655 038 1942	78	1208.004 193 8991	138	31536.719 182 7181
19	32.304 599 6937	79	1276.199 427 1848	139	33291.949 187 2568
20	35.101 543 0517	80	1348.188 020 3219	140	35144.813 860 7980
21	38.054 066 3839	81	1424.180 978 9524	141	37100.744 131 8049
22	41.170 823 8266	82	1504.401 045 9066	142	39165.473 024 1365
23	44.460 950 9019	83	1589.083 354 0851	143	41345.052 461 1041
24	47.934 091 2958	84	1678.476 115 6561	144	43645.871 004 2530
25	51.600 425 1242	85	1772.841 349 5895	145	46074.672 578 8646
26	55.470 698 7717	86	1872.455 649 6604	146	48638.576 241 0639
27	59.556 256 3909	87	1977.610 995 1728	147	51345.097 044 4731
28	63.869 073 1526	88	2088.615 606 7792	148	54202.168 067 5719
29	68.421 790 3467	89	2205.794 849 9063	149	57218.163 666 3306
30	73.227 752 4347	90	2329.492 188 4324	150	60401.924 020 2703
31	78.301 046 1639	91	2460.070 191 4139	151	63762.781 043 8978
32	83.656 541 8568	92	2597.911 595 8113	152	67310.585 739 4646
33	89.309 936 9976	93	2743.420 428 3283	153	71055.737 071 2224
34	95.277 802 2431	94	2897.023 189 6541	154	75009.212 445 8091
35	101.577 629 9928	95	3059.170 104 5786	155	79182.599 888 1072
36	108.227 885 6612	96	3230.336 441 6458	156	83588.132 006 8832
37	115.248 061 8011	97	3411.023 906 2123	157	88238.721 849 7661
38	122.658 735 2388	98	3601.762 110 9954	158	93148.000 752 6593
39	130.481 627 3864	99	3803.110 128 4195	159	98330.358 294 5260
40	138.739 667 9098	100	4015.658 129 3129	160	103800.984 474 6590
41	147.457 061 9373	101	4240.029 112 7559	161	109575.914 236 0619
42	156.659 361 0076	102	4476.880 732 1529	162	115672.074 465 4428
43	166.373 537 9636	103	4726.907 222 8789	163	122107.333 607 5831
44	176.628 066 0128	104	4990.841 437 1516	164	128900.554 039 5049
45	187.453 002 1848	105	5269.456 992 0931	165	136071.647 357 9524
46	198.880 075 4313	106	5563.570 537 2783	166	143641.632 742 2385
47	210.942 779 6272	107	5874.044 148 4144	167	151632.698 563 5255
48	223.676 471 7440	108	6201.787 854 1700	168	160068.267 421 1216
49	237.118 475 4847	109	6547.762 303 5582	169	168973.064 796 4215
50	251.308 190 6836	110	6912.981 581 6936	170	178373.191 525 7224
51	266.287 208 7903	111	7298.516 182 1753	171	188296.200 304 3407
52	282.099 434 7793	112	7705.496 144 8088	172	198771.176 446 2697
53	298.791 215 8389	113	8135.114 367 8638	173	209828.823 136 0934
54	316.411 477 2199	114	8588.630 104 5762	174	221501.551 423 0386
55	335.011 865 6403	115	9067.372 654 1433	175	233823.575 220 9451
56	354.646 900 6665	116	9572.745 258 0300	176	246831.011 592 6102
57	375.374 134 5161	117	10106.229 213 0079	177	260561.986 612 4492
58	397.254 320 7486	118	10669.388 212 9815	178	275056.747 117 7666
59	420.351 592 3402	119	11263.872 932 3286	179	290357.778 676 1924
60	444.733 649 6641	120	11891.425 864 1894	180	306509.930 115 0556

Amount of 1 Per Period

NOMINAL INTEREST RATE COMPOUNDED

YEARLY @ $5\frac{5}{8}\%$ 5.6250% PER ANNUM		HALF-YEARLY @ $11\frac{1}{4}\%$ 11.2500% PER ANNUM		QUARTERLY @ $22\frac{1}{2}\%$ 22.5000% PER ANNUM	
Periods	Amount	Periods	Amount	Periods	Amount
1	1,000 000 0000	61	483.002 841 2145	121	13337,435 566 7443
2	2,056 250 0000	62	511.171 751 0328	122	14088,666 317 3737
3	3,171 914 0625	63	540.925 162 0284	123	14882,153 797 7259
4	4,350 334 2285	64	572.352 202 3925	124	15720,274 948 8480
5	5,595 040 5289	65	605.547 013 7770	125	16605,540 414 7207
6	6,909 761 5586	66	640.609 033 3020	126	17540,602 063 0488
7	8,298 435 6463	67	677.643 291 4252	127	18528,260 929 0953
8	9,765 222 6514	68	716.760 726 5679	128	19571,475 606 3569
9	11,314 516 4255	69	758.078 517 4373	129	20673,371 109 2144
10	12,950 957 9745	70	801.720 434 0432	130	21837,248 234 1077
11	14,679 449 3605	71	847.817 208 4581	131	23066,593 447 2763
12	16,505 168 3871	72	896.506 926 4339	132	24365,089 328 6856
13	18,433 584 1088	73	947.935 441 0458	133	25736,625 603 4242
14	20,470 473 2150	74	1002.256 809 6046	134	27185,310 793 6168
15	22,621 937 3333	75	1059.633 755 1449	135	28715,484 525 7577
16	24,894 421 3083	76	1120.258 153 8718	136	30331,730 530 3316
17	27,294 732 5069	77	1184.251 550 0271	137	32038,890 372 6627
18	29,830 061 2104	78	1251.865 699 7161	138	33842,077 956 1250
19	32,508 002 1535	79	1323.283 145 3251	139	35746,694 841 1571
20	35,336 577 2746	80	1398.717 822 2497	140	37758,446 425 9721
21	38,324 259 7463	81	1478.395 699 7512	141	39883,359 037 4331
22	41,479 999 3571	82	1562.555 457 8622	142	42127,797 983 2887
23	44,813 249 3209	83	1651.449 202 3670	143	44498,486 619 8487
24	48,333 994 5952	84	1745.343 220 0001	144	47002,526 492 2152
25	52,052 781 7912	85	1844.518 776 1251	145	49647,418 607 4023
26	55,980 750 7669	86	1949.272 957 2822	146	52441,085 904 0686
27	60,129 667 9976	87	2059.919 561 1293	147	55391,896 986 1725
28	64,511 961 8224	88	2176.790 036 4428	148	58508,691 191 6447
29	69,140 759 6749	89	2300.234 475 9927	149	61800,805 071 1747
30	74,029 927 4066	90	2430.622 665 2673	150	65278,100 356 4283
31	79,194 110 8233	91	2568.345 190 1886	151	68950,993 501 4774
32	84,648 779 5571	92	2713.814 607 1367	152	72830,486 885 9355
33	90,410 273 4072	93	2867.466 678 7881	153	76928,201 773 2694
34	96,495 851 2863	94	3029.761 679 4700	154	81256,413 123 0158
35	102,923 742 9212	95	3201.185 773 9401	155	85828,086 361 1854
36	109,713 203 4605	96	3382.252 473 7243	156	90656,916 219 0021
37	116,884 571 1551	97	3573.504 175 3713	157	95757,367 756 3209
38	124,459 328 2826	98	3775.513 785 2359	158	101144,719 692 6140
39	132,460 165 4985	99	3988.886 435 6554	159	106835,110 175 3235
40	140,911 049 8078	100	4214.261 297 6610	160	112845,585 122 6855
41	149,837 296 3595	101	4452.313 495 6545	161	119194,149 285 8365
42	159,265 644 2797	102	4703.756 129 7850	162	125899,820 183 1649
43	169,224 336 7705	103	4969.342 412 0855	163	132982,685 068 4679
44	179,743 205 7138	104	5249.867 922 7653	164	140463,961 103 5692
45	190,853 761 0352	105	5546.172 993 4208	165	148366,058 915 6450
46	202,589 285 0934	106	5859.145 224 3007	166	156712,649 729 6500
47	214,984 932 3799	107	6189.722 143 1676	167	165528,736 276 9428
48	228,077 834 8263	108	6538.894 013 7208	168	174840,727 692 5208
49	241,907 213 0353	109	6907.706 801 9926	169	184676,518 625 2251
50	256,514 493 7685	110	7297.265 309 6047	170	195065,572 797 8940
51	271,943 434 0430	111	7708.736 483 2700	171	206039,011 267 7756
52	288,240 252 2079	112	8143.352 910 4539	172	217629,705 651 5880
53	305,453 766 3946	113	8602.416 511 6669	173	229872,376 594 4898
54	323,635 540 7543	114	9087.302 440 4482	174	242803,697 777 9298
55	342,840 039 9217	115	9599.463 202 7234	175	256462,405 777 9384
56	363,124 792 1673	116	10140.433 007 8766	176	270889,416 102 9474
57	384,550 561 7267	117	10711.832 364 5697	177	286127,945 758 7382
58	407,181 530 8239	118	11315.372 935 0767	178	302223,642 707 6672
59	431,085 491 9327	119	11952.862 662 6748	179	319224,722 609 9735
60	456,334 050 8539	120	12626.211 187 4502	180	337182,113 256 7845

NOMINAL INTEREST RATE COMPOUNDED

YEARLY	HALF-YEARLY	QUARTERLY
@	@	@
$5\frac{11}{16}\%$	$11\frac{3}{8}\%$	$22\frac{3}{4}\%$
5.6875%	11.3750%	22.7500%
PER ANNUM	PER ANNUM	PER ANNUM

Periods	Amount	Periods	Amount	Periods	Amount
1	1,000 000 0000	61	495,893 065 0496	121	14170,941 228 2155
2	2,056 875 0000	62	525,096 983 1243	122	14977,913 510 5703
3	3,173 859 7656	63	555,961 874 0395	123	15830,782 341 4840
4	4,354 373 0398	64	588,582 205 6255	124	16732,158 087 1559
5	5,602 028 0064	65	623,057 818 5705	125	17684,799 578 3629
6	6,920 643 3493	66	659,494 232 0017	126	18691,622 554 3823
7	8,314 254 9398	67	698,002 966 4468	127	19755,708 587 1628
8	9,787 128 1895	68	738,701 885 1634	128	20880,314 513 0576
9	11,343 771 1053	69	781,715 554 8821	129	22068,882 400 9878
10	12,988 948 0869	70	827,175 627 0660	130	23325,050 087 5440
11	14,727 694 5093	71	875,221 240 8554	131	24652,662 311 2730
12	16,565 332 1345	72	925,999 448 9291	132	26055,782 480 2267
13	18,507 485 3997	73	979,665 667 5869	133	27538,705 108 7896
14	20,560 098 6318	74	1036,384 152 4309	134	29105,968 961 8520
15	22,729 454 2415	75	1096,328 501 1004	135	30762,370 946 5573
16	25,022 191 9515	76	1159,682 184 6005	136	32512,980 794 1428
17	27,445 329 1187	77	1226,639 108 8497	137	34363,156 576 8096
18	30,006 282 2123	78	1297,404 208 1655	138	36318,561 107 1157
19	32,712 889 5132	79	1372,194 072 5049	139	38385,179 270 0829
20	35,573 435 1042	80	1451,237 610 3786	140	40569,336 341 0689
21	38,596 674 2258	81	1534,776 749 4689	141	42877,717 345 4671
22	41,791 860 0724	82	1623,067 177 0949	142	45317,387 519 4906
23	45,168 772 1140	83	1716,379 122 7922	143	47895,813 934 6616
24	48,737 746 0280	84	1814,998 185 4010	144	50620,888 352 1955
25	52,509 705 3333	85	1919,226 207 1957	145	53500,951 377 2266
26	56,496 194 8241	86	2029,382 197 7299	146	56544,817 986 8064
27	60,709 415 9048	87	2145,803 310 2258	147	59761,804 509 8060
28	65,162 263 9343	88	2268,845 873 4949	148	63161,757 141 3012
29	69,868 367 6956	89	2398,886 482 5500	149	66755,082 078 7127
30	74,842 131 1083	90	2536,323 151 2450	150	70552,777 371 9395
31	80,098 777 3151	91	2681,576 530 4720	151	74566,466 584 9686
32	85,654 395 2749	92	2835,091 195 6426	152	78808,434 371 9886
33	91,525 989 0061	93	2997,337 007 3948	153	83291,664 076 8955
34	97,731 529 6309	94	3168,810 549 6904	154	88029,877 471 2689
35	104,290 010 3786	95	3350,036 649 7040	155	93037,576 752 4473
36	111,221 504 7189	96	3541,569 984 1560	156	98330,088 930 2428
37	118,547 227 7998	97	3743,996 777 0048	157	103923,612 738 1503
38	126,289 601 3809	98	3957,936 593 6970	158	109835,268 212 6326
39	134,472 322 4594	99	4184,044 237 4635	159	116083,149 092 2261
40	143,120 435 7993	100	4423,011 753 4692	160	122686,378 196 8465
41	152,260 410 5854	101	4675,570 546 9478	161	129665,165 956 7921
42	161,920 221 4374	102	4942,493 621 8054	162	137040,872 270 5847
43	172,129 434 0317	103	5224,597 946 5456	163	144836,071 880 9742
44	182,919 295 5922	104	5522,746 954 7554	164	153074,623 469 2046
45	194,322 830 5291	105	5837,853 187 8071	165	161781,742 679 0156
46	206,374 941 5154	106	6170,881 087 8636	166	170984,079 293 8846
47	219,112 516 3141	107	6522,849 949 7359	167	180709,798 803 7243
48	232,574 540 6794	108	6894,837 040 6271	168	190988,668 610 6861
49	246,802 217 6806	109	7287,980 897 3128	169	201852,149 137 9189
50	261,839 093 8112	110	7703,484 810 8475	170	213333,490 120 1380
51	277,731 192 2717	111	8142,620 509 4644	171	225467,832 370 7209
52	294,527 153 8321	112	8606,732 050 9402	172	238292,315 336 8056
53	312,278 385 7063	113	9097,239 936 3374	173	251846,190 771 5865
54	331,039 218 8934	114	9615,645 457 7166	174	266170,942 871 7204
55	350,867 074 4679	115	10163,535 293 1242	175	281310,415 247 5495
56	371,822 639 3283	116	10742,586 362 9207	176	297310,945 114 7539
57	393,970 051 9401	117	11354,570 962 3118	177	314221,505 118 1555
58	417,377 098 6442	118	12001,362 185 7933	178	332093,853 221 7506
59	442,115 421 1296	119	12684,939 660 1103	179	350982,691 123 7377
60	468,260 735 7063	120	13407,395 603 2790	180	370945,831 681 4003

Amount of 1 Per Period

NOMINAL INTEREST RATE COMPOUNDED

	YEARLY	HALF-YEARLY	QUARTERLY
	@	@	@
	$5\frac{3}{4}\%$	$11\frac{1}{2}\%$	23%
	5.7500%	11.5000%	23.0000%
	PER ANNUM	PER ANNUM	PER ANNUM

Periods	Amount	Periods	Amount	Periods	Amount
1	1,000 000 0000	61	509,153 211 9722	121	15057,620 365 4744
2	2,057 500 0000	62	539,429 521 6606	122	15924,433 536 4892
3	3,175 806 2500	63	571,446 719 1561	123	16841,088 464 8373
4	4,358 415 1094	64	605,304 905 5076	124	17810,451 051 5654
5	5,609 023 9782	65	641,109 937 5743	125	18835,551 987 0304
6	6,931 542 8569	66	678,973 758 9848	126	19919,596 226 2847
7	8,330 106 5712	67	719,014 750 1264	127	21065,973 009 2961
8	9,809 087 6990	68	761,358 098 2587	128	22278,266 457 3306
9	11,373 110 2417	69	806,136 188 9086	129	23560,266 778 6271
10	13,027 064 0806	70	853,489 019 7708	130	24915,982 118 3982
11	14,776 120 2653	71	903,564 638 4077	131	26349,651 090 2061
12	16,625 747 1805	72	956,519 605 1161	132	27865,756 027 8929
13	18,581 727 6434	73	1012,519 482 4103	133	29469,036 999 4967
14	20,650 176 9829	74	1071,739 352 6489	134	31164,506 626 9678
15	22,837 562 1594	75	1134,364 365 4262	135	32957,465 758 0185
16	25,150 721 9836	76	1200,590 316 4382	136	34853,520 039 1045
17	27,596 888 4976	77	1270,624 259 6334	137	36858,597 441 3530
18	30,183 709 5862	78	1344,685 154 5623	138	38978,966 794 2308
19	32,919 272 8874	79	1423,004 550 9496	139	41221,257 384 8991
20	35,812 131 0785	80	1505,827 312 6292	140	43592,479 684 5308
21	38,871 328 6155	81	1593,412 383 1054	141	46100,047 266 3913
22	42,106 430 0109	82	1686,033 595 1340	142	48751,799 984 2088
23	45,527 549 7365	83	1783,980 526 8542	143	51556,028 483 3008
24	49,145 383 8463	84	1887,559 407 1483	144	54521,500 121 0906
25	52,971 243 4175	85	1997,094 073 0593	145	57657,486 378 0533
26	57,017 089 9140	86	2112,926 982 2602	146	60973,791 844 7914
27	61,295 572 5841	87	2235,420 283 7402	147	64480,784 875 8669
28	65,820 068 0076	88	2364,956 950 0552	148	68189,430 006 2292
29	70,604 721 9181	89	2501,941 974 6834	149	72111,322 231 5874
30	75,664 493 4284	90	2646,803 638 2277	150	76258,723 259 9037
31	81,015 201 8005	91	2799,994 847 4258	151	80644,599 847 3482
32	86,673 575 9040	92	2961,994 551 1528	152	85282,664 338 5707
33	92,657 306 5185	93	3133,309 237 8441	153	90187,417 538 0385
34	98,985 101 6433	94	3314,474 519 0201	154	95374,194 046 4757
35	105,676 744 9878	95	3506,056 803 8638	155	100859,210 204 1481
36	112,753 157 8246	96	3708,655 070 0859	156	106659,614 790 8866
37	120,236 464 3995	97	3922,902 736 6159	157	112793,542 641 3626
38	128,150 061 1025	98	4149,469 643 9713	158	119280,171 343 2409
39	136,518 689 6159	99	4389,064 148 4996	159	126139,781 195 4773
40	145,368 514 2688	100	4642,435 337 0384	160	133393,818 614 2172
41	154,727 203 8393	101	4910,375 368 9181	161	141064,963 184 5347
42	164,624 018 0600	102	5193,721 952 6309	162	149177,198 567 6454
43	175,089 899 0985	103	5493,360 964 9071	163	157755,887 485 2851
44	186,157 568 2966	104	5810,229 220 3893	164	166827,851 015 6889
45	197,861 628 4737	105	6145,317 400 5617	165	176421,452 449 0911
46	210,238 672 1109	106	6499,673 151 0940	166	186566,685 964 9138
47	223,327 395 7573	107	6874,404 357 2819	167	197295,270 407 8963
48	237,168 721 0134	108	7270,682 607 8256	168	208640,748 456 3504
49	251,805 922 4716	109	7689,746 857 7756	169	220638,591 492 5905
50	267,284 763 0138	110	8132,907 302 0977	170	233326,310 503 4145
51	283,653 636 8870	111	8601,549 471 9683	171	246743,573 357 3608
52	300,963 721 0081	112	9097,138 566 6065	172	260932,328 825 4091
53	319,269 134 9660	113	9621,224 034 1863	173	275936,937 732 8701
54	338,627 110 2266	114	10175,444 416 1520	174	291804,311 652 5101
55	359,098 169 0646	115	10761,532 470 0808	175	308584,059 572 5294
56	380,746 313 7858	116	11381,320 587 1104	176	326328,642 997 9499
57	403,639 226 8285	117	12036,746 520 8693	177	345093,539 970 3320
58	427,848 482 3711	118	12729,859 445 8193	178	364937,418 518 6261
59	453,449 770 1075	119	13462,826 363 9539	179	385922,320 083 4471
60	480,523 131 8886	120	14237,938 879 8812	180	408113,853 488 2453

Amount of 1 Per Period

NOMINAL INTEREST RATE COMPOUNDED

YEARLY	HALF-YEARLY	QUARTERLY
@	@	@
$5\frac{13}{16}\%$	$11\frac{5}{8}\%$	$23\frac{1}{4}\%$
5.8125%	11.6250%	23.2500%
PER ANNUM	PER ANNUM	PER ANNUM

Periods	Amount	Periods	Amount	Periods	Amount
1	1,000 000 0000	61	522.794 178 1450	121	16000.898 033 8932
2	2,058 125 0000	62	554.181 589 7497	122	16931.950 232 1132
3	3,177 753 5156	63	587.393 394 6539	123	17917.119 839 3548
4	4,362 460 4387	64	622.535 635 7182	124	18959.552 430 0173
5	5,616 028 4517	65	659.720 519 5443	125	20062.576 415 0120
6	6,942 460 1055	66	699.066 774 7428	126	21229.713 669 1346
7	8,345 990 5991	67	740.700 031 0247	127	22464.690 776 1531
8	9,831 101 3027	68	784.753 220 3280	128	23771.450 927 5169
9	11,402 534 0659	69	831.367 001 2596	129	25154.166 512 6789
10	13,065 306 3585	70	880.690 208 2078	130	26617.252 441 2283
11	14,824 727 2906	71	932.880 326 5599	131	28165.380 239 3747
12	16,686 414 5643	72	988.103 995 5412	132	29803.492 965 7884
13	18,656 312 4109	73	1046.537 540 2820	133	31536.820 994 4248
14	20,740 710 5698	74	1108.367 534 8109	134	33370.898 714 7258
15	22,946 264 3716	75	1173.791 397 7718	135	35311.582 202 5192
16	25,280 015 9882	76	1243.018 022 7673	136	37365.067 918 0406
17	27,749 416 9176	77	1316.268 445 3406	137	39537.912 490 7768
18	30,362 351 7759	78	1393.776 548 7261	138	41837.053 654 3031
19	33,127 163 4729	79	1475.789 810 6208	139	44269.832 397 9595
20	36,052 679 8497	80	1562.570 093 3631	140	46844.016 406 0909
21	39,148 241 8660	81	1654.394 480 0398	141	49567.824 859 6950
22	42,423 733 4244	82	1751.556 159 1921	142	52449.954 679 6647
23	45,889 612 9297	83	1854.365 360 9452	143	55499.608 295 4202
24	49,556 946 6813	84	1963.150 347 5501	144	58726.523 027 5915
25	53,437 444 2071	85	2078.258 461 5015	145	62141.002 178 5703
26	57,543 495 6517	86	2200.057 234 5762	146	65753.947 930 1997
27	61,888 211 3364	87	2328.935 561 3360	147	69576.896 153 6425
28	66,485 463 6203	88	2465.304 940 8386	148	73622.053 242 5730
29	71,349 931 1933	89	2609.600 790 5249	149	77902.335 087 2976
30	76,497 145 9439	90	2762.283 836 4741	150	82431.408 314 2467
31	81,943 542 5519	91	2923.841 584 4692	151	87223.733 922 5123
32	87,706 510 9627	92	3094.789 876 5665	152	92294.613 456 7584
33	93,804 451 9124	93	3275.674 538 1419	153	97660.237 863 9324
34	100,256 835 6798	94	3467.073 120 6714	154	103337.739 189 7735
35	107,084 264 2537	95	3669.596 745 8104	155	109345.245 280 1791
36	114,308 537 1135	96	3883.892 056 6606	156	115701.937 662 0895
37	121,952 720 8332	97	4110.643 282 4540	157	122428.112 788 6985
38	130,041 222 7316	98	4350.574 423 2467	158	129545.246 844 5416
39	138,599 868 8029	99	4604.451 561 5979	159	137076.064 317 3806
40	147,655 986 1771	100	4873.085 308 6158	160	145044.610 555 8283
41	157,238 490 3736	101	5157.333 392 1791	161	153476.328 544 3858
42	167,377 977 6266	102	5458.103 395 5995	162	162398.140 141 0282
43	178,106 822 5761	103	5776.355 655 4687	163	171838.532 036 7255
44	189,459 281 6383	104	6113.106 327 9428	164	181827.646 711 3602
45	201,471 602 3836	105	6469.430 633 2545	165	192397.378 676 4580
46	214,182 139 2721	106	6846.466 288 8124	166	203581.476 312 0271
47	227,631 476 1173	107	7245.417 141 8496	167	215415.649 622 6637
48	241,862 555 6666	108	7667.557 013 2196	168	227937.684 256 9810
49	256,920 816 7147	109	8114.233 764 6130	169	241187.562 154 4180
50	272,854 339 1863	110	8586.873 602 1812	170	255207.589 204 6436
51	289,713 997 6515	111	9086.985 630 3079	171	270042.530 327 1635
52	307,553 623 7650	112	9616.166 670 0696	172	285739.752 402 4299
53	326,430 178 1463	113	10176.106 357 7674	173	302349.375 510 8211
54	346,403 932 2511	114	10768.592 539 8126	174	319924.432 962 3876
55	367,538 660 8132	115	11395.516 981 1892	175	338521.040 628 3264
56	389,901 845 4729	116	12058.881 405 7208	176	358198.576 114 8478
57	413,564 890 2411	117	12760.803 887 4284	177	379019.868 351 5234
58	438,603 349 4863	118	13503.525 613 3851	178	401051.398 199 4556
59	465,097 169 1752	119	14289.418 039 6632	179	424363.510 719 7990
60	493,130 942 1335	120	15120.990 463 2186	180	449030.639 780 3873

Amount of 1 Per Period

NOMINAL INTEREST RATE COMPOUNDED

YEARLY	HALF-YEARLY	QUARTERLY
@	@	@
$5\frac{7}{8}\%$	$11\frac{3}{4}\%$	$23\frac{1}{2}\%$
5.8750%	11.7500%	23.5000%
PER ANNUM	PER ANNUM	PER ANNUM

Periods	Amount	Periods	Amount	Periods	Amount
1	1,000 000 0000	61	536,827 183 7182	121	17004,420 870 5454
2	2,058 750 0000	62	569,355 780 7616	122	18004,430 596 6899
3	3,179 701 5625	63	603,816 020 3814	123	19063,190 894 2454
4	4,366 509 0293	64	640,290 211 5788	124	20184,153 359 2824
5	5,623 041 4348	65	678,907 261 5090	125	21370,972 369 1402
6	6,953 395 1191	66	719,793 063 1227	126	22627,516 995 8272
7	8,361 907 0823	67	763,080 905 5811	127	23957,883 619 3320
8	9,853 169 1234	68	808,911 908 7840	128	25366,409 281 9678
9	11,432 042 8094	69	857,435 483 4251	129	26857,685 827 2834
10	13,103 675 3244	70	908,809 818 0763	130	28436,574 869 6363
11	14,873 516 2498	71	963,202 394 8883	131	30108,223 643 2274
12	16,747 335 3294	72	1020,790 535 5880	132	31878,081 782 2670
13	18,731 241 2800	73	1081,761 979 5538	133	33751,919 086 9752
14	20,831 701 7052	74	1146,315 495 8526	134	35735,844 333 3350
15	23,055 564 1804	75	1214,661 531 2339	135	37836,325 187 9185
16	25,410 078 5760	76	1287,022 896 1939	136	40060,209 292 7087
17	27,902 920 6924	77	1363,635 491 3453	137	42414,746 588 6553
18	30,542 217 2830	78	1444,749 076 4618	138	44907,612 950 7388
19	33,336 572 5484	79	1530,628 084 7039	139	47546,935 211 5947
20	36,295 096 1856	80	1621,552 484 6803	140	50341,317 655 2759
21	39,427 433 0865	81	1717,818 693 1553	141	53299,870 067 5233
22	42,743 794 7804	82	1819,740 541 3781	142	56432,237 433 9903
23	46,254 992 7237	83	1927,650 298 1841	143	59748,631 383 2373
24	49,972 473 5462	84	2041,899 753 2024	144	63259,863 477 0025
25	53,908 356 3671	85	2162,861 363 7031	145	66977,380 456 2764
26	58,075 472 3036	86	2290,929 468 8206	146	70913,301 558 0826
27	62,487 406 3015	87	2426,521 575 1138	147	75080,458 024 6200
28	67,158 541 4217	88	2570,079 717 6518	148	79492,434 933 5664
29	72,104 105 7302	89	2722,071 901 0638	149	84163,615 485 9134
30	77,340 221 9419	90	2882,993 625 2513	150	89109,227 895 7108
31	82,883 959 9809	91	3053,369 500 7348	151	94345,395 034 5838
32	88,753 392 6298	92	3233,754 958 9030	152	99889,186 992 8656
33	94,967 654 4468	93	3424,738 062 7385	153	105758,676 728 6965
34	101,547 004 1456	94	3626,941 423 9244	154	111972,998 986 5074
35	108,512 890 6391	95	3841,024 232 5800	155	118552,412 676 9647
36	115,888 022 9642	96	4067,684 406 2440	156	125518,366 921 7364
37	123,696 444 3133	97	4307,660 865 1109	157	132893,570 978 3884
38	131,963 610 4167	98	4561,735 940 9362	158	140702,068 273 3687
39	140,716 472 5287	99	4830,737 927 4662	159	148969,314 784 4291
40	149,983 565 2898	100	5115,543 780 7048	160	157722,262 028 0143
41	159,795 099 7506	101	5417,081 977 8212	161	166989,444 922 1602
42	170,183 061 8609	102	5736,335 544 0182	162	176801,074 811 3371
43	181,181 316 7452	103	6074,345 257 2293	163	187189,137 956 5031
44	192,825 719 1040	104	6432,213 041 0915	164	198187,499 811 4477
45	205,154 230 1014	105	6811,105 557 2556	165	209832,015 425 3702
46	218,207 041 1198	106	7212,258 008 7444	166	222160,646 331 6107
47	232,026 704 7856	107	7636,978 166 7581	167	235213,584 303 5929
48	246,658 273 6918	108	8086,650 634 0551	168	249033,382 381 4290
49	262,149 447 2712	109	8562,741 358 8059	169	263665,093 596 3379
50	278,550 727 2983	110	9066,802 413 6357	170	279156,417 845 1228
51	295,915 582 5271	111	9600,477 055 4368	171	295557,857 393 5237
52	314,300 623 0006	112	10165,505 082 4437	172	312922,881 515 3932
53	333,765 784 6019	113	10763,728 506 0373	173	331308,100 804 4226
54	354,374 524 4472	114	11397,097 555 7670	174	350773,451 726 6824
55	376,194 027 7585	115	12067,677 037 1683	175	371382,392 015 6250
56	399,295 426 8893	116	12777,653 063 1019	176	393202,107 546 5430
57	423,754 033 2191	117	13529,340 180 5592	177	416303,731 364 9024
58	449,649 582 6707	118	14325,188 916 1670	178	440762,575 582 5904
59	477,066 495 6526	119	15167,793 764 9918	179	466658,376 898 0676
60	506,094 152 2722	120	16059,901 648 6851	180	494075,556 540 8291

Amount of 1 Per Period

NOMINAL INTEREST RATE COMPOUNDED

	YEARLY @ $5\frac{15}{16}\%$ 5.9375% PER ANNUM		HALF-YEARLY @ $11\frac{7}{8}\%$ 11.8750% PER ANNUM		QUARTERLY @ $23\frac{3}{4}\%$ 23.7500% PER ANNUM
Periods	Amount	Periods	Amount	Periods	Amount
1	1,000 000 0000	61	551,263 782 4715	121	18072,071 446 0520
2	2,059 375 0000	62	584,995 069 5557	122	19146,100 688 1614
3	3,181 650 3906	63	620,729 151 8106	123	20283,900 416 5209
4	4,370 560 8826	64	658,584 945 1993	124	21489,257 003 7519
5	5,630 062 9350	65	698,688 426 3205	125	22766,181 638 3496
6	6,964 347 9217	66	741,173 051 6333	126	24118,923 673 1267
7	8,377 856 0796	67	786,180 201 5740	127	25551,984 766 2186
8	9,875 291 2843	68	833,859 651 0425	128	27070,133 861 7128
9	11,461 636 7043	69	884,370 067 8231	129	28678,423 059 7520
10	13,142 171 3836	70	937,879 540 6001	130	30382,204 428 9247
11	14,922 487 8095	71	994,566 138 3233	131	32187,147 816 8922
12	16,808 510 5232	72	1054,618 502 7862	132	34099,259 718 5201
13	18,806 515 8356	73	1118,236 476 3891	133	36124,903 264 3073
14	20,923 152 7133	74	1185,631 767 1748	134	38270,819 395 6255
15	23,165 464 9056	75	1257,028 653 3508	135	40544,149 297 2408
16	25,540 914 3844	76	1332,664 729 6435	136	42952,458 161 7644
17	28,057 406 1760	77	1412,791 697 9660	137	45503,760 365 1192
18	30,723 314 6677	78	1497,676 205 0328	138	48206,546 136 7982
19	33,547 511 4761	79	1587,600 729 7066	139	51069,809 813 6705
20	36,539 394 9700	80	1682,864 523 0329	140	54103,079 771 3572
21	39,708 921 5463	81	1783,784 604 0880	141	57316,450 132 7816
22	43,066 638 7631	82	1890,696 814 9557	142	60720,614 359 4155
23	46,623 720 4397	83	2003,956 938 3437	143	64326,900 837 0058
24	50,392 003 8408	84	2123,941 881 5579	144	68147,310 574 2030
25	54,384 029 0688	85	2251,050 930 7754	145	72194,557 139 5463
26	58,613 080 7948	86	2385,707 079 7902	146	76482,108 969 7068
27	63,093 232 4670	87	2528,358 437 6527	147	81024,234 189 7832
28	67,839 393 1447	88	2679,479 719 8883	148	85836,048 094 8016
29	72,867 357 1127	89	2839,573 828 2567	149	90933,563 450 4304
30	78,193 856 4413	90	3009,173 524 3094	150	96333,743 780 2997
31	83,836 616 6674	91	3188,843 202 3153	151	102054,559 817 2550
32	89,814 415 7821	92	3379,180 767 4528	152	108115,049 306 4045
33	96,147 146 7191	93	3580,819 625 5203	153	114535,380 358 9723
34	102,855 883 5556	94	3794,430 790 7856	154	121336,918 567 7863
35	109,962 951 6417	95	4020,725 118 9885	155	128542,298 107 7486
36	117,492 001 8954	96	4260,455 672 9284	156	136175,497 057 8962
37	125,468 089 5080	97	4514,420 228 5085	157	144261,917 195 7087
38	133,917 757 3225	98	4783,463 929 5762	158	152828,468 529 2040
39	142,869 124 1635	99	5068,482 100 3948	159	161903,658 848 1254
40	152,351 978 4107	100	5370,423 225 1058	160	171517,688 592 2329
41	162,397 877 1289	101	5690,292 104 0964	161	181702,551 352 3967
42	173,040 251 0834	102	6029,153 197 7771	162	192492,140 338 9453
43	184,314 515 9915	103	6388,134 168 8951	163	203922,361 171 5701
44	196,258 190 3785	104	6768,429 635 1733	164	216031,251 366 1321
45	208,911 020 4322	105	7171,305 144 7617	165	228859,106 915 9962
46	222,315 112 2704	106	7598,101 387 7319	166	242448,616 389 1335
47	236,515 072 0614	107	8050,238 657 6285	167	256845,002 987 2383
48	251,558 154 4651	108	8529,221 577 9252	168	272096,175 039 6056
49	267,494 419 8864	109	9036,644 109 1145	169	288252,885 432 5821
50	284,376 901 0672	110	9574,194 853 0932	170	305368,900 505 1417
51	302,261 779 5680	111	10143,662 672 4956	171	323501,178 972 6345
52	321,208 572 7299	112	10746,942 643 6750	172	342710,061 474 1347
53	341,280 331 7357	113	11386,042 363 1432	173	363059,471 374 1614
54	362,543 851 4325	114	12063,088 628 4549	174	384617,127 487 0023
55	385,069 892 6113	115	12780,334 515 7694	175	407454,769 431 5430
56	408,933 417 4851	116	13540,166 877 6432	176	431648,396 366 5409
57	434,213 839 1483	117	14345,114 286 0032	177	457278,519 900 8042
58	460,995 285 8478	118	15197,855 446 7347	178	484430,432 019 9145
59	489,366 880 9450	119	16101,228 113 8846	179	513194,488 921 0969
60	519,423 039 5011	120	17058,238 533 1465	180	543666,411 700 7870

Amount of 1 Per Period

NOMINAL INTEREST RATE COMPOUNDED

YEARLY	HALF-YEARLY	QUARTERLY
@	@	@
6%	12%	24%
6.0000%	12.0000%	24.0000%
PER ANNUM	PER ANNUM	PER ANNUM

Periods	Amount	Periods	Amount	Periods	Amount
1	1,000 000 0000	61	566,115 871 7422	121	19207,983 545 0856
2	2,060 000 0000	62	601,082 824 0467	122	20361,462 557 7907
3	3,183 600 0000	63	638,147 793 4895	123	21584,150 311 2581
4	4,374 616 0000	64	677,436 661 0989	124	22880,199 329 9336
5	5,637 092 9600	65	719,082 860 7649	125	24254,011 289 7296
6	6,975 318 5376	66	763,227 832 4107	126	25710,251 967 1134
7	8,393 837 6499	67	810,021 502 3554	127	27253,867 085 1402
8	9,897 467 9088	68	859,622 792 4967	128	28890,099 110 2486
9	11,491 315 9834	69	912,200 160 0465	129	30624,505 056 8636
10	13,180 794 9424	70	967,932 169 6493	130	32462,975 360 2754
11	14,971 642 6389	71	1027,008 099 8283	131	34411,753 881 8919
12	16,869 941 1973	72	1089,628 585 8180	132	36477,459 114 8054
13	18,882 137 6691	73	1156,006 300 9670	133	38667,106 661 6937
14	21,015 065 9292	74	1226,366 679 0251	134	40988,133 061 3953
15	23,275 969 8850	75	1300,948 679 7666	135	43448,421 045 0791
16	25,672 528 0781	76	1380,005 600 5526	136	46056,326 307 7838
17	28,212 879 7628	77	1463,805 936 5857	137	48820,705 886 2508
18	30,905 652 5485	78	1552,634 292 7808	138	51750,948 239 4259
19	33,759 991 7015	79	1646,792 350 3477	139	54857,005 133 7914
20	36,785 591 2035	80	1746,599 891 3686	140	58149,425 441 8189
21	39,992 726 6758	81	1852,395 884 8507	141	61639,390 968 3281
22	43,392 290 2763	82	1964,539 637 9417	142	65338,754 426 4277
23	46,995 827 6929	83	2083,412 016 2182	143	69260,079 692 0134
24	50,815 577 3545	84	2209,416 737 1913	144	73416,684 473 5342
25	54,864 511 9957	85	2342,981 741 4228	145	77822,685 541 9463
26	59,156 382 7155	86	2484,560 645 9082	146	82493,046 674 4630
27	63,705 765 6784	87	2634,634 284 6626	147	87443,629 474 9308
28	68,528 111 6191	88	2793,712 341 7424	148	92691,247 243 4267
29	73,639 798 3162	89	2962,335 082 2469	149	98253,722 078 0323
30	79,058 186 2152	90	3141,075 187 1818	150	104149,945 402 7142
31	84,801 677 3881	91	3330,539 698 4127	151	110399,942 126 8771
32	90,889 778 0314	92	3531,372 080 3174	152	117024,938 654 4897
33	97,343 164 7133	93	3744,254 405 1365	153	124047,434 973 7591
34	104,183 754 5961	94	3969,909 669 4447	154	131491,281 072 1846
35	111,434 779 8719	95	4209,104 249 6113	155	139381,757 936 5157
36	119,120 866 6642	96	4462,650 504 5880	156	147745,663 412 7066
37	127,268 118 6640	97	4731,409 534 8633	157	156611,403 217 4690
38	135,904 205 7839	98	5016,294 106 9551	158	166009,087 410 5172
39	145,058 458 1309	99	5318,271 753 3724	159	175970,632 655 1482
40	154,761 965 6188	100	5638,368 058 5748	160	186529,870 614 4571
41	165,047 683 5559	101	5977,670 142 0892	161	197722,662 851 3245
42	175,950 544 5692	102	6337,330 350 6146	162	209587,022 622 4040
43	187,507 577 2434	103	6718,570 171 6515	163	222163,243 979 7482
44	199,758 031 8780	104	7122,684 381 9506	164	235494,038 618 5331
45	212,743 513 7907	105	7551,045 444 8676	165	249624,680 935 6451
46	226,508 124 6181	106	8005,108 171 5597	166	264603,161 791 7838
47	241,098 612 0952	107	8486,414 661 8532	167	280480,351 499 2909
48	256,564 528 8209	108	8996,599 541 5644	168	297310,172 589 2483
49	272,958 400 5502	109	9537,395 514 0583	169	315149,782 944 6032
50	290,335 904 5832	110	10110,639 244 9018	170	334059,769 921 2794
51	308,756 058 8582	111	10718,277 599 5959	171	354104,356 116 5562
52	328,281 422 3897	112	11362,374 255 5716	172	375351,617 483 5495
53	348,978 307 7331	113	12045,116 710 9059	173	397873,714 532 5625
54	370,917 006 1970	114	12768,823 713 5603	174	421747,137 404 5163
55	394,172 026 5689	115	13535,953 136 3739	175	447052,965 648 7872
56	418,822 348 1630	116	14349,110 324 5564	176	473877,143 587 7145
57	444,951 689 0528	117	15211,056 944 0297	177	502310,772 202 9774
58	472,648 790 3959	118	16124,720 360 6715	178	532450,418 535 1560
59	502,007 717 8197	119	17093,203 582 3118	179	564398,443 647 2654
60	533,128 180 8889	120	18119,795 797 2505	180	598263,350 266 1013

Present Value of 1 per period

The present value of a periodical payment of 1

$$a_{\overline{n}|} = \frac{1-v^n}{i} = \frac{(1+i)^n-1}{i\,(1+i)^n}$$

Effective Rates	*Number of periods*
3% increasing by $\frac{1}{16}$% to 6%	180

NOTE

Nominal annual rates at these effective rates, compounded half yearly and quarterly, are shown in the heading to each table.

Present Value of 1 per period

NOMINAL INTEREST RATE COMPOUNDED

YEARLY	HALF-YEARLY	QUARTERLY
@	@	@
3%	6%	12%
3.0000%	6.0000%	12.0000%
PER ANNUM	PER ANNUM	PER ANNUM

Periods	Present Value	Periods	Present Value	Periods	Present Value
1	.970 873 7864	61	27.840 353 0739	121	32.400 992 8205
2	1.913 469 6955	62	28.000 342 7902	122	32.428 148 3694
3	2.828 611 3549	63	28.155 672 6118	123	32.454 512 9800
4	3.717 098 4028	64	28.306 478 2639	124	32.480 109 6893
5	4.579 707 1872	65	28.452 891 5184	125	32.504 960 8634
6	5.417 191 4439	66	28.595 040 3091	126	32.529 088 2169
7	6.230 282 9552	67	28.733 048 8438	127	32.552 512 8320
8	7.019 692 1895	68	28.867 037 7124	128	32.575 255 1767
9	7.786 108 9219	69	28.997 123 9926	129	32.597 335 1230
10	8.530 202 8368	70	29.123 421 3521	130	32.618 771 9641
11	9.252 624 1134	71	29.246 040 1476	131	32.639 584 4311
12	9.954 003 9936	72	29.365 087 5220	132	32.659 790 7098
13	10.634 955 3336	73	29.480 667 4971	133	32.679 408 4561
14	11.296 073 1394	74	29.592 881 0651	134	32.698 454 8118
15	11.937 935 0868	75	29.701 826 2768	135	32.716 946 4192
16	12.561 102 0260	76	29.807 598 3270	136	32.734 899 4361
17	13.166 118 4718	77	29.910 289 6379	137	32.752 329 5496
18	13.753 513 0795	78	30.009 989 9397	138	32.769 251 9899
19	14.323 799 1063	79	30.106 786 3492	139	32.785 681 5436
20	14.877 474 8605	80	30.200 763 4458	140	32.801 632 5666
21	15.415 024 1364	81	30.292 003 3455	141	32.817 118 9967
22	15.936 916 6372	82	30.380 585 7723	142	32.832 154 3658
23	16.443 608 3857	83	30.456 588 1284	143	32.846 751 8114
24	16.935 542 1220	84	30.550 085 5616	144	32.860 924 0888
25	17.413 147 6913	85	30.631 151 0307	145	32.874 683 5813
26	17.876 842 4187	86	30.709 855 3696	146	32.888 042 3120
27	18.327 031 4745	87	30.786 267 3491	147	32.901 011 9534
28	18.764 108 2277	88	30.860 453 7370	148	32.913 603 8382
29	19.188 454 5900	89	30.932 479 3563	149	32.925 828 9691
30	19.600 441 3495	90	31.002 407 1421	150	32.937 698 0283
31	20.000 428 4946	91	31.070 298 1962	151	32.949 221 3867
32	20.388 765 5288	92	31.136 211 8409	152	32.960 409 1133
33	20.765 791 7755	93	31.200 205 6708	153	32.971 270 9838
34	21.131 836 6752	94	31.262 335 6027	154	32.981 816 4891
35	21.487 220 0731	95	31.322 655 9250	155	32.992 054 8438
36	21.832 252 4981	96	31.381 219 3446	156	33.001 994 9940
37	22.167 235 4351	97	31.438 077 0336	157	33.011 645 6252
38	22.492 461 5874	98	31.493 278 6734	158	33.021 015 1701
39	22.808 215 1334	99	31.546 872 4985	159	33.030 111 8156
40	23.114 771 9742	100	31.598 905 3383	160	33.038 943 5103
41	23.412 399 9750	101	31.649 422 6586	161	33.047 517 9712
42	23.701 359 1990	102	31.698 468 6006	162	33.055 842 6905
43	23.981 902 1349	103	31.746 086 0200	163	33.063 924 9422
44	24.254 273 9174	104	31.792 316 5242	164	33.071 771 7886
45	24.518 712 5412	105	31.837 200 5090	165	33.079 390 0860
46	24.775 449 0691	106	31.880 777 1932	166	33.086 786 4912
47	25.024 707 8341	107	31.923 084 6536	167	33.093 967 4672
48	25.266 706 6350	108	31.964 159 8578	168	33.100 939 2886
49	25.501 656 9272	109	32.004 038 6969	169	33.107 708 0472
50	25.729 764 0070	110	32.042 756 0164	170	33.114 279 6574
51	25.951 227 1913	111	32.080 345 6470	171	33.120 659 8616
52	26.166 239 9915	112	32.116 840 4340	172	33.126 854 2345
53	26.374 990 2830	113	32.152 272 2660	173	33.132 868 1889
54	26.577 660 4690	114	32.186 672 1029	174	33.138 706 9795
55	26.774 427 6398	115	32.220 070 0028	175	33.144 375 7082
56	26.965 463 7279	116	32.252 495 1484	176	33.149 879 3284
57	27.150 935 6582	117	32.283 975 8722	177	33.155 222 6489
58	27.331 005 4934	118	32.314 539 6818	178	33.160 410 3388
59	27.505 830 5761	119	32.344 213 2833	179	33.165 446 9308
60	27.675 563 6661	120	32.373 022 6051	180	33.170 336 8261

Present Value of 1 per period

NOMINAL INTEREST RATE COMPOUNDED

YEARLY	HALF-YEARLY	QUARTERLY
@	@	@
$3\frac{1}{16}\%$	$6\frac{1}{8}\%$	$12\frac{1}{4}\%$
3.0625%	6.1250%	12.2500%
PER ANNUM	PER ANNUM	PER ANNUM

Periods	Present Value	Periods	Present Value	Periods	Present Value
1	.970 285 0212	61	27.467 654 2161	121	31.804 384 1493
2	1.911 738 0436	62	27.621 738 4753	122	31.829 602 5706
3	2.825 215 8095	63	27.771 244 1240	123	31.854 071 6270
4	3.711 549 6029	64	27.916 307 2155	124	31.877 813 5859
5	4.571 546 0064	65	28.057 059 7603	125	31.900 850 0530
6	5.405 987 6351	66	28.193 629 8463	126	31.923 201 9920
7	6.215 633 8485	67	28.326 141 7551	127	31.944 889 7436
8	7.001 221 4418	68	28.454 716 0753	128	31.965 933 0442
9	7.763 465 3165	69	28.579 469 8123	129	31.986 351 0434
10	8.503 059 1307	70	28.700 516 4946	130	32.006 162 3223
11	9.220 675 9303	71	28.817 966 2774	131	32.025 384 9095
12	9.916 968 7620	72	28.931 926 0423	132	32.044 036 2979
13	10.592 571 2669	73	29.042 499 4953	133	32.062 133 4606
14	11.248 098 2578	74	29.149 787 2604	134	32.079 692 8666
15	11.884 146 2780	75	29.253 886 9719	135	32.096 730 4952
16	12.501 294 1448	76	29.354 893 3627	136	32.113 261 8510
17	13.100 103 4759	77	29.452 898 3507	137	32.129 301 9779
18	13.681 119 2004	78	29.547 991 1226	138	32.144 865 4728
19	14.244 870 0549	79	29.640 258 2147	139	32.159 966 4988
20	14.791 869 0648	80	29.729 783 5922	140	32.174 618 7981
21	15.322 614 0107	81	29.816 648 7250	141	32.188 835 7046
22	15.837 587 8818	82	29.900 932 6622	142	32.202 630 1561
23	16.337 259 3153	83	29.982 712 1040	143	32.216 014 7057
24	16.822 083 0227	84	30.062 061 4715	144	32.229 001 5338
25	17.292 500 2040	85	30.139 052 9742	145	32.241 602 4585
26	17.748 938 9487	86	30.213 756 6759	146	32.253 828 9470
27	18.191 814 6258	87	30.286 240 5588	147	32.265 692 1256
28	18.621 530 2615	88	30.356 570 5847	148	32.277 202 7902
29	19.038 476 9063	89	30.424 810 7553	149	32.288 371 4156
30	19.443 033 9903	90	30.491 023 1707	150	32.299 208 1655
31	19.835 569 6692	91	30.555 268 0856	151	32.309 722 9016
32	20.216 441 1587	92	30.617 603 9642	152	32.319 925 1926
33	20.585 995 0600	93	30.678 087 5335	153	32.329 824 3227
34	20.944 567 6750	94	30.736 773 8348	154	32.339 429 3004
35	21.292 485 3123	95	30.793 716 2739	155	32.348 748 8664
36	21.630 064 5844	96	30.848 966 6696	156	32.357 791 5016
37	21.957 612 6956	97	30.902 575 3010	157	32.366 565 4352
38	22.275 427 7216	98	30.954 590 9531	158	32.375 078 6515
39	22.583 798 8809	99	31.005 060 9612	159	32.383 338 8977
40	22.883 006 7977	100	31.054 031 2540	160	32.391 353 6910
41	23.173 323 7576	101	31.101 546 3956	161	32.399 130 3248
42	23.455 013 9552	102	31.147 649 6258	162	32.406 675 8761
43	23.728 333 7346	103	31.192 382 8995	163	32.413 997 2115
44	23.993 531 8225	104	31.235 786 9250	164	32.421 100 9935
45	24.250 849 5549	105	31.277 901 2007	165	32.427 993 6869
46	24.500 521 0963	106	31.318 764 0516	166	32.434 681 5640
47	24.742 773 6532	107	31.358 412 6638	167	32.441 170 7109
48	24.977 827 6805	108	31.396 883 1183	168	32.447 467 0331
49	25.205 897 0824	109	31.434 210 4241	169	32.453 576 2601
50	25.427 189 4068	110	31.470 428 5497	170	32.459 503 9516
51	25.641 906 0345	111	31.505 570 4545	171	32.465 255 5018
52	25.850 242 3621	112	31.539 668 1184	172	32.470 836 1449
53	26.052 387 9802	113	31.572 752 5709	173	32.476 250 9593
54	26.248 526 8456	114	31.604 853 9196	174	32.481 504 8725
55	26.438 837 4487	115	31.636 001 3775	175	32.486 602 6659
56	26.623 492 9763	116	31.666 223 2892	176	32.491 548 9784
57	26.802 661 4688	117	31.695 547 1575	177	32.496 348 3114
58	26.976 505 9734	118	31.723 999 6677	178	32.501 005 0323
59	27.145 184 6922	119	31.751 606 7121	179	32.505 523 3788
60	27.308 851 1265	120	31.778 393 4138	180	32.509 907 4628

NOMINAL INTEREST RATE COMPOUNDED

YEARLY	HALF-YEARLY	QUARTERLY
@	@	@
$3\frac{1}{8}\%$	$6\frac{1}{4}\%$	$12\frac{1}{2}\%$
3.1250%	6.2500%	12.5000%
PER ANNUM	PER ANNUM	PER ANNUM

Periods	Present Value	Periods	Present Value	Periods	Present Value
1	.969 696 9697	61	27.102 794 5596	121	31.227 122 5614
2	1.910 009 1827	62	27.251 194 7245	122	31.250 543 0898
3	2.821 827 0863	63	27.395 097 9147	123	31.273 253 9053
4	3.706 014 1443	64	27.534 640 4021	124	31.295 276 5142
5	4.563 407 6551	65	27.669 954 3293	125	31.316 631 7714
6	5.394 819 5443	66	27.801 167 8345	126	31.337 339 8995
7	6.201 037 1339	67	27.928 405 1728	127	31.357 420 5086
8	6.982 823 8874	68	28.051 786 8343	128	31.376 892 6144
9	7.740 920 1332	69	28.171 429 6575	129	31.395 774 6564
10	8.476 043 7656	70	28.287 446 9406	130	31.414 084 5153
11	9.188 890 9242	71	28.399 948 5484	131	31.431 839 5300
12	9.880 136 6537	72	28.509 041 0167	132	31.449 056 5139
13	10.550 435 5430	73	28.614 827 6525	133	31.465 751 7711
14	11.200 422 3447	74	28.717 408 6328	134	31.481 941 1114
15	11.830 712 5767	75	28.816 881 0984	135	31.497 639 8656
16	12.441 903 1047	76	28.913 339 2470	136	31.512 862 8999
17	13.034 572 7076	77	29.006 874 4213	137	31.527 624 6302
18	13.609 282 6255	78	29.097 575 1964	138	31.541 939 0354
19	14.166 577 0914	79	29.185 527 4632	139	31.555 819 6707
20	14.706 983 8462	80	29.270 814 5098	140	31.569 279 6807
21	15.231 014 6388	81	29.353 517 1004	141	31.582 331 8115
22	15.739 165 7103	82	29.433 713 5519	142	31.594 988 4233
23	16.231 918 2646	83	29.511 479 8079	143	31.607 261 5014
24	16.709 738 9232	84	29.586 889 5107	144	31.619 162 6680
25	17.173 080 1680	85	29.660 014 0709	145	31.630 703 1932
26	17.622 380 7689	86	29.730 922 7355	146	31.641 894 0056
27	18.058 066 2002	87	29.799 682 6526	147	31.652 745 7024
28	18.480 549 0426	88	29.866 358 9358	148	31.663 268 5599
29	18.890 229 3746	89	29.931 014 7257	149	31.673 472 5429
30	19.287 495 1512	90	29.993 711 2491	150	31.683 367 3143
31	19.672 722 5708	91	30.054 507 8779	151	31.692 962 2442
32	20.046 276 4323	92	30.113 462 1847	152	31.702 266 4186
33	20.408 510 4798	93	30.170 629 9972	153	31.711 288 6484
34	20.759 767 7380	94	30.226 065 4519	154	31.720 037 4772
35	21.100 380 8369	95	30.279 821 0442	155	31.728 521 1900
36	21.430 672 3267	96	30.331 947 6793	156	31.736 747 8206
37	21.750 954 9834	97	30.382 494 7193	157	31.744 725 1594
38	22.061 532 1051	98	30.431 510 0308	158	31.752 460 7606
39	22.362 697 7989	99	30.479 040 0299	159	31.759 961 9497
40	22.654 737 2596	100	30.525 129 7260	160	31.767 235 8300
41	22.937 927 0396	101	30.569 822 7646	161	31.774 289 2897
42	23.212 535 3111	102	30.613 161 4687	162	31.781 129 0082
43	23.478 822 1199	103	30.655 186 8787	163	31.787 761 4625
44	23.737 039 6314	104	30.695 938 7915	164	31.794 192 9333
45	23.987 432 3698	105	30.735 455 7978	165	31.800 429 5111
46	24.230 237 4495	106	30.773 775 3191	166	31.806 477 1017
47	24.465 684 7995	107	30.810 933 6427	167	31.812 341 4319
48	24.693 997 3814	108	30.846 965 9566	168	31.818 028 0552
49	24.915 391 4001	109	30.881 906 3821	169	31.823 542 3566
50	25.130 076 5092	110	30.915 788 0069	170	31.828 889 5579
51	25.338 256 0089	111	30.948 642 9158	171	31.834 074 7228
52	25.540 127 0390	112	30.980 502 2214	172	31.839 102 7615
53	25.735 880 7650	113	31.011 396 0935	173	31.843 978 4354
54	25.925 702 5600	114	31.041 353 7876	174	31.848 706 3616
55	26.109 772 1794	115	31.070 403 6728	175	31.853 291 0173
56	26.288 263 9316	116	31.098 573 2585	176	31.857 736 7440
57	26.461 346 8427	117	31.125 889 2204	177	31.862 047 7518
58	26.629 184 8172	118	31.152 377 4258	178	31.866 228 1230
59	26.791 936 7924	119	31.178 062 9584	179	31.870 281 8162
60	26.949 756 8896	120	31.202 970 1414	180	31.874 212 6703

Present Value of 1 per period

NOMINAL INTEREST RATE COMPOUNDED

YEARLY	HALF-YEARLY	QUARTERLY
@	@	@
$3\frac{3}{16}\%$	$6\frac{3}{8}\%$	$12\frac{3}{4}\%$
3.1875%	6.3750%	12.7500%
PER ANNUM	PER ANNUM	PER ANNUM

Periods	Present Value	Periods	Present Value	Periods	Present Value
1	,969 109 6305	61	26,745 572 6711	121	30,668 388 2220
2	1,908 283 1065	62	26,888 501 6801	122	30,690 140 0092
3	2,818 445 1668	63	27,027 015 5591	123	30,711 219 8757
4	3,700 491 9848	64	27,161 250 6933	124	30,731 648 5773
5	4,555 292 0507	65	27,291 339 2546	125	30,751 446 2288
6	5,383 687 0267	66	27,417 409 3321	126	30,770 632 3234
7	6,186 492 5759	67	27,539 585 0584	127	30,789 225 7526
8	6,964 499 1650	68	27,657 986 7313	128	30,807 244 8238
9	7,718 472 8431	69	27,772 730 9328	129	30,824 707 2793
10	8,449 155 9957	70	27,883 930 6436	130	30,841 630 3131
11	9,157 268 0758	71	27,991 695 3541	131	30,858 030 5881
12	9,843 506 3121	72	28,096 131 1730	132	30,873 924 2525
13	10,508 546 3958	73	28,197 340 9308	133	30,889 326 9558
14	11,153 043 1455	74	28,295 424 2818	134	30,904 253 8639
15	11,777 631 1525	75	28,390 477 8019	135	30,918 719 6743
16	12,382 925 4052	76	28,482 595 0836	136	30,932 738 6304
17	12,969 521 8948	77	28,571 866 8285	137	30,946 324 5359
18	13,537 998 2021	78	28,658 380 9361	138	30,959 490 7676
19	14,088 914 0663	79	28,742 222 5910	139	30,972 250 2897
20	14,622 811 9358	80	28,823 474 3462	140	30,984 615 6653
21	15,140 217 5029	81	28,902 216 2047	141	30,996 599 0700
22	15,641 640 2209	82	28,978 525 6981	142	31,008 212 3028
23	16,127 573 8058	83	29,052 477 9630	143	31,019 466 7986
24	16,598 496 7228	84	29,124 145 8152	144	31,030 373 6389
25	17,054 872 6568	85	29,193 599 8209	145	31,040 943 5628
26	17,497 150 9697	86	29,260 908 3667	146	31,051 186 9779
27	17,925 767 1420	87	29,326 137 7267	147	31,061 113 9701
28	18,341 143 2024	88	29,389 352 1276	148	31,070 734 3138
29	18,743 688 1429	89	29,450 613 8123	149	31,080 057 4816
30	19,133 798 3214	90	29,509 983 1010	150	31,089 092 6533
31	19,511 857 8523	91	29,567 518 4504	151	31,097 848 7252
32	19,878 238 9847	92	29,623 276 5116	152	31,106 334 3188
33	20,233 302 4685	93	29,677 312 1856	153	31,114 557 7892
34	20,577 397 9101	94	29,729 678 6778	154	31,122 527 2337
35	20,910 864 1164	95	29,780 427 5496	155	31,130 250 4990
36	21,234 029 4284	96	29,829 608 7701	156	31,137 735 1898
37	21,547 212 0445	97	29,877 270 7645	157	31,144 988 6758
38	21,850 720 3338	98	29,923 460 4622	158	31,152 018 0989
39	22,144 853 1400	99	29,968 223 3432	159	31,158 830 3805
40	22,429 900 0751	100	30,011 603 4822	160	31,165 432 2282
41	22,706 141 8051	101	30,053 643 5927	161	31,171 830 1424
42	22,973 850 3259	102	30,094 385 0686	162	31,178 030 4227
43	23,233 289 2317	103	30,133 868 0253	163	31,184 039 1740
44	23,484 713 9738	104	30,172 131 3389	164	31,189 862 3128
45	23,728 372 1127	105	30,209 212 6846	165	31,195 505 5727
46	23,964 503 5616	106	30,245 148 5738	166	31,200 974 5102
47	24,193 340 8229	107	30,279 974 3901	167	31,206 274 5102
48	24,415 109 2166	108	30,313 724 4241	168	31,211 410 7912
49	24,630 027 1027	109	30,346 431 9070	169	31,216 388 4106
50	24,838 306 0959	110	30,378 129 0438	170	31,221 212 2695
51	25,040 151 2741	111	30,408 847 0442	171	31,225 887 1176
52	25,235 761 3801	112	30,438 616 1543	172	31,230 417 5580
53	25,425 329 0176	113	30,467 465 6856	173	31,234 808 0513
54	25,609 040 8408	114	30,495 424 0442	174	31,239 062 9207
55	25,787 077 7379	115	30,522 518 7587	175	31,243 186 3557
56	25,959 615 0095	116	30,548 776 5076	176	31,247 182 4161
57	26,126 822 5410	117	30,574 223 1448	177	31,251 055 0368
58	26,288 864 9701	118	30,598 883 7260	178	31,254 808 0309
59	26,445 901 8487	119	30,622 782 5328	179	31,258 445 0935
60	26,598 087 8000	120	30,645 943 0966	180	31,261 969 8059

Present Value of 1 per period

NOMINAL INTEREST RATE COMPOUNDED

YEARLY	HALF-YEARLY	QUARTERLY
@	@	@
3¼%	6½%	13%
3.2500%	6.5000%	13.0000%
PER ANNUM	PER ANNUM	PER ANNUM

Periods	Present Value	Periods	Present Value	Periods	Present Value
1	,968 523 0024	61	26,395 792 9218	121	30,127 401 7645
2	1,906 559 8086	62	26,533 455 6143	122	30,147 604 6145
3	2,815 070 0326	63	26,666 785 0986	123	30,167 171 5395
4	3,694 983 0824	64	26,795 917 7710	124	30,186 122 5564
5	4,547 199 1113	65	26,920 985 7347	125	30,204 477 0522
6	5,372 589 9383	66	27,042 116 9343	126	30,222 253 8036
7	6,171 999 9402	67	27,159 435 2875	127	30,239 470 9962
8	6,946 246 9155	68	27,273 060 8111	128	30,256 146 2433
9	7,696 122 9206	69	27,383 109 7444	129	30,272 296 6037
10	8,422 395 0804	70	27,489 694 6677	130	30,287 938 5992
11	9,125 806 3733	71	27,592 924 6176	131	30,303 088 2317
12	9,807 076 3906	72	27,692 905 1987	132	30,317 760 9992
13	10,466 902 0732	73	27,789 738 6912	133	30,331 971 9121
14	11,105 958 4244	74	27,883 524 1561	134	30,345 735 5081
15	11,724 899 2004	75	27,974 357 5362	135	30,359 065 8674
16	12,324 357 5791	76	28,062 331 7542	136	30,371 976 6270
17	12,904 946 8079	77	28,147 536 8079	137	30,384 480 9947
18	13,467 260 8309	78	28,230 059 8624	138	30,396 591 7624
19	14,011 874 8967	79	28,309 985 3389	139	30,408 321 3195
20	14,539 346 1469	80	28,387 395 0014	140	30,419 681 6654
21	15,050 214 1859	81	28,462 368 0400	141	30,430 684 4217
22	15,545 001 6328	82	28,534 981 1526	142	30,441 340 8442
23	16,024 214 6565	83	28,605 308 6224	143	30,451 661 8346
24	16,488 343 4930	84	28,673 422 3945	144	30,461 657 9512
25	16,937 862 9472	85	28,739 392 1497	145	30,471 339 4201
26	17,373 232 8786	86	28,803 285 3750	146	30,480 716 1453
27	17,794 898 6718	87	28,865 167 4334	147	30,489 797 7195
28	18,203 291 6918	88	28,925 101 6304	148	30,498 593 4329
29	18,598 829 7257	89	28,983 149 2789	149	30,507 112 2837
30	18,981 917 4099	90	29,039 369 7616	150	30,515 362 9866
31	19,352 946 6440	91	29,093 820 5923	151	30,523 353 9822
32	19,712 296 9917	92	29,146 557 4744	152	30,531 093 4452
33	20,060 336 0695	93	29,197 634 3578	153	30,538 589 2932
34	20,397 419 9220	94	29,247 103 4942	154	30,545 849 1944
35	20,723 893 3869	95	29,295 015 4908	155	30,552 880 5757
36	21,040 090 4474	96	29,341 419 3615	156	30,559 690 6302
37	21,346 334 5738	97	29,386 362 5778	157	30,566 286 3246
38	21,642 939 0545	98	29,429 891 1165	158	30,572 674 4064
39	21,930 207 3167	99	29,472 049 5075	159	30,578 861 4106
40	22,208 433 2365	100	29,512 880 8789	160	30,584 853 6664
41	22,477 901 4397	101	29,552 427 0014	161	30,590 657 3040
42	22,738 887 5929	102	29,590 728 3306	162	30,596 278 2606
43	22,991 658 6857	103	29,627 824 0490	163	30,601 722 2863
44	23,236 473 3033	104	29,663 752 1056	164	30,606 994 9504
45	23,473 581 8918	105	29,698 549 2548	165	30,612 101 6469
46	23,703 227 0139	106	29,732 251 0943	166	30,617 047 5999
47	23,925 643 5970	107	29,764 892 1010	167	30,621 837 8691
48	24,141 059 1738	108	29,796 505 6668	168	30,626 477 3551
49	24,349 694 1151	109	29,827 124 1325	169	30,630 970 8039
50	24,551 761 8548	110	29,856 778 8208	170	30,635 322 8125
51	24,747 469 1088	111	29,885 500 0686	171	30,639 537 8330
52	24,937 016 0860	112	29,913 317 2577	172	30,643 620 1772
53	25,120 596 6934	113	29,940 258 8452	173	30,647 574 0215
54	25,298 398 7346	114	29,966 352 3925	174	30,651 403 4107
55	25,470 604 1013	115	29,991 624 5932	175	30,655 112 2621
56	25,637 388 9601	116	30,016 101 3009	176	30,658 704 3701
57	25,798 923 9323	117	30,039 807 5554	177	30,662 183 4093
58	25,955 374 2685	118	30,062 767 6081	178	30,665 552 9388
59	26,106 900 0180	119	30,085 004 9473	179	30,668 816 4056
60	26,253 656 1917	120	30,106 542 3219	180	30,671 977 1483

Present Value of 1 per period

NOMINAL INTEREST RATE COMPOUNDED

YEARLY	HALF-YEARLY	QUARTERLY
@	@	@
$3\frac{5}{16}\%$	$6\frac{5}{8}\%$	$13\frac{1}{4}\%$
3.3125%	6.6250%	12.2500%
PER ANNUM	PER ANNUM	PER ANNUM

Periods	Present Value	Periods	Present Value	Periods	Present Value
1	.967 937 0841	61	26.053 265 3069	121	29.603 422 0897
2	1.904 839 2828	62	26.185 858 7362	122	29.622 187 1406
3	2.811 701 6652	63	26.314 200 8336	123	29.640 350 5294
4	3.689 487 3952	64	26.438 427 9091	124	29.657 931 5469
5	4.539 128 7552	65	26.558 671 9024	125	29.674 948 8657
6	5.361 528 1357	66	26.675 060 5225	126	29.691 420 5596
7	6.157 558 9940	67	26.787 717 3842	127	29.707 364 1231
8	6.928 066 7819	68	26.896 762 1384	128	29.722 796 4894
9	7.673 869 8433	69	27.002 310 5997	129	29.737 734 0490
10	8.395 760 2839	70	27.104 474 8697	130	29.752 192 6669
11	9.094 504 8120	71	27.203 363 4552	131	29.766 187 6994
12	9.770 845 5531	72	27.299 081 3844	132	29.779 734 0103
13	10.425 500 8378	73	27.391 730 3176	133	29.792 845 9869
14	11.059 165 9652	74	27.481 408 6559	134	29.805 537 5554
15	11.672 513 9409	75	27.568 211 6451	135	29.817 822 1952
16	12.266 196 1921	76	27.652 231 4774	136	29.829 712 9536
17	12.840 843 2591	77	27.733 557 3889	137	29.841 222 4596
18	13.397 065 4656	78	27.812 275 7546	138	29.852 362 9373
19	13.935 453 5662	79	27.888 470 1799	139	29.863 146 2188
20	14.456 579 3744	80	27.962 221 5897	140	29.873 583 7569
21	14.960 996 3697	81	28.033 608 3143	141	29.883 686 6370
22	15.449 240 2852	82	28.102 706 1723	142	29.893 465 5894
23	15.921 829 6772	83	28.169 588 5516	143	29.902 931 0000
24	16.379 266 4752	84	28.234 326 4867	144	29.912 092 9220
25	16.822 036 5156	85	28.296 988 7348	145	29.920 961 0860
26	17.250 610 0574	86	28.357 641 8486	146	29.929 544 9108
27	17.665 442 2818	87	28.416 350 2467	147	29.937 853 5132
28	18.066 973 7755	88	28.473 176 2823	148	29.945 895 7176
29	18.455 630 9987	89	28.528 180 3096	149	29.953 680 0654
30	18.831 826 7380	90	28.581 420 7473	150	29.961 214 8243
31	19.195 960 5450	91	28.632 954 1414	151	29.968 507 9969
32	19.548 419 1603	92	28.682 835 2246	152	29.975 567 3292
33	19.889 576 9246	93	28.731 116 9748	153	29.982 400 3186
34	20.219 796 1763	94	28.777 850 6713	154	29.989 014 2225
35	20.539 427 6359	95	28.823 085 9492	155	29.995 416 0653
36	20.848 810 7788	96	28.866 870 8523	156	30.001 612 6464
37	21.148 274 1961	97	28.909 251 8836	157	30.007 610 5470
38	21.438 135 9430	98	28.950 274 0555	158	30.013 416 1375
39	21.718 703 8770	99	28.989 980 9370	159	30.019 035 5838
40	21.990 275 9850	100	29.028 414 7000	160	30.024 474 8542
41	22.253 140 6994	101	29.065 616 1646	161	30.029 739 7258
42	22.507 577 2045	102	29.101 624 8417	162	30.034 835 7903
43	22.753 855 7333	103	29.136 478 9756	163	30.039 768 4600
44	22.992 237 8544	104	29.170 215 5844	164	30.044 542 9740
45	23.222 976 7495	105	29.202 870 4991	165	30.049 164 4032
46	23.446 317 4829	106	29.234 478 4021	166	30.053 637 6558
47	23.662 497 2611	107	29.265 072 8635	167	30.057 967 4829
48	23.871 745 6853	108	29.294 686 3772	168	30.062 158 4832
49	24.074 284 9949	109	29.323 350 3954	169	30.066 215 1077
50	24.270 330 3036	110	29.351 095 3615	170	30.070 141 6651
51	24.460 089 8280	111	29.377 950 7431	171	30.073 942 3255
52	24.643 765 1088	112	29.403 945 0629	172	30.077 621 1258
53	24.821 551 2245	113	29.429 105 9290	173	30.081 181 9729
54	24.993 636 9989	114	29.453 460 0644	174	30.084 628 6489
55	25.160 205 2016	115	29.477 033 3352	175	30.087 964 8144
56	25.321 432 7420	116	29.499 850 7781	176	30.091 194 0128
57	25.477 490 8574	117	29.521 936 6274	177	30.094 319 6736
58	25.628 545 2945	118	29.543 314 3399	178	30.097 345 1166
59	25.774 756 4859	119	29.564 006 6206	179	30.100 273 5551
60	25.916 279 7201	120	29.584 035 4464	180	30.103 108 0993

Present Value of 1 per period

NOMINAL INTEREST RATE COMPOUNDED					
YEARLY @ $3\frac{3}{8}\%$ 3.3750% PER ANNUM		HALF-YEARLY @ $6\frac{3}{4}\%$ 6.7500% PER ANNUM		QUARTERLY @ $13\frac{1}{2}\%$ 13.5000% PER ANNUM	
Periods	Present Value	Periods	Present Value	Periods	Present Value
1	.967 351 8742	61	25.717 805 2714	121	29.095 744 2929
2	1.903 121 5228	62	25.845 519 0050	122	29.113 174 6486
3	2.808 340 0463	63	25.969 063 1245	123	29.130 035 9357
4	3.684 004 8815	64	26.088 573 7601	124	29.146 346 7335
5	4.531 080 9011	65	26.204 182 5975	125	29.162 125 0142
6	5.350 501 4763	66	26.316 017 0229	126	29.177 388 1637
7	6.143 169 5055	67	26.424 200 2640	127	29.192 153 0000
8	6.909 958 4092	68	26.528 851 5251	128	29.206 435 7920
9	7.651 713 0923	69	26.630 086 1186	129	29.220 252 2776
10	8.369 250 8753	70	26.728 015 5923	130	29.233 617 6809
11	9.063 362 3945	71	26.822 747 8523	131	29.246 546 7288
12	9.734 812 4735	72	26.914 387 2815	132	29.259 053 6675
13	10.384 340 9659	73	27.003 034 8552	133	29.271 152 2781
14	11.012 663 5704	74	27.088 788 2517	134	29.282 855 8918
15	11.620 472 6195	75	27.171 741 9605	135	29.294 177 4044
16	12.208 437 8423	76	27.251 987 3862	136	29.305 129 2908
17	12.777 207 1026	77	27.329 612 9492	137	29.315 723 6187
18	13.327 407 1125	78	27.404 704 1830	138	29.325 972 0616
19	13.859 644 1234	79	27.477 343 8288	139	29.335 885 9121
20	14.374 504 5933	80	27.547 611 9263	140	29.345 476 0939
21	14.872 555 8339	81	27.615 585 9021	141	29.354 753 1743
22	15.354 346 6350	82	27.681 340 6550	142	29.363 727 3754
23	15.820 407 8694	83	27.744 948 6384	143	29.372 408 5856
24	16.271 253 0780	84	27.806 479 9404	144	29.380 806 3706
25	16.707 379 0356	85	27.866 002 3608	145	29.388 929 9836
26	17.129 266 2980	86	27.923 581 4856	146	29.396 788 3759
27	17.537 379 7321	87	27.979 280 7600	147	29.404 390 2065
28	17.932 169 0274	88	28.033 161 5574	148	29.411 743 8515
29	18.314 069 1922	89	28.085 283 2478	149	29.418 857 4138
30	18.683 501 0323	90	28.135 703 2627	150	29.425 738 7316
31	19.040 871 6153	91	28.184 477 1586	151	29.432 395 3873
32	19.386 574 7186	92	28.231 658 6782	152	29.438 834 7156
33	19.720 991 2634	93	28.277 299 8096	153	29.445 063 8120
34	20.044 489 7349	94	28.321 450 8437	154	29.451 089 5400
35	20.357 426 5875	95	28.364 160 4292	155	29.456 918 5393
36	20.660 146 6385	96	28.405 475 6268	156	29.462 557 2327
37	20.952 983 4471	97	28.445 441 9606	157	29.468 011 8333
38	21.236 259 6828	98	28.484 103 4685	158	29.473 288 3514
39	21.510 287 4804	99	28.521 502 7507	159	29.478 392 6012
40	21.775 368 7839	100	28.557 681 0164	160	29.483 330 2067
41	22.031 795 6797	101	28.592 678 1295	161	29.488 106 6086
42	22.279 850 7180	102	28.626 532 6525	162	29.492 727 0700
43	22.519 807 2242	103	28.659 281 8888	163	29.497 196 6820
44	22.751 929 6002	104	28.690 961 9238	164	29.501 520 3695
45	22.976 473 6157	105	28.721 607 6651	165	29.505 702 8968
46	23.193 686 6899	106	28.751 252 8804	166	29.509 748 8723
47	23.403 808 1643	107	28.779 930 2350	167	29.513 662 7544
48	23.607 069 5665	108	28.807 671 3277	168	29.517 448 8555
49	23.803 694 8648	109	28.834 506 7257	169	29.521 111 3475
50	23.993 900 7156	110	28.860 465 9982	170	29.524 654 2660
51	24.177 896 7019	111	28.885 577 7492	171	29.528 081 5149
52	24.355 885 5641	112	28.909 869 6486	172	29.531 396 8705
53	24.528 063 4236	113	28.933 368 4629	173	29.534 603 9860
54	24.694 619 9986	114	28.956 100 0851	174	29.537 706 3952
55	24.855 738 8137	115	28.978 089 5623	175	29.540 707 5165
56	25.011 597 4014	116	28.999 361 1244	176	29.543 610 6568
57	25.162 367 4983	117	29.019 938 2098	177	29.546 419 0151
58	25.308 215 2342	118	29.039 843 4920	178	29.549 135 6857
59	25.449 301 3148	119	29.059 098 9039	179	29.551 763 6621
60	25.585 781 1993	120	29.077 725 6628	180	29.554 305 8400

Present Value of 1 per period

NOMINAL INTEREST RATE COMPOUNDED

YEARLY	HALF-YEARLY	QUARTERLY
@	@	@
$3\frac{7}{16}\%$	$6\frac{7}{8}\%$	$13\frac{3}{4}\%$
3.4375%	6.8750%	13.7500%
PER ANNUM	PER ANNUM	PER ANNUM

Periods	Present Value	Periods	Present Value	Periods	Present Value
1	.966 767 3716	61	25.389 233 5412	121	28.603 697 7117
2	1.901 406 5224	62	25.512 249 9492	122	28.619 889 0264
3	2.804 985 1576	63	25.631 178 1986	123	28.635 542 2612
4	3.678 535 4998	64	25.746 154 1497	124	28.650 675 2979
5	4.523 055 4681	65	25.857 309 1478	125	28.665 305 4239
6	5.339 509 8181	66	25.964 770 1731	126	28.679 449 3524
7	6.128 831 2441	67	26.068 659 9861	127	28.693 123 2410
8	6.891 921 4444	68	26.169 097 2675	128	28.706 342 7103
9	7.629 652 1517	69	26.266 196 7541	129	28.719 122 8620
10	8.342 866 1285	70	26.360 069 3695	130	28.731 478 2956
11	9.032 378 1303	71	26.450 822 3512	131	28.743 423 1256
12	9.698 975 8359	72	26.538 559 3727	132	28.754 970 9976
13	10.343 420 7477	73	26.623 380 6625	133	28.766 135 1034
14	10.966 449 0613	74	26.705 383 1178	134	28.776 928 1966
15	11.568 772 5064	75	26.784 660 4160	135	28.787 362 6070
16	12.151 079 1602	76	26.861 303 1212	136	28.797 450 2545
17	12.714 034 2334	77	26.935 398 7879	137	28.807 202 6630
18	13.258 280 8299	78	27.007 032 0608	138	28.816 630 9733
19	13.784 440 6815	79	27.076 284 7717	139	28.825 745 9560
20	14.293 114 8582	80	27.143 236 0331	140	28.834 558 0240
21	14.784 884 4551	81	27.207 962 3281	141	28.843 077 2437
22	15.260 311 2557	82	27.270 537 5981	142	28.851 313 3474
23	15.719 938 3741	83	27.331 033 3275	143	28.859 275 7437
24	16.164 290 8752	84	27.389 518 6248	144	28.866 973 5287
25	16.593 876 3749	85	27.446 060 3019	145	28.874 415 4960
26	17.009 185 6192	86	27.500 722 9505	146	28.881 610 1472
27	17.410 693 0457	87	27.553 569 0156	147	28.888 565 7012
28	17.798 857 3252	88	27.604 658 8670	148	28.895 290 1039
29	18.174 121 8854	89	27.654 050 8684	149	28.901 791 0370
30	18.536 915 4179	90	27.701 801 4438	150	28.908 075 9270
31	18.887 652 3677	91	27.747 965 1420	151	28.914 151 9536
32	19.226 733 4069	92	27.792 594 6992	152	28.920 026 0578
33	19.554 545 8919	93	27.835 741 0990	153	28.925 704 9502
34	19.871 464 3063	94	27.877 453 6304	154	28.931 195 1180
35	20.177 850 6889	95	27.917 779 9448	155	28.936 502 8331
36	20.474 055 0467	96	27.956 766 1098	156	28.941 634 1589
37	20.760 415 7551	97	27.994 456 6620	157	28.946 594 9572
38	21.037 259 9445	98	28.030 894 6582	158	28.951 390 8952
39	21.304 903 8738	99	28.066 121 7239	159	28.956 027 4516
40	21.563 653 2919	100	28.100 178 1017	160	28.960 509 9230
41	21.813 803 7868	101	28.133 102 6965	161	28.964 843 4301
42	22.055 641 1231	102	28.164 933 1204	162	28.969 032 9233
43	22.289 441 5692	103	28.195 705 7358	163	28.973 083 1887
44	22.515 472 2119	104	28.225 455 6962	164	28.976 998 8531
45	22.733 991 2623	105	28.254 216 9873	165	28.980 784 3897
46	22.945 248 3502	106	28.282 022 4651	166	28.984 444 1230
47	23.149 484 8099	107	28.308 903 8937	167	28.987 982 2337
48	23.346 933 9552	108	28.334 891 9818	168	28.991 402 7637
49	23.537 821 3464	109	28.360 016 4175	169	28.994 709 6205
50	23.722 365 0479	110	28.384 305 9021	170	28.997 906 5818
51	23.900 775 8771	111	28.407 788 1833	171	29.000 997 2996
52	24.073 257 6455	112	28.430 490 0866	172	29.003 985 3047
53	24.240 007 3915	113	28.452 437 5459	173	29.006 874 0106
54	24.401 215 6050	114	28.473 655 6335	174	29.009 666 7172
55	24.557 066 4460	115	28.494 168 5883	175	29.012 366 6148
56	24.707 737 9538	116	28.513 999 8437	176	29.014 976 7878
57	24.853 402 2514	117	28.533 172 0543	177	29.017 500 2178
58	24.994 225 7415	118	28.551 707 1220	178	29.019 939 7876
59	25.130 369 2970	119	28.569 626 2207	179	29.022 298 2841
60	25.261 988 4442	120	28.586 949 8206	180	29.024 578 4015

Present Value of 1 per period

NOMINAL INTEREST RATE COMPOUNDED

YEARLY @ $3\frac{1}{2}\%$ 3.5000% PER ANNUM		HALF-YEARLY @ 7% 7.0000% PER ANNUM		QUARTERLY @ 14% 14.0000% PER ANNUM	
Periods	Present Value	Periods	Present Value	Periods	Present Value
1	.966 183 5749	61	25.067 375 9597	121	28.126 644 0855
2	1.899 694 2752	62	25.185 870 4924	122	28.141 685 1067
3	2.801 636 9809	63	25.300 357 9637	123	28.156 217 4944
4	3.673 079 2086	64	25.410 973 8780	124	28.170 258 4487
5	4.515 052 3755	65	25.517 849 1575	125	28.183 824 5881
6	5.328 553 0198	66	25.621 110 2971	126	28.196 931 9692
7	6.114 543 9805	67	25.720 879 5141	127	28.209 596 1055
8	6.873 955 5367	68	25.817 274 8928	128	28.221 831 9860
9	7.607 686 5089	69	25.910 410 5245	129	28.233 654 0928
10	8.316 605 3226	70	26.000 396 6420	130	28.245 076 4181
11	9.001 551 0363	71	26.087 339 7507	131	28.256 112 4813
12	9.663 334 3346	72	26.171 342 7543	132	28.266 775 3442
13	10.302 738 4875	73	26.252 505 0766	133	28.277 077 6273
14	10.920 520 2778	74	26.330 922 7794	134	28.287 031 5239
15	11.517 410 8964	75	26.406 688 6757	135	28.296 648 8154
16	12.094 116 8081	76	26.479 892 4403	136	28.305 940 8844
17	12.651 320 5876	77	26.550 620 7153	137	28.314 918 7289
18	13.189 681 7271	78	26.618 957 2128	138	28.323 592 9748
19	13.709 837 4175	79	26.684 982 8143	139	28.331 973 8887
20	14.212 403 3020	80	26.748 775 6660	140	28.340 071 3901
21	14.697 974 2048	81	26.810 411 2715	141	28.347 895 0629
22	15.167 124 8355	82	26.869 962 5812	142	28.355 454 1670
23	15.620 410 4691	83	26.927 500 0784	143	28.362 757 6493
24	16.058 367 6030	84	26.983 091 8632	144	28.369 814 1539
25	16.481 514 5923	85	27.036 803 7326	145	28.376 632 0327
26	16.890 352 2631	86	27.088 699 2585	146	28.383 219 3553
27	17.285 364 5054	87	27.138 839 8633	147	28.389 583 9182
28	17.667 018 8458	88	27.187 284 8921	148	28.395 733 2543
29	18.035 767 0008	89	27.234 091 6832	149	28.401 674 6418
30	18.392 045 4114	90	27.279 315 6359	150	28.407 415 1129
31	18.736 275 7598	91	27.323 010 2762	151	28.412 961 4617
32	19.068 865 4684	92	27.365 227 3200	152	28.418 320 2529
33	19.390 208 1820	93	27.406 016 7343	153	28.423 497 8288
34	19.700 684 2338	94	27.445 426 7965	154	28.428 500 3177
35	20.000 661 0955	95	27.483 504 1512	155	28.433 333 6403
36	20.290 493 8121	96	27.520 293 8659	156	28.438 003 5172
37	20.570 525 4223	97	27.555 839 4839	157	28.442 515 4756
38	20.841 087 3645	98	27.590 183 0763	158	28.446 874 8556
39	21.102 499 8691	99	27.623 365 2911	159	28.451 086 8170
40	21.355 072 3373	100	27.655 425 4020	160	28.455 156 3450
41	21.599 103 7075	101	27.686 401 3546	161	28.459 088 2560
42	21.834 882 8092	102	27.716 329 8112	162	28.462 887 2039
43	22.062 688 7046	103	27.745 246 1944	163	28.466 557 6849
44	22.282 791 0189	104	27.773 184 7289	164	28.470 104 0434
45	22.495 450 2598	105	27.800 178 4820	165	28.473 530 4767
46	22.700 918 1254	106	27.826 259 4029	166	28.476 841 0403
47	22.899 437 8023	107	27.851 458 3603	167	28.480 039 6524
48	23.091 244 2535	108	27.875 805 1790	168	28.483 130 0990
49	23.276 564 4961	109	27.899 328 6754	169	28.486 116 0377
50	23.455 617 8706	110	27.922 056 6912	170	28.489 001 0026
51	23.628 616 3001	111	27.944 016 1268	171	28.491 788 4083
52	23.795 764 5412	112	27.965 232 9727	172	28.494 481 5539
53	23.957 260 4263	113	27.985 732 3408	173	28.497 083 6269
54	24.113 295 0978	114	28.005 538 4935	174	28.499 597 7072
55	24.264 053 2346	115	28.024 674 8730	175	28.502 026 7702
56	24.409 713 2702	116	28.043 164 1285	176	28.504 373 6911
57	24.550 447 6040	117	28.061 028 1434	177	28.506 641 2474
58	24.686 422 8058	118	28.078 288 0613	178	28.508 832 1231
59	24.817 799 8124	119	28.094 964 3104	179	28.510 948 9112
60	24.944 734 1182	120	28.111 076 6284	180	28.512 994 1171

Present Value of 1 per period

NOMINAL INTEREST RATE COMPOUNDED

YEARLY	HALF-YEARLY	QUARTERLY
@	@	@
$3\frac{9}{16}\%$	$7\frac{1}{8}\%$	$14\frac{1}{4}\%$
3.5625%	7.1250%	14.2500%
PER ANNUM	PER ANNUM	PER ANNUM

Periods	Present Value	Periods	Present Value	Periods	Present Value
1	,965 600 4828	61	24,752 063 3298	121	27,663 975 8216
2	1,897 984 7752	62	24,866 204 7843	122	27,677 948 8923
3	2,798 295 4981	63	24,976 419 8279	123	27,691 441 2961
4	3,667 635 9668	64	25,082 843 5273	124	27,704 469 5678
5	4,507 071 5430	65	25,185 606 3028	125	27,717 049 6731
6	5,317 630 9408	66	25,284 834 0884	126	27,729 197 0290
7	6,100 307 4866	67	25,380 648 4860	127	27,740 926 5217
8	6,856 060 3370	68	25,473 166 9147	128	27,752 252 5254
9	7,585 815 6544	69	25,562 502 7541	129	27,763 188 9202
10	8,290 467 7411	70	25,648 765 4837	130	27,773 749 1082
11	8,970 880 1362	71	25,732 060 8171	131	27,783 946 0308
12	9,627 886 6735	72	25,812 490 8313	132	27,793 792 1843
13	10,262 292 5031	73	25,890 154 0917	133	27,803 299 6348
14	10,874 875 0784	74	25,965 145 7736	134	27,812 480 0336
15	11,466 385 1089	75	26,037 557 7777	135	27,821 344 6311
16	12,037 547 4799	76	26,107 478 8439	136	27,829 904 2907
17	12,589 062 1411	77	26,174 994 6592	137	27,838 169 5022
18	13,121 604 9643	78	26,240 187 9630	138	27,846 150 3944
19	13,635 828 5714	79	26,303 138 6486	139	27,853 856 7478
20	14,132 363 1348	80	26,363 923 8611	140	27,861 298 0063
21	14,611 817 1488	81	26,422 618 0916	141	27,868 483 2891
22	15,074 778 1763	82	26,479 293 2689	142	27,875 421 4017
23	15,521 813 5679	83	26,534 018 8474	143	27,882 120 8465
24	15,953 471 1579	84	26,586 861 8925	144	27,888 589 8337
25	16,370 279 9352	85	26,637 887 1624	145	27,894 836 2909
26	16,772 750 6919	86	26,687 157 1875	146	27,900 867 8729
27	17,161 376 6487	87	26,734 732 3477	147	27,906 691 9714
28	17,536 634 0603	88	26,780 670 9452	148	27,912 315 7237
29	17,898 982 7982	89	26,825 029 2772	149	27,917 746 0217
30	18,248 866 9143	90	26,867 861 7040	150	27,922 989 5201
31	18,586 715 1858	91	26,909 220 7160	151	27,928 052 6446
32	18,912 941 6399	92	26,949 156 9980	152	27,932 941 6001
33	19,227 946 0615	93	26,987 719 4911	153	27,937 662 3779
34	19,532 114 4830	94	27,024 955 4531	154	27,942 220 7632
35	19,825 819 6577	95	27,060 910 5160	155	27,946 622 3423
36	20,109 421 5162	96	27,095 628 7420	156	27,950 872 5091
37	20,383 267 6077	97	27,129 152 6779	157	27,954 976 4723
38	20,647 693 5258	98	27,161 523 4065	158	27,958 939 2611
39	20,903 023 3200	99	27,192 780 5977	159	27,962 765 7319
40	21,149 569 8926	100	27,222 962 5566	160	27,966 460 5740
41	21,387 635 3821	101	27,252 106 2707	161	27,970 028 3152
42	21,617 511 5337	102	27,280 247 4552	162	27,973 473 3279
43	21,839 480 0567	103	27,307 420 5964	163	27,976 799 8338
44	22,053 812 9697	104	27,333 658 9947	164	27,980 011 9096
45	22,260 772 9339	105	27,358 994 8048	165	27,983 113 4914
46	22,460 613 5753	106	27,383 459 0752	166	27,986 108 3804
47	22,653 579 7951	107	27,407 081 7866	167	27,989 000 2466
48	22,839 908 0701	108	27,429 891 8881	168	27,991 792 6340
49	23,019 826 7424	109	27,451 917 3331	169	27,994 488 9646
50	23,193 556 2992	110	27,473 185 1134	170	27,997 092 5428
51	23,361 309 6432	111	27,493 721 2924	171	27,999 606 5591
52	23,523 292 3531	112	27,513 551 0367	172	28,002 034 0945
53	23,679 702 9360	113	27,532 698 6474	173	28,004 378 1239
54	23,830 733 0704	114	27,551 187 5895	174	28,006 641 5197
55	23,976 567 8410	115	27,569 040 5210	175	28,008 827 0559
56	24,117 385 9660	116	27,586 279 3202	176	28,010 937 4106
57	24,253 360 0155	117	27,602 925 1130	177	28,012 975 1702
58	24,384 656 6233	118	27,618 998 2986	178	28,014 942 8318
59	24,511 436 6911	119	27,634 518 5744	179	28,016 842 8068
60	24,633 855 5859	120	27,649 504 9602	180	28,018 677 4236

Present Value of 1 per period

NOMINAL INTEREST RATE COMPOUNDED

YEARLY	HALF-YEARLY	QUARTERLY
@	@	@
$3\frac{5}{8}\%$	$7\frac{1}{4}\%$	$14\frac{1}{2}\%$
3.6250%	7.2500%	14.5000%
PER ANNUM	PER ANNUM	PER ANNUM

Periods	Present Value	Periods	Present Value	Periods	Present Value
1	.965 018 0941	61	24.443 131 2614	121	27.215 114 3611
2	1.896 278 0160	62	24.553 082 0375	122	27.228 095 8853
3	2.794 960 6910	63	24.659 186 5259	123	27.240 623 2910
4	3.662 205 7331	64	24.761 579 2771	124	27.252 712 4642
5	4.499 112 8908	65	24.860 390 1348	125	27.264 378 7350
6	5.306 743 4411	66	24.955 744 4003	126	27.275 636 8975
7	6.086 121 5354	67	25.047 762 9918	127	27.286 501 2280
8	6.838 235 4986	68	25.136 562 5976	128	27.296 985 5035
9	7.564 039 0819	69	25.222 255 8240	129	27.307 103 0190
10	8.264 452 6725	70	25.304 951 3380	130	27.316 866 6046
11	8.940 364 4608	71	25.384 754 0053	131	27.326 288 6414
12	9.592 631 5665	72	25.451 765 0232	132	27.335 381 0773
13	10.222 081 1257	73	25.536 082 0490	133	27.344 155 4425
14	10.829 511 3397	74	25.607 799 3235	134	27.352 622 8637
15	11.415 692 4870	75	25.677 007 7911	135	27.360 794 0784
16	11.981 367 9006	76	25.743 795 2145	136	27.368 679 4484
17	12.527 254 9101	77	25.808 246 2866	137	27.376 288 9731
18	13.054 045 7516	78	25.870 442 7374	138	27.383 632 3021
19	13.562 408 4455	79	25.930 463 4378	139	27.390 718 7475
20	14.052 987 6434	80	25.988 384 4997	140	27.397 557 2956
21	14.526 405 4460	81	26.044 279 3724	141	27.404 156 6182
22	14.983 262 1915	82	26.098 218 9360	142	27.410 525 0839
23	15.424 137 2174	83	26.150 271 5908	143	27.416 670 7685
24	15.849 589 5946	84	26.200 503 3446	144	27.422 601 4654
25	16.260 158 8368	85	26.248 977 8959	145	27.428 324 6952
26	16.656 365 5843	86	26.295 756 7149	146	27.433 847 7155
27	17.038 712 2647	87	26.340 899 1218	147	27.439 177 5300
28	17.407 683 7295	88	26.384 462 3612	148	27.444 320 8975
29	17.763 747 8693	89	26.426 501 6754	149	27.449 284 3402
30	18.107 356 2068	90	26.467 070 3744	150	27.454 074 1522
31	18.438 944 4698	91	26.505 219 9029	151	27.458 696 4074
32	18.758 933 1433	92	26.543 999 9063	152	27.463 156 9673
33	19.067 728 0032	93	26.580 458 2932	153	27.467 461 4884
34	19.365 720 6303	94	26.615 641 2962	154	27.471 615 4291
35	19.653 288 9075	95	26.649 593 5307	155	27.475 624 0570
36	19.930 797 4981	96	26.682 358 0513	156	27.479 492 4555
37	20.198 598 3094	97	26.713 976 4066	157	27.483 225 5300
38	20.457 030 9379	98	26.744 488 6915	158	27.486 828 0145
39	20.706 423 1005	99	26.773 933 5986	159	27.490 304 4772
40	20.947 091 0500	100	26.802 348 4667	160	27.493 659 3266
41	21.179 339 9758	101	26.829 769 3285	161	27.496 896 8170
42	21.403 464 3917	102	26.856 230 9563	162	27.500 021 0538
43	21.619 748 5082	103	26.881 766 9060	163	27.503 035 9988
44	21.828 466 5942	104	26.906 409 5595	164	27.505 945 4754
45	22.029 883 3237	105	26.930 190 1659	165	27.508 753 1728
46	22.224 254 1121	106	26.953 138 8815	166	27.511 462 6517
47	22.411 825 4399	107	26.975 284 8072	167	27.514 077 3479
48	22.592 835 1652	108	26.996 656 0263	168	27.516 600 5769
49	22.767 512 8253	109	27.017 279 6394	169	27.519 035 5387
50	22.936 079 9279	110	27.037 181 7991	170	27.521 385 3208
51	23.098 750 2320	111	27.056 387 7434	171	27.523 652 9031
52	23.255 730 0188	112	27.074 921 8272	172	27.525 841 1610
53	23.407 218 3535	113	27.092 807 5534	173	27.527 952 8695
54	23.553 407 3375	114	27.110 067 6028	174	27.529 990 7063
55	23.694 482 3522	115	27.126 723 8628	175	27.531 957 2558
56	23.830 622 2941	116	27.142 797 4550	176	27.533 855 0117
57	23.961 999 8013	117	27.158 308 7624	177	27.535 686 3804
58	24.088 781 4729	118	27.173 277 4546	178	27.537 453 6843
59	24.211 128 0800	119	27.187 722 5135	179	27.539 159 1646
60	24.329 194 7696	120	27.201 662 2567	180	27.540 804 9839

Present Value of 1 per period

NOMINAL INTEREST RATE COMPOUNDED

YEARLY @ $3\frac{11}{16}\%$ 3.6875% PER ANNUM		HALF-YEARLY @ $7\frac{3}{8}\%$ 7.3750% PER ANNUM		QUARTERLY @ $14\frac{3}{4}\%$ 14.7500% PER ANNUM	
Periods	Present Value	Periods	Present Value	Periods	Present Value
1	.964 436 4075	61	24.140 420 0234	121	26.779 508 6379
2	1.894 573 9915	62	24.246 336 3698	122	26.791 569 5121
3	2.791 632 5416	63	24.348 485 9504	123	26.803 201 4584
4	3.656 788 4669	64	24.447 002 7249	124	26.814 419 7308
5	4.491 176 3393	65	24.542 015 8890	125	26.825 239 0411
6	5.295 890 3815	66	24.633 650 0436	126	26.835 673 5780
7	6.071 985 9014	67	24.722 025 3585	127	26.845 737 0252
8	6.820 480 6765	68	24.807 257 7297	128	26.855 442 5800
9	7.542 356 2883	69	24.889 458 9316	129	26.864 802 9705
10	8.238 559 4101	70	24.968 736 7635	130	26.873 830 4718
11	8.910 003 0477	71	25.045 195 1908	131	26.882 536 9228
12	9.557 567 7374	72	25.118 934 4818	132	26.890 933 7411
13	10.182 102 7003	73	25.190 051 3387	133	26.899 031 9384
14	10.784 426 9563	74	25.258 639 0246	134	26.906 842 1347
15	11.365 330 3979	75	25.324 787 4861	135	26.914 374 5723
16	11.925 574 8262	76	25.388 583 4706	136	26.921 639 1294
17	12.465 894 9499	77	25.450 110 6407	137	26.928 645 3328
18	12.986 999 3489	78	25.509 449 6837	138	26.935 402 3704
19	13.489 571 4034	79	25.566 678 4170	139	26.941 919 1034
20	13.974 270 1901	80	25.621 871 8910	140	26.948 204 0780
21	14.441 731 3467	81	25.675 102 4868	141	26.954 265 5364
22	14.892 567 9052	82	25.726 440 0114	142	26.960 111 4275
23	15.327 371 0960	83	25.775 951 7892	143	26.965 749 4177
24	15.746 711 1234	84	25.823 702 7503	144	26.971 186 9008
25	16.151 137 9128	85	25.869 755 5156	145	26.976 431 0074
26	16.541 181 8328	86	25.914 170 4792	146	26.981 488 6147
27	16.917 354 3896	87	25.957 005 8871	147	26.986 366 3553
28	17.280 148 8990	88	25.998 317 9141	148	26.991 070 6260
29	17.630 041 1322	89	26.038 160 7369	149	26.995 607 5959
30	17.967 489 9407	90	26.076 586 6058	150	26.999 983 2149
31	18.292 937 8572	91	26.113 645 9128	151	27.004 203 2211
32	18.606 811 6766	92	26.149 387 2576	152	27.008 273 1487
33	18.909 523 0154	93	26.183 857 5119	153	27.012 198 3351
34	19.201 468 8515	94	26.217 101 8801	154	27.015 983 9278
35	19.483 032 0449	95	26.249 163 9591	155	27.019 634 8912
36	19.754 581 8395	96	26.280 085 7954	156	27.023 156 0132
37	20.016 474 3480	97	26.309 907 9401	157	27.026 551 9114
38	20.269 053 0179	98	26.338 669 5022	158	27.029 827 0394
39	20.512 649 0830	99	26.366 408 1998	159	27.032 985 6920
40	20.747 581 9968	100	26.393 160 4097	160	27.036 032 0115
41	20.974 159 8523	101	26.418 961 2149	161	27.038 969 9931
42	21.192 679 7852	102	26.443 844 4508	162	27.041 803 4894
43	21.403 428 3643	103	26.467 842 7494	163	27.044 536 2164
44	21.606 681 9668	104	26.490 987 5823	164	27.047 171 7578
45	21.802 707 1409	105	26.513 309 3018	165	27.049 713 5699
46	21.991 760 9557	106	26.534 837 1808	166	27.052 164 9861
47	22.174 091 3376	107	26.555 599 4510	167	27.054 529 2211
48	22.349 937 3961	108	26.575 623 3403	168	27.056 809 3753
49	22.519 529 7371	109	26.594 935 1082	169	27.059 008 4391
50	22.683 090 7651	110	26.613 560 0802	170	27.061 129 2963
51	22.840 834 9754	111	26.631 522 6814	171	27.063 174 7282
52	22.992 969 2349	112	26.648 846 4679	172	27.065 147 4172
53	23.139 693 0535	113	26.665 554 1583	173	27.067 049 9503
54	23.281 198 8461	114	26.681 667 6632	174	27.068 884 8225
55	23.417 672 1843	115	26.697 208 1140	175	27.070 654 4400
56	23.549 292 0403	116	26.712 195 8905	176	27.072 361 1236
57	23.676 231 0214	117	26.726 650 6479	177	27.074 007 1113
58	23.798 655 5963	118	26.740 591 3422	178	27.075 594 5619
59	23.916 726 3135	119	26.754 036 2552	179	27.077 125 5570
60	24.030 598 0118	120	26.767 003 0189	180	27.078 602 1044

Present Value of 1 per period

NOMINAL INTEREST RATE COMPOUNDED

YEARLY	HALF-YEARLY	QUARTERLY
@	@	@
$3\frac{3}{4}\%$	$7\frac{1}{2}\%$	15%
3.7500%	7.5000%	15.0000%
PER ANNUM	PER ANNUM	PER ANNUM

Periods	Present Value	Periods	Present Value	Periods	Present Value
1	.963 855 4217	61	23.843 774 4009	121	26.356 633 6252
2	1.892 872 6956	62	23.945 806 6515	122	26.367 839 6388
3	2.788 311 0319	63	24.044 150 9894	123	26.378 640 6157
4	3.651 384 1271	64	24.138 940 7126	124	26.389 051 1958
5	4.483 261 8093	65	24.230 304 3013	125	26.399 085 4900
6	5.285 071 6234	66	24.318 365 5916	126	26.408 757 0988
7	6.057 900 3599	67	24.403 243 9438	127	26.418 079 1313
8	6.802 795 5276	68	24.485 054 4036	128	26.427 064 2230
9	7.520 766 7736	69	24.563 907 8589	129	26.435 724 5523
10	8.212 787 2517	70	24.639 911 1893	130	26.444 071 8576
11	8.879 794 9414	71	24.713 167 4114	131	26.452 117 4531
12	9.522 693 9194	72	24.783 775 8182	132	26.459 872 2440
13	10.142 355 5850	73	24.851 832 1139	133	26.467 346 7412
14	10.739 619 8409	74	24.917 428 5435	134	26.474 551 0758
15	11.315 296 2322	75	24.980 654 0179	135	26.481 495 0128
16	11.870 165 0431	76	25.041 594 2341	136	26.488 187 9642
17	12.404 978 3548	77	25.100 331 7919	137	26.494 639 0016
18	12.920 461 0649	78	25.156 946 3054	138	26.500 856 8690
19	13.417 311 8698	79	25.211 514 5113	139	26.506 849 9942
20	13.896 204 2118	80	25.264 110 3723	140	26.512 626 5005
21	14.357 787 1921	81	25.314 805 1781	141	26.518 194 2173
22	14.802 686 4502	82	25.363 667 6416	142	26.523 560 6914
23	15.231 505 0123	83	25.410 763 9919	143	26.528 733 1965
24	15.644 824 1082	84	25.456 158 0645	144	26.533 718 7436
25	16.043 203 9597	85	25.499 911 3874	145	26.538 524 0903
26	16.427 184 5395	86	25.542 083 2650	146	26.543 155 7496
27	16.797 286 3031	87	25.582 730 8578	147	26.547 619 9997
28	17.154 010 8946	88	25.621 909 2606	148	26.551 922 8912
29	17.497 841 8261	89	25.659 671 5764	149	26.556 070 2566
30	17.829 245 1336	90	25.695 068 9893	150	26.560 067 7172
31	18.148 670 0083	91	25.731 150 8331	151	26.563 920 6913
32	18.456 549 4056	92	25.764 964 6584	152	26.567 634 4013
33	18.753 300 6319	93	25.797 556 2973	153	26.571 213 8807
34	19.039 325 9102	94	25.828 969 9251	154	26.574 663 9814
35	19.315 012 9255	95	25.859 248 1205	155	26.577 989 3797
36	19.580 735 3499	96	25.888 431 9234	156	26.581 194 5828
37	19.836 853 3493	97	25.916 560 8900	157	26.584 283 9353
38	20.083 714 0716	98	25.943 673 1470	158	26.587 261 6243
39	20.321 652 1172	99	25.969 805 4429	159	26.590 131 6861
40	20.550 989 9925	100	25.994 993 1980	160	26.592 898 0107
41	20.772 038 5470	101	26.019 270 5523	161	26.595 564 3477
42	20.985 097 3947	102	26.042 670 4118	162	26.598 134 3110
43	21.190 455 3202	103	26.065 224 4933	163	26.600 611 3841
44	21.388 390 6701	104	26.086 963 3671	164	26.602 998 9244
45	21.579 171 7302	105	26.107 916 4984	165	26.605 300 1681
46	21.763 057 0893	106	26.128 112 2876	166	26.607 518 2343
47	21.940 295 9897	107	26.147 578 1085	167	26.609 656 1295
48	22.111 128 6648	108	26.166 340 3456	168	26.611 716 7513
49	22.275 786 6649	109	26.184 424 4295	169	26.613 702 8928
50	22.434 493 1709	110	26.201 854 8718	170	26.615 617 2461
51	22.587 463 2973	111	26.218 655 2981	171	26.617 462 4059
52	22.734 904 3829	112	26.234 848 4801	172	26.619 240 8731
53	22.877 016 2727	113	26.250 456 3664	173	26.620 955 0585
54	23.013 991 5882	114	26.265 500 1121	174	26.622 607 2853
55	23.146 015 9886	115	26.280 000 1081	175	26.624 199 7930
56	23.273 268 4227	116	26.293 976 0078	176	26.625 734 7403
57	23.395 921 3713	117	26.307 446 7545	177	26.627 214 2075
58	23.514 141 0808	118	26.320 430 6068	178	26.628 640 2000
59	23.628 087 7887	119	26.332 945 1631	179	26.630 014 6506
60	23.737 915 9409	120	26.345 007 3862	180	26.631 339 4222

Present Value of 1 per period

NOMINAL INTEREST RATE COMPOUNDED

YEARLY	HALF-YEARLY	QUARTERLY
@	@	@
$3\frac{13}{16}\%$	$7\frac{5}{8}\%$	$15\frac{1}{4}\%$
3.8125%	7.6250%	15.2500%
PER ANNUM	PER ANNUM	PER ANNUM

Periods	Present Value	Periods	Present Value	Periods	Present Value
1	.963 275 1355	61	23.553 043 5566	121	25.945 988 9656
2	1.891 174 1221	62	23.651 336 3579	122	25.956 401 1710
3	2.784 996 1441	63	23.746 019 3694	123	25.966 430 9895
4	3.645 992 6734	64	23.837 225 1602	124	25.976 092 4643
5	4.475 369 2218	65	23.925 081 4307	125	25.985 399 1228
6	5.274 287 0288	66	24.009 711 1915	126	25.994 363 9954
7	6.043 864 6876	67	24.091 232 9358	127	26.002 999 6344
8	6.785 179 7111	68	24.169 760 8051	128	26.011 318 1306
9	7.499 270 0408	69	24.245 404 7491	129	26.019 331 1313
10	8.187 135 4999	70	24.318 270 6794	130	26.027 049 8555
11	8.849 739 1932	71	24.388 460 6183	131	26.034 485 1107
12	9.488 008 8555	72	24.456 072 8413	132	26.041 647 3071
13	10.102 838 1510	73	24.521 202 0145	133	26.048 546 4728
14	10.695 087 9239	74	24.583 939 3276	134	26.055 192 2676
15	11.265 587 4041	75	24.644 372 6214	135	26.061 593 9965
16	11.815 135 3682	76	24.702 586 5107	136	26.067 760 6228
17	12.344 501 2578	77	24.758 662 5028	137	26.073 700 7805
18	12.854 426 2567	78	24.812 679 1116	138	26.079 422 7868
19	13.345 624 3292	79	24.864 711 9679	139	26.084 934 6531
20	13.818 783 2190	80	24.914 833 9245	140	26.090 244 0969
21	14.274 565 4126	81	24.963 115 1591	141	26.095 358 5521
22	14.713 609 0669	82	25.009 623 2718	142	26.100 285 1796
23	15.136 528 9025	83	25.054 423 3804	143	26.105 030 8774
24	15.543 917 0644	84	25.097 578 2111	144	26.109 602 2901
25	15.936 343 9513	85	25.139 148 1865	145	26.114 005 8183
26	16.314 359 0139	86	25.179 191 5102	146	26.118 247 6275
27	16.678 491 5245	87	25.217 764 2482	147	26.122 333 6568
28	17.029 251 3180	88	25.254 920 4077	148	26.126 269 6273
29	17.367 129 5056	89	25.290 712 0122	149	26.130 061 0498
30	17.692 599 1625	90	25.325 189 1749	150	26.133 713 2328
31	18.006 115 9904	91	25.358 400 1685	151	26.137 231 2898
32	18.308 118 9552	92	25.390 391 4928	152	26.140 620 1468
33	18.599 030 9021	93	25.421 207 9401	153	26.143 884 5483
34	18.879 259 1471	94	25.450 892 6576	154	26.147 029 0652
35	19.149 196 0478	95	25.479 487 2078	155	26.150 058 1002
36	19.409 219 5524	96	25.507 031 6270	156	26.152 975 8942
37	19.659 693 7289	97	25.533 564 4811	157	26.155 786 5326
38	19.900 969 2753	98	25.559 122 9198	158	26.158 493 9508
39	20.133 384 0099	99	25.583 742 7283	159	26.161 101 9393
40	20.357 263 3449	100	25.607 458 3777	160	26.163 614 1499
41	20.572 920 7416	101	25.630 303 0730	161	26.166 034 0998
42	20.780 658 1497	102	25.652 308 8000	162	26.168 365 1774
43	20.980 766 4296	103	25.673 506 3697	163	26.170 610 6465
44	21.173 525 7600	104	25.693 925 4614	164	26.172 773 6511
45	21.359 206 0301	105	25.713 594 6648	165	26.174 857 2196
46	21.538 067 2174	106	25.732 541 5194	166	26.176 864 2693
47	21.710 359 7519	107	25.750 792 5533	167	26.178 797 6104
48	21.876 324 8663	108	25.768 373 3205	168	26.180 659 9498
49	22.036 194 9345	109	25.785 308 4363	169	26.182 453 8951
50	22.190 193 7960	110	25.801 621 6124	170	26.184 181 9579
51	22.338 537 0702	111	25.817 335 6892	171	26.185 846 5579
52	22.481 432 4577	112	25.832 472 6687	172	26.187 450 0257
53	22.619 080 0315	113	25.847 053 7447	173	26.188 994 6063
54	22.751 672 5168	114	25.861 099 3326	174	26.190 482 4624
55	22.879 395 5611	115	25.874 629 0983	175	26.191 915 6772
56	23.002 427 9938	116	25.887 661 9851	176	26.193 296 2574
57	23.120 942 0771	117	25.900 216 2409	177	26.194 626 1360
58	23.235 103 7468	118	25.912 309 4434	178	26.195 907 1749
59	23.345 072 8446	119	25.923 958 5246	179	26.197 141 1679
60	23.451 003 3421	120	25.935 179 7949	180	26.198 329 8427

Present Value of 1 per period

NOMINAL INTEREST RATE COMPOUNDED

	YEARLY @ $3\frac{7}{8}\%$ 3.8750% PER ANNUM		HALF-YEARLY @ $7\frac{3}{4}\%$ 7.7500% PER ANNUM		QUARTERLY @ $15\frac{1}{2}\%$ 15.5000% PER ANNUM
Periods	Present Value	Periods	Present Value	Periods	Present Value
1	.962 695 5475	61	23.268 080 8971	121	25.547 097 6781
2	1.889 478 2648	62	23.362 773 4268	122	25.556 772 7346
3	2.781 687 8602	63	23.453 933 5035	123	25.566 086 8685
4	3.640 614 0652	64	23.541 692 9035	124	25.575 053 5437
5	4.467 498 4984	65	23.626 178 4872	125	25.583 685 7219
6	5.263 536 4605	66	23.707 512 3823	126	25.591 995 8815
7	6.029 878 6623	67	23.785 812 1611	127	25.599 996 0352
8	6.767 632 8879	68	23.861 191 0095	128	25.607 697 7475
9	7.477 865 5961	69	23.933 757 8912	129	25.615 112 1516
10	8.161 603 4619	70	24.003 617 7051	130	25.622 249 9654
11	8.819 834 8611	71	24.070 871 4369	131	25.629 121 5070
12	9.453 511 2983	72	24.135 616 3051	132	25.635 736 7095
13	10.063 548 7829	73	24.197 945 9014	133	25.642 105 1355
14	10.650 829 1532	74	24.257 950 3263	134	25.648 235 9909
15	11.216 201 3509	75	24.315 716 3189	135	25.654 138 1380
16	11.760 482 6483	76	24.371 327 3828	136	25.659 820 1088
17	12.284 459 8299	77	24.424 863 9065	137	25.665 290 1168
18	12.788 890 3296	78	24.476 403 2794	138	25.670 556 0691
19	13.274 503 3257	79	24.526 020 0042	139	25.675 625 5780
20	13.742 000 7949	80	24.573 785 8043	140	25.680 505 9716
21	14.192 058 5270	81	24.619 769 7274	141	25.685 204 3048
22	14.625 327 1018	82	24.664 038 2454	142	25.689 727 3692
23	15.042 432 8297	83	24.706 655 3505	143	25.694 081 7032
24	15.443 978 6567	84	24.747 682 6479	144	25.698 273 6012
25	15.830 545 0365	85	24.787 179 4445	145	25.702 309 1227
26	16.202 690 7692	86	24.825 202 8346	146	25.706 194 1012
27	16.560 953 8091	87	24.861 807 7830	147	25.709 934 1528
28	16.905 852 0425	88	24.897 047 2039	148	25.713 534 6838
29	17.237 884 0361	89	24.930 972 0374	149	25.717 000 8990
30	17.557 529 7580	90	24.963 631 3236	150	25.720 337 8089
31	17.865 251 2712	91	24.995 072 2731	151	25.723 550 2372
32	18.161 493 4019	92	25.025 340 3351	152	25.726 642 8276
33	18.446 684 3821	93	25.054 479 2636	153	25.729 620 0507
34	18.721 236 4689	94	25.082 531 1804	154	25.732 486 2100
35	18.985 546 5405	95	25.109 536 6357	155	25.735 245 4489
36	19.239 996 6695	96	25.135 534 6674	156	25.737 901 7558
37	19.484 954 6758	97	25.160 562 8567	157	25.740 458 9707
38	19.720 774 6578	98	25.184 657 3831	158	25.742 920 7901
39	19.947 797 5045	99	25.207 853 0764	159	25.745 290 7727
40	20.166 351 3882	100	25.230 183 4670	160	25.747 572 3443
41	20.376 752 2390	101	25.251 680 8347	161	25.749 768 8032
42	20.579 304 2012	102	25.272 376 2548	162	25.751 883 3244
43	20.774 300 0733	103	25.292 299 6436	163	25.753 918 9645
44	20.962 021 7313	104	25.311 479 8013	164	25.755 878 6662
45	21.142 740 5355	105	25.329 944 4537	165	25.757 765 2623
46	21.316 717 7237	106	25.347 720 2924	166	25.759 581 4799
47	21.484 204 7882	107	25.364 833 0131	167	25.761 329 9446
48	21.645 443 8394	108	25.381 307 3532	168	25.763 013 1837
49	21.800 667 9561	109	25.397 167 1270	169	25.764 633 6305
50	21.950 101 5221	110	25.412 435 2607	170	25.766 193 6275
51	22.093 960 5508	111	25.427 133 8250	171	25.767 695 4296
52	22.232 452 9971	112	25.441 284 0674	172	25.769 141 2078
53	22.365 779 0586	113	25.454 906 4427	173	25.770 533 0520
54	22.494 131 4644	114	25.468 020 6428	174	25.771 872 9742
55	22.617 695 7539	115	25.480 645 6248	175	25.773 162 9114
56	22.736 650 5453	116	25.492 799 6388	176	25.774 404 7282
57	22.851 167 7933	117	25.504 500 2540	177	25.775 600 2197
58	22.961 413 0381	118	25.515 764 3841	178	25.776 751 1140
59	23.067 545 6443	119	25.526 608 3120	179	25.777 859 0749
60	23.169 719 0319	120	25.537 047 7131	180	25.778 925 7039

Present Value of 1 per period

NOMINAL INTEREST RATE COMPOUNDED

YEARLY	HALF-YEARLY	QUARTERLY
@	@	@
$3\frac{15}{16}\%$	$7\frac{7}{8}\%$	$15\frac{3}{4}\%$
3.9375%	7.8750%	15.7500%
PER ANNUM	PER ANNUM	PER ANNUM

Periods	Present Value	Periods	Present Value	Periods	Present Value
1	,962 116 6566	61	22,988 743 9436	121	25,159 504 9382
2	1,887 785 1176	62	23,079 970 1201	122	25,168 495 4306
3	2,778 386 1625	63	23,167 740 3441	123	25,177 145 3331
4	3,635 248 2622	64	23,252 185 5385	124	25,185 467 5484
5	4,459 649 5607	65	23,333 431 6666	125	25,193 474 4903
6	5,252 819 7818	66	23,411 599 9198	126	25,201 178 1025
7	6,015 942 0631	67	23,486 806 8982	127	25,208 589 8762
8	6,750 154 7209	68	23,559 164 7848	128	25,215 720 8670
9	7,456 552 9486	69	23,628 781 5127	129	25,222 581 7121
10	8,136 190 4496	70	23,695 760 9262	130	25,229 182 6454
11	8,790 081 0099	71	23,760 202 9356	131	25,235 533 5134
12	9,419 200 0095	72	23,822 203 6663	132	25,241 643 7892
13	10,024 485 8780	73	23,881 855 6019	133	25,247 522 5873
14	10,606 841 4942	74	23,939 247 7229	134	25,253 178 6769
15	11,167 135 5326	75	23,994 465 6384	135	25,258 620 4949
16	11,706 203 7596	76	24,047 591 7146	136	25,263 856 1586
17	12,224 850 2798	77	24,098 705 1974	137	25,268 893 4780
18	12,723 848 7358	78	24,147 882 3307	138	25,273 739 9668
19	13,203 943 4620	79	24,195 196 4697	139	25,278 402 8544
20	13,665 850 5948	80	24,240 718 1909	140	25,282 889 0962
21	14,110 259 1412	81	24,284 515 3971	141	25,287 205 3842
22	14,537 832 0059	82	24,326 653 4188	142	25,291 358 1568
23	14,949 206 9811	83	24,367 195 1113	143	25,295 353 6084
24	15,344 997 6967	84	24,406 200 9489	144	25,299 197 6990
25	15,725 794 5369	85	24,443 729 1150	145	25,302 896 1626
26	16,092 165 5195	86	24,479 835 5887	146	25,306 454 5161
27	16,444 657 1445	87	24,514 574 2285	147	25,309 878 0672
28	16,783 795 2081	88	24,547 996 8524	148	25,313 171 9227
29	17,110 085 5881	89	24,580 153 3156	149	25,316 340 9960
30	17,424 014 9976	90	24,611 091 5845	150	25,319 390 0142
31	17,726 051 7114	91	24,640 857 8083	151	25,322 323 5254
32	18,016 646 2648	92	24,669 496 3880	152	25,325 145 9054
33	18,296 232 1249	93	24,697 050 0426	153	25,327 861 3641
34	18,565 226 3378	94	24,723 559 8726	154	25,330 473 9523
35	18,824 030 1506	95	24,749 065 4216	155	25,332 987 5668
36	19,073 029 6097	96	24,773 604 7351	156	25,335 405 9573
37	19,312 596 1368	97	24,797 214 4175	157	25,337 732 7310
38	19,543 087 0830	98	24,819 929 6861	158	25,339 971 3587
39	19,764 846 2614	99	24,841 784 4244	159	25,342 125 1798
40	19,978 204 4608	100	24,862 811 2321	160	25,344 197 4069
41	20,183 479 9382	101	24,883 041 4741	161	25,346 191 1311
42	20,380 978 8942	102	24,902 505 3268	162	25,348 109 3264
43	20,570 995 9295	103	24,921 231 8238	163	25,349 954 8540
44	20,753 814 4842	104	24,939 248 8984	164	25,351 730 4669
45	20,929 707 2608	105	24,956 583 4260	165	25,353 438 8136
46	21,098 936 6310	106	24,973 261 2637	166	25,355 082 4424
47	21,261 755 0268	107	24,989 307 2892	167	25,356 663 8051
48	21,418 405 3174	108	25,004 745 4376	168	25,358 185 2605
49	21,569 121 1713	109	25,019 598 7373	169	25,359 649 0780
50	21,714 127 4047	110	25,033 889 3444	170	25,361 057 4413
51	21,853 640 3172	111	25,047 638 5755	171	25,362 412 4510
52	21,987 868 0142	112	25,060 866 9397	172	25,363 716 1284
53	22,117 010 7172	113	25,073 594 1693	173	25,364 970 4182
54	22,241 261 0628	114	25,085 839 2489	174	25,366 177 1913
55	22,360 804 3900	115	25,097 620 4439	175	25,367 338 2478
56	22,475 819 0162	116	25,108 955 3279	176	25,368 455 3196
57	22,586 476 5039	117	25,119 860 8085	177	25,369 530 0730
58	22,692 941 9159	118	25,130 353 1531	178	25,370 564 1111
59	22,795 374 0622	119	25,140 448 0126	179	25,371 558 9764
60	22,893 925 7364	120	25,150 160 4451	180	25,372 516 1529

Present Value of 1 per period

NOMINAL INTEREST RATE COMPOUNDED

YEARLY	HALF-YEARLY	QUARTERLY
@	@	@
4%	8%	16%
4.0000%	8.0000%	16.0000%
PER ANNUM	PER ANNUM	PER ANNUM

Periods	Present Value	Periods	Present Value	Periods	Present Value
1	.961 538 4615	61	22.714 894 2062	121	24.782 776 9269
2	1.886 094 6746	62	22.802 782 8906	122	24.791 131 6605
3	2.775 091 0332	63	22.887 291 2410	123	24.799 165 0581
4	3.629 895 2243	64	22.968 549 2702	124	24.806 889 4790
5	4.451 822 3310	65	23.046 681 9905	125	24.814 316 8067
6	5.242 136 8567	66	23.121 809 6063	126	24.821 458 4680
7	6.002 054 6699	67	23.194 047 6984	127	24.828 325 4500
8	6.732 744 8750	68	23.263 507 4023	128	24.834 928 3173
9	7.435 331 6105	69	23.330 295 5791	129	24.841 277 2282
10	8.110 895 7794	70	23.394 514 9799	130	24.847 381 9502
11	8.760 476 7109	71	23.456 264 4038	131	24.853 251 8752
12	9.385 073 7605	72	23.515 638 8498	132	24.858 896 0338
13	9.985 647 8466	73	23.572 729 6632	133	24.864 323 1094
14	10.563 122 9295	74	23.627 624 6762	134	24.869 541 4514
15	11.118 387 4322	75	23.680 408 3425	135	24.874 559 0879
16	11.652 295 6079	76	23.731 161 8678	136	24.879 383 7383
17	12.165 668 8537	77	23.779 963 3344	137	24.884 022 8253
18	12.659 296 9747	78	23.826 887 8215	138	24.888 483 4859
19	13.133 939 3988	79	23.872 007 5207	139	24.892 772 5826
20	13.590 326 3450	80	23.915 391 8468	140	24.896 896 7140
21	14.029 159 9471	81	23.957 107 5450	141	24.900 862 2250
22	14.451 115 3337	82	23.997 218 7933	142	24.904 675 2164
23	14.856 841 6671	83	24.035 787 3013	143	24.908 341 5542
24	15.246 963 1414	84	24.072 872 4050	144	24.911 866 8790
25	15.622 079 9437	85	24.108 531 1587	145	24.915 256 6144
26	15.982 769 1766	86	24.142 818 4218	146	24.918 515 9754
27	16.329 585 7467	87	24.175 786 9441	147	24.921 649 9764
28	16.663 063 2180	88	24.207 487 4462	148	24.924 663 4388
29	16.983 714 6327	89	24.237 968 6983	149	24.927 560 9989
30	17.292 033 3007	90	24.267 277 5945	150	24.930 347 1143
31	17.588 493 5583	91	24.295 459 2255	151	24.933 026 0714
32	17.873 551 4984	92	24.322 556 9476	152	24.935 601 9918
33	18.147 645 6715	93	24.348 612 4496	153	24.938 078 8382
34	18.411 197 7611	94	24.373 665 8169	154	24.940 460 4214
35	18.664 613 2318	95	24.397 755 5932	155	24.942 750 4052
36	18.908 281 9537	96	24.420 918 8396	156	24.944 952 3127
37	19.142 578 8016	97	24.443 191 1919	157	24.947 069 5314
38	19.367 864 2323	98	24.464 606 9153	158	24.949 105 3187
39	19.584 484 8388	99	24.485 198 9570	159	24.951 062 8064
40	19.792 773 8834	100	24.504 998 9972	160	24.952 945 0062
41	19.993 051 8110	101	24.524 037 4973	161	24.954 754 8136
42	20.185 626 7413	102	24.542 343 7474	162	24.956 495 0131
43	20.370 794 9436	103	24.559 945 9109	163	24.958 168 2818
44	20.548 841 2919	104	24.576 871 0682	164	24.959 777 1941
45	20.720 039 7038	105	24.593 145 2579	165	24.961 324 2251
46	20.884 653 5613	106	24.608 793 5172	166	24.962 811 7549
47	21.042 936 1166	107	24.623 839 9204	167	24.964 242 0720
48	21.195 130 8814	108	24.638 307 6158	168	24.965 617 3769
49	21.341 472 0013	109	24.652 218 8613	169	24.966 939 7855
50	21.482 184 6167	110	24.665 595 0589	170	24.968 211 3322
51	21.617 485 2083	111	24.678 456 7874	171	24.969 433 9733
52	21.747 581 9311	112	24.690 823 8341	172	24.970 609 5897
53	21.872 674 9337	113	24.702 715 2251	173	24.971 739 9901
54	21.992 956 6671	114	24.714 149 2549	174	24.972 826 9135
55	22.108 612 1799	115	24.725 143 5143	175	24.973 872 0322
56	22.219 819 4037	116	24.735 714 9176	176	24.974 876 9541
57	22.326 749 4267	117	24.745 879 7285	177	24.975 843 2251
58	22.429 566 7564	118	24.755 653 5851	178	24.976 772 3318
59	22.528 429 5735	119	24.765 051 5241	179	24.977 665 7037
60	22.623 489 9745	120	24.774 088 0039	180	24.978 524 7151

Present Value of 1 per period

NOMINAL INTEREST RATE COMPOUNDED

YEARLY	HALF-YEARLY	QUARTERLY
@	@	@
$4\frac{1}{16}\%$	$8\frac{1}{8}\%$	$16\frac{1}{4}\%$
4.0625%	8.1250%	16.2500%
PER ANNUM	PER ANNUM	PER ANNUM

Periods	Present Value	Periods	Present Value	Periods	Present Value
1	,960 960 9610	61	22.446 397 0630	121	24.416 499 7442
2	1,884 406 9295	62	22.531 072 2528	122	24.424 264 0184
3	2,771 802 4547	63	22.612 441 8044	123	24.431 725 1829
4	3,624 554 9115	64	22.690 634 7670	124	24.438 895 0706
5	4,444 016 7317	65	22.765 775 1515	125	24.445 785 0528
6	5,231 487 5500	66	22.837 982 1276	126	24.452 406 0568
7	5,988 216 2643	67	22.907 370 2127	127	24.458 768 5831
8	6,715 403 0167	68	22.974 049 4536	128	24.464 882 7225
9	7,414 201 0971	69	23.038 125 6011	129	24.470 758 1718
10	8,085 718 7720	70	23.099 700 2773	130	24.476 404 2491
11	8,731 021 0422	71	23.158 871 1374	131	24.481 829 9091
12	9,351 131 3318	72	23.215 732 0239	132	24.487 043 7565
13	9,947 033 1117	73	23.270 373 1161	133	24.492 054 0603
14	10,519 671 4587	74	23.322 881 0725	134	24.496 868 7666
15	11,069 954 5549	75	23.373 339 1688	135	24.501 495 5115
16	11,598 755 1278	76	23.421 827 4294	136	24.505 941 6327
17	12,106 911 8345	77	23.468 422 7550	137	24.510 214 1815
18	12,595 230 5917	78	23.513 199 0439	138	24.514 319 9342
19	13,064 485 8539	79	23.556 227 3094	139	24.518 265 4022
20	13,515 421 8416	80	23.597 575 7928	140	24.522 056 8430
21	13,948 753 7217	81	23.637 310 0712	141	24.525 700 2695
22	14,365 168 7415	82	23.675 493 1615	142	24.529 201 4602
23	14,765 327 3192	83	23.712 185 6207	143	24.532 565 9678
24	15,149 864 0905	84	23.747 445 6415	144	24.535 799 1282
25	15,519 388 9158	85	23.781 329 1450	145	24.538 906 0691
26	15,874 487 8470	86	23.813 889 8690	146	24.541 891 7181
27	16,215 724 0572	87	23.845 179 4537	147	24.544 760 8102
28	16,543 638 7337	88	23.875 247 5231	148	24.547 517 8957
29	16,858 751 9362	89	23.904 141 7639	149	24.550 167 3472
30	17,161 563 4222	90	23.931 908 0014	150	24.552 713 3667
31	17,452 553 4388	91	23.958 590 2716	151	24.555 159 9920
32	17,732 183 4847	92	23.984 230 8916	152	24.557 511 1034
33	18,000 897 0424	93	24.008 870 5265	153	24.559 770 4297
34	18,259 120 2809	94	24.032 548 2537	154	24.561 941 5541
35	18,507 262 7324	95	24.055 301 6252	155	24.564 027 9198
36	18,745 717 9411	96	24.077 166 7269	156	24.566 032 8359
37	18,974 864 0875	97	24.098 178 2360	157	24.567 959 4819
38	19,195 064 5886	98	24.118 369 4761	158	24.569 810 9136
39	19,406 668 6737	99	24.137 772 4695	159	24.571 590 0671
40	19,610 011 9387	100	24.156 417 9887	160	24.573 299 7642
41	19,805 416 8781	101	24.174 335 6048	161	24.574 942 7163
42	19,993 193 3963	102	24.191 553 7343	162	24.576 521 5292
43	20,173 639 2998	103	24.208 099 6846	163	24.578 038 7067
44	20,347 040 7686	104	24.223 999 6969	164	24.579 496 6551
45	20,513 672 8106	105	24.239 278 9880	165	24.580 897 6866
46	20,673 799 6979	106	24.253 961 7903	166	24.582 244 0232
47	20,827 675 3854	107	24.268 071 3901	167	24.583 537 8000
48	20,975 543 9139	108	24.281 630 1647	168	24.584 781 0691
49	21,117 639 7971	109	24.294 659 6177	169	24.585 975 8021
50	21,254 188 3936	110	24.307 180 4134	170	24.587 123 8939
51	21,385 406 2641	111	24.319 212 4093	171	24.588 227 1654
52	21,511 501 5151	112	24.330 774 6876	172	24.589 287 3661
53	21,632 674 1286	113	24.341 885 5857	173	24.590 306 1776
54	21,749 116 2797	114	24.352 562 7250	174	24.591 285 2157
55	21,861 012 6412	115	24.362 823 0390	175	24.592 226 0332
56	21,968 540 6762	116	24.372 682 8002	176	24.593 130 1219
57	22,071 870 9201	117	24.382 157 6459	177	24.593 998 9160
58	22,171 167 2505	118	24.391 262 6026	178	24.594 833 7931
59	22,266 587 1477	119	24.400 012 1107	179	24.595 636 0775
60	22,358 281 9437	120	24.408 420 0463	180	24.596 407 0414

Present Value of 1 per period

NOMINAL INTEREST RATE COMPOUNDED

YEARLY	HALF-YEARLY	QUARTERLY
@	@	@
$4\frac{1}{8}\%$	$8\frac{1}{4}\%$	$16\frac{1}{2}\%$
4.1250%	8.2500%	16.5000%
PER ANNUM	PER ANNUM	PER ANNUM

Periods	Present Value	Periods	Present Value	Periods	Present Value
1	.960 384 1537	61	22,183 121 6425	121	24,060 278 3831
2	1,882 721 8763	62	22,264 702 6578	122	24,067 494 2455
3	2,768 520 4094	63	22,343 051 7722	123	24,074 424 2454
4	3,619 227 2839	64	22,418 297 0202	124	24,081 079 7074
5	4,436 232 6856	65	22,490 561 3639	125	24,087 471 5078
6	5,220 871 7269	66	22,559 962 8945	126	24,093 610 0915
7	5,974 426 6285	67	22,626 615 0247	127	24,099 505 4900
8	6,698 128 8149	68	22,690 626 6744	128	24,105 167 3373
9	7,393 160 9266	69	22,752 102 4484	129	24,110 604 8858
10	8,060 658 7531	70	22,811 142 8076	130	24,115 827 0212
11	8,701 713 0882	71	22,867 844 2330	131	24,120 842 2772
12	9,317 371 5133	72	22,922 299 3834	132	24,125 658 8497
13	9,908 640 1088	73	22,974 597 2470	133	24,130 284 6096
14	10,476 485 0985	74	23,024 823 2864	134	24,134 727 1160
15	11,021 834 4283	75	23,073 059 5788	135	24,138 993 6288
16	11,545 579 2829	76	23,119 384 9496	136	24,143 091 1201
17	12,048 575 5418	77	23,163 875 1017	137	24,147 026 2858
18	12,531 645 1782	78	23,206 602 7387	138	24,150 805 5566
19	12,995 577 6021	79	23,247 637 6842	139	24,154 435 1084
20	13,441 130 9504	80	23,287 046 9957	140	24,157 920 8724
21	13,869 033 3257	81	23,324 895 0739	141	24,161 268 5449
22	14,279 983 9863	82	23,361 243 7684	142	24,164 483 5966
23	14,674 654 4886	83	23,396 152 4787	143	24,167 571 2812
24	15,053 689 7850	84	23,429 678 2508	144	24,170 536 6446
25	15,417 709 2773	85	23,461 875 8711	145	24,173 384 5327
26	15,767 307 8293	86	23,492 797 9555	146	24,176 119 5992
27	16,103 056 7389	87	23,522 495 0353	147	24,178 746 3138
28	16,425 504 6712	88	23,551 015 6401	148	24,181 268 9688
29	16,735 178 5557	89	23,578 406 3771	149	24,183 691 6867
30	17,032 584 4473	90	23,604 712 0068	150	24,186 018 4266
31	17,318 208 3527	91	23,629 975 5167	151	24,188 252 9907
32	17,592 517 0254	92	23,654 238 1913	152	24,190 399 0307
33	17,855 958 7279	93	23,677 539 6795	153	24,192 460 0535
34	18,108 963 9644	94	23,699 918 0596	154	24,194 439 4272
35	18,351 946 1843	95	23,721 409 9012	155	24,196 340 3862
36	18,585 302 4579	96	23,742 050 3252	156	24,198 166 0372
37	18,809 414 1252	97	23,761 873 0615	157	24,199 919 3634
38	19,024 647 4192	98	23,780 910 5032	158	24,201 603 2302
39	19,231 354 0640	99	23,799 193 7606	159	24,203 220 3891
40	19,429 871 8502	100	23,816 752 7112	160	24,204 773 4830
41	19,620 525 1863	101	23,833 616 0492	161	24,206 265 0497
42	19,803 625 6291	102	23,849 811 3318	162	24,207 697 5267
43	19,979 472 3929	103	23,865 365 0245	163	24,209 073 2549
44	20,148 352 8383	104	23,880 302 5446	164	24,210 394 4825
45	20,310 542 9420	105	23,894 648 3021	165	24,211 663 3686
46	20,466 307 7474	106	23,908 425 7403	166	24,212 881 9866
47	20,615 901 7982	107	23,921 657 3736	167	24,214 052 3281
48	20,759 569 5541	108	23,934 364 8246	168	24,215 176 3055
49	20,897 545 7902	109	23,946 568 8592	169	24,216 255 7556
50	21,030 055 9810	110	23,958 289 4206	170	24,217 292 4423
51	21,157 316 6685	111	23,969 545 6620	171	24,218 288 0599
52	21,279 535 8160	112	23,980 355 9779	172	24,219 244 2352
53	21,396 913 1487	113	23,990 738 0340	173	24,220 162 5308
54	21,509 640 4789	114	24,000 708 7962	174	24,221 044 4473
55	21,617 902 0206	115	24,010 284 5582	175	24,221 891 4260
56	21,721 874 6896	116	24,019 480 9682	176	24,222 704 8509
57	21,821 728 3934	117	24,028 313 0547	177	24,223 486 0513
58	21,917 626 3082	118	24,036 795 2506	178	24,224 236 3037
59	22,009 725 1459	119	24,044 941 4172	179	24,224 956 8343
60	22,098 175 4102	120	24,052 764 8664	180	24,225 648 8205

Present Value of 1 per period

NOMINAL INTEREST RATE COMPOUNDED

YEARLY	HALF-YEARLY	QUARTERLY
@	@	@
$4\frac{3}{16}\%$	$8\frac{3}{8}\%$	$16\frac{3}{4}\%$
4.1875%	8.3750%	16.7500%
PER ANNUM	PER ANNUM	PER ANNUM

Periods	Present Value	Periods	Present Value	Periods	Present Value
1	,959 808 0384	61	21,924 940 7100	121	23,713 735 7613
2	1,881 039 5090	62	22,003 542 3731	122	23,720 442 2424
3	2,765 244 8796	63	22,078 984 8812	123	23,726 879 1769
4	3,613 912 3020	64	22,151 395 2069	124	23,733 057 3983
5	4,428 470 1159	65	22,220 895 2196	125	23,738 987 3049
6	5,210 289 2534	66	22,287 601 8905	126	23,744 678 8769
7	5,960 685 5461	67	22,351 627 4893	127	23,750 141 6935
8	6,680 921 9399	68	22,413 079 7738	128	23,755 384 9488
9	7,372 210 6202	69	22,472 062 1704	129	23,760 417 4673
10	8,035 715 0524	70	22,528 673 9488	130	23,765 247 7191
11	8,672 551 9399	71	22,583 010 3888	131	23,769 883 8336
12	9,283 793 1037	72	22,635 162 9407	132	23,774 333 6135
13	9,870 467 2861	73	22,685 219 3791	133	23,778 604 5481
14	10,433 561 8822	74	22,733 263 9512	134	23,782 703 8254
15	10,974 024 6020	75	22,779 377 5176	135	23,786 638 3447
16	11,492 765 0649	76	22,823 637 6894	136	23,790 414 7280
17	11,990 656 3311	77	22,866 118 9580	137	23,794 039 3310
18	12,468 536 3706	78	22,906 892 8211	138	23,797 518 2541
19	12,927 209 4738	79	22,946 027 9027	139	23,800 857 3524
20	13,367 447 6054	80	22,983 590 0686	140	23,804 062 2459
21	13,789 991 7028	81	23,019 642 5373	141	23,807 138 3284
22	14,195 552 9241	82	23,054 245 9867	142	23,810 090 7771
23	14,584 813 8444	83	23,087 458 6555	143	23,812 924 5611
24	14,958 429 6047	84	23,119 336 4420	144	23,815 644 4498
25	15,317 029 0147	85	23,149 932 9977	145	23,818 255 0208
26	15,661 215 6110	86	23,179 299 8178	146	23,820 760 6678
27	15,991 568 6728	87	23,207 486 3278	147	23,823 165 6080
28	16,308 644 1971	88	23,234 539 9667	148	23,825 473 8889
29	16,612 975 8340	89	23,260 506 2668	149	23,827 689 3955
30	16,905 075 7855	90	23,285 428 9303	150	23,829 815 8565
31	17,185 435 6669	91	23,309 349 9031	151	23,831 856 8508
32	17,454 527 3348	92	23,332 309 4451	152	23,833 815 8136
33	17,712 803 6807	93	23,354 346 1981	153	23,835 696 0419
34	17,960 699 3936	94	23,375 497 2507	154	23,837 500 7001
35	18,198 631 6915	95	23,395 798 2010	155	23,839 232 8255
36	18,427 001 0236	96	23,415 283 2164	156	23,840 895 3334
37	18,646 191 7443	97	23,433 985 0907	157	23,842 491 0219
38	18,856 572 7600	98	23,451 935 3000	158	23,844 022 5765
39	19,058 498 1500	99	23,469 164 0552	159	23,845 492 5749
40	19,252 307 7624	100	23,485 700 3529	160	23,846 903 4912
41	19,438 327 7864	101	23,501 572 0244	161	23,848 257 7000
42	19,616 871 3006	102	23,516 805 7823	162	23,849 557 4805
43	19,788 238 8009	103	23,531 427 2655	163	23,850 805 0203
44	19,952 718 7051	104	23,545 461 0827	164	23,852 002 4190
45	20,110 587 8393	105	23,558 930 8532	165	23,853 151 6919
46	20,262 111 9034	106	23,571 859 2472	166	23,854 254 7733
47	20,407 545 9180	107	23,584 268 0237	167	23,855 313 5196
48	20,547 134 6544	108	23,596 178 0672	168	23,856 329 7129
49	20,681 113 0456	109	23,607 609 4226	169	23,857 305 0634
50	20,809 706 5825	110	23,618 581 3294	170	23,858 241 2126
51	20,933 131 6928	111	23,629 112 2538	171	23,859 139 7362
52	21,051 596 1059	112	23,639 219 9197	172	23,860 002 1463
53	21,165 299 2018	113	23,648 921 3386	173	23,860 829 8945
54	21,274 432 3473	114	23,658 232 8385	174	23,861 624 3738
55	21,379 179 2175	115	23,667 170 0909	175	23,862 386 9215
56	21,479 716 1056	116	23,675 748 1377	176	23,863 118 8208
57	21,576 212 2190	117	23,683 981 4159	177	23,863 821 3037
58	21,668 829 9642	118	23,691 883 7825	178	23,864 495 5525
59	21,757 725 2206	119	23,699 468 5375	179	23,865 142 7018
60	21,843 047 6022	120	23,706 748 4463	180	23,865 763 8410

Present Value of 1 per period

NOMINAL INTEREST RATE COMPOUNDED

YEARLY @ $4\frac{1}{4}\%$ 4.2500% PER ANNUM		HALF-YEARLY @ $8\frac{1}{2}\%$ 8.5000% PER ANNUM		QUARTERLY @ 17% 17.0000% PER ANNUM	
Periods	Present Value	Periods	Present Value	Periods	Present Value
1	.959 232 6139	61	21.671 730 5580	121	23.376 511 8058
2	1.879 359 8215	62	21.747 463 3650	122	23.382 745 1374
3	2.761 975 8480	63	21.820 108 7434	123	23.388 724 3524
4	3.608 609 9261	64	21.889 792 5596	124	23.394 459 8105
5	4.420 728 9459	65	21.956 635 5488	125	23.399 961 4489
6	5.199 739 9961	66	22.020 753 5240	126	23.405 238 7999
7	5.946 992 8020	67	22.082 257 5770	127	23.410 301 0071
8	6.663 782 0642	68	22.141 254 2705	128	23.415 156 8414
9	7.351 349 7019	69	22.197 845 8230	129	23.419 814 7159
10	8.010 887 0042	70	22.252 130 2859	130	23.424 282 7011
11	8.643 536 6947	71	22.304 201 7131	131	23.428 568 5383
12	9.250 394 9110	72	22.354 150 3243	132	23.432 679 6530
13	9.832 513 1041	73	22.402 062 6612	133	23.436 623 1683
14	10.390 899 8600	74	22.448 021 7374	134	23.440 405 9169
15	10.926 522 6475	75	22.492 107 1821	135	23.444 034 4526
16	11.440 309 4940	76	22.534 395 3785	136	23.447 515 0625
17	11.933 150 5938	77	22.574 959 5957	137	23.450 853 7770
18	12.405 899 8501	78	22.613 870 1158	138	23.454 056 3808
19	12.859 376 3551	79	22.651 194 3557	139	23.457 128 4228
20	13.294 365 8082	80	22.686 996 9839	140	23.460 075 2257
21	13.711 621 8784	81	22.721 340 0325	141	23.462 901 8952
22	14.111 867 5092	82	22.754 283 0048	142	23.465 613 3287
23	14.495 796 1719	83	22.785 882 9782	143	23.468 214 2242
24	14.864 073 0666	84	22.816 194 7033	144	23.470 709 0879
25	15.217 336 2749	85	22.845 270 6986	145	23.473 102 2426
26	15.556 197 8656	86	22.873 161 3416	146	23.475 397 8347
27	15.881 244 9550	87	22.899 914 9560	147	23.477 599 8414
28	16.193 040 7243	88	22.925 577 8954	148	23.479 712 0781
29	16.492 125 3950	89	22.950 194 6239	149	23.481 738 2044
30	16.779 017 1654	90	22.973 807 7927	150	23.483 681 7308
31	17.054 213 1083	91	22.996 458 3144	151	23.485 546 0248
32	17.318 190 0320	92	23.018 185 4334	152	23.487 334 3163
33	17.571 405 3064	93	23.039 026 7947	153	23.489 049 7039
34	17.814 297 6561	94	23.059 018 5081	154	23.490 695 1596
35	18.047 287 9195	95	23.078 195 2116	155	23.492 273 5344
36	18.270 779 7789	96	23.096 590 1310	156	23.493 787 5630
37	18.485 160 4594	97	23.114 235 1377	157	23.495 239 8686
38	18.690 801 3999	98	23.131 160 8035	158	23.496 632 9675
39	18.888 058 8968	99	23.147 396 4542	159	23.497 969 2733
40	19.077 274 7211	100	23.162 970 2199	160	23.499 251 1015
41	19.258 776 7109	101	23.177 909 0838	161	23.500 480 6729
42	19.432 879 3390	102	23.192 238 9293	162	23.501 660 1179
43	19.599 884 2580	103	23.205 984 5845	163	23.502 791 4800
44	19.760 080 8230	104	23.219 169 8652	164	23.503 876 7194
45	19.913 746 5928	105	23.231 817 6165	165	23.504 917 7165
46	20.061 147 8109	106	23.243 949 7520	166	23.505 916 2748
47	20.202 539 8666	107	23.255 587 2921	167	23.506 874 1245
48	20.338 167 7377	108	23.266 750 4001	168	23.507 792 9252
49	20.468 266 4151	109	23.277 458 4174	169	23.508 674 2688
50	20.593 061 3094	110	23.287 729 8968	170	23.509 519 6823
51	20.712 768 6421	111	23.297 582 6348	171	23.510 330 6305
52	20.827 595 8198	112	23.307 033 7024	172	23.511 108 5184
53	20.937 741 7936	113	23.316 099 4748	173	23.511 854 6940
54	21.043 397 4039	114	23.324 795 6592	174	23.512 570 4498
55	21.144 745 7112	115	23.333 137 3230	175	23.513 257 0262
56	21.241 962 3129	116	23.341 138 9190	176	23.513 915 6127
57	21.335 215 6478	117	23.348 814 3107	177	23.514 547 3503
58	21.424 667 2881	118	23.356 176 7969	178	23.515 153 3336
59	21.510 472 2188	119	23.363 239 1337	179	23.515 734 6126
60	21.592 779 1068	120	23.370 013 5575	180	23.516 292 1943

Present Value of 1 per period

NOMINAL INTEREST RATE COMPOUNDED

	YEARLY @ $4\frac{5}{16}\%$ 4.3125% PER ANNUM		HALF-YEARLY @ $8\frac{5}{8}\%$ 8.6250% PER ANNUM		QUARTERLY @ $17\frac{1}{4}\%$ 17.2500% PER ANNUM
Periods	Present Value	Periods	Present Value	Periods	Present Value
1	.958 657 8790	61	21.423 370 8996	121	23.048 262 5890
2	1.877 682 8079	62	21.496 341 1859	122	23.054 056 4064
3	2.758 713 2969	63	21.566 294 7259	123	23.059 610 6952
4	3.603 320 1169	64	21.633 356 2381	124	23.064 935 3579
5	4.413 009 0995	65	21.697 645 2852	125	23.070 039 8877
6	5.189 223 8222	66	21.759 276 4867	126	23.074 933 3855
7	5.933 348 1818	67	21.818 359 7236	127	23.079 624 5757
8	6.646 708 8621	68	21.875 000 3342	128	23.084 121 8221
9	7.330 577 6989	69	21.929 299 3018	129	23.088 433 1428
10	7.986 173 9474	70	21.981 353 4349	130	23.092 566 2244
11	8.614 666 4565	71	22.031 255 5398	131	23.096 528 4356
12	9.217 175 7521	72	22.079 094 5858	132	23.100 326 8406
13	9.794 776 0356	73	22.124 955 8641	133	23.103 968 2115
14	10.348 497 0983	74	22.168 921 1400	134	23.107 459 0404
15	10.879 326 1577	75	22.211 068 7981	135	23.110 805 5510
16	11.388 209 6179	76	22.251 473 9826	136	23.114 013 7097
17	11.876 054 7566	77	22.290 208 7310	137	23.117 089 2364
18	12.343 731 3424	78	22.327 342 1028	138	23.120 037 6143
19	12.792 073 1863	79	22.362 940 3023	139	23.122 864 1000
20	13.221 879 6273	80	22.397 066 7967	140	23.125 573 7328
21	13.633 916 9585	81	22.429 782 4294	141	23.128 171 3436
22	14.028 919 7924	82	22.461 145 5285	142	23.130 661 5636
23	14.407 592 3714	83	22.491 212 0106	143	23.133 048 8327
24	14.770 609 8228	84	22.520 035 4805	144	23.135 337 4070
25	15.118 619 3628	85	22.547 667 3270	145	23.137 531 3669
26	15.452 241 4503	86	22.574 156 8144	146	23.139 634 6237
27	15.772 070 8930	87	22.599 551 1702	147	23.141 650 9275
28	16.078 677 9082	88	22.623 895 6694	148	23.143 583 8729
29	16.372 609 1391	89	22.647 233 7154	149	23.145 436 9064
30	16.654 388 6294	90	22.669 606 9171	150	23.147 213 3314
31	16.924 518 7580	91	22.691 055 1632	151	23.148 916 3153
32	17.183 481 1341	92	22.711 616 6933	152	23.150 548 8943
33	17.431 737 4563	93	22.731 328 1662	153	23.152 113 9789
34	17.669 730 3356	94	22.750 224 7249	154	23.153 614 3597
35	17.897 884 0844	95	22.768 340 0598	155	23.155 052 7115
36	18.116 605 4734	96	22.785 706 4684	156	23.156 431 5988
37	18.326 284 4562	97	22.802 354 9128	157	23.157 753 4800
38	18.527 294 8651	98	22.818 315 0751	158	23.159 020 7118
39	18.719 995 0774	99	22.833 615 4106	159	23.160 235 5535
40	18.904 728 6542	100	22.848 283 1977	160	23.161 400 1711
41	19.081 824 9531	101	22.862 344 5873	161	23.162 516 6410
42	19.251 599 7154	102	22.875 824 6493	162	23.163 586 9536
43	19.414 355 6289	103	22.888 747 4170	163	23.164 613 0173
44	19.570 382 8677	104	22.901 135 9300	164	23.165 596 6612
45	19.719 959 6096	105	22.913 012 2756	165	23.166 539 6393
46	19.863 352 5316	106	22.924 397 6279	166	23.167 443 6326
47	20.000 817 2862	107	22.935 312 2856	167	23.168 310 2530
48	20.132 598 9562	108	22.945 775 7082	168	23.169 141 0454
49	20.258 932 4924	109	22.955 806 5507	169	23.169 937 4911
50	20.380 043 1324	110	22.965 422 6969	170	23.170 701 0100
51	20.496 146 8015	111	22.974 641 2912	171	23.171 432 9635
52	20.607 450 4988	112	22.983 478 7693	172	23.172 134 6564
53	20.714 152 6651	113	22.991 950 8872	173	23.172 807 3399
54	20.816 443 5375	114	23.000 072 7499	174	23.173 452 2132
55	20.914 505 4884	115	23.007 858 8375	175	23.174 070 4261
56	21.008 513 3501	116	23.015 323 0318	176	23.174 663 0807
57	21.098 634 7275	117	23.022 478 6404	177	23.175 231 2338
58	21.185 030 2960	118	23.029 338 4210	178	23.175 775 8982
59	21.267 854 0884	119	23.035 914 6037	179	23.176 298 0450
60	21.347 253 7696	120	23.042 218 9131	180	23.176 798 6051

Present Value of 1 per period

NOMINAL INTEREST RATE COMPOUNDED

YEARLY @ $4\frac{3}{8}\%$ 4.3750% PER ANNUM	HALF-YEARLY @ $8\frac{3}{4}\%$ 8.7500% PER ANNUM	QUARTERLY @ $17\frac{1}{2}\%$ 17.5000% PER ANNUM

Periods	Present Value	Periods	Present Value	Periods	Present Value
1	.958 083 8323	61	21.179 744 7653	121	22.728 659 5120
2	1.876 008 4621	62	21.250 054 8649	122	22.734 045 0415
3	2.755 457 2092	63	21.317 417 8347	123	22.739 204 8301
4	3.598 042 8352	64	21.381 957 2069	124	22.744 148 3402
5	4.405 310 5008	65	21.443 791 3359	125	22.748 884 6374
6	5.178 740 5995	66	21.503 033 6152	126	22.753 422 4071
7	5.919 751 4726	67	21.559 792 6853	127	22.757 769 9708
8	6.629 702 0097	68	21.614 172 6326	128	22.761 935 3014
9	7.309 894 1410	69	21.666 273 1809	129	22.765 926 0373
10	7.961 575 2249	70	21.716 189 8739	130	22.769 749 4968
11	8.585 940 3353	71	21.764 014 2505	131	22.773 412 6915
12	9.184 134 4529	72	21.809 834 0124	132	22.776 922 3392
13	9.757 254 5657	73	21.853 733 1856	133	22.780 284 8759
14	10.306 351 6797	74	21.895 792 2736	134	22.783 506 4679
15	10.832 432 7470	75	21.936 088 4058	135	22.786 593 0231
16	11.336 462 5121	76	21.974 695 4787	136	22.789 550 2018
17	11.819 365 2811	77	22.011 684 2909	137	22.792 383 4269
18	12.282 026 6166	78	22.047 122 6739	138	22.795 097 8940
19	12.725 294 9620	79	22.081 075 6157	139	22.797 698 5811
20	13.149 983 1971	80	22.113 605 3804	140	22.800 190 2573
21	13.556 870 1290	81	22.144 771 6219	141	22.802 577 4921
22	13.946 701 9200	82	22.174 651 4940	142	22.804 864 6630
23	14.320 193 4563	83	22.203 239 7548	143	22.807 055 9646
24	14.678 029 6587	84	22.230 648 8668	144	22.809 155 4152
25	15.020 866 7389	85	22.256 909 0940	145	22.811 166 8648
26	15.349 333 4025	86	22.282 068 5930	146	22.813 094 0022
27	15.664 032 0024	87	22.306 173 5023	147	22.814 940 3614
28	15.965 539 6430	88	22.329 268 0262	148	22.816 709 3283
29	16.254 409 2388	89	22.351 394 5161	149	22.818 404 1469
30	16.531 170 5282	90	22.372 593 5483	150	22.820 027 9252
31	16.796 331 0450	91	22.392 903 9984	151	22.821 583 6409
32	17.050 377 0491	92	22.412 363 1123	152	22.823 074 1470
33	17.293 774 4183	93	22.431 006 5746	153	22.824 502 1767
34	17.526 969 5026	94	22.448 868 5745	154	22.825 870 3490
35	17.750 389 9426	95	22.465 981 8678	155	22.827 181 1726
36	17.964 445 4540	96	22.482 377 8374	156	22.828 437 0516
37	18.169 528 5787	97	22.498 086 5508	157	22.829 640 2890
38	18.366 015 4047	98	22.513 136 8151	158	22.830 793 0913
39	18.554 266 2560	99	22.527 556 2301	159	22.831 897 5725
40	18.734 626 3531	100	22.541 371 2384	160	22.832 955 7580
41	18.907 426 4460	101	22.554 607 1745	161	22.833 969 5885
42	19.072 983 4214	102	22.567 288 3109	162	22.834 940 9232
43	19.231 600 8827	103	22.579 437 9027	163	22.835 871 5431
44	19.383 569 7080	104	22.591 078 2301	164	22.836 763 1551
45	19.529 168 5825	105	22.602 230 6396	165	22.837 617 3941
46	19.668 664 5102	106	22.612 915 5829	166	22.838 435 8267
47	19.802 313 3032	107	22.623 152 6542	167	22.839 219 9537
48	19.930 360 0510	108	22.632 960 6268	168	22.839 971 2131
49	20.053 039 5698	109	22.642 357 4868	169	22.840 690 9827
50	20.170 576 8333	110	22.651 360 4664	170	22.841 380 5822
51	20.283 187 3852	111	22.659 986 0756	171	22.842 041 2763
52	20.391 077 7343	112	22.668 250 1323	172	22.842 674 2767
53	20.494 445 7335	113	22.676 167 7914	173	22.843 280 7442
54	20.593 480 9423	114	22.683 753 5726	174	22.843 861 7908
55	20.688 364 9746	115	22.691 021 3869	175	22.844 418 4822
56	20.779 271 8320	116	22.697 984 5623	176	22.844 951 8393
57	20.866 368 2223	117	22.704 655 8681	177	22.845 462 8400
58	20.949 813 8656	118	22.711 047 5383	178	22.845 952 4216
59	21.029 761 7874	119	22.717 171 2942	179	22.846 421 4817
60	21.106 358 5987	120	22.723 038 3657	180	22.846 870 8807

Present Value of 1 per period

NOMINAL INTEREST RATE COMPOUNDED

YEARLY	HALF-YEARLY	QUARTERLY
@	@	@
$4\frac{7}{16}\%$	$8\frac{7}{8}\%$	$17\frac{3}{4}\%$
4.4375%	8.8750%	17.7500%
PER ANNUM	PER ANNUM	PER ANNUM

Periods	Present Value	Periods	Present Value	Periods	Present Value
1	.957 510 4728	61	20.940 738 4037	121	22.417 388 5330
2	1.874 336 7782	62	21.008 486 8019	122	22.422 394 7653
3	2.752 207 5674	63	21.073 356 6026	123	22.427 188 2852
4	3.592 778 0418	64	21.135 470 1162	124	22.431 778 1306
5	4.397 633 0742	65	21.194 944 4560	125	22.436 172 9557
6	5.168 290 1967	66	21.251 891 7592	126	22.440 381 0467
7	5.906 202 4624	67	21.306 419 3984	127	22.444 410 3380
8	6.612 761 1848	68	21.358 630 1839	128	22.448 268 4266
9	7.289 298 5612	69	21.408 622 5579	129	22.451 962 5868
10	7.937 090 1843	70	21.456 490 7796	130	22.455 499 7839
11	8.557 357 4475	71	21.502 325 1031	131	22.458 886 6871
12	9.151 269 8480	72	21.546 211 9480	132	22.462 129 6825
13	9.719 947 1914	73	21.588 234 0615	133	22.465 234 8845
14	10.264 461 7033	74	21.628 470 6753	134	22.468 208 1479
15	10.785 840 0510	75	21.666 997 6543	135	22.471 055 0788
16	11.285 065 2793	76	21.703 887 6403	136	22.473 781 0449
17	11.763 078 6636	77	21.739 210 1882	137	22.476 391 1860
18	12.220 781 4852	78	21.773 031 8977	138	22.478 890 4235
19	12.659 036 7303	79	21.805 416 5388	139	22.481 283 4695
20	13.078 670 7172	80	21.836 425 1718	140	22.483 574 8362
21	13.480 474 6544	81	21.866 116 2627	141	22.485 768 8437
22	13.865 206 1323	82	21.894 545 7931	142	22.487 869 6290
23	14.233 590 5516	83	21.921 767 3662	143	22.489 881 1528
24	14.586 322 4910	84	21.947 832 3076	144	22.491 807 2079
25	14.924 067 0171	85	21.972 789 7619	145	22.493 651 4259
26	15.247 460 9380	86	21.996 686 7858	146	22.495 417 2839
27	15.557 114 0041	87	22.019 568 4364	147	22.497 108 1115
28	15.853 610 0578	88	22.041 477 8565	148	22.498 727 0966
29	16.137 508 1343	89	22.062 456 3557	149	22.500 277 2918
30	16.409 343 5158	90	22.082 543 4884	150	22.501 761 6199
31	16.669 628 7404	91	22.101 777 1284	151	22.503 182 8796
32	16.918 854 5689	92	22.120 193 5400	152	22.504 543 7507
33	17.157 490 9098	93	22.137 827 4471	153	22.505 846 7990
34	17.385 987 7054	94	22.154 712 0977	154	22.507 094 4814
35	17.604 775 7801	95	22.170 879 3276	155	22.508 289 1503
36	17.814 267 6530	96	22.186 359 6195	156	22.509 433 0583
37	18.014 858 3153	97	22.201 182 1611	157	22.510 528 3623
38	18.206 925 9752	98	22.215 374 8999	158	22.511 577 1272
39	18.390 832 7709	99	22.228 964 5959	159	22.512 581 3307
40	18.566 925 4539	100	22.241 976 8722	160	22.513 542 8660
41	18.735 536 0421	101	22.254 436 2631	161	22.514 463 5462
42	18.896 982 4460	102	22.266 366 2603	162	22.515 345 1070
43	19.051 569 0686	103	22.277 789 3575	163	22.516 189 2108
44	19.199 587 3787	104	22.288 727 0928	164	22.516 997 4490
45	19.341 316 4607	105	22.299 200 0888	165	22.517 771 3455
46	19.477 023 5411	106	22.309 228 0922	166	22.518 512 3596
47	19.606 964 4918	107	22.318 830 0105	167	22.519 221 8883
48	19.731 384 3129	108	22.328 023 9478	168	22.519 901 2695
49	19.850 517 5946	109	22.336 827 2391	169	22.520 551 7840
50	19.964 588 9595	110	22.345 256 4827	170	22.521 174 6586
51	20.073 813 4861	111	22.353 327 5717	171	22.521 771 0675
52	20.178 397 1142	112	22.361 055 7239	172	22.522 342 1352
53	20.278 537 0333	113	22.368 455 5107	173	22.522 888 9386
54	20.374 422 0546	114	22.375 540 8839	174	22.523 412 5085
55	20.466 232 9667	115	22.382 325 2030	175	22.523 913 8322
56	20.554 142 8766	116	22.388 821 2596	176	22.524 393 8549
57	20.638 317 5359	117	22.395 041 3019	177	22.524 853 4816
58	20.718 915 6538	118	22.400 997 0575	178	22.525 293 5791
59	20.796 089 1957	119	22.406 699 7558	179	22.525 714 9770
60	20.869 983 6704	120	22.412 160 1492	180	22.526 118 4699

Present Value of 1 per period

NOMINAL INTEREST RATE COMPOUNDED

YEARLY	HALF-YEARLY	QUARTERLY
@	@	@
$4\frac{1}{2}\%$	9%	18%
4.5000%	9.0000%	18.0000%
PER ANNUM	PER ANNUM	PER ANNUM

Periods	Present Value	Periods	Present Value	Periods	Present Value
1	.956 937 7990	61	20.706 241 1849	121	22.114 149 4375
2	1.872 667 7503	62	20.771 522 6650	122	22.118 803 2895
3	2.748 964 3543	63	20.833 992 9808	123	22.123 256 7363
4	3.587 525 6979	64	20.893 773 1874	124	22.127 518 4080
5	4.389 976 7444	65	20.950 979 1267	125	22.131 596 5627
6	5.157 872 4827	66	21.005 721 6523	126	22.135 499 1030
7	5.892 700 9404	67	21.058 106 8443	127	22.139 233 5914
8	6.595 886 0674	68	21.108 236 2147	128	22.142 807 2645
9	7.268 790 4951	69	21.156 206 9040	129	22.146 227 0474
10	7.912 718 1771	70	21.202 111 8699	130	22.149 499 5669
11	8.528 916 9159	71	21.246 040 0668	131	22.152 631 1645
12	9.118 580 7808	72	21.288 076 6190	132	22.155 627 9086
13	9.682 852 4218	73	21.328 302 9847	133	22.158 495 6063
14	10.222 825 2840	74	21.366 797 1145	134	22.161 239 8146
15	10.739 545 7263	75	21.403 633 6024	135	22.163 865 8513
16	11.234 015 0491	76	21.438 883 8301	136	22.166 378 8051
17	11.707 191 4346	77	21.472 616 1053	137	22.168 783 5455
18	12.159 991 8034	78	21.504 895 7946	138	22.171 084 7326
19	12.593 293 5918	79	21.535 785 4494	139	22.173 286 8254
20	13.007 936 4515	80	21.565 344 9276	140	22.175 394 0913
21	13.404 723 8770	81	21.593 631 5097	141	22.177 410 6137
22	13.784 424 7627	82	21.620 700 0093	142	22.179 340 3002
23	14.147 774 8925	83	21.646 602 8797	143	22.181 186 8901
24	14.495 478 3660	84	21.671 390 3155	144	22.182 953 9619
25	14.828 208 9627	85	21.695 110 3497	145	22.184 644 9396
26	15.146 611 4476	86	21.717 808 9471	146	22.186 263 1001
27	15.451 302 8206	87	21.739 530 0929	147	22.187 811 5790
28	15.742 873 5126	88	21.760 315 8784	148	22.189 293 3771
29	16.021 888 5288	89	21.780 206 5822	149	22.190 711 3656
30	16.288 888 5443	90	21.799 240 7485	150	22.192 068 2924
31	16.544 390 9515	91	21.817 455 2617	151	22.193 366 7870
32	16.788 890 8627	92	21.834 885 4179	152	22.194 609 3656
33	17.022 862 0695	93	21.851 564 9932	153	22.195 798 4360
34	17.246 757 9613	94	21.867 526 3093	154	22.196 936 3024
35	17.461 012 4031	95	21.882 800 2960	155	22.198 025 1697
36	17.666 040 5772	96	21.897 416 5512	156	22.199 067 1481
37	17.862 239 7868	97	21.911 403 3983	157	22.200 064 2565
38	18.049 990 2266	98	21.924 787 9409	158	22.201 018 4273
39	18.229 655 7192	99	21.937 596 1157	159	22.201 931 5094
40	18.401 584 4203	100	21.949 852 7423	160	22.202 805 2721
41	18.566 109 4931	101	21.961 581 5716	161	22.203 641 4087
42	18.723 549 7542	102	21.972 805 3317	162	22.204 441 5394
43	18.874 210 2911	103	21.983 545 7719	163	22.205 207 2148
44	19.018 383 0536	104	21.993 823 7052	164	22.205 939 9185
45	19.156 347 4198	105	22.003 659 0480	165	22.206 641 0703
46	19.288 370 7366	106	22.013 070 8594	166	22.207 312 0290
47	19.414 708 8389	107	22.022 077 3774	167	22.207 954 0947
48	19.535 606 5444	108	22.030 696 0549	168	22.208 568 5117
49	19.651 298 1286	109	22.038 943 5932	169	22.209 156 4705
50	19.762 007 7785	110	22.046 835 9744	170	22.209 719 1105
51	19.867 950 0273	111	22.054 388 4922	171	22.210 257 5221
52	19.969 330 1697	112	22.061 615 7820	172	22.210 772 7484
53	20.066 344 6600	113	22.068 531 8488	173	22.211 265 7879
54	20.159 181 4928	114	22.075 150 0946	174	22.211 737 5961
55	20.248 020 5673	115	22.081 483 3441	175	22.212 189 0872
56	20.333 034 0357	116	22.087 543 8699	176	22.212 621 1361
57	20.414 386 6370	117	22.093 343 4162	177	22.213 034 5800
58	20.492 236 0163	118	22.098 893 2213	178	22.213 430 2201
59	20.566 733 0299	119	22.104 204 0395	179	22.213 808 8230
60	20.638 022 0382	120	22.109 286 1622	180	22.214 171 1225

Present Value of 1 per period

NOMINAL INTEREST RATE COMPOUNDED

YEARLY	HALF-YEARLY	QUARTERLY
@	@	@
$4\frac{9}{16}\%$	$9\frac{1}{8}\%$	$18\frac{1}{4}\%$
4.5625%	9.1250%	18.2500%
PER ANNUM	PER ANNUM	PER ANNUM

Periods	Present Value	Periods	Present Value	Periods	Present Value
1	.956 365 8099	61	20.476 145 5069	121	21.818 655 1487
2	1.871 001 3723	62	20.539 051 2917	122	21.822 981 6126
3	2.745 727 5527	63	20.599 212 2336	123	21.827 119 2948
4	3.582 285 7647	64	20.656 748 1014	124	21.831 076 4326
5	4.382 341 4367	65	20.711 773 4383	125	21.834 860 9038
6	5.147 487 3273	66	20.764 397 7892	126	21.838 480 2428
7	5.879 246 6968	67	20.814 725 9191	127	21.841 941 6548
8	6.579 076 3388	68	20.862 858 0219	128	21.845 252 0309
9	7.248 369 4813	69	20.908 889 9193	129	21.848 417 9614
10	7.888 458 5595	70	20.952 913 2522	130	21.851 445 7491
11	8.500 617 8692	71	20.995 015 6626	131	21.854 341 4217
12	9.086 066 1032	72	21.035 280 9684	132	21.857 110 7440
13	9.645 968 7778	73	21.073 789 3302	133	21.859 759 2292
14	10.181 440 5525	74	21.110 617 4108	134	21.862 292 1498
15	10.693 547 4501	75	21.145 838 5280	135	21.864 714 5486
16	11.183 308 9780	76	21.179 522 8002	136	21.867 031 2479
17	11.651 700 1583	77	21.211 737 2865	137	21.869 246 8599
18	12.099 653 4688	78	21.242 546 1198	138	21.871 365 7955
19	12.528 060 6994	79	21.272 010 6346	139	21.873 392 2730
20	12.937 774 7274	80	21.300 189 4892	140	21.875 330 3269
21	13.329 611 2157	81	21.327 138 7822	141	21.877 183 8153
22	13.704 350 2362	82	21.352 912 1647	142	21.878 956 4282
23	14.062 737 8230	83	21.377 560 9465	143	21.880 651 6947
24	14.405 487 4578	84	21.401 134 1987	144	21.882 272 9895
25	14.733 281 4898	85	21.423 678 8511	145	21.883 823 5405
26	15.046 772 4947	86	21.445 239 7859	146	21.885 306 4344
27	15.346 584 5735	87	21.465 859 9267	147	21.886 724 6235
28	15.633 314 5951	88	21.485 580 3244	148	21.888 080 9310
29	15.907 533 3845	89	21.504 440 2386	149	21.889 378 0571
30	16.169 786 8590	90	21.522 477 2156	150	21.890 618 5842
31	16.420 597 1156	91	21.539 727 1637	151	21.891 804 9819
32	16.660 463 4698	92	21.556 224 4244	152	21.892 939 6121
33	16.889 863 4499	93	21.572 001 8404	153	21.894 024 7337
34	17.109 253 7477	94	21.587 090 8217	154	21.895 062 5068
35	17.319 071 1275	95	21.601 521 4075	155	21.896 054 9975
36	17.519 733 2959	96	21.615 322 3263	156	21.897 004 1817
37	17.711 639 7330	97	21.628 521 0533	157	21.897 911 9491
38	17.895 172 4883	98	21.641 143 8644	158	21.898 780 1067
39	18.070 696 9404	99	21.653 215 8895	159	21.899 610 3830
40	18.238 562 5252	100	21.664 761 1615	160	21.900 404 4308
41	18.399 103 4311	101	21.675 802 6649	161	21.901 163 8310
42	18.552 639 2647	102	21.686 362 3813	162	21.901 890 0954
43	18.699 475 6865	103	21.696 461 3330	163	21.902 584 6699
44	18.839 905 0199	104	21.706 119 6251	164	21.903 248 9371
45	18.974 206 8332	105	21.715 356 4854	165	21.903 884 2196
46	19.102 648 4956	106	21.724 190 3028	166	21.904 491 7820
47	19.225 485 7100	107	21.732 638 6638	167	21.905 072 8340
48	19.342 963 0221	108	21.740 718 3874	168	21.905 628 5322
49	19.455 314 3069	109	21.748 445 5588	169	21.906 159 9830
50	19.562 763 2343	110	21.755 835 5613	170	21.906 668 2443
51	19.665 523 7148	111	21.762 903 1070	171	21.907 154 3281
52	19.763 800 3250	112	21.769 662 2661	172	21.907 619 2020
53	19.857 788 7149	113	21.776 126 4948	173	21.908 063 7915
54	19.947 675 9975	114	21.782 308 6621	174	21.908 488 9817
55	20.033 641 1213	115	21.788 221 0755	175	21.908 895 6191
56	20.115 855 2266	116	21.793 875 5056	176	21.909 284 5132
57	20.194 481 9860	117	21.799 283 2092	177	21.909 656 4382
58	20.269 677 9304	118	21.804 454 9520	178	21.910 012 1346
59	20.341 592 7607	119	21.809 401 0300	179	21.910 352 3104
60	20.410 369 6457	120	21.814 131 2899	180	21.910 677 6429

Present Value of 1 per period

NOMINAL INTEREST RATE COMPOUNDED

YEARLY	HALF-YEARLY	QUARTERLY
@	@	@
$4\frac{5}{8}\%$	$9\frac{1}{4}\%$	$18\frac{1}{2}\%$
4.6250%	9.2500%	18.5000%
PER ANNUM	PER ANNUM	PER ANNUM

Periods	Present Value	Periods	Present Value	Periods	Present Value
1	.955 794 5042	61	20.250 346 7054	121	21.530 631 0755
2	1.869 337 6384	62	20.310 964 5929	122	21.534 653 3577
3	2.742 497 1454	63	20.368 902 8367	123	21.538 497 8329
4	3.577 058 2035	64	20.424 279 8918	124	21.542 172 3612
5	4.374 727 0762	65	20.477 208 9766	125	21.545 684 4552
6	5.137 134 6009	66	20.527 798 3050	126	21.549 041 2952
7	5.865 839 5230	67	20.576 151 3070	127	21.552 249 7446
8	6.562 331 6827	68	20.622 366 8406	128	21.555 316 3628
9	7.228 035 0611	69	20.666 539 3937	129	21.558 247 4196
10	7.864 310 6916	70	20.708 759 2771	130	21.561 048 9076
11	8.472 459 4424	71	20.749 112 8097	131	21.563 726 5545
12	9.053 724 6761	72	20.787 682 4943	132	21.566 285 8347
13	9.609 294 7920	73	20.824 547 1869	133	21.568 731 9805
14	10.140 305 6554	74	20.859 782 2575	134	21.571 069 9934
15	10.647 842 9204	75	20.893 459 7443	135	21.573 304 6531
16	11.132 944 2489	76	20.925 648 5012	136	21.575 440 5287
17	11.596 601 4326	77	20.956 414 3380	137	21.577 481 9868
18	12.039 762 4207	78	20.985 820 1558	138	21.579 433 2012
19	12.463 333 2575	79	21.013 926 0749	139	21.581 298 1613
20	12.868 179 9355	80	21.040 789 5578	140	21.583 080 6798
21	13.255 130 1653	81	21.066 465 5272	141	21.584 784 4013
22	13.624 975 0684	82	21.091 006 4776	142	21.586 412 8089
23	13.978 470 7942	83	21.114 462 5831	143	21.587 969 2319
24	14.316 340 0661	84	21.136 881 7999	144	21.589 456 8525
25	14.639 273 6594	85	21.158 309 9640	145	21.590 878 7120
26	14.947 931 8130	86	21.178 790 8856	146	21.592 237 7176
27	15.242 945 5800	87	21.198 366 4378	147	21.593 536 6476
28	15.524 918 1170	88	21.217 076 6431	148	21.594 778 1578
29	15.794 425 9183	89	21.234 959 7544	149	21.595 964 7865
30	16.052 019 9936	90	21.252 052 3340	150	21.597 098 9596
31	16.298 226 9951	91	21.268 389 3276	151	21.598 182 9960
32	16.533 550 2940	92	21.284 004 1363	152	21.599 219 1121
33	16.758 471 0098	93	21.298 928 6846	153	21.600 209 4261
34	16.973 448 9938	94	21.313 193 4859	154	21.601 155 9629
35	17.178 923 7695	95	21.326 827 7046	155	21.602 060 6574
36	17.375 315 4308	96	21.339 859 2158	156	21.602 925 3596
37	17.563 025 5014	97	21.352 314 6627	157	21.603 751 8371
38	17.742 437 7552	98	21.364 219 5103	158	21.604 541 7798
39	17.913 919 0014	99	21.375 598 0983	159	21.605 296 8027
40	18.077 819 8341	100	21.386 473 6901	160	21.606 018 4494
41	18.234 475 3492	101	21.396 868 5210	161	21.606 708 1953
42	18.384 205 8295	102	21.406 803 8433	162	21.607 367 4507
43	18.527 317 3998	103	21.416 299 9697	163	21.607 997 5634
44	18.664 102 6521	104	21.425 376 3151	164	21.608 599 8217
45	18.794 841 2446	105	21.434 051 4362	165	21.609 175 4568
46	18.919 800 4727	106	21.442 343 0692	166	21.609 725 6457
47	19.039 235 8162	107	21.450 268 1665	167	21.610 251 5132
48	19.153 391 4611	108	21.457 842 9310	168	21.610 754 1345
49	19.262 500 7992	109	21.465 082 8492	169	21.611 234 5371
50	19.366 786 9048	110	21.472 002 7232	170	21.611 693 7034
51	19.466 462 9915	111	21.478 616 7008	171	21.612 132 5719
52	19.561 732 8473	112	21.484 938 3043	172	21.612 552 0401
53	19.652 791 2519	113	21.490 980 4581	173	21.612 952 9654
54	19.739 824 3746	114	21.496 755 5155	174	21.613 336 1677
55	19.823 010 1549	115	21.502 275 2836	175	21.613 702 4303
56	19.902 518 6666	116	21.507 551 0477	176	21.614 052 5020
57	19.978 512 4651	117	21.512 593 5939	177	21.614 387 0987
58	20.051 146 9200	118	21.517 413 2320	178	21.614 706 9044
59	20.120 570 5329	119	21.522 019 8155	179	21.615 012 5729
60	20.186 925 2405	120	21.526 422 7627	180	21.615 304 7292

Present Value of 1 per period

NOMINAL INTEREST RATE COMPOUNDED					
YEARLY @ $4\frac{11}{16}\%$ 4.6875% PER ANNUM		HALF-YEARLY @ $9\frac{3}{8}\%$ 9.3750% PER ANNUM		QUARTERLY @ $18\frac{3}{4}\%$ 18.7500% PER ANNUM	
Periods	Present Value	Periods	Present Value	Periods	Present Value
1	.955 223 8806	61	20.028 742 9659	121	21.249 814 4951
2	1.867 676 5427	62	20.087 157 4600	122	21.253 554 1446
3	2.739 273 1154	63	20.142 956 3797	123	21.257 126 3471
4	3.571 842 9759	64	20.196 256 8403	124	21.260 538 6002
5	4.367 133 5889	65	20.247 170 7131	125	21.263 798 0658
6	5.126 814 1745	66	20.295 804 8603	126	21.266 911 5853
7	5.852 479 2114	67	20.342 261 3591	127	21.269 885 6934
8	6.545 651 7841	68	20.386 637 7162	128	21.272 726 6325
9	7.207 786 7788	69	20.429 027 0721	129	21.275 440 3654
10	7.840 273 9380	70	20.469 518 3973	130	21.278 032 5878
11	8.444 440 7766	71	20.508 196 6780	131	21.280 508 7406
12	9.021 555 3687	72	20.545 143 0954	132	21.282 874 0209
13	9.572 829 0089	73	20.580 435 1956	133	21.285 133 3931
14	10.099 418 7547	74	20.614 147 0525	134	21.287 291 5994
15	10.602 429 8553	75	20.646 349 4233	135	21.289 353 1695
16	11.082 918 0707	76	20.677 109 8969	136	21.291 322 4306
17	11.541 891 8884	77	20.706 493 0358	137	21.293 203 5158
18	11.980 314 6397	78	20.734 560 5118	138	21.295 000 3733
19	12.399 106 5215	79	20.761 371 2352	139	21.296 716 7745
20	12.799 146 5280	80	20.786 981 4784	140	21.298 356 3219
21	13.181 274 2954	81	20.811 444 9943	141	21.299 922 4567
22	13.546 291 8643	82	20.834 813 1289	142	21.301 418 4661
23	13.894 965 3629	83	20.857 134 9291	143	21.302 847 4901
24	14.228 026 6153	84	20.878 457 2457	144	21.304 212 5278
25	14.546 174 6773	85	20.898 824 8317	145	21.305 516 4445
26	14.850 077 3037	86	20.918 280 4362	146	21.306 761 9768
27	15.140 372 3498	87	20.936 864 8943	147	21.307 951 7390
28	15.417 669 1102	88	20.954 617 2125	148	21.309 088 2283
29	15.682 549 5978	89	20.971 574 6507	149	21.310 173 8301
30	15.935 569 7651	90	20.987 772 8007	150	21.311 210 8227
31	16.177 260 6711	91	21.003 245 6604	151	21.312 201 3829
32	16.408 129 5963	92	21.018 025 7054	152	21.313 147 5897
33	16.628 661 1069	93	21.032 143 9574	153	21.314 051 4289
34	16.839 318 0723	94	21.045 630 0489	154	21.314 914 7978
35	17.040 542 6362	95	21.058 512 2855	155	21.315 739 5083
36	17.232 757 1450	96	21.070 817 7056	156	21.316 527 2915
37	17.416 365 0341	97	21.082 572 1366	157	21.317 279 8009
38	17.591 751 6743	98	21.093 800 2499	158	21.317 998 6158
39	17.759 285 1815	99	21.104 525 6119	159	21.318 685 2449
40	17.919 317 1883	100	21.114 770 7337	160	21.319 341 1295
41	18.072 183 5828	101	21.124 557 1188	161	21.319 967 6460
42	18.218 205 2134	102	21.133 905 3075	162	21.320 566 1097
43	18.357 688 5621	103	21.142 834 9206	163	21.321 137 7764
44	18.490 926 3877	104	21.151 364 7003	164	21.321 683 8461
45	18.618 198 3405	105	21.159 512 5495	165	21.322 205 4649
46	18.739 771 5491	106	21.167 295 5697	166	21.322 703 7277
47	18.855 901 1812	107	21.174 730 0964	167	21.323 179 6802
48	18.966 830 9791	108	21.181 831 7339	168	21.323 634 3214
49	19.072 793 7711	109	21.188 615 3876	169	21.324 068 6055
50	19.174 011 9604	110	21.195 095 2956	170	21.324 483 4441
51	19.270 697 9920	111	21.201 285 0585	171	21.324 879 7078
52	19.363 054 7984	112	21.207 197 6678	172	21.325 258 2283
53	19.451 276 2253	113	21.212 845 5334	173	21.325 619 8002
54	19.535 547 4391	114	21.218 240 5096	174	21.325 965 1822
55	19.616 045 3150	115	21.223 393 9196	175	21.326 295 0995
56	19.692 938 8083	116	21.228 316 5799	176	21.326 610 2443
57	19.766 389 3094	117	21.233 018 8226	177	21.326 911 2781
58	19.836 550 9821	118	21.237 510 5171	178	21.327 198 8328
59	19.903 571 0874	119	21.241 801 0910	179	21.327 473 5119
60	19.967 590 2925	120	21.245 899 5496	180	21.327 735 8920

Present Value of 1 per period

NOMINAL INTEREST RATE COMPOUNDED

YEARLY	HALF-YEARLY	QUARTERLY
@	@	@
$4\frac{3}{4}\%$	$9\frac{1}{2}\%$	19%
4.7500%	9.5000%	19.0000%
PER ANNUM	PER ANNUM	PER ANNUM

Periods	Present Value	Periods	Present Value	Periods	Present Value
1	.954 653 9379	61	19.811 235 2395	121	20.975 953 9699
2	1.866 018 0792	62	19.867 527 6749	122	20.979 430 9975
3	2.736 055 4455	63	19.921 267 4701	123	20.982 750 3557
4	3.566 640 0435	64	19.972 570 3772	124	20.985 919 1939
5	4.359 560 9007	65	20.021 546 8995	125	20.988 944 3379
6	5.116 525 9195	66	20.068 302 5293	126	20.991 832 3035
7	5.839 165 5556	67	20.112 937 9755	127	20.994 589 3112
8	6.529 036 3299	68	20.155 549 3799	128	20.997 221 2995
9	7.187 624 1813	69	20.196 228 5250	129	20.999 733 9374
10	7.816 347 6671	70	20.235 063 0310	130	21.002 132 6372
11	8.416 561 0187	71	20.272 136 5451	131	21.004 422 5653
12	8.989 557 0585	72	20.307 528 9214	132	21.006 608 6542
13	9.536 569 9842	73	20.341 316 3927	133	21.008 695 6126
14	10.058 778 0279	74	20.373 571 7353	134	21.010 687 9357
15	10.557 305 9932	75	20.404 364 4251	135	21.012 589 9147
16	11.033 227 6785	76	20.433 760 7877	136	21.014 405 6465
17	11.487 568 1895	77	20.461 824 1410	137	21.016 139 0420
18	11.921 306 1475	78	20.488 614 9317	138	21.017 793 8349
19	12.335 375 7971	79	20.514 190 8656	139	21.019 373 5894
20	12.730 669 0187	80	20.538 607 0316	140	21.020 881 7082
21	13.108 037 2494	81	20.561 916 0206	141	21.022 321 4399
22	13.468 293 3168	82	20.584 168 0388	142	21.023 695 8853
23	13.812 213 1903	83	20.605 411 0155	143	21.025 008 0051
24	14.140 537 6518	84	20.625 690 7070	144	21.026 260 6254
25	14.453 973 8920	85	20.645 050 7942	145	21.027 456 4443
26	14.753 197 0329	86	20.663 532 9778	146	21.028 598 0375
27	15.038 851 5827	87	20.681 177 0671	147	21.029 687 8639
28	15.311 552 8236	88	20.698 021 0664	148	21.030 728 2711
29	15.571 888 1371	89	20.714 101 2568	149	21.031 721 4998
30	15.820 418 2693	90	20.729 452 2737	150	21.032 669 6896
31	16.057 678 5387	91	20.744 107 1826	151	21.033 574 8826
32	16.284 179 9892	92	20.758 097 5490	152	21.034 439 0288
33	16.500 410 4909	93	20.771 453 5074	153	21.035 263 9893
34	16.706 835 7908	94	20.784 203 8257	154	21.036 051 5411
35	16.903 900 5163	95	20.796 375 9672	155	21.036 803 3805
36	17.092 029 1325	96	20.807 996 1501	156	21.037 521 1270
37	17.271 626 8568	97	20.819 089 4034	157	21.038 206 3265
38	17.443 080 5316	98	20.829 679 6214	158	21.038 860 4549
39	17.606 759 4573	99	20.839 789 6147	159	21.039 484 9211
40	17.763 016 1884	100	20.849 441 1596	160	21.040 081 0703
41	17.912 187 2920	101	20.858 655 0450	161	21.040 650 1864
42	18.054 594 0735	102	20.867 451 1169	162	21.041 193 4954
43	18.190 543 2683	103	20.875 848 3217	163	21.041 712 1674
44	18.320 327 7024	104	20.883 864 7462	164	21.042 207 3197
45	18.444 226 9236	105	20.891 517 6575	165	21.042 680 0188
46	18.562 507 8029	106	20.898 823 5394	166	21.043 131 2829
47	18.675 425 1102	107	20.905 798 1283	167	21.043 562 0839
48	18.783 222 0622	108	20.912 456 4470	168	21.043 973 3498
49	18.886 130 8470	109	20.918 812 8373	169	21.044 365 9664
50	18.984 373 1236	110	20.924 880 9902	170	21.044 740 7794
51	19.078 160 4999	111	20.930 673 9764	171	21.045 098 5961
52	19.167 694 9880	112	20.936 204 2734	172	21.045 440 1872
53	19.253 169 4396	113	20.941 483 7932	173	21.045 766 2885
54	19.334 767 9614	114	20.946 523 9076	174	21.046 077 6024
55	19.412 666 3116	115	20.951 335 4726	175	21.046 374 7994
56	19.487 032 2784	116	20.955 928 8522	176	21.046 658 5197
57	19.558 026 0414	117	20.960 313 9400	177	21.046 929 3744
58	19.625 800 5169	118	20.964 500 1814	178	21.047 187 9469
59	19.690 501 6867	119	20.968 496 5932	179	21.047 434 7942
60	19.752 268 9134	120	20.972 311 7835	180	21.047 670 4479

Present Value of 1 per period

NOMINAL INTEREST RATE COMPOUNDED

YEARLY	HALF-YEARLY	QUARTERLY
@	@	@
$4\frac{13}{16}\%$	$9\frac{5}{8}\%$	$19\frac{1}{4}\%$
4.8125%	9.6250%	19.2500%
PER ANNUM	PER ANNUM	PER ANNUM

Periods	Present Value	Periods	Present Value	Periods	Present Value
1	.954 084 6750	61	19.597 727 1600	121	20.708 808 7949
2	1.864 362 2421	62	19.651 975 8235	122	20.712 041 7841
3	2.732 844 1189	63	19.703 733 6420	123	20.715 126 3295
4	3.561 449 3681	64	19.753 114 9834	124	20.718 069 2469
5	4.352 008 9379	65	19.800 228 9645	125	20.720 877 0394
6	5.106 269 7082	66	19.845 179 6918	126	20.723 555 9112
7	5.825 898 3501	67	19.888 066 4919	127	20.726 111 7817
8	6.512 485 0090	68	19.928 984 1306	128	20.728 550 2986
9	7.167 546 8184	69	19.968 023 0226	129	20.730 876 8502
10	7.792 531 2519	70	20.005 269 4313	130	20.733 096 5774
11	8.388 819 3220	71	20.040 805 6589	131	20.735 214 3851
12	8.957 728 6316	72	20.074 710 2291	132	20.737 234 9530
13	9.500 516 2854	73	20.107 058 0600	133	20.739 162 7458
14	10.018 381 6677	74	20.137 920 6297	134	20.741 002 0235
15	10.512 469 0926	75	20.167 366 1345	135	20.742 756 8501
16	10.983 870 3328	76	20.195 459 6393	136	20.744 431 1032
17	11.433 627 0319	77	20.222 263 2218	137	20.746 028 4825
18	11.862 733 0060	78	20.247 836 1090	138	20.747 552 5176
19	12.272 136 4398	79	20.272 234 8089	139	20.749 006 5761
20	12.662 741 9819	80	20.295 513 2345	140	20.750 393 8711
21	13.035 412 7436	81	20.317 722 8236	141	20.751 717 4679
22	13.390 972 2062	82	20.338 912 6522	142	20.752 980 2914
23	13.730 206 0405	83	20.359 129 5429	143	20.754 185 1319
24	14.053 863 8431	84	20.378 418 1686	144	20.755 334 6518
25	14.362 660 7924	85	20.396 821 1507	145	20.756 431 3911
26	14.657 279 2295	86	20.414 379 1539	146	20.757 477 7733
27	14.938 370 1653	87	20.431 130 9757	147	20.758 476 1105
28	15.206 554 7194	88	20.447 113 6322	148	20.759 428 6087
29	15.462 425 4926	89	20.462 362 4397	149	20.760 337 3726
30	15.706 547 8761	90	20.476 911 0934	150	20.761 204 4104
31	15.939 461 3010	91	20.490 791 7408	151	20.762 031 6378
32	16.161 680 4303	92	20.504 035 0539	152	20.762 820 8828
33	16.373 696 2960	93	20.516 670 2959	153	20.763 573 8894
34	16.575 977 3844	94	20.528 725 3867	154	20.764 292 3214
35	16.768 970 6709	95	20.540 226 9640	155	20.764 977 7664
36	16.953 102 6079	96	20.551 200 4427	156	20.765 631 7390
37	17.128 780 0671	97	20.561 670 0706	157	20.766 255 6842
38	17.296 391 2388	98	20.571 658 9821	158	20.766 850 9807
39	17.456 306 4890	99	20.581 189 2494	159	20.767 418 9440
40	17.608 879 1785	100	20.590 281 9315	160	20.767 960 8291
41	17.754 446 4434	101	20.598 957 1201	161	20.768 477 8334
42	17.893 329 9401	102	20.607 233 9846	162	20.768 971 0992
43	18.025 836 5558	103	20.615 130 8141	163	20.769 441 7166
44	18.152 259 0872	104	20.622 665 0582	164	20.769 890 7255
45	18.272 876 8870	105	20.629 853 3650	165	20.770 319 1179
46	18.387 956 4814	106	20.636 711 6184	166	20.770 727 8406
47	18.497 752 1587	107	20.643 254 9728	167	20.771 117 7966
48	18.602 506 5319	108	20.649 497 8870	168	20.771 489 8477
49	18.702 451 0740	109	20.655 454 1558	169	20.771 844 8159
50	18.797 806 6299	110	20.661 136 9405	170	20.772 183 4857
51	18.888 783 9045	111	20.666 558 7983	171	20.772 506 6053
52	18.975 583 9280	112	20.671 731 7098	172	20.772 814 8888
53	19.058 398 5001	113	20.676 667 1053	173	20.773 109 0173
54	19.137 410 6143	114	20.681 375 8906	174	20.773 389 6409
55	19.212 794 8616	115	20.685 868 4705	175	20.773 657 3795
56	19.284 717 8167	116	20.690 154 7721	176	20.773 912 8248
57	19.353 338 4059	117	20.694 244 2667	177	20.774 156 5412
58	19.418 808 2585	118	20.698 145 9909	178	20.774 389 0674
59	19.481 272 0415	119	20.701 868 5662	179	20.774 610 9170
60	19.540 867 7796	120	20.705 420 2182	180	20.774 822 5803

Present Value of 1 per period

NOMINAL INTEREST RATE COMPOUNDED

YEARLY	HALF-YEARLY	QUARTERLY
@	@	@
$4\frac{7}{8}\%$	$9\frac{3}{4}\%$	$19\frac{1}{2}\%$
4.8750%	9.7500%	19.5000%
PER ANNUM	PER ANNUM	PER ANNUM

Periods	Present Value	Periods	Present Value	Periods	Present Value
1	.953 516 0906	61	19,388 124 9651	121	20,448 148 4750
2	1,862 709 0256	62	19,440 405 2111	122	20,451 154 6842
3	2,729 639 1186	63	19,490 255 2668	123	20,454 021 1530
4	3,556 270 9116	64	19,537 788 0971	124	20,456 754 3771
5	4,344 477 6273	65	19,583 111 4156	125	20,459 360 5502
6	5,096 045 4134	66	19,626 327 9290	126	20,461 845 5783
7	5,812 677 3906	67	19,667 535 5700	127	20,464 215 0925
8	6,495 997 5119	68	19,706 827 7187	128	20,466 474 4625
9	7,147 554 2426	69	19,744 293 4147	129	20,468 628 8081
10	7,768 824 0692	70	19,780 017 5587	130	20,470 683 0113
11	8,361 214 8455	71	19,814 081 1049	131	20,472 641 7271
12	8,926 068 9826	72	19,846 561 2442	132	20,474 509 3941
13	9,464 666 4911	73	19,877 531 5797	133	20,476 290 2447
14	9,978 227 8819	74	19,907 062 2929	134	20,477 988 3144
15	10,467 916 9315	75	19,935 220 3032	135	20,479 607 4511
16	10,934 843 3196	76	19,962 069 4190	136	20,481 151 3241
17	11,380 065 1439	77	19,987 670 4829	137	20,482 623 4318
18	11,804 591 3172	78	20,012 081 5094	138	20,484 027 1102
19	12,209 383 8543	79	20,035 357 8158	139	20,485 365 5401
20	12,595 360 0518	80	20,057 552 1486	140	20,486 641 7546
21	12,963 394 5666	81	20,078 714 8020	141	20,487 858 6456
22	13,314 321 3985	82	20,098 893 7325	142	20,489 018 9708
23	13,648 935 7792	83	20,118 134 6675	143	20,490 125 3595
24	13,967 995 9754	84	20,136 481 2086	144	20,491 180 3189
25	14,272 225 0064	85	20,153 974 9307	145	20,492 186 2397
26	14,562 312 2826	86	20,170 655 4762	146	20,493 145 4014
27	14,838 915 1681	87	20,186 560 6448	147	20,494 059 9775
28	15,102 660 4702	88	20,201 726 4790	148	20,494 932 0405
29	15,354 145 8596	89	20,216 187 3458	149	20,495 763 5667
30	15,593 941 2248	90	20,229 976 0151	150	20,496 556 4402
31	15,822 589 9641	91	20,243 123 7331	151	20,497 312 4579
32	16,040 610 2161	92	20,255 660 2938	152	20,498 033 3329
33	16,248 496 0344	93	20,267 614 1061	153	20,498 720 6988
34	16,446 718 5072	94	20,279 012 2585	154	20,499 376 1133
35	16,635 726 8245	95	20,289 880 5802	155	20,500 001 0616
36	16,815 949 2963	96	20,300 243 6999	156	20,500 596 9598
37	16,987 794 3230	97	20,310 125 1012	157	20,501 165 1583
38	17,151 651 3211	98	20,319 547 1763	158	20,501 706 9448
39	17,307 891 6054	99	20,328 531 2766	159	20,502 223 5468
40	17,456 869 2304	100	20,337 097 7608	160	20,502 716 1353
41	17,598 921 7930	101	20,345 266 0413	161	20,503 185 8262
42	17,734 371 1971	102	20,353 054 6281	162	20,503 633 6841
43	17,863 524 3834	103	20,360 481 1710	163	20,504 060 7238
44	17,986 674 0247	104	20,367 562 4992	164	20,504 467 9131
45	18,104 099 1892	105	20,374 314 6596	165	20,504 856 1746
46	18,216 065 9731	106	20,380 752 9531	166	20,505 226 3881
47	18,322 828 1030	107	20,386 891 9696	167	20,505 579 3927
48	18,424 627 5118	108	20,392 745 6206	168	20,505 915 9883
49	18,521 694 8861	109	20,398 327 1710	169	20,506 236 9376
50	18,614 250 1894	110	20,403 649 2691	170	20,506 542 9679
51	18,702 503 1603	111	20,408 723 9753	171	20,506 834 7727
52	18,786 653 7882	112	20,413 562 7893	172	20,507 113 0133
53	18,866 892 7658	113	20,418 176 6764	173	20,507 378 3202
54	18,943 401 9221	114	20,422 576 0919	174	20,507 631 2946
55	19,016 354 6337	115	20,426 771 0054	175	20,507 872 5098
56	19,085 916 2181	116	20,430 770 9229	176	20,508 102 5123
57	19,152 244 3081	117	20,434 584 9086	177	20,508 321 8234
58	19,215 489 2091	118	20,438 221 6053	178	20,508 530 9401
59	19,275 794 2399	119	20,441 689 2542	179	20,508 730 3362
60	19,333 296 0571	120	20,444 995 7132	180	20,508 920 4636

Present Value of 1 per period

NOMINAL INTEREST RATE COMPOUNDED

YEARLY	HALF-YEARLY	QUARTERLY
@	@	@
$4\frac{15}{16}\%$	$9\frac{7}{8}\%$	$19\frac{3}{4}\%$
4.9375%	9.8750%	19.7500%
PER ANNUM	PER ANNUM	PER ANNUM

Periods	Present Value	Periods	Present Value	Periods	Present Value
1	.952 948 1834	61	19.182 337 4190	121	20.193 752 2303
2	1.861 058 4238	62	19.232 721 7811	122	20.196 547 6882
3	2.726 440 4277	63	19.280 735 4674	123	20.199 211 6147
4	3.551 104 6362	64	19.326 490 0225	124	20.201 750 1987
5	4.336 966 8958	65	19.370 091 7427	125	20.204 169 3376
6	5.085 852 9084	66	19.411 641 9228	126	20.206 474 6517
7	5.799 502 4738	67	19.451 237 0914	127	20.208 671 4966
8	6.479 573 5307	68	19.488 969 2354	128	20.210 764 9759
9	7.127 646 0090	69	19.524 926 0135	129	20.212 759 9532
10	7.745 225 4999	70	19.559 190 9599	130	20.214 661 0632
11	8.333 746 7540	71	19.591 843 6782	131	20.216 472 7225
12	8.894 577 0139	72	19.622 960 0269	132	20.218 199 1400
13	9.429 019 1913	73	19.652 612 2949	133	20.219 844 3264
14	9.938 314 8935	74	19.680 869 3697	134	20.221 412 1037
15	10.423 647 3076	75	19.707 796 8979	135	20.222 906 1144
16	10.886 143 9501	76	19.733 457 4369	136	20.224 329 8290
17	11.326 879 2854	77	19.757 910 6010	137	20.225 686 5554
18	11.746 877 2225	78	19.781 213 1993	138	20.226 979 4453
19	12.147 113 4938	79	19.803 419 3680	139	20.228 211 5023
20	12.528 517 9214	80	19.824 580 6961	140	20.229 385 5889
21	12.891 976 5779	81	19.844 746 3453	141	20.230 504 4325
22	13.238 333 8443	82	19.863 963 1641	142	20.231 570 6325
23	13.568 394 3722	83	19.882 275 7966	143	20.232 586 6659
24	13.882 924 9526	84	19.899 726 7866	144	20.233 554 8931
25	14.182 656 2979	85	19.916 356 6757	145	20.234 477 5634
26	14.468 284 7390	86	19.932 204 0983	146	20.235 356 8204
27	14.740 473 8430	87	19.947 305 8710	147	20.236 194 7067
28	14.999 855 9552	88	19.961 697 0777	148	20.236 993 1690
29	15.247 033 6678	89	19.975 411 1521	149	20.237 754 0622
30	15.482 581 2201	90	19.988 479 9544	150	20.238 479 1540
31	15.707 045 8321	91	20.000 933 8457	151	20.239 170 1288
32	15.920 948 9764	92	20.012 801 7589	152	20.239 828 5921
33	16.124 787 5892	93	20.024 111 2652	153	20.240 456 0735
34	16.319 035 2250	94	20.034 888 6386	154	20.241 054 0307
35	16.504 143 1566	95	20.045 158 9171	155	20.241 623 8530
36	16.680 541 4238	96	20.054 945 9603	156	20.242 166 8641
37	16.848 639 8321	97	20.064 272 5054	157	20.242 684 3255
38	17.008 828 9049	98	20.073 160 2195	158	20.243 177 4394
39	17.161 480 7909	99	20.081 629 7506	159	20.243 647 3514
40	17.306 950 1283	100	20.089 700 7748	160	20.244 095 1533
41	17.445 574 8691	101	20.097 392 0427	161	20.244 521 8852
42	17.577 677 0641	102	20.104 721 4225	162	20.244 928 5386
43	17.703 563 6108	103	20.111 705 9416	163	20.245 316 0582
44	17.823 526 9668	104	20.118 361 8264	164	20.245 685 3443
45	17.937 845 8290	105	20.124 704 5398	165	20.246 037 2549
46	18.046 785 7811	106	20.130 748 8170	166	20.246 372 6074
47	18.150 599 9105	107	20.136 508 6999	167	20.246 692 1809
48	18.249 529 3965	108	20.141 997 5699	168	20.246 996 7180
49	18.343 804 0705	109	20.147 228 1786	169	20.247 286 9260
50	18.433 642 9499	110	20.152 212 6776	170	20.247 563 4792
51	18.519 254 7468	111	20.156 962 6469	171	20.247 827 0201
52	18.600 838 3531	112	20.161 489 1215	172	20.248 078 1609
53	18.678 583 3025	113	20.165 802 6173	173	20.248 317 4851
54	18.752 670 2109	114	20.169 913 1553	174	20.248 545 5486
55	18.823 271 1956	115	20.173 830 2849	175	20.248 762 8814
56	18.890 550 2757	116	20.177 563 1066	176	20.248 969 9882
57	18.954 663 7529	117	20.181 120 2921	177	20.249 167 3503
58	19.015 760 5746	118	20.184 510 1057	178	20.249 355 4261
59	19.073 982 6797	119	20.187 740 4223	179	20.249 534 6526
60	19.129 465 3291	120	20.190 818 7467	180	20.249 705 4462

Present Value of 1 per period

	NOMINAL INTEREST RATE COMPOUNDED				
	YEARLY @ 5% 5.0000% PER ANNUM		HALF-YEARLY @ 10% 10.0000% PER ANNUM		QUARTERLY @ 20% 20.0000% PER ANNUM
Periods	**Present Value**	**Periods**	**Present Value**	**Periods**	**Present Value**
1	,952 380 9524	61	18,980 275 7382	121	19,945 408 5276
2	1,859 410 4308	62	19,028 834 0363	122	19,948 008 1215
3	2,723 248 0294	63	19,075 080 0346	123	19,950 483 9252
4	3,545 950 5042	64	19,119 123 8425	124	19,952 841 8336
5	4,329 476 6706	65	19,161 070 3262	125	19,955 087 4605
6	5,075 692 0673	66	19,201 019 3583	126	19,957 226 1529
7	5,786 373 3974	67	19,239 066 0555	127	19,959 263 0027
8	6,463 212 7594	68	19,275 301 0052	128	19,961 202 8598
9	7,107 821 6756	69	19,309 810 4812	129	19,963 050 3426
10	7,721 734 9292	70	19,342 676 6487	130	19,964 809 8501
11	8,306 414 2183	71	19,373 977 7607	131	19,966 485 5715
12	8,863 251 6364	72	19,403 788 3435	132	19,968 081 4967
13	9,393 572 9871	73	19,432 179 3748	133	19,969 601 4254
14	9,898 640 9401	74	19,459 218 4522	134	19,971 048 9766
15	10,379 658 0382	75	19,484 969 9545	135	19,972 427 5968
16	10,837 769 5602	76	19,509 495 1947	136	19,973 740 5683
17	11,274 066 2478	77	19,532 852 5664	137	19,974 991 0175
18	11,689 586 9027	78	19,555 097 6823	138	19,976 181 9214
19	12,085 320 8597	79	19,576 283 5069	139	19,977 316 1156
20	12,462 210 3425	80	19,596 460 4828	140	19,978 396 3006
21	12,821 152 7072	81	19,615 676 6503	141	19,979 425 0482
22	13,163 002 5783	82	19,633 977 7622	142	19,980 404 8078
23	13,488 573 8841	83	19,651 407 3925	143	19,981 337 9122
24	13,798 641 7943	84	19,668 007 0405	144	19,982 226 5830
25	14,093 944 5660	85	19,683 816 2291	145	19,983 072 9362
26	14,375 185 3010	86	19,698 872 5991	146	19,983 878 9869
27	14,643 033 6200	87	19,713 211 9992	147	19,984 646 6542
28	14,898 127 2571	88	19,726 868 5706	148	19,985 377 7659
29	15,141 073 5782	89	19,739 874 8292	149	19,986 074 0627
30	15,372 451 0269	90	19,752 261 7421	150	19,986 737 2026
31	15,592 810 5018	91	19,764 058 8020	151	19,987 368 7644
32	15,802 676 6684	92	19,775 294 0971	152	19,987 970 2518
33	16,002 549 2080	93	19,785 994 3782	153	19,988 543 0970
34	16,192 904 0076	94	19,796 185 1221	154	19,989 088 6638
35	16,374 194 2929	95	19,805 890 5925	155	19,989 608 2512
36	16,546 851 7076	96	19,815 133 8976	156	19,990 103 0964
37	16,711 287 3405	97	19,823 937 0453	157	19,990 574 3775
38	16,867 892 7053	98	19,832 320 9955	158	19,991 023 2167
39	17,017 040 6717	99	19,840 305 7100	159	19,991 450 6825
40	17,159 086 3540	100	19,847 910 2000	160	19,991 857 7929
41	17,294 367 9562	101	19,855 152 5715	161	19,992 245 5171
42	17,423 207 5773	102	19,862 050 0681	162	19,992 614 7781
43	17,545 911 9784	103	19,868 619 1124	163	19,992 966 4554
44	17,662 773 3128	104	19,874 875 3452	164	19,993 301 3861
45	17,774 069 8217	105	19,880 833 6621	165	19,993 620 3677
46	17,880 066 4968	106	19,886 508 2496	166	19,993 924 1597
47	17,981 015 7113	107	19,891 912 6187	167	19,994 213 4854
48	18,077 157 8203	108	19,897 059 6368	168	19,994 489 0337
49	18,168 721 7336	109	19,901 961 5589	169	19,994 751 4607
50	18,255 925 4606	110	19,906 630 0561	170	19,995 001 3911
51	18,338 976 6291	111	19,911 076 2439	171	19,995 239 4201
52	18,418 072 9801	112	19,915 310 7085	172	19,995 466 1144
53	18,493 402 8382	113	19,919 343 5319	173	19,995 682 0137
54	18,565 145 5602	114	19,923 184 3161	174	19,995 887 6321
55	18,633 471 9621	115	19,926 842 2058	175	19,996 083 4592
56	18,698 544 7258	116	19,930 325 9103	176	19,996 269 9611
57	18,760 518 7865	117	19,933 643 7241	177	19,996 447 5820
58	18,819 541 7014	118	19,936 803 5467	178	19,996 616 7448
59	18,875 754 0013	119	19,939 812 9016	179	19,996 777 8522
60	18,929 289 5251	120	19,942 678 9539	180	19,996 931 2878

Present Value of 1 per period

NOMINAL INTEREST RATE COMPOUNDED

YEARLY	HALF-YEARLY	QUARTERLY
@	@	@
$5\frac{1}{16}\%$	$10\frac{1}{8}\%$	$20\frac{1}{4}\%$
5.0625%	10.1250%	20.2500%
PER ANNUM	PER ANNUM	PER ANNUM

Periods	Present Value	Periods	Present Value	Periods	Present Value
1	.951 814 3962	61	18.781 853 5186	121	19.702 914 6363
2	1.857 765 0410	62	18.828 652 9624	122	19.705 332 1940
3	2.720 061 9070	63	18.873 197 3467	123	19.707 633 2602
4	3.540 808 4778	64	18.915 595 3330	124	19.709 823 4481
5	4.322 006 8795	65	18.955 950 3467	125	19.711 908 1005
6	5.065 562 7645	66	18.994 360 8297	126	19.713 892 3027
7	5.773 289 9603	67	19.030 920 4804	127	19.715 780 8949
8	6.446 914 8938	68	19.065 718 4822	128	19.717 578 4842
9	7.088 080 8031	69	19.098 839 7213	129	19.719 289 4555
10	7.698 351 7460	70	19.130 364 9935	130	19.720 917 9826
11	8.279 216 4150	71	19.160 371 2014	131	19.722 468 0382
12	8.832 091 7692	72	19.188 931 5421	132	19.723 943 4034
13	9.358 326 4906	73	19.216 115 6855	133	19.725 347 6772
14	9.859 204 2742	74	19.241 989 9446	134	19.726 684 2853
15	10.335 946 9594	75	19.266 617 4369	135	19.727 956 4881
16	10.789 717 5104	76	19.290 058 2385	136	19.729 167 3890
17	11.221 622 8535	77	19.312 369 5310	137	19.730 319 9419
18	11.632 716 5768	78	19.333 605 7404	138	19.731 416 9584
19	12.024 001 5008	79	19.353 818 6702	139	19.732 461 1145
20	12.396 432 1245	80	19.373 057 6278	140	19.733 454 9573
21	12.750 916 9537	81	19.391 369 5446	141	19.734 400 9112
22	13.088 320 7174	82	19.408 799 0907	142	19.735 301 2837
23	13.409 466 4770	83	19.425 388 7835	143	19.736 158 2712
24	13.715 137 6343	84	19.441 179 0920	144	19.736 973 9643
25	14.006 079 8422	85	19.456 208 5349	145	19.737 750 3526
26	14.283 002 8243	86	19.470 513 7750	146	19.738 489 3303
27	14.546 582 1052	87	19.484 129 7085	147	19.739 192 6999
28	14.797 460 6593	88	19.497 089 5501	148	19.739 862 1772
29	15.036 250 4788	89	19.509 424 9138	149	19.740 499 3953
30	15.263 534 0667	90	19.521 165 8906	150	19.741 105 9086
31	15.479 865 8577	91	19.532 341 1213	151	19.741 683 1968
32	15.685 773 5706	92	19.542 977 8668	152	19.742 232 6680
33	15.881 759 4961	93	19.553 102 0743	153	19.742 755 6626
34	16.068 301 7215	94	19.562 738 4407	154	19.743 253 4563
35	16.245 855 2971	95	19.571 910 4730	155	19.743 727 2636
36	16.414 853 3464	96	19.580 640 5454	156	19.744 178 2402
37	16.575 708 1227	97	19.588 949 9540	157	19.744 607 4862
38	16.728 812 0145	98	19.596 858 9687	158	19.745 016 0488
39	16.874 538 5028	99	19.604 386 8828	159	19.745 404 9245
40	17.013 243 0722	100	19.611 552 0598	160	19.745 775 0619
41	17.145 264 0783	101	19.618 371 9783	161	19.746 127 3641
42	17.270 923 5724	102	19.624 863 2750	162	19.746 462 6904
43	17.390 528 0880	103	19.631 041 7847	163	19.746 781 8588
44	17.504 369 3877	104	19.636 922 5791	164	19.747 085 6479
45	17.612 725 1757	105	19.642 520 0039	165	19.747 374 7987
46	17.715 859 7746	106	19.647 847 7134	166	19.747 650 0166
47	17.814 024 7706	107	19.652 918 7040	167	19.747 911 9730
48	17.907 459 6270	108	19.657 745 3459	168	19.748 161 3068
49	17.996 392 2684	109	19.662 339 4131	169	19.748 398 6264
50	18.081 039 6368	110	19.666 712 1124	170	19.748 624 5105
51	18.161 608 2206	111	19.670 874 1106	171	19.748 839 5103
52	18.238 294 5586	112	19.674 835 5603	172	19.749 044 1502
53	18.311 285 7191	113	19.678 606 1252	173	19.749 238 9294
54	18.380 759 7564	114	19.682 195 0032	174	19.749 424 3231
55	18.446 886 1453	115	19.685 610 9489	175	19.749 600 7834
56	18.509 826 1942	116	19.688 862 2952	176	19.749 768 7409
57	18.569 733 4389	117	19.691 956 9734	177	19.749 928 6052
58	18.626 754 0168	118	19.694 902 5327	178	19.750 080 7664
59	18.681 027 0237	119	19.697 706 1585	179	19.750 225 5957
60	18.732 684 8530	120	19.700 374 6898	180	19.750 363 4462

Present Value of 1 per period

NOMINAL INTEREST RATE COMPOUNDED		
YEARLY	HALF-YEARLY	QUARTERLY
@	@	@
$5\frac{1}{8}\%$	$10\frac{1}{4}\%$	$20\frac{1}{2}\%$
5.1250%	10.2500%	20.5000%
PER ANNUM	PER ANNUM	PER ANNUM

Periods	Present Value	Periods	Present Value	Periods	Present Value
1	.951 248 5137	61	18.586 986 6665	121	19.466 076 2087
2	1.856 122 2484	62	18.632 091 9539	122	19.468 324 5743
3	2.716 882 0437	63	18.674 998 2915	123	19.470 463 3287
4	3.535 678 5196	64	18.715 812 8813	124	19.472 497 8156
5	4.314 557 4502	65	18.754 637 6992	125	19.474 433 1183
6	5.055 464 8754	66	18.791 569 7495	126	19.476 274 0721
7	5.760 251 9623	67	18.826 701 3075	127	19.478 025 2767
8	6.430 679 6312	68	18.860 120 1498	128	19.479 691 1074
9	7.068 422 9548	69	18.891 909 7739	129	19.481 275 7265
10	7.675 075 3434	70	18.922 149 6066	130	19.482 783 0930
11	8.252 152 5265	71	18.950 915 2025	131	19.484 216 9731
12	8.801 096 3391	72	18.978 278 4328	132	19.485 580 9494
13	9.323 278 3249	73	19.004 307 6650	133	19.486 878 4299
14	9.820 003 1628	74	19.029 067 9334	134	19.488 112 6563
15	10.292 511 9266	75	19.052 621 1019	135	19.489 286 7123
16	10.741 985 1858	76	19.075 026 0185	136	19.490 403 5313
17	11.169 545 9556	77	19.096 338 6620	137	19.491 465 9037
18	11.576 262 5023	78	19.116 612 2825	138	19.492 476 4839
19	11.963 151 0129	79	19.135 897 5339	139	19.493 437 7968
20	12.331 178 1336	80	19.154 242 6006	140	19.494 352 2443
21	12.681 263 3851	81	19.171 693 3181	141	19.495 222 1111
22	13.014 281 4603	82	19.188 293 2871	142	19.496 049 5706
23	13.331 064 4093	83	19.204 083 9830	143	19.496 836 6902
24	13.632 403 7187	84	19.219 104 8590	144	19.497 585 4366
25	13.919 052 2889	85	19.233 393 4449	145	19.498 297 6805
26	14.191 726 3152	86	19.246 985 4411	146	19.498 975 2014
27	14.451 107 0775	87	19.259 914 8072	147	19.499 619 6922
28	14.697 842 6421	88	19.272 213 8475	148	19.500 232 7631
29	14.932 549 4812	89	19.283 913 2913	149	19.500 815 9459
30	15.155 814 0130	90	19.295 042 3699	150	19.501 370 6976
31	15.368 194 0671	91	19.305 628 8893	151	19.501 898 4044
32	15.570 220 2779	92	19.315 699 3002	152	19.502 400 3847
33	15.762 397 4106	93	19.325 278 7635	153	19.502 877 8927
34	15.945 205 6224	94	19.334 391 2138	154	19.503 332 1214
35	16.119 101 6622	95	19.343 059 4186	155	19.503 764 2059
36	16.284 520 0116	96	19.351 305 0356	156	19.504 175 2256
37	16.441 873 9706	97	19.359 148 6664	157	19.504 566 2074
38	16.591 556 6903	98	19.366 609 9086	158	19.504 938 1284
39	16.733 942 1548	99	19.373 707 4041	159	19.505 291 9176
40	16.869 386 1164	100	19.380 458 8862	160	19.505 628 4591
41	16.998 226 9835	101	19.386 881 2235	161	19.505 948 5936
42	17.120 786 6668	102	19.392 990 4623	162	19.506 253 1212
43	17.237 371 3834	103	19.398 801 8666	163	19.506 542 8026
44	17.348 272 4218	104	19.404 329 9564	164	19.506 818 3615
45	17.453 766 8697	105	19.409 588 5435	165	19.507 080 4866
46	17.554 118 3065	106	19.414 590 7667	166	19.507 329 8327
47	17.649 577 4616	107	19.419 349 1241	167	19.507 567 0227
48	17.740 382 8410	108	19.423 875 5045	168	19.507 792 6495
49	17.826 761 3232	109	19.428 181 2171	169	19.508 007 2765
50	17.908 928 7260	110	19.432 277 0199	170	19.508 211 4402
51	17.987 090 3457	111	19.436 173 1461	171	19.508 405 6506
52	18.061 441 4704	112	19.439 879 3304	172	19.508 590 3930
53	18.132 167 8672	113	19.443 404 8328	173	19.508 766 1289
54	18.199 446 2470	114	19.446 758 4616	174	19.508 933 2974
55	18.263 444 7059	115	19.449 948 5961	175	19.509 092 3162
56	18.324 323 1447	116	19.452 983 2067	176	19.509 243 5826
57	18.382 233 6691	117	19.455 869 8756	177	19.509 387 4745
58	18.437 320 9695	118	19.458 615 8151	178	19.509 524 3515
59	18.489 722 6820	119	19.461 227 8859	179	19.509 654 5555
60	18.539 569 7332	120	19.463 712 6144	180	19.509 778 4119

Present Value of 1 per period

NOMINAL INTEREST RATE COMPOUNDED

	YEARLY	HALF-YEARLY	QUARTERLY
	@	@	@
	$5\frac{3}{16}\%$	$10\frac{3}{8}\%$	$20\frac{3}{4}\%$
	5.1875%	10.3750%	20.7500%
	PER ANNUM	PER ANNUM	PER ANNUM

Periods	Present Value	Periods	Present Value	Periods	Present Value
1	.950 683 3036	61	18.395 593 3301	121	19.234 706 8812
2	1.854 482 0474	62	18.439 066 7428	122	19.236 797 9857
3	2.713 708 4230	63	18.480 396 1905	123	19.238 785 9638
4	3.530 560 5923	64	18.519 687 4063	124	19.240 675 9014
5	4.307 128 3111	65	18.557 040 9091	125	19.242 472 6336
6	5.045 398 2756	66	18.592 552 2606	126	19.244 180 7568
7	5.747 259 2043	67	18.626 312 3095	127	19.245 804 6411
8	6.414 506 6708	68	18.658 407 4244	128	19.247 348 4407
9	7.048 847 6965	69	18.688 919 7142	129	19.248 816 1052
10	7.651 905 1185	70	18.717 927 2387	130	19.250 211 3894
11	8.225 221 7407	71	18.745 504 2079	131	19.251 537 8628
12	8.770 264 2811	72	18.771 721 1721	132	19.252 798 9189
13	9.288 427 1241	73	18.796 645 2022	133	19.253 997 7838
14	9.781 035 8874	74	18.820 340 0616	134	19.255 137 5247
15	10.249 350 8139	75	18.842 866 3687	135	19.256 221 0574
16	10.694 569 9954	76	18.864 281 7528	136	19.257 251 1538
17	11.117 832 4377	77	18.884 641 0008	137	19.258 230 4492
18	11.520 220 9747	78	18.903 996 1981	138	19.259 161 4491
19	11.902 765 0383	79	18.922 396 8609	139	19.260 046 5350
20	12.266 443 2925	80	18.939 890 0638	140	19.260 887 9715
21	12.612 186 1367	81	18.956 520 5598	141	19.261 687 9111
22	12.940 878 0859	82	18.972 330 8946	142	19.262 448 4004
23	13.253 360 0342	83	18.987 361 5160	143	19.263 171 3848
24	13.550 431 4050	84	19.001 650 8768	144	19.263 858 7140
25	13.832 852 1973	85	19.015 235 5335	145	19.264 512 1464
26	14.101 344 9291	86	19.028 150 2398	146	19.265 133 3537
27	14.356 596 4864	87	19.040 428 0354	147	19.265 723 9251
28	14.599 259 8801	88	19.052 100 3308	148	19.266 285 3714
29	14.829 955 9169	89	19.063 196 9871	149	19.266 819 1291
30	15.049 274 7873	90	19.073 746 3929	150	19.267 326 5636
31	15.257 777 5756	91	19.083 775 5370	151	19.267 808 9731
32	15.455 997 6951	92	19.093 310 0767	152	19.268 267 5918
33	15.644 442 2533	93	19.102 374 4045	153	19.268 703 5929
34	15.823 593 3483	94	19.110 991 7096	154	19.269 118 0919
35	15.993 909 3032	95	19.119 184 0376	155	19.269 512 1492
36	16.155 825 8379	96	19.126 972 3471	156	19.269 886 7728
37	16.309 757 1840	97	19.134 376 5629	157	19.270 242 9213
38	16.456 097 1446	98	19.141 415 6272	158	19.270 581 5057
39	16.595 220 1018	99	19.148 107 5482	159	19.270 903 3922
40	16.727 481 9744	100	19.154 469 4457	160	19.271 209 4044
41	16.853 221 1283	101	19.160 517 5954	161	19.271 500 3250
42	16.972 759 2426	102	19.166 267 4704	162	19.271 776 8984
43	17.086 402 1320	103	19.171 733 7805	163	19.272 039 8321
44	17.194 440 5296	104	19.176 930 5103	164	19.272 289 7988
45	17.297 150 8302	105	19.181 870 9545	165	19.272 527 4379
46	17.394 795 7982	106	19.186 567 7524	166	19.272 753 3575
47	17.487 625 2389	107	19.191 032 9197	167	19.272 968 1355
48	17.575 876 6383	108	19.195 277 8797	168	19.273 172 3213
49	17.659 775 7702	109	19.199 313 4923	169	19.273 366 4374
50	17.739 537 2741	110	19.203 150 0818	170	19.273 550 9803
51	17.815 365 2042	111	19.206 797 4634	171	19.273 726 4221
52	17.887 453 5512	112	19.210 264 9681	172	19.273 893 2118
53	17.955 986 7391	113	19.213 561 4670	173	19.274 051 7759
54	18.021 140 0966	114	19.216 695 3935	174	19.274 202 5202
55	18.083 080 3057	115	19.219 674 7651	175	19.274 345 8302
56	18.141 965 8284	116	19.222 507 2039	176	19.274 482 0727
57	18.197 947 3116	117	19.225 199 9561	177	19.274 611 5962
58	18.251 167 9730	118	19.227 759 9108	178	19.274 734 7319
59	18.301 763 9672	119	19.230 193 6169	179	19.274 851 7951
60	18.349 864 7341	120	19.232 507 3007	180	19.274 963 0850

Present Value of 1 per period

NOMINAL INTEREST RATE COMPOUNDED

YEARLY	HALF-YEARLY	QUARTERLY
@	@	@
$5\frac{1}{4}\%$	$10\frac{1}{2}\%$	21%
5.2500%	10.5000%	21.0000%
PER ANNUM	PER ANNUM	PER ANNUM

Periods	Present Value	Periods	Present Value	Periods	Present Value
1	.950 118 7648	61	18.207 593 8342	121	19.008 627 8970
2	1.852 844 4322	62	18.249 495 3294	122	19.010 572 8238
3	2.710 541 0282	63	18.289 306 7263	123	19.012 420 7352
4	3.525 454 6586	64	18.327 132 2815	124	19.014 176 4705
5	4.299 719 3906	65	18.363 071 0513	125	19.015 844 6275
6	5.035 362 8414	66	18.397 217 1509	126	19.017 429 5748
7	5.734 311 4883	67	18.429 660 0009	127	19.018 935 4630
8	6.398 395 7133	68	18.460 484 5614	128	19.020 366 2357
9	7.029 354 5970	69	18.489 771 5548	129	19.021 725 6396
10	7.628 840 4722	70	18.517 597 6767	130	19.023 017 2348
11	8.198 423 2515	71	18.544 035 7974	131	19.024 244 4036
12	8.739 594 5382	72	18.569 155 1519	132	19.025 410 3597
13	9.253 771 5328	73	18.593 021 5220	133	19.026 518 1565
14	9.742 300 7437	74	18.615 697 4081	134	19.027 570 6950
15	10.206 461 5142	75	18.637 242 1929	135	19.028 570 7316
16	10.647 469 3722	76	18.657 712 2973	136	19.029 520 8851
17	11.066 479 2135	77	18.677 161 3275	137	19.030 423 6438
18	11.464 588 3263	78	18.695 640 2163	138	19.031 281 3718
19	11.842 839 2649	79	18.713 197 3551	139	19.032 096 3152
20	12.202 222 5795	80	18.729 878 7222	140	19.032 870 6083
21	12.543 679 4105	81	18.745 728 0021	141	19.033 606 2787
22	12.868 103 9529	82	18.760 786 7003	142	19.034 305 2529
23	13.176 345 7985	83	18.775 094 2521	143	19.034 969 3614
24	13.469 212 1601	84	18.788 688 1255	144	19.035 600 3434
25	13.747 469 9859	85	18.801 603 9197	145	19.036 199 8512
26	14.011 847 9676	86	18.813 875 4582	146	19.036 769 4548
27	14.263 038 4490	87	18.825 534 8771	147	19.037 310 6459
28	14.501 699 2389	88	18.836 612 7099	148	19.037 824 8417
29	14.728 455 3339	89	18.847 137 9666	149	19.038 313 3888
30	14.943 900 5548	90	18.857 138 2106	150	19.038 777 5666
31	15.148 599 1019	91	18.866 639 6300	151	19.039 218 5906
32	15.343 087 0327	92	18.875 667 1069	152	19.039 637 6157
33	15.527 873 6653	93	18.884 244 2821	153	19.040 035 7394
34	15.703 442 9124	94	18.892 393 6172	154	19.040 414 0042
35	15.870 254 5486	95	18.900 136 4534	155	19.040 773 4007
36	16.028 745 4143	96	18.907 493 0673	156	19.041 114 8700
37	16.179 330 5599	97	18.914 482 7243	157	19.041 439 3064
38	16.322 404 3325	98	18.921 123 7286	158	19.041 747 5595
39	16.458 341 4085	99	18.927 433 4713	159	19.042 040 4366
40	16.587 497 7753	100	18.933 428 4763	160	19.042 318 7046
41	16.710 211 6630	101	18.939 124 4430	161	19.042 583 0923
42	16.826 804 4304	102	18.944 536 2879	162	19.042 834 2919
43	16.937 581 4066	103	18.949 678 1833	163	19.043 072 9615
44	17.042 832 6903	104	18.954 563 5946	164	19.043 299 7259
45	17.142 833 9101	105	18.959 205 3155	165	19.043 515 1790
46	17.237 846 9454	106	18.963 615 5017	166	19.043 719 8850
47	17.328 120 6132	107	18.967 805 7023	167	19.043 914 3800
48	17.413 891 3190	108	18.971 786 8906	168	19.044 099 1734
49	17.495 383 6760	109	18.975 569 4922	169	19.044 274 7491
50	17.572 811 0936	110	18.979 163 4130	170	19.044 441 5669
51	17.646 376 3359	111	18.982 578 0646	171	19.044 600 0635
52	17.716 272 0532	112	18.985 822 3892	172	19.044 750 6542
53	17.782 681 2857	113	18.988 904 8829	173	19.044 893 7332
54	17.845 777 9436	114	18.991 833 6179	174	19.045 029 6752
55	17.905 727 2623	115	18.994 616 2641	175	19.045 158 8363
56	17.962 686 2350	116	18.997 260 1084	176	19.045 281 5547
57	18.016 804 0238	117	18.999 772 0745	177	19.045 398 1517
58	18.068 222 3504	118	19.002 158 7406	178	19.045 508 9328
59	18.117 075 8673	119	19.004 426 3568	179	19.045 614 1879
60	18.163 492 5105	120	19.006 580 8616	180	19.045 714 1928

Present Value of 1 per period

NOMINAL INTEREST RATE COMPOUNDED		
YEARLY @ $5\frac{5}{16}\%$ 5.3125% PER ANNUM	HALF-YEARLY @ $10\frac{5}{8}\%$ 10.6250% PER ANNUM	QUARTERLY @ $21\frac{1}{4}\%$ 21.2500% PER ANNUM

Periods	Present Value	Periods	Present Value	Periods	Present Value
1	.949 554 8961	61	18.022 910 6166	121	18.787 667 7485
2	1.851 209 3969	62	18.063 297 9149	122	18.789 476 7938
3	2.707 379 8428	63	18.101 647 8717	123	18.791 194 5817
4	3.520 360 6816	64	18.138 063 2609	124	18.792 825 7155
5	4.292 330 6175	65	18.172 641 6721	125	18.794 374 5667
6	5.025 358 4499	66	18.205 475 7717	126	18.795 845 2859
7	5.721 408 6171	67	18.236 653 5518	127	18.797 241 8145
8	6.382 346 4613	68	18.266 258 5655	128	18.798 567 8951
9	7.009 943 2274	69	18.294 370 1512	129	18.799 827 0814
10	7.605 880 8094	70	18.321 063 6451	130	18.801 022 7479
11	8.171 756 2582	71	18.346 410 5829	131	18.802 158 0989
12	8.709 086 0612	72	18.370 478 8917	132	18.803 236 1770
13	9.219 310 2064	73	18.393 333 0723	133	18.804 259 8713
14	9.703 796 0417	74	18.415 034 3713	134	18.805 231 9253
15	10.163 841 9387	75	18.435 640 9460	135	18.806 154 9439
16	10.600 680 7727	76	18.455 208 0200	136	18.807 031 4007
17	11.015 483 2263	77	18.473 788 0308	137	18.807 863 6446
18	11.409 360 9270	78	18.491 430 7711	138	18.808 653 9059
19	11.783 369 4263	79	18.508 183 5215	139	18.809 404 3023
20	12.138 511 0279	80	18.524 091 1777	140	18.810 116 8449
21	12.475 737 4746	81	18.539 196 3705	141	18.810 793 4432
22	12.795 952 4981	82	18.553 539 5803	142	18.811 435 9105
23	13.100 014 2415	83	18.567 159 2454	143	18.812 045 9684
24	13.388 737 5587	84	18.580 091 8651	144	18.812 625 2519
25	13.662 896 1982	85	18.592 372 0974	145	18.813 175 3134
26	13.923 224 8766	86	18.604 032 8521	146	18.813 697 6270
27	14.170 421 2478	87	18.615 105 3789	147	18.814 193 5924
28	14.405 147 7724	88	18.625 619 3509	148	18.814 664 5387
29	14.628 033 4931	89	18.635 602 9445	149	18.815 111 7282
30	14.839 675 7205	90	18.645 082 9146	150	18.815 536 3591
31	15.040 641 6337	91	18.654 084 6667	151	18.815 939 5695
32	15.231 469 8005	92	18.662 632 3245	152	18.816 322 4399
33	15.412 671 6207	93	18.670 748 7947	153	18.816 685 9963
34	15.584 732 6962	94	18.678 455 8288	154	18.817 031 2131
35	15.748 114 1329	95	18.685 774 0808	155	18.817 359 0154
36	15.903 253 7760	96	18.692 723 1628	156	18.817 670 2817
37	16.050 567 3838	97	18.699 321 6976	157	18.817 965 8461
38	16.190 449 7413	98	18.705 587 3686	158	18.818 246 5008
39	16.323 275 7187	99	18.711 536 9672	159	18.818 512 9978
40	16.449 401 2759	100	18.717 186 4377	160	18.818 766 0513
41	16.569 164 4163	101	18.722 550 9201	161	18.819 006 3395
42	16.682 886 0926	102	18.727 644 7906	162	18.819 234 5064
43	16.790 871 0672	103	18.732 481 7003	163	18.819 451 1633
44	16.893 408 7285	104	18.737 074 6115	164	18.819 656 8910
45	16.990 773 8668	105	18.741 435 8329	165	18.819 852 2407
46	17.083 227 4106	106	18.745 577 0520	166	18.820 037 7360
47	17.171 017 1258	107	18.749 509 3669	167	18.820 213 8739
48	17.254 378 2797	108	18.753 243 3158	168	18.820 381 1266
49	17.333 534 2715	109	18.756 788 9052	169	18.820 539 9421
50	17.408 697 2311	110	18.760 155 6370	170	18.820 690 7462
51	17.480 068 5874	111	18.763 352 5336	171	18.820 833 9430
52	17.547 839 6082	112	18.766 388 1625	172	18.820 969 9162
53	17.612 191 9129	113	18.769 270 6587	173	18.821 099 0302
54	17.673 297 9588	114	18.772 007 7472	174	18.821 221 6311
55	17.731 321 5039	115	18.774 606 7629	175	18.821 338 0473
56	17.786 418 0452	116	18.777 074 6710	176	18.821 448 5909
57	17.838 735 2358	117	18.779 418 0852	177	18.821 553 5582
58	17.888 413 2803	118	18.781 643 2857	178	18.821 653 2303
59	17.935 585 3107	119	18.783 756 2356	179	18.821 747 8745
60	17.980 377 7431	120	18.785 762 5976	180	18.821 837 7443

Present Value of 1 per period

NOMINAL INTEREST RATE COMPOUNDED		
YEARLY	HALF-YEARLY	QUARTERLY
@	@	@
$5\frac{3}{8}\%$	$10\frac{3}{4}\%$	$21\frac{1}{2}\%$
5.3750%	10.7500%	21.5000%
PER ANNUM	PER ANNUM	PER ANNUM

Periods	Present Value	Periods	Present Value	Periods	Present Value
1	.948 991 6963	61	17.841 468 1664	121	18.571 661 8379
2	1.849 576 9360	62	17.880 396 8364	122	18.573 344 5674
3	2.704 224 8503	63	17.917 339 8210	123	18.574 941 4637
4	3.515 278 6243	64	17.952 398 4067	124	18.576 456 9051
5	4.284 961 9210	65	17.985 668 7133	125	18.577 895 0463
6	5.015 384 9784	66	18.017 241 9581	126	18.579 259 8305
7	5.708 550 3947	67	18.047 204 7052	127	18.580 554 9993
8	6.366 358 6189	68	18.075 639 1034	128	18.581 784 1037
9	6.990 613 1615	69	18.102 623 1111	129	18.582 950 5136
10	7.583 025 5388	70	18.128 230 7105	130	18.584 057 4269
11	8.145 219 9656	71	18.152 532 1096	131	18.585 107 8784
12	8.678 737 8084	72	18.175 593 9355	132	18.586 104 7482
13	9.185 041 8111	73	18.197 479 4169	133	18.587 050 7693
14	9.665 520 1054	74	18.218 248 5569	134	18.587 948 5356
15	10.121 490 0170	75	18.237 958 2984	135	18.588 800 5082
16	10.554 201 6769	76	18.256 662 6794	136	18.589 609 0232
17	10.964 841 4490	77	18.274 412 9816	137	18.590 376 2973
18	11.354 535 1829	78	18.291 257 8710	138	18.591 104 4339
19	11.724 351 3005	79	18.307 243 5312	139	18.591 795 4296
20	12.075 303 7253	80	18.322 413 7900	140	18.592 451 1787
21	12.408 354 6622	81	18.336 810 2396	141	18.593 073 4792
22	12.724 417 2358	82	18.350 472 3508	142	18.593 664 0372
23	13.024 357 9936	83	18.363 437 5808	143	18.594 224 4719
24	13.308 999 2822	84	18.375 741 4765	144	18.594 756 3197
25	13.579 121 5015	85	18.387 417 7713	145	18.595 261 0388
26	13.835 465 2446	86	18.398 498 4781	146	18.595 740 0131
27	14.078 733 3282	87	18.409 013 9768	147	18.596 194 5558
28	14.309 592 7195	88	18.418 993 0978	148	18.596 625 9129
29	14.528 676 3649	89	18.428 463 2008	149	18.597 035 2673
30	14.736 584 9252	90	18.437 450 2498	150	18.597 423 7412
31	14.933 888 4225	91	18.445 978 8848	151	18.597 792 3998
32	15.121 127 8031	92	18.454 072 4885	152	18.598 142 2536
33	15.298 816 4205	93	18.461 753 2513	153	18.598 474 2620
34	15.467 441 4429	94	18.469 042 2313	154	18.598 789 3353
35	15.627 465 1890	95	18.475 959 4129	155	18.599 088 3371
36	15.779 326 3952	96	18.482 523 7607	156	18.599 372 0874
37	15.923 441 4190	97	18.488 753 2724	157	18.599 641 3641
38	16.060 205 3798	98	18.494 665 0271	158	18.599 896 9055
39	16.189 993 2430	99	18.500 275 2334	159	18.600 139 4121
40	16.313 160 8475	100	18.505 599 2725	160	18.600 369 5488
41	16.430 045 8813	101	18.510 651 7414	161	18.600 587 9467
42	16.540 968 8079	102	18.515 446 4924	162	18.600 795 2044
43	16.646 233 7442	103	18.519 996 6713	163	18.600 991 8903
44	16.746 129 2946	104	18.524 314 7533	164	18.601 178 5436
45	16.840 929 3424	105	18.528 412 5773	165	18.601 355 6760
46	16.930 893 8006	106	18.532 301 3782	166	18.601 523 7732
47	17.016 269 3244	107	18.535 991 8180	167	18.601 683 2961
48	17.097 289 9876	108	18.539 494 0147	168	18.601 834 6819
49	17.174 177 9242	109	18.542 817 5703	169	18.601 978 3458
50	17.247 143 9375	110	18.545 971 5970	170	18.602 114 6817
51	17.316 388 0783	111	18.548 964 7421	171	18.602 244 0633
52	17.382 100 1930	112	18.551 805 2119	172	18.602 366 8453
53	17.444 460 4441	113	18.554 500 7942	173	18.602 483 3645
54	17.503 639 8046	114	18.557 058 8795	174	18.602 593 9402
55	17.559 800 5263	115	18.559 486 4811	175	18.602 698 8756
56	17.613 096 5849	116	18.561 790 2549	176	18.602 798 4585
57	17.663 674 1019	117	18.563 976 5171	177	18.602 892 9618
58	17.711 671 7456	118	18.566 051 2618	178	18.602 982 6447
59	17.757 221 1109	119	18.568 020 1773	179	18.603 067 7529
60	17.800 447 0803	120	18.569 888 6617	180	18.603 148 5200

Present Value of 1 per period

NOMINAL INTEREST RATE COMPOUNDED

YEARLY	HALF-YEARLY	QUARTERLY
@	@	@
$5\frac{7}{16}\%$	$10\frac{7}{8}\%$	$21\frac{3}{4}\%$
7.4375%	10.8750%	21.7500%
PER ANNUM	PER ANNUM	PER ANNUM

Periods	Present Value	Periods	Present Value	Periods	Present Value
1	.948 429 1642	61	17.663 192 9644	121	18.360 452 1557
2	1.847 947 0437	62	17.700 716 5044	122	18.362 017 4565
3	2.701 076 0343	63	17.736 304 9242	123	18.363 502 0334
4	3.510 208 4499	64	17.770 058 0194	124	18.364 910 0495
5	4.277 613 2305	65	17.802 070 4393	125	18.366 245 4530
6	5.005 442 3051	66	17.832 431 9519	126	18.367 511 9886
7	5.695 736 6261	67	17.861 227 6959	127	18.368 713 2079
8	6.350 431 8920	68	17.888 538 4194	128	18.369 852 4794
9	6.971 363 9758	69	17.914 440 7060	129	18.370 932 9976
10	7.560 274 0730	70	17.939 007 1900	130	18.371 957 7926
11	8.118 813 5844	71	17.962 306 7599	131	18.372 929 7381
12	8.648 548 7463	72	17.984 404 7516	132	18.373 851 5596
13	9.150 965 0232	73	18.005 363 1313	133	18.374 725 8419
14	9.627 471 2727	74	18.025 240 6699	134	18.375 555 0368
15	10.079 403 6967	75	18.044 093 1072	135	18.376 341 4694
16	10.508 029 5879	76	18.061 973 3085	136	18.377 087 3450
17	10.914 550 8836	77	18.078 931 4129	137	18.377 794 7552
18	11.300 107 5363	78	18.095 014 9737	138	18.378 465 6836
19	11.665 780 7102	79	18.110 269 0919	139	18.379 102 0118
20	12.012 595 8129	80	18.124 736 5424	140	18.379 705 5239
21	12.341 525 3708	81	18.138 457 8944	141	18.380 277 9124
22	12.653 491 7566	82	18.151 471 6248	142	18.380 820 7824
23	12.949 369 7750	83	18.163 814 2262	143	18.381 335 6561
24	13.229 989 1168	84	18.175 520 3094	144	18.381 823 9773
25	13.496 136 6846	85	18.186 622 7001	145	18.382 287 1154
26	13.748 558 7998	86	18.197 152 5312	146	18.382 726 3691
27	13.987 963 2956	87	18.207 139 3301	147	18.383 142 9701
28	14.215 021 5015	88	18.216 611 1015	148	18.383 538 0866
29	14.430 370 1259	89	18.225 594 4057	149	18.383 912 8267
30	14.634 613 0418	90	18.234 114 4334	150	18.384 268 2411
31	14.828 322 9797	91	18.242 195 0761	151	18.384 605 3264
32	15.012 043 1343	92	18.249 858 9933	152	18.384 925 0280
33	15.186 288 6870	93	18.257 127 6760	153	18.385 228 2424
34	15.351 548 2508	94	18.264 021 5065	154	18.385 515 8197
35	15.508 285 2408	95	18.270 559 8165	155	18.385 788 5664
36	15.656 939 1733	96	18.276 760 9404	156	18.386 047 2473
37	15.797 926 8982	97	18.282 642 2671	157	18.386 292 5878
38	15.931 643 7683	98	18.288 220 2889	158	18.386 525 2760
39	16.058 464 7477	99	18.293 510 6474	159	18.386 745 9642
40	16.178 745 4631	100	18.298 528 1778	160	18.386 955 2713
41	16.292 823 2015	101	18.303 286 9499	161	18.387 153 7843
42	16.401 017 8556	102	18.307 800 3081	162	18.387 342 0598
43	16.503 632 8210	103	18.312 080 9087	163	18.387 520 6257
44	16.600 955 8468	104	18.316 140 7552	164	18.387 689 9829
45	16.693 259 8428	105	18.319 991 2319	165	18.387 850 6062
46	16.780 803 6447	106	18.323 643 1364	166	18.388 002 9460
47	16.863 832 7395	107	18.327 106 7091	167	18.388 147 4295
48	16.942 579 9544	108	18.330 391 6624	168	18.388 284 4619
49	17.017 266 1097	109	18.333 507 2080	169	18.388 414 4274
50	17.088 100 6376	110	18.336 462 0823	170	18.388 537 6905
51	17.155 282 1696	111	18.339 264 5712	171	18.388 654 5968
52	17.218 999 0939	112	18.341 922 5335	172	18.388 765 4741
53	17.279 430 0831	113	18.344 443 4224	173	18.388 870 6335
54	17.336 744 5957	114	18.346 834 3069	174	18.388 970 3696
55	17.391 103 3510	115	18.349 101 8916	175	18.389 064 9623
56	17.442 658 7798	116	18.351 252 5350	176	18.389 154 6767
57	17.491 555 4521	117	18.353 292 2679	177	18.389 239 7645
58	17.537 930 4822	118	18.355 226 8101	178	18.389 320 4643
59	17.581 913 9131	119	18.357 061 5864	179	18.389 397 0023
60	17.623 629 0818	120	18.358 801 7417	180	18.389 469 5932

Present Value of 1 per period

NOMINAL INTEREST RATE COMPOUNDED

YEARLY	HALF-YEARLY	QUARTERLY
@	@	@
5½%	**11%**	**22%**
5.5000%	11.0000%	22.0000%
PER ANNUM	PER ANNUM	PER ANNUM

Periods	Present Value	Periods	Present Value	Periods	Present Value
1	.947 867 2986	61	17.488 013 4254	121	18.153 886 9754
2	1.846 319 7143	62	17.524 183 3416	122	18.155 343 1046
3	2.697 933 3785	63	17.558 467 6224	123	18.156 723 3219
4	3.505 150 1218	64	17.590 964 5710	124	18.158 031 5847
5	4.270 284 4756	65	17.621 767 3659	125	18.159 271 6443
6	4.995 530 3086	66	17.650 964 3278	126	18.160 447 0562
7	5.682 967 1172	67	17.678 639 1733	127	18.161 561 1907
8	6.334 565 9879	68	17.704 871 2543	128	18.162 617 2424
9	6.952 195 2492	69	17.729 735 7861	129	18.163 618 2392
10	7.537 625 8286	70	17.753 304 0626	130	18.164 567 0514
11	8.092 536 3304	71	17.775 643 6613	131	18.165 466 3994
12	8.618 517 8487	72	17.796 818 6363	132	18.166 318 8620
13	9.117 078 5296	73	17.816 889 7026	133	18.167 126 8834
14	9.589 647 8954	74	17.835 914 4101	134	18.167 892 7805
15	10.037 580 9435	75	17.853 947 3081	135	18.168 618 7493
16	10.462 162 0317	76	17.871 040 1025	136	18.169 306 8714
17	10.864 608 5609	77	17.887 241 8033	137	18.169 959 1198
18	11.246 074 4653	78	17.902 598 8657	138	18.170 577 3647
19	11.607 653 5216	79	17.917 155 3229	139	18.171 163 3789
20	11.950 382 4849	80	17.930 952 9127	140	18.171 718 8425
21	12.275 244 0615	81	17.944 031 1969	141	18.172 245 3484
22	12.583 169 7266	82	17.956 427 6748	142	18.172 744 4061
23	12.875 042 3949	83	17.968 177 8908	143	18.173 217 4465
24	13.151 698 9525	84	17.979 315 5363	144	18.173 665 8261
25	13.413 932 6564	85	17.989 872 5463	145	18.174 090 8304
26	13.662 495 4089	86	17.999 879 1908	146	18.174 493 6781
27	13.898 099 9136	87	18.009 364 1619	147	18.174 875 5243
28	14.121 421 7191	88	18.018 354 6558	148	18.175 237 4638
29	14.333 101 1555	89	18.026 876 4510	149	18.175 580 5344
30	14.533 745 1711	90	18.034 953 9820	150	18.175 905 7198
31	14.723 929 0722	91	18.042 610 4095	151	18.176 213 9524
32	14.904 198 1727	92	18.049 867 6867	152	18.176 506 1160
33	15.075 069 3580	93	18.056 746 6225	153	18.176 783 0484
34	15.237 032 5668	94	18.063 266 9407	154	18.177 045 5435
35	15.390 552 1960	95	18.069 447 3372	155	18.177 294 3540
36	15.536 068 4322	96	18.075 305 5329	156	18.177 530 1934
37	15.673 998 5140	97	18.080 858 3250	157	18.177 753 7378
38	15.804 737 9279	98	18.086 121 6351	158	18.177 965 6282
39	15.928 661 5431	99	18.091 110 5546	159	18.178 166 4723
40	16.046 124 6854	100	18.095 839 3882	160	18.178 356 8457
41	16.157 464 1568	101	18.100 321 6950	161	18.178 537 2945
42	16.262 999 2007	102	18.104 570 3270	162	18.178 708 3361
43	16.363 032 4177	103	18.108 597 4663	163	18.178 870 4607
44	16.457 850 6329	104	18.112 414 6600	164	18.179 024 1334
45	16.547 725 7184	105	18.116 032 8531	165	18.179 169 7947
46	16.632 915 3729	106	18.119 462 4200	166	18.179 307 8623
47	16.713 663 8606	107	18.122 713 1943	167	18.179 438 7320
48	16.790 202 7114	108	18.125 794 4970	168	18.179 562 7791
49	16.862 751 3853	109	18.128 715 1630	169	18.179 680 3594
50	16.931 517 9007	110	18.131 483 5669	170	18.179 791 8098
51	16.996 699 4320	111	18.134 107 6463	171	18.179 897 4501
52	17.058 482 8739	112	18.136 594 9254	172	18.179 997 5830
53	17.117 045 3781	113	18.138 952 5359	173	18.180 092 4957
54	17.172 554 8608	114	18.141 187 2379	174	18.180 182 4604
55	17.225 170 4841	115	18.143 305 4387	175	18.180 267 7350
56	17.275 043 1129	116	18.145 313 2121	176	18.180 348 5640
57	17.322 315 7468	117	18.147 216 3147	177	18.180 425 1791
58	17.367 123 9307	118	18.149 020 2036	178	18.180 497 8001
59	17.409 596 1428	119	18.150 730 0508	179	18.180 566 6352
60	17.449 854 1638	120	18.152 350 7590	180	18.180 631 8817

Present Value of 1 per period

NOMINAL INTEREST RATE COMPOUNDED

YEARLY	HALF-YEARLY	QUARTERLY
@	@	@
$5\frac{9}{16}\%$	$11\frac{1}{8}\%$	$22\frac{1}{4}\%$
5.5625%	11.1250%	22.2500%
PER ANNUM	PER ANNUM	PER ANNUM

Periods	Present Value	Periods	Present Value	Periods	Present Value
1	.947 306 0983	61	17.315 859 8421	121	17.951 820 5641
2	1.844 694 9421	62	17.350 725 7237	122	17.953 175 1940
3	2.694 796 8664	63	17.383 754 3860	123	17.954 458 4431
4	3.500 103 6035	64	17.415 042 6392	124	17.955 674 0728
5	4.262 975 5865	65	17.444 682 1922	125	17.956 825 6462
6	4.985 648 8682	66	17.472 759 9216	126	17.957 916 5387
7	5.670 241 6750	67	17.499 358 1258	127	17.958 949 9479
8	6.318 760 6158	68	17.524 554 7669	128	17.959 928 9027
9	6.933 106 5632	69	17.548 423 6987	129	17.960 856 2725
10	7.515 080 2256	70	17.571 034 8833	130	17.961 734 7756
11	8.066 387 4251	71	17.592 454 5964	131	17.962 566 9870
12	8.588 644 0972	72	17.612 745 6212	132	17.963 355 3459
13	9.083 381 0276	73	17.631 967 4328	133	17.964 102 1630
14	9.552 048 3387	74	17.650 176 3721	134	17.964 809 6275
15	9.996 019 7406	75	17.667 425 8113	135	17.965 479 8129
16	10.416 596 5571	76	17.683 766 3103	136	17.966 114 6836
17	10.815 011 5402	77	17.699 245 7646	137	17.966 716 1006
18	11.192 432 4833	78	17.713 909 5461	138	17.967 285 8265
19	11.549 965 6444	79	17.727 800 6358	139	17.967 825 5313
20	11.888 658 9882	80	17.740 959 7497	140	17.968 336 7969
21	12.209 505 2582	81	17.753 425 4586	141	17.968 821 1220
22	12.513 444 8864	82	17.765 234 3006	142	17.969 279 9261
23	12.801 368 7497	83	17.776 420 8887	143	17.969 714 5541
24	13.074 120 7812	84	17.787 018 0118	144	17.970 126 2798
25	13.332 500 4440	85	17.797 056 7311	145	17.970 516 3100
26	13.577 265 0743	86	17.806 566 4711	146	17.970 885 7881
27	13.809 132 1011	87	17.815 575 1059	147	17.971 235 7969
28	14.028 781 1497	88	17.824 109 0405	148	17.971 567 3623
29	14.236 856 0329	89	17.832 193 2888	149	17.971 881 4563
30	14.433 966 6386	90	17.839 851 5465	150	17.972 178 9995
31	14.620 690 7174	91	17.847 106 2608	151	17.972 460 8639
32	14.797 575 5760	92	17.853 978 6958	152	17.972 727 8758
33	14.965 139 6812	93	17.860 488 9954	153	17.972 980 8178
34	15.123 874 1800	94	17.866 656 2420	154	17.973 220 4313
35	15.274 244 3386	95	17.872 498 5122	155	17.973 447 4187
36	15.416 690 9069	96	17.878 032 9305	156	17.973 662 4452
37	15.551 631 4098	97	17.883 275 7186	157	17.973 866 1411
38	15.679 461 3710	98	17.888 242 2438	158	17.974 059 1034
39	15.800 555 4728	99	17.892 947 0634	159	17.974 241 8979
40	15.915 268 6540	100	17.897 403 9677	160	17.974 415 0601
41	16.023 937 1500	101	17.901 626 0203	161	17.974 579 0978
42	16.126 879 4790	102	17.905 625 5965	162	17.974 734 4917
43	16.224 397 3750	103	17.909 414 4194	163	17.974 881 6973
44	16.316 776 6726	104	17.913 003 5945	164	17.975 021 1461
45	16.404 288 1445	105	17.916 403 6419	165	17.975 153 2467
46	16.487 188 2956	106	17.919 624 5276	166	17.975 278 3865
47	16.565 720 1142	107	17.922 675 6922	167	17.975 396 9321
48	16.640 113 7850	108	17.925 566 0790	168	17.975 509 2311
49	16.710 587 3629	109	17.928 304 1601	169	17.975 615 6127
50	16.777 347 4130	110	17.930 897 9611	170	17.975 716 3886
51	16.840 589 6157	111	17.933 355 0845	171	17.975 811 8542
52	16.900 499 3399	112	17.935 682 7325	172	17.975 902 2893
53	16.957 252 1870	113	17.937 887 7276	173	17.975 987 9591
54	17.011 014 5051	114	17.939 976 5330	174	17.976 069 1146
55	17.061 943 8770	115	17.941 955 2710	175	17.976 145 9937
56	17.110 189 5815	116	17.943 829 7417	176	17.976 218 8218
57	17.155 893 0316	117	17.945 605 4391	177	17.976 287 8122
58	17.199 188 1886	118	17.947 287 5681	178	17.976 353 1673
59	17.240 201 9549	119	17.948 881 0592	179	17.976 415 0785
60	17.279 054 5458	120	17.950 390 5830	180	17.976 473 7274

Present Value of 1 per period

NOMINAL INTEREST RATE COMPOUNDED

YEARLY	HALF-YEARLY	QUARTERLY
@	@	@
$5\frac{5}{8}\%$	$11\frac{1}{4}\%$	$22\frac{1}{2}\%$
5.6250%	11.2500%	22.5000%
PER ANNUM	PER ANNUM	PER ANNUM

Periods	Present Value	Periods	Present Value	Periods	Present Value
1	.946 745 5621	61	17.146 664 3306	121	17.754 112 9081
2	1.843 072 7215	62	17.180 273 9225	122	17.755 373 1675
3	2.691 666 4819	63	17.212 093 6544	123	17.756 566 3124
4	3.495 068 8586	64	17.242 218 8444	124	17.757 695 9171
5	4.255 686 4934	65	17.270 739 7344	125	17.758 765 3653
6	4.975 797 8636	66	17.297 741 7604	126	17.759 777 8606
7	5.657 560 1075	67	17.323 305 8086	127	17.760 736 4361
8	6.303 015 4864	68	17.347 508 4579	128	17.761 643 9632
9	6.914 097 5019	69	17.370 422 2086	129	17.762 503 1604
10	7.492 636 6882	70	17.392 115 7005	130	17.763 316 6015
11	8.040 366 0953	71	17.412 653 9176	131	17.764 086 7234
12	8.558 926 4808	72	17.432 098 3835	132	17.764 815 8328
13	9.049 871 2244	73	17.450 507 3454	133	17.765 506 1139
14	9.514 670 9817	74	17.467 935 9483	134	17.766 159 6344
15	9.954 718 0892	75	17.484 436 4007	135	17.766 778 3521
16	10.371 330 7353	76	17.500 058 1309	136	17.767 364 1203
17	10.765 756 9092	77	17.514 847 9345	137	17.767 918 6938
18	11.139 178 1389	78	17.528 850 1155	138	17.768 443 7338
19	11.492 713 0309	79	17.542 106 6183	139	17.768 940 8131
20	11.827 420 6210	80	17.554 657 1534	140	17.769 411 4206
21	12.144 303 5465	81	17.566 539 3168	141	17.769 856 9663
22	12.444 311 0499	82	17.577 788 7023	142	17.770 278 7847
23	12.728 341 8224	83	17.588 439 0081	143	17.770 678 1393
24	12.997 246 6958	84	17.598 522 1379	144	17.771 056 2266
25	13.251 831 1913	85	17.608 068 2962	145	17.771 414 1790
26	13.492 857 9325	86	17.617 106 0792	146	17.771 753 0689
27	13.721 048 9302	87	17.625 662 5602	147	17.772 073 9114
28	13.937 087 7446	88	17.633 763 3706	148	17.772 377 6676
29	14.141 621 5333	89	17.641 432 7769	149	17.772 665 2474
30	14.335 262 9901	90	17.648 693 7533	150	17.772 937 5123
31	14.518 592 1800	91	17.655 568 0505	151	17.773 195 2779
32	14.692 158 2769	92	17.662 076 2608	152	17.773 439 3164
33	14.856 481 2089	93	17.668 237 8800	153	17.773 670 3587
34	15.012 053 2156	94	17.674 071 3657	154	17.773 889 0970
35	15.159 340 3224	95	17.679 594 1924	155	17.774 096 1865
36	15.298 783 7372	96	17.684 822 9040	156	17.774 292 2476
37	15.430 801 1713	97	17.689 773 1636	157	17.774 477 8675
38	15.555 788 0912	98	17.694 459 7999	158	17.774 653 6024
39	15.674 118 9029	99	17.698 896 8519	159	17.774 819 9786
40	15.786 148 0738	100	17.703 097 6113	160	17.774 977 4945
41	15.892 211 1941	101	17.707 074 6616	161	17.775 126 6221
42	15.992 625 9826	102	17.710 839 9163	162	17.775 267 8079
43	16.087 693 2379	103	17.714 404 6545	163	17.775 401 4749
44	16.177 697 7401	104	17.717 779 5545	164	17.775 528 0236
45	16.262 909 1030	105	17.720 974 7262	165	17.775 647 8330
46	16.343 582 5827	106	17.723 999 7408	166	17.775 761 2620
47	16.419 959 8416	107	17.726 863 6599	167	17.775 868 6504
48	16.492 269 6726	108	17.729 575 0626	168	17.775 970 3199
49	16.560 728 6841	109	17.732 142 0711	169	17.776 066 5751
50	16.625 541 9494	110	17.734 572 3750	170	17.776 157 7042
51	16.686 903 6208	111	17.736 873 2545	171	17.776 243 9803
52	16.744 997 5108	112	17.739 051 6019	172	17.776 325 6618
53	16.799 997 6433	113	17.741 113 9426	173	17.776 402 9934
54	16.852 068 7748	114	17.743 066 4545	174	17.776 476 2068
55	16.901 366 8873	115	17.744 914 9865	175	17.776 545 5212
56	16.948 039 6567	116	17.746 665 0760	176	17.776 611 1444
57	16.992 226 8939	117	17.748 321 9654	177	17.776 673 2728
58	17.034 060 9646	118	17.749 890 6182	178	17.776 732 0926
59	17.073 667 1854	119	17.751 375 7332	179	17.776 787 7799
60	17.111 164 1992	120	17.752 781 7592	180	17.776 840 5017

Present Value of 1 per period

NOMINAL INTEREST RATE COMPOUNDED

YEARLY	HALF-YEARLY	QUARTERLY
@	@	@
$5\frac{11}{16}\%$	$11\frac{3}{8}\%$	$22\frac{3}{4}\%$
5.6875%	11.3750%	22.7500%
PER ANNUM	PER ANNUM	PER ANNUM

Periods	Present Value	Periods	Present Value	Periods	Present Value
1	.946 185 6889	61	16.980 360 7783	121	17.560 629 4517
2	1.841 453 0469	62	17.012 760 0505	122	17.561 801 9649
3	2.688 542 2088	63	17.043 415 7781	123	17.562 911 3802
4	3.490 045 8510	64	17.072 421 7889	124	17.563 961 0930
5	4.248 417 1269	65	17.099 866 8611	125	17.564 954 3163
6	4.965 977 1751	66	17.125 834 9957	126	17.565 894 0899
7	5.644 922 2236	67	17.150 405 6731	127	17.566 783 2903
8	6.287 330 3121	68	17.173 654 0964	128	17.567 624 6389
9	6.895 167 6519	69	17.195 651 4217	129	17.568 420 7110
10	7.470 294 6440	70	17.216 464 9762	130	17.569 173 9430
11	8.014 471 5733	71	17.236 158 4636	131	17.569 886 6403
12	8.529 363 9960	72	17.254 792 1595	132	17.570 560 9843
13	9.016 547 8377	73	17.272 423 0960	133	17.571 199 0390
14	9.477 514 2167	74	17.289 105 2357	134	17.571 802 7572
15	9.913 674 0075	75	17.304 889 6375	135	17.572 373 9867
16	10.326 362 1597	76	17.319 824 6127	136	17.572 914 4759
17	10.716 841 7832	77	17.333 955 8724	137	17.573 425 8790
18	11.086 308 0149	78	17.347 326 6682	138	17.573 909 7613
19	11.435 891 6758	79	17.359 977 9238	139	17.574 367 6039
20	11.766 662 7329	80	17.371 948 3608	140	17.574 800 8079
21	12.079 633 5734	81	17.383 274 6169	141	17.575 210 6994
22	12.375 762 1038	82	17.393 991 3584	142	17.575 598 5328
23	12.655 954 6813	83	17.404 131 3858	143	17.575 965 4953
24	12.921 068 8882	84	17.413 725 7347	144	17.576 312 7099
25	13.171 916 1568	85	17.422 803 7702	145	17.576 641 2394
26	13.409 264 2525	86	17.431 393 2776	146	17.576 952 0893
27	13.633 839 6239	87	17.439 520 5465	147	17.577 246 2111
28	13.846 329 6264	88	17.447 210 4520	148	17.577 524 5049
29	14.047 384 6258	89	17.454 486 5306	149	17.577 787 8225
30	14.237 619 9889	90	17.461 371 0520	150	17.578 036 9698
31	14.417 617 9670	91	17.467 885 0877	151	17.578 272 7095
32	14.587 929 4780	92	17.474 048 5750	152	17.578 495 7629
33	14.749 075 7923	93	17.479 880 3784	153	17.578 706 8130
34	14.901 550 1287	94	17.485 398 3474	154	17.578 906 5055
35	15.045 819 1638	95	17.490 619 3707	155	17.579 095 4516
36	15.182 324 4601	96	17.495 559 4282	156	17.579 274 2298
37	15.311 483 8180	97	17.500 233 6400	157	17.579 443 3872
38	15.433 692 5540	98	17.504 656 3122	158	17.579 603 4414
39	15.549 324 7110	99	17.508 840 9814	159	17.579 754 8825
40	15.658 734 2032	100	17.512 800 4555	160	17.579 898 1739
41	15.762 255 8990	101	17.516 546 8532	161	17.580 033 7541
42	15.860 206 6460	102	17.520 091 6411	162	17.580 162 0382
43	15.952 886 2410	103	17.523 445 6687	163	17.580 283 4187
44	16.040 578 3475	104	17.526 619 2016	164	17.580 398 2673
45	16.123 551 3637	105	17.529 621 9530	165	17.580 506 9353
46	16.202 059 2442	106	17.532 463 1135	166	17.580 609 7555
47	16.276 342 2772	107	17.535 151 3788	167	17.580 707 0425
48	16.346 627 8199	108	17.537 694 9770	168	17.580 799 0940
49	16.413 130 9946	109	17.540 101 6932	169	17.580 886 1918
50	16.476 055 3467	110	17.542 378 8936	170	17.580 968 6026
51	16.535 593 4682	111	17.544 533 5481	171	17.581 046 5784
52	16.591 927 5867	112	17.546 572 2513	172	17.581 120 3580
53	16.645 230 1235	113	17.548 501 2431	173	17.581 190 1673
54	16.695 664 2209	114	17.550 326 4275	174	17.581 256 2198
55	16.743 384 2421	115	17.552 053 3909	175	17.581 318 7177
56	16.788 536 2433	116	17.553 687 4189	176	17.581 377 8524
57	16.831 258 4206	117	17.555 233 5129	177	17.581 433 8047
58	16.871 681 5334	118	17.556 696 4049	178	17.581 486 7460
59	16.909 929 3042	119	17.558 080 5723	179	17.581 536 8384
60	16.946 118 7976	120	17.559 390 2518	180	17.581 584 2350

Present Value of 1 per period

NOMINAL INTEREST RATE COMPOUNDED

	YEARLY @ $5\frac{3}{4}\%$ 5.7500% PER ANNUM		HALF-YEARLY @ $11\frac{1}{2}\%$ 11.5000% PER ANNUM		QUARTERLY @ 23% 23.0000% PER ANNUM
Periods	Present Value	Periods	Present Value	Periods	Present Value
1	.945 626 4775	61	16.816 884 7925	121	17.371 240 8498
2	1.839 835 9126	62	16.848 118 0071	122	17.372 331 7729
3	2.685 424 0308	63	16.877 652 9618	123	17.373 363 3786
4	3.485 034 5445	64	16.905 581 9970	124	17.374 338 8923
5	4.241 167 4180	65	16.931 992 4321	125	17.375 261 3639
6	4.956 186 6836	66	16.956 966 8389	126	17.376 133 6774
7	5.632 327 8332	67	16.980 583 2992	127	17.376 958 5602
8	6.271 704 8068	68	17.002 915 6493	128	17.377 738 5912
9	6.876 316 6022	69	17.024 033 7110	129	17.378 476 2092
10	7.448 053 5246	70	17.044 003 5092	130	17.379 173 7203
11	7.988 703 0965	71	17.062 887 4791	131	17.379 833 3052
12	8.499 955 6468	72	17.080 744 6611	132	17.380 457 0262
13	8.983 409 5951	73	17.097 630 8852	133	17.381 046 8333
14	9.440 576 4493	74	17.113 598 9458	134	17.381 604 5705
15	9.872 885 5312	75	17.128 698 7667	135	17.382 131 9815
16	10.281 688 4456	76	17.142 977 5572	136	17.382 630 7154
17	10.668 263 3055	77	17.156 479 9595	137	17.383 102 3314
18	11.033 818 7286	78	17.169 248 1887	138	17.383 548 3039
19	11.379 497 6157	79	17.181 322 1642	139	17.383 970 0273
20	11.706 380 7241	80	17.192 739 6352	140	17.384 368 8202
21	12.015 490 0464	81	17.203 536 2981	141	17.384 745 9292
22	12.307 792 0061	82	17.213 745 9083	142	17.385 102 5335
23	12.584 200 4786	83	17.223 400 3861	143	17.385 439 7480
24	12.845 579 6488	84	17.232 529 9160	144	17.385 758 6270
25	13.092 746 7128	85	17.241 163 0411	145	17.386 060 1674
26	13.326 474 4329	86	17.249 326 7528	146	17.386 345 3119
27	13.547 493 5535	87	17.257 046 5748	147	17.386 614 9522
28	13.756 495 0861	88	17.264 346 6428	148	17.386 869 9311
29	13.954 132 4691	89	17.271 249 7804	149	17.387 111 0460
30	14.141 023 6115	90	17.277 777 5702	150	17.387 339 0506
31	14.317 752 8241	91	17.283 950 4210	151	17.387 554 6578
32	14.484 872 6469	92	17.289 787 6321	152	17.387 758 5416
33	14.642 905 5762	93	17.295 307 4535	153	17.387 951 3396
34	14.792 345 6986	94	17.300 527 1428	154	17.388 133 6545
35	14.933 660 2351	95	17.305 463 0192	155	17.388 306 0562
36	15.067 291 0024	96	17.310 130 5146	156	17.388 469 0839
37	15.193 655 7943	97	17.314 544 2219	157	17.388 623 2472
38	15.313 149 6872	98	17.318 717 9403	158	17.388 769 0281
39	15.426 146 2763	99	17.322 664 7190	159	17.388 906 8823
40	15.532 998 8429	100	17.326 396 8974	160	17.389 037 2410
41	15.634 041 4590	101	17.329 926 1441	161	17.389 160 5116
42	15.729 590 0321	102	17.333 263 4932	162	17.389 277 0795
43	15.819 943 2928	103	17.336 419 3789	163	17.389 387 3092
44	15.905 383 7284	104	17.339 403 6680	164	17.389 491 5454
45	15.986 178 4666	105	17.342 225 6908	165	17.389 590 1138
46	16.062 580 1103	106	17.344 894 2703	166	17.389 683 3228
47	16.134 827 5274	107	17.347 417 7496	167	17.389 771 4636
48	16.203 146 5980	108	17.349 804 0186	168	17.389 854 8119
49	16.267 750 9201	109	17.352 060 5377	169	17.389 933 6283
50	16.328 842 4777	110	17.354 194 3619	170	17.390 008 1591
51	16.386 612 2720	111	17.356 212 1625	171	17.390 078 6375
52	16.441 240 9192	112	17.358 120 2482	172	17.390 145 2837
53	16.492 899 2143	113	17.359 924 5846	173	17.390 208 3061
54	16.541 748 6660	114	17.361 630 8129	174	17.390 267 9017
55	16.587 942 0010	115	17.363 244 2675	175	17.390 324 2569
56	16.631 623 6416	116	17.364 769 9929	176	17.390 377 5479
57	16.672 930 1575	117	17.366 212 7593	177	17.390 427 9413
58	16.711 990 6927	118	17.367 577 0773	178	17.390 475 5946
59	16.748 927 3690	119	17.368 867 2126	179	17.390 520 6569
60	16.783 855 6681	120	17.370 087 1987	180	17.390 563 2689

Present Value of 1 per period

NOMINAL INTEREST RATE COMPOUNDED

YEARLY	HALF-YEARLY	QUARTERLY
@	@	@
$5\frac{13}{16}\%$	$11\frac{5}{8}\%$	$23\frac{1}{4}\%$
5.8125%	11.6250%	23.2500%
PER ANNUM	PER ANNUM	PER ANNUM

Periods	Present Value	Periods	Present Value	Periods	Present Value
1	.945 067 9268	61	16.656 173 6511	121	17.185 822 7331
2	1.838 221 3129	62	16.686 283 4269	122	17.186 837 7868
3	2.682 311 9319	63	16.714 739 2103	123	17.187 797 0814
4	3.480 034 9032	64	16.741 631 8585	124	17.188 703 6800
5	4.233 937 2977	65	16.767 047 2378	125	17.189 560 4773
6	4.946 426 2707	66	16.791 066 4976	126	17.190 370 2089
7	5.619 776 7473	67	16.813 766 3297	127	17.191 135 4602
8	6.256 138 6862	68	16.835 219 2130	128	17.191 858 6748
9	6.857 543 9444	69	16.855 493 6449	129	17.192 542 1616
10	7.425 912 7649	70	16.874 654 3602	130	17.193 188 1031
11	7.963 059 9078	71	16.892 762 5377	131	17.193 798 5617
12	8.470 700 4445	72	16.909 875 9954	132	17.194 375 4866
13	8.950 455 2340	73	16.926 049 3755	133	17.194 920 7197
14	9.403 856 0983	74	16.941 334 3182	134	17.195 436 0021
15	9.832 350 7131	75	16.955 779 6274	135	17.195 922 9790
16	10.237 307 2303	76	16.969 431 4258	136	17.196 383 2052
17	10.620 018 6465	77	16.982 333 3026	137	17.196 818 1502
18	10.981 706 9311	78	16.994 526 4525	138	17.197 229 2028
19	11.323 526 9284	79	17.006 049 8075	139	17.197 617 6754
20	11.646 570 0446	80	17.016 940 1606	140	17.197 984 8084
21	11.951 867 7326	81	17.027 232 2841	141	17.198 331 7740
22	12.240 394 7857	82	17.036 959 0399	142	17.198 659 6801
23	12.513 072 4496	83	17.046 151 4849	143	17.198 969 5737
24	12.770 771 3640	84	17.054 838 9697	144	17.199 262 4441
25	13.014 314 3428	85	17.063 049 2331	145	17.199 539 2266
26	13.244 479 0009	86	17.070 808 4896	146	17.199 800 8048
27	13.462 000 2371	87	17.078 141 5141	147	17.200 048 0140
28	13.667 572 5809	88	17.085 071 7204	148	17.200 281 6434
29	13.861 852 4096	89	17.091 621 2360	149	17.200 502 4392
30	14.045 460 0445	90	17.097 810 9732	150	17.200 711 1061
31	14.218 981 7313	91	17.103 660 6953	151	17.200 908 3106
32	14.382 971 5122	92	17.109 189 0800	152	17.201 094 6822
33	14.537 952 9944	93	17.114 413 7791	153	17.201 270 8160
34	14.684 421 0225	94	17.119 351 4746	154	17.201 437 2744
35	14.822 843 2581	95	17.124 017 9323	155	17.201 594 5889
36	14.953 661 6733	96	17.128 428 0518	156	17.201 743 2618
37	15.077 293 9618	97	17.132 595 9143	157	17.201 883 7678
38	15.194 134 8723	98	17.136 534 8274	158	17.202 016 5555
39	15.304 557 4694	99	17.140 257 3679	159	17.202 142 0489
40	15.408 914 3243	100	17.143 775 4216	160	17.202 260 6487
41	15.507 538 6408	101	17.147 100 2212	161	17.202 372 7336
42	15.600 745 3192	102	17.150 242 3827	162	17.202 478 6614
43	15.688 831 9614	103	17.153 211 9388	163	17.202 578 7704
44	15.772 079 8218	104	17.156 018 3709	164	17.202 673 3802
45	15.850 754 7046	105	17.158 670 6400	165	17.202 762 7928
46	15.925 107 8129	106	17.161 177 2144	166	17.202 847 2939
47	15.995 376 5509	107	17.163 546 0975	167	17.202 927 1531
48	16.061 785 2814	108	17.165 784 8529	168	17.203 002 6255
49	16.124 546 0427	109	17.167 900 6289	169	17.203 073 9520
50	16.183 859 2252	110	17.169 900 1809	170	17.203 141 3604
51	16.239 914 2117	111	17.171 789 8933	171	17.203 205 0660
52	16.292 889 9815	112	17.173 575 7999	172	17.203 265 2721
53	16.342 955 6825	113	17.175 263 6030	173	17.203 322 1709
54	16.390 271 1707	114	17.176 858 6916	174	17.203 375 9441
55	16.434 987 5210	115	17.178 366 1586	175	17.203 426 7635
56	16.477 247 5095	116	17.179 790 8173	176	17.203 474 7912
57	16.517 186 0692	117	17.181 137 2166	177	17.203 520 1807
58	16.554 930 7211	118	17.182 409 6554	178	17.203 563 0769
59	16.590 601 9809	119	17.183 612 1965	179	17.203 603 6167
60	16.624 313 7445	120	17.184 748 6795	180	17.203 641 9295

Present Value of 1 per period

NOMINAL INTEREST RATE COMPOUNDED

YEARLY	HALF-YEARLY	QUARTERLY
@	@	@
$5\frac{7}{8}\%$	$11\frac{3}{4}\%$	$23\frac{1}{2}\%$
5.8750%	11.7500%	23.5000%
PER ANNUM	PER ANNUM	PER ANNUM

Periods	Present Value	Periods	Present Value	Periods	Present Value
1	.944 510 0354	61	16.498 166 2547	121	17.004 255 4847
2	1.836 609 2424	62	16.527 193 6290	122	17.005 199 9855
3	2.679 205 8960	63	16.554 610 2753	123	17.006 092 0761
4	3.475 046 8912	64	16.580 505 5729	124	17.006 934 6645
5	4.226 726 6977	65	16.604 963 9414	125	17.007 730 4978
6	4.936 695 8184	66	16.628 065 1158	126	17.008 482 1703
7	5.607 268 7777	67	16.649 884 4069	127	17.009 192 1325
8	6.240 631 6672	68	16.670 492 9463	128	17.009 862 6989
9	6.838 849 2725	69	16.689 957 9186	129	17.010 496 0557
10	7.403 871 8040	70	16.708 342 7803	130	17.011 094 2675
11	7.937 541 2552	71	16.725 707 4666	131	17.011 659 2845
12	8.441 597 4075	72	16.742 108 5871	132	17.012 192 9488
13	8.917 683 5018	73	16.757 599 6100	133	17.012 697 0000
14	9.367 351 5956	74	16.772 231 0366	134	17.013 173 0815
15	9.792 067 6227	75	16.786 050 5659	135	17.013 622 7452
16	10.193 216 1726	76	16.799 103 2499	136	17.014 047 4571
17	10.572 105 0036	77	16.811 431 6410	137	17.014 448 6017
18	10.929 969 3069	78	16.823 075 9301	138	17.014 827 4869
19	11.267 975 7326	79	16.834 074 0780	139	17.015 185 3477
20	11.587 226 1937	80	16.844 461 9391	140	17.015 523 3508
21	11.888 761 4580	81	16.854 273 3782	141	17.015 842 5982
22	12.173 564 5412	82	16.863 540 3808	142	17.016 144 1305
23	12.442 563 9114	83	16.872 293 1578	143	17.016 428 9308
24	12.696 636 5161	84	16.880 560 2435	144	17.016 697 9276
25	12.936 610 6410	85	16.888 368 5889	145	17.016 951 9977
26	13.163 268 6101	86	16.895 743 6495	146	17.017 191 9695
27	13.377 349 3366	87	16.902 709 4682	147	17.017 418 6253
28	13.579 550 7311	88	16.909 288 7539	148	17.017 632 7039
29	13.770 531 9775	89	16.915 502 9553	149	17.017 834 9034
30	13.950 915 6812	90	16.921 372 3309	150	17.018 025 8827
31	14.121 289 8996	91	16.926 916 0150	151	17.018 206 2647
32	14.282 210 0586	92	16.932 152 0803	152	17.018 376 6373
33	14.434 200 7638	93	16.937 097 5965	153	17.018 537 5558
34	14.577 757 5101	94	16.941 768 6862	154	17.018 689 5451
35	14.713 348 2976	95	16.946 180 5772	155	17.018 833 1004
36	14.841 415 1571	96	16.950 347 6526	156	17.018 968 6899
37	14.962 375 5911	97	16.954 283 4972	157	17.019 096 7555
38	15.076 623 9349	98	16.958 000 9419	158	17.019 217 7148
39	15.184 532 6422	99	16.961 512 1056	159	17.019 331 9620
40	15.286 453 4991	100	16.964 828 4351	160	17.019 439 8697
41	15.382 718 7713	101	16.967 960 7415	161	17.019 541 7895
42	15.473 642 2870	102	16.970 919 2364	162	17.019 638 0539
43	15.559 520 4599	103	16.973 713 5645	163	17.019 728 9765
44	15.640 633 2561	104	16.976 352 8354	164	17.019 814 8538
45	15.717 245 1062	105	16.978 845 6533	165	17.019 895 9658
46	15.789 605 7673	106	16.981 200 1448	166	17.019 972 5769
47	15.857 951 1380	107	16.983 423 9856	167	17.020 044 9369
48	15.922 504 0264	108	16.985 524 4256	168	17.020 113 2816
49	15.983 474 8774	109	16.987 508 3123	169	17.020 177 8339
50	16.041 062 4580	110	16.989 382 1131	170	17.020 238 8041
51	16.095 454 5058	111	16.991 151 9368	171	17.020 296 3911
52	16.146 828 3407	112	16.992 823 5531	172	17.020 350 7827
53	16.195 351 4434	113	16.994 402 4114	173	17.020 402 1560
54	16.241 182 0009	114	16.995 893 6589	174	17.020 450 6786
55	16.284 469 4223	115	16.997 302 1572	175	17.020 496 5087
56	16.325 354 8263	116	16.998 632 4980	176	17.020 539 7957
57	16.363 971 5006	117	16.999 889 0181	177	17.020 580 6807
58	16.400 445 3371	118	17.001 075 8141	178	17.020 619 2970
59	16.434 895 2416	119	17.002 196 7547	179	17.020 655 7705
60	16.467 433 5222	120	17.003 255 4944	180	17.020 690 2201

Present Value of 1 per period

NOMINAL INTEREST RATE COMPOUNDED

YEARLY	HALF-YEARLY	QUARTERLY
@	@	@
$5\frac{15}{16}\%$	$11\frac{7}{8}\%$	$23\frac{3}{4}\%$
5.9375%	11.8750%	23.7500%
PER ANNUM	PER ANNUM	PER ANNUM

Periods	Present Value	Periods	Present Value	Periods	Present Value
1	,943 952 8024	61	16,342 803 0806	121	16,826 424 0279
2	1,834 999 6954	62	16,370 787 5687	122	16,827 302 9172
3	2,676 105 9072	63	16,397 203 6046	123	16,828 132 5472
4	3,470 070 4729	64	16,422 139 0958	124	16,828 915 6787
5	4,219 535 5496	65	16,445 677 0226	125	16,829 654 9180
6	4,926 995 2091	66	16,467 895 7146	126	16,830 352 7249
7	5,594 803 7372	67	16,488 869 1111	127	16,831 011 4218
8	6,225 183 4687	68	16,508 667 0075	128	16,831 633 2005
9	6,820 232 1829	69	16,527 355 2873	129	16,832 220 1303
10	7,381 930 0841	70	16,544 996 1414	130	16,832 774 1643
11	7,912 146 3921	71	16,561 648 2751	131	16,833 297 1462
12	8,412 645 5619	72	16,577 367 1033	132	16,833 790 8165
13	8,885 093 1557	73	16,592 204 9353	133	16,834 256 8179
14	9,331 061 3859	74	16,606 211 1484	134	16,834 696 7013
15	9,752 034 3466	75	16,619 432 3524	135	16,835 111 9304
16	10,149 412 9526	76	16,631 912 5451	136	16,835 503 8871
17	10,524 519 6012	77	16,643 693 2579	137	16,835 873 8757
18	10,878 602 5734	78	16,654 813 6948	138	16,836 223 1275
19	11,212 840 1873	79	16,665 310 8623	139	16,836 552 8048
20	11,528 344 7196	80	16,675 219 6930	140	16,836 864 0045
21	11,826 166 1070	81	16,684 573 1616	141	16,837 157 7623
22	12,107 295 4402	82	16,693 402 3944	142	16,837 435 0559
23	12,372 668 2622	83	16,701 736 7735	143	16,837 696 8079
24	12,623 167 6811	84	16,709 604 0340	144	16,837 943 8895
25	12,859 627 3096	85	16,717 030 3565	145	16,838 177 1228
26	13,082 834 0385	86	16,724 040 4546	146	16,838 397 2841
27	13,293 530 6559	87	16,730 657 6562	147	16,838 605 1059
28	13,492 418 3182	88	16,736 903 9823	148	16,838 801 2799
29	13,680 158 8844	89	16,742 800 2193	149	16,838 986 4589
30	13,857 377 1181	90	16,748 365 9887	150	16,839 161 2592
31	14,024 662 7663	91	16,753 619 8123	151	16,839 326 2623
32	14,182 572 5228	92	16,758 579 1739	152	16,839 482 0175
33	14,331 631 8799	93	16,763 260 5771	153	16,839 629 0431
34	14,472 336 8778	94	16,767 679 6008	154	16,839 767 8283
35	14,605 155 7548	95	16,771 850 9506	155	16,839 898 8350
36	14,730 530 5060	96	16,775 788 5080	156	16,840 022 4991
37	14,848 878 3538	97	16,779 505 3762	157	16,840 139 2322
38	14,960 593 1363	98	16,783 013 9245	158	16,840 249 4227
39	15,066 046 6184	99	16,786 325 8284	159	16,840 353 4374
40	15,165 589 7282	100	16,789 452 1094	160	16,840 451 6223
41	15,259 553 7258	101	16,792 403 1711	161	16,840 544 3042
42	15,348 251 3046	102	16,795 188 8341	162	16,840 631 7916
43	15,431 977 6326	103	16,797 818 3685	163	16,840 714 3756
44	15,511 011 3346	104	16,800 300 5248	164	16,840 792 3309
45	15,585 615 4191	105	16,802 643 5632	165	16,840 865 9171
46	15,656 038 1537	106	16,804 855 2809	166	16,840 935 3790
47	15,722 513 8914	107	16,806 943 0381	167	16,841 000 9477
48	15,785 263 8503	108	16,808 913 7822	168	16,841 062 8415
49	15,844 496 8499	109	16,810 774 0717	169	16,841 121 2663
50	15,900 410 0058	110	16,812 530 0972	170	16,841 176 4166
51	15,953 189 3860	111	16,814 187 7024	171	16,841 228 4758
52	16,003 010 6298	112	16,815 752 4034	172	16,841 277 6173
53	16,050 039 5326	113	16,817 229 4074	173	16,841 324 0045
54	16,094 432 5971	114	16,818 623 6294	174	16,841 367 7919
55	16,136 337 5548	115	16,819 939 7091	175	16,841 409 1251
56	16,175 893 8571	116	16,821 182 0263	176	16,841 448 1417
57	16,213 233 1394	117	16,822 354 7151	177	16,841 484 9715
58	16,248 479 6596	118	16,823 461 6780	178	16,841 519 7371
59	16,281 750 7111	119	16,824 506 5987	179	16,841 552 5542
60	16,313 157 0135	120	16,825 492 9545	180	16,841 583 5320

Present Value of 1 per period

NOMINAL INTEREST RATE COMPOUNDED

YEARLY @ 6% 6.0000% PER ANNUM	HALF-YEARLY @ 12% 12.0000% PER ANNUM	QUARTERLY @ 24% 24.0000% PER ANNUM

Periods	Present Value	Periods	Present Value	Periods	Present Value
1	,943 396 2264	61	16,190 026 1370	121	16,652 217 6247
2	1,833 392 6664	62	16,217 005 7896	122	16,653 035 4950
3	2,673 011 9495	63	16,242 458 2921	123	16,653 807 0708
4	3,465 105 6127	64	16,266 470 0869	124	16,654 534 9724
5	4,212 363 7856	65	16,289 122 7235	125	16,655 221 6721
6	4,917 324 3260	66	16,310 493 1354	126	16,655 869 5020
7	5,582 381 4396	67	16,330 653 9013	127	16,656 480 6622
8	6,209 793 8110	68	16,349 673 4918	128	16,657 057 2285
9	6,801 692 2745	69	16,367 616 5017	129	16,657 601 1590
10	7,360 087 0514	70	16,384 543 8695	130	16,658 114 3009
11	7,886 874 5768	71	16,400 513 0844	131	16,658 598 3971
12	8,383 843 9404	72	16,415 578 3816	132	16,659 055 0916
13	8,852 682 9626	73	16,429 790 9260	133	16,659 485 9355
14	9,294 983 9270	74	16,443 198 9868	134	16,659 892 3920
15	9,712 248 9877	75	16,455 848 1007	135	16,660 275 8415
16	10,105 895 2715	76	16,467 781 2271	136	16,660 637 5863
17	10,477 259 6901	77	16,479 038 8935	137	16,660 978 8550
18	10,827 603 4812	78	16,489 659 3335	138	16,661 300 8066
19	11,158 116 4917	79	16,499 678 6165	139	16,661 604 5345
20	11,469 921 2186	80	16,509 130 7703	140	16,661 891 0703
21	11,764 076 6213	81	16,518 047 8965	141	16,662 161 3871
22	12,041 581 7182	82	16,526 460 2797	142	16,662 416 4029
23	12,303 378 9794	83	16,534 396 4903	143	16,662 656 9839
24	12,550 357 5278	84	16,541 883 4814	144	16,662 883 9471
25	12,783 356 1583	85	16,548 946 6806	145	16,663 098 0633
26	13,003 166 1870	86	16,555 610 0760	146	16,663 300 0597
27	13,210 534 1387	87	16,561 896 2981	147	16,663 490 6223
28	13,406 164 2818	88	16,567 826 6963	148	16,663 670 3984
29	13,590 721 0206	89	16,573 421 4116	149	16,663 839 9985
30	13,764 831 1515	90	16,578 699 4450	150	16,663 999 9986
31	13,929 085 9920	91	16,583 678 7217	151	16,664 150 9421
32	14,084 043 3887	92	16,588 376 1525	152	16,664 293 3416
33	14,230 229 6119	93	16,592 807 6910	153	16,664 427 6807
34	14,368 141 1433	94	16,596 988 3878	154	16,664 554 4158
35	14,498 246 3616	95	16,600 932 4413	155	16,664 673 9772
36	14,620 987 1336	96	16,604 653 2465	156	16,664 786 7709
37	14,736 780 3147	97	16,608 163 4401	157	16,664 893 1801
38	14,846 019 1648	98	16,611 474 9435	158	16,664 993 5661
39	14,949 074 6838	99	16,614 599 0033	159	16,665 088 2699
40	15,046 296 8715	100	16,617 546 2295	160	16,665 177 6131
41	15,138 015 9165	101	16,620 326 6316	161	16,665 261 8992
42	15,224 543 3175	102	16,622 949 6525	162	16,665 341 4143
43	15,306 172 9410	103	16,625 424 2004	163	16,665 416 4286
44	15,383 182 0198	104	16,627 758 6797	164	16,665 487 1968
45	15,455 832 0942	105	16,629 961 0186	165	16,665 553 9593
46	15,524 369 9002	106	16,632 038 6967	166	16,665 616 9427
47	15,589 028 2077	107	16,633 998 7705	167	16,665 676 3610
48	15,650 026 6110	108	16,635 847 8967	168	16,665 732 4161
49	15,707 572 2746	109	16,637 592 3554	169	16,665 785 2982
50	15,761 860 6364	110	16,639 238 0711	170	16,665 835 1870
51	15,813 076 0721	111	16,640 790 6331	171	16,665 882 2518
52	15,861 392 5208	112	16,642 255 3143	172	16,665 926 6527
53	15,906 974 0762	113	16,643 637 0889	173	16,665 968 5403
54	15,949 975 5436	114	16,644 940 6499	174	16,666 008 0569
55	15,990 542 9657	115	16,646 170 4245	175	16,666 045 3367
56	16,028 814 1186	116	16,647 330 5891	176	16,666 080 5063
57	16,064 918 9798	117	16,648 425 0841	177	16,666 113 6852
58	16,098 980 1696	118	16,649 457 6265	178	16,666 144 9860
59	16,131 113 3676	119	16,650 431 7231	179	16,666 174 5151
60	16,161 427 7052	120	16,651 350 6822	180	16,666 202 3727

SUPPLEMENTARY TABLES OF VALUES OF THE ANNUITY

at rates of interest or for periods not given
in the main tables.

	Effective Rates %	Nominal Annual Rates %
For Quarterly Compounding: 5, 10, 15, 20, 25 and 30 years.	$\frac{25}{32}$ to $1\frac{15}{32}$ at intervals of $\frac{1}{16}$	$3\frac{1}{8}$ to $5\frac{7}{8}$ at intervals of $\frac{1}{4}$
In conjunction with the main tables interest intervals of $\frac{1}{8}$% nominal annual are provided, from 3% to 6%.		
For Monthly Compounding: 5, 10, 15, 20, 25 and 30 years.	$\frac{1}{4}$ to $\frac{1}{2}$ at intervals of $\frac{1}{96}$	3 to 6 at intervals of $\frac{1}{8}$

The values are given to 8 decimal places.

REPAYMENT OF A LOAN OF 1

Quarterly payments to

$1+i$	INTEREST RATE % Effective/ Quarterly	INTEREST RATE % Nominal Annual	5 Years 20 Quarters	10 Years 40 Quarters
1·0078125	$\frac{25}{32}$	$3\frac{1}{8}$	·05420260	·02920611
1·0084375	$\frac{27}{32}$	$3\frac{3}{8}$	·05454749	·02955994
1·0090625	$\frac{29}{32}$	$3\frac{5}{8}$	·05489366	·02991630
1·0096875	$\frac{31}{32}$	$3\frac{7}{8}$	·05524111	·03027520
1·0103125	$1\frac{1}{32}$	$4\frac{1}{8}$	·05558984	·03063663
1·0109375	$1\frac{3}{32}$	$4\frac{3}{8}$	·05593983	·03100057
1·0115625	$1\frac{5}{32}$	$4\frac{5}{8}$	·05629110	·03136703
1·0121875	$1\frac{7}{32}$	$4\frac{7}{8}$	·05664364	·03173600
1·0128125	$1\frac{9}{32}$	$5\frac{1}{8}$	·05699745	·03210746
1·0134375	$1\frac{11}{32}$	$5\frac{3}{8}$	·05735253	·03248140
1·0140625	$1\frac{13}{32}$	$5\frac{5}{8}$	·05770886	·03285783
1·0146875	$1\frac{15}{32}$	$5\frac{7}{8}$	·05806646	·03323673

BY WAY OF ANNUITY
include principal and interest

15 Years 60 Quarters	20 Years 80 Quarters	25 Years 100 Quarters	30 Years 120 Quarters
·02094083	·01685774	·01444687	·01287142
·02130860	·01724051	·01484482	·01328439
·02168014	·01762819	·01524875	·01370434
·02205541	·01802075	·01565861	·01413115
·02243441	·01841815	·01607433	·01456471
·02281711	·01882035	·01649581	·01500489
·02320350	·01922729	·01692300	·01545157
·02359354	·01963895	·01735580	·01590462
·02398723	·02005526	·01779413	·01636391
·02438452	·02047618	·01823791	·01682929
·02478541	·02090166	·01868704	·01730064
·02518987	·02133165	·01914143	·01777780

REPAYMENT OF A LOAN OF 1

Monthly payments to

1 + *i*	INTEREST RATE % Effective/ Monthly	INTEREST RATE % Nominal Annual	5 Years 60 Months	10 Years 120 Months
1·0025	$\frac{1}{4}$	3	·01796869	·00965607
1·00260416	$\frac{25}{96}$	$3\frac{1}{8}$	·01802429	·00971388
1·00270833	$\frac{13}{48}$	$3\frac{1}{4}$	·01808000	·00977190
1·0028125	$\frac{9}{32}$	$3\frac{3}{8}$	·01813582	·00983014
1·00291666	$\frac{7}{24}$	$3\frac{1}{2}$	·01819175	·00988859
1·00302833	$\frac{29}{96}$	$3\frac{5}{8}$	·01825181	·00995148
1·003125	$\frac{5}{16}$	$3\frac{3}{4}$	·01830392	·01000612
1·00322916	$\frac{31}{96}$	$3\frac{7}{8}$	·01836016	·01006521
1·00333333	$\frac{1}{3}$	4	·01841652	·01012451
1·0034375	$\frac{11}{32}$	$4\frac{1}{8}$	·01847299	·01018403
1·00354166	$\frac{17}{48}$	$4\frac{1}{4}$	·01852956	·01024375
1·00364583	$\frac{35}{96}$	$4\frac{3}{8}$	·01858623	·01030369
1·00375	$\frac{3}{8}$	$4\frac{1}{2}$	·01864302	·01036384
1·00385416	$\frac{37}{96}$	$4\frac{5}{8}$	·01869991	·01042420
1·00395833	$\frac{19}{48}$	$4\frac{3}{4}$	·01875691	·01048477
1·0040625	$\frac{13}{32}$	$4\frac{7}{8}$	·01881402	·01054556
1·00416666	$\frac{5}{12}$	5	·01887123	·01060655
1·00427083	$\frac{41}{96}$	$5\frac{1}{8}$	·01892856	·01066776
1·004375	$\frac{7}{16}$	$5\frac{1}{4}$	·01898598	·01072917
1·00447916	$\frac{43}{96}$	$5\frac{3}{8}$	·01904352	·01079079
1·00458333	$\frac{11}{24}$	$5\frac{1}{2}$	·01910116	·01085263
1·0046875	$\frac{15}{32}$	$5\frac{5}{8}$	·01915891	·01091467
1·00479166	$\frac{23}{48}$	$5\frac{3}{4}$	·01921677	·01097692
1·00489533	$\frac{47}{96}$	$5\frac{7}{8}$	·01927473	·01103938
1·005	$\frac{1}{2}$	6	·01933280	·01110205

BY WAY OF ANNUITY
include principal and interest

15 Years 180 Months	20 Years 240 Months	25 Years 300 Months	30 Years 360 Months
·00690582	·00554598	·00474211	·00421604
·00696609	·00560875	·00480738	·00428375
·00702669	·00567196	·00487316	·00435206
·00708760	·00573557	·00493945	·00442096
·00714883	·00579960	·00500624	·00449045
·00721481	·00586869	·00507839	·00456558
·00727222	·00592888	·00514131	·00463116
·00733439	·00599414	·00520959	·00470237
·00739688	·00605980	·00527837	·00477415
·00745968	·00612587	·00534763	·00484650
·00752278	·00619234	·00541738	·00491940
·00758620	·00625922	·00548761	·00499285
·00764993	·00632649	·00555832	·00506685
·00771397	·00639416	·00562951	·00514139
·00777832	·00646224	·00570117	·00521647
·00784297	·00653070	·00577330	·00529208
·00790794	·00659956	·00584590	·00536822
·00797320	·00666881	·00591896	·00544487
·00803878	·00673844	·00599248	·00552204
·00810465	·00680847	·00606645	·00559971
·00817083	·00687887	·00614087	·00567789
·00823732	·00694966	·00621575	·00575656
·00830410	·00702084	·00629106	·00583573
·00837118	·00709238	·00636682	·00591538
·00843857	·00716431	·00644301	·00599551